Western Civilization
An Urban Perspective

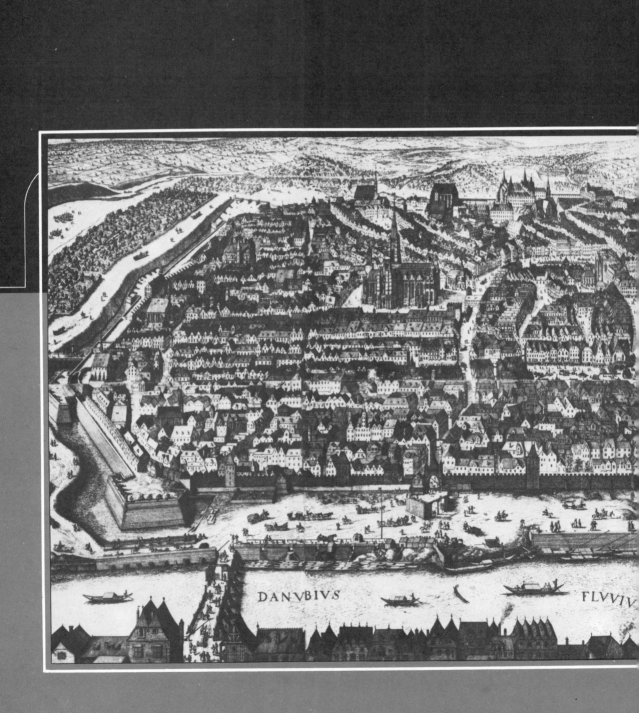

DANVBIVS   FLVVIV

SECOND EDITION

Western Civilization
An Urban Perspective

Volume I
*From Ancient Times
Through the Seventeenth Century*

F. Roy Willis

University of California, Davis

D. C. HEATH AND COMPANY
Lexington, Massachusetts   Toronto

Cover illustration: *The Piazzetta, Venice, Looking North,* by Giovanni Antonio Canaletto. The Norton Simon Foundation.

Title page illustration: Plan of Vienna in 1609, by Jakob Hufnagel. Bildarchiv d. Ost Nationalbibliothek.

Maps and plans prepared by Richard D. Pusey.

Contents

Preface to the Second Edition

In the first edition of this book, we adopted a new approach to the study of Western civilization. We wanted above all to avoid the sense of superficiality and perhaps even monotony in the study of past society that assails a reader made to move relentlessly through the vast complexities of human history while feeling little personal involvement in the details comprising events. Too often, it seemed, the study of Western civilization was like an infinitely long train ride with no stopovers allowed, a kind of Orient Express in which Paris, Vienna, and Istanbul were viewed as little more than names on railroad stations. In a way, this book was to be an invitation to the student to stop and explore the intricacies of the great cities that might otherwise have flashed by largely unobserved. Better yet, as historians we could visit the city as it was at the time of its greatness. Modern research has greatly facilitated the task of presenting the city in this manner. The lives of the elite, whether rulers, economic movers, artists, or thinkers, are already well documented. But in the past few years, historians have adopted the techniques of other social scientists to broaden our understanding of urban life, to give insight into classes previously mute, to enable us to apply modern economic concepts to the structure of past cities, and to help us grasp with a new sympathy such questions as family structure, social morality, and the position of minorities. It thus became possible to attempt to reconstruct the life of a great city, seen not only in its position in the evolution of Western civilization but understood also as a unique creation in itself. Ten great cities were chosen, to cover the evolution of our civilization from Athens in the fifth century B. C. to New York City in the twentieth century. Narrative chapters, with an urban focus, linked the studies of individual cities, enabling the reader to place the cities in a wider historical focus.

The enthusiastic response of so many students and teachers to this approach justifies us in seeking to enhance, in this second edition, the originality of the first edition, in these ways:

1. The book now opens with a totally new chapter studying the origins of civilization in Mesopotamia, Palestine, and Egypt. Here, in cities like Ur, Babylon, Jerusalem, and Thebes, we are able to follow the progress in social and economic organization, in religion, in artistic creativity and military capacity, that are the first distinctively urban achievements.

2. At the beginning of each chapter which studies a city in depth, a chart is provided that summarizes the basic characteristics of the city. The reader is thus able to compare such features as area, population, form of government, and so on, of the major cities studied. On the page opposite this chart, there is a city plan indicating most of the principal buildings mentioned in the chapter. Many of these plans have been specially drawn for this edition.

3. A large number of new maps have been added, and most of the maps from the first edition have been clarified and enlarged for easier reference.

4. Several chapters have been expanded and rewritten. The more important changes include revised sections on feudalism and manorialism, in Chapter 7; extensive rewriting of Chapter 11 on Renaissance Florence, to give greater coverage to social structure; and increased coverage of the political history of the nineteenth century, especially concerning the Second Empire in France and Austria-Hungary under Francis Joseph.

5. The bibliographies for Suggested Reading at the end of each chapter have been updated to provide reference to the large number of new books, particularly in urban history, that have appeared in the past four years.

6. Time charts of significant events have been provided at several places in the text, to enable the reader rapidly to relate events in urban history to the wider context of Western history.

7. Many new illustrations have been added, directly related, as in the first edition, to material in the text.

A new teacher's manual, completely rewritten by Rosemary M. Southard of the University of California, Davis, is available to accompany the text. The manual provides many thought-provoking discussion questions as well as an abundance of objective test questions.

Introduction: Civilization and the City

Cities have been a major driving force in the development of Western civilization. The highest achievements of man, Sophocles proclaimed in his play *Antigone,* are "language, and wind-swift thought, and city-dwelling habits." The city, from the time of its earliest appearance some five thousand years ago, has focused and magnified human energies in the task of mastering the environment, enriched our understanding by providing a multiplicity of human contacts, and provided the stimulus to the highest creativity in all forms of science and art. It has at the same time been responsible for many of the darkest features of Western civilization—the spoliation of the environment; the coercion of vast numbers of individuals by governments, armies, and economic exploiters; the exclusion of vast segments of the population from intellectual and social advancement; and perhaps even the glorification of war. The city has always been at the extremes of the Western experience.

In recent years, the process of urbanization has been expolored with considerable success by a large range of social scientists, including the urban geographer, the political scientist, the sociologist, the social anthropologist, the economist, and the historian. Their findings have thrown much light on such basic concerns as the impact of population growth, the spatial patterns of city development, the occupational structure of cities at varying stages of development, class relationships, family structure and mores, the functioning of political systems, and relationship to environment. All of this is enormously helpful to historians of civilization. But historians must always remember the one task that distinguishes them from the other social scientists: to respect the uniqueness of each period of civilization.

This book seeks to meet that challenge by focusing on the achievements of the great cities of Western civilization. Over half of the book is devoted to studies of ten great cities at the height of their creativity.

Several questions have been asked about each city. The first and most basic is, *How did the city produce its wealth?* The city was a provider of services—religious, governmental, legal, military, and commercial; a manufacturer of goods itself, by artisans in the pre-industrial age and by factory production after the industrial revolution of the eighteenth century; and often an exploiter, using military force to acquire economic wealth. Secondly we ask, *What social relationships developed inside this economic system?* We shall be interested in the distribution of wealth, the status accorded to birth or profession, the relationship between classes, the extent of mobility within the social structure, and the distincitve ways of life developed within each stratum of society. Thirdly, we turn to the political superstructure to ask, *How did the citizens conceive the relationship of the individual to the state in theory and carry it out in practice?* Underlying all political systems is a theory or theories of government, though these assumptions are not always explicitly formulated. In times of dissatisfaction with an established political system, theorists construct new formulas based on their own conception of man and the ideal form of state; and as we shall see, these theories are occasionally put into practice, usually as the result of revolution. Political theory will therefore accompany the analysis of the distribution of power within the city and, since most of these cities are also capitals, within the state.

Fourthly, we consider, *How did the city spend its wealth?* The consumption habits of different social classes have been subject to a vast amount of detailed research, and it is increasingly possible to re-create the way of life of the less privileged classes as well as that of the elite. Public expenditure as well as private must be assessed, especially that used for the beautification of the city or the improvement of its amenities; but we must also consider the waste of a city's resources, from military adventuring to the ravaging of the natural surroundings. Fifthly, we examine the city's intellectual life, asking, *To what goals was the intellectual activity of its citizens directed?* In cities as multifaceted as these, we must emphasize the most salient features of each city's contribution to the intellectual advance of Western civilization—the contribution of Athens to philosophy and drama, of Rome to law, of Vienna to music, for example. But in each case the contribution of the environment of the city must be explained: why Paris was a magnet for Europe's theologians in the thirteenth century and for its artists and writers in the late nineteenth century; why tiny Lisbon could attract the continent's cartographers and maritime technologists; why Berlin could be transformed in months from the center of military science to an incubator of avant-garde artistic talent and then in an even shorter time back to its military preoccupations.

Finally, we ask, *How did the cultural and scientific achievements of the city reflect the citizens' conception of human nature, of God, and of beauty?* Much of this creation was the possession of an elite, but that is hardly a reason for excluding it from a history of civilization. Hence, we shall consider what the Parthenon tells us of the Greek concept of beauty, how a Botticelli Venus reveals the Florentine conception of the divine, how Newton's laws of motion justify a naturally ordered universe.

City and countryside, however, cannot be isolated from each other, and should not. As late as 1800, only three percent of the world's population lived in cities of more than 5,000 people; and even in 1950, only thirty percent did so. Throughout the development of Western civilization, most people have lived on the land; the city depends on outside supplies for food. We are therefore concerned throughout the book with the life of the rural population as well as the urban, with agrarian technology and the nature of bulk transportation of agricultural products, with the social structure of the countryside and its impact upon the city, and with the needs, values, and aspirations of the inhabitants of the countryside. We must thus consider the farms of the Roman campagna as well as Rome, the decaying aristocratic estates as well as prerevolutionary Paris, the turnips and clover of the agricultural revolution as well as the cotton mills of Manchester.

This book is undisguisedly enthusiastic about cities, with a few notable exceptions that will be evident to the reader. I only wish that one could show the same admiration for all man's urban creations that Wordsworth did about London, one bright morning at the beginning of the last century:

Earth has not anything to show more fair:
Dull would he be of soul who could pass by
A sight so touching in its majesty:
This city now doth, like a garment, wear
The beauty of the morning; silent, bare,
Ships, towers, domes, theatres, and temples lie
Open unto the fields, and to the sky;
All bright and glittering in the smokeless air.
Never did sun more beautifully steep
In his first splendor, valley, rock, or hill;
Ne'er saw I, never felt, a calm so deep!
The river glideth at his own sweet will:
Dear God! the very houses seem asleep;
And all that mighty heart is lying still!"[1]

---

[1] "Composed upon Westminster Bridge, September 3, 1802."

Chronicles of Events

Maps and Plans

Chronicle of Events

From Prehistory to the Roman Republic

3,000,000–27 B. C.

All dates are B. C. Major cities are capitalized.

Prehistory

3,000,000	Possible appearance of first hominids
2,000,000–12,000	Paleolithic (Old Stone) Age
600,000–10,000	Glacial periods
40,000	Appearance of homo sapiens
12,000–8000	Mesolithic (Middle Stone) Age
8000–4000	Neolithic (New Stone) Age

	Mesopotamia	Syria-Palestine	Asia Minor, Greece and Italy	Egypt
8000		JERICHO		
6000			ÇATAL HÜYÜK	
		AGE OF COPPER AND BRONZE		
4000	Sumerian city-states formed			Pre-Dynastic period Union of Upper and Lower Egypt Archaic period (3100–2700) MEMPHIS
3000				
2800	2800–2630 Domination of UR			Old Kingdom (2700–2181) MEMPHIS: GIZAH 2650–2500 Building of pyramids
2600				

2400	Akkadian empire (2370–2230)						
2200	Guti invasion / Sumerian revival	Middle Kingdom (2050–1786) THEBES					
2000	Rise of BABYLON		First Hittite empire HATTUSAS	Abraham to Palestine / First wave of Indo-European invaders			
1800	Babylonian empire (1790–1595) Hammurabi (c. 1790–1750)						
1600	Sack of BABYLON	Hyksos invasion / New Kingdom (1550–1090) THEBES; TELL-EL-AMARNA		Hebrews in Egypt / Canaanite UGARIT			
1400			Second Hittite empire	Moses leads exodus from Egypt			
1200	Rise of Assyria		AGE OF IRON	Second wave of Indo-European invaders / Phoenician trading dominance			
1000			c. 814 Foundation of CARTHAGE / MILETUS / Rise of ATHENS / Age of Homer and Hesiod (?)	TYRE; SIDON / Hebrew kingdom under Saul and David / JERUSALEM / 925 Division of Hebrew kingdom			

	Mesopotamia	Syria-Palestine	Asia Minor, Greece and Italy	Egypt
800	Assyrian empire ASSUR; NIMRUD; NINEVEH Sennacherib (705–681)	722 Assyrians conquer Hebrew northern kingdom	753 Traditional date for foundation of ROME Greek colonies in Aegean and Western Mediterranean— AGRIGENTO, PAESTUM	Necropolis paintings in Etruria
700			Age of lawgivers and tyrants begins in Greece Etruscan Dominance in Italy— TARQUINIA, CERVETERI	

	Greece/Eastern Mediterranean		Rome/Western Mediterranean	
	Main Events	Culture	Main Events	Culture
600	612 Sack of NINEVEH New Babylonian empire (612–539) BABYLON Babylonian Captivity of Hebrews of southern kingdom Reforms of Solon, ATHENS Tyranny of Pisistratus, ATHENS (546–527) 508 Reforms of Cleisthenes, ATHENS	Dionysian Festival begun First Parthenon built in ATHENS Aeschylus (525–456)	Roman Republic (509–27) 509 Expulsion of Etruscans from ROME	

500			
490 Battle of Marathon 490–479 Persian Wars 480 Battle of Thermopylae 480 Battle of Salamis 470 Battle of Platea Pericles, general (461–429) 431–404 Peloponnesian War 429 Death of Pericles 415–413 Expedition to Sicily	Phidias (500–431) Sophocles (496–406) Herodotus (484–428?) Euripides (480–406) Thucydides (471–c. 400) Rebuilding of ATHENS begun Socrates (469–399) 454 Treasury of Delian League to ATHENS Parthenon begun Sophist philosophy taught Plato (427–347)	c. 500–275 Conquest of Italian peninsula 471 Secession by plebians Twelve Tables of Law	Greek temples in Sicily and Southern Italy
400			
Greek mercenaries in Persia Philip of Macedon (359–336) 338 Battle of Chaeronea Alexander the Great (336–323) 332 ALEXANDRIA founded	Anabasis of Xenophon 395 Completion of Acropolis temples Aristotle (384–322) 351–340 Philippics of Demosthenes Skeptic philosophers Epicurus (342–270) Zeno (335–263)	390 Gauls sack ROME	Servian wall built at ROME

Greece/Eastern Mediterranean		Rome/Western Mediterranean	
Main Events	Culture	Main Events	Culture
300 Division of Alexander's empire Seleucid rule in Syria–Persia (c. 305–264) Ptolemies' rule in Egypt (c. 304–31)	Euclid (c. 300) c. 280 Museum in ALEXANDRIA founded Eratosthenes (275–194)	282 Capture of NAPLES 280–275 Invasion of Pyrrhus	
Antigonid rule in Macedon (276–167)		264–241 First Punic War Scipio Africanus (237–183) 218–202 Second Punic War	Cato the Elder (234–149)
200 146 Sack of CORINTH Roman conquest of Greece		149–146 Third Punic War 148 Annexation of Macedon 146 Destruction of CARTHAGE 135 Slave revolt in Sicily 133 Tiberius Gracchus tribune 123–121 Gaius Gracchus tribune 107–100 Marius consul	Terence (190–159)
100		88 Sulla's march on ROME	Cicero (106–43) Lucretius (c. 96–55) Cato the Younger (95–46) Catullus (c. 84–54)

Virgil (70–16)
Horace (65–8)
Livy (59 B.C.–A.D. 17)
Caesar wrote *Gallic Wars*

c. 29–19 Virgil wrote *Aeneid*

82–79 Sulla, consul
73–71 Slave revolt under
Spartacus

59 Julius Caesar, consul
58–50 Caesar's conquest of
Gaul
49–45 Caesar defeats Pompey
in the Civil Wars
31 Battle of Actium

Roman Empire (27 B.C.–A.D.
476)
27 Octavian becomes
Emperor Augustus

c. 8–4 Birth of Jesus Christ

31 Antony and Cleopatra
defeated at ACTIUM
Egypt annexed by ROME

1 / The Civilization
of the Ancient Near East

The progress of humanity toward civilization has been of ever-increasing acceleration. The consensus among scientists is that the Earth is about five billion years old, and that life first appeared about two billion years ago. Human beings with physical characteristics similar to our own, known to anthropologists as *homo sapiens*, appeared only about forty thousand years ago. Jericho, the oldest human settlement yet excavated that deserves to be called a city, existed about ten thousand years ago. From that point on, there was a dramatic change in the pace of humanity's concerted progress both toward control and exploitation of the physical environment and development of human physical and mental abilities. As Lewis Mumford has pointed out, the appearance of the city "resulted in an enormous expansion of human capabilities in every direction. The city effected a mobilization of manpower, a command over long-distance transportation, an intensification of communication over long distances in space and time, an outburst of inventiveness along with a large-scale development of civil engineering, and not least, it promoted a tremendous rise in agricultural productivity." [1]

The geographical area that proved most encouraging to the advance of organized city life was the "Fertile Crescent," which sweeps in an arc from the valleys of the Tigris and Euphrates rivers under the Taurus mountains to the oases and river valleys of the eastern Mediterranean shore, and the

[1] Lewis Mumford, *The City in History* (New York: Harcourt, Brace, and World, 1961), p. 30.

The Great Sphinx and Pyramid of Pharoah Chephren, Gizah   Trans World Airlines photo

Nile valley of Egypt. The Sumerians at Ur, the Akkadians at Babylon, the Assyrians at Nineveh, the Phoenicians at Tyre, the Hebrews at Jerusalem, the Egyptians at Memphis and Thebes, and the inhabitants of many other cities worked out a new way of life that has had profound consequences on the rest of our history. Large numbers of laborers were organized, often unwillingly, to carry out massive projects for taming nature through irrigation or flood control, for defense through the erection of city walls and citadels, for war in trained armies, for piety in the erection of temples and tombs, for governmental glorification or efficiency through palace buildings. Differentiation of occupation took place, especially with the rise of commerce and of a merchant class; and social divisions became sharper. Kings and priests united to compel advances in architectural techniques in the building of tomb and temple, palace and citadel, and to develop law that would regulate citizens' relations to god and each other. Writing developed from a system of pictures to the final invention of the alphabet by the Phoenicians. Astronomy made possible the calendar. Arithmetic, geometry, medicine, geography, biology, botany, and geology made great progress. The worship of god or gods gave encouragement to the earliest literature and to a profound examination of the human being's moral and spiritual nature.

Much of these achievements has been lost, because the rulers of the Near East took as much pride in the destruction of rival cities as in the creation of their own. Many of the languages and even some of the cities themselves were forgotten for more than two thousand years, only to be rediscovered in this century through the concerted efforts of archaeologist and linguist. Thus, the influence of the Near East upon the development of Western civilization was rarely direct. Nevertheless, this influence did survive in those peoples who inherited their achievements and acted to transmit them to the West. Newer powers like the Carthaginians and the Persians absorbed much of the material progress. The Hebrews passed on to Judaism, Christianity, and Islam a heritage of religion and philosophy. And the Greeks learned from all alike in their multifaceted search for the realization of the potential of the individual human being.

The Solitariness of the Paleolithic Age

Skeleton remains found recently in East Africa indicate the existence of hominids, or "near-human" creatures, as much as three million years ago. By 600,000 B. C. such beings are known to have lived in various parts of the world. They used stone and wood tools, still however resembling the ape in stance and size of the cranium. Not until 40,000 B. C. did beings resembling modern men and women appear: they are known collectively to the anthropologist as *homo sapiens.* All other forms of humanity, such as the beings known as Neanderthal who lived at the same period, eventually died out.

Homo sapiens spread throughout the globe, acquiring different racial and cultural characteristics according to the areas settled.

The first period of human history, known to us almost exclusively from the tools used, is called the Stone Age; it is divided into periods according to the degree of skill achieved in working and utilizing stone tools. The Paleolithic or Old Stone Age lasted from about 2,000,000 to 12,000 B. C. During this time, human beings advanced from the use of primitive tools of chipped stone to the invention of a wide array of devices such as stone drills and small stone tools called microliths that could be incorporated in other more complex tools such as the harpoon. Geologically, this period is known as the Pleistocene or Ice Age. From about 600,000 to about 10,000 B. C., much of Europe, Asia, and North America was intermittently covered by the polar ice cap, which advanced and retreated four times, bringing vast changes not only in climate but also in topography and ecology, and thus presenting enormous problems of adaptation for survival. During the Mesolithic or Middle Stone Age, from 12,000 to 8000 B. C., which corresponded to the final retreat of the glaciers, more effective tools such as fishhooks, arrowheads, and possibly bows-and-arrows, and means of transportation such as dug-out canoes, were developed. From 8000 to 4000 B. C., in the Neolithic or New Stone Age, human beings ceased to be food gatherers and hunters, and began to practice agriculture and animal husbandry: only then was the birth of the city possible.

The scarcity of human remains of the Paleolithic Age is a good indication of the precarious and marginal existence led by our predecessors. Only a few dozen skulls have been found from the first three million years of the existence of a hominid population. By the end of the Paleolithic Age, the total human population of the planet could not have been more than ten million. Human life was dictated by the necessity of obtaining food, which consisted mostly of wild grains, nuts, berries, roots, and to some extent the catch from hunting and fishing. It has been calculated that such a way of life would permit the survival of no more than 1.7 persons per square mile of relatively fertile land. The basic social unit was the family group and perhaps a loose association of several families, brought together by both the difficulty of hunting large savage animals with primitive weapons and by the need to pass on to children during the exceptionally long period of infancy the skills necessary for human survival. These groups sought shelter, where possible, in caves but when necessary also in simple lean-to constructions of stone or wood, or in holes in the ground that could be covered with a roof of skins. Food was cooked, often in hearths set aside for a family group, and was stored in special pits; and in the eighth millenium B. C. clay pottery was invented. Clothes were made from animal skins, stitched with bone needles, or from woven fibres. Sea shells found far inland and widely diffused flint tools indicate the probability of long-distance trade.

In wall paintings in caves of the Dordogne region in France, we possess a still mystifying glimpse into the mind of the Paleolithic people. The paint-

Paleolithic Cave Paintings, France
On the walls and ceiling of limestone caves at Lascaux [above] and Font de Gaume [below], about 14,000 B. C., skilled artists invoked magic to aid the tribal hunt for bison, antelope, and reindeer.
Courtesy French Government Tourist Office and American Museum of Natural History

ings, of astonishing realism, color, and design, were executed about 14,000 B. C. on the walls of limestone caves often as deep as two miles in the earth, by specialized artists; they depicted the animals of the hunt—reindeer, bison, rhinoceros, and woolly mammoths. Drawn by the light of a feeble flame of fat in uninhabited caves, the paintings indicate perhaps a tradition in the group of calling upon magical ritual to aid them in the hunt, and also a willingness to devote part of their meager surplus to the support of the artist who could invoke such magic on their behalf. But the aesthetic awareness that led to the embellishment of hunting equipment with tiny sculptures and to the development of beads and bracelets for personal adornment proves that the aesthetic sense fulfilled far more than services to gods now unknown; it also became a means to mundane luxury sought after by a society reaching beyond the pure necessities of life.

It can be argued that at the end of the Paleolithic Age humanity had already developed many of the social characteristics that were to be at the basis of city life, though in a very elementary form—respect for leadership, in obedience to the commands of the most skillful hunter; a sense of the supernatural or the religious, and provision and respect for the guardians of the secrets of the supernatural; a differentiation of occupation, accompanied by provision of part of the surplus for a class not actively engaged in the production of the group's economic livelihood; and recognition of the importance to the enrichment of life of non-material benefits of art. But the Paleolithic Age lacked that most essential urban characteristic—the determination to manipulate the natural environment.

The Neolithic Revolution, c. 8000–4000 B. C.

The last four thousand years of the Stone Age were marked not only by greater sophistication in the manufacture and use of stone tools and weapons but by the far more important change from food gathering and hunting to food production and animal rearing. Agriculture probably developed almost at the same time in several parts of the world. One of the most important parts was the upland plateau stretching from Anatolia to Iran, on the edge of the "Fertile Crescent." Here, in the years when the retreat of the ice cap was leaving continental Europe covered with vast deciduous forests, the

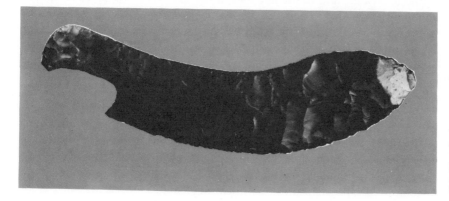

Flint Knife, 3rd millenium B. C. *The working of flint reached its highest perfection in Egypt in the third millenium B. C. Although later replaced by copper for everyday use, flint knives were retained for ritual slaughter of animals for over a thousand years.* Lowie Museum of Anthropology, University of California, Berkeley

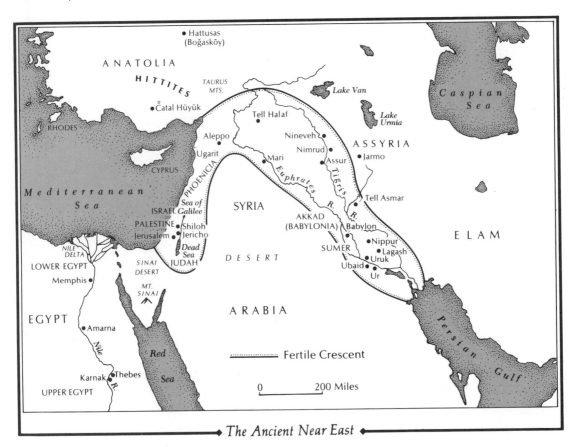

→ The Ancient Near East ←

land proved ideal for the transformation of the nomad into permanent set-
tler. Since the area lay to the north of the dessicating winds then creating
the deserts of Africa and Asia, adequate rainfall nurtured wild cereal grains,
especially barley and two basic forms of wheat, usually found in the foothills at altitudes of 2000 to 3000 feet above sea level. At first seeds were collected and eaten, and in the late Paleolithic Age stone sickles were used in
the harvesting. Then, once it had been noticed that seeds scattered on the
ground would reproduce themselves many times over at the next harvest,
areas near favorite hunting grounds were probably sown, to be reaped
when the nomads returned. Finally, probably about nine or eight thousand
years ago, certain nomad groups settled in agricultural villages amid fields
sown with cereal grain. The hunters, however, probably turned to the domestication of animals only when pressure of population growth and declining numbers of their prey forced them to find other ways of providing
an adequate supply of meat. The first animal to be domesticated was the
dog, which was used to help in the hunt in Paleolithic times. But in the Near
East, the large numbers of wild sheep, goats, pigs, and cattle were relatively
easy to herd into enclosures, in which they could be used for milk, wool,

and meat. Neolithic people thus enjoyed not only a fuller but also a more varied diet. The wheat or barley was cooked into porridge or flat cakes, and was varied with such products as millet, rice, and corn, and even squash and yams. Special ovens were constructed for baking bread, and, by 8000 B. C. at the latest, the fermentation of cereals for brewing beer had begun. Moreover, food could now be cooked or preserved in pottery containers, and cloth could be made from thread of flax or woven animal hair or wool. In these vastly improved material conditions of life in the eighth century B. C., several agricultural villages expanded to such an extent that we are justified in describing them as the first true cities.

The oldest city thus far discovered by the archaeologist is Jericho, in the south of Palestine, whose lowest level of settlement was found only in 1957.

Brewer Straining Mash
This stone servant figure, buried in a royal or aristocratic tomb at Gizah, Egypt, in the third millenium B. C., represents a brewer straining the mash made from fermented barley bread into a beer vat.
Lowie Museum of Anthropology, University of California, Berkeley

Ruins of Jericho
In the eighth millenium
B. C., *the three thousand*
inhabitants of Jericho ir-
rigated their fields from
deep springs, producing a
food surplus for export to
other cities of the Fertile
Crescent. Courtesy of the
Oriental Institute, University
of Chicago

Excavation down to the rock foundations on which the earliest buildings
were erected on the site proved, through the use of Carbon-14* testing, that
the city had been founded around 8000 B. C. It covered a site of more than
eight acres, and must have had a population of over three thousand. The inhabitants lived in round houses, with mud-brick walls rising from a stone
foundation, roofed in wattle and mud plaster. The more ambitious houses
had three rooms. Storage buildings for grain indicated a solid agricultural
surplus from the oasis-fed fields. Obsidian and other stones from Anatolia
and turquoise matrix from the Sinai found in the ruins are considered to be
proof of a flourishing export trade in such products of the area as salt and
sulphur. Above all, the extraordinary walls, rising to twenty feet in height
and encircled by a rock-cut ditch 25 feet wide and 6 feet deep, and a tall defense tower with winding inner staircase of yard-long stones, were proof of
the existence of some central authority capable of both planning elaborate
defense works and commanding the labor needed to carry them out.

Jericho was not, however, an isolated phenomenon. Other excavation
has found cities somewhat similar in size and complexity at Jarmo in Iraq,
at Tell Halaf on a tributary of the Euphrates river, and especially at Čatal
Hüyük in Anatolia. Čatal Hüyük, whose foundation has been dated at c.
6500 B. C., proved even more impressive than Jericho. Three times larger in
area, its houses were square, one-story high, with doorways opening onto
inner courtyards. Entrance was by ladder through a hole in the roof, and
much of the social life seems to have taken place on the flat roofs of the

---

* Scientists believe they can date objects containing organic matter to within less than a hundred years, by measuring the residual radioactivity emitted by the radioactive isotope of car-
bon C-14, which decays at a known rate after the organic matter has died.

houses. The householder not only had a storage room and a separate kitchen, but covered the floor with rushes and woven rush mats. The diet had considerably improved, the basic cereals now being accompanied with vegetable oil, almonds, pistachios, peas, and apples. Wine may have been made from hackberries. Honey was used for sweetening. Yogurt was made from sheep's milk. Other amenities abounded. Obsidian found extensively at the site was made into hand-held mirrors set in lime-plaster. Jewelry was made from sea-shells and rare stones. Above all, the skill in working flints by pressure-flaking for the manufacture of spearheads, arrowheads, daggers, and lances was superior to any other part of the Near East.

Most fascinating to archaeologists thirsty for some glimpse of the religious and artistic ideas of these peoples were the elaborate shrines uncovered. A room devoted to the worship of cult statues of a goddess, depicted either as a young or old woman or as a mother giving birth, was linked to every four or five rooms. Here many of the dead were buried, wrapped in cloth once their flesh had been removed. Wall paintings or monumental reliefs depicted vultures, often attacking headless corpses. Bulls' or rams' heads were modeled in plaster, or the horns were set in benches. Throughout, the statues and paintings emphasize the goddess as the source of fertility. Here in short is spectacular, if still somewhat mystifying evidence of the enormous advances toward a developed urban society that had been made as a result of the development of agriculture, by peoples whose technology was still in the Stone Age.

The Age of Copper, c. 4000–2500 B. C.

Between about 4000 and 3000 B. C. the inhabitants of the Near East carried through an enormously productive series of inventions and discoveries that totally transformed the economy of their societies and made possible what archaeologist V. Gordon Childe has termed the "Urban Revolution." These technological advances were the development of metallurgy, the use of the wheel, the invention of the plow, the harnessing of oxen, the design of the sailing ship, and the development of writing.

Copper and to a much smaller degree gold and silver were the first metals to be worked. Copper had been known since 7000 B. C. but only after 4000 B. C. were its properties fully exploited. Copper could be hammered when cold, but when heated it turned liquid and could be poured into a mould of any desired shape. Then, when cooled, it became as hard as stone and could be given a sharp cutting edge that was far more durable than flints. About 2500 B. C., it was found that alloys of copper, especially the fusion of copper and tin that produced bronze, were even stronger than pure copper itself. Thus, for farming implements, for all kinds of tools, and especially for weapons, copper and bronze provided far more effective means of production and destruction than any possessed in the Neolithic Age. To produce copper or bronze, societies had to specialize. Copper and, even more so, tin were located in distant mines, often in barren mountains, and had to be dug and transported. The ore had to be reduced to produce ingots, and the ingots worked into metal of the shapes desired. Specialization was required at all stages of the metal's manufacture. Hence the larger agricultural cities, with their ability to set aside part of their surplus for the support of the new manufacture, were the natural organizations where the bronzesmith would work.

Rough carts with either two or four wooden wheels bound in leather seem to have been widely used in the Fertile Crescent by 3000 b. c. For transport of goods or people they were a great advance over the use of sleds or even of rollers. But the wheel was also applied to the making of pottery, enabling one man to throw large numbers of symmetrical pots in one day and thus creating a new source of tradable surplus and a new professional class.

The new carts could be dragged by goats, donkeys, or cows, but heavier loads were pulled by oxen, which were also harnessed for dragging the newly invented plow in the fields. The so-called traction plow, a flat share breaking the ground a little below the surface, pulled by one animal and directed by a man (replacing the women who had previously dug the fields), was in wide use in the Near East by 3000 b. c., vastly expanding the amount of ground that could be effectively farmed by one family as well as increasing the yield of the ground tilled.

While animal power was being harnessed for agriculture and land transportation, the wind was harnessed for transport by sea. Rough sails, perhaps copied from those developed in the Persian Gulf, were in use on the Nile and in the Fertile Crescent by 3000 b. c. and far more elaborate techniques of carpentry were being used in the construction of even bigger boats. The ability to transport bulky goods by water encouraged the development of trade over wide distances, while further specialization of occupation was encouraged for both the trading and the shipbuilding classes.

Finally, in Mesopotamia, writing passed from the pictographic stage reached in the late Paleolithic Age, in which the symbol was an actual picture of an object, through an intermediate ideographic stage, in which the symbol represented an action or an idea, to a final stage, in which the symbol represented a sound in the language. The pen was a wedge-shaped reed, cut into a triangle at the end, which produced lines and triangles when jabbed into wet mud, which was later dried hard, although for monumental work stone or metal could be used. The writing was later known as cuneiform, after the Latin word *cuneus,* which means wedge. At first cuneiform employed about 2000 signs, which made it the exclusive possession of a learned class of scribes, but by 2000 b. c. it had been reduced to 600 signs, and about five hundred years later to a mere 30. Writing, like law, was originally developed to settle property rights, but it soon developed many more

Cuneiform Tablet, Assur
The clay tablet records the sale of a female slave named Likanu.   Lowie Museum of Anthropology, University of California, Berkeley

uses in the Mesopotamian states, from validating commercial transactions and legal documents to commemorating the deeds of kings to recording early scientific observations and literary epics.

As Childe has pointed out, the rich potential of these new inventions could easily be ignored by those Neolithic societies of Mediterranean Europe or the northern plateaus from Anatolia to Iran who were satisfied with the relatively abundant sustenance provided by their settled agriculture. The inventions could only be turned to full advantage when exploited by a new political and economic organization. Just such an organization was created at this time in the challenging environment of the great alluvial river valleys of the Tigris and Euphrates in Mesopotamia and the Nile in Egypt.

The City Civilization of Mesopotamia

The Land of the Two Rivers

The word Mesopotamia, derived from the Greek, means literally "between the rivers," but it is generally used to denote the whole plain between and on either side of the Tigris and Euphrates rivers. The plain was bordered to the north and east by mountain ranges, in whose foothills, as we have seen, agriculture was first practiced. To the southwest lay the forbidding deserts of Syria and Arabia. Each year the two great rivers were swollen with the winter snows of the northern mountains, and each year at flood stage they spread a thick layer of immensely fertile silt across the flood plain where they approached the Persian Gulf. This delta, a land of swamp rich in fish, wildlife, and date palms, was the most challenging and rewarding of the three natural units into which the river valleys were divided; and it was here, between 3500 and 3000 B. C., that agricultural settlers created the rich city-states of Sumer, of which the best known is Ur. The delta could only be made habitable by large-scale irrigation and flood control, which was managed first by a priestly class and then by godlike kings. Except for the period 2370–2230 B. C., when the Sumerian city-states were subdued by the rulers of Akkad, the region immediately to the north, the Sumerians remained prosperous and powerful until the beginning of the second millenium B. C.

Immediately to the north of Sumer, where the two rivers came most closely together, the plain was less subject to flooding but made fertile by rainfall and irrigation. This area, known first as Akkad, was inhabited by Semitic peoples who subdued the Sumerians in the middle of the third millenium; but when a new Semitic people called the Amorites conquered the area about 2000 B. C. and founded a great new capital city of Babylon, the area henceforth came to be known as Babylonia. Except for invasions of Hittites and Kassites, who were Indo-European peoples from Asia, Babylonia continued to dominate Mesopotamia for a thousand years.

The third natural region, called Assyria, stretched from the north of Babylonia to the Taurus range. Its rolling hills were watered by a large number of streams flowing from the surrounding mountains as well as by the headwaters of the two great rivers themselves. The Assyrians, a viciously warlike Semitic people, were able to conquer the whole of Mesopotamia in the eighth and seventh centuries B. C. Thus the history of Mesopotamia can be envisaged as a shift of the center of power northwards, from Sumer to Babylonia and then to Assyria.

The Rise of the Sumerian City States

Little is known about the origins of the Sumerian people, who spoke a language totally distinct from that of the Semitic inhabitants of the valleys to the north. The Sumerians probably moved down into the swamps of the delta under pressure of over-population of the foothills after 3900 B. C. Although at first they formed small agricultural villages, they soon found not only that the richness of the alluvial land permitted greater density of settlement but also that the vast engineering works in canals and dikes necessary to harness the annual floods required work forces of hundreds of men. Moreover, the layout and clearing of the canals required expert planning, while the division of the irrigated land, the water, and the crops demanded political control. By 3000 B. C. the Sumerians had solved this problem by forming "temple-communities," in which a class of priest-bureaucrats controlled the political and economic life of the city in the name of the city gods.

All Sumerian cities recognized a number of gods in common, including Anu the sky god, Enlil the lord of storms, and Ishtar the morning and evening star. The gods seemed hopelessly violent and unpredictable, and one's life a period of slavery to their whims. The epic poem, *The Creation*, emphasizes that mortals were created to enable the gods to give up working. Each city moreover had its own god, who was considered literally to inhabit the temple and who was in theory the owner of all property within the city. Hence the priests who interpreted the will of the god and controlled the distribution of the economic produce of the city were venerated for their supernatural and material functions alike. When, after 3000 B. C., the growing warfare among the cities made military leadership vital, the head of the army who became king assumed an intermediate position between the god, whose agent he was, and the priestly class, whom he had both to use and to conciliate. Thus, king and priests represented the upper class in a hierarchical society. Below them were the scribes, the secular attendants of the temple, who supervised every aspect of the city's economic life and who developed a rough judicial system. Outside the temple officials, society was divided between an elite or noble group of large landowners and military leaders; a heterogeneous group of merchants, artisans, and craftsmen; free peasants who composed the majority of the population; and slaves.

Temple Oval and Surrounding Walls, Khafaje, Iraq
In most Sumerian cities the temple compound, where the priests lived and worked, was separated from the rest of the city by a high, defensible wall.   Courtesy of the Oriental Institute, University of Chicago

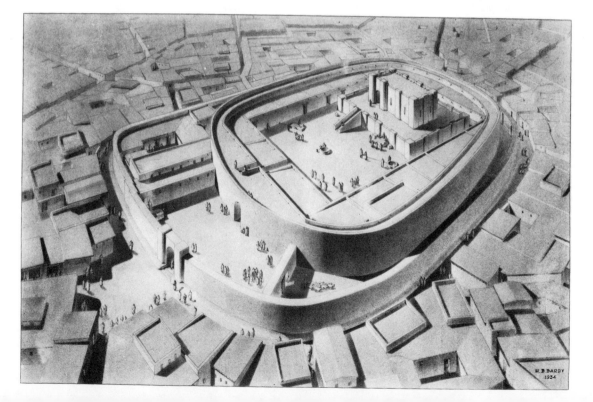

The Sumerian Achievement

The priests and scribes of the temples must be credited with the great advances made by the Sumerians in both arts and science. Following the invention of cuneiform writing, a rich epic literature was created, of which the three most impressive survivals are the story of the creation, an epic of the flood which parallels in many details the Biblical story of Noah, and the *Epic of Gilgamesh*. Gilgamesh, two-thirds god and one-third man, is the classic hero of Mesopotamian literature, a majestic, almost overly powerful figure pressing the gods in vain for the secret of immortality. He is also a great lover of his city Uruk; and throughout the poem we find, perhaps for the first time in literature, the celebration of the appeal of the civilized life of a great city. Gilgamesh, we are told at the start of the poem, has built the great rampart which still today runs seven miles around the ruins of his city:

> *Of ramparted Uruk the wall he built.*
> *Of hallowed Eanna, the pure sanctuary.*
> *Behold its outer wall, whose cornice is like copper.*
> *Peer at the inner wall, which none can equal.*
> *Seize upon the threshold which is of old.*
> *Draw near to Eanna the dwelling of Ishtar*
> *Which no future kin, no man, can equal.*

The Temple of Anu, Uruk
According to Sumerian legend, the great walls of Uruk in the Euphrates valley were built by the mythical hero Gilgamesh. Anu, the sky god, was one of three divinities controlling the universe. Reconstruction from Walter Andrae, *Alte Feststrassen in Nahen Osten* (Leipzig: J. C. Hinrichs Verlag, 1941)

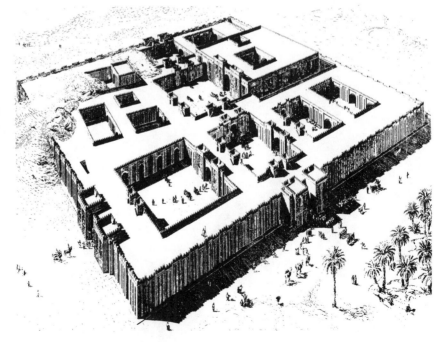

Sumerian Fertility Cult Statuettes
These painted stone fig-ures from a shrine at Tell Asmar probably represent a god and goddess sur-rounded by priests and worshippers.   Courtesy of the Oriental Institute, Uni-versity of Chicago

Go up and walk on the walls of Uruk,
Inspect the base terrace, examine the brickwork:
Is it not the brickwork of burnt brick?
Did not the Seven Sages lay its foundation? [2]

Sculpture, too, advanced to serve the needs of the temples and then of the kings. The earliest statues surviving show bearded figures with wide staring eyes and piously clasped hands who represent some form of fertility cult. Later work in limestone or alabaster shows the female goddess bring-ing water, once again the symbol of fertility, while the achievements of the Akkadian rulers during their brief hegemony are recorded on enormous sandstone tablets. Few portrait busts cast in antiquity rival the expressive dignity of the head of Sargon of Akkad. Even more demanding in artistic technique were the small cylinder seals used to roll one's signature into the wet clay of a tablet recording a commercial transaction. Thousands of these tablets have been found in the temple compounds, proving that the bureau-crats of Sumer had developed a complex commercial system, including con-tracts, grants of credit, loans with interest, and business partnerships. Moreover, the planning of the vast public works under their control led the priests to develop a useful mathematical notation, including both a decimal

Sargon I of Akkad (Reigned c. 2800 B. C.)
The superbly cast bronze head, found at Nineveh, was probably damaged by thieves gouging out gems inset in the eye sockets.
Hirmer Fotoarchiv

[2] James B. Pritchard, ed., *Ancient Near Eastern Texts Relating to the Old Testament* (Princeton: Princeton University Press, 1969), p. 73.

notation and a system based upon 60, which has given us our sixty-second minute, our sixty-minute hour, and our division of the circle into 360 degrees. They invented mathematical tables and used quadratic equations. Both for religious and agricultural purposes, they studied the heavens, and they created a lunar calendar with a day of 24 hours and a week of seven days. Much of this science was transmitted to the West by the Greeks and later by the Arabs. It is not surprising, however, that the achievement which the Sumerians themselves admired most was the city itself.

The Physical Appearance of the Sumerian City

All of the Sumerian cities were built beside rivers, either on the Tigris or Euphrates or on one of their tributaries. The city rose, inside its brown brick walls, amid well-watered gardens and pastures won from the swamps. In all directions, the high levees of the irrigation canals led to grain and vegetable fields. The trading class lived and worked in the harbor area, where the river boats brought such goods as stone, copper, and timber from the north. Most citizens lived within the walls in small, one-story houses constructed along narrow alleyways, although the more elaborate homes were colonnaded and built around an inner courtyard. By far the most impressive section of the city was the temple compound, which was surrounded by its own wall. Here were the workshops and homes of large numbers of temple craftsmen, such as glaziers, jewelers, carpenters, and weavers, the offices and schoolrooms of the scribes, and the commercial and legal offices of the bureaucrat-priests. The king's palace and graveyard was located near the temple; and, as Leonard Woolley's excavations at Ur proved, an increasingly lavish form of ceremonial life was organized here as the kings gained greater control over the city's surplus. Woolley himself described the growing horror his archaeological party felt as they slowly uncovered the royal graves, because they discovered not only elaborate golden daggers, headdresses of gold, lapis lazuli and carnelian, fantastically worked heads of bulls, harps and lyres, sledges and chariots, but also lines of elegantly costumed skeletons laid carefully in rows. In a gigantic mass suicide, probably through the drinking of a drug, the king's courtiers and some of his soldiers had gone to their deaths with their master.

The most elaborate of the Sumerian buildings was the temple or ziggurat. Normally a huge platform or terrace was first constructed, upon which the temple could be built; but in later times, as the terraces grew to be like artificial mountains, they were built in huge steps or levels mounted by an elaborate stairway clearly symbolizing the ascent toward heaven. The purpose of these ziggurats is still unclear. We do know that they were not burial chambers like the pyramids of Egypt, nor were they for human sacrifice like the pyramids of Aztec Mexico. It has been suggested that they were a nostalgic re-creation of the mountains the original settlers had left, or an attempt to raise the city's god above the material life of the streets below, or

an attempt to reach closer to heaven. We do know that the creation of a temple was regarded as a god-imposed task for every ruler of any ambition. Gudea, ruler of Lagash about 2000 B. C., built fifteen large temples with the aid of the gods: "Inscrutable as the sky, the wisdom of the Lord, of Ningirsu, the son of Enlil, will soothe thee," he was told. "He will reveal to thee the plan of His temple, and the Warrior whose decrees are great will build it for thee." The task proved enormous.

> [Gudea] *purified the holy city and encircled it with fires. . . . He collected clay in a very pure place; in a pure place he made with it the brick and put the brick into the mold. He followed the rites in all their splendor: he purified the foundations of the temple, surrounded it with fires, anointed the platform with an aromatic balm. . . .*
>
> *Gudea, the great en-priest of Ningirsu, made a path in the Cedar mountains which nobody had entered before; he cut its cedars with great axes. . . . Like giant snakes, cedars were floating down the water. . . .*
>
> *In the quarries which nobody had entered before, Gudea, the great en-priest of Ningirsu, made a path, and then the stones were delivered in large blocks. . . . Many other precious metals were carried to the ensi. From the Cop-*

Gudea of Lagash (Reigned c. 2000 B. C.)
The pious posture and simple robe emphasize Gudea's conception of his own role as the in-strument of the gods.   The Metropolitan Museum of Art, Harris Brisbane Dick Fund, 1959

per mountain of Kimash . . . its copper was mined in clusters; gold was deliv-ered from its mountains as dust. . . . For Gudea, they mined silver from its mountains, delivered red stone from Meluhha in great amount. . . .

Finally, when the temple was finished, Gudea declared proudly: "Re-spect for the temple pervades the country; the fear of it fills the strangers; the brilliance of the Eninnu enfolds the universe like a mantle." [3]

The Fall of the Sumerian Cities

Around 2000 B. C. both Sumer and Akkad were attacked by barbarian in-vaders. The Amorites from Syria seized control in Akkad, and built a pow-erful new state around the city of Babylon. The Elamites from Iran took the city of Ur, sacked it, and burnt it down. When Ur was later rebuilt under

[3] Cited in Georges Roux, *Ancient Iraq* (London: George Allen and Unwin, 1964), p. 141.

Babylonian rule, its inhabitants remembered with terror the Elamite destruction of their beloved city:

O Father Nanna, that city into ruins was made . . .
Its people, not potsherds, filled its sides;
Its walls were breached; the people groan.
In its lofty gates, where they were wont to promenade, dead bodies were
*   lying about;*
In its boulevards, where the feasts were celebrated, scattered they lay.
In all its streets, where they were wont to promenade, dead bodies were ly-
*   ing about;*
In its places, where the festivities of the land took place, the people lay in
*   heaps . . .*
Ur—its weak and its strong perished through hunger;
Mothers and fathers who did not leave their houses were overcome by fire;
The young, lying on their mothers' laps, like fish were carried off by the
*   waters;*
In the city the wife was abandoned, the son was abandoned, the posses-
*   sions were scattered about. . .*
O Nanna, Ur has been destroyed, its people have been dispersed.[4]

Hammurabi and the Old Babylonian Kingdom

The whole of Mesopotamia was eventually reunited under the Babylonian king Hammurabi (perhaps c. 1792–1750), who in thirty years of war linked together the whole of the Tigris and Euphrates valleys from Assyria to the Persian Gulf. Like Sargon of Akkad, who had united Mesopotamia once before, Hammurabi and his successors accepted and absorbed the civilization of Sumeria. They took the religious myths in their entirety, satisfied merely to insert their own god Marduk as the creator of the world. They accepted the Sumerian form of writing, their mathematics and science, and their forms of art. But in many ways they were more efficient or more ruthless than the Sumerians. The private ownership of land and the individual control of trade and banking begun under the Sumerians was permitted to expand into a system of semi-capitalism. Even the achievement for which Hammurabi is most remembered, his formulation of a written law code, was a working-out of legal precedents established under the Sumerians.

Nevertheless, the law code of Hammurabi is precious to us as the earliest complete system of laws that has survived from antiquity and for the light it throws upon the rules of conduct enforced by the state. The code recognized three different classes, for whom different forms of punishment were prescribed. Punishment was largely by mutilation or death, or occasionally by corporal punishment, and frequently the principle applied was

[4] Pritchard, *Ancient Near Eastern Texts,* pp. 459–60.

to make the criminal suffer identically with his victim. An architect who de-signed a house that collapsed on its owner and killed him was put to death. In many ways, however, the code set out, as Hammurabi claimed, "to de-stroy the wicked and the evil that the strong may not oppress the weak." The rights of women and children were clearly laid down, including many detailed provisions for the rights of woman in divorce cases. Perhaps the most significant feature of the code was that it was set up in a public place so that it was publicly known and thus was proof of the king's determina-tion not to change the law capriciously.

At the end of the stele, Hammurabi added with pride:

> *The laws of justice, which Hammurabi, the efficient king, set up and by which he caused the land to take the right way and have good govern-ment. . . .*
>
> *I made an end of war;*
> *I promoted the welfare of the land;*
> *I made the peoples rest in friendly habitations;*
> *I did not let them have anyone to terrorize them. . . .*
> *My benign shadow is spread over my city.*
> *In my bosom I carried the peoples of the land of Sumer and Akkad. . . .*
> *I am the king who is preeminent among kings;*
> *My words are choice; my ability has no equal.*[5]

The Indo-European Invasions, c. 1750–1500 B. C.

In the eighteenth century B. C. the stability of the Near Eastern states was broken by waves of nomadic invaders who are called Indo-Europeans. These people, whose original home is unknown, had established them-selves in Asia to the north of the Black and Caspian seas by around 2500 B. C. Their languages, although already differentiated, were all offshoots of one common language, which is known as Indo-European, because these languages deriving from the common stock are found all the way from northern India to western Europe. Hence the peoples are called Indo-Eu-ropean because of linguistic and not because of racial affinity. From this original language they were to develop Latin, Greek, Persian, Sanskrit, Cel-tic, the Germanic languages, and the romance languages derived from Latin. In the first wave of invasions (c. 1750–1500 B. C.) they penetrated into the Near East, Greece, northern India, and north Africa. In a second wave, (c. 1200–900 B. C.) they moved into western Europe, Italy, and once again into Greece.

Babylon was sacked about 1600 B. C. by a raiding army of Hittites, an Indo-European people that established a military empire in Asia Minor, western Mesopotamia, and Syria which lasted for almost five hundred years

---

[5] Ibid., pp.177–78.

THE INDO-EUROPEAN LANGUAGES

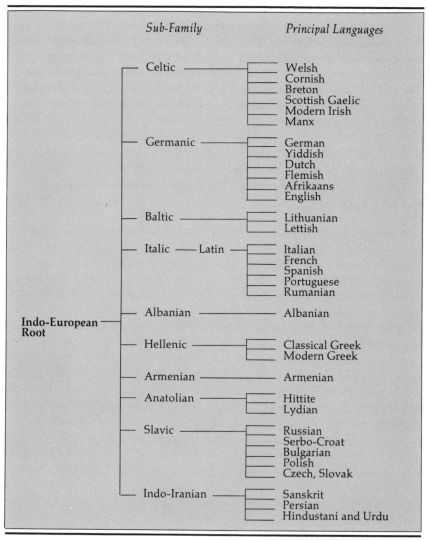

Sub-Family	Principal Languages
Celtic	Welsh, Cornish, Breton, Scottish Gaelic, Modern Irish, Manx
Germanic	German, Yiddish, Dutch, Flemish, Afrikaans, English
Baltic	Lithuanian, Lettish
Italic — Latin	Italian, French, Spanish, Portuguese, Rumanian
Albanian	Albanian
Hellenic	Classical Greek, Modern Greek
Armenian	Armenian
Anatolian	Hittite, Lydian
Slavic	Russian, Serbo-Croat, Bulgarian, Polish, Czech, Slovak
Indo-Iranian	Sanskrit, Persian, Hindustani and Urdu

Indo-European Root

(c. 1700–1200 B. C.). The Hittites were almost completely unknown to historians until 1906 when German archaeologists rediscovered their capital city of Hattusas in Anatolia, a fortified city with two defense walls, huge many-roomed temples, and vast state archives of clay tablets written in cuneiform and hieroglyphics. It was then possible to reconstruct with some exactness the vicissitudes of an empire whose successes were based upon professional military leadership, horsedrawn chariots, iron weapons, and the weakness of their neighbors. But for law, religion, literature, and science the Hittites were satisfied to draw upon the achievements of more creative peoples in

Mesopotamia and Egypt, while exerting little lasting influence of their own. Babylon, weakened by the Hittite attack, was then easily conquered by the Kassite people from Iran, who established a conservative, uncreative rule that lasted more than five hundred years. The period is usually regarded by historians, with some justification, as one of backwardness after the great triumphs of the Sumerian cities. The somnolence of the Kassites, however, was broken with calamitous speed by the rise of Assyria, the most egregiously bloodthirsty of the military empires of the ancient Near East.

Assyria and New Babylonia

The Foundation of Assyrian Power

The Assyrians were a Semitic people who, like the people of Prussia at a later age, seemed destined by geography to become disciplined militarists. Their northern borders were exposed to continual raids from the savage nomads of the high mountains overlooking their valleys. To the south lay the rich and powerful cities of Babylonia and Sumer, against whom no natural barrier could be found on the level plains between the Tigris and Euphrates. To the west the open steppes of Syria, with their trade routes to the Mediterranean and their easy access for invaders, required constant defense over wide distances. As a result, the rulers of Assyria built an autocratic state, based upon a large, highly trained army and an obedient people which, under King Tiglath-Pileser I (c. 1115–1077 B. C.) was able to establish control over northern Syria as far as the Mediterranean. From the start, the secret of Assyrian success was a combination of military preparedness and well-publicized ruthlessness. The armies began their assault with waves of arrows, followed it up with charges of pikemen and cavalry, and completed their conquest with skillfully constructed siege weapons like assault ladders

Storming of Nimrud by Tiglath-Pileser III
Assyrian siege techniques included the use of battering rams, scaling ladders, and massed formations of archers. Prisoners were ruthlessly slaughtered.
Courtesy of the Trustees of the British Museum

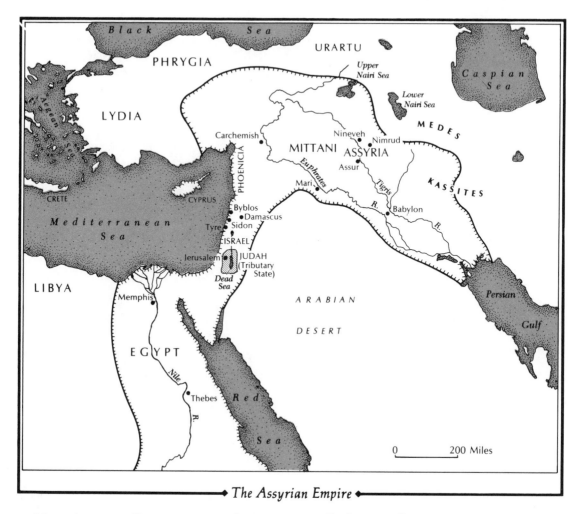

◆ *The Assyrian Empire* ◆

and battering rams. Once a city was taken, it was usually dramatically destroyed, its population tortured and then slaughtered or removed hundreds of miles for resettlement. The policy was carried to its extremes by the later Assyrian conquerors, especially Sennacherib (705–681 B. C.) and Assurbanipal (669–633 B. C.). By the end of the seventh century B. C. the empire of the Assyrians included the whole of the Fertile Crescent and even, for a brief period, Egypt also.

The Cities of the Assyrians

The Assyrians owe it to their own boasting, in their historic annals and in the superb surviving friezes of their palaces, that they are regarded most of all as the destroyers rather than the constructors of cities. Sennacherib was merely embroidering a refrain found again and again for five hundred years

Assyrian Winged Bull
Entrances to the royal palaces in Assyria were lined with terrifying statues of winged bulls or lions with human heads, to create an aura of supernatural power around the monarch.   Courtesy of the Oriental Institute, University of Chicago

of royal self-praise in Assyria, when he described how he destroyed the city of Babylon:

The city and its houses, from its foundation to its top, I destroyed, I devastated, I burned with fire. The wall and the outer wall, temples, and gods, temple towers of brick and earth, as many as they were, I razed and dumped them into the Arakhtu Canal. Through the midst of that city I dug canals, I flooded its site with water, and the very foundations thereof I destroyed. I made its destruction more complete than that by a flood.[6]

Yet the kings of Assyria were almost equally proud of their city-building. One early king, after recording the destruction of a neighboring royal city, noted with equal satisfaction: "At that time I rebuilt the walls of my city Assur from their foundations to the summits." For the Assyrian kings, cities served a double purpose. Provincial cities were the administrative and military centers through which they exerted close control over their subject populations; but their capital cities were themselves part of their enormous propaganda effort to create around themselves an aura of overwhelming power and terror that would weaken their enemies' will to resist. They built successively three capital cities: Assur, Nimrud, and Nineveh. Assur was an

[6] Cited Mumford, *City in History,* p. 68.

old fortress, commanding the upper Tigris; but the Nimrud of Assurnasir-pal II (reigned 884–859 B. C.) and the Nineveh of Sennacherib were each the creation of a single ruler as an expression of his own might. At Nimrud thousands of captives raised a wall five miles in circumference, protected it with a wide canal, and built an artificial hill for the ziggurat and royal palace. According to Assurnasirpal, no expense was spared:

A palace of cedar, cypress, juniper, boxwood, mulberry, pistachio-wood and tamarisk, for my royal dwelling and for my lordly pleasure for all time I founded therein. Beasts of the mountains and of the seas of white limestone and alabaster I fashioned and set them up in its gates. . . . Door-leaves of cedar, cypress, juniper and mulberry I hung in the gates thereof and silver, gold, lead, copper and iron, the spoil of my hand from the lands which I had brought under my sway, in great quantities I took and placed therein.[7]

Sennacherib was even more ambitious. Nineveh's wall was eight miles long, with outer and inner courses broken by fifteen gates, and sheltered a population of 300,000. His palace was decorated with huge pillars of copper resting on bronze lions; the walls were paved with gigantic limestone slabs sculpted with the exploits of the king; and a park filled with flowering bushes and fruit trees freshened the air. About 612 B. C. all the cities of Assyria were destroyed by fire after their armies had been defeated by the Medes, a newly powerful Indo-European people from Iran, allied with the reviving Babylonians.

[7] Cited Roux, *Ancient Iraq*, p. 242.

The Gugurri Gate, Assur
Assur, the first capital of the Assyrians, was founded as a fortress commanding the upper valley of the Tigris river. Etching from Walter Andrae, *Das Wiedererstandene Assur* (Leipzig: J. C. Hinrichs Verlag, 1938), p. 6

The joy of the subject peoples of the Near East at the final overthrow of the savage rule of the Assyrians is most graphically felt in the prediction of the Israelite prophet Nahum of the coming destruction of Nineveh:

And it shall come to pass that all they that look upon thee shall flee from thee, and say, Nineveh is laid waste; who will bemoan her? . . . . The gates of thy land shall be set wide open unto thine enemies; the fire shall devour thy bars . . . . There shall the fire devour thee; the sword shall cut thee off, it shall eat thee up like the cankerworm . . . . Thy shepherds slumber, O king of Assyria: thy nobles shall dwell in the dust: thy people is scattered upon the mountains, and no man gathered them.

There is no healing of thy bruise; thy wound is grievous: all that hear the bruit of thee shall clap the hands over thee: for upon whom hath not thy wickedness passed continually? [8]

The Neo-Babylonian Resurgence, 612–539 B. C.

The Medes left control of Mesopotamia to their Babylonian allies who completed their conquest of the Tigris and Euphrates valleys and of Syria and Palestine. Under King Nebuchadnezzar II (604–562 B. C.), the city of Babylon experienced a rebirth of science, literature, and architecture that was firmly grounded on a basis of economic prosperity. Astronomers discovered several planets, although the greatest effort was devoted to astrology. For example, they divided the sky into twelve parts, and denoted each by one of the signs of the zodiac. However, the most impressive achievement by far, to contemporaries at least, was the rebuilding of the city of Babylon itself. Tales spread by such esteemed writers as the Greek historian Herodotus, with enraptured descriptions of acres of hanging gardens and sky-high towers, were discounted, even by the archaeologists digging in the ruins, until 1902. Then a discouraged German team excavating Babylon made one of archaeology's most spectacular finds, the forty-foot high Ishtar Gate that spanned the Processional Way where the god Marduk was carried into the city at the climax of the New Year festival. The gateway was lined with brightly colored enameled bricks of bulls and dragons, six hundred of which had been placed there at Nebuchadnezzar's orders. With this discovery the magnitude and splendor of the ancient city became credible. Covering 500 acres, the city of 250,000 people was surrounded by a double wall of burnt brick so thick that chariots could pass along its top. The Processional Way was one of the most magnificent streets of antiquity, 63 feet wide and paved with red and white stone. The huge, stepped ziggurat, which was seven stories tall, rose from a base 300 feet wide, and was probably the Biblical Tower of Babel. The palace, referred to euphonically in Babylonian descriptions as "the House, the marvel of mankind, the center

---

[8] Nahum 3:7–19.

of the Land, the shining Residence, the dwelling of Majesty," consisted of five courtyards surrounded by offices and reception rooms. The river facade was terraced, and by use of subterranean waterworks a vast park was created on the rooftops overlooking the Euphrates. This was undoubtedly the famous Hanging Gardens which an Alexandrian historian later called one of the Seven Wonders of the World.

Babylon fell to the armies of Cyrus the Great, ruler of the powerful new Persian empire, in 539 B. c. The following year, Cyrus ended the famous Babylonian Captivity (586–538 B. c.), by returning the Jews to Palestine, from which they had been removed by Nebuchadnezzar. In the 137th Psalm, the Jews had lamented their exile, in the well-known lines: "By the river of Babylon, there we sat down, yea, we wept, when we remembered Zion . . . If I forget thee, O Jerusalem, let my right hand forget her cunning. . . . O daughter of Babylon, who art to be destroyed: happy shall he be, that rewardeth thee as thou hast served us."

The Mediterranean Lands of the Fertile Crescent

The Peoples of Syria and Palestine

The settling and civilizing of the lands in the western part of the Fertile Crescent, that narrow band of valleys and oases that lay between the Eastern Mediterranean Sea and the Syrian desert, lagged hundreds of years behind the progress of Mesopotamia. Topography accounted in part for this delay. In the north the Lebanon and anti-Lebanon mountain ranges provided rugged barriers to east-west travelers. In Palestine, the land rises to 2500 feet above sea level between the Mediterranean and Jerusalem and then plunges to 1290 feet below sea level at the Dead Sea. The soil, though fertile along the valleys of rivers like the Jordan, near the linked oases, and along the coastal plain, lacks the abundant promise of the Sumerian Delta or the Nile valley. Nevertheless, the low hills offered grazing to nomadic tribes, the plains the possibility of agriculture to more sedentary peoples, and the fine harbors of the coast, especially at Tyre and Sidon, an invitation to sea commerce to the west. By the second millenium B. c. the area was being settled by groups of Semitic tribes who had penetrated northwards from the Arabian desert, notably by the Canaanites along the northern coast, by the Aramaeans inland, and somewhat later by the Hebrew tribes.

Apart from Biblical references the Canaanites were little known until 1928, when archaeologists discovered the city of Ugarit at Ras Shamra on the northern coast of Syria. They found a royal palace of some sixty rooms covering 9000 square yards, and best of all the royal archives that gave proof that in the fifteenth and fourteenth centuries B. c. Ugarit was a powerful, prosperous state with close ties to the Hittites and the Egyptians. Far

◆ *Palestine in the 9th Century* B.C. ◆

more important for the development of Western civilization, however, was the contribution of the Phoenicians, who were descendants of the original Canaanite peoples. By about 1000 B. C., in the area of present-day Lebanon, the Phoenicians had founded a great trading empire, based upon export of cedar, glass, and woven cloth dyed purple. Their skill at navigation enabled them to explore the Mediterranean and then, in feats unparalleled until the Portuguese voyages of the fifteenth century, to sail past Gibralter up the coasts of Spain and Africa and perhaps even to southern Britain and to the Azores. They founded important colonies, both to advance their trade and to create an outlet for their excess population, at Palermo in Sicily, Cadiz in Spain, and especially Carthage in North Africa. They thus made a network of trade routes that acted as a stimulant to the growth of the economy of many other Mediterranean peoples, including the Greeks and Romans. Although the prophet Ezekiel predicted the fall of Tyre, he showed remarkable admiration of its achievement:

Thy borders are in the midst of the seas, thy builders have perfected thy beauty.

They have made all thy ship boards of fir trees of Senir: they have taken cedars from Lebanon to make masts for thee. . . .

Syria was thy merchant by reason of the multitude of the wares of thy making: they occupied in thy fairs with emeralds, purple, and broidered work, and fine linen, and coral and agate. . . .

The ships of Tarshish did sing of thee in thy market: and thou wast replenished, and made very glorious in the midst of the seas.[9]

Nevertheless the most lasting achievement of the Phoenicians was their adoption from the north Canaanites of the alphabet, which they apparently found necessary to handle the vast volume of their commercial transactions but which proved equally suitable for expressing abstract or scientific thought as well. They broke with the Babylonian cuneiform writing, which was in use throughout the Near East, because it required hundreds of symbols, each symbol representing only one word or syllable. Instead they used twenty-nine and later only twenty-two signs which represented consonants. Vowel signs had to be supplied by the reader from the context. The Phoenician traders carried their alphabet throughout the Mediterranean, the Greeks adopting it from them, but substituting five Phoenician consonantal signs as vowel signs.

The Aramaeans established an inland trading network that stretched from their principal city of Damascus as far east as India. They exercised an influence in the East similar to that of the Canaanites in the West because their traders brought to that area a common system of weights and measures, their alphabet and their language. Aramaic was widely used throughout the Near East as a kind of lingua franca, not least by the Hebrews. Part of the Old Testament was written in Aramaic, and Jesus himself spoke the language.

[9] Ezekiel 27:4–5, 16, 25.

ANCIENT ISRAEL

EVENTS IN BIBLICAL TRADITION

c. 1950	Abraham brings family tribe from Ur into Palestine; Covenant with Jehovah
c. 1600	Hebrew tribes migrate to Egypt
c. 1570–c. 1350	"Bondage" in Egypt
c. 1350–1310	Moses leads Exodus into Sinai; Ten Commandments
c. 1300	Under Joshua, Hebrews penetrate into Palestine, capture Jericho
c. 1300–1020	Rule of "Judges"

HISTORICALLY ESTABLISHED EVENTS

1020–1005	Union of Hebrew tribes under Saul
c. 1005–965	Reign of King David
c. 965–925	Reign of King Solomon; building of temple in Jerusalem
c. 925	Division of kingdom into Israel (capital Samaria) and Judah (capital Jerusalem)
722	Assyrians capture Israel
586	New Babylonian conquest of Judah
586–538	Babylonian Captivity
538	Persian king Cyrus permits Hebrews to return to Palestine
A. D. 70	Sack of Jerusalem by Roman Emperor Titus

The Political History of the Hebrews, c. 2000–539 B. C.

The early history of the Hebrews is based upon the traditional stories preserved in the Old Testament, and modern archaeological discoveries have shown many of these legends to be factually accurate within certain chronological limitations. The Semitic tribes whom the Bible calls Hebrews were nomads who, around 2000 B. C., were scattered around the edges of the Arabian desert and in the Tigris and Euphrates valleys. According to Biblical legend, Abraham led his family to find a new home, after the destruction of the Sumerian city of Ur by the Elamites. Before going, he made the first covenant of Israel with its god and received the promise of future greatness for his people: "I will make of thee a great nation, and I will bless thee, and make thy name great; and be thou a blessing: and I will bless them that bless thee, and him that curseth thee will I curse."

Abraham settled in Palestine, and there his grandson Jacob's twelve sons founded the twelve tribes of Israel. By about 1600 B. C. some of these tribes had wandered into Egypt, where the reviving Egyptian monarchy brought all foreigners living there into virtual slavery after about 1570 B. C. The bondage was ended when the Hebrew tribes followed Moses into the Sinai desert in c. 1350 B. C., where God renewed his convenant with his chosen people by handing them the tablets containing the Ten Commandments. Only under Moses's successor Joshua were these Hebrews able to fight their way back into Palestine, which recent research shows had been infiltrated for several centuries by Hebrew pastoral nomads from the bordering deserts. Joshua's followers established a loose tribal federation with a religious center at Shiloh where their "holy ark" containing the tablets of the Ten Commandments was kept. Here they found themselves under constant attack by the Philistines, one of the so-called "Sea Peoples" that had been marauding throughout the eastern Mediterranean since about 1200 B. C. The Philistines had settled permanently on the southern coast of Palestine, which owes its name to their state of Palesit; and from their flourishing cities of Gaza, Ashkelon, and Ashdod, they traded with the Aegean cities and made war on the Hebrews. The temporary military leaders called Judges whom the Hebrews appointed to hold off these raids were ineffective, and the fiercely independent Hebrew tribes resigned themselves to banding together under a king for their mutual defense. The first king, Saul (reigned c. 1020–1005), after bringing the tribes into some kind of organized cooperation, was described in the Bible as turning pathologically moody and suspicious. After Saul's death in battle with the Philistines, David succeeded him as king, defeated the Philistines, captured Jerusalem, and built there a new capital city.

The Jerusalem of David and Solomon

The period of the rule of David (reigned 1005–965 B. C.) and his son Solomon (965–925 B. C.) is regarded as the golden age of the Hebrew kingdom. David had brought peace, based upon the combination of military force and treaties of friendship with neighboring states. He built a small but effective bureaucracy, which helped end the old tribalism; and he governed within the limits laid down by a kind of federal constitution. The economy was bolstered by close ties with Tyre, and by the export of copper from mines at Aqaba. To consolidate this kingdom, David planned to make of Jerusalem not only the Hebrew administrative and religious capital but also a symbol of their union as a people that would bind them together emotionally for all time.

The city that David took from the Jebusites was a small, rough fortress with few urban pretensions, but it commanded the only north-south route through the inland hills of Palestine. Located in a neutral position between the quarreling northern and southern tribes of Hebrews, it was ideally positioned as a seat of the unifying administration that David created. After strengthening the city's fortifications, David brought into Jerusalem royal officials rather than the heads of the tribes to act as the tribal representatives to the royal government; and he strengthened the royal control through increased taxation based upon an accurate census. A small permanent army, with professional officer corps, was also stationed in Jerusalem under the king's direct command. To house his new court bureaucracy, David constructed a few buildings and began a palace with the help of men

Jerusalem
The Moslem Dome of the Rock, built in the seventh century, stands on the foundation terrace, on which Solomon's Temple had originally been built.

The Wailing Wall, Jerusalem
Jews bewail the Roman destruction of the Temple in A. D. 70 at the Wailing Wall, the only remaining part of the foundation of the Temple Mount begun by Solomon and extended by Herod in the first century B. C.

and materials supplied by the neighboring ruler of Tyre. Here he led the exciting life of loves, violence, cunning, grandeur, and repentance that made him one of the most human characters portrayed in ancient chronicles. The description of David in the Bible (II Samuel 18:33) is at its most moving when the king laments over the death of his son Absalom who has led a revolt against him: "And the king was much moved, and went up to the chamber over the gate, and wept: and as he went, thus he said, O my son Absalom, my son, my son Absalom! would God I had died for thee, O Absalom, my son, my son!"

By far the most important monument was to be the national shrine of the Temple, which was to house the Ark of the Covenant and centralize in the royal capital the worship of the Hebrew's god Jehovah. David is credited with forming a special priesthood for the Temple, laying down the order of the Temple services, and enlisting musical guilds for the worship. But he made little progress on the Temple, which was almost entirely to be the work of his son Solomon.

Solomon had grandiose ideas of kingship, and he drew unstintingly on the new riches of his people. According to I Kings 9:15, he paid for the building program with a one-time tax or levy: "And this is the reason of the levy which king Solomon raised; for to build the house of the Lord, and his own house, and Millo, and the wall of Jerusalem, and Hazor, and Megiddo, and Gezer." As the site of the temple, a huge stone platform was built on the northwestern edge of the city; and on it was erected a stone-dressed temple of simple design, comprising one main hall, three side temples, and a rear room for the Holy of Holies. Turning again to Tyre for help with cedar and carpenters, Solomon lavished vast wealth upon the interior decoration. All has disappeared, but the biblical detail in I Kings 5–7 and II Chronicles 2–4 is long and explicit. The chronicler describes a temple lined throughout with cedar of Lebanon, over which a layer of gold had been placed. The Holy of Holies contained two cherubims of olive wood, fifteen feet high, while the main hall had huge bronze pillars with intricate capitals, basins of bright brass, and candlesticks, lamps, tongs, and even door hinges in gold. For the dedication ceremony, the elders of all the tribes were assembled to see the Ark brought to its resting place, and Solomon declared in prayer: "I have surely built thee an house to dwell in, a settled place for thee to abide in for ever."

Solomon's palace, built on a similar munificent scale, took thirteen years to complete, and he built yet another palace for his principal wife, the daughter of the Egyptian Pharaoh. But the cost of these programs had to be borne largely by the small farmers who comprised the majority of the population. Forced labor and high taxes as well as growing corruption in the bureaucracy provoked disaffection among the northern tribes, even during the reign of Solomon. After his death, the kingdom broke apart. The ten northern tribes established their own kingdom of Israel with its capital at Samaria; the two southern tribes formed the kingdom of Judah with Jerusa-

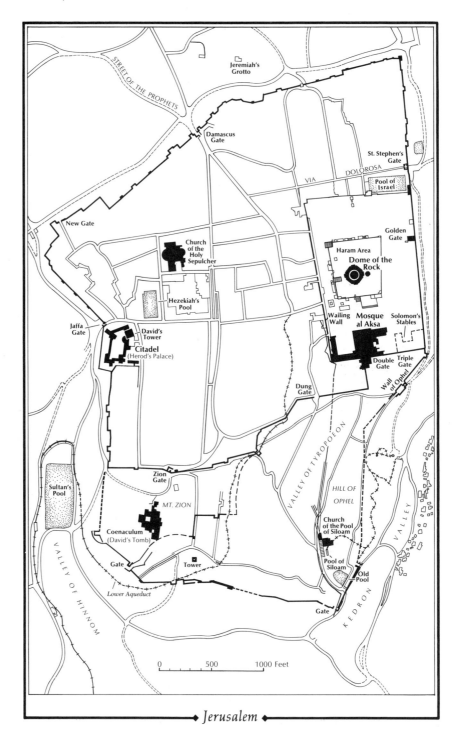

◆ *Jerusalem* ◆

lem as capital. Neither Israel nor Judah alone enjoyed power or prosperity for long. Israel fell to the Assyrians in 722 B. C. Jerusalem was captured by Nebuchadnezzar in 586 B. C., its temple and fortifications razed, and the major part of the population deported to Babylon.

Although Cyrus of Persia permitted the return of the Hebrews to Jerusalem from Babylon in 538 B. C., they remained under Persian rule for two centuries. Then in the third century B. C., after Alexander the Great of Macedon had defeated the Persians, the Hebrews passed under Greek rule for a further two centuries. After a century of independence under the Maccabees, the Hebrews passed first under the influence and then under the direct rule of Rome. A series of revolts against Roman rule culminated in the unsuccessful rebellion of A. D. 70, in which Jerusalem was besieged by a Roman army under the Emperor Titus for five months. After the last frantic resistance was overcome, the Romans burned the Temple, and then systematically sacked and burned the rest of the city. Titus carried back to Rome the sacred furnishings of the Temple, including the seven-branched candlestick, which he displayed in his triumphal procession. As a result of the political troubles of these five hundred years, many Hebrews had already been driven out or had voluntarily left Palestine, thus beginning the dispersion or *Diaspora* of the Hebrews. After the revolt of A. D. 70, large numbers of Hebrews were forcibly removed to other parts of the Roman empire. In A. D. 135, the Emperor Hadrian determined to obliterate Jerusalem as a Jewish city, and thus to end its sacred role in Hebrew aspirations, by building upon the site a totally new Roman city called Aelia Capitolina, with a temple of Jupiter Capitolinus on the foundations of the Hebrew temple. A vast Hebrew uprising was savagely suppressed, and half a million Jews may have been killed.

The Hebrew Religious Tradition

Throughout this troubled history, and especially following their dispersion, the Hebrews drew continually for inspiration and unity upon their distinctive religious faith. Those teachings, contained in the Old Testament of the Bible, played a vital role in the spiritual, moral, and even literary development of Western civilization and, as accepted by Mohammed, influenced to a lesser degree those peoples who worship in the Moslem religion.

During their nomadic wanderings, the Hebrews distinguished themselves from their neighbors by recognizing the existence of one God only, in the doctrine of monotheism, which was coupled with a strong insistence upon a set of moral precepts laid down by God or Yahweh. These ideas are embodied in the Ten Commandments or Decalogue traditionally assumed to have been handed to Moses upon two stone tablets that were henceforth kept in an oblong chest known as the Ark of the Covenant. This god was not to be represented in any physical form, a prohibition that prevented the

Hebrews from developing any type of artistic tradition in painting or sculpture. When the Hebrews first settled in Palestine, a priestly class, drawn from the tribe of Levi, administered religious festivals deriving from their past experiences: Passover, when lambs were sacrificed and unleavened bread eaten in memory of the flight from Egypt; the Feast of Weeks, to celebrate the grain harvest; the Feast of Tabernacles, the vintage; and, most solemn of all, the expiatory fast of Yom Kippur, on the tenth day of the Hebrew New Year. The emphasis on the ritual observance of these festivals as part of the Hebrew fulfilment of the Covenant of the Chosen People with Yahweh acted as a social cement.

During the period of the divided monarchy and especially at the time of the Babylonian Captivity, the prophetic movement reached its most subtle form. Where the priests stood for respect for form, the prophets called for moral regeneration. They unswervingly called kings to repentance, reminding them of a higher law then their own. They told the Hebrews that their sufferings were inflicted upon them, not by their conquerors but by God, who was merely using the Assyrians or the Babylonians as his instruments, to bring his people back from sin. And they emphasized that God would maintain the covenant throughout their tribulations and eventually restore a golden age. Finally, in a prophecy critical for the development of Christianity, the prophets foretold the coming of a Messiah or savior from the family of David: "And the spirit of the Lord shall rest upon him, the spirit of wisdom and understanding, the spirit of counsel and might, the spirit of knowledge and the fear of the Lord. . . . And he shall set up an ensign for the nations, and shall assemble the outcasts of Israel, and gather together the dispersed of Judah from the four corners of the earth." (Isaiah 11:2, 12)

The Civilization of the Egyptians

The Valley of the Nile

The territory of Egypt, or at least its habitable portion, had the most unusual shape of any country of the ancient world. Its southern stretch, called Upper Egypt, was a strip of fertile land between the First Cataract at Aswan and the beginning of the Nile Delta just north of present-day Cairo, six hundred miles long but never more than thirteen miles wide. Lower Egypt comprised the flat, marshy plains of the Delta where the Nile split into seven branches as it meandered to the Mediterranean. Lower Egypt was less than 150 miles in length, but contained twice as much cultivable land as Upper Egypt. The fertility of the "Black Land" of Upper Egypt was dependent upon the annual floods of the Nile, which was fed by the tropical rain-

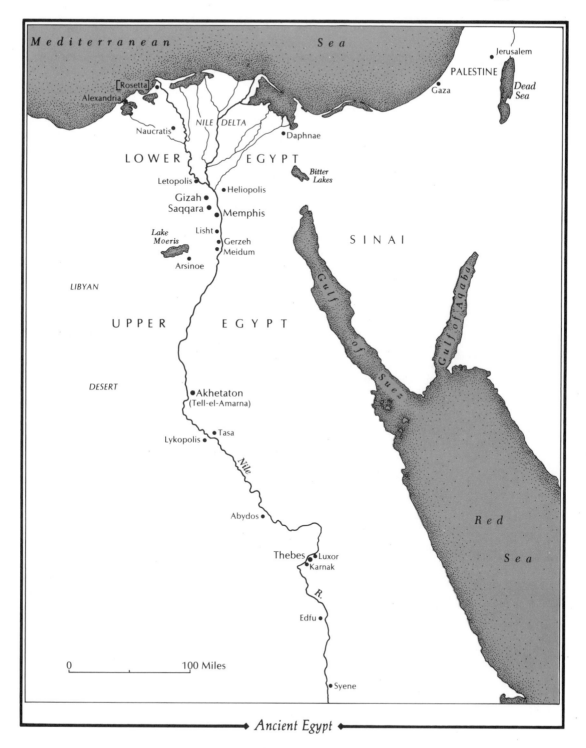

Mediterranean   Sea

Jerusalem

[Rosetta]

PALESTINE

Alexandria   Dead
                                         Sea

Gaza

Naucratis   NILE DELTA

LOWER   EGYPT   Daphnae

Letopolis

Bitter
Lakes

Gizah   Heliopolis

Saqqara   Memphis   S I N A I

Lisht

Lake   Gerzeh
Moeris   Meidum

Arsinoe

LIBYAN

UPPER   EGYPT

Gulf of Suez   Gulf of Aqaba

DESERT

Akhetaton
(Tell-el-Amarna)

Tasa
Lykopolis

Nile

Abydos   Red

Thebes   Luxor   Sea
         Karnak

R.

Edfu

0   100 Miles

Syene

◆ *Ancient Egypt* ◆

fall of regions over a thousand miles to the south of Aswan but, as in Sumeria, these floods could only be utilized through canals and dykes requiring organized human labor. The Delta by contrast required drainage works only.

This elongated state was sheltered from invasion by the Libyan desert to the west which, in ancient times, supported a thin population of nomads and shepherds, and by the harsher Arabian desert to the east. In the north the salt ponds and mud flats of the Delta were an equally effective barrier. In their isolation, the Egyptians were proud of their superiority over their neighbors, whom they habitually despised. They felt that their gods had given them a land which satisfied almost all their wants. For food they had the native barley and rough wheat, lentils, beans, onions, cucumbers, dates, figs, and grapes. They loved beef from their domesticated African cattle but also kept pigs, goats, and sheep and hunted wild duck and geese. Even in their stone, they saw a cause for pride, their quarries in the hills near the river supplying them with limestone for the pyramids, sandstone for the temples of the later dynasties, red granite, and especially alabaster and diorite. In the eastern desert they had large quantities of gold available to them. Only wood was lacking, and convoys were forced to seek cedar and pine from the forests of Lebanon. Indeed it seemed at times that the main internal problem of the Egyptians was to maintain a harmonious relationship between the Delta and the valley; and for that a powerful ruler was the obvious solution.

The Archaic Age, c. 3100–2700 B. C.; The Old Kingdom, 2700–2181 B. C.

The excavations at Jericho and other Neolithic sites in Mesopotamia have indicated that city life may have begun earlier in Mesopotamia than in Egypt, although some experts have disputed this finding. Nevertheless, we are sure that in Egypt the transition from hunting and food gathering to settled agriculture was complete by at least 3300 B. C., by which time the whole valley had been divided into agricultural districts called *nomes* and loosely organized into the confederations of Upper and Lower Egypt. Around 3100 B. C. a conqueror named Menes from Upper Egypt succeeded in unifying the two regions. He established a new capital city at Memphis, on the southern edge of the Delta, and called himself King of Upper and Lower Egypt. (The title of pharaoh, which means "great house," was not used until the fifteenth century B. C.) The first four dynasties, who controlled Egypt during the formative period of its civilization, are rather artificially divided into an Archaic Period (c. 3100–2700 B. C.) and an Old Kingdom (c. 2700–2181 B. C.) Those rulers forged a form of religion, politics, social life, and cultural expression that lasted with little profound change for almost three thousand years.

Religion was central to all Egyptian life. Many gods were worshipped, some of them deriving from the Neolithic times when animal figures were

Funeral Stele of Lady Nofert
In this grave carving from the mid-third millenium, found at Giza, the wife of a leading nobleman sits before an offering stand containing loaves of bread.   Lowie Museum of Anthropology, University of California, Berkeley

worshipped as totems and when gods were associated with specific geographic locations. Horus, always represented as a human body with a falcon head, was the god of the western Delta, for example. Others took human form. Osiris was the god of agriculture. But he also represented the cycle of death and resurrection, seen in the fall of the Nile waters and their replenishment in the spring with the new floods, and his role developed until he was also judge of the resurrected souls in the afterlife. Re, whose temple was the center of an important cult at Heliopolis, was the Sun-God; and his attributes and name were later compounded with those of Amun, the god of Thebes in Upper Egypt, to become Amun-Re. The pharaoh was himself regarded as a god and not, as in Mesopotamia, an agent of the gods. Egypt was his personal possession; but in his actions as a god he expressed the harmony, or *ma'at*, of this basically just universe.

Above all, the Egyptians believed that the soul or *ka* of a dead person returns periodically to the body after the judgment is completed, to enjoy again the material life that it had known on earth. For this reason, the pharaoh and later the wealthier nobles, too, ensured that the body would be ready to receive the *ka* by embalming it and burying it in several coffins in a hidden burial chamber in a sealed tomb. Within the burial chamber were placed all the necessities of life, including tables, chairs, beds, clothing, jewels, food, wine, cosmetics, and weapons. At first dead servants and then later models of courtiers, workers, and boatmen were buried with the pharaoh, while the walls were decorated with engravings and paintings illustrating the religious myths, the exploits of his reign, and joyful scenes of daily life. Curiously, none of this appears morbid. It is rather a determination to continue to enjoy in the afterlife those pleasures, of work and play, that were delightful in this life.

These tombs became more elaborate under the Old Kingdom, and absorbed an increasing share of the labor and wealth of the country. While the buildings, even the palaces, for the living in all the great cities of Egypt were built of mud-bricks and have vanished, the tombs for the dead and the temples for the gods were built of the hardest stone. The most impressive of all Egyptian monuments were the great series of pyramids built by the pharaohs of the Fourth Dynasty between about 2650 and 2500 B. C. The first of the great pyramids was the Step Pyramid at Saqqara, designed by the Chancellor Imhotep who is credited with being the first architect in Egypt to build entirely in stone. The greatest height of any pyramid was reached in the Great Pyramid of Khufu (often called Cheops) at Gizah, completed about 2600 B. C., which reached the height of 481 feet. It was built of over two million limestone blocks, some of them weighing up to 15 tons, by conscripted workers, whose numbers have been estimated by different sources to have been as few as 2500 and as many as 100,000.

Inside these gigantic tombs and in the temples and vestibules that adjoined them, artists and sculptors depicted scenes of the public and private

(Below) **Nile River Boat** *This form of vessel was traditionally used in the funerary voyage to and from the sanctuary of Osiris at Abydos. A model of the boat was buried in the tomb, because without a boat the spirit might be barred from eternal life.* Lowie Museum of Anthropology, University of California, Berkeley

(Opposite Page) **A Hunting Expedition Along the Nile** *Ti, a royal overseer of the Old Kingdom, is portrayed hunting by boat beneath overhanging trees filled with wild fowl.* Hirmer Fotoarchiv

A Herdsman and His Cattle
Slaves, often from conquered territories to the south of the settled areas of the Nile, worked the great farming estates for the Egyptian aristocracy, as in this scene from the tomb of the royal overseer Ti in Saqqara.
Copyright 1958 by Hirmer Verlag Munchen

life of the pharaoh and his people with extraordinary vivacity and variety. The most elaborate statues were of the pharaoh himself. He was depicted in painted wood and precious metals on one or more of the interlocking coffins in which his mummified body was placed, and also in stone either seated on his throne or standing to look through eyeholes cut from the wall of the tomb into the adjacent room where the funeral offerings were laid out. Although the sculptors were compelled to work within strict stylistic conventions for the poses permitted in representations of gods or pharaohs, nevertheless they attained a skill in the presentation of personality traits that endured for more than two thousand years. Less inhibited by convention, the artists who presented the scenes of daily life in bas-relief or wall painting achieved a sense of delight which is only to be compared with the great Etruscan tombs (see pp. 140–42). There are realistic scenes of boatmen fighting with their poles, while the hieroglyphics, like a modern cartoon, call out slang expressions like "Slosh him." Animals appear frequently, not the dying lions of the Assyrian friezes but soulful asses, newborn calves carried on a drover's back, or geese fluttering through the reeds of the Nile bank. Musicians and acrobats recall past—and, it was implied, future—pleasures in a world strewn with flowers. It is this sense of joy in living that so amazes the visitor to the tombs of the dead and imparts to Egyptian civilization a sense of humanity that links them immediately with the Greeks.

The Middle Kingdom, c. 2050–1786 B. C.

The stability of the Old Kingdom broke down during the so-called First Intermediate Period (c. 2181–2050 B. C.). The excessive expenditures of the pharaohs on their tombs and funerary temples reduced their revenues and as a result their power, and they were compelled to buy support from the priestly class by ever more generous land grants and from the nobility by decentralizing power. Chaos followed, during which the literature shows that the poorer classes suffered greatly. In the complaint of the writer Ipuwer, the confusion seems universal:

Why really! The desert is spread throughout the land. The nomes [provinces] are destroyed. Barbarians from outside have come to Egypt.

Why really! Laughter has disappeared, and is no longer made. It is wailing that pervades the land, mixed with lamentation . . .

Why really! The ways are not guarded roads. Men sit in the bushes until the benighted traveler comes, to take away his burden and steal what is on him . . . Ah, would that it were the end of men, no conception, no birth! Then the earth would cease from noise, without wrangling![10]

Prosperity was restored by the pharaohs of the Middle Kingdom (c. 2050–1786) who enforced their rule from their new capital city of Thebes in Upper Egypt. Tough, ruthless, and expansionist, they not only brought the local provincial rulers in Egypt back under their control but also sent their armies to the South into Nubia and across Sinai into Syria as well. With the empire cowed and exploited, they created a new center of royal power in the Fayum region of the Nile, just south of the Delta. Here huge irrigation works created a flourishing agricultural region where another capital, Lisht, was built. All the arts that had flourished in the Old Kingdom were revived to decorate the tombs of the new dynasties of pharaohs, and once again Egyptians rejoiced in the love of their land. One papyrus fragment remarkably preserved tells the story of the nobleman Sinuhe who, after years in exile, was permitted to return to receive the greatest blessing any Egyptian could hope for, the welcome of the pharaoh himself and provision of a tomb to prepare for the afterlife:

Gilded Mummy Mask, Probably from Middle Kingdom   Lowie Museum of Anthropology, University of California, Berkeley

And there was constructed for me a pyramid out of stone within the precinct of the pyramids. The chief architect began the building of it, the painter designed in it, the master-sculptor carved in it, the master-builders of the necropolis bus-

[10] Pritchard, *Ancient Near Eastern Texts*, pp. 441–442.

ied themselves with it. . . . And my statue was overlaid with gold and its apron was of fine gold. It was his majesty who caused it to be made. There is no humble man for whom the like had been done.[11]

The Middle Kingdom was destroyed by invaders from Asia known as the Hyksos, or "shepherd kings," who controlled Egypt during the Second Intermediate Period (c. 1786–1550), although the extent of their power is disputed among scholars. The Hyksos had been able to conquer Egypt by use of the horse, the war-chariot, and the long-range bow; but eventually the rulers of Thebes were able to adopt these weapons themselves and to drive out the Hyksos. The pharaohs of Thebes quickly consolidated their own power, and brought Egypt four hundred years of effective government during the New Kingdom.

Thebes, Capital of the New Kingdom (c. 1550–1090 B. C.)

During the New Kingdom, Egyptian civilization reached its greatest vigor and variety and, perhaps for the first time Egyptian cities, notably Thebes and Amarna, rivaled in splendor those of Mesopotamia. Once more the Egyptian empire was extended to Palestine and Syria and south into Nubia, and tribute was exacted from the conquered provinces. Trade flourished, bringing into Egypt luxuries from all the surrounding lands of Europe and Asia.

The wealth of this empire was poured into the great capital city of Thebes, which expanded from a rural town into a metropolis. Its inhabitants were convinced that it was the greatest city in the world, the standard of comparison by which all other cities would be judged. They called it Waset, or the City of Amun, but usually simply called it "The City." A very long poem in the praise of Thebes "the Mistress of every city" has survived:

> *Waset (Thebes) is the pattern for every city.*
> *Both the flood and the earth were in her from the beginning of time.*
> *The sands came to delimit her soil,*
> *To create her ground upon the mound when earth came into being.*
> *Then mankind came into being within her,*
> *To found every city in her true name (The City),*
> *Since all are called "city"*
> *After the example of Waset.*[12]

---

[11] Adolf Erman, ed., *The Ancient Egyptians: A Sourcebook of Their Writings* (New York: Harper and Row, 1966), pp. 28–29.

[12] Cited Charles F. Nims, *Thebes of the Pharaohs: Pattern for Every City* (New York: Stein and Day, 1965), p. 69.

Temple of Amun, Karnak
The entrance to the great temple is flanked to the left by the obelisk of the Pharoah Thutmose I and to the right by the obelisk of Queen Hatshepsut.   Hirmer Fotoarchiv

Although Thebes was continually embellished for hundreds of years by the different pharaohs, three rulers stand out for leaving their indelible imprints on the city. Queen Hatshepsut (c. 1504–1482 B. C.) was one of the most remarkable women in Egyptian history. Named regent for her stepson, she took power herself, claimed that she was the son of the god Amun, and had herself crowned king. She picked skillful advisers and excellent

(Right) **Tomb of Queen Hatshepsut, Thebes** *The elaborate tomb, with side chapels for the worship of the queen and her ancestors, was cut into the cliffs of the west bank of the Nile.* Hirmer Fotoarchiv

(Below) **Queen Hatshepsut** *After seizing power, Hatshepsut took the title of king and had herself portrayed in the traditional pose and costume of a male ruler.* The Metropolitan Museum of Art, Rogers Fund and contributions from Edward S. Harkness, 1929

generals, using the wealth her army's conquests sent to Thebes to build a vast funeral temple in the cliffs on the western side of the river. Rising in two stepped terraces from the river valley, the temple cut deeply into the rock walls, providing room after room where painters and sculptors extolled the glories of her reign. On the right bank, where the main city of Thebes was situated, she continued the embellishment of the great temple of Amun at Karnak which was the principal center of worship and religious festivals. Her stepson Thutmose III showed his hatred for Hatshepsut by defacing her name on all the monuments she had erected, and by walling in at roof height the two huge obelisks she had brought to the Karnak temple. His own obelisks have suffered a different fate. Of the two he erected in Heliopolis, one is in New York's Central Park, the other on the river embankment in London; the two he erected in Thebes are now in Rome and Constantinople.

The wealth that Thutmose's conquests in Asia brought to Thebes is proven by the sumptuousness of the tombs of his officials which surrounded the royal tombs in the Valley of the Kings. The third great builder in Thebes was Amunhotep III (c. 1473–1379), who created a new temple complex for the god Amun at Luxor, which he joined to the temple of Karnak with a mile-long road lined on each side with statues of rams between whose legs the king is standing. The king's taste for the grandiose reached extravagant proportions. On the west bank, he raised two seventy-foot high statues in front of his funerary temple, the so-called Colossi of Memnon; the fingers alone are over four feet long. A new palace built in the necropolis covered eighty acres. His tomb nearby was so large that it was never finished.

When Pharaoh Amunhotep IV adopted monotheism, he found it necessary first to break the power of the priests. He declared that there was only one god, Aton or the solar disc, and that all other gods must be repudiated.

Tomb of Djeserkareseneb, Thebes
The daughters of a high bureaucrat are presenting him with a decorative neckband and a bowl of liquor.   Hirmer Fotoarchiv

Temple of Amun, Karnak
Later additions to the temple, at the end of the New Kingdom, were overwhelmingly massive in scale and style, as in this entrance hall of the Pharaoh Sethos I (reigned 1312–1298 B. C.*).* Hirmer Fotoarchiv

He changed his own name to Akhenaton, which meant "Pleasing to Aton," and celebrated Aton's glory in the beautiful hymn:

Thou appearest beautifully on the horizon of heaven,
Thou living Aton, the beginning of life! . . .
At daybreak, when thou arisest on the horizon,
When thou shinest as the Aton by day,
Thou drivest away the darkness and givest thy rays . . .
Trees and plants are flourishing . . .

The ships are sailing north and south as well,
For every way is open at thy appearance.
The fish in the river dart before thy face;
Thy rays are in the midst of the great green sea . . .
O sole god, like whom there is no other.[13]

Like the Roman Emperor Constantine and the Russian Tsar Peter the Great, he decided to abandon his capital city where the old ways and vested interests would oppose his revolution in his country's way of life. Further north on the Nile he created a new capital city called Tell-el-Amarna, with two royal palaces, a temple to Aton, and quarters for bureaucrats and merchants. This city flourished only during the reign of Akhenaton, with the result that its well-preserved remains have given much evidence of city planning in ancient Egypt. His successor Tutenkhamen returned to Thebes and to the worship of the traditional gods. His unlooted tomb, discovered in 1922, provided graphic proof of the luxury of life in the restored capital.

Egyptian power lasted only two more centuries after the disruption caused by Akhenaton's experiment with monotheism. Under the pressure of the second wave of Indo-European invaders (c. 1200–900 B.C.), the Egyptians were forced to retreat from Asia. The kingdom broke apart once more in 1085 B.C., and then for a thousand years Egypt passed almost continuously under the rule of one foreign conqueror after another—first the Assyrians, then the Persians, then the Greeks under Alexander of Macedon, and finally the Romans.

The Achievement of the Ancient Near East

The ancient Near East played a vitally important role in the transmission of civilization to the West. As a result of the Neolithic revolution, the practice of agriculture was brought to Europe, possibly in three distinct currents of migration through Turkey and Russia, Greece and the Danube valley, and the southern Mediterranean coast, between about 6000 and 3000 B.C. Metallurgy reached eastern Europe by 2500 B.C., after which the use of copper and bronze spread gradually westwards. The use of iron reached Europe about 750 B.C.

Most of the Near East's achievements were passed into the civilization of the West through intermediaries, however. The clearest example is the religious tradition of the Hebrews, which exerted its greatest influence with the Christianization of the Roman Empire. The alphabet developed by the Phoenicians was made far more serviceable by the Greeks, with their addition of vowels to the consonants that the Phoenicians had developed. The

[13] Pritchard, *Ancient Near Eastern Texts,* p. 370.

monumental sculpture and the massive architecture of pillar and lintel created by the Egyptians were absorbed by the Greeks who made it infinitely more flexible and expressive. The commercial achievements of the Sumerians and the later cities of Mesopotamia, with their concomitant advances in science and mathematics, had to be taken up by the Phoenicians and by the Persians before they could be brought to the West. Above all, the unique capacity of the city for the mobilization of human talent had been conclusively demonstrated. In the Greek city-state that capacity was soon to be turned to the creative development of the individual.

SUGGESTED READING

The study of human development before the invention of writing is the sphere of the anthropologist and archaeologist. The work of the former is described in Marvin Harris, *The Rise of Anthropological Theory* (1968) and William Howells, *Mankind in the Making* (rev. ed., 1967). Prominent archaeologists have devoted much energy to popularizing their methods as well as their discoveries. See for example, Leonard Woolley, *Digging Up the Past* (1956); Mortimer Wheeler, *Archaeology from the Earth* (1954); and Kathleen Kenyon, *Beginning in Archaeology* (1961).

Louis S. Leakey describes the problems of the study of hominids in *Adam's Ancestors: The Evolution of Man and His Culture* (1960). Good surveys of prehistory include the brief but perceptive study by Glyn Daniel, *The Idea of Prehistory* (1963); Jacquetta Hawkes and Leonard Woolley, *History of Mankind*, Vol. I (1963), in the series on the scientific and cultural development of man commissioned by UNESCO; François Bordes, *The Old Stone Age* (1968); and John Clark and S. Piggott, *Prehistoric Societies* (1965).

Neolithic man's development of agriculture is analyzed in V. Gordon Childe's perceptive survey, *What Happened in History?* (rev. ed., 1954), in which he also presents his concept of the urban revolution in Mesopotamia in the fourth millennium B. C.

The best introduction to the Sumerians is Leonard Woolley's personal description, written in 1929, of the excavation at Ur, in *Ur of the Chaldees* (1950), while his description of the royal tombs is illustrated with fine photographs in Shirley Glubok, ed., *Discovering the Royal Tombs at Ur* (1969). Rich quotations from Sumerian writing are skillfully presented in Samuel N. Kramer, *History Begins at Sumer* (1959) and Edward Chiera, *They Wrote on Clay* (1938). A popularized version of the legends, including that of Gilgamesh, is narrated by Theodor H. Gaster, *The Oldest Stories in the World* (1952), but for a more scholarly version one must turn to the invaluable collection edited by James B. Pritchard, *Ancient Near Eastern Texts Relating to the Old Testament* (1969). A scholarly survey of the history of Babylon, broadly interpreted to include most of Mesopotamia, is H. W. F. Saggs, *The Greatness That Was Babylon* (1962), which is especially useful for social life and economics. Descriptions of the archaeologists' work, intermingled with surveys of the civilizations they were uncovering, are given in popular but reliable form in C. W. Ceram, *Gods, Graves and Scholars* (1951) and James Wellard, *By the Waters of Babylon* (1972). George Roux's *Ancient Iraq* (1964) makes evocative use of contemporary writings to illustrate the whole historical development of the Tigris and Euphrates valleys.

Assyria receives more than usual sympathy, and perhaps more than it deserves, in Jorgen Laessoe, *People of Ancient Assyria* (1963).

The planning of the Mesopotamian city is described with many plans and photographs in Paul Lampl, *Cities and Planning in the Ancient Near East* (1968), while fuller economic and social analysis of the role of the city is provided in Mason Hammond's invaluable *The City in the Ancient World* (1972). Extremely provocative and thoughtful judgments on the city's role in the shaping of civilization, for good and less than good purposes, are trenchantly given in Lewis Mumford, *The City in History* (1961).

For a good introduction to the peoples of Syria and Palestine, see Sabatino Moscati's *The Face of the Ancient Orient* (1962), which uses the literary evidence to the fullest. The recent archaeological evidence concerning the Canaanites and their descendants the Phoenicians is summarized in John Gray, *The Canaanites* (1967) and Donald B. Harden, *The Phoenicians* (1963). The extraordinary difficulties of excavating in Palestine and the painstaking progress in verifying the evidence of the Bible can be followed in three excellent books by Kathleen Kenyon, one of the foremost archaeologists to work in Jericho and Jerusalem. See her *Digging Up Jerusalem* (1974) and especially her well-illustrated *Jerusalem* (1967) and *Royal Cities of the Old Testament* (1971).

Well-documented surveys of Hebrew history include Giuseppe Ricciotti's *The History of Israel* (1958), which sticks closely to the narrative and eschews analysis, and the short introduction by Harry M. Orlinsky, *Ancient Israel* (1954). For the significance of the Hebrew religious tradition, see J. A. Bewer, *The Literature of the Old Testament in Its Historical Development* (1962) and R. H. Pfeiffer, *The Books of the Old Testament* (1957).

For a good general introduction to the history of ancient Egypt, see Alan Gardiner, *Egypt of the Pharaohs* (1961) or Cyril Aldred, *The Egyptians* (1961). Aldred's beautifully illustrated *Egypt to the End of the Old Kingdom* (1965) is particularly useful for his study of Egyptian architecture, sculpture, and painting during the formative years. The complicated events of the Middle Kingdom are unraveled in H. L. Winlock, *The Rise and Fall of the Middle Kingdom at Thebes* (1947). The New Kingdom's great city of Thebes is analyzed from the point of view of its rulers in Elizabeth Riefstahl, *Thebes in the Time of Amunhotep III* (1964), which is not restricted to that one great builder-king. The development of the city's architecture can be followed in Charles F. Nims, *Thebes of the Pharaohs: Pattern for Every City* (1965). The rich remains found in the tomb of Tutankhamen, which are perhaps the best introduction to the art of the later years of the New Kingdom, are discussed with beautiful photographs in Christiane Desroches-Noblécourt, *Tutankhamen: Life and Death of a Pharaoh* (1963). A wide variety of the surviving literature can be sampled in Adolf Erman, ed., *The Ancient Egyptians: A Sourcebook of Their Writings* (1966) and in William K. Simpson, ed., *The Literature of Ancient Egypt: An Anthology of Stories, Instructions, and Poetry* (1972). More mundane details can be found in J. M. White, *Everyday Life in Ancient Egypt* (1963), more elevated matters in Henri Frankfort, *Ancient Egyptian Religion* (1961). The noted Egyptologist John A. Wilson argues that the Egyptians had no real cities, in "Egypt Through the New Kingdom: Civilization Without Cities," in Carl H. Kraeling and Robert M. Adams, eds., *City Invincible* (1960), pp. 124–264.

I would have you day by day fix your eyes upon the greatness of Athens, until you become filled with the love of her; and when you are impressed by the spectacle of her glory, reflect that this empire has been acquired by men who knew their duty and had the courage to do it. . . . —Pericles, Funeral Oration

2 / The Athens of Pericles

Few cities in the whole history of the world have been loved as Athens has; for the reasoned adoration of its own citizens has been shared by generation after generation of peoples who believed themselves to be part of a Western tradition of civilization. Athens during its centuries of greatness was far more than an economic machine or an imperialist oppressor or a system of class and racial exploitation or an educational magnet or a commercial hub or a constitutional laboratory, although it was all these things. Athens was an attitude of mind and an achievement of the mind, a unique combination of the physical and the intellectual. And Western civilization owes an important part of its character, perhaps the finest part, to its nourishment for centuries from the Greek achievement that reached its height in Athens.

Looking back in later centuries, Greeks called the period of Athenian greatness, between the defeat

Pericles
Courtesy of the Trustees of the British Museum

Parthenon Greek National Tourist Office

of the Persians in 479 B. C. and the beginning of the Peloponnesian war with Sparta in 431 B. C., the Pentekontaetia, or "the time of fifty years." Only a special word could describe that unique half-century of human achievement. During the Pentekontaetia, the Athenians saw the Parthenon and its subsidiary temples rise on the Acropolis. They turned out by the thousands to see plays like the *Oresteia* of Aeschylus, the *Antigone* of Sophocles, or the *Medea* of Euripides. Socrates wandered through the streets and colonnades, talking of the eternal problems of justice and human goodness. Direct democracy became a way of life, with most citizens participating in the making of laws and the administration of justice. Whereas few people in history have ever caught what they were pursuing, it can be said for Athens that at no other time have a greater proportion of a city's population come closer to

The Athens of Pericles

Period Surveyed	End of Persian wars (479 B. C.) to Peloponnesian War (431–404 B. C.)
Population	Between 200,000 and 250,000 (Attica); about 100,000–125,000 (city of Athens)
Area:	0.7 square miles (city of Athens)
Form of Government	Direct, or participatory, democracy
Main Institutions	Assembly *(Ecclesia)*; Council of 500 *(Boulē)*; Ten Generals *(Strategoi)*; Juries
Political Leaders	Pericles (ruled 461–429)
Economic Base	Small farming (wheat, olives, grapes); artisan crafts (pottery, woolen textiles, weapons); tribute from empire; seaborne commerce
Intellectual Life	Drama (Aeschylus, Sophocles, Euripides, Aristophanes); philosophy (Socrates); architecture and sculpture (Phidias, Ictinus); history (Herodotus, Thucydides)
Principal Buildings	Acropolis (Parthenon, Erectheion); Agora (Hephaestaeion)
Religion	Polytheism: Zeus, Hera, Apollo, Poseidon, Athena, and many others

achieving their ideals. The sense of having lived through great events inspired Thucydides to write, in the first paragraph of his history of the Peloponnesian war: "Judging from the evidence which I am able to trust after most careful enquiry, I should imagine that former ages were not greater either in their wars or in anything else."

Yet there was a contrast, which thoughtful Athenians recognized and many deplored, between their ideal of Athens and the material realities of its social and political life. No one was more sensitive than Pericles, the great statesman who dominated the government of Athens for much of the Pentekontaetia, to the glaring irony of the coexistence of one Athens of the Acropolis and drama festivals and democratic assemblies, and another Athens of imperialist expansion and political demagoguery and war profi-

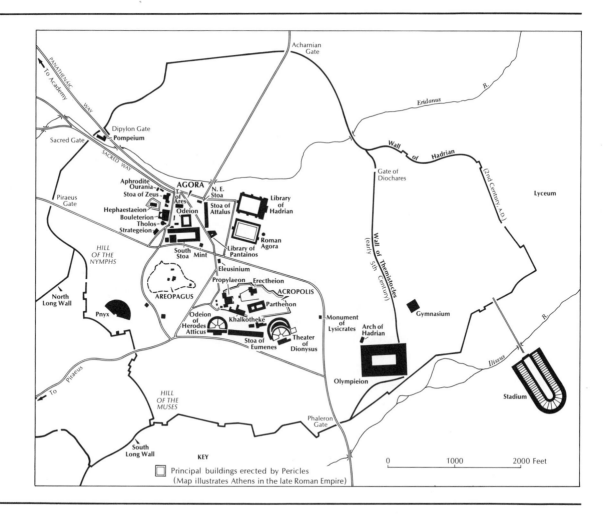

KEY

☐ Principal buildings erected by Pericles
(Map illustrates Athens in the late Roman Empire)

teering. This seeming contradiction, which as we shall see occurs again and again in cities at the height of their greatness, between superb achievements of the human intellect and the continuance of social injustice and political self-seeking, was recognized by Pericles as a problem of the utmost importance. But far from separating the ideal Athens from the less satisfactory reality of the city's daily life, as many of the later admirers of Athens have done, Pericles affirmed that both formed a unity. In a concrete sense, the empire, the money-making, the class of slaves were all necessary to provide the citizens with the wealth and the time to create the ideal city. But it was the greatness of Pericles to remind the Athenians that it was the pursuit of their ideal city that mattered, and that without that ideal the rest of the city's activities would degenerate into individual self-seeking. The true well-being of the individual Athenian citizens, he constantly urged, lay in the greatness of their city.

Greece and Its Invaders

Too much emphasis has been placed on the physical attraction of Greece, mostly by Englishmen and Germans whose misery in the North European drizzle has led them to equate a good climate with civilization. "The preponderance of sunshine," comments one author, "combined with the mildness of winter and the dry warmth of summer, stimulates the energy of the population and encourages an open-air life."[1] "It was perhaps the greatest boon conferred upon Attica by her climate," remarks another, "that her big assemblies could be held in the open air. However democratic the instincts of the Athenian might be, Athenian democracy could not have developed as it did—nor for that matter Athenian Drama—if a roof and walls had been necessary."[2] The scenery too was held to have exercised the same fascination on the wandering tribes from the north, the original Greek settlers, that it does on the modern tourist. "When they emerged at length out of the last rough Balkan defile," wrote Alfred Zimmern, one of the finest Greek scholars, "and pitched camp one evening on level Greek ground between the mountains and the sea, it was the sheer beauty of this new world which made them feel that they had found a home."[3]

It is very tempting to assume that the achievements of the Greeks were determined by this unparalleled setting. But for every beneficial effect of the setting an equally malignant one can be deduced, and the balance of evidence is that the Greeks had to master rather than enjoy their environment.

[1] N. G. L. Hammond, *A History of Greece to 322 B. C.* (Oxford: Oxford University Press, 1967), p. 1.
[2] H. D. F. Kitto, *The Greeks* (Harmondsworth, England: Penguin, 1951), p. 37.
[3] Alfred Zimmern, *The Greek Commonwealth* (Oxford: Oxford University Press, 1931), p. 18.

Minoan Civilization, c. 2000–1400 B. C.

Details about the origin of the first settlers in Greece are still open to dispute, although it has been asserted that two waves of invaders, who were not Greek, but who came from North Africa and Asia Minor, penetrated the islands in the Neolithic period after 6000 B. C. Whoever they were, by 2000 B. C. these early immigrants had produced a magnificent civilization that we call Minoan, after its mythical king, Minos. The focal point of the Minoans was the palace of Cnossus in North Crete, a sprawling, five-story-tall labyrinth of frescoed assembly halls, storage chambers, lavatories, bathrooms, and colonnaded stairwells. Cnossus ruled Crete and the neighboring islands, and its culture influenced the small towns springing up on the mainland of Greece; and its riches—the vast stores of precious metals and of oil, wine, and grain; the homes and palaces; the pottery thin as eggshell—were a prize for a people strong enough to seize them. The eventual conquerors of Cnossus were the first wave of Greeks, who entered the peninsula around the year 2000 B. C. and probably settled in the mainland towns of Mycenae and Tiryns four hundred years later.

Minoan Statuette of a Snake Goddess, 16th Century B. C.
The Snake Goddess was a common figure in the art of Cnossus. She wears the elaborate flounced dress, with bared breasts, of the royal court.   Courtesy Museum of Fine Arts, Boston. Gift of Mrs. W. Scott Fitz.

Minoan Double Axe
This double-headed axe in gold, found near Cnossus, was used in Minoan religious ritual.   Courtesy, Museum of Fine Arts, Boston

Mycenaean Civilization, c. 1600–1100 B. C.

These Greeks were wandering tribesmen, organized in clans under kings. Their language was one of the Indo-European group, and they worshipped male gods of the sky. Fighting on horseback with battle-axes, they had little difficulty in subduing the original inhabitants of the mainland, whom they used as slaves to build the enormous Cyclopean walls of their citadels. After first taking the best that Minoan culture had to offer, and creating a rival Mycenaean civilization, they finally captured Cnossus itself about 1450 B. C., and ruled it until its destruction fifty years later. Mycenae itself, from which the culture received its name, then enjoyed two hundred years of hegemony. During that time, its most grandiose effort was the destruction of Troy on the coast of Asia Minor (c. 1260 B. C.), until it too succumbed, possibly owing to internal political disputes or to attack by a new wave of Greek invaders, the Dorians.

Walls of Tiryns
Constructed about 1300 B. C. these Cyclopean walls of rough-hewn rock encircled the palace or citadel of one of the lesser Mycenaean rulers. Tiryns was captured and laid waste by the Dorian Greeks, probably in the twelfth century B. C.   Author's photo

Lion Gate, Mycenae
The main entrance gate in the massive fortifications of Mycenae built around 1400 B. C. Roger Viollet

The Dorian Invasion, 1200–1000 B. C., and the Dark Age, 1000–800 B. C.

The Dorian invaders felt little attraction for the palace culture of the Mycenaens, laid their towns in ruins, and forgot many, if not most, of their cultural achievements. They came to settle, beginning as nomadic herders and turning later to agriculture on the richer plains. Along the south and east coasts of the Peloponnesus, where the mountain fingers reach to the sea, leaving in their cracks a series of fertile valleys, the Dorians founded a series of rough villages, two of which were to develop into the powerful city-states of Sparta and Argos. From the Peloponnesus, the Dorians spread across the southern islands of the Aegean, including Crete and Rhodes, and settled part of southern Asia Minor.

By the end of the Dark Age (1000–800 B. C.), two hundred years of chaos about which little is known, the inhabitants of Greece were easily distinguishable from one another by the dialect of Greek they spoke. In the central highlands of the Peloponnesus, where three rugged mountain chains and a savage winter climate discouraged Dorian expansion, the original inhabitants kept their Arcadian dialect along with their claim to have been there before the birth of the moon. Northern Greece was divided between a pre-Dorian branch of Greeks called the Aeolians and the last wave of invaders called, for want of a better label, the North-West Greeks. Finally, the

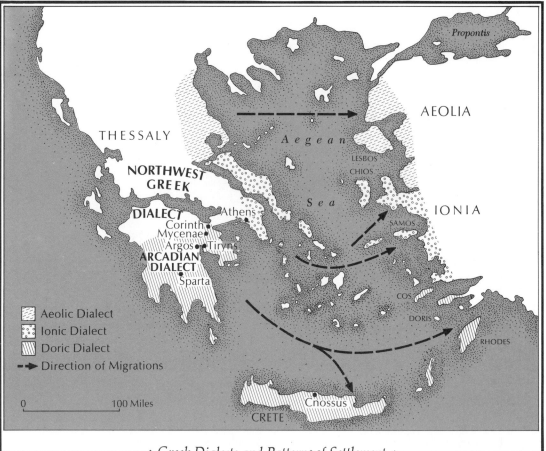

→ *Greek Dialects and Patterns of Settlement* ←

Ionic dialect was spoken by the lively, versatile people who lived in the central Aegean islands, the central coast of Asia Minor and in the small peninsula shaped like a horse's head that juts from the mainland of Greece. The peninsula was called Attica and its most important town was the Mycenaean settlement of Athens.

The Archaic Age, 800–500 B. C.

Class Antagonism in the Countryside, 800–600 B. C.

By 800 B. C. the great movement of peoples, both of invaders and of those seeking refuge, had come to an end. In many parts of Greece, the control of political power was exercised by the richest of the landowners, who had become a kind of territorial aristocracy replacing the tribal kings, taking to themselves nearly all of the duties of governor, judge, jury, bureaucrat, and military overseer. Society was split into two sharply antagonistic classes; and the fascination from a social point of view of the two great works of literature that have survived from the eighth and seventh centuries B. C., the epic poems of Homer, the *Iliad* and the *Odyssey*, and *The Works and Days* of Hesiod, is that they illustrate two differing concepts of society. At one point in the *Odyssey*, Homer makes it clear through Odysseus that the position of the king is beyond criticism. When an unpopular warrior named Thersites dares to criticize King Agamemnon, Odysseus beats him black and blue with his staff in front of all the other warriors: "Thersites, this might be eloquence," he shouted, "but we have had enough of it. You driveling fool, how dare you stand up to the king. It is not for you, the meanest wretch of all who followed the Atreidae to Ilium, to hold forth with the kings' names on your tongue."[4] Hesiod, by contrast, in giving homely advice to his brother on farming, was furious at the "gift-hungry" nobility, whom he likened to a hawk with a nightingale in its claws.

> *Now I will tell you a fable for the barons; they understand it.*
> *This is what the hawk said when he had caught a nightingale*
> *With spangled neck in his claws and carried her high among the clouds.*
> *She, spitted on the clawhooks, was wailing pitifully, but the hawk in his*
> *masterful manner, gave her an answer:*
> *"What is the matter with you? Why scream? Your master has you.*
> *You shall go wherever I take you, for all your singing.*
> *If I like, I can let you go. If I like, I can eat you for dinner.*
> *He is a fool who tries to match his strength with the stronger.*
> *He will lose his battle, and with the shame will be hurt also."*
> *So spoke the hawk, the bird who flies so fast on his long wings.*[5]

Changes in Military Technique, 800–600 B. C.

During the next two centuries, the predominance of the aristocracy was undermined by vitally important changes in the methods of fighting and by the development of commerce. For the first two hundred years after the Dorian invasions, the rich nobles developed military predominance, probably because they were owners of horses and the main instrument of fighting was the cavalry. Sometime during the seventh century, however, a great change took place in military technique; and many historians have argued that this change brought about significant social and political consequences. The new technique was to arm the infantry in breastplates and helmets of heavy armor, with large strong shields and long spears. These armed men,

---

[4] Cited in W. G. Forrest, *The Emergence of Greek Democracy 800–400 B. C.* (London: Weidenfeld and Nicolson, 1966), p. 63.

[5] Hesiod *The Works and Days*, trans. Richmond Lattimore (Ann Arbor: University of Michigan Press, 1962), p. 43.

Combat of Greeks and Amazons. Detail, Athenian Red-figured Pottery, 5th–4th Century B. C.
Combats of Greeks with the legendary female warriors of Pontus were used to illustrate the barbarism of the natives of Asia Minor. The Greek soldiers are wearing greaves on their legs and carrying the round shield and thrusting sword of the hoplite. The Metropolitan Museum of Art. Fletcher Fund, 1944

called hoplites, were trained to attack in coordinated lines, each man's shield protecting the right side of his neighbor and all charging forward in coordination in response to the battle cry or paean of their leader. This infantry formation, called the phalanx, destroyed the predominance of the cavalry and thus, in the view of these historians, also ended the privileged position of the aristocracy. Whatever its social consequences, the development of the phalanx caught the Greek imagination. Greek vases of the seventh and sixth centuries B. C. have thousands of pictures of the phalanx—

the thrusting spears, the iron helmet with the semicircular protective band, the round shield protecting the whole body from thigh to cheekbone, and the metal greaves that covered the leg from knee to ankle. The vases show, above all, the perfect discipline of the advancing line, firmly in step, rumbling inexorably forward like a wall in motion.

Commercial Revolution and the New Wave of Colonization

The phalanx, however, would not have been possible had there not also occurred an economic revolution. The phalanx presupposed the existence of sufficient numbers of what we must call middle-class people who could afford not the highly expensive horse of a cavalryman but the still moderately expensive shield, spear, and helmet of the hoplite. At the same time it presupposed the existence of mining, ore refining, and metalwork on a sufficient scale to provide equipment for thousands of soldiers. The economic pattern was fairly simple. In the more favored areas of Greece, farmers began to concentrate on goods that could be used for export as well as nourishment, notably wine and olive oil. Growing numbers of artisans in the cities produced manufactured goods like vases, cloth, metalwork, and even perfume, for sale abroad. In return, the Greeks imported grain from the Black Sea coast, Asia Minor, and Sicily, and metals from Etruria and Asia. Hand in hand with the development of the export trade was a new wave of colonization from Greece in 750–550 B. C. precipitated by overpopulation in the cities of the Greek mainland. A comparatively small number of mother

Temples of Paestum
Founded by Greek colonists from Sybaris about 600 B. C., the flourishing city of Paestum south of Naples contained some of the most beautiful Hellenic temples. In the foreground, the Doric basilica, probably dedicated to Poseidon. Italian State Tourist Office photo

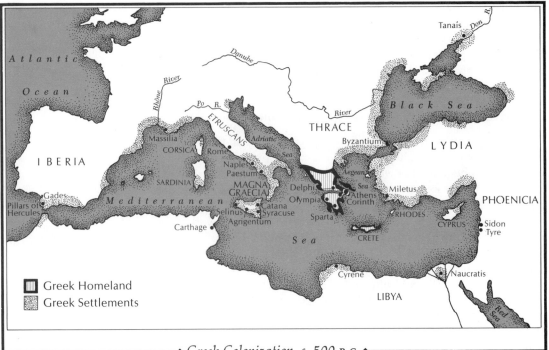

Greek Colonization, c. 500 B.C.

cities sponsored colonies, but the colonists were usually joined by the inhabitants of other cities. They settled the islands of the Aegean, the west coast of Asia Minor, the shores of the Black Sea as far as the river Don, the coast of Libya, and the coasts of Sicily and southern Italy. These colonists founded independent city-states, whose ties with their mother cities were of tradition and commerce, not of law or might; and their foundation further encouraged the specialization of trades and the ambition of the middle classes.

Lawgivers and Tyrants, 650–500 B. C.

These military and economic changes made possible a remedy for the grievances that were tearing aristocratic society apart, especially the accumulation of land in the hands of the aristocrats and the burden of debt on the poor. Occasionally, the warring groups would agree to call in an arbiter or "lawgiver," or the newly prosperous groups and the peasantry would throw their support to one man who promised to break the power of the landowners. Tyranny, or one-man rule, became the normal form of government in most Greek states between about 650 and 500 B. c..

It is easy to understand why most Greeks saw the value of the tyrant when one glances at Sparta, the most important state that avoided tyranny. From the time of their conquest of Laconia the Spartans had a society of three classes: the Spartans themselves, the neighbors, or perioikoi, who were freeholders not allowed citizenship, and the subordinate population of slaves, called helots. Most of the land was owned by the Spartans and worked by the helots. When the Spartans became too numerous for Laconia, they conquered the neighboring area of Messenia, thereby spreading the control of the Spartan minority so thin that to maintain their predominance, they created a unique system of society. The Spartans devoted themselves entirely to being soldiers, following a system of laws that they believed had been laid down in the ninth century by a mythical lawgiver named Lycurgus. The state took over the total education of a youth from age seven to thirty, training him harshly for hoplite warfare. As an adult, he ate with all the other males in common messes, to which he had to contribute from the farm assigned to him. Food was of the most meager and rough kind, especially a famous black broth that horrified more sensitive palates from other cities. The only money permitted was a cumbersome iron "spit."

Sparta had an extraordinary mixture of institutions: two kings, who could thus check each other; five ephors, chosen annually by lot and acting as the real executive; a boulē, or council; and an assembly of all the citizens. Sparta went through a period of economic troubles by strengthening the austerity of its social life, so that by the beginning of the fifth century, the Spartans were admired, if not envied, by most other Greeks for their extraordinary devotion to an ideal of discipline and subordination of individual desires. Plutarch tells the story of an old man looking for a seat at the Olympic Games who was being jeered at by those already seated. When he reached the Spartans, every young Spartan and most of the older ones offered him their seats, whereupon the crowd applauded them. The old man commented: "All Greeks *know* what is right, but only the Spartans *do* it."

Spartan Warrior, Sixth Century B. C.
Courtesy Wadsworth Atheneum, Hartford

The Rise of Athens

The Physical Character of Attica

Whereas Sparta avoided the institution of tyranny by establishing a self-denying oligarchy, Athens passed in the sixth century B. C. under the beneficent rule of a lawgiver, Solon, and then under a succession of tyrants, to emerge with Cleisthenes's reforms in 508 B. C. as the most famous example in history of direct or participatory democracy.

In part, Athenians attributed their unique evolution to the character of their own region, Attica. All ancient writers were agreed that the poverty of Attica was its preservation. "Attica, whose soil was poor and thin, enjoyed a long freedom from civil strife, and therefore retained its original inhabitants," the historian Thucydides wrote.[6] The mountains of Attica, once

---

[6] *Thucydides,* trans. Benjamin Jowett (Boston: D. Lothrop, 1883), p. 2.

Acropolis of Athens
Easily defensible in times of danger, the rocky plateau was revered as the sanctuary of the Goddess Athena, and thus was the spiritual center of the city.   TWA photo

covered with thick forest that was cut down by the early settlers, displayed grey ribs of bare limestone—like a body wasted with disease, Plato commented; and even the plains lacked topsoil. Thus, the first advantages of Attica were that it did not attract invaders, and it did not need large armies of slaves to till the fields. Yet there were natural benefits. The plain around Athens was broad and flat, nine miles by thirteen in size and thus large by Greek standards and divisible into family farms. There was water in a couple of tiny rivers, though they tended to be torrential in winter and almost dry in summer; and hard work made possible market-gardening. The surface of the plain was of high-quality clay, which had superb qualities of color and brightness when turned into the pottery that was one of Athens' chief exports. At the southern tip of Attica, the hills behind Cape Sounion held large deposits of lead and copper; and just at the crucial moment of the Persian invasion at the beginning of the fifth century, an easily exploitable vein of silver was found, which was used to pay for the ships that turned back the Persian invasion. From the land, the Athenian plain was defended by a semicircle of mountains, broken only by three rough passes that were guarded with border fortresses. Should the invader get past these barriers, the Athenian plain offered a last vital refuge to its inhabitants—a long, anvil-shaped rock three hundred feet high and some nine hundred feet in length, with springs of water, impassable rock faces on three sides, and the protection of the goddess Athena. To this Acropolis, the Athenians withdrew in times of trouble. In times of prosperity, however, it was the sea that beckoned. The sea was three miles from the Acropolis; offshore the island of Salamis protected the harbor mouth; and beyond Cape Sounion, lines of islands allowed sailors, who avoided the open sea, to be easily within sight of land the whole way to Asia. The sea provided fish—tunny, anchovy, and sardine; a road to new lands where colonies could be settled in times of over-population; and in imperialist days, the temptation of an empire of islands and coastal ports to an Athens that became too powerful for its own safety.

The Reforms of Solon

The whole of Attica was united under Athens, probably peacefully, in a process that took several centuries. The area escaped conquest during the Dorian invasions, but in the eighth and seventh centuries b. c. was plunged into internal social conflict. The basic trouble was the growing subjection of the poor to the upper class of the "well-born." Many peasants held their land as sharecroppers and could be sold into slavery for not producing what was owing. A man could also be sold into slavery for personal debts, since his liberty was accepted as security for his loan. As a result there was widespread demand for the end of sharecropping, for redistribution of the land, for cancellation of debts, and for the freeing of persons sold into slavery for debt. Even the upper classes realized the need to face the problem and, in 594 b. c. in an extraordinary agreement, they entrusted Solon, one of their most admired citizens, with power to remedy the situation. Solon was a poet, philosopher, and political theorist, who, though a well-to-do merchant with a good understanding of problems of agriculture and of commerce,

Man and Woman in Oxcart, c. 600 b. c.
The simple dignity of the working people is magnified by the so-called geometric style: the rhythm of the statue is based almost entirely upon the crossing of horizontal and diagonal lines. Courtesy Museum of Fine Arts, Boston. John Michael Rodocanachi Fund

was from an aristocratic family. He canceled all debts and all mortgages on land, freed those in slavery for debt, and even bought back from abroad those sold into debt slavery there. Having restored the freedom of the peasantry of Attica, he set about making a constitution that would break the political power of the rich. He divided the population of citizens into four classes according to wealth. He permitted all citizens to take part in the assembly and gave it the right to elect a Council of Four Hundred, which could act to check the old aristocratic Areopagus, or council of the well born. Even the poorest were given the right to take part in the juries. He finally set out to improve Athenian morality. He controlled the extent of women's wardrobes, ordered fathers to teach their sons a trade, forbade immoral people to speak before the assembly, and punished those persistently idle. Solon was regarded by Athenians as the doctor who helped give Athens the economic and political good health that made its cultural achievement of the fifth century possible.

Perhaps the most moving commentary on Solon's reforms was written by himself:

Aye, many brought I back to their God-built birthplace, many that had been sold, some justly, some unjustly, and others that had been exiled through urgent penury, men that no longer spake the Attic speech because they had wandered so far and wide; and those that suffered shameful servitude at home, trembling before the whims of their owners, these made I free men.[7]

After ruling as archon for twenty-two years, Solon set off to travel around Egypt and the Near East, enjoining the Athenians to allow ten years in which to test his constitutional reforms. Apparently, Solon continued to give free advice wherever he went, because when asked by the rich king Croesus of Lydia, "Who is the happiest of men?" he is reported to have replied:

I know God is envious of human prosperity and likes to trouble us; and you question me about the lot of man. Listen, then; as the years lengthen out, there is much both to see and to suffer which one would wish otherwise. Take seventy years as the span of a man's life: those seventy years contain 25,200 days, without counting intercalary months. Add a month every other year, to make the seasons come round with proper regularity, and you will have thirty-five additional months, which will make 1,050 additional days. Thus the total of days for your seventy years is 26,250 and not a single one of them is like the next in what it brings. You can see from that, Croesus, what a chancy thing life is. You are very rich, and you rule a numerous people; but the question you asked me I will not answer, until I know that you have died happily. Great wealth can make a man no happier than moderate means, unless he has

[7] Cited in André Bonnard, *Greek Civilization* (London: Macmillan, 1957), I, 110.

the luck to continue in prosperity to the end. . . . Though the rich have the means to satisfy their appetites and to bear calamities, the poor have not; the poor, if they are lucky, are more likely to keep clear of trouble, and will have besides the blessings of a sound body, health, freedom from trouble, fine children and good looks.[8]

Croesus realized the wisdom of this advice when the Persian king later captured him and was about to burn him alive; for then he sighed, "Ah, Solon! Solon!" and was set free to explain what he meant by his sigh.

The Tyranny of Pisistratus and Hippias

Fortunate in the mediation of Solon, Athens was even luckier in its tyrants, Pisistratus (c. 605–527 B. C.) and his son Hippias (died 490 B. C.). In the 560s B. C., Athens, far from becoming the harmonious place envisaged by Solon, was split between two factions, the old aristocracy of the plain and the new mercantile middle class of the coast. Intervening in their dispute, Pisistratus put together a third group, the discontented poor and the smaller landholders from "beyond the hills" in Eastern Attica. He displayed considerable bravado as well as a sense of humor in making himself tyrant. On the first occasion, he rushed into the assembly covered with self-inflicted wounds, presumably superficial, which he blamed on his enemies and demanded a bodyguard; given the bodyguard, he seized the Acropolis. Driven out later by the factions of the coast and the plain, he returned with a procession led by a very tall, lovely woman whom he had dressed as the Goddess Athena in a complete suit of armor. According to Herodotus, the Athenians, who must have been quite gullible, thought that Athena herself was speaking when the armored beauty told them: "Men of Athens, give kind welcome to Pisistratus whom Athena herself honors above all other men, and is now conducting to her own citadel." Driven out again shortly afterwards, he returned with a strong army and a good supply of silver; and with such effective means, for the next quarter-century, from 546 B. C. Pisistratus and his son gave Athens a period of prosperity that the citizens themselves recognized as a golden age.

Pisistratus allowed the existing constitutional machinery to go on working, intervening only when necessary to make his own policies respected. In a period of calm, the Athenians got used to running the machinery of government that Solon had created. The grievances of the poor farmers were partially removed by grants to them of state lands and of estates confiscated from disloyal aristocrats. Farmers in trouble were granted loans. By planting strategic colonies on the Dardanelles, Pisistratus safeguarded the vitally important route to the southern grainlands of Russia on the Black Sea. Above all, he and his son set out to make the Athenians proud of their own

[8] Aubrey de Selincourt, trans., *The Histories of Herodotus* (Harmondsworth, England: Penguin, 1954), p. 25.

state. Religion was used to cement loyalty to the state. Athena's head and her owl appeared on the coinage of Athens, which soon became the most important currency of the eastern Mediterranean region. Athena was glorified by the embellishment of her temple on the Acropolis, and the Acropolis was turned into the shrine of the city. The Panathenaic Festival, the four-yearly festival in honor of the goddess, was built up into the greatest festival in the life of Athens and a rival to the national festivals like the Olympic Games. Public reading of the Iliad and the Odyssey played an important role in impressing the two masterpieces into the citizens' consciousness. To the tyranny is due also the creation of the festival in honor of Dionysus, the god of wine, music, and fertility. For the Dionysian Festival, the first Greek plays, both in tragedy and in comedy, were created. Thus, under Pisistratus, music, drama, and poetry became Athenian institutions, open to the whole body of the citizens, and under constant improvement by the introduction of the competitive spirit that appealed so forcefully to the Greeks. By the end of the tyranny, the average Athenian had the protection of a lawcode and a constitution requiring his participation while, at the same time, the growing physical beauty of the city was strengthening his emotional identification with the well-being of the city.

Maidens Preparing for the Dionysian Festival, Athens. Red-figured Pottery Vase, c. 330 B. C. The Metropolitan Museum of Art. Rogers Fund, 1906

The Reforms of Cleisthenes, 508 B. C.

A third and far more democratic remodeling of the Athenian constitution, carried out by Cleisthenes in 508 B. C., gave the city the system of direct democracy that lasted throughout its period of greatest achievement in the fifth century. Cleisthenes made the unit of local government the "deme," which was the equivalent of a village or city ward, and of which there were about one hundred seventy altogether in Attica. He then divided Attica into three areas—the city, inland, and the coast—and formed ten completely new tribes, each of which was composed of demes from all three new divisions. Deme and tribe were basic to the new Athenian democracy. In the deme, everyone was eligible for office. The small local assemblies became a training ground for participation in the larger assemblies. Naturalized citizens were admitted through the deme, and became indistinguishable from other citizens, since everyone was designated not only by his name but by that of the deme in which he lived. The tribe was now composed of citizens of all parts of Attica, who thus came to feel a new loyalty to their country as a whole.

All Athenian citizens, who numbered between thirty and fifty thousand, were eligible to sit in the assembly, or *ecclesia,* which met about forty times a year, and was the supreme legislative and judicial body. Anyone could speak who could make the others listen, and proceedings were frequently emotional, tempestuous, and chaotic. After 500 B. C. the assembly was given the power of ostracism. Once a year, a majority of the members of the assembly could order one of its leading citizens into exile by writing his name on a broken piece of pottery. The business of the assembly was prepared by the Council of Five Hundred, or *boulē,* whose members were chosen by lot from the ten tribes. The Council members served in groups of fifty, called "prytanies," for one-tenth of the year, maintaining a permanent executive between full meetings of the Council. Juries, which numbered from 101 to 1001 members, were also chosen by lot from a list of 6,000 volunteers from the assembly, while magistrates were elected from the whole assembly and reported back to it at the end of their term of office. Thus, because of the use of election by lot, the majority of citizens would have served in the Council and been directly responsible for the technical administration of the city. The only position where strong leadership could be perpetuated was the office of general. The ten generals were elected annually for their competence, a test which applied in no other office in the Athenian state. It was as general that Pericles was able to guide Athenian policy for more than thirty years.

This system worked because it was in harmony with the economic and social structure of Athens. The Athenian population numbered between two hundred and two hundred fifty thousand, of whom one-third were slaves and one-tenth resident aliens. The aliens, who were not allowed to own land and were still liable for taxes and military service, took care of a large part of the city's commerce and banking, as well as many menial manufacturing jobs the Athenian looked down on. The slaves did all the tough, painful work in the lead and silver mines, most of the domestic work not done by women, and about one-third of the labor on the farms. Although conditions in the mines were ghastly, slaves worked beside Athenians in most other occupations, and there was never a fear in Athens, as there was in Sparta and later in Rome, of slave revolt or indeed of excessive reliance on slave labor.

The majority of the citizens were independent small farmers, growing olives, vines, figs, and a little grain. With the help of two or three slaves, they could feed their families and share in a small way in the export of oil and wine. When Pericles introduced payment for service in the administration of the juries, it became easier for farmers to take more of a share in the city's political life. The citizens who lived in Athens itself tended either to be larger landowners, who could afford to leave a bailiff to manage their estates while they devoted themselves to politics, or tradesmen and artisans who made and sold the staple items of the Athenian export trade in manufactures, such as pottery, woolen textiles, weapons, or silver goods. Among the citizens of Athens, therefore, division by wealth did obtain, but the poorer citizen felt a sense of social independence from the wealthier, since the farmer's livelihood was derived from his own farm or trade. This feeling was the essential basis of the system of direct democracy, in which all citizens met on equal terms in the assemblies and the juries.

The Persian Wars, 490–479 B. C.

The Athenian citizens quickly used the power given them by the reforms of Cleisthenes to reject his foreign policy of friendship with the Persian Empire. By the beginning of the fifth century, the Persians had extended their control over all the territory from the eastern Mediterranean and the Black Sea as far as northern India. Although the Persian empire was well governed, the Ionian cities in Asia Minor preferred their independence. In 499 B. C. they revolted and succeeded in burning Sardis, one of the great cities of the Persian Empire. Although aided by Athens, the Ionian rebels were put down after five years of fighting; and the Persian king Darius decided to prevent a second intervention from the Greek mainland by punishing Athens.

Battle of Marathon, 490 B. C.

The Persians did not expect the Greeks to put up much resistance, and Darius sent a fleet of only one hundred ships, carrying about twenty thousand men including the former tyrant Hippias, who was to be reinstated in

power. Aided only by one other city, the Athenians met the Persian army on the plain of Marathon. The Athenians had perhaps half the number of soldiers of the Persians. Their hoplites, however, broke through the un-disciplined Persian line, and if the traditional figures are to be believed, killed more than six thousand Persians for the loss of one hundred ninety-two Athenians. Three days later, a small Spartan army arrived, found no one to fight, and, said Herodotus, "praised the Athenians and their achieve-ment, and then went home." Many reasons were adduced for the Athenian victory—the lack of large-scale preparations by Darius, the effectiveness of the Athenian phalanx and the skill of its general, the fact that the Athenians were defending their own city—but undoubtedly the sense of defending their new liberties against Persian autocracy played a vital role. In a famous passage, Herodotus characterized the Athenians' spirit after the end of the tyranny:

Thus Athens went from strength to strength and proved, if proof were needed, how noble a thing freedom is, not in one respect only but in all; for while they were oppressed under a despotic government, they had no better success in war than any of their neighbors, yet, once the yoke was flung off, they proved the

Palace of Darius, Persepolis

Persepolis was the ceremo-nial capital of the Persian kings Darius and Xerxes, while the administrative capitals were Susa and Babylon.   Courtesy of the Oriental Institute, University of Chicago

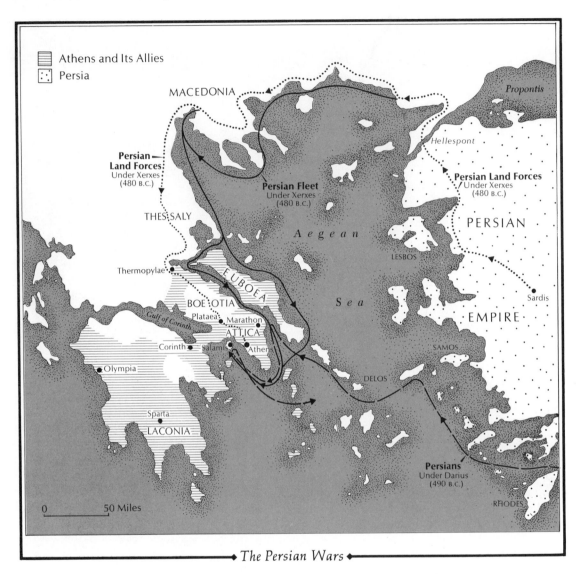

Athens and Its Allies
Persia

MACEDONIA
Propontis
Hellespont

Persian Land Forces
Under Xerxes
(480 B.C.)

Persian Land Forces
Under Xerxes
(480 B.C.)

THESSALY

Persian Fleet
Under Xerxes
(480 B.C.)

A e g e a n

PERSIAN

LESBOS

Thermopylae

E U B O E A

S e a

Sardis

BOEOTIA

EMPIRE

Plataea   Marathon
Gulf of Corinth
ATTICA
Corinth   Salamis   Athens
SAMOS

Olympia

DELOS

Sparta

LACONIA

Persians
Under Darius
(490 B.C.)

0   50 Miles

RHODES

◆ The Persian Wars ◆

finest fighters in the world. This clearly shows that, so long as they were held down by authority, they deliberately shirked their duty in the field, as slaves shirk working for their masters; but when freedom was won, then every man amongst them longed to distinguish himself.[9]

Invasion of Xerxes, 480–479 B.C.

The Athenians had won only a temporary respite. Ten years later, Xerxes, the son of Darius, returned with a far larger and better-equipped expedi-

[9] Selincourt, *Histories of Herodotus*, p. 339.

tion. To get his soldiers to Greece, he built a bridge of boats across the Hellespont; and he dug a canal across the Mount Athos peninsula to allow his ships to sail safely near the coastline. As the vast army advanced slowly through the north of Greece, the Greek cities there submitted and put their armies at his disposition. So clear was the threat to all the remaining Greek city-states that almost all united in preparation to hold off the Persians in the mountains north of Athens; but the Persians were delayed only for a short while in the pass at Thermopylae by three hundred soldiers under Spartan king Leonidas. Fortunately for the Athenians, they had just used the silver from the newly discovered mines near Sounion to build a new navy of two hundred ships, which now became their final line of defense, the "wooden walls" behind which the Oracle at Delphi had advised them to find safety. The first sortie of the Athenian fleet taught them that they were no match for the Persians except in narrow straits, where the faster Persian ships could not maneuver. This meant that they had to lure the Persians into the waters between the island of Salamis and the Athenian mainland. So, as the Persian army flooded southwards, the whole Athenian population, abandoning Attica to the Persians, fled to the island of Salamis with whatever possessions they could carry with them. From the hills of Salamis, the Athenians saw their city go up in flames, and the sacred temples on the Acropolis ruined. Perhaps tempted by a trick, perhaps overconfident, the Persian fleet allowed itself to meet the Greeks in the straits at Salamis. Xerxes, sitting on the shore, saw his ships first rammed, then turn tail, and finally sink in the universal chaos.

The next year, the Persians occupying central Greece were driven out at the battle of Plataea by a large Spartan army. By the end of 479 B. C., the Persians had withdrawn from the Greek mainland, and all the Greeks

Boat Race. Black-figured Amphora
Greek ships were propelled by banks of oars and a single, large sail.
Courtesy of the Louvre, Paris

exulted in the extraordinary achievement by which so small a people had humiliated the greatest military empire of the time. The Spartans were quietly proud of their achievement. At Thermopylae, they put up an understated memorial to their dead:

> *Stranger, go to the Spartans and say,*
> *Here we lie, obedient to their command.*

The Athenians, however, felt they had made the greatest sacrifices and the greatest contribution for victory. In the words of Herodotus:

> *The Athenians through fear of the approaching danger had abandoned their country, or if they had stayed there and submitted to Xerxes, there would have been no attempt to resist the Persians by sea, . . . the Spartans would have been left alone to perform prodigies of valor and to die nobly. . . . In view of this, therefore, one is surely right in saying that Greece was saved by the Athenians.*[10]

A more fascinating insight into the attitude of the Athenians can be found in Aeschylus' play, *The Persians*. Aeschylus had fought at Marathon and at Salamis, and had seen the devastation of the Persian occupation of Athens. Yet only eight years later *The Persians* portrays the greatness of the triumph of Athens, not by vilifying the Persians but by ennobling them. The play opens in the palace of Xerxes at Susa, where the chorus of Persian nobles are uncertain of the fate of the vast army that had left for Greece. Slowly the doom is revealed. A messenger arrives, with a long list of Persian leaders killed. Then he describes the ruined navy; then the last battle on land. But it is for the queen to seek out the reasons for this disaster. At first, she displays her ignorance of even the whereabouts of Athens.

Queen: My friends, where is Athens said to be?

Chorus: Far toward the dying flames of sun.

Queen: Yet my son lusts to track it down?

Chorus: Then all Hellas would be subject to the king.

Queen: So rich in numbers are they?

Chorus: So great a host as dealt to Persians many woes.

Queen: Who commands them? Who is shepherd of their host?

Chorus: They are slaves to none, nor are they subject.

Then she cannot understand how the city of Athens could have fallen without the Persians winning a victory.

---

[10] Ibid., p. 460.

Herald: The gods saved the city of the goddess.

Queen: What? Athens still stands unsacked?

Herald: As long as there are men the city stands.[11]

After the messenger's description of the losses at Salamis, the chorus brings home to her the meaning of the battle. The Persian power to enforce submission and crush liberty is ended:

> They throughout the Asian land
> No longer Persian laws obey,
> No longer lordly tribute yield,
> Exacted by necessity;
> Nor suffer rule as suppliants,
> To earth obeisance never make:
> Lost is the kingly power.
>
> Nay, no longer is the tongue
> Imprisoned kept, but loose are men,
> When loose the yoke of power's bound,
> To bawl their liberty.
> But Ajax's isle, spilled with blood
> Its earth, and washed round by sea,
> Hold the remains of Persia.[12]

Finally her husband Darius himself, from the grave, warns the queen and all Persia with her to leave Greece unmolested in the future, and emphasizes the message of Aeschylus, that the Greeks are the instrument of the gods to punish excessive ambition.

> And corpses, piled up like sand, shall witness,
> Mute, even to the century to come,
> Before the eyes of men, that never, being
> Mortal, ought we cast our thoughts too high.
> Insolence, once blossoming, bears
> Its fruit, a tasseled field of doom, from which
> A weeping harvest's reaped, all tears.
> Behold the punishment of these! remember
> Greece and Athens! lest you disdain
> Your present fortune, and lust after more,
> Squandering great prosperity.[13]

Only by bearing in mind the nobility of this approach can one understand the quality that the Athenians sought to achieve during the next, and greatest, half-century of their history.

---

[11] David Grene and Richmond Lattimore, eds., *The Complete Greek Tragedies* (Chicago: University of Chicago Press, 1959), I, 228–29.

[12] Ibid. I, 232–33.

[13] Ibid. I, 249.

Pericles and the Reconstruction of Athens

When the Athenians abandoned their city to the Persians and fled to Salamis, they were knowingly sacrificing what was already becoming a beautiful city. The Acropolis was ringed with hewn stone walls and embellished with the two fine temples erected by Pisistratus. The marketplace, or agora, of Solon was lined with temples and public buildings. Elaborate fountains supplied mountain water brought by a long new aqueduct. The Persians left everything in ruins, except for a few houses where their leaders had lodged, and thus compelled the Athenians to rebuild their city.

Fearing both a return of the Persians and a possible attack from their rivals the Spartans, the whole Athenian population set to work in enormous haste pulling down the ruined buildings and using the stone for erection of new walls. According to Thucydides:

In such hurried fashion did the Athenians build the walls of their city, to this day the structure shows evidence of haste. The foundations are made up of all sorts of stones, in some places unwrought, and laid just as each worker brought them; there were many columns too, taken from sepulchers, and many old stones already cut, inserted in the work. The circuit of the city was extended in every direction, and the citizens, in their ardor to complete the design, spared nothing.[14]

After the wallbuilding was complete, however, the rest of the city rose haphazardly, as a confusion of tiny uncomfortable houses of unbaked brick and narrow broiling streets, while the temples on the Acropolis were left in ruins as a reminder of the Persian invasions. For Pericles, it was intolerable that the physical beauty of Athens was not commensurate with its political and economic achievements or with its position as the head of a wealthy empire. Once in power, he determined to realize his ambition of making Athens a model for the rest of Greece.

Pericles (c. 495–429 B. C.)

Although an aristocrat by birth, Pericles had risen to power in 461 B. C. through leadership of the democratic party in Athens. He was a man of broad culture and varied talents and had studied music, literature, and philosophy. His oratory was so calm and impressive that his nickname was the "Olympian." Although personally incorruptible, he was determined to make permanent the supremacy of the democratic party over the aristocratic supporters of oligarchy; and he slowly introduced the constitutional reforms needed for that goal—abolition of the power of the Areopagus, reduction of property qualifications for office, and establishment of pay for

---

[14] Jowett, *Thucydides,* pp. 58–59.

jurors, expense allowance for Council members, and most criticized, pay for soldiers and sailors. The conservatives felt that he had destroyed the moral fiber of Athens; but he had built such strong political support that, by creating democracy, he had brought about one-man rule.

Pericles' ambitions for Athens were unbounded, even by moral scruple, or perhaps he regarded the cause of Athens as the highest morality. By founding colonies, he attempted to expand Athenian influence in Italy and the Black Sea, but without much success. His principal effort was to expand, and exploit, the Athenian empire in the Aegean Sea. At the end of the Persian wars, Athens had formed the Delian League as a means of maintaining the protection against Persia that Athens had extended to the Aegean islands and the Ionian cities in Asia Minor. All members agreed to contribute either ships and men, or money, which was stored in the sanctuary on the island of Delos. The voluntary character of the league soon disappeared. Cities that refused to join or that attempted to leave the league were besieged by the Athenian fleet, disarmed, and forced to pay monetary recompense. Pericles himself was no less aggressive. He attacked Egypt, fought briefly with Sparta, tried to break down the sphere of influence of Corinth, stationed garrisons in the lands of recalcitrant members of the league, and finally in 454 B. C. announced that he was moving the treasury from Delos to the Acropolis in Athens. With the surplus from the treasury, he planned an enormous building program that would make Athens the strongest and most beautiful city of the Mediterranean.

Goals of Pericles' Building Program

The program Pericles envisaged was to include the reconstruction of the sanctuaries and theater on the Acropolis, the public buildings in the agora, the port of Piraeus, and the defense walls that linked Athens to the Piraeus. Not only would the program bring Athens eternal honor, he told the assembly, according to Plutarch, but it would bring immediate economic benefits. It would provide work for the unemployed, stimulate the economy, and involve the citizen in the life of his polis.

"We shall need stone, bronze, ivory, gold, ebony, and cypress wood," he explained, "and to fashion them, carpenters, masons, dyers, goldsmiths, ivory-carvers, painters, and sculptors. Our shipwrights and seamen will work to bring the materials we need from overseas and our wagoners will find employment hauling materials we need for the hinterland. Every auxiliary craft will be stimulated, from metallurgy to cobbling and every trade will be organized under a chief, becoming part and parcel of the services of the state. In a word, all the different needs will be carefully planned and catered for and prosperity will spread to every citizen of whatever age and trade."

Pericles was overly sanguine since many of the artisans had to be brought in from the outside. Nevertheless, by the end of the century, the work was almost completed, and Athens had achieved the beauty it had been the genius of Pericles to conceive. Contemporaries were well aware of the greatness of what had been accomplished, and they came by the thousands to see for themselves, to wander over the Acropolis, to study in the schools, to attend the theaters, and to watch the Athenians in their assemblies. Perhaps for the first time in history, as Pericles himself noted, a city proudly threw itself open to the inspection of the world.

The Face of the City

Most visitors to fifth-century Athens came by sea to one of the three harbors of the Piraeus. After its reconstruction by the town planner Hippodamus of Miletus, whom Pericles had called in for the task, the Piraeus had

City Plan of Miletus
Miletus, on the coast of Asia Minor, is traditionally regarded as the city where the checkerboard city plan, incorporating straight streets crossing at right angles and blocks of uniform size, was first fully developed.

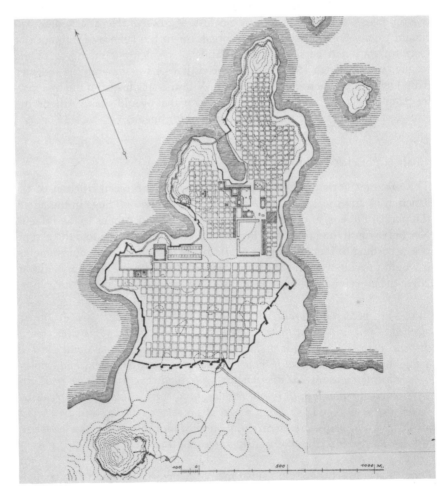

a checkerboard appearance, with warehouses and business offices crowded around the waterfront and the more imposing religious and civic buildings set around the marketplace in the center of town. It was a pleasant place whose exotic sights and brilliant festivals made an attractive excursion for Athenian citizens.

One road to Athens lay between the Long Walls, tall stone defense-works six thousand yards in length that linked the walls of the Piraeus with those of Athens, but most people preferred the pathway to the north of the Walls, where they could avoid military traffic and enjoy the fields and olive groves that stretched from the little river Cephissus all the way to the sub-urb of Colonus on the edge of the city. Contrasting with the little farms and the grey-green olive groves, one saw the long, grey outline of the Acropolis of Athens, crowned with its golden complex of temples, high above the or-ange and white houses of the city. This was the excitement and the charm of Athens, the combination of a countryside teeming with gods and flowers on the edge of the urban clamor. The poet Sophocles, at the age of ninety, turned back to the beauty of Colonus after the horror of the Peloponnesian war:

> *Of all the land far famed for goodly steeds,*
> *Thou com'st, O stranger, to the noblest spot,*
>   *Colonus, glistening bright,*
> *Where evermore, in thickets freshly green,*
>   *The clear-voiced nightingale*
>   *Still haunts, and pours her song,*
>   *By purpling ivy hid,*
> *And the thick leafage sacred to the God,*
>   *With all its myriad fruits.*
>   *By mortal's foot untouched,*
>   *By sun's hot ray unscathed,*
>   *Sheltered from every blast;*
> *There wanders Dionysus evermore,*
>   *In full, wild revelry,*
> *And waits upon the Nymphs who nursed his youth.*
>
> *And in it grows a marvel such as ne'er*
>   *On Asia's soil I heard,*
> *Nor the great Dorian isle from Pelops named,*
>   *A plant self-sown, that knows*
>   *No touch of withering age,*
>   *Terror of hostile swords,*
>   *Where here on this our ground*
>   *Its high perfection gains,*
> *The grey-green foliage of the olive-tree,*
>   *Rearing a goodly race:*

And never more shall man,
Or young, or bowed with years,
Give forth the fierce command,
And lay it low in dust.
For lo! the eye of Zeus,
Zeus of our olive groves,
That sees eternally,
Casteth its glance thereon,
And she, Athena, with the clear, grey eyes.[15]

By contrast with the quiet beauty of these Athenian suburbs, the streets inside the city walls at once brought home the simplicity, and at times the meanness, of everyday Athenian life. All the streets were narrow and winding, dusty in summer and muddy in winter; and the lack of sanitation was evident to even the least sensitive nose. Most of the houses were one story, with two or three rooms and whitewashed walls of sunbaked brick or even mud and wattle. When there was a second floor, one reached it by an outer wooden staircase. Usually, it would be rented out to a peasant, or occasionally to a visitor from out of town. The walls were so thin that burglars entered by making a hole in the wall rather than prying the door. From place to place, the owner of a house might be seen removing the door or taking off the tile from the roof, the normal method of ousting people who couldn't pay the rent. Smoke poured above the flat roofs of the houses from simple braziers where the women or slaves prepared the meal, or got ready charcoal for heating the inside of the house. The few better-built houses were little more comfortable. Some might have a colonnaded courtyard, and even a few wallpaintings or tapestries. But even the richest homes had little furniture—a few tables, sofas for reclining while eating or for sleeping, a sideboard for jewels or vases. With the rats, flies, and mosquitoes that abounded, it was hardly surprising that the Athenians spent most of their time out of doors, and even when possible slept on the roof rather than in the bedroom. It was perhaps symbolic that Athenian doors opened out onto the street, not inwards; one knocked on going out so as not to hit the people in the street as the door swung open.

Most of the city's activity was concentrated in the *agora*. One passed a stone inscribed, "I am the boundary of the Agora," performed a rite of purification since the agora was a sacred place, and entered an open spacious square. On the north side was an impressive line of government buildings. On the extreme left was the circular tholos, where the fifty members of the prytany on duty ate at public expense before beginning work, and where one-third of them slept every night on constant readiness. Next to it was the bouleterion, or council house, where the full five hundred met. Inside, it

---

[15] *Oedipus at Colonus,* trans. R. H. Plumptre, cited in Charles A. Robinson, Jr., *Athens in the Age of Pericles* (Norman: University of Oklahoma Press, 1959), pp. 49–50.

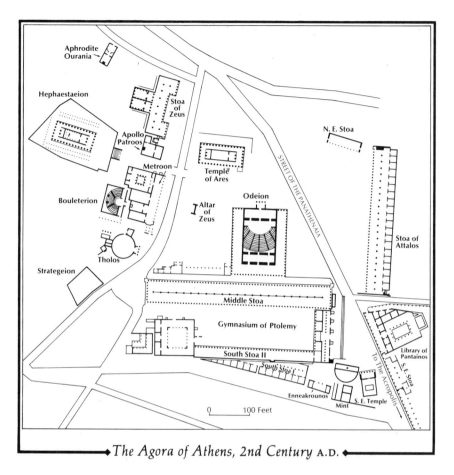

Aphrodite
Ourania

Hephaestaeion

Stoa
of
Zeus

Apollo
Patroos

N. E. Stoa

Metroon

Temple
of Ares

Bouleterion

Altar
of
Zeus

Odeion

STREET OF THE PANATHENAIA

Stoa of
Attalos

Tholos

Strategeion

Middle Stoa

Gymnasium of Ptolemy

South Stoa II

South Stoa I

To The Acropolis

Library of
Pantainos

S. E. Stoa

Enneakrounos

Mint

S. E. Temple

0   100 Feet

The Agora of Athens, 2nd Century A.D.

had a semicircular theater cut in the rock, with a large annex for storage of
documents. This council chamber was similar to the parliament buildings of
modern-day France or to the United States Senate—roofed, with seats for
the members, a public gallery, and offices nearby. In spite of the constant
assertion that Greek democracy was dependent on meetings in the open air,
the basic work of government was done indoors in Athens as anywhere
else. Next came a small Doric temple of the god Apollo, and finally a fine
marble *stoa*. The stoa was essential to Greek city life. It was a colonnade,
roofed over, which usually served as entrance to a line of shops and offices.
It suited the climate perfectly, providing shade in summer and protection
from rain or wind. It was used for gossiping and more serious discussions
(in the fourth century, the followers of the philosopher Zeno, who met
there, were known as Stoics), for meetings of the Areopagus acting as a
court, and for business transactions and banking. Behind this line of buildings, set high on its own pedestal, stood one of the great Doric temples built

Foot Race. Detail from Black-figured Amphora, Late 6th Century B. C. *The foot race was the main event at the Olympic Games, which were held every four years at Olympia from at least the eighth century* B. C.   The Metropolitan Museum of Art. Rogers Fund. 1914

by Pericles, the Hephaestaeion, which is still preserved in almost perfect condition today.

This superb architectural ensemble looked out over a scene of swirling confusion. Scattered over the agora were altars, shrines, fountain buildings, tiny temples, minor stoas, metalsmiths' fires, fishmongers' stands, and tombs for heroes. Most Athenians thrived on this excitement, notably Socrates, who drew many of his celebrated metaphors from the craftsmen he watched at work there. Others however were less admiring. Aristophanes, the comic playwright, constantly portrayed the agora as a place for decent people to avoid, suggesting that they would do better to go out of town to the gymnasium. "Brilliant and fresh like a flower," one of his characters advises, "you should spend your time in the gymnasium, instead of indulging in the artful chattering of the agora, or undoing yourself in some minor legal affair, full of chicanery, argumentation, and roguery."

The Acropolis: Athenian Architecture and Sculpture

The great rock of the Acropolis was the natural choice for a fortress and sanctuary. It rose about three hundred feet above the city. On three sides, it fell away so sharply that it was impregnable, and could only be reached on the fourth side by a steep winding pathway. For Pericles, it was natural that the most beautiful of the new shrines should be Athena's on the Acropolis. The planner was to be Ictinus, the best architect of his day. The great statue of gold and ivory of Athena was to be sculpted by Phidias, the finest sculptor. To ensure harmony in the architecture and decoration of the building, the supervision of all the work was given to Phidias. The temple to Athena, called the Parthenon, was completed in the astonishing time of only eleven years. The workmen then began the triumphal gateway to the rock, called the Propylaeon, which was almost completed during the Peloponnesian War, when the workmen turned to the two other buildings on the Acropolis, the tiny jewel of the temple of Athena Nike and the temple to Athena and Poseidon, the Erectheion. Work was finished in 395 B. C.

The Architecture of the Acropolis

The Acropolis was the greatest achievement of Greek architecture and sculpture in the creation of urban beauty and especially in the harmonization of buildings with their natural setting. In the spring and autumn, the Acropolis reaches its highest beauty. In the days of early fall, the sky is full of pastel shades, muted grays, creamy blues, and soft pinks, with a mild wind rustling clouds that seem more like the embellishments of a Corot painting than the brazen dome of the Mediterranean sky. Against that pale wash of the heavens, the buildings of the Acropolis assume shades of pink and gold of incredible complexity, contrasting with the rough greens and browns of the pine and aloes below. In Pericles' time, the contrast must have been even more startling, since the marble was painted in vivid, and even gaudy, colors. The slope of the cliffside was also used for dramatic effect. The complex of temples on the plateau of the Acropolis was reached

Propylaeon of the Acropolis, Athens
The massive gateway of the Acropolis, built in 437–432 B. C., provided a dramatic entrance to the sacred rock.   Author's photo

West Front of Parthenon Seen from the Propylaeon Gate
Greek National Tourist Office photo

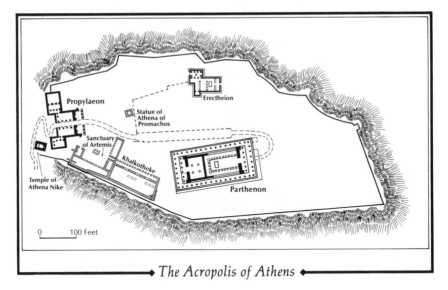

Propylaeon

Statue of Athena of Promachos

Erectheion

Sanctuary of Artemis

Khalkotheke

Temple of Athena Nike

Parthenon

0   100 Feet

◆ *The Acropolis of Athens* ◆

by a meandering path up the west slope. As one approached the fortresslike gateway of the Propylaeon, it was impossible to see the Parthenon. The two square porticoes on either side of the gate were bare and unadorned. The gateway itself was narrow, barely six feet across. The excitement grew as one reached the narrow gate, knowing but not seeing what lay beyond. Af-

Theater of Dionysus, Athens
This theater at the base of the Acropolis was constructed in the time of Pericles for presentation of the dramas of the Dionysian Festival. The original wooden benches were replaced with marble in the fourth century B. C. TAP

ter crossing through the heavy Doric gateway, the pediment of the Parthenon could be glimpsed above two older buildings, the Sanctuary of the goddess Artemis, who protected childbirth, and the Khalkotheke which housed several prized bronze statues. But only when the Street of the Panethenaia swung to the right, around a high stone wall, did one see, across the rocky surface of the Acropolis with its tones of pink and blue, the glorious west front of the Parthenon.

Since the Parthenon, like all Greek temples, consisted only of one main room, the *cella*, where the statue of the goddess was housed, and a secondary room for storage of treasures of the goddess, it appears deceptively simple as architecture. Why do architects regard this as "the most perfect example ever achieved of architecture finding its fulfillment in bodily beauty?"[16] A little knowledge of the technical details of the temple enables one to gain a growing feeling for the achievement.

Many of the elements of the classical Greek temple had been invented centuries earlier. Temples consisting of forests of huge stone colonnades serving as frames for mammoth statues of pharaohs had been built in Egypt around the fifteenth century B. C. The ground plan had already been used in the palaces of the Mycenaean kings. But in the two centuries before the erection of the Parthenon, Greek architects had advanced far beyond these earlier buildings. Using wood, they had transformed the simplest of build-

[16]Nikolaus Pevsner, *An Outline of European Architecture* (Harmondsworth, England: Penguin, 1961), p. 10.

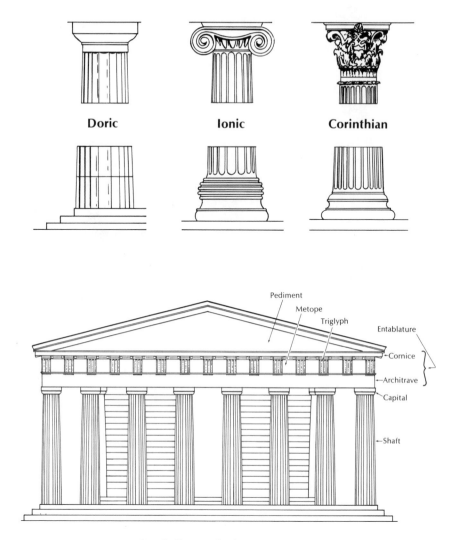

Greek Doric Architecture

ing devices, the lintel laid across a post, into the Doric column and entablature. To protect the fragile brick walls of their temple they had surrounded it with a colonnade and covered it with a sloping roof, thereby creating a triangular pediment in the facade of the building, into which sculpture could be inserted. By increasing the size of the lintel above the columns, they had left space free for a decorative alternation between rectangular spaces filled with sculpture, known as metopes, and blocks decorated only with perpendicular grooves, called triglyphs. Finally, in the sixth century they had mastered the technique of building in marble and limestone. The Parthenon was the final perfection of the style.

Temple of Athena Nike of the Acropolis, Athens *The delicate little temple was built during a temporary truce in the Peloponnesian War. Its elegant Ionic columns contrast with the power of the Doric Parthenon and Propylaeon.* Author's photo

The base of the Parthenon consists of three steps. In Doric temples like the Parthenon, the columns sit directly on the top step. The column itself is composed of a series of circular stones placed one on top of the other and joined at the center by a small square wooden post. The columns are fluted with sharp edges. On the top of the column is placed a simple round capital, on which a series of flat stone blocks are laid to create the entablature. Above the entablature at each end of the building is the depressed triangle of the pediment, the tiny fragment remaining indicative of the place where the Athenians lavished their greatest compositions of sculpture. The three steps at the base lift the temple from the ground, without one's even being aware of their existence, so that the columns seem to rise suspended in the air. The columns themselves, so strong that the heavy weight of the entablature seems slight by comparison, are not crass but delicate in appearance. It was once thought that the curve in the line of the entablature and the bulges in the columns, which are clearly visible to the eye, were deliberately used by the architects to avoid the effects of foreshortening that a perfectly straight building produces. We now feel, however, that the Greeks exaggerated the curves to such an extent that, far from negating illusory optical effects, the curves endowed the architecture with an aspect of lightness.

After creating a totally harmonious building, the architects of the Acropolis proceeded to erect a series of sharply contrasting buildings. The little temple of Athena Nike was built in the second of the classical Greek styles, known as Ionic because it was developed under Eastern influences in the Greek cities of Ionia in Asia Minor. The Ionic style was more delicate and elegant than the Doric. The column was placed on a circular, molded base; it was deeply fluted, and much slimmer than the Doric column; and most important of all, its capital was decorated with two swirls, like rolled up parchment, called volutes. The effect was of softness and charm, contrasting with the robust self-assertion of the Doric colonnade. Finally, a few yards away on the north side of the Acropolis was the Erectheion, set at an angle from the Parthenon, so that the buildings might catch the light at different angles. The Erectheion also contrasts with the Parthenon by the change in the character of the architecture, again Ionic and thus much lighter in character.

The Sculpture of the Acropolis

The Porch of Maidens of the Erectheion provides the odd spectacle of a group of girls acting as the columns of a projecting porch. Yet their flowing garments provide a quick glimpse of the character of classical Greek sculpture. There is perfection of technique in the handling of clothes, and there is deliberate exclusion of all individuality. These women represent all Greek women. There is perfection, and yet something basically human is lacking. It was this determination to exclude the emotional and the individual that led English art critic Eric Newton to complain that Greek sculpture had made the mistake of "pursuing an aim that was attainable. Beyond a certain point nothing more could be done. . . . When we see a headless Greek statue, we do not wonder what the head was like: we know that the head would tell us nothing. It would not alter the statue's mood, for the statue has hardly any mood. An armless Greek Venus is not incomplete; it arouses no curiosity as to what she was doing with her arms. We know perfectly well she was doing nothing. She was just being Venus—and even that in the mildest way." [17]

---

[17] Eric Newton, *European Painting and Sculpture* (Harmondsworth, England: Penguin, 1951), p. 86.

In short, as soon as Greek artists had mastered the technical problems of presenting the human anatomy and clothing naturalistically, they agreed on principle not to represent the peculiarities of each individual (even though they were capable of doing so), but to idealize him. The great bronze *Diadoumenos* of Polykleitos, cast in 440 B. C., shows both technical mastery and deliberate abstraction. The face was apparently what all Greeks wanted to look like, and did look like in most of the statues carved for the next hundred years. The face does not represent emotions, such as determination or excitement but rather qualities of character, such as intelligence or self-control. It is hard to say why the Greeks adopted this method of portrayal during the classical age—perhaps most sculpture was dedicated to the gods, or perhaps the individual was expected to subordinate himself to group or state or eternal laws of justice. Whatever the reason, when Phidias sought in the frieze of the Parthenon to represent the procession that culminated the great Panathenaic Festival of Athens, he

Porch of Maidens, the Erectheion of the Acropolis, Athens
The last of the great fifth-century temples on the Acropolis completed as part of Pericles' reconstruction, it was used to guard many of the sacred treasures, such as Athena's olive tree and the mark of the trident of Poseidon.   Greek National Tourist Office photo

Diadoumenos of Polykleitos
This Roman copy in marble of a bronze statue cast in 440 B. C. by the Argos sculptor Polykleitos portrays the Greek ideal of manly beauty as embodied in a victorious athlete. The Metropolitan Museum of Art. Fletcher Fund, 1925

chose to present not any one but all Panathenaic processions. For one hundred and seventy-three yards, the stone procession wound around the outer wall of the inner cella of the temple—charioteers and prancing horses, maidens bearing the robe of the goddess, young men with sacrifices, and older folk seated to watch. The frieze represented the unity of the Athenian people. The metopes, outside, showed the mythical fights of Greeks with giants, Amazons, and barbarians, the achievement of a united people. The pediments portrayed the birth of Athena and her contest with Poseidon for possession of Attica, the symbol of the city itself. In this way, the great sculptural achievements of the Parthenon realized Pericles' goal of focusing the patriotism of the Athenian citizens in the love of their goddess and her temple.

Panathenaic Procession, North Frieze of the Parthenon
The sculptures of Phidias wound around all four inner walls of the Parthenon, representing the great procession of all Athenian citizens—the culminating point of the Panathenaic festival.   Photo copyright by the Trustees of the British Museum

The Drama of Man's Fate

For Pericles, the city was far more than the buildings he was erecting. It was the character of the citizens and of their way of life. After the physical setting, the form of government that allowed all to participate, and the economic prosperity that filled Athens with the products of faraway countries, what most impressed foreigners was the intellectual vigor of the Athenian population. To get the Spartans to act against Athens, the Corinthians insulted them by contrasting their sluggishness with Athenian vivacity:

Have you never considered what manner of men these Athenians are with whom you will have to fight, and how utterly unlike yourselves? They are revolutionary, quick in the conception and in the execution of every plan. . . .

*Their bodies they devote to their country as though they belonged to other men.
Their true self is their mind, which is most truly their own when employed in
her service. . . . If a man should say of them, in a word, that they were born
neither to have peace themselves, nor to allow peace to others, he would simply
speak the truth.*[18]

Athens was a city bubbling with talk. Strangers were astonished to be
asked the most impertinent personal questions. They were even more
astonished to see leading men called to account before an assembly of thousands who all seemed to have opinions on the matters discussed. Teachers
called Sophists were paid handsomely to teach questioning that would find
the flaws in an opponent's arguments and even one's own. Thousands sat
breathless while their favorite playwrights explored the most difficult questions of human fate: Does duty to the state take precedence over duty to the
gods, or one's own conscience? Is a man responsible for acts committed in
ignorance? Why do the gods permit so much suffering in the world? From
the questions asked in Athens came our modern theater, our logic and
metaphysics, our political science and history.

Two superb instruments developed by the Athenians for asking the
most profound questions about man and his fate were the theater and the
philosophic dialogue. The former reached its height in the tragedies of
Aeschylus, Sophocles, and Euripides; the latter achieved its greatest subtlety in the conversations of Socrates, as reported and developed by Plato.

Origin of Athenian Drama

Theater as we know it was invented in Athens at the beginning of the fifth
century. Before then there had been epic songs, like those of Homer, and
poetry, both performed in public, and religious ritual dances. But the
Athenians hit on the idea of letting the playwright take an ancient religious
myth and embroider it, presenting his own version of the situations and
characters of the myth. At first there was only one actor, who talked to a
chorus. Aeschylus added a second actor, and Sophocles a third; by changing
their masks and costumes, these actors were allowed to play more than one
role. The plays were written for the five-day festival of Dionysus, the god of
wine and revelry, which was held in the spring. On the first day there was a
procession and the sacrifice of a bull, and a competition for the recital of
poems between ten choruses, each of fifty performers. Five comic plays
were produced on the second day. On each of the last three days one playwright chosen by a jury was permitted to stage three tragedies. Plays were
almost never repeated, so that throughout the fifth century nine new tragedies were produced at each festival. Of the twelve hundred plays we know
were written at this time, only forty-seven have survived! And of these we

---

[18]Jowett, *Thucydides,* p. 44.

Theater of Epidaurus
The sacred precinct of As-
clepius outside the city of
Epidaurus on the Pelopon-
nesus was visited by
invalids who wished to re-
ceive medical advice from
the god. Its theater, built
in the fourth century B. C.,
was the site of regular
dramatic festi-
vals.   Author's photo

have seven plays each by Aeschylus and Sophocles and nineteen by Euripides.

Comedy took the form of a ribald satirical probing of the character of democracy, of the foibles of rulers, or of the teachings of Sophists. It dealt exclusively with contemporary vices, personalities, and policies, and only a self-confident, democratic people could stomach many of the criticisms hurled at it and its heroes. But it required even greater moral and intellectual stamina to face, year after year, the harsh questions of man's destiny that were raised by the writers of tragedy. One symptom of the decline of Athens after the Peloponnesian War was that almost no new tragedies were written, and contemporary playwrights concentrated on bawdy, mindless comedy intended to divert the audience from weighty or worrying questions.

Aeschylus (525–456 B. C.)

Aeschylus excelled in the dramatic presentation of nemesis, the vengeance that is dealt out by the jealous gods to men who have transgressed. But he enhanced the tragic impact of his presentation by showing that the punishment was the result of either an action that was both good and bad at the same time, or a tragic flaw in an otherwise admirable or even awesome character. Aeschylus also made it clear that he did not like this state of affairs, and he raged against the injustice of the gods. The great trilogy of the *Oresteia*, which Aeschylus produced in 458 B. C., illustrates his technique perfectly.

Agamemnon, the first play in the triad, opens with quiet portents of coming doom, which intensify as the play progresses. Clytemnestra is waiting to murder her husband, Agamemnon, on his return from the siege of Troy. The trap has already been laid. Beacon fires will be lighted all the way from Troy across the islands of the Aegean to Argos to tell her when the soldiers will return. Dressed in her finest robes she meets him at the harbor and takes him inside the palace to bathe. But the audience is warned by the prophetess Cassandra that she will hack him to death with an axe:

> See there, see there! Keep from his mate the bull.
> Caught in the folded web's
> entanglement she pinions him and with the black horn
> strikes. And he crumples in the watered bath.
> Guile, I tell you, and death there in the cauldron wrought.[19]

The play ends with Clytemnestra standing with one foot on her murdered husband's body, with her lover by her side; and as the chorus warns that her son Orestes will avenge his father, Clytemnestra turns superbly to her lover and sneers,

> These are howls of impotent, bitter rage; forget them, dear, you and I
> Have the power; we two shall bring good order to our house at least.[20]

This is the terrible fate that Agamemnon suffers for the sins of his family that go back through generations of murder and sadism. The revenge of the gods is visited on the children as well as on the fathers who commit the

---

[19] Grene and Lattimore, *Complete Greek Tragedies*, I, 70.
[20] Ibid., I,90.

sins. Why can this be? asks Aeschylus. He then goes on to show, however, that Agamemnon too is guilty of the crime of *hubris*, of offending against the gods by excessive ambition. He has already made several bad choices. He has gone to war unjustly:

> For one woman's promiscuous sake
> The struggling masses, legs tired,
> Knees grinding in dust,
> Spears broken in the onset.[21]

Worse, he has compounded this error by giving in to the bloodlust of the army leaders, who wanted to get the fleet moving, sacrificing his own daughter to make the storm cease. Finally, Clytemnestra tempts him to one last act of sacrilege. She places before the palace a purple carpet whose use was reserved to persons carrying images of the gods; and Agamemnon, after a brief hesitation, strides across it. He has thus sealed his own doom.

In the second play, *The Coëphoroe*, or *The Bearers of Libations*, Clytemnestra has to be punished even if her husband was guilty in the eyes of the gods. But the tragedy is that Orestes has to kill the murderer of his father, knowing that he himself will then be punished for killing his mother. After he has stabbed her to death, he displays her body to the chorus, which tries to console him: "What you did was well done." But they have not understood what Orestes knew all along, that his punishment must come next in this endless cycle of killing. Suddenly, Orestes sees the avenging Furies, and is driven mad:

> They come like gorgons, they
> Wear robes of black, and they are wreathed in a tangle
> Of snakes. . . .
> Ah, Lord Apollo, how they grow and multiply
> Repulsive for the blood drops of their dripping eyes.[22]

But Aeschylus refuses to accept this endless violence, and in the final play of the series, *The Eumenides*, or "The Kindly Ones," Orestes, still pursued by the Furies, is permitted by the gods to be tried by mortals, by the court of the Areopagus in Athens. When the jury divides equally, Athena herself casts the deciding vote in favor of acquittal. The chain of vengeance is finally broken; the gods come out in favor of justice; the Furies are converted into the Kindly Ones, who will live in Athens and promote respect for marriage. The play ends beautifully with the apotheosis of Athens, which has reconciled destiny and justice through the intervention of Athena:

---

[21] Ibid., I, 37.
[22] Ibid., I, 130–31.

Chorus: What song then shall I chant over the land?

Athena: A song of faultless victory: from earth and sea
    From skies above may gentle breezes blow,
    And, breaking sunshine, float from shore to shore;
    That corn and cattle may continually
    Increase and multiply, and that no harm
    Befall the offspring of humanity;
    And prosper too the fruit of righteous hearts;
    For I, as one who tends flowers in a garden,
    Delight in those, the seed that bring no sorrow.[23]

Most experts on Aeschylus lean over backwards to find the ending of the *Oresteia* a stroke of genius; but one knows that the gods have not changed, just as one knows in the earlier trilogy on Prometheus that the Titan who stole fire from the gods will remain chained to a rock by Zeus until his final destruction. The real answer of Aeschylus to the question of why men seem to be punished by implacable and often unjust gods is that men grow nobler through suffering. Like Prometheus, the man of character accepts his fate and grows stronger by refusing to be cowed. As the thunder crashes around him, Prometheus hurls back threat for threat:

> Worship him, pray; flatter whatever king
> is king today; but I care less than nothing
> for Zeus. Let him do what he likes,
> let him be king for his short time: he shall not
> be king for long.[24]

Sophocles (496–406 B. C.)

Although Sophocles used many of the same stories as Aeschylus, he never attempted to present the tragedy of man as a result of the cruelty or lack of feeling in the gods, or chance. So he did not put on the great spectacles of approaching cataclysm that terrified the audiences of Aeschylus. Sophocles was interested in the character that determined the decisions a man or woman made when faced with a moral dilemma. He posed his questions from two points of view: that of the character in the play who has to make a decision—for example, Should I obey my conscience or the state?—and that of the audience—for example, What drives a woman to sacrifice herself and the man she is to marry, in order to satisfy her conscience?

    Oedipus the King is the story of a man who, in complete ignorance, murders his father, marries his mother, and on discovering what he has done, gouges out his own eyes. Piece by piece, the evidence is put together before

---

[23] *Oresteia of Aeschylus,* edited by George Thomson (Cambridge: Cambridge University Press, 1938), p. 343.

[24] Grene and Lattimore, *Complete Greek Tragedies,* I, 345.

Oedipus. His wife admits that she had once exposed to the elements to die
a son by her first husband. A shepherd confesses that he gave the child to
the neighboring king for adoption. A messenger tells Oedipus that he was
adopted as a child by that king. The wife of Oedipus says that her first husband was killed on the road by robbers; Oedipus tells her that he killed an
old man on the road to Thebes. The queen then rushes from the stage and
hangs herself. Finally, Oedipus, realizing in a moment of terrible anguish,
that he has killed his father and married his mother, screams:

> O, O, O, they will all come,
> all come out clearly! Light of the sun, let me
> look upon you no more after today!
> I who first saw the light bred of a match
> accursed, and accursed in my living,
> with them I lived with, cursed in my killing.[25]

What has also been revealed by Sophocles, however, is far more than the
web of an archaic murder mystery. It is the imperfection, the violent rage,
that Oedipus has never been able to master. On the road to Thebes, he
loses his temper when the old man in a chariot hits him with a stick, and,
knocking the old man from the chariot, beats him to death. The man proves
to be his father. Twice during the play he threatens to torture old men who
refuse to tell him the truth they fear will hurt him. "You blame my temper,"
says a seer, "but you do not see your own that lives within you." The man
who cannot control himself is ready therefore for his final outburst of rage;
but this time the victim is himself.

Antigone presents a far more complex set of questions. Antigone's two
brothers have fought and killed each other for the control of Thebes. Creon,
the ally of the younger brother, has made himself king, and has ordered under pain of death that the body of the older brother should not be buried so
that, as the Greeks believed, his spirit would be endlessly in torment. His
punishment after death would, in Creon's view, preserve civil order. Antigone decides that her moral and religious duty is to bury her brother even
though she will herself be executed. For Sophocles, the story is complicated
from a psychological point of view. Why does one disobey the state? he
asks. The answer seems easy: Because there is a higher law than that of the
state. As Antigone explains to Creon:

> For me it was not Zeus who made [your] order.
> Nor did that Justice who lives with the gods below
> mark out such laws to hold among mankind.
> Nor did I think your orders were so strong
> that you, a mortal man, could over-run
> the gods' unwritten and unfailing laws.[26]

---

[25] Ibid., II, 63.
[26] Ibid., II, 174.

Sophocles, however, wants to know why a particular human being has the will power to follow through the consequences of such an opinion. To make Antigone's case more difficult, she is bethrothed to the son of Creon, and by sacrificing herself, she knows she will be causing terrible pain. To explain Antigone's actions, Sophocles presents her as hard and inflexible, "a rigid spirit." She betrays little feeling for her fiancé, Haemon, and scorns the weakness of her sister. One is left with the uncomfortable feeling that Antigone was a woman who welcomed martyrdom as a way of showing how worthless other people were. Sophocles now shows that he is as interested in the man enforcing the questionable decree as in the woman opposing it. Creon believes almost as strongly as Antigone that his decision is morally right, that it is necessary for the well-being of the state for which he is responsible, and that he must sacrifice his niece Antigone and the happiness of his son to maintain the rule of the law. It is the dilemma that all governments, just or unjust, believe they have to face. Creon's first speech explains his concept of the state:

> For I believe that [he] who controls the state
> and does not hold to the best plans of all,
> but locks his tongue up through some kind of fear,
> that he is worst of all who are or were.
> And he who counts another greater friend
> than his own fatherland, I put him nowhere.[27]

Like any state official, he is faced with down-to-earth disrespect, and has to stomach it, when a guard comes to tell him of Antigone's action:

Guard: May I say something? Or just turn and go?

Creon: Aren't you aware your speech is most unwelcome?

Guard: Does it annoy your hearing or your mind?

Creon: Why are you out to allocate my pain?

Guard: The doer [Antigone] hurts your mind. I hurt your ears.[28]

When confronted with Antigone, he becomes petty and overbearingly male. "No woman rules me while I live," he snaps. Finally, Creon can stand the pressures upon him no longer, and he gives orders that Antigone shall be freed from the cave where she has been entombed. But Antigone has hanged herself; his son has stabbed himself over her body; and Creon, now seen to be a weak, changeable man, who has not even had the strength to uphold a decree he believed to be just, is broken in spirit. His breakdown is ignominious and pitiable, and he goes off with a whimper:

---

[27] Ibid., II, 165.
[28] Ibid., II, 168.

Servants, take me away, out of the sight of men.
I who am nothing more than nothing now.[29]

Antigone is a great play because it contrasts absolutes, political and moral, but shows that there is no comparable absolute in the human character that carries them out.

Euripides (c. 480–406 B. C.)

Euripides faced the basic question, Is there something wrong with our society and with us as human beings? And with a little subterfuge, he gave the answer, Yes, far too much: our religion preaches injustice, if not at times flagrant immorality; our wars are cruel and nonsensical; our women are oppressed; our slaves are men like us, not the debased creatures we pretend them to be. Worse yet, in some human beings are character traits that will bring inevitable suffering to those around them. The Athenians listened in fascination, but rarely gave him the festival prize; and near the end of his life, annoyed at being twice prosecuted, though unsuccessfully, he went to live in Macedon. After his death, and the sufferings of the Peloponnesian War, he became the favorite tragic playwright of Athens, because only then was his message accepted.

The greatest moments in Euripides' plays occur when he shows that love and jealousy can become "blind and irrational forces in human nature," destroying the person they control and causing dreadful suffering to all who come near. "Love when it comes in too great strength, has never brought good renown or virtue to mortals." The great example is the play *Medea*. Jason, a nasty boorish fellow, has been helped to find the Golden Fleece by the barbarian princess Medea, who has borne him two sons. Back home, Jason decides to marry a younger, less exacting woman from his own people, and he has Medea exiled. Medea first breaks into the famous lament on the misery of women:

> Of all things upon earth that bleed and grow
> A herb most bruised is woman. We must pay
> Our store of gold, hoarded for that one day,
> To buy us some man's love; and lo, they bring
> A master of our flesh! . . .
> Home never taught her that—how best to guide
> Toward peace the thing that sleepeth at her side.
> And she who, laboring long, shall find some way
> Whereby her lord may bear with her, nor fray
> His yoke too fiercely, blessed is the breath
> That woman draws! Else let her pray for death.[30]

[29] Ibid., II, 203.
[30] *The Medea*, trans. Gilbert Murray (New York: Oxford University Press, 1912), p. 15.

But Medea is not one to writhe in self-pity. She has a savage strength that compels her to plan revenge. She sends a magic robe as a gift to the would-be bride of Jason, who is immediately burned to death in its folds. With a frightful insight into abnormal psychology, Euripides then changes the traditional legend, and has Medea take revenge on Jason himself by murdering their own two sons. There are few more terrible moments in all literature than when Medea wavers in her resolve to carry through this hideous plan.

> O children, my children, for you there will be a city, a home where you will always live, robbed of your mother, while for me there can only be my misery to live with. . . . Never again, from that other life, shall your dear eyes behold your mother. Woe, woe! Why do you look at me like that, my sons? Are you trying to smile at me for the last time? . . . Come, my sons, give me your right hands and let me hold them. O dearest hands, O lips I love, the form and noble features of my children! Go, go away. I've no strength left to look upon my sons: I am borne down by evil. Too well I know what horror I intend, but passion overwhelms my mind, worst cause of man's worst ills.[31]

The Search for Reality in Athenian Philosophy

While the Athenian playwrights were struggling with problems concerning man and the nature of the universe, the Athenian philosophers were seeking a method of inquiry by which answers to these problems could be found. Philosophy began only in the sixth century B. C., in the Ionian cities of Asia Minor, when, for the first time, men tried to explain the nature of the world without using myths. Instead of saying, "The physical world is controlled by gods," the Ionian philosophers asked more scientific questions, such as, Is there a material explanation of the nature of matter? Their answers were necessarily less satisfactory than their questions. One philosopher held that water was the basic element; another, air and earth. Soon, however, the philosophers turned from their study of the nature of the material universe to concentrate on the nature of human beings, particularly their knowledge of right and wrong, and on the type of state in which they can achieve the most ethical way of life.

In Athens, the philosophers most in public view were the Sophists, "the teachers of wisdom" who, for money, taught well-to-do young men the principles of rhetoric and, probably to a lesser degree, of the search for a theory of knowledge. One, a friend of Pericles who was later exiled for impiety, proclaimed: "Man is the measure of all things, of things that are what they are, and of things that are not what they are not." Another, apparently overwhelmed with the need to rely on man as the source of knowledge, fell

---

[31] Cited in *Literary History of Greece* by Robert Flacelière, published by Elek Books Ltd. London, 1962, p. 213.

into total skepticism: "There is nothing; even if there is anything, we cannot know it; even if we could know it, we could not communicate our knowledge to anyone else." But the philosopher who most upset traditional Athenian thinking by his questioning was Socrates.

Socrates (469–399 B. C.)

The reputation of Socrates has survived unblemished longer than that of any other person in history. In the fourth century B. C., Plato called him "the best and the wisest and the most righteous man of our time." Twenty-four hundred years later, a fine classical scholar still could describe him as "the most noble man who has ever lived." Yet the evidence of his life is very sparse. He was the son of a stonemason and a midwife, and he later claimed to have followed both professions. After a little stonecutting, he said, he became a midwife; but "I attend men and not women, and I practise on their souls when they are in labor, and not on their bodies; and the triumph of my art is in examining whether the thought which the mind of the young man is bringing to birth is a false idol or a noble and true creation." In city affairs he did only what he had to, serving as a hoplite and in a few minor city offices. He was ugly and pot-bellied, looked like a satyr, and apparently could become immobilized for hours in mystical trances. He avowed his own ignorance: "The only thing I know is that I know nothing." Nonetheless, wherever he went, he talked, and his talk began a revolution in philosophy. Part of the effect was due to his personal magnetism; he was like a torpedo-fish whose touch makes a man torpid, said one of the Sophists. But his real contribution was to teach a new method for seeking truth through discussion.

Bust of Socrates
The sculptor has caught the humorous irreverence in Socrates' character that led him to challenge the most deeply rooted assumptions of all who engaged him in philosophical discussion. Courtesy of the Louvre, Paris

He began by destroying preconceptions. "Justice is nothing else than that which is advantageous to the stronger," an unwary young man tells him at the beginning of Plato's *Republic*. Socrates replies:

I must first learn what you mean. As yet I do not know. You say to me that what is advantageous to the stronger is just. Now what do you mean by that, Thrasymachus? For example, you surely do not mean to assert that if Polydamus, the athlete, is stronger than we and it is to his bodily advantage to eat meat, then for us also who are weaker, this diet is advantageous, and consequently just.[32]

The second step is inductive inquiry, that is, to take a series of individual examples of something that might be beautiful or just in order to discover what they have in common. What they have in common would then be beauty or justice, and one would thus have reached the third step in the Socratic dialogue, which is definition. The definition that Socrates sought, of the good man, for example, had always a moral purpose. We shall see as

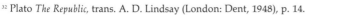

[32] Plato *The Republic*, trans. A. D. Lindsay (London: Dent, 1948), p. 14.

we explore the political thinking of later cities that one can crudely classify political philosophers into those who believe in the goodness of humanity, and who therefore seek a state that will bring out that goodness, and those who believe either in the selfishness or in the morally neutral character of human beings, whom the state must therefore mold so that they may become good according to that particular state's conception of goodness. Socrates believed in the essential goodness of human nature. He considered that it was necessary to know oneself better to achieve that goodness.

The irony of Socrates' life, and the disgrace of Athenian democracy, is that the philosopher who sought goodness should have been tried and condemned to death for impiety. In 399 B. C., Socrates was accused of corrupting the young and introducing new gods. In his trial, far from defending himself, Socrates asserted that Athens needed him as a "gadfly."

I think that no better piece of fortune has ever befallen you in Athens than my service to God. For I spend my whole life in going about and persuading you all to give your first and chiefest care to the perfection of your soul, and not till you have done that to think of your bodies, or your wealth; and telling you that virtue does not come from wealth, but that wealth, and every other good thing which men have, whether in public or private, comes from virtue. . . . Either acquit me, or do not acquit me: but be sure that I shall not alter my way of life; no, not if I have to die for it many times.[33]

The jury was even less impressed by his suggestion that instead of condemning him to death they should give him a state pension. On being condemned, he refused an escape plan dreamed up by his friends, talked to them a long last time about the problem of immortality, drank hemlock, and died in front of them. His death was a measure of the debasement of Athenian democracy under the impact of the Peloponnesian War.

Plato (427–347 B. C.)

In Plato, who was twenty-eight years old at the time of the trial, the views of Socrates achieved a flowering that the master never dreamed of and would probably have disapproved. With an aristocratic background, the shock of the brutality of the Peloponnesian War, and especially the degradation of Athenian democracy displayed in the treatment of Socrates, Plato was led to reject the polis of Pericles. Although many of his dialogues have left us in an idealized form the splendor of the intellectual sparring of fifth-century Athenians, yet he rejected the political system in which this mental give-and-take thrived. Plato's greatest book, *The Republic,* proclaims the ideal of a city-state that is far closer to the military oligarchy of Sparta than the Athens that Socrates had loved. The purpose of *The Republic* is to define the meaning of justice. At the heart of his argument was his theory of

---

[33] Benjamin Jowett, trans. (1875), cited in G. Lowes Dickinson, *Plato and His Dialogues* (Harmondsworth, England: Penguin, 1950), p. 32.

knowledge expounded in the marvelous simile of the cave. Human beings, he says, are like prisoners in an underground cave, chained by their legs and necks, so that they can only see the back wall along which shadows cast by a fire behind them are moving. The prisoners believe that the shadows are real objects because they have never seen anything else. When one of them is released, and goes to the mouth of the cave, he is first dazzled and wants to return to the shadows. Then he becomes used to the light, and perceives the objects that have been casting the shadows. The purpose of education is to bring people out of the cave to a perception of reality. But what does Plato mean by the real objects one finds outside the cave? To understand this we must glance at his theory of "ideas."

What is it that a side chair and an armchair and a rocking chair have in common? They all resemble the idea of a perfect chair, Plato would reply. The idea of a chair exists, for otherwise we would not know that these three objects are all chairs. So also the idea of goodness or justice or of the perfect state exists. These are the real objects to be found outside the cave. Plato felt, however, that not everyone is capable of perceiving all reality. Some can get as far as perceiving the idea of a chair but are incapable of perceiving the idea of the perfect state. He therefore held that the few who were capable of perceiving all the ultimate ideas should rule the state. Then, they could bring the state in which they were living as close as possible to the ideal state that they alone could perceive. These rulers would of course be the philosophers: "Unless philosophers bear kingly rule in cities, or those who are now called kings and princes become genuine and adequate philosophers . . . , there will be no respite in evil for cities or for humanity." A second group were to be the Guardians, and live much like Spartan soldiers. The rest were to be Workers. To fortify his argument, Plato launched a telling attack on democracy, in which all people are free to do as they want. Such a democratic city would be devoted to the pursuit of pleasure and the avoidance of pain, and would inevitably decline into a tyranny. Unfortunately Plato himself ends with the justification of all authoritarian states, that the rulers have the duty to force the populace to lead good lives for their own benefit. Plato accepted too easily a blanket condemnation of Periclean democracy. Instead of appreciating its vitality, and seeking a method to cure the ills within the political system, he rejected it. As he himself remarked, "Plato was born late in the day for his country."

Aristotle (384–322 B. C.)

Aristotle, Plato's most famous pupil, exercised far greater influence than his master, since his views on almost every one of the many subjects he studied came to be accepted as final truth by the medieval Christian Church. Only when Aristotle had been displaced as the ultimate authority was progress possible in medicine, biology, political theory, ethics, and logic. The reasons for the longevity of Aristotle's teachings were their encyclopedic volume and their internal consistency, even more than the fact that they repre-

Aristotle
After tutoring Alexander the Great for seven years, Aristotle returned to Athens in 336 B.C. to continue his many-sided research and to teach at his school in the Lyceum.
Museo Nazionale delle Terme, Rome/Alinari-Scala

sented the most up-to-date research of the day. Aristotle was an experimenter; he studied embryology by breaking open eggs at regular intervals to inspect the development of the chicken, and he dissected fish and shellfish. But he was above all a collector and classifier. To write a book on politics, he collected 158 constitutions; he broke down his collection of data on living things into a form of classification similar to the modern one that is organized into species and genera. In his logic, he developed a method of establishing truth by the use of classified forms of arguments called syllogisms. Here is one of the most common examples. "All men are mortal. Socrates is a man. Therefore Socrates is mortal." The final results of his work were so voluminous and so impressive that he eventually came to be known as The Philosopher.

The Politics provides a good example of Aristotle's method of work, some of his most basic ideas, and examples of his disagreement with Plato. From his classification of the 158 constitutions he had collected, Aristotle determined that there were only three types of states, each of which could be good or bad. Good rule by one man was monarchy; bad was tyranny; good rule by the few, aristocracy; bad, oligarchy; good rule by the many, polity; bad (usually by the poor or a mob), democracy. Unlike Plato, Aristotle felt that there was no such thing as an ideal state that would suit everyone. Observation had shown him that, while the state was the natural unit in which to achieve the good life, different states suited different people. Tradition and habit molded the citizens in the working of a particular state; education was necessary to train an individual in the spirit of the constitution; the most successful state was run by a large middle class whose members possessed a "moderate and adequate property." The ideal in politics as in ethics was the golden mean—a state of moderate size, with sufficient natural resources and a temperate climate, a balanced distribution of age groups, and a wide sharing of wealth. Only then could the citizen pursue one of the few absolutes of which Aristotle approved, "the energy, and practice of goodness, to a degree of perfection, and in an absolute mode."

The disillusionment of Aristotle and the outright disgust of Plato with Periclean democracy can, however, only be understood by consideration of the disastrous effects of the Peloponnesian War, which many felt to be the result of the failings of Athenian political leadership.

The Peloponnesian War: The Hubris of the Periclean Empire

The Peloponnesian War left Athens its buildings, but impaired its nobility of thought. And for this Pericles must take a large share of the blame. Pericles had argued that the Athenians owed no responsibility to their empire beyond extending protection. They could use their power at sea to enforce obedience in their league, and, worse, they could challenge the land power of the rival Peloponnesian League headed by Sparta. By 431 B. C., Pericles had succeeded in making enemies of every important city in Greece. Moreover, Pericles felt that he had made Athens impregnable. His fleet and colonies controlled the grain route to the Black Sea. Construction of the Long Walls had made Athens and the Piraeus into an enormous fortress. The annual tribute from the empire, which was as great as the revenue of Athens itself, had been used for a vast war treasury. With a land army of over twenty thousand hoplites, and a navy of three hundred triremes, Pericles believed he could neutralize any opponents by land and defeat them at sea.

He had recognized that war was a probable consequence of his policy. "Do not imagine that what we are fighting for is simply a question of freedom and slavery," he is said by Thucydides to have told the Athenians at the beginning of the war. "There is also involved the loss of our empire and the dangers arising from the hatred which we have incurred in administering it. . . . In fact, you hold your empire down by force; it may have been wrong to take it; it is certainly dangerous to let it go." The Spartans were finally persuaded by the Corinthians to take the lead in a war against Athens. At first it appeared that there would be a stalemate. Pericles called the inhabitants of the countryside into Athens and abandoned the fields to the Spartans. The Athenian fleet was sent to ravage the coasts of the Peloponnesus. In the pages of Thucydides' account of the Peloponnesian War, which is not only a superb reconstruction of the events but a telling portrayal of the character of men at war, Pericles blossoms into a great war leader. When the headstrong young men would have rushed out of the walls at the sight of the Spartan army burning the fields only six miles from the city, he ignored the anger of the people and forced them to stay with his wise but unpopular strategy. A year later, when the even more disastrous progress of the war led them to blame him personally for their troubles, he appeared before the assembly and called on them to remember their highest traditions:

You, in your private afflictions, are angry with me that I persuaded you to declare war. Therefore you are angry also with yourselves, that you voted with me. . . . I have not changed: it is you who have changed. A calamity has befallen you, and you cannot persevere in the policy you chose when all was well: it is the weakness of your resolution that makes my advice seem to have been wrong. It is the unexpected that most breaks a man's spirit.

You have a great polis, and a great reputation; you must be worthy of them.[34]

Above all, in the great funeral speech that he had given in memory of those who had died in the first year of the war, he had reminded Athenians of the ideal of Athens for which they were fighting.

[34] Cited in Kitto, *The Greeks,* p. 142, from Thucydides II. 60–64.

It is true that we are called a democracy, for the administration is in the hands of the many and not of the few. But while the law secures equal justice to all alike in their private disputes, the claim of excellence is also recognized; and when a citizen is in any way distinguished, he is preferred to the public service, not as a matter of privilege, but as the reward of merit. Neither is poverty a bar, but a man may benefit his country whatever be the obscurity of his condition. There is no exclusiveness in our public life, and in our private intercourse we are not suspicious of one another, nor angry with our neighbor if he does what he likes. . . . And we have not forgotten to provide for our weary spirits many relaxations from toil; we have regular games and sacrifices throughout the year; our homes are beautiful and elegant; and the delight which we daily feel in all these things helps to banish melancholy. Because of the greatness of our city the fruits of the whole earth flow in upon us; so that we enjoy the goods of other countries as freely as our own. . . .

We are lovers of the beautiful, yet simple in our tastes, and we cultivate the mind without loss of manliness. Wealth we employ, not for talk and ostentation, but when there is a real use for it. To avow poverty with us is no disgrace, the true disgrace is doing nothing to avoid it. . . . We alone regard a man who takes no interest in public affairs, not as harmless, but as a useless character. . . . The great impediment to action is, in our opinion, not discussion, but the want of that knowledge which is gained by discussion preparatory to action. . . . To sum up: I say that Athens is the school of Hellas, and that the individual Athenian in his own person seems to have the power of adapting himself to the most varied forms of action with the utmost versatility and grace. . . .

I have dwelt upon the greatness of Athens because I want to show you that we are contending for a higher prize than those who enjoy none of these privileges, and to establish by manifest proof the merit of these men whom I am now commemorating. Their loftiest praise has been already spoken. For in praising the city I have praised them, and men like them whose virtues made her glorious.[35]

In 430 B. C., the weakness of Athens' military position was exposed when plague, probably typhus, brought from Egypt hit the city. During the next months, about one-third of the population of Athens died in terrible suffering. Thucydides himself caught the plague, recovered, and described it in the medical terms of his day, with his usual didactic conclusions.

Internally, the throat and the tongue were quickly suffused with blood, and the breath became unnatural and fetid. There followed sneezing and hoarseness; in a short time the disorder, accompanied by a violent cough, reached the chest, then fastening lower down, it could move the stomach and bring on all the vomits of bile to which physicians have ever given names. . . .
Men who had hitherto concealed what they took pleasure in, now grew bolder.

---

[35] Selected from Jowett, *Thucydides*, pp. 117–22, from Thucydides II. 36–43.

For, seeing the sudden change—how the rich died in a moment, and those who had nothing immediately inherited their property—they reflected that life and riches were alike transitory, and they resolved to enjoy themselves while they could, and to think only of pleasure.[36]

Pericles himself died of the plague in 429 B. C. Lacking his resolute leadership, the city divided into warring factions of those who had done well out of the war, the commercial and manufacturing classes, and those who had suffered, the aristocrats and the peasants together. Demagogic leaders appeared, playing on the passions of the assembly. For Thucydides, the breakdown of morality was complete. The whole of Greece was engaging in a civil war of city against city and class against class. He used the waves of murder inside the city of Corcyra as an example of the degradation that war had brought. "In peace and prosperity," he commented, "both states and individuals are actuated by higher motives because they do not fall under the dominion of imperious necessities. But war, which takes away the comfortable provision of daily life, is a hard master, and tends to assimilate men's characters to their conditions." By now, neither side was willing to give up without complete victory. After a long truce, the Athenians struck out foolishly to conquer the rich city of Syracuse in Sicily, and lost both fleet and army. Athens itself was seized by an oligarchy that persecuted the leaders of the democratic party, and then by the democrats, who banished the oligarchs. With political chaos in the city, the Athenians' ability to fight lessened year by year. The Persians entered the war on the side of the Spartans; and finally, in 404 B. c., the Athenians fearfully accepted the peace terms imposed by Sparta: destruction of the Long Walls and the walls of Piraeus, surrender of their fleet except for twelve ships, return of the banished oligarchs, and recognition of Spartan leadership. So happy were the people of Athens at the coming of peace that they rushed with great enthusiasm to pull down the walls, to the accompaniment of female flute players. It was a suitably ignoble end to a war that had poisoned the soul of Athens.

SUGGESTED READING

Among the innumerable general histories of Greece, H. D. F. Kitto, *The Greeks* (1963) is a lively, idiosyncratic overview by a British scholar who has devoted his life to Greek literature. Anthony Andrewes, *The Greeks* (1967) is more political in focus. Moses I. Finley, *The Ancient Greeks* (1963) is readable, reliable, and too short. Evocation through color photography is successfully practiced by the magazine *Horizon, The Horizon Book of Ancient Greece* (1965); by contrast, N. G. L. Hammond, *A History of Greece to 322 B. C.* (1967) is based on vast research, extremely detailed, and very dull. R. M. Cook, *The Greeks Till Alexander* (1961) is easy to use for individual topics, such as religion or war, but is not integrated as a book. Latest findings of

---

[36] Ibid., pp. 125, 128, from Thucydides II. 49, 53.

scholarship are surveyed in Victor Ehrenberg, *From Solon to Socrates* (1968), which is hard to read but useful. The classical, rather romanticized account of Alfred Zimmern, *The Greek Commonwealth* (1931) is still worth reading, as is the similarly dated Werner Jaeger, *Paideia: The Ideals of Greek Culture,* 3 vols. (1939–44).

The Minoan age in Crete is assessed in R. W. Hutchinson, *Prehistoric Crete* (1962), and the buildings described in J. Walter Graham, *The Palaces of Crete* (1961).

The Mycenaean age is best understood by reading the poems of Homer, especially the *Iliad,* which is well translated by E. V. Rieu (1946); but the recent advances made by archaeologists in accurate reconstruction of that age can be admired in John Chadwick's *The Decipherment of Linear B* (1960) which tells how Michael Ventris worked out the Mycenaean script from thousands of clay tablets, and in William A. MacDonald, *Progress into the Past: The Rediscovery of Mycenaean Civilization* (1967). Alan E. Samuel, *The Mycenaeans in History* (1966) is a reliable introduction. Emily Vermeule, *Greece in the Bronze Age* (1964) is up to date, thorough, and amusing. The finest history of the Dark Age is Chester G. Starr, *The Origins of Greek Civilization, 1100–650* B. C. (1961), which can be supplemented with A. R. Burn, *The World of Hesiod* (1937); A. M. Snodgrass, *The Dark Age of Greece* (1971), and V. R. d'A. Desborough, *The Greek Dark Age* (1972).

For the defeated side in the Trojan War, see C. W. Blegen, *Troy and the Trojans* (1963).

The political development of the seventh and sixth centuries B. C. is freshly treated in an exciting new analysis by W. G. Forrest, *The Emergence of Greek Democracy 800–400* B. C. (1966) and in A. Andrewes, *The Greek Tyrants* (1956). The great colonization movement throughout the Mediterranean from the Greek cities is described in J. Boardman, *The Greeks Overseas* (1964); A. J. Graham, *Colony and Mother City in Ancient Greece* (1964); and T. J. Dunbabin, *The Western Greeks* (1948). On the troubled relationship with Persia, see A. T. Olmstead, *History of the Persian Empire* (1948); C. Hignett, *Xerxes' Invasion of Greece* (1963); and the popular but reliable account of Peter Green, *Xerxes at Salamis* (1970).

For a good reference work to the topography of Athens, see John Travlos, *Pictorial Dictionary of Ancient Athens* (1971). The achievements of Athens are well synthesized in C. M. Bowra, *Periclean Athens* (1971). Thin on facts but long on excerpts from primary sources, Charles A. Robinson, Jr.'s *Athens in the Age of Pericles* (1959) is an evocative introduction. Angelou Procopiou, *Athens City of the Gods* (1964) is a beautifully illustrated history of classical Athens, with emphasis on the physical appearance of the city. R. E. Wycherley explains in *How the Greeks Built Cities* (1962) why Athens looked as it did; this is a clear, layman's account based on the latest documentation, with detailed study of the different parts of the city, such as the agora, shrines, and gymnasium. Roland Martin, *Living Architecture: Greece* (1967) is part of a fine Swiss series, providing a simplified introduction to the technical aspects of Greek architecture by a prime authority. Martin's *L'Urbanisme dans la Grèce Antique* (1956) is the definitive work on Greek town planning. The vitally important findings of the American excavation team are given in Homer A. Thompson and R. E. Wycherley, *The Agora of Athens: The History, Shape and Uses of an Ancient City Center* (1972).

For the political life of fifth-century Athens, one might begin with Frank J. Frost, *Democracy and the Athenians* (1961), and then focus on its leading statesman, in A. R. Burn, *Pericles and Athens* (1962). P. J. Rhodes, *The Athenian Boule* (1972) gives a detailed study of the working of the Council of Five Hundred. The best book on the Athenian empire is Russell Meiggs, *The Athenian Empire* (1972) which attempts to explain the motivation for Periclean imperialism. W. Robert Connor attempts a prosopographic approach in *The New Politicians of Fifth Century Athens* (1971).

Social life in fifth-century Athens is described in a juvenile way in Marjorie Quennell and C. H. B. Quennell, *Everyday Things in Classical Greece* (1932), which has a few insights, into women's hairstyle, for example; but fortunately Robert Flacelière, *Daily Life in the Athens of Pericles* (1964) is excellent on social structure, education, and details of daily life, and makes fine use of primary sources and photographs.

The economic structure of the city can be pieced together from the old-fashioned H. Michell, *The Economics of Ancient Greece* (1957) or the even more antique George M. Calhoun, *The Business Life of Ancient Athens* (1926), which does have some interesting details on the grain trade. A short but reliable analysis of the economy of the whole Greek world is made by Frank Frost in *Greek Society* (1971). Commerce and industry are treated in the collaborative study edited by Carl Roebuck, *The Muses at Work* (1969). The controversy over the economic value of slavery is illustrated in W. L. Westermann, *The Slave Systems of Greek and Roman Antiquity* (1955) and Moses I. Finley, *Slavery in Classical Antiquity* (1960). The conditions of skilled labor are analyzed in Alison Burford, *Craftsmen in Greek and Roman Society* (1972). Moses I. Finley provides a stimulating series of lectures on both Greece and Rome in his *The Ancient Economy* (1973).

Greek and Roman ideas on city planning can be compared in J. B. Ward-Perkins, *Cities of Ancient Greece and Italy: Planning in Classical Antiquity* (1974).

The evolution of Greek architecture can be followed in A. W. Lawrence, *Greek Architecture* (1957) or the rather more complete D. S. Robertson, *A Handbook of Greek and Roman Architecture* (2nd ed., 1954). Eric Newton disparages Greek sculpture quite effectively in *European Painting and Sculpture* (1951), but more appreciative views can be found in R. Lullies and M. Hirmer, *Greek Sculpture* (2nd ed., 1960), Rhys Carpenter, *Greek Sculpture* (1960), and J. J. Pollitt, *Art and Experience in Classical Greece* (1972).

For superbly literate introductions to Greek literature, see the limpid treatment of C. M. Bowra, *Landmarks in Greek Literature* (1966) and the penetrating analysis of H. D. F. Kitto, *Greek Tragedy* (1955), which perhaps gives too much attention to the form of the tragedies and too little to their meaning. Or better yet, read the tragedies in the translations edited for the University of Chicago Press by David Grene and Richmond Lattimore. Aubrey de Selincourt has a fine new translation of *The Histories of Herodotus* (1954), and Benjamin Jowett's translation of *The Peloponnesian War* of Thucydides is still exciting. A fascinating guidebook of Greece by Pausanias, one of Baedeker's forerunners in the second century A. D., called *Description of Greece*, provides marvelous descriptions of the antiquities that would appeal to a tourist-minded Roman. Greek philosophy before Socrates is discussed in F. M. Cornford, *Before and After Socrates* (1950) and J. Burnet, *Early Greek Philosophy* (rev. ed., 1958), Greek religion in Edith Hamilton, *Mythology* (1942) and W. K. C. Guthrie, *The Greeks and Their Gods* (1950).

It is also instructive to compare Athens with Sparta, by consulting K. M. T. Chrimes, *Ancient Sparta* (1949), W. G. Forrest, *A History of Sparta, 950–192 B. C.* (1969), or H. Mitchell, *Sparta* (1952).

Finally, for the catastrophe that brought the golden age to an end, see Donald Kagan, *The Outbreak of the Peloponnesian War* (1969).

3 / The Hellenistic Age

The vicious struggles of the Peloponnesian War destroyed the precarious harmony of fifth-century Greece. That harmony had been a balancing of tensions—of city with city, class with class, even philosophy with philosophy; but the wars bred the intolerance that destroys civic harmony. When Athens surrendered to the Spartan commander Lysander in the spring of 404 B. C., it was a city that had lost confidence in itself.

During the next two centuries, however, the Greeks succeeded in salvaging a good deal from the wreckage of the wars, and with the restoration of political calm displayed continuing virtuosity in the creation of a distinctly different culture, which we call Hellenistic, or Greek-like. This culture spread throughout the eastern Mediterranean area and the Near East, as a result of the conquests of Alexander the Great (reigned 336–323 B. C.) of Macedon. Within this vast empire during the brief reign of Alexander, and in the Seleucid, Antigonid, and Ptolemaic empires into which it broke after his death, a new form of city life was created. With little independent political life, the large cosmopolitan cities lived largely for commerce and manufacturing, and the cultural life grew out of the patronage of the great dynasties and of the prosperous middle classes. Although Athens remained intellectually vigorous, it was no longer the school of the Mediterranean world whose attention was focused on the newer centers of wealth and learning like Antioch in Syria and especially Alexandria in Egypt.

Laocoön with His Sons (Hellenistic Sculpture, 1st Century B.C.) Courtesy Boston Public Library

The rise of the city of Rome under its republican institutions, from the fifth century B. C. on, transformed the whole character of the Mediterranean world and, from the third century B. C., western Europe as well. The Romans had developed under the beneficial cultural influences of the Etruscan cities to the north and the Greek cities on the Italian peninsula and Sicily to the south. Between about 500 and 275 B. C. they conquered Italy. By 30 B. C. they were masters of the Mediterranean and of most of western Europe. During this expansion they had absorbed much of Hellenistic cultural inheritance, which was thus given new and enduring life. Through Macedon and then through Rome, Greek culture was transmitted to become a permanent part of Western civilization. But the Greek culture that left its lasting stamp upon the Roman republic was not from the time of Pericles; it was that lighter, flashier, more superficial, yet attractive mode of thought created in the renewed vigor that came with convalescence from the Peloponnesian War.

In examining the period from the end of the Peloponnesian War in 404 B. C. to the end of the Roman republic in 27 B. C., we shall therefore consider first the establishment and character of the empire of Alexander the Great and its successor states; second, the influence of the Etruscan and Greek cities of Italy on Rome during its early years; and third, the expansion of Rome, and the influence of imperialism on Roman society during the period of the republic.

Alexander and the Spread of Hellenistic Culture

The Greek cities remained blind to the lessons of the Peloponnesian War. Unity had enabled them to hold off Persia at the beginning of the fifth century. Unity, Xenophon told them at the beginning of the fourth century, would enable them to conquer the Persian Empire itself. Xenophon, a young Athenian aristocrat who had studied with Socrates, had turned mercenary soldier in the service of Persia after the defeat of Athens. Leading ten thousand Greek mercenaries on an exciting trek from Babylon across Armenia to the Black Sea, which he described in the great adventure story *Anabasis,* Xenophon became convinced that the weaknesses of the Persian armies were so great that the empire lay open to Greek conquest. Their duty, Xenophon told his soldiers at the beginning of their march, was not "to live in idleness and luxury, and to consort with the tall and beautiful women of these Medes and Persians," but to get back home "to point out to the Greeks that it is by their own choice that they are poverty-stricken, for they could bring their poor here and make them rich." Evidently the dreams of empire were hard for some Athenians to relinquish. More than half a century passed, however, before the Greek cities followed Alexander into Persia.

Philip of Macedon (Reigned 359–336 B. C.)

Instead, the Greek city-states continued their internecine struggles, dominated now by Sparta, now by Thebes. The result of their fighting, Xenophon commented despairingly forty years after the *Anabasis,* was "the opposite of what all men believed would happen. . . . While each party claimed to be victorious, neither was found to be any better off, as regards either additional territory, or city, or sway, than before the battle took place; but there was even more confusion and disorder in Greece after the battle than before." [1]

Both in Greece itself and among the Greek cities on the coasts of Italy and Sicily, political life had degenerated into petty squabbles by the middle of the fourth century B. c. In Greece, the way was open for Macedon; in Italy for the expansion of Rome. Macedon, a large tribal state in the north of Greece, influenced by Greek culture but run despotically by its kings, had both a tougher climate and people than the rest of Greece. The Macedonians were sturdy peasants and mountaineers with little love for the city-states that had treated them for decades like poor relatives in the Greek family. Thus, when Philip of Macedon seized the throne in 359 B. c., he decided to bring Greece under his control by bribery and guile, and if necessary, by force. His citizen army, with an infantry of peasants and cavalry of nobles, was a professional force easily superior to the mercenaries being used by most Greek cities. Moreover, many sincere Greeks were beginning to wonder if Philip might not be their salvation, bringing efficiency and discipline that the bickering city governments could not supply; and many refused to see in Philip, as the great Athenian orator Demosthenes begged them to do, the embodiment of military autocracy. Nor were they stirred by Demosthenes' passionate demand, in his first great attack on Philip, known as the *First Philippic:* "Are you content to run around and ask one another, 'Is there any news today?' Could there be any news more startling than that a Macedonian is triumphing over Athenians and settling the destiny of Hellas?" [2] With his victory over the Greeks at Chaeronea in 338 B. c., Philip ended forever the dominance of the polis. The influence of Greek civilization in the future was to be spread by empires—by Alexander and the heirs to his divided empire and by the Romans.

Far from destroying Athens, as Demosthenes had forecast, Philip seemed determined to fulfill the hopes of his admirers, "to put an end to the madness and the imperialism with which the Greeks have treated one another, reconcile and bring them into concord, and declare war on Persia." The first troops sent against Persia had already crossed the Hellespont

---

[1] Xenophon *Hellenica* VII. 26–27, trans. Carleton L. Brownson, in Loeb edition, Vol. II (London: W. Heinemann, 1921), p. 227. Loeb editions, to which subsequent footnotes refer for original text, are now published by the Harvard University Press.

[2] Demosthenes *First Philippic* 10, in Loeb edition (London: W. Heinemann, 1930), p. 75.

when Philip, at the age of forty-six, was murdered by a disaffected noble; but his twenty-year-old son, Alexander, was immediately acclaimed king. No one could have been better prepared. Aristotle, his tutor since he was thirteen, had given him a broad training in ethics, metaphysics, politics, science, and medicine, as well as a genuine love of Greek poetry. Alexander's favorite poem was the *Iliad,* since it portrayed the exploits of one of his own fabled ancestors, "swift-footed Achilles." He had already subdued an uprising, commanded the left wing at Chaeronea, and governed Macedon in Philip's absence. He quickly put an end to Athens' rejoicing over the death of Philip, whose ruthless suppression of opposition to his rule had earned him much hatred, broke an incipient rebellion of the Greek cities, and within two years was ready to take up again the invasion of Persia.

Conquests of Alexander the Great

During the eleven years of life he had left—he died at Babylon in 323 B.C. at the age of thirty-three—Alexander proved conclusively that he was one of the greatest generals who ever lived. Setting out with an army of thirty thousand men and five thousand horses, he took most of Asia Minor within a year. Syria fell in 333 B. C., and Egypt shortly after. Finally, with the whole

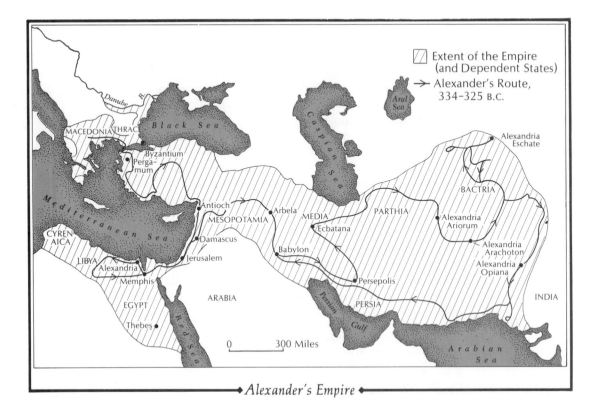

◆*Alexander's Empire* ◆

coast of the eastern Mediterranean secure, he struck inland to defeat the main Persian army in Mesopotamia. Then the beautiful Persian cities fell to him one by one—Babylon, Susa, Persepolis, Ecbatana. By the spring of 330 B. C., with a sullen army rebellious at campaigning endlessly in the wastes of central Persia and with his empire on the point of revolt, he should have withdrawn to a defensible frontier on the Euphrates. Instead, declaring he was "King of Asia," he plunged deep into Central Asia, past the southern shore of the Caspian Sea, up through Afghanistan near to Bokhara, over the Khyber Pass into northern India, and finally down the Indus River and back to Babylon. On his death he was planning to capture Arabia, as the link of his Indian and Near Eastern provinces. In thirteen years, he had marched twenty thousand miles, won every battle he had fought, caused the death of thousands of soldiers in battle and from disease, and created an empire that stretched from Greece to India. But the fascination of Alexander's career goes beyond the rapidity and scale of his conquests; for like Napoleon, with whom he is often compared, Alexander had far-reaching plans for his empire.

Vaulting ambition was undoubtedly his driving force, as his biographer Arrian testified:

Alexander had no small or mean conceptions, nor would ever have remained contented with any of his possessions so far, not even if he had added Europe to Asia, and the Britannic islands to Europe; but would always have searched far beyond for something unknown, being always the rival, if of no other, yet of himself. In this connection I applaud the Indian wise men, some of whom, the story goes, were found by Alexander in the open air in a meadow, where they used to have their disputations, and who, when they saw Alexander and his army, did nothing further than beat with their feet the ground on which they stood. Then when Alexander enquired by interpreters what this action of theirs meant, they replied: "O King Alexander, each man possesses so much of the earth as this on which we stand; and you being a man like other men, save that you are full of activity and relentless, are roaming over all the earth far from your home, troubling yourself and troubling others. But not so long hence you will die, and will possess just so much of the earth as suffices for your burial." On that occasion Alexander applauded their remarks and the speakers, but he always acted diametrically opposite to what he then applauded.[3]

According to one story, which though apocryphal, has the ring of verity, he showed no more understanding for the philosopher Diogenes, who lived in a barrel to show his freedom of material possessions. When Alexander, conqueror of half the known world, asked Diogenes what he could do for him, the philosopher retorted, "Don't block my light."

---

[3] *Arrian* in Loeb edition (London: W. Heinemann, 1923–1933), vol. 2, VII, 4–2.1.

Alexander at the Battle of Issus, 333 B. C.
In this mosaic from Pompeii, which copies a Greek original, Alexander (at the left) is seen defeating the Persian Emperor Darius III (in the chariot). Museo Nazionale, Naples. Alinari—Art Reference Bureau photo

Alexander however wanted more than territorial conquests. He sincerely felt that he had a mission to bring peace, justice, and unity to this vast war-torn area, a mission that was used to justify his willing acceptance of deification as the son of the god Amun-Re in Egypt and his later attempts to be deified in Greece. He met the racial problem directly, ordering Greeks and Persians to be associated equally in the government and armies of the empire, and encouraging intermarriage. He saw the integrating function of trade, which he tried to develop by creating an empirewide coinage, new sea routes, and great ports like Alexandria at the mouth of the Nile. Above all, however, he believed that his foreign subjects would be best served by exposure to his own native culture, Hellenism. The seventy cities he founded (mostly named Alexandria) were to spread Greek learning and Greek military and administrative skills among the upper classes of Asia and the Near East. At the time of his premature death, however, only Alexander's personality and the power of his troops were holding his empire together. He left only a posthumous son as heir and no provision for future administration; and by the end of the century, three of his generals and their descendants had split up most of the empire among them. These three absolute dynasties—the Seleucids in Syria, Mesopotamia, and Persia; the Ptolemies in Egypt; and the Antigonids in Macedonia—continued to hold power until they were defeated by Rome, in the second and first centuries B. C.

Urban Centers of the Hellenistic Age

In spite of this political disunity, Alexander's empire remained united by what we call Hellenistic culture, a culture that the Romans swallowed whole as they penetrated the area from 200 B. C. on. The pins on which the unifying web was stretched were the cities, which were predominantly of Greek culture and often even of Greek nationality. The bureaucrats who lived there were able to make the administrative language, the law, the calendar, and the coinage Greek. Teachers were readily available to assist in Hellenizing the local inhabitants, who found it advisable for their own advancement to develop a veneer of Greek culture. And the merchants and bankers who ran the flourishing commerce were deeply inbued with Greek ideas.

Trade and the cities expanded together, until the great urban agglomerations of Hellenistic days created a totally different way of life from that of the tiny city-states of the classical age. The basis of the trade was the long-distance commerce in luxury goods. The exotic products of Asia and Africa, such as spices, ivory, incense, pearls, and rare woods, were exchanged for the native manufactures of Syria and Egypt, such as glass, metals, and linen. Greece continued to export its pottery, wine, and olive oil. Sicily and Egypt were the main exporters of wheat. Large profits were made from the sale of

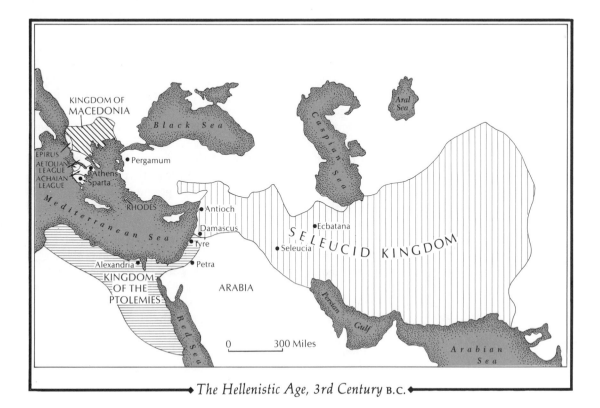

The Hellenistic Age, 3rd Century B.C.

slaves, from both Africa and Asia. The vast returns brought by the sale of the more exotic products produced some extraordinary voyages of discovery, such as the one of Pytheas that took him all around Britain and up into the North Sea, and of Eudoxus, who sailed across the open ocean from the Red Sea to India. Great caravan routes stretched across Afghanistan to India and through the Sudan to Ethiopia. Contact was made even with China. At the nodal points of these routes, several cities became vast boiling caldrons of human activity. Rhodes dominated the export trade of the eastern Mediterranean. Alexandria on the delta in Egypt was the export center of the Ptolemies. The pink city of Petra in the Jordanian desert dominated the caravan routes from Arabia, while the trade of the Seleucid empire brought prosperity to their newly created cities of Antioch and Seleucia.

Both the comforts and discomforts of this rich material life formed Hellenistic culture. The cities themselves, existing primarily for trade rather than defense or administration, were no longer built around an acropolis but almost always adopted the more functional rectangular or gridiron plan, sometimes called Milesian, after Miletus where it was first used. To create a whole city in rectangular blocks made colonization, or the expansion of existing cities, easy to carry out, providing the planners ignored any topographical features that interfered with their rectangles. Towns and army camps were laid out on the same basis. Several important changes in the appearance of the city resulted. The street, which in Periclean Athens had been a rough, rambling inconvenience, became uniform in size, averaging eighteen to nineteen feet, although a few main thoroughfares where big processions took place were considerably wider. The rectangular blocks were ready-made lots for public buildings, such as temples that were no longer to grace high cliffs above the city, the public baths, and especially the marketplace, or agora. In the Hellenistic city, the agora was built with lines of shops on three sides, and often with a long colonnaded porch in front that provided the shopper or talker with shelter from the rain or sun. One of the finest of these, the stoa built by Attalos, king of Pergamum (reigned 159–138 B. C.), in the agora of Athens, has been recently reconstructed. The rectangular plan also introduced to town planning one of the most characteristic features of the later European city—the vista. Long rows of relatively uniform houses, or the repetitive columns of the stoa arcades, drew the eye into the orderly distance in a search for some grandiose, monumental apotheosis, which the architects were willing and the rulers able to provide.

The absolute monarchs, controlling the public purse, indulged their populations with a spree of public building that literally dwarfed Pericles'. Every city had to have its colonnaded market squares, aqueducts and public fountains, baths, gymnasium, stadium, theater, libraries, and harbor facilities. The rich middle classes were little less lavish. With no time lost on politics or military service, they flung themselves into the making and spending of money. For themselves, they bought ever greater luxuries—improved sanitation, better diet and medical care, sculptured busts of them-

The Stoa of Attalos, Athens
Originally built in the mid-second century B. C. and now reconstructed, the Stoa of Attalos dominated the agora, or marketplace, of Athens. Author's photo

selves, mosaic floors. But they also made ostentatious public gifts of temples or bridges or public banquets. The cities themselves, as one ancient writer related, were incapable of providing these functions themselves:

The folk of Myme in Aiolis raised a sum of money by mortgaging one of their public colonnades. As the loan was not repaid, the mortgagees took possession of the property, kindly allowing the people to shelter from the rain. As this was announced by a crier shouting "Come under shelter!" a story grew up that the inhabitants were so stupid they didn't know when to seek shelter unless told.[4]

Alexandria Under the Ptolemies

Alexandria was the archetype of the great cosmopolitan city of the Hellenistic age. Founded by Alexander in 332–331, B. C., it was chosen as capital of the strong state founded by Alexander's general Ptolemy in 323 B. C. For two centuries, it remained the center of Mediterranean commerce and learning; and even after the defeat of Cleopatra, the last of the Ptolemaic

[4] Strabo, cited in Jack Lindsay, *The Ancient World* (London: Weidenfeld and Nicolson, 1968), p. 155.

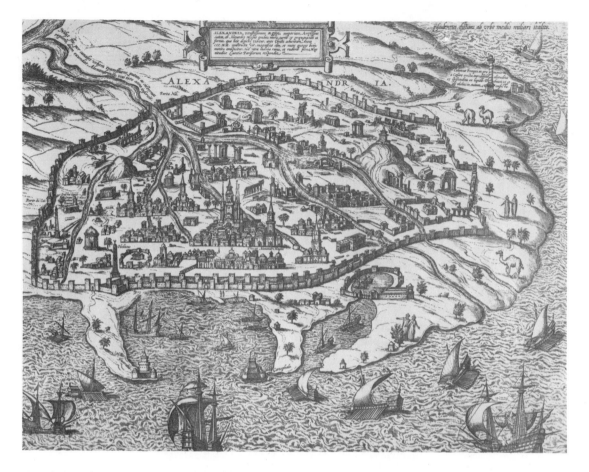

Plan of Alexandria, Sixteenth Century
This city plan is taken from the great series of drawings called Civitates Orbis Terrarum *(cities of all the lands of the earth), which portrayed almost every city in Europe and several in Asia and Africa.*

dynasty, by the Roman armies of the future emperor Augustus in 31 B. C., it continued to flourish within the empire of Rome.

Most of the northern ports of Egypt had been founded within the Delta, since the sandy northern coast along the Mediterranean provided almost no natural harbors. Just to the west of the extreme edge of the Nile Delta, however, a ridge of clay separated a large inland lake from the Mediterranean itself, while a line of reefs running parallel to shore broke the force of the seas. The most important of these reefs had been called by the Greeks the island of Pharos, a corruption of the word Pharaoh, and was later chosen as the site for one of the greatest buildings of the classical world, the vast fortress-lighthouse which gave its name of Pharos to every other lighthouse in the Mediterranean. By joining the island of Pharos to the mainland by a mole, Alexander was able to create a double harbor with specialization of ports, although two openings with bridges permitted passage from one harbor to the other. For protection against attack either from the Delta or from the desert that lay to the west, a wall supposedly nine miles long was built. Within the wall, Alexander commissioned his Greek city planner, Dinocrates of Rhodes, to lay out the city. Following the rectangular Milesian plan, Dinocrates laid out a magnificent main street, called Canopus street, with a marketplace or agora that Alexander intended as the center of the new city. When Ptolemy I succeeded in purloining the corpse of Alexander, it was wrapped in gold and placed in a glass coffin in the Royal Tomb beside the marble colonnades of Canopus street.

The source of the city's prosperity was and remained its intermediary position in Mediterranean commerce. Canals were built to link the lake Mareotis to the Nile Delta, thus enabling Alexandria to supply not only its own needs in wheat but to exercise a virtual monopoly over the export of some 300,000 tons of wheat annually. The ruling Ptolemy controlled this trade by the size of his purchases and by his control of sea transport, and he also monopolized the lucrative trade in the products of Africa and the East, such as ivory, ebony, and some of the spice trade. The artisans of Alexandria were highly skilled in working these raw materials into luxury articles. The spices, herbs, and aromatic leaves were turned into medicines or perfume. Furniture was inlaid with ivory. Gold and silver were worked into elaborate jewelry. And the plentiful sands of the nearby desert were used in the most subtle glass-making industry of the Mediterranean. As a result of this commercial and industrial expansion, migrants moved into the city from all over the eastern Mediterranean. Egyptians continued to work in agriculture and textiles and to dominate the occupations connected with the temples, such as those of scribe or embalmer. Greeks provided much of the artisan crafts, especially in luxury goods of the Aegean style, and worked in international commerce and in education. Jews settled in large numbers, overflowing the section of the city reserved for them, although they were often subject to mob violence. Alexandria thus was a multiracial, cosmopolitan community far different in character from any of the inland cities of Egypt and in fact very different from the Greek cities of the Aegean.

The wealth produced by this flourishing commerce flowed above all into the royal quarter of the city. The royal palaces were grouped on a low hill overlooking the Great Port and the Mediterranean, where they could

The Royal Palaces and Great Port, Alexandria

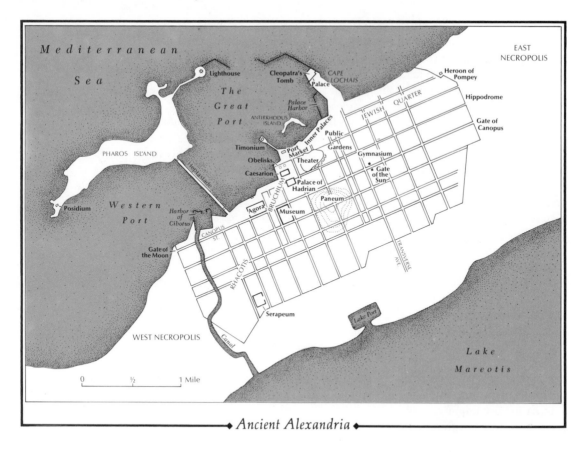

◆ *Ancient Alexandria* ◆

receive the north breeze in the sultry summer months. Here, amid large public gardens, each Pharoah added new buildings, as the geographer Strabo explained:

And the city contains the most beautiful public precincts and also the royal palaces, which constitute one-fourth or even one-third of the whole circuit of the city. It was customary for each of the kings, from love of splendor, to add some embellishment to the public monuments; but it was also customary for each of them to endow, at his own expense, a residence for himself, in addition to those already built, so that now, to quote Homer's words, 'there is building upon building.' All, however, are connected with one another and with the harbor, even those that lie outside the harbor. The Museum is also part of the royal palaces; it has a public walk, an exedra with seats, and a large house in which there is the common room of the scholars who were fellows of the Museum.[5]

---

[5] Strabo XVII. 8, trans. H. L. Jones, in Loeb edition, Vol. VIII (London: W. Heinemann, 1932), pp. 33–35, cited in Claire Preaux, "Alexandria Under the Ptolemies," in Arnold Toynbee, ed., *Cities of Destiny* (New York: McGraw-Hill, 1973), p. 113.

The Museum mentioned by Strabo was the most famous institution of learning in the Hellenistic world. Begun under the first Ptolemy, it was a kind of research university to which scholars were attracted from many countries by high salaries, fine working conditions, and royal encouragement. The greatest library ever assembled up to that time, comprising some 700,000 works, was at their disposal. Its purpose was the collection of all works written in the Greek language, the translation of important works in foreign languages into Greek, and the classification of scientific knowledge. The achievements of the scholars in the Museum were very great. As a result of the development of textual criticism of Greek manuscripts, they are credited with beginning the science of philology. Geometry was advanced by the work of Euclid. Collection of the reports of travelers in Asia and Africa gave Eratosthenes the raw material on which he based his map of the world, while doctors and surgeons were able to carry on profitable experiments in anatomy and physiology.

Alexandria, in short, had become the intellectual and commercial hub of the eastern Mediterranean, the model of urban organization that was followed by all the other great cities of the Hellenistic age, a city whose influence can be seen in the character of the other cosmopolitan centers that rose later—Rome and Constantinople.

Hellenistic Culture

For learning and art, the outpouring of royal and bourgeois patronage was a great stimulant. In the new libraries, scholars worked on textual criticism of the Greek classics, and issued carefully revised texts of the great writers. In the museums, important advances were made in science and mathematics. Hellenistic scientists laid the basis of plane and solid geometry, surmised that the earth moved around the sun, measured the earth's circumference with an error of only 200 miles, and came near to discovering the circulation of the blood, among other achievements. Aristotle and Theophrastus, Euclid and Archimedes, Hipparchus and Ptolemy laid down the scientific theories that, accepted by medieval Christianity as dogma, remained unchallenged and largely undeveloped until the sixteenth century. Only creative literature fell behind. Drama was rough and dirty, mired in stereotypes of slaves, prostitutes, cuckolds, and misunderstood youth. Poetry was stiff and elegiac, although occasionally a moving lyric survived, including that best known of all Hellenistic poems:

> *They told me, Heraclitus, they told me you were dead,*
> *They brought me bitter news to hear, and bitter tears to shed.*
> *I wept as I remembered, how often you and I*
> *Had tired the sun with talking and sent him down the sky.*
> *And now that you are lying, my dear old Carian guest,*
> *A handful of grey ashes, long long ago at rest,*

(Right) **A Gaul Commits Suicide After Killing His Wife;** (Opposite Page) **Old Market Woman** *Hellenistic sculptors struck directly at the emotions of their audience by detailed, realistic portrayals of the desperation of military defeat, or the ravages of age and poverty.* E. Richter—Rome; The Metropolitan Museum of Art. Rogers Fund, 1909

Still are they pleasant voices, they Nightingales awake,
For Death, he taketh all away, but them he cannot take.[6]

Sculpture, like everything else in the Hellenistic age, often reflected this
down-to-earth quality, the abandonment of the idealization of the classic
age. Realistic or sentimental figures of dogs, babies with toys, drunken old
women, fishermen, and the like were popular for homes. Portrait sculpture
sold by the ton. There were so many public statues in Rhodes that old ones
had to be removed to make room for new ones. Kings usually wanted to
look like Alexander, young, tough, and brilliant; but some were content to
look tough and mean. The ceremonial pieces on a larger scale, celebrating
the gods or the victories of the cities, also displayed an emotional idealism
that at times can create in the onlooker almost the physical pangs of a
sword between the shoulder blades or a noose around the throat.

[6] "Heraclitus," by William J. Cory, in Arthur Quiller-Couch, ed., *The Oxford Book of English*
Verse 1250–1918 (Oxford: The Clarendon Press, 1939), p. 768.

Within this prosperous city world, however, there were many dangerous signs of discontent. Some were disgusted at the obsession with money. "When I saw people's lives wholly absorbed in moneymaking," a character remarks in one comedy, "when I watched them scheming and calculating, by Hephaistus, I grew bitter. Not one of them, I thought, has any true kindly feeling for another. This idea struck me down." Children were disgusted with their parents and their superficial ideals. One daughter remarks:

All this pedigree stuff is killing me, mother. Don't keep bringing it up at every word, if you love me. People who have no good quality in themselves, all take refuge in family monuments, their pedigrees. You reel off a list of grandfathers, and that's all you have to say. We can take for granted that they exist. We can't be born without them. Some folk, through a change of home or a lack of friends, can't give the names; but are they any worse-born than the others? The man whose natural bent is to goodness is the nobly born one, even if he's a black African.[7]

As for the parents, perhaps in despair with the younger generation, they were refusing to have more than one or two children; and infanticide, especially of girls and usually through exposure, continued to be extremely common.

Thus, over all this busy life loomed the specter of unknown but ever threatening calamity, the dark forces prowling outside the little circle of civilization. The old city cults and the worship of the Olympian gods degenerated into dry routine; and emotional outlets were found in the worship of the mystery religions. The alienated—slaves, foreigners, women, freedmen, out-of-luck shopkeepers—began to form private groups of one hundred to two hundred members. They often met secretly, in the dark, for the worship of the gods of the East. Some adopted the Egyptian god Serapis, some the star worship of Babylon. Others followed Dionysus, the god of natural fertility, who was now treated as a glorification of the many-sidedness of life, or Fortune, the goddess who watched over man's fate. All the religions had in common a rejection of the crass material life of the city, of the injustice and violence and impersonality on which it was based. All sought to give the individual a meaning for his life in the identification with a wider power than himself.

Skeptics, Cynics, Epicureans, and Stoics

Even the philosophers of the Hellenistic age sought to provide an answer to the alienation with politics and the city, and a guide to spiritual survival in a hostile world. The most blunt answer was given by the Skeptics, who told

[7] Lindsay, *Ancient World,* p. 158.

the individual to be indifferent to everything, since nothing could be known, and by the Cynics who dressed in filthy rags, lived in the streets on handouts, and deliberately shocked the conventional not only with their questioning but with their public behavior, which included defecation and more. Epicurus (342–270 B. C.), the founder of Epicureanism, was far less severe with the material world. He accepted man's need for pleasure but held that reason should dictate which pleasures he should seek, so that he would achieve the ideal of imperturbability, or absence of displeasure. Man should not embark on the usual sources of mental anguish, such as marriage or moneymaking, but live, like Epicurus himself, in a little vegetable garden surrounded by a group of like-minded friends, in the conviction that man can carve out a peaceful life for himself in a purely mechanistic world.

Head of Epicurus
This life-sized bust is a good example of the Hellenistic sculptor's desire to display the human qualities of the person portrayed.   The Metropolitan Museum of Art. Rogers Fund, 1911

Zeno (335–263 B. C.) taught while walking up and down in the Painted Stoa in Athens, and hence his disciples were later called Stoics. His philosophy was far more demanding than that of Epicurus. The universe was rationally organized, he felt, and one had to understand how to fit into the pattern. To live in accordance with this "law of Nature," one had to realize that all human beings were related, sharing in a living community both with nature and with humanity. One should follow the cardinal principle of wisdom, which was to have complete control over the material self, and to seek temperance, courage, and fairness. The wise person, it turned out, had to be "a monster, passionless, pitiless, perfect; he would do good, but without feeling for others, for his calm must remain unruffled. . . . Unhappiness usually arose from wanting something you had not got or could not get; the way to be happy, then, was to want what you got, that is, to go in accord with the Divine Will." [8]

Here, then, was a complex civilization, rich in material things, vastly inventive intellectually, yet disturbed by fears for its own spiritual health. At this point, in the last two centuries before Christ, it was faced by Rome, a new puritanical, military power, supremely confident in its own virtues and goal, prepared to gobble up the inheritance of Alexander and to digest the whole rich meal of Hellenism.

Tarquinia and the Etruscan Inheritance

Until recently, the birth and early growth of the city of Rome was treated by historians as a unique phenomenon, the tale of a people of giants marked by geography or racial genius or historical necessity for an unparalleled rise to greatness and for an equally impressive decline and fall. As Livy remarked at the beginning of his history of Rome, "If any people should be permitted to consecrate its own origins and attribute them to the gods, the

[8] W. W. Tarn and G. T. Griffith, *Hellenistic Civilization* (London: E. Arnold, 1961), pp. 333–34.

military glory of the Roman people is such that when they call Mars their father and the father of their founder, the nations of men might as well put up with it as calmly as they endure Rome's domination." Divine intervention apart, we now know that the Latin people, an Indo-European group who had penetrated into Italy during the Bronze Age (c. 1500–1000 B.C.), were influenced during the crucial centuries from about 800 to 500 B.C., when they were creating the city-state of Rome, by the higher civilization to the south of the Greek colonies in Italy and to the north by the still mysterious Etruscans. During this period, a relatively unified cultural area existed in the whole of western Italy, from the Po down to Sicily; and Rome began its history with a cultural inheritance ready-made.

The Temple of Concord, Agrigento
This superbly preserved temple, built in 450–440 B.C. in the flourishing colony of Acragas, was built of volcanic rock and originally covered with stucco. Italian State Tourist Office photo

Greek Settlement in Italy

The Greek colonies, founded mostly from 750 to 600 B.C., stretched like inset pearls along the glorious coast of southern Italy and Sicily. Lovely in themselves, with temples and theaters that rivaled those of Athens, these cities beamed throughout Italy the brightness of Greek art and learning. Although they conquered them, the Romans never ceased to admire these Greek cities so miraculously planted on Italian soil.

Virgil even gives Aeneas, whose descendants according to legend were

to found Rome, a glimpse of the transcendently lovely temples of Agrigento and Selinunte on the Sicilian coast, as he sails to the Italian mainland:

> *Thence Pachynus' cliffs and jutting rocks*
> *We round the point, and lo! before our eyes*
> *Stands Camarina, that the Fates forbade*
> *E'er to disturb; and then the plains of Gela,*
> *Gela, named from its river's furious stream.*
> *Then lofty Acragas [Agrigento] displays afar*
> *Her mighty walls, where long ago*
> *High-mettled horses were reared. Then with favoring breeze*
> *Palmy Selinus [Selinunte], leaving thee, I thread*
> *The Channels dangerous with sunken reefs*
> *Of Lilybaeu, till I come at last*
> *To port at Drepanum on that joyless shore.*[9]

What does it matter if the temples Virgil describes were built after Aeneas had supposedly passed by? Virgil was creating a past that would be an emotional cement for the Roman people; and Agrigento's glory remains to this day.

Etruscan Economy and Society

The Romans were far less grateful to the Etruscans, although their debt to them may well have been greater. No one is sure where the Etruscans came from, or even if they came by land or sea; but they probably conquered the rolling hill country between the Arno and the Tiber, which is called Etruria, between 800 and 600 B. C. and captured the infant city of Rome; and for brief periods they even extended their control to the Po valley and the Bay of Naples.

Although they were small in number and lived as a landowning aristocracy, controlling, and highly unpopular with, the native populations, they rapidly became wealthy; and wealth, combined with a regimented labor force, paid for their cultural achievements. Fortunately for them, Etruria contained almost all of Italy's mineral resources in copper, zinc, tin, lead, and especially the iron of Elba. Fertile soil and an equable climate gave them fine harvests of wheat, olives, and grapes. A powerful fleet made them not only trading partners but maritime rivals and occasional predators of the Greeks and Phoenicians. The wealth of the towns was proven by excavation that brought out quantities of gold and silver and jewelry, as well as huge numbers of vases imported from Greece, and by the grandeur of such

---

[9] Reprinted from *Greek City-States* by Kathleen Freeman, p. 84. By permission of W. W. Norton & Company, Inc. Copyright 1950 by Kathleen Freeman. Also by permission of John Farquharson Ltd. on behalf of the late Kathleen Freeman. Original source—Virgil *Aeneid* III. 699–708.

city walls as still remain. But it is only when one visits the well preserved "cities of the dead" that one realizes the powerful influence that the advanced culture of the Etruscans must have exerted on the Romans during the century of Etruscan rule (traditionally dated 616–509 B. C.), in which they converted Rome from a collection of villages into a genuine city.

Etruscan Cities

The Etruscans lived in cities, for pleasure and for protection. Most of their cities stood high on defensible hilltops, ringed by sharp ravines and with uninterrupted views on all sides over the land they dominated and the plains from which invaders would appear. They had fine gates and walls, efficient drainage channels, porticoed temples with projecting revetments of brightly colored terra cotta, and tightly packed houses of brick and wood. But, one ravine away, paralleling the town of the living, the Etruscans built an ever expanding city of the dead, a necropolis; and in these acres of tombs we have rediscovered much of their lost civilization.

Cerveteri, about 25 miles from Rome, was a powerful Etruscan city in 600 B. C. with a population of 25,000, three distinct harbors, and a necropolis that covered 140 acres. The original road of hewn boulders, with deep indentations left by the wheels of the funeral processions, still leads through the huge, beehive-shaped mounds in which the Etruscans expected to enjoy unrestrained luxury for all eternity. The tombs were carved in solid rock, often several rooms deep, with molded doorways, beamed ceilings, and stone beds around the walls. Here the dead were laid, reclining, on their funeral couches, dressed in their finest clothes and jewelry, with all

The Necropolis of Cerveteri
The city of the dead at Cerveteri (Caere) covers 140 acres. Its beehive-shaped tombs were carved from solid rock.
Italian State Tourist Office photo

they might need: silver bowls, bronze vases, jars of honey and eggs, bronze beds, and even triumphal chariots. And in the Etruscan necropolis at Tarquinia, on the walls, painted on a thin stucco base, were superbly vigorous scenes of everyday life, or of the last ceremonies of the funeral itself. D. H. Lawrence described the impression these paintings make on us today, and the greatness of the artists' achievement:

Etruscan Tomb Sculpture, Cerveteri
The Etruscan dead were often portrayed reclining in life-like posture on the top of their coffins.
Photo courtesy of the Louvre, Paris

The walls of this little tomb are a dance of real delight. The room seems inhabited still by Etruscans of the sixth century before Christ, a vivid, life-accepting people who must have lived with real fullness. On come the dancers and music players, moving in a broad frieze towards the front wall of the tomb, the wall facing us as we enter from the dark stairs and where the banquet is going on in all its glory. Above the banquet, in the gable angle are the two spotted leopards, heraldically facing each other across a little tree. And the ceiling of rock has chequered slopes of red and black and yellow squares, with a roof-beam painted with coloured circles, dark red and blue and yellow. So that all is colour, and we do not seem to be underground at all, but in some gay chamber of the past.

The dancers on the right wall move with a strange, powerful alertness onwards. The men are dressed only in a loose coloured scarf, or in the gay handsome chlamys draped as a mantle. The subulo plays the double flute the Etruscans loved so much, touching the stops, with big, exaggerated hands, the man behind him touches the seven-stringed lyre, the man in front turns round

Tomb of the Leopards, Tarquinia

The procession of musicians, painted in the fifth century B. C. on the walls of an underground tomb in the necropolis of Tarquinina illustrates the Etruscan belief that in the afterlife they would enjoy the most worthwhile pleasures of life on earth. Alinari–Art Reference Bureau

and signals with his left hand, holding a big wine bowl in his right. And so they move on, on their long sandalled feet past the little berried olive trees, swiftly going with their limbs full of life, full of life to the tips.

This sense of vigorous, strong-bodied liveliness is characteristic of the Etruscans, and is somehow beyond art. You cannot think of art, but only of life itself, as if this were the very life of the Etruscans, dancing in their coloured wraps with massive yet exuberant naked limbs, ruddy from the air and the sea light, dancing and fluting along through the little olive trees, out in the fresh day.[10]

Here then were a people who had not only mastered the Greek styles of sculpture in their own terra cotta and bronze, but had even enlivened it with a fierce realism of their own or a primitive impressionism recently revived by twentieth-century Italian sculptors. Their wall painting achieved a color and passion that is not found again until Pompeii, and their technique in the minor arts of working ivory, gold, and jewels has never been surpassed. They developed granulation, for example, by which tiny gold balls two hundredths of a millimeter in size were soldered to a jewel. Their architecture and town building, their technical advances in agriculture, and their widespread commercial contracts—all made the Etruscans ideal teachers for a people that could learn fast. In their early days, the Romans were voracious students.

[10] From *Etruscan Places* by D. H. Lawrence. Originally published by The Viking Press, Inc. in 1932. All rights reserved. Reprinted by permission of The Viking Press, Inc.

Republican Rome and Its Imperial Conquests

Origins of Rome

In the eighth century B. C. Rome was a few scattered villages of thatched wooden huts inhabited by several hundred shepherds of a mixed Indo-European stock. Five hundred years later, the Romans were in control of all Italy up to the Po. Of their position by the mid-second century, the Greek historian Polybius pointed out, "The Romans have subjected to their rule not portions, but nearly the whole of the world, and possess an empire which is not only immeasurably greater than any which preceded it, but need not fear rivalry in the future." This empire was the conquest of a single city; and part of the fascination of Roman history lies in the double question of how the Romans did it, and even more intriguing, why they did it? "Who is so worthless or indolent," Polybius asked, "as not to wish to know by what means and under what system of government the Romans in less than fifty-three years have succeeded in subjecting nearly the whole inhabited world to their sole government—a thing unique in history?" [11]

Looking back, the Romans themselves decided that their heroic ancestry had got them off to a triumphant start. According to the hallowed legend that Virgil immortalized in the *Aeneid,* Trojans led by Aeneas fled after the fall of their city to the Greeks, and after many tribulations, settled in the hills of Latium. Several generations later, the daughter of one of Aeneas' descendants bore twins to the god Mars (which surprised no one since Aeneas himself had been the son of the goddess Venus); their names were Romulus and Remus. The twins were thrown in the Tiber by their great-uncle, but after being washed up on the Palatine hill, they were looked after by a she-wolf until adopted by shepherds. The Roman historian Livy has a lively story of how the pair as adults appealed to omens to decide who should be the founder of Rome:

Remus was the first to receive an omen; he saw six vultures. He had just pointed it out, when Romulus saw double the number. Each was proclaimed king by his own side. Remus based his claim on priority, Romulus on the larger number of birds. They argued, came to blows; tempers were roused and degenerated into bloodlust. Remus was killed during the fighting. On the other hand, according to more popular tradition, Remus, to make fun of his brother, jumped the newly built walls at one bound and Romulus, angered, killed him, adding: "So shall perish all who attempt to pass over our walls." Thus, the power fell into Romulus' hands alone, and after its foundation the town took the name of its founder. [12]

[11] Polybius *The Histories* in the Loeb edition, (London: W. Heinemann, 1922–1927), I. 1. 7–8, p. 7; I. 1. 5, pp. 3–5.

[12] Livy I. 7. 1–2, cited in Raymond Bloch, *The Origins of Rome* (New York: Praeger, 1966), p. 48.

Archaeologists have not found any evidence of the arrival of seaborne emigrants from Troy or from Greece; but they have agreed that the traditional founding date of 753 B. C. is nearly correct. The legends, however, came to have a power of their own, giving the Romans a common pride in their divine origins and their heroic ancestors and a desire to emulate the first Romulus's gifts as warrior and statesman. Moreover, around the Palatine Hill, the Romans were able to foster a civic religion in such hallowed places as the she-wolf's cave, the fig tree where the twins were fed, and the sacrosanct area around the line where, in Etruscan fashion, Romulus had ploughed the boundary furrow.

In reality, early Rome owed much of its prosperity to its location. The seven tiny hills of Rome lay in the middle of a coastal plain, fringed by a circle of volcanic hills. The plain was well watered, and suitable for pasture and tilling. Along the coast and on the hillsides there was timber for building. The river Tiber was navigable with difficulty as far as Rome, which was the lowest point for fording and bridging the river. The steep slopes of several of the hills, especially the Capitol and the Palatine, made them easily defensible. And best of all, the site commanded the principal routes throughout central Italy, giving Rome a strategic and commercial importance it never lost. Any topographical map shows how the contorted mountain chains of Italy must have dictated the routes that men should follow, and directed travel through Rome, a fact that the Romans enhanced through their road system. Romulus, Cicero concluded, "must at the very beginning have had a divine intimation that the city would one day be the seat and

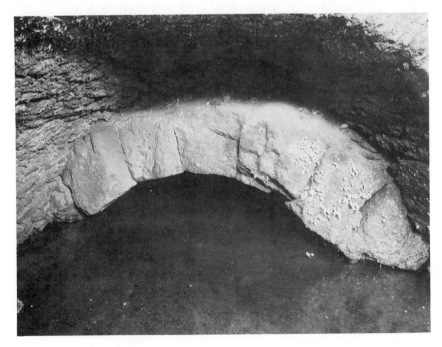

The Cloaca Maxima, Rome
The oldest of all Roman engineering works, this great sewer was built in the sixth century B. C. to drain the Forum. Water running off the Capitol and Palatine hills was fed into the Tiber through this outlet, which is still in use today. The arch was added in c. 200 B. C.
Alinari photo

hearthstone of a mighty empire, for scarcely could a city placed upon any other site in Italy have more easily maintained our own present widespread dominion." [13]

The natural advantages of the site were reinforced by its intermediate position between the Etruscan and Greek civilizations; and the Romans profited from being part of the cultural and commercial boom that enriched all of western Italy from the eighth to the fifth centuries. By 500 B. C., Rome had become, under Etruscan rule, a fairly prosperous city. Its huts had disappeared; and temples with polychrome terra cotta friezes and substantial homes graced the hills. A defense wall, six miles long, of cut stone and earth surrounded the settlements; and the earliest surviving Roman monument, the great sewer called the Cloaca Maxima, had drained the lowlying land between the Palatine and the Capitol hills; and this area, called the Forum, had been paved. Traders were bringing in the finest of Greek goods. A powerful army, based on legions, had been created.

Foundation of the Roman Republic

At that point, around the turn of the sixth century, political upheavals swept through the world of the central Mediterranean. In Rome, the power of the king was replaced by an aristocratic, or patrician, form of government, in the hands of a jealously restricted group of landowning elders who had usually sat in the highest advisory body of the kingdom, the senate. In a short time, the patricians worked out an effective form of constitution to replace the kings. The core of the system was the election annually by the patrician assembly of two consuls as the highest executive; and the consuls were allowed to veto each other's decisions, as a clumsy system of checks and balances. Other officers were added later as needed—a praetor to supervise justice; aediles for markets and roads; and many others. The main assembly, the senate, though advisory in theory, was extremely powerful since it included the wealthiest members of the oligarchy, all of whom had large numbers of dependents, called clients. With the early decline of the power of the comitia curiata, the assembly which was supposed to represent the whole citizen body, the key problem facing the oligarchy was to make constitutional provision for the peaceful expression of the will of the nonpatrician, or plebeian, majority of the population. This internal political struggle was closely affected by the wars of conquest and the economic system that grew up during them.

Roman Conquest of Italy, c. 500–275 B. C.

The Romans easily persuaded themselves that their early wars were necessary for their own or their neighbors' protection. "According to Livy," Edward Gibbon remarked, "the Romans conquered neighbors' world in self-

---

[13] Cicero *De Re Publica* in the Loeb edition (London: W. Heinemann, 1928), II. v. 10, p. 121.

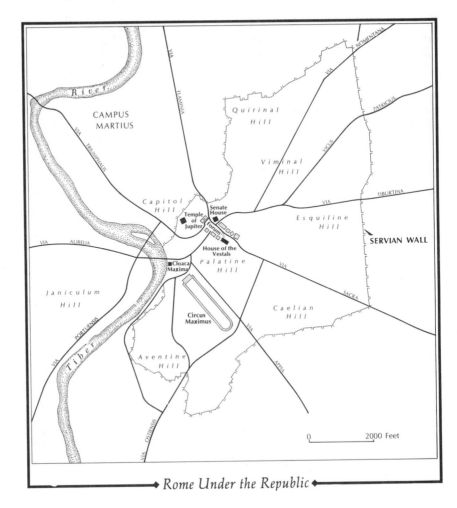

◆ Rome Under the Republic ◆

defense." This was probably true of their early wars. At first, the Romans drove up into the surrounding hills, where they brought the local tribes under their control. Interrupted by an incursion of Celts or Gauls from the north, who even sacked Rome and left it in ruins in 390 B. C., they picked off the Etruscan cities one by one; and around 340 B. C. they turned to the assault of the coastal plain around the Bay of Naples. In subsequent campaigns, they reorganized their legions for hill fighting, replacing the clumsy phalanx with mobile groupings that could operate independently, and that were armed with javelins for hurling; and they built superb all-weather roads of shaped lava blocks to enable the rapid movement of troops southward. With this means, they conquered an empire, first in Italy and then in the Mediterranean. The area round Naples was in their hands by 282 B. C. Then, using the excuse that a small Greek city had asked for their aid, the Romans drove their legions even further south to complete the conquest of the peninsula, defeating the coastal cities, the inland tribes, and the elephants of the king of Epirus, who had unwisely chosen to use the confusion of battling alliances as the chance to hack out a dominion in Italy for himself. This king, Pyrrhus, exhausted his resources in men and money and elephants, while winning only inconclusive "pyrrhic" victories, and finally withdrew to Greece in 275 B. C. leaving Rome victorious.

The mainland of Italy was not governed by Rome as an empire, but a subtle system called the Roman Confederacy was created to hold the defeated peoples under control. Ultimately, about half the population in Italy were classified as "allies," who were nominally autonomous except in foreign policy, but who provided troops for the Roman army. The rest were either full or half (nonvoting) citizens. The Romans thereby avoided the formation of a united opposition to their rule; and in most cases, the peoples of Italy gratefully accepted the blessing of internal peace and the conveniences of a common currency, written law, and language. Nevertheless, the hard-bitten Romans trusted little in the gratitude of the defeated, especially after they had stripped them of most of their valuables and one-third of their land. To ensure loyalty and at the same time to resettle Latin farmers and reward soldiers, the Romans founded new cities, called colonies. One of the first was a new port for Rome itself, Ostia. Others followed along the coast; and much larger cities, of up to six thousand people, were planted at strategic crossroads, mountain passes, fords, or frontiers. From this point, Rome became a city-building empire, thereby transforming the face of Europe.

Acquisition of a Mediterranean Empire, 264–30 B. C.

With Italy secured, Rome moved rapidly against its only rival in the western Mediterranean, Carthage. This city on the coast of North Africa near Tunis had been founded as a Phoenician colony, by the city of Tyre, a little earlier than Rome. Profiting from their superb location at the narrow central straits of the Mediterranean and their skill as sailors and merchants, the Carthaginians had expanded their own colonies and direct military control to large parts of the western Mediterranean by the third century. In particular, they held western Sicily and Sardinia, granaries that Rome coveted. With typical enterprise, the Romans decided, once the war had begun, to become a sea power, built themselves a fleet by copying a Carthaginian ship that had been grounded, and practiced rowing on dry land while their ships were being constructed. To adapt the ships to Roman techniques of fighting, they added a spiked gangplank for grappling enemy ships and put legionaries on their decks; and they quickly won a series of naval battles. It still took twenty-three years of exhausting fighting, however, before the Carthaginians handed over Sicily. By then, they were so worn down by a rebellion of their own mercenaries, aided by Rome, that they could not prevent Rome from taking Sardinia and Corsica as well three years later.

The acquisition of these islands marked a vitally important change in

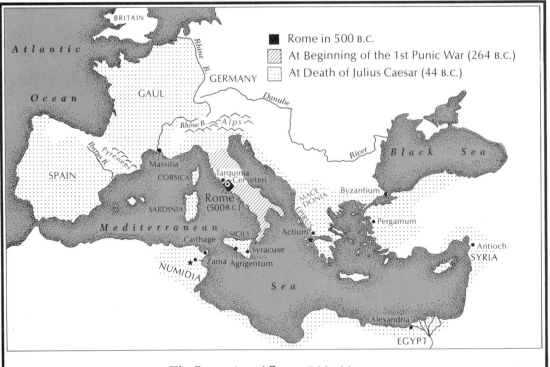

The Expansion of Rome, 500–44 B.C.

Legend:
- Rome in 500 B.C.
- At Beginning of the 1st Punic War (264 B.C.)
- At Death of Julius Caesar (44 B.C.)

Ship Mosaic, Square of the Corporations, Ostia
The seventy mercantile and commercial companies in Ostia, the port of Rome, advertised their services with mosaics, laid on the pavement outside their offices in the main square of the city. E. Richter-Rome

Roman policy. Instead of their being offered the position of allies, like many states of peninsular Italy, they were made into overseas provinces that were governed directly by Roman officials, and they paid tribute, usually one-tenth of their wheat harvest, directly to Rome. Rome had ceased to extend the Confederacy, and had created the pattern for the acquisition of an empire and its spoils.

New annexations extended the imperial system for the next two hundred years. Carthage remained the immediate enemy, since under vigorous new leaders it had acquired new wealth in the mines of Spain; and matching Rome's feat of creating a navy to defeat Carthage by sea, it was forming a new army to attack Rome by land. This Second Punic War (218–202 B. C.) fascinated Polybius by its dramatic fusion of the whole Mediterranean world. "Previously the doings of the world had been, so to say, dispersed," he wrote.

But ever since this date history has been an organic whole, and the affairs of Italy and Africa have been interlinked with those of Greece and Asia, all leading up to one end. . . . The Romans, feeling that the chief and most essential step in their scheme of universal conquest had now been taken, were first emboldened to reach out their hands to grasp the rest and to cross with an army to Greece and Asia.[14]

Victory was again costly for the Romans, because the Carthaginian general Hannibal brought his army across the Alps to defeat several Roman armies in Italy itself. Although he laid waste much of central Italy, he failed to take Rome; and when the Romans counterattacked at Carthage itself, he returned home to be defeated at the decisive battle of Zama (202 B. C.). The Romans then annexed Spain, and at once began exploiting its rich resources of copper, gold, silver, lead, and iron.

No other war was so costly or so risky. The Hellenistic monarchies, which were Rome's next prey, were torn by internal dissensions and their armies were no match for the Roman legions. After half a century of wars, during which the Romans showed surprising reluctance to annex the states they defeated, they finally lost patience. Victorious in a Third Punic War (149–146 B. C.) with Carthage, they completed the ruin of their rival by leveling the city and spreading salt on its site. The Carthaginian territories, roughly the area of modern Tunisia, were made into the Roman province of Africa. Macedon was annexed in 148 B. C., and the Greek cities were punished for revolting against Rome with the total destruction of Corinth. The Seleucid kingdom, after numerous defeats by Rome, was finally overthrown in the middle of the first century; and the kings of Pergamum were so terrified by fear of internal revolution that their last king, Attalos III, bequeathed his kingdom to Rome. Rome thus acquired the richest part of

Scipio Africanus (237–183 B. C.**)** *Scipio, one of the greatest of Roman generals, was given the surname Africanus after he defeated the Carthaginian general Hannibal at Zama on the North African coast in 202 B. C.* Museo Capitolino. Alinari photo

[14] Polybius *The Histories* I. 3. 3–6, pp. 7–9.

Roman Temple, Nîmes, France
The best preserved of all Roman temples, built in the first century B. C. and known erroneously as the Maison Çarrée (Square House), overlooked the forum of the important provincial city of Southern Gaul. French Government Tourist Office photo

Asia Minor, which became its sixth province, Asia. The rest of the republic's conquests were mostly cleaning-up operations, to protect what had already been taken—southern Gaul to link Spain and Italy; Syria to protect Asia Minor; northern Gaul, to subdue its dangerous tribes. The last of the great Hellenistic monarchies, Egypt, finally fell to Rome in 30 B. c., completing Rome's possession of the whole shoreline of the Mediterranean. The territory it then held was more than one hundred times larger than at the beginning of the wars with Carthage; and its problems had correspondingly increased.

The Economics of Empire Building

The acquisition of an empire transformed the economic basis of the city of Rome, revolutionized its social structure, and changed for the worse the Romans' image of themselves. Throughout the history of the republic, leading

Romans preached a civic ethic of service and self-denial that they thought derived from the honest peasant farmers they honored as their ancestors. Livy, writing his history of Rome at the time of Augustus, sought "to turn [his gaze] away from the troubles which our age has been witnessing for so many years . . . absorbed in the recollection of the brave days of old." His reader should imagine the change in Rome, "how, with the gradual relaxation of discipline, morals first gave way, as it were, then sank lower and lower, and finally began the downward plunge which has brought us to the present time, when we can endure neither our vices nor their cure." [15]

Economic Power of the Patrician Class

The economic base of Roman life at the beginning of the Republic, traditionally dated in 509 B. C., was of necessity quite simple. Rome controlled only about 400 square miles of territory, and already the population was too large for the land available. Famines were frequent, and the hunger for wheat became a fixed goal of all Roman policy. There were very few slaves until the beginning of the overseas wars of conquest—perhaps less than twenty thousand as late as 300 B. C. It is amazing that none of the Roman historians who deplored the corruption of the moral standards of the city thought to connect it with the introduction of enormous numbers of slaves after the wars with Carthage. The bulk of the Roman population, even of the city itself, engaged in small-scale agriculture, feeding their own families; and it was part of the accepted belief of Roman patricians that small farmers possessed the Stoic virtues of thrift and frugality that the state should encourage and were, moreover, ideal soldiers. From the third century B. C. on, the great families dominating the Senate concentrated on increasing the size of their own estates, giving themselves not only larger incomes to spend on life in the city but greater political leverage within the oligarchy; and they tended to gain ever greater shares of the small holdings (especially when the continuous wars often compelled the new draftee to sell his land for a song), as well as to take for themselves a large part of the lands confiscated in the conquest of peninsular Italy. In short, there was a social conflict based on rivalry for land at the heart of Rome's political troubles. In this conflict, the small holders and the expropriated farmers were joined by the remaining freemen of Rome—the artisans, such as woodworkers and builders, the small shopkeepers, the traders, and the manual laborers.

The victories over Carthage ensured the predominance of the senatorial oligarchy, who had become agricultural capitalists on their huge estates, or latifundia, and began the process of converting the frugal farmer into the debauched proletarian of Augustan days. The acquisition of the great wheat-producing regions of Sicily, Sardinia, North Africa, and Spain made it less profitable to grow cereals than to raise animals in central Italy, especially as the wheat of the conquered regions was exacted as tribute and sold

---

[15] Livy *History* in the Loeb edition, (London: W. Heinemann, 1919), preface, 5, 9–10, pp. 5–7.

by the government below the market price or given away free. Hannibal's sixteen-year campaign in Italy itself drove many more peasants off the land, and the government distributed the vacant lands in large estates to those with the capital to care for them. Finally, the victories over Carthage and the Hellenistic monarchies brought vast numbers of slaves into Roman possession, and thereby transformed the whole character of Rome.

Impact of Slavery

Probably seventy-five thousand prisoners were put on sale during and after the First Punic War, and afterwards the numbers increased rapidly, supplied not only from conquests of the campaigns and by pirates but even from the children of desperate peasants. By the time of Augustus, it has been calculated, one-quarter of Rome's one million population were slaves; and they were permitted to wear the same clothes as freemen so, it has been suggested, that they would not realize their own numbers. The great slave markets, like the island of Delos or Capua near Naples, put on sale slaves of every nationality and ability, Nubians and Syrians and Gauls, poets and businessmen and dancing girls. They were publicly displayed beneath a sign announcing their origin and special talents and, like animals, could be thoroughly inspected by prospective buyers. Prices varied according to supply and the qualifications of the slave; but they were low enough for many well-to-do Romans to own four or five hundred. Most of the slaves were put to work on the large estates, which shifted over from wheat production to cattle rearing, market gardening, and oil and wine production. The owner usually stayed in Rome, and left it to his overseer to squeeze the profits from the land. The result was misery for the slaves. They lived in huge barracks surrounded by armed guards, could be chained, tortured, or even killed, and had no hope for anything but backbreaking work until they were dead.

Cato's description of how to get the most profit out of your slaves was famous in Rome for its moderation:

For laborers, 4 pecks of wheat in winter months; 4½ in summer. For overseer, house-keeper, foreman and head-shepherd, 3 pecks. The chain-gang should get 4 pounds of bread daily in winter, 5 when they start digging the vines till the figs begin to ripen, then back to 4 again.

Keep all windfall olives you can. Then keep the ripe ones for which only a small yield can be got. Issue them sparingly so as to last as long as possible. When they're finished, give the slaves fish-pickle and vinegar. A peck of salt should suffice for each man for a year.

A tunic 3½ feet long and a blanket-cloak every other year. On issuing tunic or cloak, take back the old one to make rough clothes. One good pair of clogs every second year.[16]

---

[16] Cited in Lindsay, *Ancient World*, p. 184. Original source—Cato *De agricultura* 56, 58, 59, in the Loeb edition, pp. 70–73.

Part of the fear in which Romans came to live from the second century on was the knowledge that in the fields and mines of Italy, among the hundreds of thousands of enslaved human beings, many were reaching that point of desperation where they would risk torture and crucifixion to destroy their odious captors.

The small holders, dispossessed by the growing estates, poured into the cities, especially into Rome. Here again they found much of the manual work and even many of the manufacturing and commercial jobs being carried on by slaves. Almost all domestic service and even the provision of supplies for the wealthy homes, like bread or cloth, were carried out by the household slaves. Greek slaves acted as household tutors. Phoenicians or Syrians engaged in commerce for their owners and were given a share of the profits as an incentive. Even the state used large numbers of "public slaves" as petty bureaucrats or in provision of services like the baths or aqueducts. With this type of competition for jobs, the city proletariat became increasingly dependent on handouts of food by the government and by aspiring politicians and generals. Their volatile discontent added a further element of uncertainty to the fear of slave revolt.

Between the proletariat and the well-to-do, Rome did develop a fairly substantial lower middle class, however. Its basis was the large numbers of shopkeepers, bar owners, tailors, bakers, and so on whose shopfronts still open onto the excavated streets of Pompeii or Ostia. There was nothing that could be called industry in the city, since Romans bought what manufactured goods they wanted from other parts of Italy, but there was local small-scale production for the needs of the growing city, such as pottery, tiles, and bricks; textiles and shoes; and woodwork. In these trades the arti-

Interior of a Bar, Ostia
Ostia, once a flourishing port of 100,000 people, was abandoned in the fourth century because of malaria and the silting up of its harbor.   E. Richter–Rome

san class managed to preserve a precarious existence. It was however in commerce and banking that real wealth was to be made.

Structure of Roman Commerce

Rome's commerce was constructed on an unfavorable balance of trade. It produced little to sell—some pottery, oil and wine, and a few metal goods. Rome was a consumer on a scale hitherto unknown. The most significant of its imports was wheat, much of which it acquired free of payment as tribute from the conquered provinces, although it even bought wheat from Egypt before that country was expropriated. The uneasy peace within the streets of Rome depended on the regular arrival of the wheat convoys from Sicily or Africa, for any delay could bring the city poor to starvation. The shipping of this tribute in cereals to Rome was contracted out by the state to private citizens, called publicans, who were also entrusted with operating the state-owned mines, collecting rent from the public lands, constructing public works, and especially collecting taxes. They were able to form joint-stock companies, in which many poorer citizens invested with considerable success. The Roman state was itself thus the principal importer, paying for its purchases with tribute, taxation, customs dues, the sale of slaves, and the products of its mines. But the empire had also brought vast wealth in gold and silver to other groups. Many people were growing wealthy from landed estates and from taking positions within the provincial governments. A year's service as provincial governor was regarded as the opportunity to amass a personal fortune, although the rapacity was less great in the early days of empire. Successful generals were permitted to pocket a share of the booty they exacted, and they in turn made large distributions to their soldiers. The prosperous trading class, called equestrians because they could afford to equip themselves as cavalry, not only engaged in banking at high rates of interest, but also were permitted minor administrative plums themselves, such as local governorships. The equestrians frequently became wealthier than senators. In short, Rome's oligarchy drew from the land of Italy, the bodies of its slaves, and the conquered territories of the empire an abundance of ready cash that they spent in providing themselves with all the luxuries of the known world.

To grace their tables they bought fish from Spain and the Black Sea; cattle from Sicily, Spain, and Gaul; geese from Belgium; figs, dates, pomegranates and nuts from Asia Minor and Syria; ginger, cinnamon, and myrrh from Arabia; and cheese and poultry from Gaul. Huge sums were paid for a special sturgeon. To make the home a match for his menu, the wealthy Roman brought statues from Greece, marbles from Africa, rare woods from Lebanon and Syria, granite and porphyry from Egypt. For adornment, silk was obtained from China, through India or Persia, and after manufacture in Greece, was sold in Rome to the leaders of fashion. The Mediterranean became a single commercial unit, patrolled with increasing effectiveness by

Pompeii
*The home of a well-to-do
Roman was usually built
around an open court-
yard, or atrium, in the
center of which was a
fountain and reflecting
pool. The prosperous trading city of Pompeii was
buried in lava and cinders
from the eruption of
Vesuvius in A. D. 79.*
Foto ENIT

the warships of Rome, and from the Mediterranean the trade routes
branched out through the empire to Britain, Germany, Parthia, China, India,
Arabia, and Ethiopia. "By the lowest reckoning," Pliny complained, "India,
China, and the Arabian peninsula take from our empire 100 million sesterces every year—that is the sum which our luxuries and our women cost
us." It was hardly surprising that vast tensions were building within this
empire, particularly in the city of Rome itself, which were to erupt with
enormous force from 133 B. C. on and eventually destroy the Republic itself.

The City During the Destruction of the Republic

The narrative of the so-called Roman Revolution in the years from the murder of the aristocratic reformer Tiberius Gracchus in 133 B. C. to the establishment of imperial rule by Augustus in 27 B. C. is a complicated sequence
of political confrontations and frequently resultless bloodletting. But if one
concentrates on the central experiences of the city, several vital features
stand out. First, the acquisition of empire produced extremes of wealth and
poverty of a magnitude previously unknown in Rome; and the result was a
slow sapping of the civic morality, or at least of the publicly displayed rectitude, of all classes of society. Second, the constitutional process disintegrated into a series of struggles among major family groupings within

the oligarchy for control of power. And third, the manipulation of violence, either through the pressure of the city mob or of legions loyal to a single general, became the principal instrument in the transfer of power. This unfortunate combination of corruption, family ambition, and violence destroyed the republican form of government.

Many of Rome's social problems had arisen from the acquisition of empire. From the empire came much of the wealth of many older senatorial families and the newer business class called the equites, usually as the result of war booty, indemnities, payments both legal and illegal to imperial administrators, and tax collecting. The empire provided many of the luxuries, which more austere Romans felt were weakening the self-control of the city's noble youth. From the empire came the slaves who drove the free peasantry from the land of Italy and the educated urban citizens from professional jobs as secretaries, doctors, and teachers in the cities. Thus the economic spoils of empire created for the Roman ruling class a range of new, profound problems.

Cato the Elder (234–149 B. C.)

To Cato and conservatives among the oligarchy who supported him, the most deleterious effect of the new wealth was the decay of the ancient standards of probity of the ruling class. Cato was an unpleasant newcomer in Roman politics, a rough blunt farmer from the hills near Rome with a genius for scathing oratory. Throughout his political career he campaigned against the superficial luxuries he claimed were weakening ancient Roman virtue. As censor, he taxed luxury goods at ten times their market value, fined senators for flouting laws against public extravagance, and tried unsuccessfully to tighten sexual morality. Achieving little in his campaign for universal frugality, he turned his barbs against those who were seeking to introduce Greek culture and ways of life into Rome. Latin was better than Greek, he said; Roman religion sounder than Greek philosophy; his own prescriptions better than Greek medicine. Rome, he declared, would lose its empire when it became infected with Greek letters. Although he set an example as consul in Spain by refusing to fill his own pockets, leading a life of ostentatious simplicity, he did make a fortune from farming by careful management and by squeezing every possible scrap of work from his slaves. Since his appeals for a changed morality went largely unheeded, it was not surprising that he was still prosecuting his enemies in the courts at the age of eighty-five with undiminished acerbity. Later critics of the oligarchy's morality had no more success. His great-great-grandson, Cato the Younger (95–46 B. C.), was soon shunted aside when he preached his implacable ancestor's message. Another great admirer of Cato the Elder, Cicero (106–43 B. C.), after distinguishing himself by denouncing individual wrongdoers among the senators, finally retired to write a justification of the Roman oligarchs as he thought they were in the earlier days of the republic.

His *De Re Publica,* copying the form of Plato's *Republic,* argued that the Romans had already achieved a fine constitution early in their history: "The greatest number of votes belonged, not to the common people but to the rich, and put into effect the principle which ought always to be adhered to in the commonwealth, that the greatest number should not have the greatest power." But, he warned, the rich should remember that "unless there is in the State an even balance of rights, duties, and functions, so that the magistrates have enough power, the counsels of the eminent citizens enough influence, and the people enough liberty, this kind of government cannot be safe from revolution." [17]

Slave Revolts

In the most immediate sense, there was the everpresent fear of a slave revolt that would find its fighting power among the most oppressed segments of the slave population and its leadership among the best treated. A great series of slave uprisings did begin in the estates of Sicily in 135 B. C. and culminated in the outbreak led by the gladiator Spartacus in 73–71 B. C. The Sicilian uprising was led by an ingenious prestidigitator who, to keep up his followers' enthusiasm, combined religious exhortation with the trick of breathing fire out of his mouth. The slaves seized the central part of the island, organized an army, and even issued their own currency. They were finally starved into surrender. In 73 B. C., a group of seventy-eight slaves broke free from a gladiators' school in Capua and established themselves on the slopes of Vesuvius. Joined by runaway slaves, the army, headed by Spartacus, soon numbered seventy thousand men and was easily able to defeat the armies Rome sent against it. When the slave army finally tried to cross the Alps to disperse to their homes, a Roman army blocked their way. Spartacus turned south, and terrified Rome with threat of attack, but he was pinned down and defeated. He himself was killed in battle. Six thousand slaves who were captured were crucified along the Appian Way between Rome and Capua. Their bodies were a warning not only to other slaves but a reminder to the Romans of the great fear with which they had to live: "Every slave we own is an enemy we harbor."

No slave revolt could long triumph against the power of the Roman armies. Far more serious problems were undermining the social structure of Rome. The plight of the independent peasant, who was being forced to sell his lands to the rich for large-scale production by slaves worried the more perspicacious of Rome's rulers. This policy was increasing the unemployed and discontented proletariat not only of Rome but of many cities of Italy and Gaul and was reducing the number and health of the farmers from whom the bulk of the Roman armies had been drawn. Moreover, Rome's allies in Italy itself were becoming increasingly dissatisfied with their treat-

---

[17] Cicero *De Re Publica* II. xxii. 39, p. 149; II. xxxiii. 57–58, p. 169.

ment, both the economic demands being made on them and the interference in their internal political affairs by an increasingly insensitive Roman government. Reformers like the Gracchi brothers realized that the
misery of the independent peasantry and the resentment of the allied
people in Italy had to be remedied together if Rome was to be secure in its
own peninsula.

The Roman Oligarchy

The ruling class that faced these problems was a tightly knit oligarchy
whose main constitutional instrument was the Senate. The Senate had three
hundred members until the constitutional reforms of 82–79 B. C. when its
numbers were increased to six hundred. They were mainly drawn from the
landed aristocracy but their decisions were controlled by an inner group of
little more than twenty families. The constitution itself, as Ronald Syme has
pointed out, was "a screen and a sham"; these great families merely used it
for their own purposes. They possessed far-reaching networks of influence
based on family relationships, wealth, and carefully cultivated networks of
influence, known as *amicitia,* that enrolled in their support vast numbers of
lesser men throughout the landowning and business classes. Occasionally,
the great families would admit into their ranks a *novus homo,* a new man
whose family had never produced a consul; and they would replenish their
finances by ties with the business class of equites whom they satisfied with
the provision of a business environment conducive to the making of money,
the grant of tax-farming privileges, or the profits of financing state commerce or military operations. The great families employed agents, often
freedmen, to scatter bribes, manage elections, and organize physical in-
timidation; and they ensured the collaboration of spiritual forces by filling
the priesthood with their own men. After 130 B. C. the great families divided
according to their political point-of-view into two groups, the Optimates
and the Populares. These groups did not represent a division between the
well-to-do and the poorer, dissatisfied classes, as has frequently been
claimed; as recent historians have shown, both groups were members of the
same class. The division was a battle between family groupings, whose
main purpose was the securing of office, not a fight between ideologies and
especially not a class war. The Optimates were united by the determination
to preserve the oligarchic system without primary economic or social reforms, and since they succeeded in gaining control of the Senate, they came
to be thought of as the senatorial party. The Populares, a word that means
"demagogue" and was applied to them by their enemies, were other members of the inner group of families who turned to the tribunate and the popular assembly for support because their opponents had won control of the
Senate. Their leaders must be divided between those like the Gracchi, who
were sincere reformers, and those like Marius, who were self-seekers court-
ing the people to break their rivals inside the oligarchy. Thus the great

struggles of the last century of the republic have to be seen, not mainly as battles of principle, but as skirmishes among the leading families of a restricted oligarchy. The Gracchi brothers were related through their mother to the Cornelii family, being the grandsons of Scipio Africanus, who defeated Hannibal; Sulla, who controlled Rome on behalf of the Optimates in 82–79 B. C., based his strength on his fourth wife's family, the Metellii; and Julius Caesar came from the ancient Claudian family.

THE DESTRUCTION OF THE ROMAN REPUBLIC, 133–31 B. C.

133	Tiberius Gracchus, Tribune. Murdered
123–121	Gaius Gracchus, Tribune. Killed, 121
107–100	Marius, Consul
106	Military reforms of Marius
88	Sulla, Consul. March on Rome
87	Seizure of Rome by Marius
82–79	Sulla, Consul. Constitutional reforms
73–71	Slave revolt of Spartacus
70	Pompey and Crassus, Consuls
63	Conspiracy of Catiline
60–53	First Triumvirate (Caesar, Pompey, Crassus)
59	Julius Caesar, Consul
58–50	Conquest of Gaul by Caesar
49	Caesar crossed Rubicon
49–45	Defeat of Pompey by Caesar in Civil Wars
46	Caesar, Consul for Life
44	Murder of Caesar
43–36	Second Triumvirate (Octavian, Mark Antony, Lepidus)
31	Octavian defeated Antony and Cleopatra at Battle of Actium

The Reform Program of the Gracchi

The character of the struggles within the oligarchy was changed by the resort to violence. At first, the violence was deployed by the controlling faction of the senate against would-be reformers. In 133 B. C., Tiberius Gracchus was elected tribune of the people. He had decided, when passing through Tuscany where he "observed the dearth of inhabitants in the country, and that those who tilled the soil or tended its flocks there were imported barbarian slaves," that Rome's main problem was the expulsion of the peasant-farmer from the land. His solution was simple: limit the holdings of public land to 500 acres, compensate present owners for amounts above that confiscated, and redistribute the land to the city poor in twenty-acre farms. What worried the senators, however, was not only the proposed agrarian reform but the revolutionary oratory with which Tiberius began to inflame the city proletariat:

The wild beasts that roam over Italy have every one of them a cave or lair to lurk in; but the men who fight and die for Italy enjoy the common air and light, indeed, but nothing else; horseless and homeless they wander about with their wives and children. . . . They fight and die to support others in wealth and luxury, and though they are styled masters of the world, they have not a single clod of earth that is their own.[18]

When he stood for reelection as tribune, a group of senators and their hangers-on, armed with clubs, beat him and three hundred of his supporters to death in the assembly, and threw their bodies into the river. In 123 B. C., his younger brother Gaius Gracchus revived and extended the reform proposals. The senate sent armed forces against him and his followers, who had barricaded themselves on the Aventine Hill. In a pitched battle fought in the heart of Rome in 121 B. C., Gaius's forces were overwhelmed. Gaius had his own slave kill him; but his head was cut off and brought to the senate, which had promised to pay its weight in gold. The head was surprisingly heavy, and it was found that the aristocrat claiming the reward had filled it with lead. In this unsavory fashion, the Optimates repelled a moderate effort to repopulate the countryside and get the mob out of Rome.

Legions as Instrument of Political Change

Far more significant was the eruption of the legions into Roman politics. Around 106 B. C., the whole character of the Roman army was changed by the reforms of Marius, an ambitious self-made general from an equestrian family. Marius created a new military force by calling for volunteers from the whole citizen body and not merely the propertied classes. He paid them well, organized them into groups of ten-cohort legions of 5000 men each, and provided generous bonuses of land and money; and his example was followed by other generals. These professional legions, composed mostly of landless peasants, owed little allegiance to the state. They followed their general loyally, for booty; and they were as prepared to attack Rome as its enemies. Marius threw in his lot with the opposition to the Optimates who picked their own man, an aristocrat named Sulla, for the military operations in northern Asia Minor and in Greece that Marius had hoped to command. When Marius attempted to use the assembly to get himself the command, Sulla set an ominous precedent, in 88 B. C., by marching on Rome and seizing the city. After Sulla had left for the front, Marius returned, reestablished his political alliances in the city, proscribed his opponents who were then executed by his soldiers, and confiscated their property. Decapitated heads were displayed on the speakers' platform in the Forum; bodies were left in the streets to be torn to pieces by birds and dogs; and Marius, apparently crazed with his new eminence in bloodshed, presided over the slaugh-

Roman Legionary
The principal unit of the Roman army was the legion, composed of about 5000 men, mainly foot-soldiers. The legionary wore a metal helmet and tough leather cuirass and carried a round shield and short thrusting sword. Photo copyright by the Trustees of the British Museum

[18] *Plutarch's Lives* (London: W. Heinemann, 1914–1954), VIII, 7, p. 163; IX, 5, pp. 165–67.

ter, giving summary judgments that were at once carried out before him. In the words of the historian Appian, "Neither reverence for gods, nor the indignation of men, nor the fear of odium for their acts, existed any longer among them. After committing savage deeds, they turned to godless sights. They killed remorselessly and severed the necks of men already dead, and they paraded these horrors before the public eye, either to inspire fear and terror, or for a godless spectacle." [19] Sulla returned five years later to carry out a similar butchery; but he followed it with a reform program aimed at restoring law and order based on the power of the senate—ending the state sale of grain, filling the assemblies with his supporters, and enacting a law that no bill could be considered by the assembly without the senate's agreement. But his main efforts were to compensate his army through confiscated property; for behind the senatorial restoration were the blood-stained swords of the legions, the one constant factor in these civil wars.

Julius Caesar (100–44 B. C.)

In the end, victory in Rome's internal political struggles went to the general who could command the finest military strength, backed by wealth and family alliances. Julius Caesar combined these assets. His patrician ancestry reached so far back that he was, he claimed, descended from Aeneas and hence from the goddess Venus. In a fairly conventional early career, he had worked his way through the lower offices of the republic until, in Spain, he had formed the first important army on whose personal loyalty he could rely. According to the historian Suetonius, he was already burning with ambition: "He saw a statue of Alexander the Great in the Temple of Hercules and was overheard to sigh impatiently: vexed, it seems, that at an age when Alexander had already conquered the whole world, he himself had done nothing in the least epoch-making." [20] To gain the financial support he needed, he struck up an alliance with the wealthy financier Crassus, who fed him the money for organization of magnificent games in Rome and for the bribery necessary to get him elected chief priest of the state religion, and in 59 B. c., consul. By then he had an unsavory reputation for debauchery, bribery, unsuccessful sedition, and pandering to the poor; but he was also building up a political alliance system of his own within the oligarchy, composed of several ancient families excluded by the dominant Optimate group in the senate, ambitious bankers from the equites class, and younger aristocrats eager for rapid advancement. The governorship of Gaul (northern Italy and southern France) in 58–50 B. c., proved him to be a superb general, a masterful propagandist in his description of his own triumphs in his book *The Gallic Wars*, and a successful fortune seeker. In nine years he

---

[19] *Appian's Roman History* in the Loeb edition (London: W. Heinemann, 1912–1913), I, 71, p. 133.

[20] Suetonius *The Twelve Caesars*, trans. Robert Graves (Harmondsworth, England: Penguin, 1969), p. 12. Original source—Suetonius *Julius* 7.1.

conquered northern France and Belgium, invaded Britain, although he withdrew almost at once, and welded his armies into the most effective fighting force in the Roman Empire. In 49 B. C., he led his forces across the river Rubicon into Italy to strike directly against his Optimate opponents who controlled the senate. In four years of fighting, he defeated the armies raised by the Optimates' leader, Pompey, destroying them one by one in Spain, north Africa, and Greece. By 45 B. C. he was master of the Roman state.

Caesar apparently had serious plans for dealing with Rome's problems. In the three years during which he was dictator, although occupied with the war against the supporters of Pompey, he almost doubled the size of the senate to dissipate its power and bring in the business classes. He attacked the land problem by founding new overseas colonies, and redistributed state lands in Italy. To control the Roman proletariat, he reduced the free grain supplies, the distribution of which had begun in the tribunate of Clodius in 58 B. C., provided work on public buildings, and organized huge free entertainments. He even attempted to cut down on corruption in the government of the empire, and he seems to have planned a vast series of campaigns to round out the empire in Europe and Asia. His senatorial opponents, however, fearing the final destruction of their political power if he remained longer at the head of the state, organized his assassination. He was stabbed to death on March 15, 44 B. C., the Ides of March, while attending the senate, unarmed and without his guards.

The murder of Caesar did not restore the power of the Optimates, as the conspirators had hoped. The Roman mob rose in fury against the conspirators, who went into hiding; and when Caesar's body was brought to the Forum for cremation, Suetonius wrote,

two divine forms (perhaps the twin brethren Castor and Pollux) suddenly appeared, javelin in hand and sword at thigh, and set fire to the couch with torches. Immediately the spectators assisted the blaze by heaping on it dry branches and the judges' chairs, and the court benches, with whatever else came to hand. . . . Veterans who had assisted at his triumphs added the arms they had then borne. Many women in the audience similarly sacrificed their jewelry together with their childrens' golden buttons and embroidered tunics.[21]

In this universal grief, Caesar was recognized to have become a god; and the precedent for deifying emperors was established. Caesar's obvious successor was his lieutenant, Mark Antony, a fine general but a poor statesman, who might well have taken over the empire with the connivance of the frightened senate had he not been challenged by Caesar's eighteen-year-old adopted son, whom Caesar's will had named as heir—Gaius Julius Caesar Octavian, later to become the Emperor Augustus. Supported by Caesar's

Busts of Marcus Brutus and Julius Caesar
Brutus, a member of one of the great patrician families of Rome, was thirty-four when he led the assassination plot against Julius Caesar. He committed suicide two years later, in 42 B. C., after his forces were defeated at the battle of Philippi. Museo Capitolino. Alinari photo; Lowie Museum of Anthropology, University of California, Berkeley

[21] Ibid., p. 47. Original source—Suetonius *Julius* 84. 3–4.

veterans, Octavian first accepted the support of the Optimates against Antony, but then broke with the senatorial conservatives and defeated their remaining forces at Philippi in Macedonia. Finally he engaged in a new civil war with Antony and his ally, Cleopatra of Egypt. His victory in the naval battle of Actium (31 B. C.) off Greece, followed the next year with the dual suicide of Antony and Cleopatra, finally brought an end to the century of civil chaos that had begun with the murder of Tiberius Gracchus. Octavian returned to a Rome in political, social, moral, and physical degradation.

SUGGESTED READING

The culture of the Hellenistic age is analyzed briefly but profoundly by W. W. Tarn and G. T. Griffith, *Hellenistic Civilization* (1961) and by Michael Grant, *The Ancient Mediterranean* (1969). The social and economic aspects are given fuller treatment in C. Bradford Welles, *Alexander and the Hellenistic World* (1970). The basic study of the economic structure of the eastern Mediterranean is still M. I. Rostovtzeff, *Social and Economic History of the Hellenistic World* (1953), while the changed character of city life is explained in A. H. M. Jones, *The Greek City from Alexander to Justinian* (1940). For Athens after the Peloponnesian War, see Claude Mossé, *Athens in Decline, 404–86 B. C.* (1973) or the older but beautifully written study of W. S. Ferguson, *Hellenistic Athens* (1911). For Hellenistic intellectual life in Greece, see T. B. L. Webster, *Art and Literature in Fourth Century Athens* (1956).

The exploits of Alexander the Great permitted Plutarch, *Life of Alexander* (many translations), to draw many obvious moral lessons. More documented modern treatments, which of necessity lack the emotive appeal so essential to appreciation of Alexander's extraordinary ambitions, are W. W. Tarn, *Alexander the Great* (1948) and A. R. Burns, *Alexander and the Hellenistic Empire* (1947). J. R. Hamilton, in contrast with Tarn, sees the power-hungry drive of the ruthless soldier in *Alexander the Great* (1973). Fortunately, however, we now have a finely researched life that reads like a novel, in Robin L. Fox, *Alexander the Great* (1974).

During the First World War, the English novelist E. M. Forster wrote a delightful guidebook to Alexandria which has been republished, as *Alexandria: A History and a Guide* (1961). The fullest scholarly treatments are André Bernand, *Alexandrie la Grande* (1966) and the massive work of P. M. Fraser, *Ptolemaic Alexandria* (1972).

Excellent introductions to the Etruscan society are provided by Raymond Bloch, *The Etruscans* (1958), Massimo Pallottino, *The Etruscans* (1975), and E. H. Richardson, *The Etruscans* (1964). On Etruscan urban life, see Luisa Banti, *The Etruscan Cities and their Culture* (1973). The finest word pictures of the tombs are still those of D. H. Lawrence, *Etruscan Places* (1957), even if some of the information is out of date. Lovely reproductions grace Raymond Bloch's *Etruscan Art* (1959); P. J. Riis, *An Introduction to Etruscan Art* (1953), by a Danish scholar, is quite useful.

Short essays on several of the Greek cities in Italy combine literary with archaeological documentation in Kathleen Freeman's *Greek City-States* (1950), while fuller treatments are J. J. Dunbabin, *The Western Greeks* (1948) and A. G. Woodhead, *The Greeks in the West* (1962). Greek influence on Roman civilization was obvious to Petronius, *Satyricon* (many translations) as well as to Cato the Elder two centuries earlier, and the Roman fascination with the Greek achievement is best illustrated in the search for the Hellenic past in Pausanias' *Description of Greece.* Greek conceptions of the city-state had profound influence on the Roman idea of the city "not as a political or legal institution, but rather as a design for a society in which men could live together," as Lidia Storoni Mazzolani shows in her book, *The Idea of the City in Roman Thought* (1970).

Raymond Bloch, *The Origins of Rome* (1960) takes the history of Rome from Romulus to the founding of the republic, while the character of republican politics, especially the nature of oligarchic family alliances, is explored at length in the magistral *Roman Revolution* (1939) of Ronald Syme, and in less compass in H. H. Scullard's *From the Gracchi to Nero* (1959). Lily Ross Taylor focuses on an even shorter period of political infighting in *Party Politics in the Age of Caesar* (1949). Syme summarizes his views on the failure of the republic in *A Roman Post-Mortem* (1950). T. P. Wiseman, *New Men in the Roman Senate, 139 B. C.–A. D. 14* (1971) studies the problem of how to gain access to power for the *novus homo*. Class relations, broken down into rural, rural-urban, and urban segments, are analyzed in Ramsay MacMullen, *Roman Social Relations, 50 B. C. to A. D. 284* (1974). W. Ward Fowler, *Social Life at Rome in the Age of Cicero* (1909) is still useful.

On Rome's great rival in the Mediterranean, see Brian H. Warmington, *Carthage* (1964). For the general who defeated Carthage, H. H. Scullard, *Scipio Africanus: Soldier and Politician* (1970) is a lively biography. The financing of the imperial achievement is discussed in the very detailed study of R. Duncan-Jones, *The Economy of the Roman Empire* (1974). B. H. Warmington, *The Dawn of Empire: Rome's Rise to World Power* (1971) is a good study of the years 264–148 B. C.

Two other reliable surveys are Jacques Heurgon, *The Rise of Rome* (1973) and R. M. Errington, *The Dawn of Empire: Rome's Rise to World Power* (1971).

For imperial diplomacy, see Ernst Badian, *Foreign Clientelae, 264–70 B. C. (1958).* The cities that were founded to hold the empire together are described in E. T. Salmon, *Roman Colonization Under the Republic* (1970). On the army, see H. M. D. Parker, *The Roman Legions* (1928, 1958).

The most impressive account of Caesar as a military leader is Julius Caesar, *The Conquest of Gaul* and *The Civil War* (many translations), but for more colorful detail one should not miss Suetonius' life in *The Twelve Caesars* (1969) as translated by Robert Graves. Finally, for the survey of Rome's early centuries that provided the picture of their own history as held by the educated of imperial Rome, see Livy, *The Early History of Rome* (1965) and *The War with Hannibal* (1965), both of which are translated by Aubrey de Selincourt.

Chronicle of Events

From the Rome of Augustus to the Constantinople of Justinian

27 B. C. –A. D. 600

	Rome/Western Europe	Eastern Mediterranean/Byzantium	Christianity
	Augustus (27 B.C.–14 A.D.)		8–4 B.C.–Birth of Jesus Christ
A.D. 1	Tiberius (14–37)		c. 29 Crucifixion of Christ
			Gospels written (first and early second centuries)
			c. 35 St. Paul begins missions
	Caligula (37–41)		
	Claudius (41–54)		
	Conquest of England	Roman frontier established on Euphrates	
	Nero (54–68)		Persecution by Nero
	Golden House built		c. 67 Death of St. Peter and St. Paul
	Burning of ROME		
	Vespasian (69–79)	70 Sack of JERUSALEM by Titus	
	POMPEII destroyed; Colosseum begun		
	Titus (79–81)		
	Domitian (81–96)		
	Palace built on Palatine		
	Nerva (96–98)		
	Trajan (98–117)	Trajan's conquest of Dacia	
	Imperial forum built	Revolt in Palestine	
100	Hadrian (117–138)		
	Wall in Scotland		
	Antoninus Pius (138–161)		
	Marcus Aurelius (161–180)	Campaigns on Danube	Tertullian (c. 150–230)
	Commodus (180–192)		
	Septimius Severus (193–211)		
200	Caracalla (211–217)		Christian catacombs in ROME
	Imperial baths constructed	First raids by Goths across Danube	
	235–285 Breakdown of imperial government		250 Persecution by emperor Decius
	Aurelian (270–275)	Withdrawal from Dacia	First monasteries founded
	Wall around ROME		
	Diocletian (284–305)	Diocletian's palace in SPALATO	
300	Constantine (306–337)	324 Foundation of CONSTANTINOPLE	Conversion of Constantine
	312 Battle of the Milvian Bridge	First Santa Sophia built	Building of first St. Peter's cathedral on Vatican Hill, ROME
		330 Transfer of capital to CONSTANTINOPLE	325 Council of Nicaea

400	Beginning of Anglo-Saxon raids on England 410 Visigoths sack ROME Visigothic kingdom in Spain (412–711) 455 Vandals from Africa sack ROME 476 Deposition of Romulus Augustulus, last Roman emperor in West Clovis (481–511) Merovingian dynasty of Franks in Gaul (481–752) Ostrogothic rule in Italy (490–554) Theodoric in RAVENNA (493–526)	378 Goths defeat Byzantine emperor at battle of Adrianople Theodosius I (379–395) Division of Empire between his sons, Arcadius (East) and Honorius (West) Theodosius II (408–450) Land Walls of CONSTANTINOPLE Collection of Roman law (Theodosian Code) Raids on central Europe by Attila the Hun Defeated at Battle of Chalons (451) Repelled from Italy (452)	St. Jerome (340–420) St. Augustine (354–430) Goths and Vandals converted to Arianism 381 Council of Constantinople 431 Council of Ephesus condemned Nestorianism c. 432 St. Patrick in Ireland Pope Leo I, the Great (440–461) 451 Council of Chalcedon condemned Monophysitism St. Benedict (480?–543) 496 Conversion of Clovis
500	533–568 Byzantine reconquest in Italy and north Africa 568 Lombards invade Italy	Justin I (518–527) Justinian (527–565) 532 Nika riots Second Santa Sophia constructed 548 Death of Theodora	529 Monastery of Monte Cassino founded c. 587 Conversion of Visigoths to Catholicism Pope Gregory the Great (590–604) 590, 601 Mission of St. Augustine in England

4 / *The Rome of Augustus*

City growth is a capricious process and, like the sorcerer's apprentice, quickly gets out of hand. Rome, at the end of the century of political turmoil that culminated in the defeat of Antony at Actium in 31 B. C. by the future emperor Augustus, was the product of more than seven hundred years

of unplanned growth. Its expansion had gone through three phases. At its foundation in the middle of the eighth century B. C., it was little more than a tribal village of rough wooden huts spreading across the summits of the Palatine and Capitol hills. During its second phase, from the beginning of Etruscan rule about the year 600 B. C. to the completion of its control over the whole of the Italian peninsula in 275 B. C., it was converted into a small metropolis, with a wall of hewn tufa stone, temple complexes on its hills, a central Forum crammed with buildings for administrators and priests, and an unregulated sprawl of tenements,

Augustus   Museo Tolosa, Rome. Alinari photo

Arch of Septimius Severus, Rome   Italian Government Travel Office photo

villas, baths, theaters, and shops. Part of the confusion was explained by the fact that the citizens were given one year to rebuild the city after its partial destruction by the Gauls in 390 B. c. They were in such a hurry, the historian Livy commented, that they did not bother to lay out streets, and the city resembled a "squatters' settlement rather than a planned community." The third phase began with the acquisition of a Mediterranean empire, from 264 to 30 B. c. During this phase, building in Rome reflected the tastes, power, and imperial spoils enjoyed by its dominant aristocratic families, who ran their empire with no clear sense of economic rationale or adminis-

The Rome of Augustus

Period Surveyed	Reign of Augustus, 27 B. c.–A. D. 14
Population	One million
Area	5.28 square miles
Form of Government	Principate (imperial power exercised by Augustus as Princeps, or First Citizen; Imperator, or Commander-in-Chief; and Pontifex Maximus, or Chief Priest). Forms of republican government (senate, popular assemblies, magistrates)
Political Leaders	Augustus; Agrippa; Maecenas
Economic Base	Unfavorable trade balance, covered by surplus from landed estates in Italy, tribute in grain from empire, taxation, slave labor. Small exports of artisan products
Intellectual Life	Poets (Virgil, Propertius, Horace, Ovid); historians (Livy)
Principal Buildings	Forum (Curia; Temple of Concord; Basilica Julia; residence of vestal virgins); Palatine hill (Temple of Apollo); Mausoleum of Augustus; Ara Pacis; Forum of Augustus
Public Entertainment	Public baths; gladiatorial games; chariot races; drama
Religion	Household deities (Janus; Vesta); State religion (deified emperors; Jupiter, Juno, Minerva, etc.); emotional religions (Dionysus, Isis, Mithras); Judaism

trative responsibility. Beautiful homes for the well-to-do, constructed around gracious open patios decorated with fountains and Greek statues, were built on the Palatine hill. Delicate temples in the Hellenistic style were erected beside the river. Warehouses and shops expanded to deal with the rising commerce of the empire. More ominously, the multistoried apartment houses of the city's slums expanded to accommodate the thousands of dispossessed farmers whose lands had been taken over by Rome's patrician families; and the city's arenas grew to provide the free games with which the poor were distracted in their idleness.

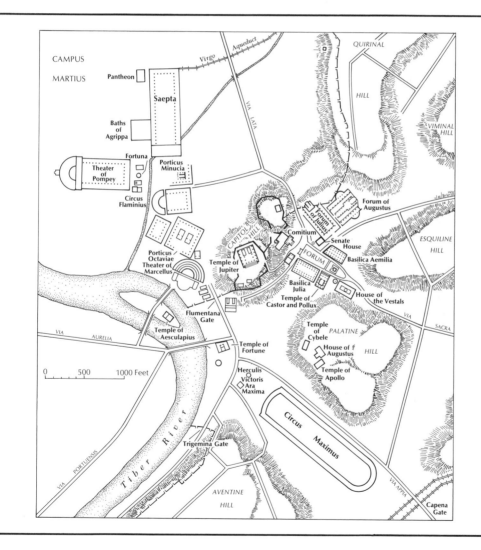

Rome was not yet a beautiful city, however. Augustus felt that "the City was architecturally unworthy of her position as capital of the Roman Empire, besides being vulnerable to fire and river floods," and he began its monumental rebuilding. In this fourth phase, which lasted from the beginning of Augustus's reign in 27 B.C. until the Emperor Constantine built a new capital at Constantinople in A.D. 324–330, almost all the emperors considered the beautification of Rome to be an essential contribution to their own prestige and reputation with posterity. Augustus must above all be credited with making Rome a true imperial capital because he gave it the administrative capacity to govern a world empire. Such a capital, in the view of Augustus and his successors, required an architectual grandeur worthy of its imperial position.

The focus of the great imperial building programs was on the two central hills of Rome, the Capitol and the Palatine, and on the drained valley of the Forum between them. Even within this small area, which is less than a mile long, clear differentiation of activity was achieved in various localities. In considering in this chapter the achievements of imperial Rome, and especially the reign of Augustus (27 B.C.–A.D. 14), we shall therefore examine the activity concentrated in each of the major divisions of the central city. In order, we shall turn to:

1. the curia and the comitium in the northern end of the Forum, where Augustus maintained the machinery of republican government as an insurance of continuing political stability

2. the imperial palaces of the Palatine hill, where the reality of political power was concentrated and where the great writers of the Augustan golden age contributed their imagination to enhance the mythology of imperial rule

3. the Basilica Julia and the Basilica Aemilia in the Forum, the outstanding law courts of Rome, where Roman lawyers practised within one of the world's most lasting and comprehensive legal traditions

4. the temples of the Capitol hill and the house of the Vestal Virgins in the Forum, which emphasize the ubiquitous role of religion, or rather religions, in Roman life

5. the Circus Maximus and the Colosseum, on the edge of the Palatine hill, where public games provided for the dispossessed masses of the city were the symbol of the deep social unrest tearing at the fiber of Roman society

It will thus become clear that life in the Rome of Augustus was not an unmixed blessing. To some, life there was decidedly unappealing. The satirist Juvenal complained:

Here in town the rich die from insomnia mostly,
Undigested food, on a stomach burning with ulcers,

Brings on listlessness, but who can sleep in a flophouse?
Who but the rich can afford sleep and a garden apartment?
That's the source of infection. The wheels creak by on the narrow
Streets of the wards, the drivers squabble and bawl when they're stopped,
More than enough to frustrate the drowsiest son of a sea cow.

When his business calls, the crowd makes way, as the rich man
Carried high in his car, rides over them, reading or writing,
Even taking a snooze, perhaps, for the motion's composing.

Still he gets where he wants before we do; for all of our hurry
Traffic gets in our way, in front, around and behind.

Somebody gives me a shove with an elbow, or two-by-four scantling.
One clunks my head with a beam, another cracks down with a beer keg.
Mud is thick on my shins, I am trampled by somebody's big feet.
Now what?—a soldier grinds his hobnails into my toes.[1]

Most inhabitants of Rome, however, like New Yorkers today, loved their city in their loathing, and could not be persuaded by any blandishment to prefer the healthy boredom of the fine provincial cities. Rome possessed an indefinable magnetism. Once out of its noise and smells, Romans looked back on it with nostalgia. "From my home [in exile], I turn to the sights of splendid Rome," the poet Ovid wrote, "and in my mind's eye, I survey them all. Now I remember the forums, the temples, the theaters covered with marble, the colonnades where the ground has been leveled—now the grass of the Campus Martius and the views over noble gardens, the lakes, the Waterway, the aqua Virgo."[2]

The Augustan Political Settlement

The Maintenance of the Forms of Republican Government

The secret of the success of the political system imposed by Augustus was to maintain the facade of republican government, and especially the functioning of the assemblies and magistrates, in their traditional locations, while keeping in his own hands the levers of power. He was able in this way to respect both the hallowed constitution and the pragmatic teaching of Rome's political theorists.

During the time of the Roman republic, the political heart of the state lay where the Roman Forum met the base of the Capitol hill near the umbi-

---

[1] From *The Satires of Juvenal*, translated by Rolfe Humphries. Copyright © 1958 by Indiana University Press. Reprinted by permission of the publishers, p. 42. Original Source—Juvenal *Sat.* III. 232–248.

[2] Ovid *Letters from Pontius* I. 8. 33–38, cited in Donald R. Dudley, ed., *Urbs Roma* (Aberdeen: Phaidon, 1967), p. 5.

THE BUILDING OF ROME

753 B.C.	Traditional date of founding. Huts on Palatine hill, digging of sacred boundary furrow
616–509 B.C.	Rule of Etruscan kings. Polychrome temples; six–mile defense wall; draining of Forum by Cloaca Maxima; Circus Maximus for chariot races
	ROMAN REPUBLIC, 509–27 B.C.
c. 500–275	Conquest of Italian mainland. Creation of road system; temples in Forum (Castor and Pollux)
c. 390 B.C.	Sack by Gauls. Hasty rebuilding; Servian wall
264–241	First Punic War
218–202	Second Punic War
	Large-scale use of slaves in city of Rome
146 B.C.	Carthage sacked
	Aristocratic homes on Palatine; Hellenistic temples near river
133–31 B.C.	Roman revolution. City plundered several times by rival legions
	ROMAN EMPIRE, 27 B.C.–A.D. 476
27 B.C.–A.D. 14	Reign of Augustus. Beautification program in Rome (use of marble). Imperial palace on Palatine hill; Altar of Peace; Mausoleum of Augustus
14–68	Julio-Claudian Emperors
	Extension of Palatine palaces; Nero's Golden House
64	Great Fire. Nero imposes urban planning statutes
	Arch of Titus
69–96	Flavian Emperors
	Building of Colosseum on site of Nero's Golden House. Flavian palace on Palatine hill. Imperial Forums
96–180	Five Good Emperors (Nerva; Trajan; Hadrian; Antoninus Pius; Marcus Aurelius). Pantheon. Columns of Trajan and Marcus Aurelius. Tomb of Hadrian
180–284	Breakdown of imperial government. Wall of Aurelian. Baths of Caracalla. Christian catacombs
284–305	Reign of Diocletian. Baths of Diocletian
305–337	Reign of Constantine. Christianization of Rome. Building of first church of St. Peter on Vatican Hill. Arch of Constantine
330	Transfer of capital from Rome to Constantinople
410	Sack of Rome by Visigoths
455	Sack of Rome by Vandals
476	Death of last Roman emperor in West (Romulus Augustulus)

licus stone from which mileages in the Roman empire were counted. The curia, where the senate usually met, was one of the most venerated of Roman buildings, constantly destroyed by fire and immediately rebuilt. It had a simple floor of white marble and three rows of uncomfortable marble seats for the senators, an extraordinarily small and simple hall for the main assembly of a world empire. The senate, although in theory a consultative body, had supreme control over finances and most legislation, and its families provided the majority of leading magistrates. The senate, however, had been compelled to recognize the power of the people, especially as they blackmailed the senators on several occasions by leaving the city en masse in a *secessio,* a kind of sit-out. The tribunes chosen by the people could veto acts of the other magistrates; all laws had to be passed and all magistrates elected by the assemblies; and there was a genuine belief that government power, or *imperium,* could only be conferred by the people's acclamation. The assemblies of the people met almost on the doorstep of the curia, in a small paved space, occasionally covered by an awning, called the comitium. Here vast crowds gathered for the voting, which was often tumultuous and violent, and in which hundreds with no legal right to vote frequently participated. Overlooking the comitium was a long stone platform about eight feet in height decorated with rostra, or beaks, of warships captured in the third century B. C. From this vantage point, with his back to the Capitol hill and with the senate house on the left, a well-trained orator could dominate the crowds massed below. This rough-and-ready system, combining aristocracy with democracy, might easily appear to be a hoax, an inexpensive method for an oligarchy to keep the masses cooperative; but at least during the years of imperial expansion, the system worked. By the time of the Gracchi, however, the poorer classes had such economic grievances that they were alienated from the traditional constitution, and in the first cen-

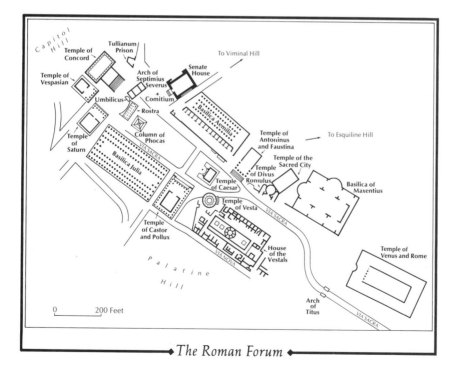

◆ *The Roman Forum* ◆

tury, a new and more potent influence for change had been the bloody intervention of the armies responsible only to their generals. A return to monarchy would have been one solution out of the constitutional chaos, as Julius Caesar had foretold. But as Brutus and his associates demonstrated, in Rome there would always be many willing to kill and to die for the traditional republic. Augustus had to come to terms with tradition.

Roman Political Theory

The success of Augustus owed much to the character of Roman theorizing about the state. The Romans did not produce ambitious blueprints for the construction of ideal states, such as appealed to the Greeks. With very few exceptions, Roman theorists ignored, or rejected as valueless, intellectual exercises like Plato's *Republic,* in which the relationship of the individual to the state was worked out painstakingly without reference to particular states or particular individuals. The closest the Romans came to the Greek model was in Cicero's *De Re Publica,* and even here Cicero had his own state clearly in mind rather than hypothetical men emerging blinded from imaginary caves. Roman thought about the state was concrete, even when it involved religious and moral concepts. The first ruler of Rome, Romulus, was held to have received authority *(imperium)* from the gods, and specifically from Jupiter, the "guarantor" of Rome. All constitutional development was a method of conferring and administering the imperium. Very early it was believed that only the assembly of the fathers, the family heads who formed the original senate, possessed the religious character necessary to exercise imperium, because its primal function was to consult the gods. Being practical as well as exclusive, the senators moved on to share out the imperium, holding that their consuls would possess it on alternate months, and later extending its possession to lower officials. But the important achievement was to create the idea of continuing state authority only temporarily embodied in certain upper-class individuals and only conferred when the mass of the people concurred. The system grew with enormous complexity, as new offices and assemblies were created and almost none discarded. In Roman thinking, the individual had a role in a specific state that had developed in time in a particular political form sanctified by the gods. Total demolition of an existing state, or at least of the existing Roman state, would not be just an act of madness or impiety; it would be impossible. The whole argument of the only important books of political theory that the Romans have left us, Cicero's *De Re Publica* and *Laws,* was the need to preserve the continuity of a great tradition. "On the customs and men of old", Cicero wrote, quoting the poet Ennius, "the Roman state is founded."

The Senate Under Augustus

Augustus satisfied the Optimates in part by restoring the old constitutional forms. "After I had brought to an end the civil wars . . . , having attained su-

Augustus as Commander-in-Chief
The official statues of Augustus usually represent him in one of his three state functions—as civic head, or **princeps**; *as religious head, or* **pontifex maximus**; *or, as here, as* **imperator**, *or commander-in-chief.* Museo Vaticano, Rome. Alinari photo

preme power by the consent of all, I transferred the state from my own power to that of the Roman Senate and People," he observed later. He carefully preserved all the republican magistrates' positions, even though he held a large number of them himself. He often attended the senate meetings and, according to Suetonius, allowed a considerable freedom of abuse there:

Augustus's speeches in the House would often be interrupted by such remarks as, "I don't understand you!" or "I'd dispute your point if I got the chance."

And it happened more than once that, exasperated by recriminations which lowered the tone of the debates, he left the House in angry haste, and was followed by shouts of: "You ought to let senators say exactly what they think about matters of public importance." [3]

He even succeeded in gaining the collaboration of the leaders of the senatorial oligarchy by sharing with them the fruits of office, especially of provincial office. He left eight rich provinces under direct control of the senate. About one hundred of the six hundred senators were abroad on provincial administration at any time, and thus able to enjoy the perquisites of their position. The sons of twenty senators each year were appointed to the senate by Augustus, a form a patronage that gave him great leverage on the leading families. He was thus able to ensure that the senate should request him to go on administering the state as *princeps,* or first citizen, and *imperator,* or commander-in-chief. The forms were undisturbed, but Augustus in fact held the reins of command.

Any spark of independence in the senate quickly died out. New men personally indebted to the emperor were appointed. Men who spoke out unwisely lost all chance of advancement and might even be tried for treason. The precedent for the senate's self-abasement was set when it proclaimed Augustus *Pater Patriae* (Father of his country).

Instead of issuing a decree or acclaiming him with shouts [the senate] chose Valerius Messala to speak for them all when Augustus entered the House. Messala's words were: "Caesar Augustus, I am instructed to wish you and your family good fortune and divine blessings; which amounts to wishing that our entire city will be fortunate and our country prosperous. The Senate agree with the People of Rome in saluting you as Father of your country." With tears in his eyes, Augustus answered—again I quote his exact words: "Fathers of the Senate, I have at last achieved my highest ambitions. What more can I ask of the immortal gods than that they may permit me to enjoy your approval until my dying day." [4]

Such affecting scenes were less common under the later emperors. Again and again, the senate assembled to ratify the army's or the guard's choice of an emperor, or to vote condemnation for treason on the flimsiest charges. Their prestige gradually diminished until the historian Tacitus finally washed his hands of them: "All readers of the history of these terrible times in my pages or another's may fairly take it for granted that the gods were thanked for each instance of banishment or murder ordered by the emperor. Indeed, such occasions, once the sign of public rejoicings, now marked only public disasters. But I shall still record senatorial decrees that

---

[3] Suetonius *The Twelve Caesars,* trans. Robert Graves (Harmondsworth, England: Penguin, 1969), p. 81. Original source—Suetonius *Aug.* 54.1.

[4] Ibid., p. 83. Original source—Suetonius *Aug.* 58.

plumbed new depths of sycophancy, or established new records of servility." [5]

The collapse of even the semblance of independent political life in Rome was symbolized by the encroachment into the Forum itself of the monstrous brick arches needed to hold up the increasingly grandiose palaces on the Palatine hill; and many a senator, crossing the black volcanic paving on his way to a yet more demeaning debate in the senate, must have looked up at the statues of the deified emperors and the towering marble porticoes of the palace, and sighed for the virtue of an earlier Rome.

The View from the Palatine

Augustus (Reigned 27 B. C.–A. D. 14)

In the days of the republic, the Palatine hill was already regarded as one of the pleasantest places to live in Rome; and a number of leading citizens had spacious homes there, where they could enjoy views over the Forum to the

[5] Cited in Donald R. Dudley, *The World of Tacitus* (London: Secker and Warburg, 1968), p. 123.

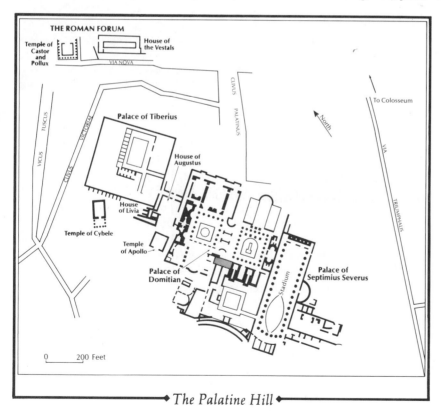

The Palatine Hill

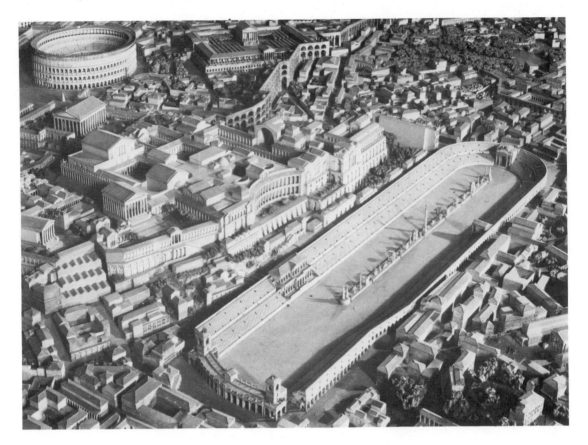

Rome in the Fourth Century

On this model of Imperial Rome, the palaces of the Palatine hill can be seen to the left of the vast oval of the Circus Maximus. In the left center, the complex of temples on the Capitol hill; in the upper left, the Colosseum. Two of the city's aqueducts cut through the close-packed apartment buildings.

Alban hills or across the river to the cypress-covered slopes of the Janiculum hill. Augustus himself was born on the Palatine, and he returned to live there as emperor, buying a house on the very edge of the hill next to the traditional site of Romulus's cabin. Beside his home he built the finest temple in Rome, dedicated to the sun god Apollo, who had helped him defeat Antony's patron god, Neptune, in the sea battle at Actium. Perhaps Augustus had the Parthenon of Athens in mind, or perhaps through worship of Apollo he was laying the basis for a new state religion. The magnificent portico of colored Numidian marble, with the enormous statue of Apollo as the restorer of peace, towered above the city as a harbinger of a new age of imperial peace and glory. Contemporaries were certainly impressed. "You ask why I come so late?" the poet Propertius gushed. "Great Caesar has opened the golden portico of Apollo: a glorious sight, with its columns of African marble, between which sit statues of the many daughters of old Danäus. And there in the middle rose the temple with its shining marble, which Apollo loves more than his home in Ortygia." [6]

[6] Propertius *Elegies* II. 31, cited in Dudley, *Urbs Roma*, p. 155.

In knowing contrast to such splendor, Augustus's home was modest. We can still see its small, painted rooms, set around a little courtyard, almost bare of marble and mosaic. Augustus slept in the same bedroom in this house for forty years, even though the Roman winters did not suit him; and when he wanted to work on secret state papers or to be alone, he retreated to a little study at the top of the house overlooking the whole city. His way of life was as simple as his house. His clothes were usually woven and sewn by the womenfolk of his house; he drank little, and was forgetful about his food. In this unpretentious setting, Augustus developed into the greatest emperor Rome was ever to know; and it pleased him especially that the senate decreed that the title *Pater Patriae* should be inscribed over the doorway of his home.

Augustus's great achievement was to restore peace at home and abroad. With the treasure of Egypt and a loyal experienced army, Augustus could act from strength. He settled part of the army on the land, but maintained a personal "praetorian" guard in Rome of 4,500 men, and a force of legions and auxiliaries of 250,000. He developed an imperial bureaucracy, but decentralized the administration of the empire to bring more effective rule to the provinces. On most of the borders of the empire, Augustus was content to hold firm, using negotiation whenever possible to prevent war. On the northern frontiers, however, there was continuous fighting, mostly in Germany and along the Danube; but after several defeats, he had to be satisfied to establish the frontier along the Rhine and Danube rivers. Finally, the coming of internal peace brought economic prosperity. The great altar built by Augustus to celebrate his achievements was an Ara Pacis, an altar of peace, showing the victory of the Pax Augusta (the Augustan Peace) over war. Augustus permitted almost total freedom of trade and industry within the empire, allowing the great capitalists of republican days to continue amassing fortunes and encouraging the smaller men of the provincial cities to emulate them. Italy in particular boomed economically during the Augustan age. Its large agricultural estates were managed on a scientific basis, and brought wealth to their owners who usually resided in the cities rather

Bust of Old Roman Woman
Roman sculptors of the Augustan age adopted the uncompromising realism developed earlier by Hellenistic artists. E. Richter-Rome

Altar to the Augustan Peace
Augustus and his family mingle with members of the aristocracy. The emperor is wearing the simple toga of a senator, to emphasize his retention of the traditional institutions of Rome. E. Richter-Rome

than on their estates. Oil and wine were sold in the cities, and formed the main items of export trade. But Italy was also transformed into a manufacturing center at this time. Pottery, bronze, glassware, jewelry, even woolen cloth were made for export, while many smaller cities like Pompeii developed workshops to provide the agricultural implements, clothing, and pottery required by their local markets. The booming economy in conditions of peace was a major reason why contemporaries agreed with the poet Horace that Augustus was a Savior of the Empire, a Mercury or Apollo or Hercules.

Even Augustus, however, did not appeal to everyone, as the historian Tacitus showed a century later:

When he had seduced the army by gifts, the common people by the provision of cheap food, and everyone by the blandishments of peace, then little by little he began to enlarge his powers, to encroach upon the proper functions of the Senate, the magistrates and the laws. No one opposed him. Men of spirit had died on the battlefield, or in the proscriptions. The remainder of the aristocracy were rewarded by wealth and position in proportion to their readiness to accept servitude.[7]

The Julio-Claudian Emperors, 14–68

The administrative structure created by Augustus had a solidity that enabled it to function in subsequent years with relative smoothness in spite of the personal deficiencies of the next four emperors. For almost half a century, the Roman provinces remained unaffected by the oddities of the Julio-Claudian dynasty, while in Rome itself the Augustan age's creativity in art and literature, architecture and engineering, and jurisprudence continued with little interruption.

Augustus finally recognized his stepson Tiberius (reigned 14–37) as his successor. The historian Tacitus probably maligned him by presenting him at fifty-six as moody, brusque, tactless, and implacable; Tiberius in fact was more a colorless administrator than a man of passion. His mother Livia, the wife of Augustus, tried to dominate him; and the desire to get out from under her scrutiny provided a motive to Tiberius for building a vast new palace on the Palatine, stretching across the hill from Augustus's home to the cliffs overhanging the Forum. Tiberius was the first emperor to have a real palace, with huge numbers of reception rooms, offices, kitchens, and baths. He governed from Rome, sternly and efficiently, for nine years; but then, wearying of the city, he retired to the island of Capri, where he had built a sumptuous villa on the tall cliffs overlooking the Bay of Naples. Roman society buzzed with scandal about the orgies of this sixty-seven year old pervert, and finally concluded that the old man had gone mad. In 37, he was smothered with his bedclothes by the prefect of the guard.

---

[7] Cited in Dudley, *World of Tacitus,* p. 77. Original source—Tacitus *Ann.* I. 2.2.

His successor, Caligula (reigned 37–41), demanded deification at the age of twenty-five, and would sit in the Temple of Castor and Pollux, between the statues of the divine twins, "offering himself for the adoration of visitors to the Temple." He finally built a bridge across from the Palatine Hill to the Capitol Hill where, Suetonius reported, he would have conversations with the statue of Jupiter, "pressing his ear to the God's mouth, and sometimes raising his voice in anger. Once he was overheard threatening the god: 'If you do not raise me up to Heaven, I will cast you down to Hell.'" His extravagances dictated his policy—war in Mauretania to seize its royal treasury, conspiracy trials for confiscation of rich men's property, heavy taxation on everything and everyone. Caligula was stabbed to death by the praetorian guard, which then picked his successor, a pedantic student of Etruscan history, Caligula's uncle Claudius. Claudius (41–54) surprised everyone by bringing a little sanity back into the government. He set up ministries headed by Greek freemen to carry on the imperial administration; citizenship was extended to many outside Italy; and he conquered most of England. His fourth wife, his niece Agrippina, however, fed him poisoned mushrooms; and like Caligula, he died in the palace of Tiberius, in agony. Nero (54–68) was dissatisfied with everything he inherited, his palaces not least. He murdered his wife and mother and Claudius's son, and married Poppea, whom he took from her husband the later emperor Otho. He cast away the last remnants of Roman dignity, and horrified the senate by performing in the public theaters and arenas as a musician, poet, actor, and charioteer; and he compelled senators to do the same. He threw off the guidance of his tutor, the philosopher Seneca, who had given him five efficient years of government at the beginning of his reign, and eventually had Seneca commit suicide for conspiracy.

Bust of Caligula
Roman sculptors displayed great skill in the delineation of character in the portrait bust. The petulant tyranny of Caligula is unerringly portrayed without, apparently, the emperor being aware of it.   Museo Nazionale, Rome. Alinari photo

The Great Fire of 64 and Nero's Rebuilding

The Roman population had no hesitation in attributing the Great Fire of 64 to Nero himself, who, it was thought, wanted the fame of founding a new city of Rome. This fire, probably the worst in Rome's history, began in shops where the Palatine overhangs the great chariot arena, the Circus Maximus, spread through the nearby slum districts, climbed the Palatine and consumed its palaces, temples, and libraries, and was halted on the sixth day just before it could destroy the Forum and the Capitol. The populace was in total panic. In Tacitus's words:

All movement was blocked by the terrified, shrieking women, by helpless old people or children, by those who sought safety or tried to help others—some carrying invalids, others waiting for them to catch up, some rushing headlong, others rooted to the spot. When people looked back, outbreaks of fire threatened them from the front or the flanks. When they reached a neighboring quarter, that too was alight. . . . Finally, utterly at a loss as to what to avoid, or where

Nero
Nero's extravagant expenditures and indiscriminate cruelty brought the armies to a state of rebellion, and he was compelled to commit suicide in 68.   E. Richter-Rome

to go, they filled the streets, or collapsed in the fields. . . . A widespread report had it that as the city was burning Nero entered his private theater and sang "The Fall of Troy," comparing the modern with the ancient calamity.[8]

With two-thirds of the city destroyed, Nero began rebuilding on an ambitious scale. For the first time, Rome had a city plan. Heights of houses, widths of streets, building materials, and street layout were prescribed by the government. The combination of large tenement houses, monumental areas, and parks was unchanged for the rest of imperial history. But for Nero the crowning achievement of the reconstruction was to be his own palace, the Golden House, of which a few fragments remain. For a site he cleared 125 acres in the heart of Rome, stretching from the Palatine across the site of the future Colosseum. It roused mixed feelings in all who saw it, but it was at least symbolic of how much the empire had changed in fifty years. According to Suetonius:

A huge statue of himself, 120 feet high, stood in the entrance hall; and the pillared arcade ran for a whole mile. An enormous pool, more like a sea than a pool, was surrounded by buildings made to resemble cities, and by a landscape garden consisting of ploughed fields, vineyards, pastures and woodlands where every variety of domestic and wild animal roamed about. Parts of the house were overlaid with gold and studded with precious stones and nacre. All the dining rooms had ceilings of fretted ivory, the panels of which could slide back

[8] Cited in Dudley, *Urbs Roma*, p. 19. Original source—Tacitus *Ann.* XV. 38.4–39.3.

The Colosseum, Rome
An amphitheater constructed by Vespasian on the site of Nero's Golden House, the Colosseum seated up to 50,000 spectators. Its floor could be flooded for miniature naval battles, but most spectacles were battles of gladiators among themselves and with wild animals.   Italian Government Travel Office photo

and let a rain of flowers or of perfume from hidden sprinklers, shower upon his guests. The main dining-room was circular, and its roof revolved slowly, day and night in time with the sky. Sea water, or sulphur water, was always on top of the baths. When the palace had been decorated throughout in this lavish style, Nero dedicated it, and condescended to remark, "Good, now I can at last begin to live like a human being." [9]

He had little time to enjoy it. He not only had squandered the revenues of the state but also had caused too many powerful people to be in danger themselves. Plots against him in Rome culminated in revolt of the army in Spain, which marched on Rome. Lacking all support Nero took a dagger and remarking, ham actor to the end, "What an artist dies in me!" had to be helped to make his suicide effective.

The Flavian Emperors (69–96)

In the chaos that followed Nero's death, several army commanders and the praetorian guard attempted to control the succession. The final victor was Vespasian, the commander of the army in the Near East, who sent a deputy to conquer Rome for him while he held up the Roman food supply from Egypt. The Flavian family (Vespasian, reigned 69–79, and his two sons, Titus, reigned 79–81, and Domitian, reigned 81–96) could not work fast enough to remove all traces of Nero. Much of the Golden House was smashed down. Earth was poured into its rooms to make a vaulted foundation for a new baths; the statues were transferred to a temple in the Forum; the lake was filled in, and the largest amphitheater in the world, the Colosseum, erected in its place. And on the Palatine, Domitian built yet another palace, which took up the rest of Palatine hill beyond the palaces of Augustus and Tiberius. Private homes were again razed and the area became a palace compound; and any future expansion had to be made by building enormous brick arches out from the sides of the hill to hold the new buildings. Domitian probably outdid Nero, with fountains, lakes, porticoes, domed dining halls, private arenas, and large baths for his concubines. Martial even wrote a poem declaring that if he received two invitations to dinner on the same night, from Domitian and from the gods, he would reply: "Please find other people who would like to be guests in heaven; I prefer my Jupiter here on earth."

Bust of Woman of Flavian Period
The restored prosperity under the Flavian emperors enabled Roman aristocrats to indulge again in an elaborate and expensive social life. Women's clothes and hair styles grew increasingly elaborate. E. Richter–Rome

For a while the solid achievements of the Flavians kept the populace quiet. The senate was replenished with provincial families of sound abilities and mores; the army was satisfied with successful campaigns in Scotland and the Near East; and the frontier regions, with their borders secure, experienced new prosperity. Finances were restored, as provincial well-being enabled the imposition of new taxes. There was even the beginning of a state-financed system of education. Domitian, however, succumbed to the

[9] Suetonius *Twelve Caesars*, pp. 224–25. Original source—Suetonius *Nero* 31.2–2.

Arch of Titus
This single-span arch commemorates the defeat of the Jews and the destruction of the Temple in Jerusalem by Titus in A. D. 70. Motyka from Monkmeyer

conspiracy complex that sooner or later affected all masters of the Palatine. He had the palace walls lined with polished, translucent stone so he could watch for assassins; and he embarked on a sadistic purge of suspected opposition. Cruelty provoked conspiracy; and Domitian in his turn was murdered in his own palace, in a plot headed by his wife and his own servants and backed by senators. Of the first ten emperors of Rome, seven had been murdered or had committed suicide!

The Five Good Emperors (96–180)

Fortunately for Rome and its empire, for the next century it was governed by the so-called Five Good Emperors, of whom three were unexceptional and two were great. Their rule provoked one of Edward Gibbon's most famous, and uncharacteristically appreciative, judgments: "If a man were called upon to fix the period in the history of the world during which the condition of the human race was most happy and prosperous, he would without hesitation name that which elapsed from the accession of Nerva to the death of Aurelius. Their united reigns are possibly the only period in which the happiness of a great people was the sole object of government." [10]

[10] Edward Gibbon, *The Decline and Fall of the Roman Empire* (many editions), chap. 3.

However, although most of the empire did not feel it, there was almost constant war. Trajan (reigned 98–117) embarked on two great wars of aggression, against the Dacians (in what is now Rumania), and against the Armenians and Mesopotamians. With the spoils from both, he indulged in extensive building in Rome, not on the Palatine but mostly in functional buildings, like aqueducts, bridges, harbors, and especially his great Forum. But the wars of the later emperors were all defensive. A strong wall was built in Britain by Trajan's successor Hadrian (reigned 117–138) to keep out the marauding Scots; an earthen rampart cut across Germany to bar the Germanic tribes; and a revolt by the Jews in Palestine provoked bloody repression. And the whole reign of Marcus Aurelius (161–180), who pre-

Marcus Aurelius Entering Rome in Triumph
Museo Nuova, Palazzo Conservatori, Rome. Alinari photo

Conflict of Roman and Barbarian
The emperor Constantine incorporated battle scenes sculpted in the second century into the triumphal arch he had built near the Colosseum in A. D. 312.
Alinari photo

ferred philosophy to war, was a long struggle to fend off attacks along all the frontiers in Europe and Asia. The defense, however, was successful, and was the foundation of the domestic achievements of these years.

Perhaps the most striking change was the new prominence of the provinces. Two of the emperors were born in Spain, the family of another had migrated from southern France. All were prepared to extend the privilege of citizenship more widely. Closer supervision, especially as the result of widespread tours by several of the emperors, helped cut corruption and emphasize efficiency. A workable compromise was reached by using the local upper classes to govern for Rome, or by permitting self-governing cities of the Hellenistic world to retain many of their privileges; and these groups frequently became the missionaries for Rome. One popular Greek philosopher, living in Asia Minor, praised Rome in effulgent terms:

The coasts and interiors have been filled with cities, some newly founded, others increased under and by you. . . . As on holiday, the whole civilized world lays down the arms which were its ancient burden, and has turned to adornment and all glad thoughts—with power to realize them. All the other rivalries have left our cities, and this one contention holds them all, how each city may appear more beautiful and attractive. . . . Cities gleam with radiance and charm, the whole earth has been beautified like a garden. . . . Thus it is right to pity only those outside your hegemony—if indeed there are any—because they lose your blessings.[11]

After Marcus Aurelius, the great days of the imperial rulers were over. Certain danger signals finally appeared: voluntary limitation of population, plague brought in by the armies, financial weakness in the provincial government and dwindling funds in Rome, growing strength in the attacks on the frontiers, and a general lethargy in the Roman ruling class. It is symbolic that the only important buildings constructed in Rome for the next two-and-a-half centuries were two public baths, a basilica for law courts, and a massive fortified wall. Commodus (reigned 180–192), the son of Marcus Aurelius, provided twelve years of indolent self-indulgence, in which he displayed his prowess as an archer, as an animal wrestler, and as a sadist. He was strangled by the praetorian guard while he was taking a bath in the palace. The throne was seized after further civil war by the commander of the armies on the Danube, Septimius Severus (reigned 193–211), a man from Leptis Magna in North Africa. Septimius was a soldier's emperor who devoted most of his reign to unproductive wars. Much of his building was done largely in his native Africa, and he recruited the praetorian guard, many senators, and most of his administrators from the provinces. The city of Rome was losing its primacy. His son, Caracalla (reigned 211–217), deprived Roman citizenship of most of its value by giving it to all freemen in the empire, built the largest baths in the world, invaded Parthia, and was murdered during the campaign. From then until the establishment of a taut, oriental-style despotism by Diocletian, there was almost uninterrupted chaos. Every emperor was picked by the army or the praetorian guard, and usually murdered by them. Thirty-seven emperors in all were proclaimed but only Aurelian made any mark on the appearance of the city—by building the great wall that helped prolong the city's safety. Order was eventually restored by two emperors from Illyria, which is now part of Yugoslavia: Diocletian (reigned 284–305), who built his home at Spalato (Split) on the Dalmatian coast, and Constantine (reigned 306–337), who built a new capital at Constantinople. After the third century of chaos, we must look to Constantinople for the continuance of Roman civilization. In Rome, we can only trace the stages of decline.

Caracalla (Reigned 211–217)
Caracalla gained absolute power by murdering his brother Geta and by persecuting Geta's followers in Rome. He himself was murdered by a rival while on military campaign.
The Metropolitan Museum of Art, Samuel D. Lee Fund, 1940

The Political Message of Rome's Poets and Historians

The most rapturous acclamation of Rome's emperors was provided by its poets, the most scathing indictment by its historians. Both saw them-

[11] Cited in Michael Grant, *The World of Rome* (Cleveland: World Publishing Co., 1960), p. 52.

selves fulfilling an important political role in imperial society; indeed, the triumphant creation of the greatest writers of Latin literature is best understood when considered in the political context in which they chose to work. The writers of the Augustan golden age were not inhabitants of some Parnassus remote from the reality of Roman life.

The Poets of the Augustan Age

Virgil (70–19 B. C.), the greatest Latin poet, began his career with the rhapsodies to the life of the countryside, first to the shepherd's idyll in the well-watered meadows of the Po valley where Virgil himself grew up, and then to the practical problems of farming. Virgil's *Georgics*, thought by some to be the finest poem ever written, talks about the diseases of cattle and the varieties of soil; but the poet, through his elegance and deep humanity, transforms the theme into a call to the debased city to restore itself with rural values, the only remedy Virgil can see to the barbarism of the civil wars.

> *This was the life which once the ancient Sabines led,*
> *And Remus and his brother; this made Etruria strong,*
> *Through this, Rome became the fairest thing on earth.*[12]

In the *Aeneid*, on which he spent the last ten years of his life, he narrowly avoided writing a poem of political propaganda in support of Augustus. What saved him was his worship of Rome and of its traditional *virtus*. For the century past, *virtus* had come to mean winning personal fame as a form of immortality, as *virtù* was to mean again at the Italian Renaissance. Virgil brought back the virtue that demands *pietas*, to do one's duty to the gods, one's own country, and one's family; and, while idolizing Augustus in the poem, he set him a high standard to follow at the same time. The *Aeneid* is a hard poem for modern readers to enjoy, with its endless references to abstruse mythology, its insufferable gods and senseless killings. But one has to see the sensitive, sick poet struggling to set standards for an empire he regards as an essential stage in the slow climb of humanity toward a universal good or even a universal divinity; and at times one glimpses a quick way into the heart of a good man's thought, as when Aeneas suddenly experiences the pity of war:

> *Yes, Aeneas drove his strong sword*
> *Right through the young man's body, and buried it there to the hilt.*
> *It penetrated his light shield, frail armor for so aggressive*
> *A lad, and the tunic his mother had woven of pliant gold,*
> *And soaked it with blood from his breast.*

---

[12] Virgil *Georgics* II. 531–34, trans. in Gilbert Highet, *Poets in a Landscape* (London: Hamish Hamilton, 1957), p. 69.

Then the soul left the body,
Passing sadly through the air to the land of shadows.
But when Aeneas beheld the dying boy's look, his face—
A face that by now was strangely grey—he felt pity for him,
And a deep sigh escaped him.[13]

Virgil had brought the Roman state back to the eternal needs and duties of man. It was not political philosophy, but it came close.

Even Horace (65–8 B. C.), the other great elegiac poet of the Augustan age, had a sharp political content in much of his poetry, and again the theme was the return to the old values and through them to internal peace. At its most blatant, it became: "I will fear neither civil war nor violent death while Caesar rules the earth." At its most scathing, it involved a splendid denunciation of the distasteful Roman population, as in his *Satires* and some of his *Odes*:

The fickle crowd, the false swearing courtesan,
They all move back, these friends, when our casks are drained
Of wine, and only dregs are left; too
Crafty are they to share our misfortunes. . . .
Alas, for shame, these wounds and these brother's woes!
From what have we refrained, this our hardened age?
What crime is left untried? From what, through
Fear of the gods, has our youth held back or
Restrained its hand? [14]

[13] Cecil Day Lewis, *The Aeneid of Virgil* (London: Hogarth Press, 1952), pp. 232–33. Reprinted by permission of the translator's Literary Estate, The Hogarth Press and A. D. Peters Company, Ltd.

[14] From *The Odes of Horace, Newly Translated from the Latin and Rendered into the Original Metres*, by Helen Rowe Henze. Copyright 1961 by the University of Oklahoma Press, p. 67.

Girls in Bikinis, Piazza Armerina, Sicily
This lively scene depicting an athletic contest is part of a large mosaic floor known as the "Room of the Ten Girls" in an imperial villa of the fourth century.   Italian Government Travel Office photo

To Horace, the answer was for youth to dedicate itself again to the service of the state, in which alone the individual can achieve virtus. He ended with the most foreboding of sentiments, to be repeated for hundreds of years on countless gravestones: *Dulce et decorum pro patria mori.*

> *Seemly and sweet is death for one's native land*
> *For death pursues the man who would flee from him,*
> *Nor spares the knees and shrinking back of*
> *Those of our youth unprepared for warfare.*[15]

Horace will, however, be better remembered for the delicate complexity of his new poetic forms; in the *Odes* he worked out an intricate craftsmanship for adapting Greek meters to the more unbending Latin tongue. For fear of tying him to nothing but riling or exhortation, one should at least taste the humor he could bring to a love poem. Here, a lover is shut out by his mistress:

> *Though you dwelt by the Don, Lisa, and drank of it*
> *And were wed to a harsh husband, you still might weep*
> *To expose me, outstretched prone by your cruel doors,*
> *To Aquilo's native winds.*

She ignores his gifts, his prayers, and his pallor, however.

> *Lady, you are no more soft than the rigid oak,*
> *Neither are you at heart gentler than Moorish snakes;*
> *Not forever will my body be lying here*
> *And enduring the rain of heaven!* [16]

The Didactic Message of Rome's Historians

The historians found no such distraction in their pursuit of the city's lost virtues. Livy (59 B. C.–A. D. 17) belonged in the tradition of ancient historians who felt that a history book should not only relate facts but be great literature. Livy wrote a *History of Rome* in 142 books, all of which celebrate the virtus of earlier Romans, whose simple conception of the individual's role was to achieve glory by performance of great deeds on behalf of the state, in peace or war: "War no less than peace has its rules and we have learned to wage both with justice no less than courage. . . . I will conquer by Roman methods, by virtus, by labor and by arms." Morals, according to Livy, declined when riches began to abound, and it was the duty of the Augustan age to restore the moral tone. There is no lament for the loss of liberty in Livy, but for the loss of duty; and Livy's ideals, which were studied from his *History* by successive generations of the Roman elite, created an idealized standard of political conduct to which all would pay lip service.

[15] Ibid., p. 119.
[16] Ibid., p. 139.

It was, however, by Tacitus (c. 56–123), the most subtly vindictive of all historians, that the emperors themselves, including Augustus, were tested and found wanting. His two great works, the *Annals,* on the Julio-Claudian emperors, and the *Histories,* on the Flavians, are a scintillating condemnation of one-man rule. "As I see it," he wrote, "the chief duty of the historian is this: to see that virtue is placed on record, and that evil men and evil deeds have cause to fear judgment at the bar of posterity." His excoriation reached its peak in his treatment of Tiberius, who symbolized in his view the almost inevitable degradation of monarchy into tyranny. Unlike the later sadists and madmen, such as Caligula and Nero, Tacitus saw in Tiberius a slow but relentless corruption by exercise of power. His last summation of Tiberius's career is a masterpiece of malice:

As a private citizen, or holding military command under Augustus, his conduct and his reputation were excellent. While Drusus and Germanicus lived, craft and equivocation provided a screen of virtues. While his mother was alive, Tiberius still showed good and bad qualities; while he had Sejanus to love (or fear), his cruelty was appalling but his perversions remained hidden. In his last phase, there was a great eruption of crime and vice: set free from shame and fear he stood out at long last in no other character but his own.[17]

But did Tacitus have an alternative to offer? He dismissed political theory very briefly. A mixed constitution in which the masses, nobility, and individuals share power, he wrote, "is easier to command than to create; or, if created, its tenure of life is brief." If the masses dominated, one should "study the character of the masses and the methods of controlling them," a strikingly modern concept. If the nobility were in power, one needed "the most exact knowledge of the temper of the senate and the aristocracy." It was this latter form of government, refreshed by an infusion of new men like himself from outside Rome, that Tacitus approved. But such a restoration of the aristocratic republic was impossible, he saw, and as a result his history of one-man rule could be nothing but a long condemnation: "A series of savage mandates, of perpetual accusations, of traitorous friendships, of ruined innocents, of various causes and identical results—everywhere monotony of subject, and satiety." This was mock modesty, of course. The venom of Tacitus is still fresh on the page today.

Attorneys and Jurisconsults

One of the principal reasons why Rome was able to survive so many interludes of political chaos inflicted upon it by the struggles for imperial power and by the ineffectiveness of so many emperors, was that it possessed and continually developed one of the most effective legal systems ever created. The establishment of social order through a just set of rules and procedures

[17] Cited in Dudley, *World of Tacitus,* p. 82. Original source—Tacitus *Ann.* 51.3.

for their administration was a permanent goal of the systematic Roman mind; and this search for a stable rational system of laws that would survive the periods of political turmoil was greatly advanced by the wiser of the Roman emperors. Rome's lawyers succeeded so well that their concepts are still basic to the law of much of the Western world.

In Rome, the center of judicial life was in two splendid basilicas, the Basilica Aemilia and the Basilica Julia, built on each side of the open courtyard of the Forum where the assemblies of the people met. These two vast buildings were similar in size and decoration. Around the outside ran a two-story portico, lined with small shops. The Basilica Aemilia, we know, had a huge central nave, twelve yards wide and over eighty yards long, paved with colored marbles and lined with columns of African marble carved in spirals of acanthus leaves; and the Basilica Julia, begun by Julius Caesar and finished by Augustus, was even more colorful. Most of the meetings of the most important jury took place there. These cases, dealing with disputes over wills and inheritances of the rich and noble, led to some of the greatest legal battles; and spectators would pour in to listen and comment. Pliny the Younger described one case in which he appeared:

One hundred and eighty judges [jurors] were sitting, that being the total of the four panels. A huge number of counsel were engaged on either side: the benches were crowded: and the court, broad as it was, was encircled by a crowd of spectators standing several rows deep. Add to this that the tribunal was crowded, and the galleries were packed with men and women; they hung over in their eagerness to hear (which was hard) and to see (which was easy).[18]

The case was enough to attract a crowd—an eighty-year old patrician had disinherited his daughter after falling hopelessly in love with a younger woman who apparently had married him for the money. With Pliny's help the stepmother's plans were foiled.

In this supercharged atmosphere, in which every citizen was frequently called on to share in the burden of the law, as judge, juror, or witness for his friends, and many indulged in litigation as a matter of habit, the Romans hammered out a consistent, effective body of law.

Evolution of Roman Law

Law in Rome, as in many primitive cultures, was originally a set of customary rules whose existence from time immemorial was simply assumed; and it was the job of the king, then of the consuls, and even later of the emperors, to make them known in specific cases. Law could therefore evolve as the rules were interpreted to meet changing circumstances. In the middle of the fifth century B. C. a first attempt was made to write down the laws, in the

---

[18] Cited in Dudley, *Urbs Roma*, p. 86. Original source—Pliny *Letters* VI. 33.3–4.

Bust of Hadrian
This bronze bust was found in the River Thames under London Bridge. Hadrian inspected the imperial defenses in Britain in 122, and ordered the erection of a stone and earthen rampart across northern England to block the incursions of the Scots. Photo copyright by the Trustees of the British Museum

Twelve Tables, which were put up for everyone to see in the Forum near the speakers' platform. The Tables were still those of a rural society with strong religious sanctions frequently involving ritual punishments. (For stealing crops by night, the criminal was beaten to death with rods!) But during the republic a vast amount of legislation was enacted by the senate and the assemblies; the decisions of the magistrates and especially of the praetors, who were to supervise justice, became more highly developed; and a number of experts, called jurisconsults, gave opinions that slowly evolved into a complex body of legal commentary that in practice came to be accepted as law. A serious attempt to bring order to this growing mass of complex rules was made in the second century B. C.; but the emperor Hadrian inaugurated the finest period of Roman jurisprudence by ordering the codification of the praetors' law in a perpetual edict to be observed by all magistrates. By the end of the second century A. D., Rome already had its legal textbooks for budding lawyers, and one way to advancement as a lawyer was to publish learned commentaries on the law.

Character of Roman Law

All this development would not concern us greatly if the Romans had not developed good law. The laws of the Assyrians or the Babylonians strike us as quaint and crude. The Romans, however, seriously tackled the problem of regulating disputes that arose between persons living side by side in a complex society, and they established many principles of lasting value. It is important to distinguish some of the differences from our way of thinking. All people were not equal before the law. A person's rights were dependent on individual status—born free, freed, Roman citizen, resident alien, child under guardianship, woman, and so on. Slaves were not considered persons and lacked legal rights, even though the emperors began to lay down some rules for their physical protection. Fathers of families exercised defined powers over their children that lasted throughout life, and in theory until Hadrian's reign the father had the right of life and death. There was little freedom of political action or guarantee of free speech, and most of the rights zealously preserved and for which there was a genuine legal remedy were the property rights of the upper classes. What the Roman lawyers achieved was first the recognition that all persons of the same status enjoyed equal rights under the law; and under the influence of Stoicism in the second century, they were moving toward the idea of *ius gentium,* an "international law" achieved by human reason and applicable to all people. They had recognized the idea that guilt as well as consequences of an act should be considered in determining punishment, and that it was better for the guilty to go free than the innocent suffer. And by the development of private property law, to which most of their efforts were directed, they provided the mechanism for the complex economic and social structure of an empire of seventy million people. The law that was elaborated in Rome in the second century was developed in Constantinople under Justinian in the sixth century, passed on to the Catholic Church in the canon law, applied through most of Europe in the Middle Ages, and absorbed into the present law of many countries of continental Europe and of their former colonies overseas.

Posterity's admiration was not however shared by all Roman citizens! One will that has survived begins: "I, Lucius Titus, have written this my testament without any lawyer, following my own natural reason rather than excessive and miserable diligence." It is hard for a layman to love the law, even for a Roman layman.

Priests and Philosophers

Roman State Religion

In spite of their grandeur, the Basilica Aemilia and the Basilica Julia were not the most prominent buildings in the Roman Forum. Temples, not law courts, dominated the heart of Rome; for religion, even more than law, helped bind the Roman state together.

From the early days, Romans had enjoyed the company of their own comfortable household gods, which were disembodied spiritual forces that accompanied all their daily actions. Vesta protected the hearth, Janus the doorway, the Penates the storeroom, and hundreds of others watched over stump, rivulet, rainstorm, or planting. In the first centuries after the city's foundation, the state authorities developed an official religion that was to be practiced in addition to the worship of the household deities. In its origins, the state religion undoubtedly represented the feeling of the government that among its many duties, one of the most important was to maintain the harmony between human beings and the divine order; this was a complicated task involving specialists employed by the state to master the difficult formulas that assured the city's well-being at the hands of the gods. Receptive as ever, the Roman state took all the native spirits and gave them official status. Vesta became the goddess of the common hearth of the whole Roman people, and a perpetual flame was kept burning in her temple in the Forum as a symbol of the Roman home. From the Etruscans, the Romans took the mighty triad of Jupiter, Juno, and Minerva. Jupiter, the most powerful god in Rome, was the god of light, thunder, and rain, the source of state authority, and the special guardian of Rome itself. Juno was a kindlier creature, the goddess of women and all their manifold functions, especially

Neptune Mosaic, Herculaneum
Neptune, associated by the Romans with Poseidon, the Greek god of the sea, was frequently portrayed in mosaic on the walls of private homes, perhaps because the Romans had originally considered him the god of fresh water rather than salt water.   Italian Government Tourist Office photo

those of marriage and childbirth. Minerva was the goddess of arts and crafts, which came to include musicians and actors, and even to extend to all wisdom. The first large temple erected on the Capitol hill was for these three deities, the so-called Capitoline Triad; and for the rest of Roman history all solemn religious processions as well as the triumphs of victorious generals wound their way across the Forum along the Via Sacra (Holy Road) and up the side of the Capitol hill to the seat of Jupiter and his accompanying goddesses.

Other gods were added as they made themselves useful. Two divine youths on horseback were seen to intervene decisively in the Romans' victory over the Etruscans in 496 B. C., and simultaneously announce the victory in Rome. A temple was at once erected to the divine twins, Castor and Pollux, across the street from Vesta's hearth. Acquaintance with the Greek cities of the south, perhaps through the Etruscans, led to the absorption of most of the Greek gods, especially of Apollo, whose invaluable capacities included archery, medicine, music, prophecy, philosophy, and purification. He helped fend off plague, and won the battle of Actium for Augustus. To simplify matters, most Roman gods were assumed to be different from Greek gods only in name—Neptune was Poseidon, Mercury was Hermes, Minerva was even Athena. The state religion, for all its staid moralistic character, permitted some extraordinary innovations. At the end of the third century B. c., the worship of Cybele, a goddess from Asia Minor, was permitted, even though her rites were carried out by eunuch priests who in a frenzy of bloodlust provoked by wild ritual dances cut themselves all over with knives. Cybele's stone was brought to the Palatine hill, and a temple erected a few yards from the site of Augustus's future home.

A large priesthood composed of nonprofessional and professional priests, administered the state religion. At its head was the *pontifex maximus,* elected by the people, who picked another eight members of the principal college of priests. But there were many other colleges for separate functions, like blessing foreign relations, or bringing in the New Year by dancing. The professional priests alone knew the ritual formulas, drew up the calendar of religious festivals, and told whether a particular day was auspicious for public business. Indeed, a well-placed bribe to a priest could close down the law courts when an inconvenient charge had been brought. The most pervasive influence of the priests however was through augury; for while many religions have specialized in consoling for past misfortune, the Roman priesthood could predict the future. The art had been a long time in the fashioning, possibly since the Babylonians; but the augurs claimed to be able to tell from the flight of birds or the appearance of the entrails of a sacrificed animal, whether a particular action would have a favorable outcome. The liver in particular was an infallible portent. Almost every natural phenomenon, however, had to be watched, for the Roman moved in a world full of supernatural powers. Julius Caesar should have known better than to go to the senate on the Ides of March, since he had

Augustus as Pontifex Maximus

As pontifex maximus, *or head priest, Augustus exercised considerable political powers through his control over auguries and by supervision of the state priesthood. The pope later assumed the title.*

E. Richter–Rome

THE ROMAN GODS

Official State Religion

	Jupiter: *God of day, controller of thunder and lightning, guardian of Rome. Greek Zeus.*
CAPITOL TRIAD	Juno: *Wife of Jupiter, goddess of women. Greek Hera.*
	Minerva: *Patroness of arts and crafts, wisdom, doctors, and musicians. Greek Athena.*

Mars: *God of agriculture, then of war, special protector of Rome. Greek Ares.*

Saturn: *God of newly sown seed, then of agriculture. Greek Cronus.*

Venus: *Goddess of fertility. Greek Aphrodite.*

Ceres: *Goddess of harvest, and of plebeians. Greek Demeter.*

Mercury: *God of merchants and robbers. Greek Hermes.*

Diana: *Goddess of light, moon, women, and hunting. Greek Artemis.*

Castor and Pollux: *Divine twins, associated with sons of Zeus and Leda. Protectors of Rome and patrons of equites.*

Household Deities

Janus: *God of beginnings, guardian of the doorway.*

Vesta: *Goddess of hearth.*

Di Penates: *Keepers of the storehouse, deities of the home.*

Di Manes: *Kindly shades, spirits of ancestors.*

N.B. Varro said the Romans had thirty thousand gods!

dreamed the night before that he was sailing in the clouds to shake hands with Jupiter, and a little wren, with a sprig of laurel in its beak, had been torn to pieces by a pursuing group of birds in Pompey's Assembly room. Caesar had been warned directly by the augur Spurinna that he was in danger until the Ides of March were over. Suetonius recorded the famous scene as Caesar entered the senate: "Several victims were then sacrificed, and despite consistently unfavorable omens, he entered the House, deriding Spurinna as a false prophet. 'The Ides of March have come,' he said. 'Ay, they have come,' replied Spurinna, 'but they have not yet gone.' "

Similarly unfortunate signs preceded the murder of Claudius, as Tacitus records:

A series of prodigies in the following year indicated changes for the worse. Standards and soldiers' tents were set on fire from the sky. A swarm of bees settled on the pediment of the Capitoline temple. Half-bestial children were born, and a pig with hawk's claws. A portent too was discerned in the losses suffered by every official post: a quaestor, aedile, tribune, praetor, and consul had all died within a few months. Agrippina was particularly frightened— because Claudius had remarked in his cups that it was his destiny first to endure his wife's misdeeds, and then to punish them. She decided to act quickly.[19]

No less important for the safety of the city were the vestal virgins, who kept alive the sacred flame of the hearth and looked after other precious objects, including a statue that had fallen from the sky at Troy and been brought to Rome by Aeneas. The vestals, usually six in number, had been chosen at an age between six and ten, and devoted thirty years of virginity to their priesthood. If they ceased to be chaste, they were buried alive. During their priesthood, they lived together in a lovely colonnaded home just below the Palatine hill, in the heart of the Forum, amid fountains and reflecting pools. They had special seats at all state functions, including the gladiatorial games; and at the end of thirty years were given a large dowry and permitted to marry. Most did not.

This whole apparatus of official religion was welcomed, even by non-believers, as the cement of the state, the supernatural stimulus to patriotism. Augustus deliberately turned it to his own advantage. He became pontifex maximus himself, repaired the ruined temples, built new ones to gods related to himself, such as Apollo, and sought to revive the veneration for the old religion that had lapsed during the civil wars. He set an important precedent, however, by erecting a temple to the deified Julius Caesar, on the spot where his body had been cremated. Emperor worship became an important asset both to future emperors and to the cohesion of the state. Augustus refused to be considered a god during his lifetime, but was deified after his death, as most other emperors were, except those the senate specifically condemned. It thus became possible to name as traitors to the state any religious sect, like the Christians, that refused to worship at the shrines of the divine emperors.

Worship of Dionysus, Isis, and Mithras

This state religion was not exclusive. The Roman state had no objection if its subjects wanted to worship other religions as well. From the second century b. c., many did, seeking an emotional release that the ritualized official religion could not give. Many simply practiced magic. To hurt your enemies, it was quite common to stick nails in images of them, or to burn part of their clothes. Others followed astrology, worshipping the sun and moon, studying the influence of the seven planets, and especially the twelve

---

[19] Tacitus *Annals* XII. 64, cited in Grant, *World of Rome*, p. 46.

signs of the zodiac. But from the second century B. C. outbreaks of religious emotionalism began to occur on such a scale that the senate clamped down on their excesses. Among the first to be introduced was worship of the Greek god Dionysus, who was identified with the Roman god of the vine, Bacchus. The initiates indulged in wild orgiastic rites, in which they submitted to thrashing for purification, and even at times went so far as human sacrifice. The great attraction was the promise of happy afterlife for all the miserable of this earth. The appeal of the worship of the Egyptian goddess Isis, which was the most popular of all Roman religions in the first two centuries of the Empire, was its promise of immortality through union with the divine. Isis, a sweet dignified woman, enjoyed musical processions, with slow lines of linen-clad priests intoning hymns and playing flutes and tambourines. She was the universal mother, the shield against demons, and the pardoner of the penitent. Her attraction is most graphically portrayed in Apuleius's novel, *The Golden Ass*, the picaresque masterpiece by an African lawyer. Lucius, roaming the world in search of magic, unfortunately uses the wrong ointment in a witch's house, and is turned into an ass. After innumerable adventures, most of them unpleasant, he gallops off to the sea and falls asleep by the shore.

Head of a Roman Priest of Isis, Second Century A. D. Los Angeles County Museum of Art. William Randolph Hearst Collection

Not long afterwards I awoke in sudden terror. A dazzling full moon was rising from the sea. It is at this secret hour that the Moon-goddess, sole sovereign of mankind, is possessed of her greatest power and majesty. She is the shining deity by whose divine influence not only all beasts, wild and tame, but all inanimate things as well, are invigorated, whose ebbs and flows control the rhythm of all bodies whatsoever, whether in the air, on earth or below the sea.

Lucius begs Isis to end his sufferings, restore him to human shape, and send him back home, or else give him the gift of death.

I had scarcely closed my eyes before the apparition of a woman began to rise from the middle of the sea with so lovely a face that the gods themselves would have fallen down in adoration of it. . . . Her long thick hair fell in tapering ringlets on her lovely neck, and was crowned with an intricate chaplet in which was woven every kind of flower. Just above her brow shone a round disc, like a mirror, or like the bright face of the moon, which told me who she was. Vipers rising from the left-hand and right-hand partings of her hair supported this disc, with ears of corn bristling beside them. . . . All the perfumes of Arabis floated into my nostrils as the Goddess deigned to address me: "You see me here, Lucius, in answer to your prayer. I am Nature, the universal mother, mistress of all elements. . . . Weep no more, lament no longer; the hour of deliverance, shone over by my watchful light, is at hand." [20]

[20] Apuleius *The Golden Ass*, trans. Robert Graves (Harmondsworth, England: Penguin, 1950), pp. 268–70. Original source—Apuleius *Golden Ass* 1.3–4.

The softness of Isis came up against a tough competitor in the first century A. D., when the cult of Mithras was brought into Italy, probably by soldiers who had served in Asia Minor. Mithras was an Iranian god, born in a cave in the rocks at the will of the sun god. His greatest deed was to slay a bull after a tremendous struggle by plunging a knife into its throat, whereupon the earth was fertilized, plants grew, and the first human beings were born. As the story became more elaborate, Mithras fought the perils that plague the earth, overcoming the evil spirit, and finally ascended to heaven in the sun's chariot. The devotees usually met in an underground cave such as the one found beneath St. Clement's in Rome, which represented the cave where Mithras was born and where a statue of Mithras killing the bull was placed. Only men could join. Vicious initiation tests, including torture, were applied. Strict rules of personal conduct had to be observed. It was a soldier's religion, and shrines to Mithras have been found in all the garrisons of the empire.

Victory over all the other emotional religions would eventually go to Christianity. (See Chapter 5.) But when the empire was at its height, the Christians were regarded by most Romans as a small, unappealing group of fanatics. Cybele, Dionysus, Isis, and Mithras held the field.

Epicureanism and Stoicism

There was always a small intellectual elite who regarded the state religion with approval only because it kept the common people obedient. "The whole base throng of gods assembled by a superstition coeval with time," wrote Seneca the Younger, "we must worship without forgetting that we do it to set an example, not because they exist." And the elite was equally repelled by the emotionalism, and also by the lack of class barriers, in the newer religions. They therefore turned to philosophy for guidance, with the same pragmatic genius they brought to all their activity. The Romans wanted something they could use, and their philosophers provided it. Once more, however, they appropriated ideas developed by that far more creative people, the Greeks, and made them practical. Lucretius (96–55 B. C.) took the ideas of Epicurus, and created the classic statement of Epicureanism, his long poem, *De Rerum Naturae* (On the Nature of Things). Fear, he argued, was destroying people's lives, especially such unwarranted fear as terror of the gods (who had no relationship to men) or of death (which was not followed by an afterlife). The only reality was physical sensation, the greatest happiness the experience of unspoiled nature—trees, grass, streams, moonlight, birdsong. In the operation of nature, mechanistically conceived as a constant flow of atoms, he saw the boundaries of human existence. The implication for one's daily life were obvious: ignore religion, shun moral causes, avoid involvement, seek mental peace and quiet. It is the passion with which Lucretius recommends dispassion that makes him a great poet, and gives his verse such a modern flavor.

Do you not see that nature is clamoring for two things only, a body free from pain, a mind released from worry and fear, for the enjoyment of pleasurable sensations? So we find that the requirements of our bodily nature are few indeed, no more than is necessary to banish pain. . . . Nature does not miss luxuries when men recline in company on the soft grass by a running stream under the branches of a tall tree and refresh their bodies pleasurably at small expense.[21]

Roman governments were of necessity unfriendly to the spread of such debilitating ideas among a people with an empire to conquer and administer. The Greek Epicureans had been expelled from Rome in the second century B. C. for enticing the youths away from the military exercises of the Campus Martius, and in the time of Augustus's religious revival it was unwise to announce one's admiration of Lucretius. He was forgotten until the Italian Renaissance rediscovered his power; but he has never been so thoroughly appreciated as in the twentieth century.

Stoicism, especially as expounded by Seneca (2 B. C.–A. D. 65), became the commonly accepted belief of the Roman upper classes in the second century A. D. Seneca, born in Spain, had moved to Rome where he had a career of sensational variety: philosophical study in the best literary circles, serious illness and years of convalescence in the hothouse atmosphere of Alexandria, promising political career interrupted by banishment to Corsica, return as tutor to the future emperor Nero followed by five years' guardianship, in which he ran the Roman Empire as a philosopher-king, dismissal, conspiracy, and state-ordered suicide. A career, in short, that required more than a normal dose of Stoicism. In all these vicissitudes, Seneca developed a noble message for the individual who must face the worst of life's challenges. The two most important things one possessed could not fall into the control of others. Money, goods, office, power, could all be taken away, and one should not become attached to them. But one's own mind and universal Nature, a kind of divine providence that existed in all things, could not be affected by the actions of others. Moreover, Nature or Providence was benevolent to humanity. It recognized an essential equality and brotherhood in all human beings, even in slaves: "We are members of one great body. Nature has made us relatives. She planted in us a mutual love, and fitted us for a social life. . . . You must live for your neighbor if you would live for yourself."[22]

In all the inhumanity of Roman life, into which we are about to plunge, the words of the Stoics blow like a clean breeze from the country. It was a pity that their ideals were not more practiced.

[21] Lucretius *De Rerum Natura* II. 16–21, 23, 29–31, trans. R. C. Trevelyan, cited in Grant, *World of Rome*, p. 19.

[22] Ibid., p. 196.

Street in Pompeii
The principal streets of Pompeii were about twenty feet wide, with raised sidewalks. The lower floors of the buildings were occupied by stores, artisan workshops, wine parlors, or bakeries; the upper floors, with sleeping quarters.   Italian State Tourist Office photo

Bread and Circuses

The Everyday Life of the Proletariat

For the great mass of Rome's inhabitants, slave or free, everyday life was a harsh struggle for survival in conditions of noisome squalor. The great intellectual achievements in law or literature and the physical achievements in engineering or architecture brought few benefits to the poor. Most Romans lived in blocks of tenement houses, six to ten stories high, housing up to two hundred people in narrow, cubicle-like rooms. Water available at city fountains had to be carried through the streets and up long flights of stairs; garbage and sewage was flung in unsanitary heaps at the bottom of stairwells. Great outbreaks of typhoid, typhus, and cholera were inevitable in these conditions, and serious plagues broke out at least two or three times a century. Malaria was ever present even until the end of the nineteenth century. Dead bodies of people and animals were piled in enormous pits on the edge of the city, poisoning the air and feeding the epidemics. Ordinary comforts were few and far between. Sleep itself was hard to obtain, since the streets reechoed all night to the sound of carts that had been forbidden to circulate in the narrow thoroughfares of the city during the day. Perhaps one-fifth of the city's population, that is, up to two hundred thousand people, relied on government handouts of bread for their main sustenance, while thousands of others sought support as clients of the great families. The destitute arrived in the morning at their patron's house with a basket, to pick up the food he would hand out; but most patrons came to prefer giving a small gift of six and a half sesterces. Work itself was in short supply for the freemen of the city's vast proletariat, especially as their numbers were constantly augmented from the countryside and the demobilized armies.

The Public Games

In these circumstances, the proletariat turned for entertainment to the free public games that, by the middle of the first century, were being held on ninety-three days a year. For a time the games had been intended as a salutary display of public punishment of criminals, who were thrown to wild animals; but the games increased rapidly in complexity and expense. Theat-

The Arenas of Arles
Roman provincial cities were provided with all the amenities of the capital itself, including baths, theaters, and especially arenas for the gladiatorial games. French Government Tourist Office photo

Gladiator Resting Before Combat
E. Richter–Rome

rical performances were given, on a competitive basis as in Athens; but the size of the theaters, which accommodated only about twenty thousand people, show that they were not the chief magnet for the Roman populace; and almost no new tragedies were written after the time of Claudius. Far more popular were the chariot races, the most important of which were held in the vast Circus Maximus below the Palatine hill. This oval arena seated two hundred fifty thousand people; and the emperor attended the games from a high balcony that Augustus had erected on the side of the Palatine hill. The crowds followed the exploits of the popular charioteers with a passion that Pliny the Younger found execrable: "Such favor, such weighty influence, hath one worthless [charioteer's] tunic—I say nothing of the vulgar herd, more worthless than the tunic—but with certain grave personages. When I observe such men thus insatiably fond of so silly, so low, so uninteresting, so common an entertainment, I congratulate myself that I am insensible to these pleasures." The attraction of the gladiatorial games was even more debased, however. Teams of gladiators, consisting mostly of slaves and the most desperate of the poor, were trained by contractors and hired out for the games both in Rome and the provincial cities. They used specialized weapons. Samnites carried a sword and shield, Thracians a dagger and buckler, others called *retiarii* specialized in net and trident. Sometimes they fought with animals, the more exotic the better. Some provinces saw whole species wiped out to provide Rome's amusement. The hippopotamus disappeared from Nubia, the elephant from North Africa, and the tiger from Hyrcania. Augustus boasted that he gave twenty-six shows of African animals, in which thirty-five hundred were slaughtered. Often the gladiators fought in duels to the death. But the slaughter was soon extended to include the massacre of such undesirables as arsonists and Christians. One of the most impressive of all Roman buildings, the Colosseum, was erected by Vespasian and Titus for these games. It could seat forty-five thousand people, who were protected from rain or sun by a huge canvas awning. Its equipment provided for every kind of spectacle, from a sea battle with real ships to the slaughter of five thousand animals in one day.

It was this city, "Babylon, the harlot of the seven hills, the great city that holds sway over the kings of the earth," that St. John the Divine assigned to damnation in his Revelation:

Her sins are piled as high as heaven, and God has not forgotten her crimes. Pay her back in her own coin, repay her twice over for her deeds! Double for her the strength of the potion she mixed! . . . The kings of the earth who committed fornication with her and wallowed in her luxury will weep and wail over her, as they see the smoke of her conflagration. They will stand at a distance, for horror at her torment, and will say, "Alas, alas for the great city, the mighty city of Babylon! In a single hour your doom has struck!" The merchants of the earth also will weep and mourn for her, because no one any longer buys their cargoes, cargoes of gold and silver, jewels and pearls, cloths of purple and scarlet, silks and fine linens; all kinds of scented woods, ivories, and every sort of thing made of costly woods, bronze, iron, or marble; cinnamon and spice, incense, perfumes and frankincense; wine, oil, flour and wheat, sheep and cattle, horses, chariots, slaves, and the lives of men. "The fruit you longed for," they will say, "is gone from you; all the glitter and the glamor are lost, never to be yours again!" [23]

---

[23] Revelation of John 18: 5–23, cited in Thomas W. Africa, *Rome of the Caesars* (New York: Wiley, 1965), p. 20.

SUGGESTED READING

Augustan Rome is successfully re-created in two short studies, Henry T. Rowell's *Rome in the Augustan Age* (1962), which deals at length with the physical appearance of the city and Thomas W. Africa, *Rome of the Caesars* (1965), which prefers to let the city come alive through an extremely variegated group of its citizens, including a wizard. The ancient historians themselves, however, are a splendidly entertaining introduction to their city, especially Suetonius (cited in chap. 3); Tacitus, in Michael Grant's translation, *The Annals of Imperial Rome* (1959); Donald R. Dudley's *The World of Tacitus* (1968) is exciting reading, while his *Urbs Roma* uses quotations from the ancient writers as background for good photographs of the imperial city. Juvenal's scathing comments are well translated by Rolfe Humphries in *The Satires of Juvenal* (1958). Many translations are available of the bawdy but revealing novel of Petronius, *The Satyricon,* and of *The Golden Ass* of Apuleius with its great evocation of the goddess Isis.

Augustus's account of his own exploits, which was carved on a number of temple walls in different parts of the empire, can be read in *Res Gestae Divi Augusti* (1967), translated and introduced by P. A. Brund and J. M. Moore. The major documents of his reign are collected in V. Ehrenburg and A. H. M. Jones, *Documents Illustrating the Reigns of Augustus and Tiberius* (2nd ed., 1955). The better biographies of Augustus include T. Rice Holmes, *The Architect of the Roman Empire* (2 vols., 1928–31); John Buchan's very popular *Augustus* (1937); and D. Earl, *The Age of Augustus* (1968). On the later emperors of the first century, see F. B. Marsh, *The Reign of Tiberius* (1931); Robin Seager, *Tiberius* (1972); J. V. P. D. Balsdon, *The Emperor Gaius* (1934) on Caligula; V. Scramuzza, *The Emperor Claudius* (1940); B. H. Warmington, *Nero: Reality and Legend* (1970); On the emperors of the second century, see Marguerite Yourcenaar, *Memoirs of Hadrian* (1963); Marcus Hammond, *The Antonine Monarchy* (1959); Anthony Birley's two biographies, *Marcus Aurelius* (1966) and *Septimius Severus* (1971); and the broader study of S. Dill, *Roman Society from Nero to Marcus Aurelius* (1904; 1964).

The administration of the empire is analyzed in several sound studies by A. H. M. Jones, including *The Cities of the Eastern Roman Provinces* (1937) and *The Later Roman Empire, 284–602* (1964), and in G. H. Stevenson, *Roman Provincial Administration* (1949). J. P. V. D. Balsdon, *Rome: The Story of an Empire* (1970) is comprehensive, up-to-date, and very well-illustrated. Studies in depth of individual provinces are often the most revealing of the pitfalls of imperial expansion, as well as Rome's great achievement in stamping its own character on distant peoples. See especially Sheppard Frere, *Britannia* (1967); J. Wilkes, *Dalmatia* (1969); O. Brogan, *Roman Gaul* (1953); D. Magie, *Roman Rule in Asia Minor* (1950); and the classic study published originally in 1886 by Theodor Mommsen, *The Provinces of the Roman Empire* (1968).

More specialized urban studies include J. S. Wacher, *The Towns of Roman Britain* (1975) and Alexander G. McKay, *Houses, Villas and Palaces in the Roman World* (1975) which links the ancient writers to the findings of modern scholarship. Norman J. G. Pounds, in *An Historical Geography of Europe, 450 B. C.–A. D. 1330* (1973) gives an excellent analysis of the effects of the lack of a centralized urban planning authority in Rome in the second century A. D.

Communication within the empire is described in Lionel Casson, *Travel in the Ancient World* (1974). The economic structure of the empire is analyzed in another classic work by M. Rostovtzeff, *Social and Economic History of the Roman Empire* (1957).

For the more important aspects of Roman commerce, see J. Innes Miller, *The Spice Trade of the Roman Empire* (1969); M. P. Charlesworth, *Trade Routes and Commerce in the Roman Empire* (1926); and Tenney Frank, ed., *Economic Survey of Ancient Rome* (1933–40), especially volume 5. The military forces are portrayed in G. Webster, *The Roman Imperial Army of the First and Second Centuries A. D.* (1969) and C. G. Starr, *The Roman Imperial Navy, 31 B. C.–A. D. 324* (1960).

Fortunately, excellent translations are available of the major Roman poets. Among them are Rolfe Humphries's edition of Virgil, *The Aeneid* (1951) or the looser translation by the English poet C. Day Lewis (1952); and Helen Rowe Henze's version of Horace, *The Odes* (1961). The best introduction to Roman poetry is Gilbert Highet's *Poets in a Landscape* (1957), a sensitive re-creation of the environment of the Augustan Age. The visual achievements of the Roman architect and engineer can be assessed in M. Wheeler, *Roman Art and Architecture* (1964) and H. Kähler, *The Art of Rome and Her Empire* (1963).

Rome's religious beliefs are described in detail by H. J. Rose, *Ancient Roman Religion* (1949) and R. M. Ogilvie, *The Romans and Their Gods* (1969), while the mystery religions are the subject of F. Cumon's *Oriental Religions in Roman Paganism* (1956).

The influence of Roman society on the evolution of its law is traced in J. Crook, *Law and Life of Rome* (1967). F. Schulz, *A History of Roman Legal Science* (1946) stays more closely to his brief.

Finally, Jerome Carcopino's *Daily Life in Ancient Rome* (1940) provides a fascinating glimpse into the down-to-earth realities of Roman life. The position of women in Roman society is described in J. P. V. D. Balsdon, *Roman Women: Their History and Habits* (1962); Susan G. Bell, ed., *Women from the Greeks to the French Revolution* (1973); and Julia O'Faolain and Lauro Martines, eds., *Not in God's Image. A History of Women from the Greeks to the Nineteenth Century* (1973). L. P. Wilkinson draws on the actual experience of specific individuals in *The Roman Experience* (1974). And Michael Grant, *The World of Rome* (1960) brings new life to a masterly synthesis of imperial politics and society.

5 / *Western Europe on the Threshold of the Middle Ages, 300–600*

The two centuries following the reigns of Diocletian and Constantine have traditionally been regarded as the period of the decline and fall of the Roman Empire. This view, however, leads us into a dangerous distortion of focus for several reasons. The first and most important reason is that, after Diocletian had divided the Roman Empire into an eastern and a western section and especially after Constantine had moved the capital from Rome to Constantinople in 330, the history of the two parts of the Empire followed totally different patterns. The eastern part of the Empire, consisting of all the provinces to the east of the Adriatic Sea, not only contained the richest, most populated, and most cultured provinces, but went from strength to strength for the next four centuries. We shall turn to the achievements of this Eastern Roman or Byzantine Empire, and particularly to its great capital city Constantinople, in Chapter 6. For the moment we should note that, while the period 300–600 does mark the decline and disappearance of the Roman Empire and especially a decline of the cities, in the West, it is the time of the ascendancy of the Roman Empire in the East.

Secondly, even in the western section of the empire, these years are far from being a time of universal decline, even though they are often referred to as the Dark Ages. During this period the Catholic Church rose to that position of influence and power from which it was able to determine in large part the distinctive character of the new period of civilization in the West that we call medieval. While Roman imperial authority was declining

Monastery of Monte Cassino   Foto ENIT

Combat of Romans and Barbarians

Although the Roman legions are portrayed as savagely triumphant in sarcophagus sculpture, like this from the third century B. C., the barbarian tribes were presented as powerful opponents.
E. Richter-Rome

in western Europe, the Catholic Church prospered, establishing the basis of a new unity of thought, a capable administration, and a central role for itself in the new society.

Third, the traditional description of the Germanic tribes that invaded Europe at this time as barbarians ignores the creative role these tribes were to play in Western civilization. There was no sudden cataclysmic descent into barbarism in most of western Europe because the Germanic tribes brought far more than flame and the sword. They brought a respect for Roman culture, a new vigor to populations too long held in subservience to a stultifying Roman bureaucracy, and many new constructive ideas—not least the ability to colonize the forest lands of central Europe and Britain.

In this chapter, we shall be seeking not only the reasons for the decline of the Roman Empire in the West, but also the origins of the new, medieval civilization that was dominant in western and central Europe for the next thousand years. The chapter begins with an analysis of the causes of the decline of the empire in the West from the third century on, and then turns to the concurrent rise of Christianity, and especially of the Catholic Church. Following a narrative of the life of Christ and the activity of his followers in the Early Church, we shall study the three major forces that enabled the Catholic Church to assume a formative role in the new society: the establishment of a highly developed theology through the writings of the Church Fathers and the pronouncements of Church Councils, the rise of the papacy in Rome as the head of a responsive church organization spread throughout western and central Europe, and the creation of disciplined and influential orders of monks, of which the most important was the order founded by Saint Benedict. Finally, we shall consider the invasions and settlement of the Germanic tribes in the fourth, fifth, and sixth centuries. While the influence of certain of the earlier invaders, such as the Visigoths and Vandals, was largely destructive, it was also ephemeral. In Italy, however, the Ostrogoths created a superb culture whose lasting memorial is the great churches of their capital city of Ravenna. In France and Britain, we shall see the settlement of the Franks and Anglo-Saxons, whose immediate cultural achievements are slight but who were to found the French and English nations that moved rapidly into the forefront of medieval civilization.

The Crisis of the Third Century

The crisis of the Roman Empire from which both medieval and Byzantine civilizations finally emerged began in the third century. The period of the Roman peace, that had begun with Augustus and survived through the reign of Marcus Aurelius, ended with Aurelius's mistake in naming his own son Commodus as emperor (reigned 180–192). The brutality and incompetence of Commodus, which led to his own murder, flung the empire back into the same sort of troubles it had undergone in the last century of the republic. During the third century, all the causes of the decline of the western part of the Roman Empire became blatant, and though they were diagnosed and temporarily checked by the authoritarian reforms of the emperors Diocletian and Constantine at the end of the century, the deep-seated sources of decay proved fatal in the fifth century to the continuance in western Europe of the Roman Empire. As a result, in the fifth century, western Europe, including Rome, ceased to be a part of the Roman Empire.

Political and Economic Problems of the Empire

The most obvious cause of decay in the empire was the breakdown of the constitutional system invented by Augustus. Augustus had struck an uneasy compromise with the senators and knights, that is, with the aristocracy and the gentry, giving them privileged status in a society governed by a largely civilian bureaucracy under an absolute emperor, in return for their collaboration in commanding the army and governing the provinces. He did not, however, make provision for an orderly succession to the position of emperor, an omission that caused much of the political chaos in the later empire. His immediate successors had only been chosen after sharp family quarrels. The murder of Domitian in 96 ended the attempt of the Flavian emperors to make the succession hereditary. The system of having each emperor "adopt" a suitable successor lasted only from 96 to the death of Marcus Aurelius in 180. During most of the third century, the army chose and overthrew the emperors, especially during the fifty-year period of military anarchy from 235 to 284, during which all but one of the twenty-six emperors who reigned died violently. One emperor supposedly advised his sons, "Stick together, pay the soldiers, and forget everything else." The emperors resembled the soldiers who picked them—tough, cruel, venal, reckless, and short-sighted. The army ceased to display a sense of the needs of the empire as a whole, but tended to break into provincial groups interested primarily in the well-being of their own region. The generals they forced into power were often incompetent to run the government, while the few who were competent were rarely in office long enough to enforce a consistent policy. The army added to the economic distress by demanding a larger and larger share of the state's revenues in wages and special gifts, and allowed internal order to break down. Even within the empire no individual felt safe. "Behold the roads closed by brigands, the seas blocked by pirates, the bloodshed and the horror and the universal strife," wrote Saint Cyprian. "The world drips with mutual slaughter, and murder, considered a crime when perpetrated by individuals, is regarded as virtuous when committed publicly."

Provincial government broke down with the collapse of the imperial authority. The success of the empire in Romanizing the western provinces had been due above all to the planting of cities, where a wealthy middle class had gladly taken over the duties of municipal administration. The grant of citizenship to almost all free-born provincials had, however, made Roman citizenship less of a privilege for the provincial elite, who were also alienated by growing taxation and administrative interference from Rome. So in the third century the urban middle class became increasingly unwilling to work for the central government in the collection of taxes, or to use their own wealth to beautify their cities or run public games and festivals. The decline of the provincial cities, on whose prosperity the Roman peace had largely depended, was accelerated by the debasement of the currency and by a general breakdown of trade. Long-distance commerce with the East—the purchases of jewels and spices from India, and silk from China especially—was reduced in volume by chaotic transport conditions and lack of money for payment. Manufacturing in the old established cities was threatened, for example in glass and pottery, with the foundation of industries in the northern provinces, such as Gaul, Britain, and Germany. No effort was made to develop a market among the poorer classes or beyond the frontiers of the empire. It was a luxury trade that declined, however, since the goods manufactured in Italy itself, such as pottery, cloth, or weapons, were mostly small-scale craft products. The real surplus of manufactured goods was produced in the eastern sections of the empire, in cities of Asia Minor and Syria, that manufactured bronze, pottery, linens, ornaments, paper, and glassware; and this trade continued within the eastern section during the western part's decline. Also, plague, brought into the empire by the Germanic tribes, as well as the older established curse of malaria, cut the population of both city and country by perhaps as much as a third.

When the western section of the empire ceased to be a civilization of cities, the imperial government was unable to find an alternative source of strength in the countryside. Most of the agricultural land had been divided up into huge estates, and small peasant farmers who had been the strength of the early Roman republic had virtually disappeared. The estate was an almost completely self-sufficient and self-governing unit. It manufactured all its own tools and clothes. It even had its own prison. The best part of the estate was kept by the landowner for himself and worked by slaves. But most of the land was leased to tenants, called *coloni,* who paid part of the harvest and certain personal services to the landlord. Under the colonate, there was no improvement in farming tools or methods, nor any production for open market; and a form of class inferiority had been institutionalized that had turned the Roman Empire into a rigid and static "caste system." One might add that the fall in agricultural production in the third century has also been attributed by some historians to a change in climate, a reduction in rainfall supposedly producing drought and impoverishment of the soil; but satisfactory proof of this has not yet been adduced.

Reforms of Diocletian

The western section of the empire was thus in such trouble that it might well have fallen to the barbarian tribes at the end of the third century had its decline not been arrested by the emperors Diocletian (reigned 284–305) and Constantine (reigned 306–337). Diocletian was a highly experienced soldier and administrator from a poor family in Spalato in what is now Yugoslavia. Although made emperor by his troops he at once distinguished himself from his predecessors who had taken power in the same time-dishonored way, by destroying this system. He threw out the little that was left of the liberal character of the principate of Augustus, and copied the Persian system of ceremonial monarchy. He wore Persian royal robes, scarlet boots, and a purple robe embroidered with gold. He forced even his most important subjects to prostrate themselves and kiss the hem of his robe. To keep an aura of mystery around himself, he appeared in public only on specially staged ceremonial occasions. To the dignity of empire he added the sanctity of theocracy. He called himself Jovius, or son of Jupiter, and declared his powers to be derived not from the Roman people but directly from the gods. Although retaining primacy himself and thus perpetuating the unity of the empire, he divided it for administrative purposes into two sections, taking the eastern part himself and giving the western part to his best general, Maximian, who like Diocletian took the title of Augustus. Later, however, he appointed as well two junior emperors, called caesars. In this way the empire was divided into four parts, although Diocletian retained supreme control. This complicated system broke down after his death, but Diocletian was faced by only two revolts during his reign, and was even able after twenty-one years of rule to retire peacefully to his own palace at Spalato.

Bust of Diocletian *Diocletian's tough and uncompromising policy restored the effectiveness of the central government of the Roman Empire.* Museo Capitolino, Rome. Alinari photo

Prefecture of Gaul

Prefecture of Orient

Prefecture of Italy

Prefecture of Illyricum

◆ *The Empire of Diocletian and Constantine* ◆

It was not, however, the ceremonial changes so much as the administrative and military reforms that broke the political power of the army. Diocletian put an end to the system whereby military officers frequently moved into civil service positions, and he made the army a purely professional body, which he doubled in size to about four hundred thousand men. He also doubled the number of provinces, so that the smaller units could be kept under control and made more quickly responsive to his wishes. The small provinces were regrouped into larger units, called *dioceses*, and at the head of each diocese was a *vicarius*, a kind of prefect. Thus Diocletian's solution to the constitutional problem was an absolute emperor governing through an efficient bureaucracy on a reorganized provincial basis. It worked so well that it became the basis of the organization of the Byzantine Empire, and was absorbed into the structure of the Catholic Church in the West.

Secondly, Diocletian turned to the economic problem. Instead of trying to change the agricultural system, he decided to perpetuate the social system built upon it. He tied large sections of the population to a hereditary profession. Sons of soldiers had to be soldiers. Gold miners' sons had to be gold miners. Even town councillorships were hereditary. But most important of all, Diocletian ordered the peasantry to stay in the places where they were registered, which meant that he bound them to the soil. To stop inflation, he fixed maximum prices for food, raw materials, and textiles, and also maximum wages. In a preamble to the law, Diocletian denounced "the tradesmen who were constantly raising prices." "Who is so dumb-witted, or so devoid of human feeling that he cannot have known or noticed that all salable objects, offered for sale or traded in towns, have increased so much in price that unbridled greed is no longer restrained even by superfluity in the market or a good harvest?" [1] In these ways, Diocletian did not reverse the economic decline and start the state toward new economic progress, but at least he stopped the decline. It was an attempt to stabilize the existing situation in the Roman Empire. Diocletian, however, had made one significant error of judgment. In 303, he began to persecute the Christian Church, in the hope of wiping it out; and he failed. The next strong emperor, Constantine, reversed the policy completely by accepting conversion himself, and giving official toleration of the religion in the empire. Christianity could then make its contribution to the end of the Roman Empire in the west, a contribution that, as we shall see, has been evaluated in the most diverse ways, from Gibbon's conviction that by Christianity "the attention of the emperors was diverted from camps to synods" to St. Augustine's view that Christianity was the only good thing left in the declining Roman Empire.

Christianity: From Christ to Constantine

The Origins of Christianity

Augustus had been ruling in Rome for over twenty years when, sometime between 8 and 4 B. C., in a small town called Bethlehem in the obscure province of Judea, a young Jewish couple named Joseph and Mary registered their first child, Jesus, who had just been born in a stable while they were in town for the tax census. Thirty years later, the young man Jesus began his meteoric three-year career as a religious and social reformer with the first of his attacks on the scribes and Pharisees who dominated the application of the Judaic religious laws. He was a sensational speaker, with the capacity to reach the uneducated in his audience through the telling of parables and the direct simplicity and kindness of his character. People attributed miracles to him, which enhanced his fame. Above all, however, he claimed to have a unique relationship to God, to be the son of God, and alone to be able to reveal the truth about the Father. Hence, his followers declared that he was

---

[1] Cited in Joseph Vogt, *The Decline of Rome: The Metamorphosis of Ancient Civilization,* trans. Janet Sondheimer (London: Weidenfeld and Nicolson, 1967), p. 77.

the Messiah, whom the Jewish people had traditionally expected to come to bring them prosperity on this earth. Jesus himself was careful to point out that although he had come to save them, he was far from being the kind of savior they had been expecting. How different they would later realize after he had been crucified.

In A. D. 29 he led his followers to Jerusalem for the celebration of the Passover, the feast of Jewish independence. In the superheated climate of a city thronged with Jews from all over Palestine, the nervous Jewish government tried him before the Jewish ecclesiastical court and found him guilty of blasphemy and deserving of the death penalty. After some hesitation, the Roman governor, Pontius Pilate, agreed to his death, and his crucifixion was carried out by the Roman occupation troops. His disciples were flung into dejection. After three days, however, they later claimed, Christ's body disappeared from the tomb in a "Resurrection," and Christ himself appeared visibly to them on several occasions during the next forty days to tell them to go forth as his witnesses and representatives throughout the world. On the fortieth day after his resurrection from the tomb, his disciples believed that they saw him ascend to heaven. Jesus, in short, had had only three years to preach his gospel, had died a horrible and ignominious death, and would probably have been quickly forgotten if a handful of people had not been convinced, by what they believed was supernatural experience after his death, that he was indeed what he had claimed to be, the son of God.

Jewish Influence on Christianity

The survival and future spread of Christianity is partly explained by the fact that Jesus was Jewish. As we saw in Chapter 1, during their disturbed history in the Fertile Crescent, the Jews had developed a unique religious tradition; and Christianity was to absorb many of its ideas. The most important was the belief in the coming of the Messiah, although there had been a good deal of debate over the kind of savior he would be. Most Jews had such expectations of material prosperity as a result of the coming of the Messiah that they could not accept Jesus as the Messiah. Secondly, the Jews believed that they were the chosen people of God, exclusively marked out for salvation, which could be immortality of the spirit or even resurrection of the body. The idea of immortality was connected with the idea of a kingdom of heaven, where the everlasting values of goodness were observed and the virtuous were rewarded, whereas the guilty were punished or perhaps banished forever. Third, there was monotheism, the belief that there was only one God, who was personal and who intervened directly in human history. This belief forced the Jews to reject all forms of polytheism as practiced in the Graeco-Roman religions, and made it impossible for them to accommodate themselves with Roman ease to the undemanding state religious ceremonies. It also posed great problems for the Christians themselves in the future. They had to decide how, for example, Christ could be treated as divine if there was only one God, that is, the relationship of father and son in a monotheistic system. Finally, from an organizational point of view, the Jews also left a great contribution to the early Christians: the habit of meeting privately in special buildings, called synagogues, for reading the scriptures and listening to a talk on their meaning. In these synagogues, the Christians first organized.

Christ had added through his teaching, however, certain doctrines of great power. First, all individuals were important in God's eyes, the poor more than the rest. All should be kindly and forgiving toward each other. Charity, self-control, and humility were desirable virtues. These views were preached by other great religions. To these ethical views, however, Christ added the claim that his father, God, had sacrificed him, his only son, to redeem the world of sin. Belief in him was necessary for this redemption. Ethics was no longer enough for personal salvation, nor indeed was a belief in God alone. There had to be a commitment to Christ, a man who lived in a particular time and place and yet was the Savior of all humankind, irrespective of time and place.

The Early Church

The immediate question for Christ's followers was whether this religion was a reformed type of Judaism that would appeal largely to Jews or a new form of religion open to everyone, and therefore probably unappealing to most Jews. The question was settled when the early Christians asked whether converts to Christianity would be required to accept circumcision and the ritual requirements of the Mosaic law. Christianity's greatest missionary, Saint Paul (died 67?), settled the matter, and with it the future of the Christian Church, by declaring that the spirit was more important than the letter of the law, and that circumcision and the Jewish culinary laws were not needed for non-Jews. Saint Paul himself carried the message to the Gentiles, traveling for more than thirty years throughout the eastern Mediterranean area to found little communities of Christians. He preached in synagogues and marketplaces, and sent long epistles to help the people understand the meaning of Christianity. He was finally arrested for provoking a riot, and after months of imprisonment sent to Rome for trial, as was his right as a Roman. He was probably acquitted after long imprisonment in Rome, and he spent the next years of his life helping to establish the Christian community in the capital.

By the reign of Nero, the Christians were established throughout the empire. They were still a fairly undisciplined group, with many fanatics and a large following among the poor and the slaves. To the dignified Tacitus, they were repellent:

Their founder, one Christos, had been put to death by the procurator Pontius Pilate in the reign of Tiberius. This checked the abominable superstition for a while, but it broke out again and spread, not merely through Judea, where it originated, but even to Rome itself, the great reservoir and collecting-ground of every kind of depravity and filth.[2]

For Nero, they were an obvious scapegoat to blame for the burning of Rome; and in the great persecution Saint Paul was arrested again and beheaded outside the walls. A church, San Paolo alle Tre Fontane, now stands where his head was supposed to have bounced three times, causing hot, tepid, and cold fountains to gush from the ground. On the same day, Saint Peter, who had been the principal companion of Jesus and had in fact been told by him that he was the rock on which Christ would build his church, was also executed in Rome. Peter, after taking part in the founding of the Christian community in Antioch, had moved to Rome as head of its Chris-

---

[2] Cited in Donald R. Dudley, *The World of Tacitus* (London: Secker and Warburg, 1968), p. 166.

The Chalice of Antioch, Early Christian Metalwork, Fourth to Fifth Century
The Metropolitan Museum of Art. The Cloisters Collection, purchase, 1950

tian congregation. When the persecutions began, legend relates, he fled from Rome along the Appian Way, but two miles out, at the point now called Quo Vadis, he met Christ hurrying in the opposite direction. "Lord, where are you going," he asked. ("*Domine, quo vadis?*") "I am going to Rome to be crucified again," said Christ. Peter returned in Christ's place, and at his own request, was crucified upside down, and buried in a little Christian graveyard on the Vatican hill, which in the fourth century was used as the site for one of the principal Christian churches, Saint Peter's. By killing Peter, the first pope, and Paul, the greatest Christian missionary, Nero had unwittingly strengthened the Roman Christian congregation's claim to superiority over the other congregations associated with Christ's original apostles. These were Antioch, with Saint Peter; Jerusalem, with Saint James; and Alexandria, with Saint Mark.

For the next two hundred fifty years, the Christian Church went underground. Veneration of the martyrs was used to help propagate the faith. Four accounts of the life of Christ, called gospels, attributed to Matthew, Mark, Luke, and John who, except for Luke, had known Christ personally; a description through the *Acts of the Apostles* of the spread of the Church after Christ's death; Paul's commentary on Christian doctrine; and a few other books were generally recognized as divinely inspired, and read in Christian worship as the New Testament of the Bible, Greek philosophy was slowly harmonized with Christian teachings, as intellectuals of the Church attempted to provide the new religion with a developed philosophical foundation. Organization remained elementary because of the persecutions; but within the local churches a professional hierarchy of bishop, priest, and deacon had been established. By the end of the third century, Christianity had progressed so far that persecution was ineffective against it. Perhaps one in ten of the population of the empire was Christian, but the Church had a solid basis not only among the poor of the cities, but among the peasantry, the army, and the educated upper classes. As early as 200, the Christian writer Tertullian warned that the Christians could paralyze the state by passive resistance alone:

We could take up the fight against you without arms and without commotion, merely by passive resistance and secession. With our numbers, the loss of so many citizens in the far corners of the earth would be enough to undermine your empire, our mere defection would hit you hard. Imagine the horror you would feel at finding yourselves thus deserted, in the uncanny stillness and torpor of a dying world. You would look in vain for your subjects—the enemy at your gates would be more multitudinous than the population of your empire.[3]

It was hardly surprising that eventually a Roman emperor would decide to enlist the Christians on his side.

---

[3] Vogt, *Decline of Rome,* p. 69.

Organization of the Church in the West

The Conversion of Constantine

After Diocletian had retired to his palace on the Dalmatian coast, his plans for assuring an easy transition of power quickly went awry, with his junior emperors and their sons fighting each other for supremacy. In twenty years of bitter fighting, control of the whole empire was won by Constantine, a violent-tempered, ruthless, but farsighted general from Niš, in southern Yugoslavia. Constantine believed that the turning point in his struggle for empire was the battle of the Milvian Bridge, which occurred just outside Rome. According to his biographer and friend, Eusebius, on the day before the battle:

Being convinced that he needed some more powerful aid than his military forces could afford him, on account of the wicked and magical enchantments which were so diligently practised by the tyrant [his rival Maxentius], he began to seek for Divine assistance. . . . He considered therefore on what god he might rely for protection and assistance. . . . While he was thus praying with fervent entreaty, a most marvellous sign appeared to him from heaven. . . . About mid-day, when the sun was beginning to decline, he saw with his own eyes the trophy of a cross of light in the heavens, above the sun, and bearing the inscription, CONQUER BY THIS. At this sight he himself was struck with amazement, and his whole army also, which happened to be following him on some expedition, and witnessed the miracle.[4]

Constantine instructed his soldiers to put a monogrammed cross of Christ on their shields, won the battle with ease, and immediately afterwards declared his own conversion to Christianity.

In Rome, where the Christians had had many graveyards in the catacombs but few churches above ground, he permitted the construction of a fine new basilican church at the Lateran, and the next year he joined with the ruler of the eastern part of the empire in granting toleration to the Christians. The transformation of Rome into the Christian city we know today was pushed rapidly. Constantine's mother went to Jerusalem, and brought back the Holy Staircase that Jesus had supposedly mounted in the house of Pontius Pilate, and also some pieces of the cross on which Christ was crucified. Constantine began a new church, San Paolo Fuori le Mura, on the spot where Saint Paul was buried, and on top of Saint Peter's tomb on the Vatican Hill he began the first great church of Saint Peter's. This vast church, with five naves and eighty-six marble columns taken from imperial buildings, covered with frescoes and mosaics, was to be the principal

---

[4] Eusebius Pamphilus, *The Life of the Blessed Emperor Constantine* (London: Samuel Bagster, 1845), pp. 25–27.

Arch of Constantine, Rome
Erected to commemorate the Battle of the Milvian Bridge, the arch was built with stone from the arches of Trajan and Marcus Aurelius. Italian Government Travel Office photo

church of the pope until the fifteenth century. Rome too was to bear a few marks of Constantine's own fame. The senate built him a triumphal arch between the Colosseum and the Forum, decorating it with sculptures taken from earlier arches, and used the same parsimony in dedicating the partly finished Basilica of Maxentius on the edge of the Forum to Constantine.

Constantine was not satisfied with transforming Rome, which in spite of all his buildings still looked like a pagan city. His desire to create a new Christian capital for the empire coincided with his conception of the administrative need for a capital more realistically located in the eastern part of the empire. He won the final battle against his rival for control of the empire at Scutari on the Bosphorus in 324, and at once began the conversion of the little Greek town of Byzantium on the opposite European shore into his new capital city of Constantinople, or New Rome. Six years later, the new capital was consecrated, and the center of government transferred there. Constantine was thus responsible for two vital changes in the history of the empire—the acceptance of Christianity as the religion of the emperor and the transfer of the capital from Rome to Constantinople.

The Elaboration of a Christian Theology

During the fourth century, Christianity became the sole tolerated religion of the empire and began to fashion a theology that would take account of its

supreme position inside the empire. Constantine had continued to tolerate the pagan religions, and was only baptized on his deathbed. After an attempt by the emperor Julian to take the empire back to paganism, Theodosius I (reigned 379–395) declared Christianity the sole religion and reversed the established procedures by persecuting pagans who would not repent and destroying their books and temples. The Church too had its problems of defining the nature of the faith that was to unify the empire spiritually. Most of the theological infighting was centered around Constantinople and the Eastern churches, especially the great patriarchates of Antioch and Alexandria, with the pope of Rome standing on the sidelines and intervening as a kind of impartial outsider, and the emperor ordering agreement from his position as a deeply concerned insider. This important process of formulation of Christian theology took two forms. On the one hand, there were the writers called the Fathers who were accepted by the Church as official exponents of its doctrines. Most of them were from the eastern part of the empire and wrote in Greek, but in the fourth century the West produced three Latin Fathers of great influence—Saint Ambrose, of Milan; Saint Jerome, of Stridon in Dalmatia; and Saint Augustine, of Hippo in North Africa. The future character of Christianity was shaped by the deep grounding of all these writers in Greek philosophy, especially in Plato's works, although they used pagan writing in their work to make Christianity comprehensible and even acceptable to the well-educated of

Door (Opposite Page) **and Nave** (Above), **Santa Sabina, Rome**
Built on the Aventine hill in the fifth century B. C., *Santa Sabina is one of the best preserved examples of the basilican form of church architecture. Its carved west door presents scenes from the Old and New Testament.*   Alinari photo; E. Richter–Rome

their own day. Through them, many of the habits of thought of the Hellen-istic world entered even into the theology of Christianity. Saint Jerome, for example, saw the entry of the Goths into Italy as a repetition of the troubles of fifth-century Greece: "The Roman world is falling yet we hold up our heads instead of bowing them. What courage, think you, have the Corin-thians now, or the Athenians, or the Lacedaemonians, or the Arcadians, or any of the Greeks over whom the barbarians bear sway? I have mentioned only a few cities, but these once were the capitals of no mean states." [5] To Saint Augustine above all, the Latin Church owed the basis of its theology for the next eight hundred years, and many of his ideas passed over into the Protestant churches through Luther and Calvin.

Saint Augustine (354–430)

Augustine had come to a sense of sin the practical way, and his *Confessions* is an edifying illustration of this. From the sense of sin, he derived man's need of salvation by direct intercession with God. In the *Confessions*, he related how "the flesh wrestled with the spirit in Augustine."

Thus was I sick and tormented, reproaching myself more bitterly than ever, rolling and writhing in my chain till it should be wholly broken, for at present, though all but snapped, it still held me fast. And Thou, O Lord, went urgent in my inmost heart, plying with austere mercy the scourges of fear and shame, lest I should fail once more. . . . [Augustine hears a voice telling him to pick up the Bible and read.] I caught it up, opened it, and read in silence the passage on which my eyes first fell, "Not in rioting and drunkenness, not in chamber-ing and wantonness, not in strife and envying: but put ye on the Lord Jesus Christ, and make not provision for the flesh to fulfill the lusts thereof." . . . As I reached the end of the sentence, the light of peace seemed to be shed upon my heart, and every shadow of doubt melted away.[6]

After his conversion, Augustine was baptized, and within eight years had been appointed Bishop of Hippo (Carthage). From Hippo, he surveyed the cataclysm of the Germanic invasions falling on the Roman Empire, and he died while the Vandals were besieging his own city. The message he preached to those suffering from the disruption of a comfortable urban life they had grown to take for granted was that God had created two cities: one the city of this earth, and another that could be called by the name of his great book, *The City of God.* The urban image was central to his theology, because he was determined to show that Rome had passed from a city-state to a cosmopolitan capital of an empire to a final and higher membership in

---

[5] Cited in Bertrand Russell, *History of Western Philosophy* (London: George Allen and Unwin, 1947), p. 363.

[6] *The Confessions of St. Augustine*, trans. C. Bigg (London, 1897), VIII, 11, 12.

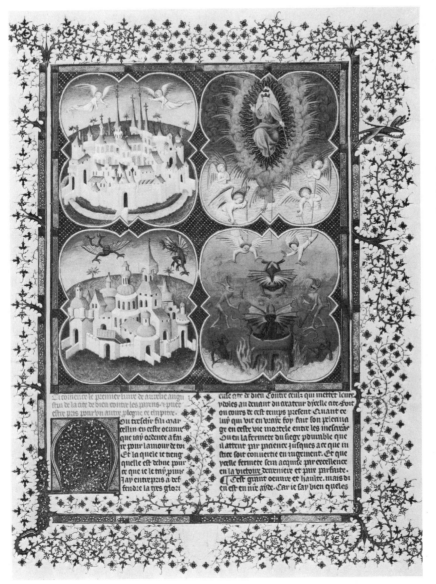

St. Augustine, The City of God
This French manuscript c. 1410 illustrated St. Augustine's great theological treatise. On the left, two earthly cities, one of the blessed and one below for the sinful. On the right, the city of God and below the regions of the eternally damned.   Philadelphia Museum of Art. Photo by A. J. Wyatt, Staff Photographer

the universal city. The earthly city, he argued, was the product of human selfishness; and even at best, when that city sought earthly peace, civic obedience and social harmony, its aim was merely things helpful in this life. The heavenly city was different in origin, since it was created by love of God, even in conflict with individual self-interest; and it was different in purpose. On this earth, it consisted of "citizens out of all nations . . . a society of pilgrims of all languages," who achieved earthly peace by faith in God and not for their material betterment; in the spiritual life beyond this earth, those who have lived righteously will receive their reward. "There the virtues shall no longer be struggling against any vice or evil, but shall enjoy the reward of victory, the eternal peace which no adversary shall disturb. This is the final blessedness, this the ultimate consummation." [7] Saint Augustine's own personal experience of the struggle between good and evil and his determination to incorporate the contributions of even such non-Christian philosophies as Neoplatonism greatly enriched the complete philosophy of history and the full statement of the Christian faith that he conceived.

Definition of Heresy by Church Councils, 325–449

While the Fathers in both West and East were defining Christian *theology* in their writings, the churches in the East were hammering out the principles of Christian *orthodoxy* in their condemnation of heresies. The questions troubling Christians in the eastern part of the empire were mainly concerned with the nature of Christ, specifically the problem of how he could be both human and divine. The intellectual problem was exacerbated by rivalries between the great patriarchates of Constantinople, Antioch, and Alexandria. Generally the theological school of Antioch would develop a new interpretation of the Scriptures, which would be opposed on theological grounds by the churchmen of Alexandria and frequently on political grounds (that is, to maintain its supremacy within a unified Church) by the patriarchate of Constantinople. The heresies also became identified with movements of the provinces to break away from the fiscal burden of rule from Constantinople and with nationalist movements, especially in Syria and Egypt. Finally, outstanding Church leaders sought to advance their own personal power by espousing or extirpating one or another interpretation of Christ's nature. Trouble began when Arius, a priest from Alexandria, claimed that Jesus was created by his Father and was not equal with him. The rapid spread of this doctrine, Arianism, with its threat to Christian unity, outraged the new convert Constantine, who ordered the calling of the first ecumenical council, a meeting of all the bishops of the Church, in Nicaea in 325. The council condemned the doctrines of Arius, and the orthodox position was stated for the benefit of the faithful in the Nicene creed, which is still used by the Roman Catholic, Greek Orthodox, and some Protestant churches:

We believe in one God the Father All-sovereign, maker of heaven and earth, and of all things visible and invisible;

    And in one Lord Jesus Christ, the only-begotten son of God, Begotten of the Father before all the ages, Light of Light, true God of true God, begotten not made, of one substance with the Father. . . . [8]

---

[7] St. Augustine, *City of God* (London: Dent, 1945), II, 245.

[8] Henry Bettenson, ed., *Documents of the Christian Church* (New York: Oxford University Press, 1947), p. 37.

Unfortunately, this statement did not settle the Arian question, since Constantine himself began to incline toward Arianism, and missionaries who went out shortly after converted the Goths and Vandals to Arianism, thus making it almost impossible for them to fuse with the Catholic populations in western Europe that they later conquered.

A new council was called at Constantinople in 381, which blasted Arianism again. This shifted the dispute to the relationship of the human and divine in Christ's nature, which pitted Nestorius, patriarch of Constantinople, against Cyril, patriarch of Alexandria. Cyril was an unscrupulous, brilliant fanatic, with a justified reputation for organizing anti-Semitic riots, who found distasteful the claim of Nestorius that Christ had two distinct natures, divine and human, which were separate within his own person. By emphasizing the human nature of Christ, Nestorius was making it difficult for those who had begun to venerate the Virgin Mary as mother of God, since according to Nestorius, she was merely the mother of the human but not of the divine part of Christ, which had a father but no mother. The Council of Ephesus in 431 was presided over by Cyril, who kept out the supporters of Nestorius by the simple expedient of locking the doors early, and thus enabled his own supporters to declare Nestorius a heretic. Nestorius was finally exiled to Egypt, and Nestorian Christian churches grew up there beyond the boundaries of the empire and in the

The Council of Nicea, by Giovanni Speranza (1480–1536)
The emperor Constantine (foreground) summoned over three hundred bishops to this first ecumenical council, which condemned the doctrine of Arianism.   Sala Sistina, Vatican. Scala, New York/Florence

province of Syria, whose disaffection prepared it for an equable acceptance of the Moslem armies two centuries later.

When a new synod was called at Ephesus in 449 to crush Nestorianism further, the Alexandrian priests persuaded it to adopt a new interpretation, Monophysitism, which held that Christ had a single divine nature that encompassed his human nature. This heresy in its turn was rejected by the Fourth Ecumenical Council at Chalcedon, which ended the ambitions of the patriarch of Alexandria. But the council indicated the arrival of a new challenger to the power of the patriarch of Constantinople, by approving a compromise text that was suggested by the pope of Rome, Leo the Great (440–461). Monophysitism, however, was adopted on a large scale in Egypt and Syria and even by the emperor's opponents in Constantinople. The gains from attempts to extirpate heresy have always been questionable. As a result of the decisions of these ecumenical councils, Syria and Egypt, the two richest sections of the Roman empire, became supporters of heretical branches of Christianity, Nestorianism and Monophysitism, and seized any chance to break away from the empire, while two of the most powerful of the barbarian peoples, the Goths and Vandals, adopted the equally heretical Arian form of Christianity and fought for it passionately when they invaded western Europe.

Origins of Papal Power

Up to this point, the pope in Rome and the patriarch of Constantinople were more or less in agreement as to what in theory constituted orthodox Christianity. In administration the Church was a hierarchy headed by the five patriarchs, of Rome, Constantinople, Alexandria, Antioch, and Jerusalem. Although the supremacy of Rome in *honor* as the original capital of the empire and the seat of the descendants of Peter was recognized, its claim to administrative supremacy in the whole Church was ignored. From the fourth century on, however, the power of the pope of Rome increased enormously in the West. His most important advantage was actual possession of the city of Rome. After Constantine the empire, while it was unified, was governed from Constantinople. When it was divided into two parts, the western section was ruled from Ravenna, or Milan, or even Trier. The pope was thus forced to exercise not only religious duties but to take on various political tasks as well, including the job of protecting the city of Rome from the barbarian invaders. In the West, moreover, the pope had no rival, like the warring patriarchs of the East. He was the recipient of vast donations, which the emperor permitted the Church to retain in perpetuity. During the invasions of the barbarians, which destroyed the military hold of the emperor on Italy, first during the Gothic invasions in the fourth and fifth centuries and again during the Lombard invasion in the sixth century, the pope's independence of action was increased. The success of the missionary movements sent out by the pope to convert the barbarians vastly increased the number of Christians recognizing the supremacy of the Latin Church.

Between the fifth and eighth centuries, the peoples converted included the pagan Irish, Anglo-Saxons, and Franks, and the Arian West Goths, East Goths, and Lombards. Thus, little by little, the popes gained the basis of wealth and power that led them to the assertion of their primacy in the Christian Church and to a permanent break with the patriarch of Constantinople. Although the division of Christianity into a Latin, or Roman Catholic, Church and a Greek Orthodox Church was recognized officially by both churches only in 1054, the alienation of the churches was evident as early as the sixth century, especially during the papacy of Gregory the Great.

Gregory the Great (Pope, 590–604)

Gregory was an autocratic Roman aristocrat who served as prefect of Rome and as papal ambassador to the court of Constantinople, which he despised. He had not wished to be pope, and he accepted his choice by acclamation reluctantly. But at a time when the Church was faced with the enormous problems provoked by the Lombard invasion, he brought to the papal duties enormous energy and also administrative and scholarly talent. Unaided by the imperial representative in Ravenna, he negotiated peace with the Lombards, who were threatening to seize Rome; and he even succeeded in converting some of them from Arianism to acceptance of the Nicene Creed. He established strict standards of administration throughout the Church, and put his instructions into a widely used book called *Pastoral Rule*. He required clerical celibacy, and demanded high standards of financial incorruptibility in the clergy. For the layman, he poured out his advice in hundreds of simple, outspoken letters, which he sent to lords, barbarian princes, and even to ladies of the Byzantine court, as well as in stories of the miracles of the saints.

The life Gregory held up as a standard was that of Saint Benedict, the founder of the order of monks to which Gregory belonged. In his dialogues, Gregory gives us a glimpse of the asceticism that was at the origin of the monastic movement:

A certain woman there was which some time he had seen, the memory of which the wicked spirit put into his mind, and by the memory of her did so mightily inflame with concupiscence the soul of God's servant, which did so increase that, almost overcome with pleasure, he was of mind to have forsaken the wilderness.

But suddenly, assisted with God's grace, he came to himself; and seeing many thick briers and nettle bushes to grow hard by, off he cast his apparel and threw himself into the midst of them, and there wallowed so long that, when he rose up, all his flesh was pitifully torn; and so by the wounds of his body, he cured the wounds of his soul.[9]

[9] Cited in Russell, *History of Western Philosophy*, p. 399.

He saw that the message of Christ was preached to the heathen, as when in 596 and 601 he sent Saint Augustine of Canterbury on a successful mission to convert the Anglo-Saxons in England. He felt that in theology he should explain the role of unquestioning faith in the achievement of salvation; and his writings earned him the recognition as last of the great Church Fathers in the West. Finally, he faced the problem of the relative standing of the pope in Rome and the patriarch of Constantinople, by refusing to recognize the patriarch's claim that his title was "ecumenical" or "worldwide." He thus established the precedent of the separation of the two churches. By the time of his death, Gregory had established the papacy as a finely honed administrative machine, a spiritual body of great prestige and influence, and as an independent center of power in western Europe.

Monasticism

Saint Benedict and the Benedictine Order

With Saint Benedict, a third important feature entered medieval Christianity, to complete its basic triad which consisted of an orthodox theology based on the Scriptures and elaborated by the fathers, the supremacy of the pope of Rome in the Latin, or western, section of Christendom, and the organization of monks into disciplined orders of great attractive and expansive power.

The first monks were simply ascetics who wandered off into the deserts of Egypt and Syria to get away from the corruption of civilized life and to devote themselves to the mortification of the flesh and the struggle with their own evil desires. Many showed great ingenuity in finding ways to mortify their bodies; Saint Simon Stylites sat on top of a pillar! Saint Pachomius in the fourth century persuaded dirty, lice-ridden hermits that the Christian life required not only cleanliness but hard work; and he organized his followers into little communities that cooperated in agricultural labor. In this form, monasticism spread to the West, but it remained chaotic and, many clergymen felt, a refuge for fanatics whose excesses brought the Church into disrepute. A form of organization that could bring the monasticism within the discipline of the Church without destroying its ascetic purpose was provided by Saint Benedict of Nursia. Benedict, born near Rome to a wealthy provincial family, had fled from the temptations he had at first enjoyed in the city; and by the age of twenty, following the hermits' example, he had spent three years in a totally secluded life at the bottom of a cave, where he too had wrestled with the temptations of the body. From this experience, he decided that "idleness is the enemy of the soul" and that what monasticism needed was less contemplation and more work. Gathering together those disciples who had been impressed by his apprenticeship in the cave, he took them south to the flat-topped mountain, Monte Cassino, which commands the long valley linking Rome to Naples. He lived there for the next fourteen years until his death in 543, making of the abbey of Monte Cassino the model for future monasteries throughout the West. The way of life of the monks was prescribed in great detail in his "Rule," which required three vows: poverty, chastity, and obedience to the abbot. Excess was to be avoided. Clothes were to be simple but warm. Two cooked dishes were to be served at the evening meal. Most of the day was to be spent in manual work, but time was set aside for reading of sacred books or lying quietly on one's bed. The monks were to sleep together in dormitories, the younger ones spread among the older: "And when they rise from the service of God, let them gently encourage one another because the sleepy ones are apt to make excuses." Guests, and especially the poor and pilgrims, were to be welcome at the monastery at all times. The rule, in short, prescribed a simple, disciplined, but not excessively hard way of life for his monks. It was the work of a practical man experienced in the everyday problems of running communal living, as can be seen in the article, "Whether all ought to receive necessaries equally."

As it is written: "It was divided among them singly, according as each had need" (Acts 4:35.): whereby we do not say—far from it—that there should be respect of persons, but a consideration for infirmities. Wherefore he who needs less, let him thank God and not be grieved; but he who needs more, let him be humiliated on account of his weakness, and not made proud on account of the indulgence that is shown him. And thus all members will be in peace. Above all, let not the evil of grumbling appear, on any account, by the least word or sign whatever. But, if such a grumbler is discovered, he shall be subjected to stricter discipline.[10]

In the centuries of turmoil that followed, thousands of men sought in the Benedictine monastries an oasis of quiet and security, so that within four centuries several hundred monasteries had been founded throughout western Europe. At first they served as agricultural colonies, opening up land that had never been colonized; but later they became centers for the preservation of learning, through the establishment of libraries, the copying of Latin books, and even through provision of schooling for the lay nobility. Medieval Christianity would have been completely different without the contribution of the monastic orders, whose success was attributable in large measure to Saint Benedict.

The Germanic Invasions

The Germanic Tribes

The purpose of the great defense walls of the Roman Empire, the *limes* that ran across central Germany, Hadrian's Wall in England, and the fortifications along the Danube, and also of most campaigns fought in Europe from

---

[10] Bettenson, *Documents of the Christian Church*, pp. 169–70.

Hadrian's Wall
Built in 121–127, the 73-mile long wall stretched across northern England from the Solway Firth in the west to the Tyne river mouth in the east. Its purpose was to repel attacks from the Celtic tribes of Scotland.
Copyright by The British Travel Association

the time of Augustus, had been to protect the area of "civilization" within the empire from the "barbarians" outside. In Scotland and Ireland, the barbarians were Celtic, an artistic, warlike, and highly emotional people, who for several centuries had been withdrawing ever further northwards to the coastal fringes of northwestern Europe from the lands they had once held in France and Germany. On the continent between the Rhine-Danube frontier, Scandinavia, and the Black Sea, lived the Germanic tribes. In spite of the danger they represented to the empire, these tall fair-haired warriors, dressed in skins and draped in gold armbands and chains, fascinated the urbanized Romans. Tacitus claimed to see in them a noble simplicity and vigor that had been lost by the effete Roman of his own day. The way of life of all the Germanic tribes, at least before the influence of Rome affected those closest to the empire, was fairly similar. They had begun to give up a nomadic life and to settle in small village communities separated from each other by the forest. Their political institutions were primitive but important for the future. Law was administered through a tribal court, called a moot, in which all the warriors of the community judged complaints brought by one member of the tribe against another. The court usually settled the matter either by allowing the defendant to take an oath of innocence provided he was supported by friends who swore to his reliability, or by putting the defendant to ordeal. In this case, he might be made to walk through fire. If he were innocent, his wounds would begin to heal in a few days. The chief was chosen by the warriors for his fitness to lead them in war. The warriors in turn swore personal allegiance to the chief, and became members of his *comitatus,* or group of warrior companions. Elective monarchy was thus accompanied by the principle of personal loyalty to one's lord, which became one of the primary social bonds in medieval European society. Beyond these facts, little is known about the German tribes before they began to press again on the weakening Roman Empire in the late fourth century.

The Visigoths

The first Germanic people to penetrate the frontiers of the empire were the West Goths, or Visigoths. The Goths had originally lived in southern Scandinavia and around the Baltic. But moving south in the second century they had split into two groups, the East Goths, or Ostrogoths, who had remained in southern Russia to live off the land as an army of conquerors, and the West Goths, or Visigoths, who drove the Romans out of Dacia

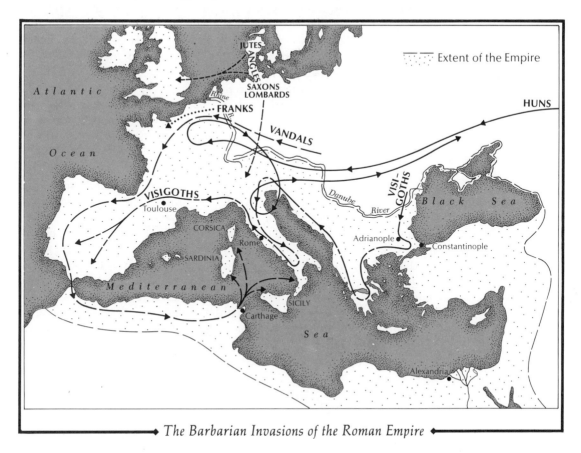

The Barbarian Invasions of the Roman Empire

(modern Rumania). The Goths were receptive to Roman ways of life, developed a taste for Roman luxuries, and adopted the Arian form of Christianity. Many were recruited into the Roman army, and even took offices of state in Constantinople itself. Thus, when the westward drive of a Mongolian people called the Huns from the steppes of Russia overwhelmed the Ostrogoths, the emperor Valens of Constantinople was not unwilling to permit the Visigoths to move into the empire in 376 to defend its Danube frontier. Apparently outraged at the treatment they had received from imperial officials, the Visigoths took up arms against the emperor, who was defeated and killed at the battle of Adrianople in 378. His successor Theodosius I placated the Visigoths with gifts of land and payment of tribute, and they in return furnished recruits to the imperial army. Relations with the Visigoths deteriorated after the death of Theodosius I in 395, when the empire was divided again between his two sons, Arcadius (reigned 395–408) who inherited the Eastern Roman Empire and Honorius (reigned 395–423) who inherited the Western Roman Empire. Furious at the conditions of military service imposed on his people, Alaric, the leader of the Visigoths, led his troops against Constantinople in 395, but was persuaded to divert his army into Greece, capturing Athens. Alaric, after declaring himself king of the Visigoths, led them north into Illyricum (Yugoslavia). In Italy, Honorius sought seclusion and luxury in the city of Ravenna, which was well protected by broad marshes, leaving his regent, the Vandal soldier Stilicho, to deal with Alaric's invasion of Italy after 403. Stilicho used strategic cunning as well as bribery to keep the Visigoths away from Rome; but, after Stilicho was unjustly executed on charges of treason, Alaric was able to besiege and finally in August 410 to capture and sack Rome. It was eight hundred years since a foreign invader had broken through the walls of Rome. "The world sinks into ruin," wrote St. Jerome. "Yes! but shameful to say our sins still live and flourish. The renowned city, the capital of the Roman Empire, is swallowed up in one tremendous fire; and there is no part of the earth where Romans are not in exile." Fortunately, Jerome was exaggerating. Few people were killed; the houses of nobles were plundered. The Forum was set ablaze, but all the churches were spared. Alaric even organized a fine procession to Saint Peter's to present the treasures he had saved for the pope. Alaric died shortly afterwards, and a river was temporarily diverted to provide a secure grave for him in its bed. The Visigoths then moved on to southern France and Spain, where they finally settled. Although they were tolerant of the Catholic worship in the areas they controlled, they were isolated from the Latin population for almost two centuries by their refusal to give up Arianism. They were finally converted toward the end of the sixth century.

The Vandals

Even before the Goths sacked Rome, another Germanic tribe, the Vandals, had pushed into the empire over the Rhine. Crossing France, they settled for a short while in Spain, from which the Visigoths expelled them. They then crossed the Straits of Gibraltar, conquered the rich province of North Africa, built themselves a fleet, and in 455 sacked Rome with greater thoroughness than the Visigoths. They took the treasures from the emperor's palaces on Palatine hill and even the tile from the roofs of the temples, and returned with their spoil to their new capital of Carthage. As Arian Christians, they persecuted their Catholic subjects, and thus, as a result of internal dissension, were so weakened that they fell easy prey to the armies of the East Roman Emperor Justinian in 533.

The Huns

The Huns, who had set in motion this vast movement of peoples, moved westward from the center they had established on the plains of Hungary. Both Romans and Germans were terrified of these savage warriors whose only interest was plunder and bloodshed. Joining momentarily together in 451, the Romans and Visigoths defeated the Hun leader, Attila, at the battle of Châlons; and within a couple of years the Huns had withdrawn from Europe. Their disappearance, however, only facilitated the entry into the empire of several more Germanic tribes: the Ostrogoths, the Franks, and the Anglo-Saxons.

The Ostrogoths

Once they had broken loose from Hun control, the Ostrogoths moved slowly toward northern Italy. Their leader was Theodoric, one of the most talented leaders of all the Germanic peoples. He had spent ten years in Constantinople as a hostage, knew both Latin and Greek, and had developed a profound admiration for the ancient civilization he had been forcibly acquainted with. He had not, however, lost his tribal skills, for after conquering most of northern Italy, he demonstrated his ability with the broadsword by slicing in two his rival for control of Italy and his ruthlessness by exterminating the rival's family. Theodoric then showed more constructive statesmanship. From 493 till his death in 526, he governed Italy and large parts of the Balkans as the regent of the emperor in Constantinople and as King of the Goths, establishing both in title and in actuality a successful policy of racial coexistence. The Goths took one-third of the land and houses and all military duties. The Romans kept the rest, and devoted themselves to peaceful pursuits. Gothic law applied to Goths, Roman law to Romans. Intermarriage was forbidden. Although Theodoric was an Arian Christian, he tolerated the Catholic religion and even the Jewish and other faiths. "Religion is not something we can command," he said. "No one can be forced into a faith against his will." He showed great concern for Roman culture. He restored monuments that had fallen into ruin, including the Colosseum in Rome, where circuses were still presented. But it was at the capital of Ravenna that the Ostrogothic king showed the heights of civilization that could be achieved with the fusion of Germanic and Roman skills.

San Vitale, Ravenna
Every available space on the walls of the Byzantine church of San Vitale, consecrated in 547, glitters with bright mosaics representing scenes from the Old Testament and the court of the Eastern Roman Emperor in Constantinople. Italian Government Travel Office

Ravenna had been made the capital of the western part of the Roman Empire because of its excellent harbor and because it was protected by wide marshes. It was a city of islands, canals, bridges, and causeways, looking across lagoons to the Adriatic Sea. Here Theodoric found that the Roman artists had brought to perfection one of the most demanding and uncompromising of all artistic forms, the art of mosaic; and it was for this achievement that his Ravenna would be principally remembered. In mosaic the artist must set enormous numbers of tiny bits of marble, enamel, glass, and colored stone into damp cement. He cannot produce those subtleties of expression possible in an oil painting, but must seek an overall effect usually visible only from a distance. But in return he is able to use the play of light not only upon the many different angles of the tiny mosaic stones but within the mosaic itself. In Ravenna, the artists were developing new materials for this art, applying gold leaf to glass cubes and covering them again with a thin film of glass, using metallic oxides to produce variations of color, or employing mother of pearl to produce just the right effect of creamy perfection. In the windows, they often used thick sheets of alabaster, so that the entering light already had a soft opacity before playing upon the planes of yellow marble and the complexity of the mosaic surface. In Ravenna, they constructed buildings as though they were galleries meant to display mosaics, with bare walls designed to permit the artist to create the largest, most complex compositions yet attempted in that exacting form of art. One last advantage is still evident today; the process is almost permanent. Unlike frescoes, which fade fairly rapidly, many of the mosaics in Ravenna have required no restoration, and shine as brightly today as in the sixth century.

The building that turned Theodoric to the use of mosaic for his churches and palaces was the tiny mausoleum of Galla Placidia, probably

The Mausoleum of Theodoric, Ravenna *Inspired by the Mausoleum of Galla Placidia, Theodoric's tomb is topped by a monolithic rock weighing three hundred tons brought from Istria on the opposite shore of the Adriatic.* Italian State Tourist Office photo

Christ as the Good Shepherd. Mausoleum of Galla Placidia, Ravenna *This early fifth-century mosaic, depicting one of the scenes most favored by artists of the early Christian Church, shows Christ without a beard, in reminiscence of the young Apollo.* Italian State Tourist Office photo

the tomb of an emperor's daughter who had been married to a Visigothic prince. The architecture was simple, a cross of unadorned brick with very small windows. Its mosaics however are the loveliest possible introduction to the art that was the glory of Ravenna and later of Constantinople itself. The mosaic over the entrance to the mausoleum represents the good shepherd, a kindly protector, not feeding his sheep but patting them benevolently on the nose. He is dressed in a stunning robe with red piping and deep blue stripes that could appear unchanged at a present-day fashion show. In the center of the tiny chapel, one turns to look upward to the dome, the Dome of Heaven, lit up by almost eight hundred golden stars; these become smaller as the dome rises, increasing the sensation of the swirling distance wherein a gold cross symbolizes Redemption.

Theodoric called on the skilled mosaic artisans to decorate one of the most beautiful basilicas in Europe, Sant' Apollinare Nuovo. The church consists of a central aisle, with a narrow nave on each side separated by a line of columns, with a small semicircular apse at the east end. As one steps inside the central nave one at once feels the rushing, forward motion built up by the long line of columns surmounted by the figures in the mosaics above. On each side are twelve columns of Greek marble, topped by delicately carved capitals. The mosaic carries on the forward motion of the pillars. On the north side is a procession of twenty-two virgin martyrs, preceded by a very lifelike group of the three Wise Men bringing gifts to the Madonna and the child Jesus. Again the clothes are amazingly modern. The three kings seem to be wearing stretch pants decorated with the most imaginative designs in orange and deep vermilion. Indeed, King Caspar seems to be wearing a pair of leopard-skin tights. We are a long way from the impersonality of Greek sculpture, and the three men, one brown-bearded, one white-bearded, and one clean-shaven, are hardly idealized pictures of piety. On the opposite side of the church, above a line of twenty-two male martyrs, there is a whole panoply of scenes, each one worth looking at in detail. Perhaps most moving of all is the scene of the paralytic being lowered on ropes from a roofless building to be healed by Christ below.

Theodoric died in 526. His successors lacked his skills, and in less than forty years, the Ostrogoths were driven from Italy by the army of the Eastern Roman emperor; they moved north of the Alps, and rather surprisingly disappeared from history. Thus, the Visigoths, the Ostrogoths, and the Vandals, who were largely responsible for the disappearance of the Roman Empire in the West, left little lasting trace. The Franks and the Anglo-Saxons, however, were to become the principal creators of medieval civilization.

The Three Kings. Sant' Apollinare Nuovo, Ravenna
After the Byzantine conquest of Ravenna in 539, the mosaic artists completed the decoration of Sant' Apollinare Nuovo begun under the Ostrogoths. Here the three kings bring their gifts to the infant Christ.
Alinari photo

◆ *The Germanic Kingdoms at Theodoric's Death in 526* ◆

The Franks

The Franks lived between the North Sea and the upper Rhine, and they never gave up this territory but expanded from it both westward and eastward. Most of France was in the hands of the Visigoths and another Germanic tribe, the Burgundians, when the Franks began their conquests in the fifth century. Under their powerful king, Clovis (reigned 481–511), they defeated both the Visigoths and the Burgundians, and established control over most of modern France. The crucial event in the reign of Clovis occurred in 496, during one of his many battles. Apparently influenced by his wife, who was Catholic, Clovis promised to give up his paganism and to become Christian if he were victorious. He kept his promise, and took three thousand of his warriors with him to be baptized in the local shrine. By his conversion to Catholicism, Clovis accepted the ecclesiastical structure of Gaul based upon the original Roman administration, won the alliance of the Catholic clergy, and took for the Frankish armies the task of crusader against non-Catholic barbarians. At the same time, he made possible the intermingling of the Germanic tribesmen with the original Romanized population of France. Once the religious barrier was removed, intermarriage was permitted. The Germanic language slowly gave way to the rough Latin that was to turn gradually into French. The constitutional ideas of Romans and Germans were combined, usually to the benefit of the absolutism of the Germanic kings. Roman agricultural practices were taken up by the Ger-

Baptism of Clovis
The bishops on the left and the nobles on the right indicate the partnership of Church and state. A dove, symbolizing the Holy Ghost, holds the holy oil for the baptism.
Bibliothèque Nationale, Paris

Barbarian Warrior. Fourth to Fifth Century
This gold figure probably represents a Frankish warrior in armor.
Courtesy of the Dumbarton Oaks Collection, Washington, D.C.

mans, who contributed their ability to open up the heavy clay soils that appeared once the forests had been cleared. What distinguished the Frankish kingdom was not the height of its culture. Clovis was no Theodoric, and his capital city of Paris was no Ravenna. The Franks were creating a new people whose culture would be a genuine fusion of Roman and Germanic elements.

The Anglo-Saxons

Whereas in France, the original Romanized inhabitants vastly outnumbered the invading Franks, in England the Germanic invaders, the Angles, Saxons, and Jutes from northern Germany and Denmark, drove most of the original Celtic inhabitants to Cornwall, Wales, and Scotland in the far western regions of the British Isles. The invaders, whom for convenience we call the Anglo-Saxons, ignored most of the Roman achievements they found. They disliked the land already being farmed, which was mostly light chalky soil on the hilltops, and preferred the clay lands of the river valleys. They paid no attention to Roman law, but introduced a wholly Germanic tribal system of government. They arrived as pagans, and were converted only at the end of the sixth century by St. Augustine's mission sent directly from Rome. The Anglo-Saxons thus received what Romanization they had from the Catholic Church. From the Roman Empire itself, they acquired only the roads. By contrast even with Clovis's Paris, life in Anglo-Saxon England was rough, drab, and dangerous.

Under the impact of these Germanic invaders, the control of the Roman Empire in western Europe disappeared. The last emperor in the West was the boy ruler Romulus Augustulus, who was killed in 476 by the Germanic chieftain Odoacer. Odoacer however did not declare that he had put an end to the Roman Empire in the West. He sent the insignia of the emperor back to Constantinople with the message that the empire needed only one emperor, and that he would act as the representative of Constantinople in Italy. Odoacer felt, in short, that he had reunited the Roman Empire. However, the Roman Empire in the West had fallen. Britain, France, the Low Countries, Spain, north Africa, and Italy itself were all in the hands of Germanic invaders, whether or not those invaders paid lip service to the emperor in faraway Constantinople.

SUGGESTED READING

Edward Gibbon's *Decline and Fall of the Roman Empire* (1776–88) can be sampled in all its suggestive grandeur in the abridgement by D. A. Saunders (1952). Several excellent shorter and more modern introductions to the problems of Roman decline can supplement the diapasons of Gibbon and correct his attribution of guilt. R. F. Arragon, *The Transition from the Ancient to the Medieval World* (1936) emphasizes economic decay in the late empire, but is useful on the cultural heritage bequeathed by Rome. H. T. L. B. Moss, *The Birth of the Middle Ages, 395–814* (1935) is vividly written and still valuable, especially on relations of barbarian invaders and Romanized populations. Although A. H. M. Jones's *The Decline of the Ancient World* (1966) is palpably a summary of a larger book, it is a good analytical summary of the problems of the empire as a whole. Hugh Trevor-Roper ventures enthusiastically and successfully out of his own field of specialization in modern history to provide a very stimulating survey in *The Rise of Christian Europe* (1965); and Solomon Katz's *The Decline of Rome and the Rise of Medieval Europe* (1955) is reliable, short, and soundly documented. Joseph Vogt, *The Decline of Rome: The Metamorphosis of Ancient Civilization* (1967) translated by Janet Sondheimer, is an important work of scholarship on the third, fourth, and fifth centuries, fascinating to expert or beginner.

On the rise of Christianity, see the basic account from the Christian point of view by Kenneth S. Latourette, *A History of Christianity* (1953). The most important primary sources on the Church are gathered in Henry Bettenson, ed., *Documents of the Christian Church* (1947). For Constantine's conversion, one can consult Eusebius, *Ecclesiastical History* (many translations available) or the short and lively *Constantine and the Conversion of Europe* (1949) by A. H. M. Jones. Charles N. Cochrane, *Christianity and Classical Culture: A Study of Thought and Action from Augustus to Augustine* (1957) is a rather difficult study of intellectual changes brought to Graeco-Roman civilization by early Christianity; it gives a parallel in intellectual history to the political and economic changes emphasized in the surveys mentioned above. The most important of the Western Church fathers, St. Augustine of Hippo, wrote a revealing autobiography, *Confessions* (many translations) and the masterpiece of political and theological theory, *The City of God* (many translations). On St. Ambrose of Milan, see E. K. Rand, *Founders of the Middle Ages* (1928; 1957). On the situation of the Jews within the Roman Empire at the time of the life of Christ and during the early work of his disciples, see Michael Grant, *The Jews in the Roman World* (1973).

On the barbarian invasions, Ferdinand Lot's classic study, *The End of the Ancient World and the Beginnings of the Middle Ages* (1961), translated by P. Leon and M. Leon, has been brought up to date in bibliography and introduction by Glanville Downey. On England, see F. M. Stenton, *Anglo-Saxon England* (2nd ed., 1947) and J. M. Wallace-Hadrill, *Early Germanic Kingship in England and on the Continent* (1970). On France, see Peter Lasko, *The Kingdom of the Franks: North-Western Europe Before Charlemagne* (1971) and S. Dill, *Roman Society in the Last Century of the Western Empire* (1966), or the contemporary account of Gregory of Tours, *History of the Franks* (several translations). On Spain, see E. A. Thompson, *The Goths in Spain* (1969) and P. D. King, *Law and Society in the Visigothic Kingdom* (1972) which is a technical study of the forms of society that can be traced through the surprisingly rich legal records remaining from that vanished kingdom. For a general survey of the new kingdoms, see J. M. Wallace-Hadrill, *The Barbarian West, 400–1000* (1952) or A. R. Lewis, *Emerging Medieval Europe, A. C. 400–1000* (1967).

On the evolution of the city of Rome itself, see Peter Llewellyn, *Rome in the Dark Ages* (1971) which includes a good survey of the architectural changes that pilgrims found between the fifth and ninth centuries.

Finally, for a fascinating change of viewpoint, see the decline of Rome as viewed from Constantinople in Walter E. Kaegi, Jr., *Byzantium and the Decline of Rome* (1968), which makes great use of contemporary writings, especially Zosimus's eyewitness account of the court of Ravenna.

O what a splendid city, how stately, how fair, how many monasteries therein, how many palaces raised by sheer labor in its broadways and streets, how many works of art, marvelous to behold; it would be wearisome to tell of the abundance of all good things; of gold and of silver, garments of manifold fashion, and such sacred relics. Ships are at all times putting in at this port, so that there is nothing that men want that is not brought hither."—Fulk of Chartres in the eleventh century

6 / *The Constantinople of Justinian*

For more than a thousand years, Christian Constantinople was the richest, most beautiful, and most cultivated city in Europe; and for several centuries, it had no rivals anywhere in the world in wealth, power, or culture. Throughout its history, from its foundation by the emperor Constantine in

324 to its capture by the Turkish sultan Mohammed II in 1453, foreigners came and marveled at its brilliancy. When the Crusaders reached Constantinople in 1204, they were dazzled by its magnificence (but not deflected from their desire to sack it). The French chronicler of their expedition commented: "Indeed you should know that they gazed well at Constantinople, those who had never seen it; for they could not believe that there could be in all the world a city so rich, when they saw those tall ramparts and the mighty towers with which it was shut all around, and those rich palaces and those tall churches, of

Justinian   Stab. D. Anderson

Santa Sophia, Constantinople   Hirmer Fotoarchiv

which there were so many that nobody could believe their eyes, had they not seen it, and the length and breadth of the city which was sovereign among all others." [1]

The appearance of this splendid city and the character of its civilization were established by the end of the emperor Justinian's reign (527–565). Constantinople enjoyed by then the three bases of its future prosperity and endurance. It was a great military bastion; it was the center of world commerce; and it enjoyed a political and ecclesiastical constitution of great resilience. In this situation of prosperous safety, the city had become the home of a new form of culture, which we call Byzantine, and which can still be admired in the buildings, paintings, mosaics, histories, and poems that have fortunately survived.

Constantinople at the Accession of Justinian

When Constantine began casting around, "on the command of God," for a place to found a new Christian capital for the Roman Empire, he knew only

The Constantinople of Justinian

Period Surveyed	Reign of Justinian, 527–565
Population	About 1 million
Area	8.14 square miles
Form of Government	Absolute emperor controlling state and church; imperial bureaucracy, with power to regulate political, social, and economic life
Political Leaders	Emperor Justinian; Empress Theodora; General Belisarius; Tribonian, codifier of laws
Economic Base	Center of world commerce (silk, spices, ivory, textiles, foodstuffs); manufacturing (silk, jewelry, icons, furnishings); customs duties; agricultural surplus from empire (wheat, wine, oil, cotton)
Intellectual Life	Historians (Procopius, Agathias); poets (Agathias, Paul the Silentiary); architects (Anthemius, Isidore)
Principal Buildings	Land and sea walls; Santa Sophia; Church of the Holy Apostles; Great Palace
Public Entertainment	Hippodrome (chariot races)
Religion	Greek Orthodox Christianity; State Church headed by semipriestly Emperor, administered by Patriarch of Constantinople

[1] G. de Villehardouin, *Chronicle of the Fourth Crusade,* trans. Frank Marzials (London: Dent. 1908), p. 31.

that it would have to be somewhere to the east of Rome. He toyed briefly with the idea of putting it in the inaccessible mountains of Yugoslavia, at his birthplace of Niš, began a few buildings at Troy, and finally decided to build it at the point where the waters from the Black Sea flowed through the narrow channel of the Bosphorus into the Sea of Marmara. Even then it took a flight of eagles to give him supernatural warning not to build on the Asiatic shore, but to choose the triangular peninsula on the European shore where Greek sailors from Megara in the seventh century B. C. had founded the colony of Byzantium. The site had only one big disadvantage, its climate. In the summer it was hot and muggy. In the winter and spring a north wind blew from the plains of southern Russia across the Black Sea and rushed with gale force down the seventeen-mile funnel of the Bosphorus. The wind not only chilled the citizens of Byzantium but often prevented ships from rounding the tip of the city to enter the superb natural harbor of the Golden Horn, a deep sheltered bay at the north of the city, seven miles long, whose existence was one of the primary reasons for Constantine's choice of the site. But all other factors were overwhelmingly favorable.

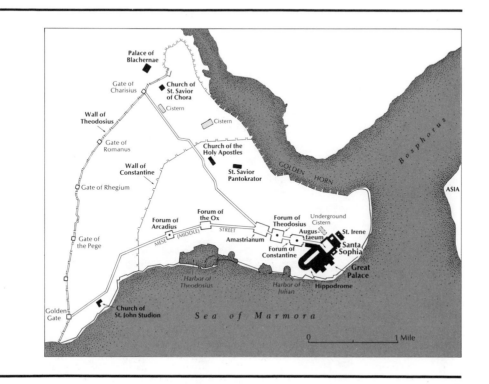

Advantages of Constantinople's Site

Constantinople lay at the intersection of two of the greatest routes of the ancient world. It controlled the trade route that led from the wheatfields of southern Russia, which had fed Athens, through the Bosphorus and the Sea of Marmara to the narrow channel of the Hellespont and out into the Aegean, and on to the cities of Greece and Italy or down the eastern shore of the Mediterranean to Syria and Egypt. It sat on the short ferry crossing on the quickest land route from Europe to Asia, and thus was ideally located to become the trading center for the exchange of European goods and money for the products of India and China. Fishing was good around its shores. Fresh water was abundant in the hills to the north. On both the European and the Asian shores the land was well suited to wheatfields and vineyards. And it was beautiful. The gentle hills on either side of the Bosphorus combined the startling colors of the Mediterranean landscape—the dark green of juniper and pine, the sharp brown of outcropping rock—with a more northern effulgence of meadow grass and wildflowers where the streams burst out into the Bosphorus. As in Hong Kong and San Francisco of later date, wherever one looked there were vistas of blue waters, over the rooftops or at the ends of streets that seemed to dip into the bay. The sixth-century historian Procopius broke off his description of the buildings of Justinian, to which we shall return, to "say a few words about the glory which the sea adds to Byzantium":

Golden Horn, Constantinople
The long ridge of the skyline of Constantinople, viewed across the calm waters of the Golden Horn, is today dominated by the sixteenth-century mosque of the Sultan Selim.   Turkish News Bureau

The two seas which are on either side of it, that is to say the Aegean and that which is called the Euxine [Black Sea], which meet at the east part of the city and dash together as they mingle their waves, separate the continent by their currents, and add to the beauty of the city while they surround it. It is therefore encompassed by three straits connected with one another, arranged so as to minister both to its elegance and its convenience, all of them most charming for sailing on, lovely to look at, and exceedingly safe for anchorage. . . . The sea encircles the city like a crown, the interval consisting of the land lying between it in sufficient quantity to form a clasp for the crown of waters. This gulf [the Golden Horn] is always calm, and never crested into waves, as though a barrier were placed there to the billows, and all storms were shut out from thence, through reverence for the city. Whenever strong winds and gales fall upon these seas and this straits, ships, when they once reach the entrance of this gulf, run the rest of their voyage unguided, and make the shore at random; . . . when a ship is moored there the stern rests on the sea and the bow on land, as though two elements contended with one another to see which of them could be of greatest service to the city.[2]

Constantine's City Plan

Constantine himself laid out his new city. The Greeks had settled only the tip of the peninsula, around a little hill they had made their Acropolis, which later became the site of the imperial palace. Constantine, with his spear in his hand, walked westward with his architects and planners, until the new Rome, like the old Rome, enclosed seven hills. When his planners expressed surprise at how far he was walking before marking the line for the defense wall, Constantine replied: "I shall keep on until He who is going before me stops." Like Romulus, he knew he was tracing a sacred boundary. The parallels with Rome did not stop there. The Acropolis became another Palatine hill, from which the courtyards, gardens, colonnades, and churches of the scattered palace buildings descended in a series of terraces to the water and the private harbor of the emperor. In front of the Great Palace was a large square called the Augustaeum, the heart of the empire, like the Forum in Rome; and here was built the milestone, or Milion, from which, like the umbilical stone in Rome, all mileages in the empire were calculated. At the southwestern corner of the Augustaeum was a huge arena, the oval Hippodrome, which combined the functions of the Roman Colosseum and the imperial chariot ring. Between the palace and the Hippodrome, Constantine again copied Rome by building a senate house. Having thus established the center of his city, Constantine laid down the plan of its streets. Leading out from the Augustaeum was the main street of the city, Middle Street or Mese, which was paved with large stone blocks. On

Bust of Constantine
This colossal head was part of a seated statue placed in the Basilica of Maxentius, which Constantine renamed after himself. The Metropolitan Museum of Art, Bequest of Mary Clark Thompson, 1926

---

[2] Procopius, *The Buildings of Justinian* (London: Palestine Pilgrims' Text Society, 1896), pp. 24–25.

either side, using a structure like the stoas of Athens, Constantine erected roofed colonnades covering the sidewalks and the shop entrances. Immediately beyond the palace of the governor of the city, the Praetorium, the street entered the hexagonal Forum of Constantine, conceived as the commercial heart of the city. In the center of the forum, Constantine erected a tall column of porphyry, on which he placed a statue of Apollo with his own head substituted for that of the god. Later emperors carried on many of these ideas. The more ambitious would build new forums named after themselves, along the main street, just as earlier emperors had done in Rome. Theodosius I, whose column had spiral reliefs, imitated Trajan's column. Arcadius built his forum near the wall, and set there one of the tallest columns in the city, one hundred forty feet high. Theodosius II found that in only a century the population had outgrown even the area planned by Constantine, and he enlarged the city by building new land walls one mile beyond those of the city's founder.

Constantinople as Fusion of Classical and Christian

Constantine had, however, done more than lay down the ground plan of the city. He had established the character of Constantinople as a combination of classical and Christian. To complete the capital within six years, he had ransacked the eastern Mediterranean for its artistic treasures. From Delphi he brought the tripod of bronze that the Greek states had set up to commemorate their final victory over the Persians, and put it in the middle of the Hippodrome. From Ephesus, Rhodes, Athens, and Rome itself he brought statues and temples, thereby setting the city's taste in sculpture with the highest examples of ancient art. He also helped himself to Christian relics. At the base of his column in his forum, he deposited what he believed to be the crosses of the two thieves crucified with Christ, part of the bread with which Christ had fed the five thousand, and one of Noah's tools used in building the Ark. He set the example to future emperors of the acquisitive passion that led to the eventual location in Constantinople of the Crown of Thorns, the Lance, most of Christ's cross, and a phial of Holy Blood. But the mark of the Christian capital was to be its churches, which were to distinguish the new capital clearly from the pagan temples of old Rome.

On the fourth side of the Augustaeum, Constantine built the Church of the Holy Wisdom, or Santa Sophia, the city's cathedral, where the emperor was to be crowned and the patriarch was to conduct the major services. Near the wall he built a second large church, a shrine to the Holy Apostles. Since he was himself known as the thirteenth apostle, he thought it suitable that he, and future emperors, should be buried in this church; and until the sack of the city by the Crusaders in 1204, one emperor after another was entombed there in a huge sarcophagus of porphyry. This habit of building a shrine where generations of rulers could lie together in sumptuous death

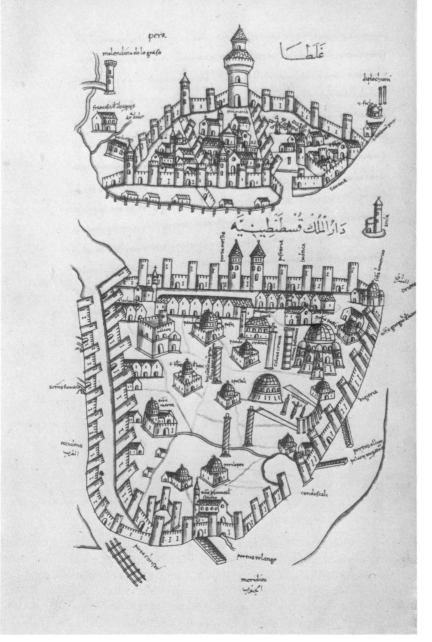

was followed by the French kings in the Abbey of Saint Denis, the English kings in Westminster Abbey, and the Russian tsars in the Cathedral of the Archangel in the Kremlin. A mausoleum of this kind became a necessity for any self-respecting ruling family, so that even the dukes of tiny Burgundy had to have their own sanctified necropolis; and as late as 1888, the emperor of a highly industrialized Germany sought respectability among his peers by burial in his own sepulcher in the park of the Charlottenburg palace in Berlin.

St. Mark's Cathedral, Venice
St. Mark's Cathedral, built in 1063–1073, was modeled upon Justinian's Church of the Holy Apostles in Constantinople, which was destroyed shortly after the Turkish conquest in 1453. Foto ENIT

To people his city, Constantine provided the same inducement that had filled Rome with a mob of dispossessed—free bread and circuses, or at least chariot races. To bring scholars, he built libraries, for storage and study of Greek manuscripts; and a knowledge of Greek and Latin was the key to rapid advancement inside his court and administration. Army recruitment brought vast numbers of Isaurians from Asia Minor and Illyricans from the Balkans and many other nationalities including even the Germanic tribes. Commercial advantages shared with all citizens of the empire brought Syrians and Egyptians, Armenians and Jews; and to persuade the highest ranks of the Roman aristocracy to move with him, Constantine created a new senate and, it was said, built homes that were exact replicas of the houses the aristocrats had had in Rome itself. Of all the great cities created by the vision and obstinacy of an absolute ruler, only St. Petersburg could rival Constantine's creation; and St. Petersburg was a capital for less than two hundred years.

By the year 330, Constantine was satisfied that his city was ready. On May 11, he dedicated it as New Rome. A solemn procession made its way from the Augustaeum, down the Mese, into the Forum of Constantine, where his statue was hoisted to the top of its enormous column, on which was inscribed: "Oh, Christ, ruler and master of the world. To you now I dedicate this subject city, and these scepters and the might of Rome. Protect her; save her from all harm."

Justinian's Attempt to Reunite the Roman Empire

In 518, the rich prize of Constantinople fell into the hands of a rough, illiterate general from a peasant family in Illyrica, who had used bribes, given him for use on behalf of another candidate, to make himself emperor of Byzantium. Justin I (reigned 518–527) was then sixty-eight years old, in bad health, and unskilled in government. Fortunately he had a nephew he had brought up almost as a son, to whom he gave the best classical and theological education available in Constantinople, and whom he pushed ahead rapidly through the ranks of the emperor's bodyguard. In gratitude, the young man copied his uncle's name, called himself Justinian, and governed from behind the throne throughout the whole of his uncle's reign. Constantinople was thus dominated from 518 to 565 by Justinian, a man who added robust health to his many other achievements.

Character of Justinian

Justinian was unusually qualified to be emperor. He had served in the army. He knew the technique of war and the qualities that make great commanders. During his uncle's reign he had learned the intricacies and the intrigues of Byzantine politics, without having to take personal responsibility for his decisions. His education had given him a wide background in classical learning and the ambition to patronize its practitioners, whatever their background. In spite of the occasional savageries in which he indulged, he had a deep love of the Christian Church and a less fortunate fascination with the complexities of theological dispute. Speaking Latin in a capital where most people talked Greek, he was convinced of the necessity of maintaining the link of the Latin and Greek parts of the empire. And as an upstart, one generation removed from the poverty of the Dalmatian swineherds, he believed that human talent should be recognized without regard to the niceties of aristocratic upbringing. Here lay his greatest skill—to be able to pick brilliant people to serve him in vast enterprises he had conceived for his empire. To see to the codification of the laws, he singled out Tribonian, a lawyer from Asia Minor who was working his way up through the bureaucracy, and who developed into one of the most subtle legal

Empress Theodora and Her Ladies. San Vitale, Ravenna
The empress appears in her ceremonial robes and crown, against an elegant background that probably represents her rooms in the palace.   Italian Government Travel Office photo

minds of all time. To command the armies in the reconquest of the West, he chose one of his youngest generals, Belisarius, a man like himself from a peasant family in Illyrica. And as his wife, he picked Theodora, the daughter of a bearkeeper in the Hippodrome, an actress with a reputation for bewitchment, literal and metaphorical; and with this brilliant, forceful woman he shared not only a lifelong if turbulent love affair but also the decision-making of empire. Theodora frequently abused her powers. She could make or break the highest public officials. Her inordinate love of ceremonial, her passion for debasing highborn aristocrats, and her countermanding of imperial orders bred hatred and disorder in the administration. But on most crucial matters her advice to Justinian, whether or not he followed it, was sound. She wanted him to accept Monophysitism, or at least come to a compromise with it, not only because she believed in it herself but because such a course might weaken the disaffection of Syria and Egypt. She finally persuaded Justinian to get rid of the unpopular finance minister, whose extortion brought the mob of Constantinople into open revolt in 532. After her death from cancer in her early fifties, Justinian began to lose himself in ever more intricate theological expositions that satisfied no one but himself.

Justinian came to the throne with a clear, ambitious program of securing, quite deliberately, his own place in the history of the Roman Empire.

He wanted to reunite the Latin-speaking and Greek-speaking parts of the empire by conquering the barbarians who had illegally entrenched themselves in his rightful dominions in western Europe and North Africa. Secondly, he wanted to make the empire economically prosperous and politically and legally efficient. And third, he wanted to patronize a new golden age of literature, art, and architecture, of which the most impressive feature would be a series of great churches scattered throughout his empire.

Justinian's War Goals

Justinian had no qualms about being constantly at war. He had received from the earlier emperors a city that was already superbly fortified; and he did little to enable the city to withstand a siege beyond keep the great land and sea walls in good repair and build magnificent underground cisterns. A small navy was maintained, which was sufficient to give superiority in the Black Sea and most of the Mediterranean then and for the next century. But to embark on a program of reconquest, he had to have a large enough army to hold firm on the eastern frontier against Persia and to defeat the Germanic warriors, whose whole economic organization was planned to enable them to embark instantly on war. He was fortunate in having a large treasury built up by his uncle's frugal predecessor and an army of one hundred fifty thousand men. The army had a tradition of scientific management and the study of military theory; and in the armored horse and rider, called the

The Cisterns of Constantinople
To safeguard the water supply of the peninsula city, Justinian constructed several vast, covered cisterns. Water was brought into the city from the small hills to the northwest by aqueducts that ran below the surface of the ground. Turkish State Tourist Office photo

cataphract, it had the foremost military weapon of the sixth century. Justinian was also aided by the fact that the Byzantine and Persian empires were both so well matched that neither could conquer the other. In sensible days, the two empires concluded truces that varied from a five-year breathing space to the Perpetual Peace of 532, which lasted eight years; they even shared the financing of border fortresses. Justinian was even prepared to pay tribute to the Persians to buy peace on his eastern border. Unfortunately for him, his reign coincided with that of one of the greatest Persian emperors, Khusru I, who hoped to profit from the disloyalty of Armenia and Syria and the absence of Justinian's finest troops in the West. To Justinian's fury, therefore, most of his reign he was forced to waste troops and finances in forcing back the incursions of the Persians, who at one time penetrated far enough into the empire to sack Antioch, the richest city of Syria.

Campaigns in Western Mediterranean

In the respite brought on by the Perpetual Peace of 532, Justinian struck westward for the first time, at the Vandal kingdom of north Africa. His advisers were appalled at the expense, at the long sea voyage, and at the strength and skill of the enemy. He raised only fifteen thousand men, but it took five hundred ships to transport them. Luck was on his side, however. Rule in north Africa had been seized by a usurper who was disliked by both his fellow Vandals and the native Libyans. The Ostrogoths allowed Belisarius to land in Sicily, so that he was able to invade Tunisia from Sicily. He was thus able to revive his forces among the rich cities of southern Sicily before making the short sea trip to Carthage. Within a few days of landing, Belisarius had defeated the Vandal ruler and was in possession of Carthage. By the spring of 534, the north African coast was under the control of Belisarius, who was back in Constantinople within a year of his departure. Victories of this kind had been rare in recent Roman history, and Justinian decided to celebrate with a triumph as grand as anything out of the Roman past. The procession set off from Belisarius's own house, and passed through the streets of Constantinople to the Hippodrome, where the emperor and empress awaited it. The display of captives and spoils outshone anything seen in Rome, or to be more accurate, it included much of the spoil that had already been seen in Rome. There was not only the Vandal king and a well-picked group of the handsomest blonde warriors of the Vandals. There were all the treasures the Vandals had brought back from their sack of Rome in 455, including jewelry, gold dinner services, chariots, and so on. Finally there was even the treasure of the Jews that had been displayed by the emperor Titus in his triumph after he had sacked Jerusalem in 70.

In 535, Belisarius was sent back to Sicily, this time with orders to defeat the Ostrogothic rulers and bring the whole peninsula under the control of

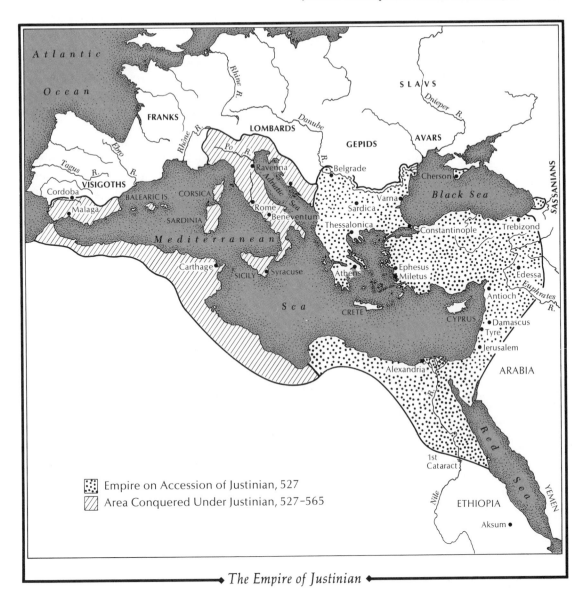

The Empire of Justinian

Constantinople. The situation again seemed hopeful. The great ruler Theodoric was dead, and rivals were fighting for the succession. The native Roman population was prepared to throw off the rule of the Ostrogoths, as
heretic Arians and alien invaders. The Catholic Franks were willing, for a
price, to invade from the north. The early campaigns went well. Although
he only had eight thousand men, Belisarius took first Sicily, then Naples,
and finally Rome itself. There, however, he was besieged by the Goths for
more than a year. "After sixty years," wrote Procopius in his history of

these campaigns, "Rome was again brought under the Romans." The war, however, brought misery for its citizens. The Goths cut the aqueducts, and for the first time since their construction, water stopped running into the great baths of Caracalla and Diocletian. A surprise attack by the Goths on the mausoleum of Hadrian was repelled only when the Roman soldiers tore down the statues on the tomb and dropped them on their attackers. For lack of food and water, plague broke out. The city was finally relieved by another army sent from Constantinople. Belisarius drove north to capture Milan in 539, and at last in May 540 he crossed the marshes to enter the Ostrogothic capital of Ravenna. The war was not over, however. For the next twelve years the Goths tried to drive out the imperial armies. Rome changed hands four times, suffering further devastation each time. But in 552, the last remnants of the Ostrogoths were retreating to oblivion across the Alps. The Gothic war that restored Italy to the empire had been a long struggle of sieges that had left the cities in shambles and the people in starvation. It did not, however, deter Justinian from sending another force against the Visigoths in Spain, which succeeded in bringing the southwest under the rule of Constantinople for seventy years.

Procopius attempted fairly successfully to copy Herodotus and Thucydides in his description of these wars. He had seen the fighting, and could describe in detail the battles and sieges. He was a subtle observer who could characterize men like the Vandal king or his hero Belisarius in their reactions to misfortune or victory. But he did not conceal the total waste of the whole enterprise. Justinian spread hatred of his rule among the provinces of the East by the extortions necessary to pay for these wars. He had failed to realize that when Rome conquered the East it was seizing rich provinces whose wealth would support the less productive West and the city of Rome, whereas when the East conquered the West it was simply winning new financial responsibilities. Above all, he could not understand that the future of the West lay in the fusion of the Germanic invader and the Romanized population of western Europe. Europe did not gain from the disappearance of the Visigoths, the Ostrogoths, and the Vandals, but might have profited greatly by their further domestication. In any case, their disappearance merely opened the way for the less civilized Franks and Lombards in Italy, and for the Arabs in north Africa and Spain. Justinian was a great ruler in spite of his wars, and not because of them.

The Economic Basis of Constantinople's Prosperity

War had made Rome prosperous; war added nothing to Constantinople's wealth, which was the product of healthier factors. Constantinople never led the kind of parasitic existence that Rome did. Although the customs duties provided a large share of the empire's income—a straight ten percent duty was applied on all imports and exports—Constantinople created its own wealth by its services as the world's greatest trading center and by its own manufacturing.

Commerce of Byzantine Empire

The basis of international trade in the sixth century was the exchange of goods between Asia and Europe, although a small amount of trade between Europe and north Africa also existed. The most prized item of international commerce was Chinese silk, whose secret had been guarded by the Chinese emperors for three thousand years, in part by imposing the death penalty on anyone guilty of trying to export the eggs of the silkworm. Only limited quantities of silk were exported, and enormously high prices were paid by such fashionable customers as Cleopatra of Egypt, who would wear nothing else, and aristocrats who found wool abrasive next to the skin. To season the food of the well-to-do, especially the dried meats and salt fish that were the staple of European diet through all the winters of the Middle Ages, came the spices of southeast Asia and India—pepper, cloves, nutmeg, aloes, cinnamon, camphor, balsam, and musk, as well as sugar and ginger. India also supplied pearls and jewels, and ivory, used by Byzantine artisans for church ornaments, furniture, book covers, and reliquary cases. Southern Russia continued to send wheat, furs, salt, and slaves. Syria shipped its manufactured goods such as textiles, enamels, and glassware, which were transshipped to China, where they were highly esteemed. The Balkans supplied flax and honey. The barbarian invasions did not provoke a complete breakdown of west European trade, as was once assumed; Italy and France continued to send to Constantinople their manufactured goods, including textiles and weapons. While Constantinople itself was a large customer for these imported goods, especially raw materials for its textile and metal workers, the great bulk of these wares were reexported, Eastern goods to the Mediterranean basin and northern Europe, and to a much smaller extent, European, Syrian, and Egyptian goods to the East. The basis of Constantinople's wealth was its position as intermediary in a commercial situation where the extraordinary difference in price between original sale and final purchase permitted enormous profits to be made without any danger of losing customers. There was never any danger that a glut in supplies would drive down prices, especially as both the Chinese and the Byzantines were careful to keep supplies low in the most profitable of all trades, the sale of raw silk and silk textiles.

It was vitally important to Constantinople that secure and rapid trade routes should be kept open. Vast difficulties faced the merchant making the long journey by land from China to Europe, a trip that under ideal circumstances took 230 days. The greatest difficulty was the existence of the Persian empire, which straddled all except two of the routes from the East; for the Persians used their favored geographical position to impose very large tolls for passage of goods across their territory, and in times of war would cut off the trade entirely. Nevertheless, the easiest trade route passed from Constantinople along the southern shore of the Black Sea to the port of Trebizond, skirted the southern slopes of the Caucasus Mountains as far as the Caspian Sea to reach the great oasis cities of Samarkand and Bokhara before crossing central Asia to enter China just south of the Great Wall. It was possible to avoid the Persians by going north of the Caspian Sea, across the steppes of Russia, crossing the Black Sea to the port of Cherson on the Crimean peninsula. Justinian spent much time and money to persuade the inhabitants of the plains of Turkestan to permit caravans to use this route, but without much success. The sea route was also a way of avoiding the Persians. Ceylon acted as the shipping point for all Asian goods, which then passed along the shore of Arabia to the Persian Gulf, and then, if relations with the Persians were good, up the Euphrates to Antioch in Syria. If relations were bad, however, the shipping could pass along the coast of Arabia and up the Red Sea to enter the Byzantine empire in the Nile valley. Again, however, the lack of many Byzantine ships in the Red Sea and difficulties with the kingdom of Ethiopia made it generally more profitable to pay the price the Persians were demanding. Constantinople was linked with the West by the old land route across the Balkan peninsula, the Roman Via Ig-

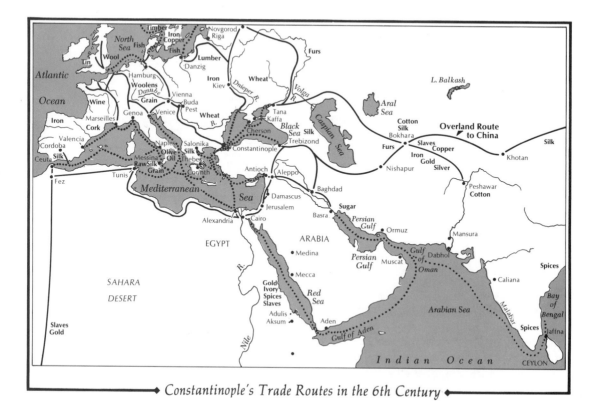

◆ *Constantinople's Trade Routes in the 6th Century* ◆

natia, and with central Europe and France by a longer and less safe route that followed the Danube River. Most European goods, however, came from the Mediterranean ports of Marseilles, Syracuse, and especially Salonica. Justinian, as emperor, did not make the mistake of later rulers, of discouraging citizens from trading outside the boundaries of the empire; but even so, the greatest volume of the shipping trade was in the hands of foreigners, most of whom came all the way to Constantinople itself to sell their goods. Special provision was made in Constantinople for lodging these foreigners, who were expected to stay apart from the native population in segregated national compounds, so that the police and customs officials could keep an eye on their activities. The great storehouses for imported goods were down at the harbor on the Golden Horn, but much of the buying and selling took place in the pandemonium of Middle Street.

An unusual insight into the experiences of the Byzantine merchants who ventured into the Indian Ocean is given in the strange book, *The Christian Topography*, of Cosmas. As part of his attempt to prove that the earth was flat, Cosmas, a sea captain who became a monk, described his own observations of the countries where he traded, especially Ethiopia and Ceylon. On the silk trade, he commented:

If Paradise did exist in this earth of ours, many a man among those who are keen to know and enquire into all kinds of subjects, would think he could not be too quick in getting there: for if there be some who to procure silk for the miserable gains of commerce, hesitate not to travel to the uttermost ends of the earth, how should they hesitate to go where they would gain a sight of Paradise itself? Now this country of silk is situated in the remotest of all the Indies, and lies to the left of those who enter the Indian sea, far beyond the Persian Gulf, and the island called by the Indians Selediba [Ceylon] . . . He who comes by land from Tzinitza [China] to Persia shortens very considerably the length of his journey. This is why there is always to be found a great quantity of silk in Persia. Beyond Tzinitza there is neither navigation nor any land to inhabit.[3]

He also described how in Ethiopia the merchants bargained with the natives for gold.

[The merchants] take along with them to the mining district oxen, lumps of salt, and iron, and when they reach its neighborhood they make halt at a certain spot and form an encampment, which they fence around with a great hedge of thorns. Within this they live, and having slaughtered the oxen, cut them in pieces, and lay the pieces on the top of the thorns, along with the lumps of salt and the iron. Then come the natives, bringing gold in nuggets like peas, . . . and lay one or two or more of these upon what pleases them—the pieces of

[3] Cosmas Indicopleustes, *The Christian Topography*, trans. J. W. McCrindle (London: Hakluyt Society, 1897), pp. 47–49.

flesh or the salt or the iron, and they retire to some distance off. Then the owner of the meat approaches, and if he is satisfied he takes the gold away, and upon seeing this its owner comes and takes the flesh or the salt or the iron. If, however, he is not satisfied, he leaves the gold, when the native seeing that he has not taken it, comes and either puts down more gold, or takes up what he has laid down, and goes away. Such is the mode in which business is traced with the people of that country.[4]

At the end of the book, he described the strange Indian animals and plants he had seen: the rhinoceros ("His skin, when dried is four fingers thick, and this some people put, instead of iron, in the plough, and with it plough the land"); the giraffe; the hippopotamus ("It had teeth so large as to weigh thirteen pounds, and these I sold here"); and cocoanuts ("Their taste is sweet and very pleasant, like that of green nuts. The nut is at first full of a very sweet water which the Indians drink, using it instead of wine"). Finally, he described the bustling trade of Ceylon.[5]

In this island they have many temples, and on one, which stands on an eminence, there is a hyacinth [ruby] as large as a great pine-cone, fiery red, and when seen flashing from a distance, especially if the sun's rays are playing round it, a matchless sight. The island being, as it is, in a central position, is much frequented by ships from all parts of India and from Persia and Ethiopia, and it likewise sends out many of its own. And from the remotest countries, I mean Tzinitza and other trading places, it receives silk, aloes, cloves, sandalwood, and other products, and these again are passed on to marts on this side, such as Male [Malabar coast of India], where pepper grows, and to Calliana [near Bombay], which exports copper and sesame-logs, and cloth for making dresses, for it also is a great place of business. And to Sindu [mouth of Indus] also where musk and castor is produced and androstachys [spikenard], and to Persia and the Homerite country, and to Adule. And the island receives imports from all these marts which we have mentioned and passes them on to the remoter ports.[6]

Manufactures of Constantinople

Industry in Constantinople was stimulated by this international trade. Possibly Justinian's most lasting contribution to the city's prosperity was to persuade two Nestorian monks to smuggle back from China in their hollow staves several silkworms and the seeds of the mulberry tree. The industry was planted in Syria, and from then on the need to import from China fell. The production of silk fabrics was a state monopoly, and the workshops

[4] Ibid., pp. 52–53.
[5] Ibid., pp. 358–62.
[6] Ibid., pp. 356–66.

were in the palace grounds, in a building called the House of Lights because it was lit up all the night. Superb quality of design and color was achieved. Designs were of animals, pagan and religious stories, and abstract patterns, often of Persian origin. Violet, peach blossom, and deep purple were the favorite colors, although later gold and silver threads were added. The silk cloth of Constantinople was so highly prized in western Europe for kings and aristocrats and especially for the vestments of the clergy that it became the city's most profitable manufacture.

The most prosperous artisans concentrated on luxury goods. The goldsmiths worked gold, silver, pearls, and jewels, to produce jewelry for personal adornment, frames for icons, covers for relic boxes, tableware for sacred or culinary use, and all the badges and insignia required for the imperial ceremonies. Trade and manufacture thus provided employment

Byzantine Silk, Alexandria, Sixth to Seventh Century
Courtesy of the Dumbarton Oaks Collection, Washington, D.C.

for a good part of the city's population. Constantinople differed from Rome in that its poorer classes could find work in the artisan shops, as porters or longshoremen, as shopkeepers in the bazaars, or in the other trades fostered by the city's growth, such as the building trade or food suppliers. Moreover, in contrast with the situation in medieval western Europe, it was no disgrace for an aristocrat, or an emperor for that matter, to engage in trade in order to make money. On the contrary, it was admired. One empress ran a perfume factory in her own bedroom. The aristocrats had to go to a shop in the palace grounds to buy their silk. It is still disputable whether the intricate regulations with which the emperors bound up every aspect of economic life acted as a hindrance or as a stabilizing factor in the development of commerce. The state's bureaucrats were everywhere ensuring that niggling regulations were respected. The state set wages and prices and supervised quality. It laid down strict rules as to what could be imported—soap for example was forbidden—and what could be exported—nobody could export ceremonial robes, raw silk, raw materials needed by the artisans, salt fish, or gold. All trade was in the hands of guilds, who were regulated minutely; there were five guilds in the silk industry alone. Probably these regulations prevented great fluctuations of economic growth and decline; and it is indisputable that until the twelfth century Constantinople remained the center of world trade. Its predominance was symbolized, and in part maintained, by the use of the Byzantine coinage based on the gold coin known as the solidus, or nomisma, throughout Asiatic as well as European commerce. Its reliability remained unchallenged until the twelfth century, when the emperors foolishly debased its value. It would be hard to find another great commercial city whose currency has kept its value for six centuries.

Weakness of Byzantine Agriculture

Byzantine agriculture did not share the prosperity of its commerce. The tax on land was so great and so mercilessly extorted that many peasants fled from the land into the cities. It was hard to make a profit from wheat since the state insisted on providing cheap bread for the cities. Worse, however, the aristocracy and the commercial middle class sought to buy up big estates, and frequently did so by force. Justinian himself protested in vain:

We are almost ashamed to refer to the conduct of these. Men of great possessions, with what insolence they range the country; how they are served by guards, so that an intolerable crowd of men follow them; how daringly they pillage everybody, among whom are many priests, but mostly women. . . .

What can be more trying than the driving-off of oxen, horses, and cattle in general, or even (to speak of small matters) of domestic fowls . . . whence a multitude appeal to us here, hustled from their homes, in beggary sometimes to die here.[7]

---

[7] Cited in Jack Lindsay, *Byzantium into Europe* (London: Bodley Head, 1952), p. 128.

The emperors made constant efforts to preserve the character of the free villages, at the same time undermining their independence by their fiscal exactions. Nevertheless, in spite of all difficulties, the more fertile agricultural areas continued to produce a surplus: wheat in Asia Minor, wine and oil in Greece, cotton in Syria, timber in the Balkans. It is doubtful whether the Byzantine empire knew the agrarian poverty that appalled visitors to the same areas in the late nineteenth century.

The Emperor as the Guarantor of Stability

The symbol of the third basis of Constantinople's greatness, the political counterpart to its military and economic power, was the vast equestrian statue of Justinian in the center of the Augustaeum. The statue stood on the top of a tall column of cut stone, bound in brass, which rose on a huge rectangular base that was used for seats by the citizens. Procopius described it graphically:

This brass is in color paler than unalloyed gold; and its value is not much short of its own weight in silver. On the summit of the column there stands an enormous horse, with his face turned towards the east—a noble sight. He appears to be walking, and proceeding swiftly forwards; he raises his left fore-foot as though to tread upon the earth before him, while the other rests upon the stone beneath it, as though it would make the next step, while he places his hind feet together, so that they may be ready when he bids them move. Upon this horse sits a colossal brass figure of the Emperor, habited as Achilles, for so his costume is called; he wears hunting-shoes, and his ankles are not covered by his greaves. He wears a corslet like an ancient hero, his head is covered by a helmet which seems to nod, and a plume glitters upon it. . . . He looks toward the east, directing his course, I imagine against the Persians; in his left hand he holds a globe, by which the sculptor signifies that all lands and seas are subject to him. He holds no sword or spear, or any other weapon, but a cross stands upon the globe, through which he has obtained his empire and victory in war; he stretches forward his right hand towards the east, and spreading his fingers seems to bid the barbarians in that quarter to remain at home and come no further.[8]

Constitutional Position of Byzantine Emperor

Justinian was determined, in short, to carry on the political ideal established by Constantine and his successors of the Christian emperor who on behalf of God rules both state and church. Without altering the essential character of this system in any way, Justinian used his half-century of rule to establish it even more firmly. He reorganized the provincial administration to

[8] Procopius, *Buildings of Justinian*, p. 2.

lessen corruption, and divided the imperial bureaucracy in the palace, making its chiefs directly responsible to the emperor. Through his changes he was able to ensure that no minister could ever aspire to the powers of a prime minister but that in fact the emperor would always be the head of his own government. While accepting the difference in duties of the civil and ecclesiastical authorities, he made clear, by his punishment of heresy, his interference in doctrinal disputes, and his control of Church appointments, that he was the ultimate authority over the Church. "Nothing will be a greater matter of concern to the emperor than the divinity and honor of the clergy," he informed the patriarch, "the more as they offer prayers to God on his behalf. . . . We therefore have the greatest concern for the true doctrines of the God-head and the dignity and honor of the clergy." But the two actions of totally different character that most contributed to the political stability were his codification of the laws and his defeat in 532 of the attempt by the factions of the Hippodrome to overthrow his rule.

Codification of the Law

Justinian's codification of the laws affected the lives of more men than any of his other deeds. Justinian's law code continued in force in Constantinople until 1453. It was regarded as the basis of the law of the Holy Roman Empire set up by Charlemagne in western Europe in 800. Many of its conceptions were embodied in the canon law of the Roman Catholic Church. After the discovery of a complete manuscript of the most important section of the law, the *Digest,* at Pisa in the eleventh century, study of Roman law became the basis of all legal faculties in the European universities. Napoleon's law code, the Code Napoleon, drew heavily on Justinian's; and many other nations modeled their codes on Napoleon's, including, for example, the Italians, the Belgians, and most Latin American states. The only Western countries little influenced by Roman law were England and its former colonies, where common law based on Germanic tribal practice was established early.

Less than six months after becoming emperor, Justinian ordered a commission of ten lawyers headed by Tribonian, of the imperial civil service, and Theophilus, a professor of law at the University of Constantinople, to draw up a codification of the law, that is, a collection of laws then in force that would supersede all codes. As an efficient man, Justinian was appalled at the confusion existing in the laws, many of which were out of date, contradictory, or repetitive. As emperor, he was aware that the continuous existence of Roman law for almost a thousand years had been one of the great bonds guaranteeing the permanence of the Roman state, and incidentally linking the Eastern and Western parts of the empire together. The new code, called the Codex Justinianus, was ready in just over a year. It was a fine, clear summation, of which any emperor could have been proud. But it only whetted Justinian's legal interests. The writings of the legal experts

Justinian Offering Money to the Church. San Vitale, Ravenna *Although the emperor occupies center stage in this sixth-century mosaic, the powerful archbishop of Ravenna, Maximianus, who commissioned the mosaic, is the only person whose name is inserted.*   Alinari photo

called jurisconsults had also come to have the force of law. Justinian decided that these writings too should be drawn up in an authoritative form. This work was more necessary than the collection of the laws, in that the writings of the jurisconsults were even more contradictory and hard to find (unless like Tribonian one owned a large library of scarce law books oneself), and to consult them was more time-consuming. Another commission headed by Tribonian set to work and produced first a collection of Fifty Decisions, corrected where necessary, which were for the use of judges. With this out of the way, the commission began to draw up its *Digest*, or summation of the jurisconsults' writings from the first to the fifth century. Although they had allowed ten years, the commission finished its work in three. It consulted 2,000 books by 39 authors, classified the quotations from their writings that were to have the force of law into separate "titles," each of which dealt with a different point of law. The greatest of the Roman legal writers, Ulpian, was quoted 2,464 times. Since the commission's work had made the original Codex Justinianus out-dated, Tribonian and his group revised the code itself. Thus the great work of clarification of the law for which Justinian is remembered was all carried out between 527 and 534, an amazingly short time for so complicated a task. From then on, all new laws, or *Novels,* issued by Justinian, were written in Greek rather than the Latin of the earlier compilation, a most important milestone in Constantinople's loss of contact with the Latin West.

Justinian took a great interest in the training of young lawyers in the universities, and he himself wrote the preface to the handbook he commissioned as the basic introduction to their studies. In it he explained what he had tried to achieve.

In the name of Our Lord Jesus Christ . . . to the youth desirous of studying the law. . . . Having removed every inconsistency from the sacred constitutions hitherto inharmonious and confused, we extended our care to the immense volumes of the older jurisprudence, and, like sailors crossing the mid-ocean, by the favor of heaven, have now completed a work of which we once despaired. When this, with God's blessing had been done, we called together Tribonian, master and exquaestor of our sacred palace, and the illustrious Theophilus and Dorotheus, professors of law . . . and specially commissioned them to compose by our authority and advice a book of Institutes *whereby you may be enabled to learn your first lesson in law no longer from ancient fables, but grasp them by the brilliant light of imperial learning. . . .*

Receive then these laws with your best powers and with the eagerness of study, and show yourselves so learned as to be encouraged to hope that when you have encompassed the whole field of law you may have the ability to govern such portions of the state as may be entrusted to you.

Given at Constantinople, the 21st day of November in the third consulate of the Emperor Justinian, ever August.[9]

However, nothing illustrates better Justinian's legislation and the modernity of some of his concerns than his *Novels*. He had arms legislation: "Arms are to be manufactured only in state arsenals and for state purposes and on no account to be sold to private individuals." He had a wage freeze: "Artisans, laborers, sailors, and the like are forbidden to demand or accept increases of wages. Offenders are to pay the treasury three times the amount concerned." And he would not allow real estate speculators to ruin the views in Constantinople.

In this our royal city one of the most pleasing amenities is the view of the sea; and to preserve it we enacted that no building should be erected within 100 feet of the sea front. This law has been circumvented by certain individuals. They first put up buildings conforming with this law; then put up in front of them awnings which cut off the sea view without breaking the law; next put up a building inside the awning; and finally remove the awning. Anyone who offends in this way must be made to demolish the buildings he has put up and further pay a fine of ten pounds of gold.[10]

---

[9] Cited in P. N. Ure, *Justinian and His Age* (Harmondsworth, England: Penguin, 1951), pp. 142–43.

[10] Ibid., p. 164.

Political Factions of the Hippodrome

If the law was the greatest contribution to continuity in Byzantine life, the activity of the factions of the Hippodrome was its most disruptive force. The Hippodrome was a huge oval arena at the south of the Augustaeum, built of brick and covered with marble. Thirty tiers of seats could accommodate a crowd of forty to sixty thousand. On the side next to the palace was the imperial box, which an emperor and his court would enter by a closed passageway. In the center of the arena was a raised barrier decorated with famous monuments, including a great obelisk brought from Egypt, which is still standing there today. While gladiator fights with wild animals, boxing and wrestling matches, and acrobats were presented, the main spectacle was the chariot race, of which twenty-four were presented in one day's spectacle. The Constantinople crowd had a passion for the sport. Charioteers and horses became public heroes. Emperors and even patriarchs would breed their own horses for the races. Statues were erected to the charioteers, with occasionally poignant inscriptions, such as "Since Constantius has entered the house of Hades, the racecourse is dark with mourning faces." What made this emotion politically dangerous, however, was

Blue Mosque and the Ruins of the Hippodrome
On the opposite side of the Hippodrome, facing Santa Sophia, the Ottoman emperors erected the Blue Mosque, so called because it is entirely covered inside with translucent blue tiles. The link between Santa Sophia and the great Ottoman mosques of the fifteenth and sixteenth centuries is evident in the use of a great dome superimposed upon four half-domes and in the placing of the windows.   Turkish State Tourist Office photo

that the crowd was split into two organized factions, or demes, called the Blues and the Greens. They became so powerful that the government found it wise to organize them, giving them the duties of a local militia for city defense, of a ceremonial escort, and of entertainment for special festivals. The factions gloried in their role as the one democratic element in the city. A new emperor would come to the Hippodrome to be acclaimed. During the race days, the factions would make demands for the redress of grievances, and would even engage in a kind of dialogue with the emperor on those occasions. The emperors found it judicious to side with one faction against the other; but befriended by an emperor or not, the factions were a dangerous element to any emperor. The young men of the factions roamed the streets at night, beating up enemies and stealing from all. They ignored the prohibition on possession of weapons, and fell on each other in the Hippodrome, often fighting to the death over the result of a chariot race. Justinian attempted to curb both factions at once, and thereby united them against him.

Nika Riots

In 532, the city prefect ordered the execution of seven faction members, both Blue and Green, for a riot in which several people had been killed. Two of the rioters, though hanged, survived and were taken to a church sanctuary, outside which the prefect posted troops. At the chariot races shortly afterwards, the factions demanded that Justinian pardon the two men, and when he ignored them, raised the seditious cry, "Long live the humane Greens and Blues," and "Nika" or "Conquer." That evening the factions besieged the prefect's palace and prison, freed the prisoners, and set fire to the building. From there, they moved on down Middle Street to the Augustaeum, starting more fires as they went. In the main square, they burned the palace gatehouse, the senate building, and finally the church of Santa Sophia. Although Justinian dismissed his most unpopular ministers on the mob's demand, the incendiarism continued. Justinian was besieged in his own palace, while the two factions united in agreeing on a new candidate for emperor to replace Justinian. Justinian again appeared in the royal box, holding a copy of the Gospels in one hand, and promised amnesty and satisfaction of all demands. The rioters refused. Justinian returned to the palace, his nerve broken, and ordered ships to be prepared for his escape. At that point Theodora made her most famous intervention, which is usually credited with saving Justinian his throne.

While it is not proper for a woman to be bold or to behave brashly among men who themselves are hesitant, I think the present crisis hardly permits us to debate this point academically from one perspective or another. . . . For my part, then, I consider flight, even though it may bring safety, to be quite useless, at any time and especially now. Once a man has come into the light of day it is impossible for him not to face death; and so also is it unbearable for someone who has been a ruler to be a fugitive. . . . So now if it is still your wish to save yourself, O Emperor, there is no problem. For we have plenty of money, the sea is there, and here are the ships. Nevertheless, consider whether, once you have managed to save yourself, you might not then gladly exchange your safety for death. But as for me, I take pleasure in an old expression that royal rank is the best burial garment.[11]

Justinian sent two forces, composed mostly of Goths, to the Hippodrome where the crowd was acclaiming its new candidate. There, the troops massacred thirty thousand people. The next day, their candidate was executed. Leading aristocrats implicated were exiled. And the bodies of the slain were laid in a mass grave near a city gate that was henceforth known as the Gate of Death. The factions were not destroyed, but they never again combined together in this way against the emperor. Future troubles were sporadic and usually unorganized. But the heart of Constantinople was a mass of burned ruins. To Justinian, however, the destruction had given the opportunity to outdo Augustus, who had found Rome brick and left it marble. Justinian expected the rebuilding of the city to usher in a second golden age of Roman culture.

Justinian as Patron of a New Golden Age

Character of Byzantine Literature

For an emperor who wanted to be remembered as the patron of a golden age of culture, Justinian was fortunate in the intellectual character that had already been imprinted on his city. Schools for both boys and girls were good; and at Justinian's accession, the great universities of the Hellenistic age, Antioch, Beiruth, Alexandria, Gaza, and Athens, and also the newer university of Constantinople, were flourishing. Constantinople was steeped in Greek culture. For example, children from the age of six studied the classics, especially Homer, whose works every educated person knew by heart. Later studies could include rhetoric, law or philosophy; and nonspecialists often also studied physics and medicine. At the same time, theological works of the Greek fathers were read side by side with the pagan classics, so that a student in Byzantium gained a thorough grounding in both Christian and pagan Greek achievements. Constantinople was felt to have the task of preserving the heritage of Greek culture. The fine libraries containing manuscripts of classical authors were patronized by the state, the church, and private families; and the continuing study of these manuscripts

[11] Procopius, *History of the Wars*, I, xxiv, 32–37, cited in John W. Barker, *Justinian and the Later Roman Empire* (Madison: University of Wisconsin Press, 1966), pp. 87–88.

was indicated by the large number of dictionaries, lexicons, grammars, anthologies, and encyclopedias that were written. Preserving and keeping alive the study of the works of classical Greece was of great importance to the Western tradition of classical culture. With the revival of interest in Greek culture in the Italian Renaissance of the fifteenth century, the students had to turn to Constantinople for their manuscripts and teachers. Unfortunately, this great admiration of classical achievements had the effect of stifling originality in Byzantine literature; and even the best works of Justinian's age were deliberate continuations of writing traditions already established, even involving copying the style of individual authors. Hence, the writers of Byzantium during its whole history produced almost no novels, no good plays, and little original poetry; and even theology, which through the sixth century profoundly considered the widest philosophical questions, descended into polemics whose intricacies have little lasting interest. The creative writing of Constantinople thus was canalized in two separate forms. Great writing was produced when the genuine religious feeling of orthodox Christians could break past the polemics, in hymns that are still in use today, for example, or in books of devotion. In history and biography, the age of Justinian came closest to rivaling the classical Greek writers so much admired. The long line of historians goes from Eusebius, the biographer of Constantine, through the fifteenth-century historians who chronicled the fall of the empire; and the foremost of all these historians was Procopius of Caesarea, who has already been quoted several times in this chapter.

Byzantine Historians

Procopius studied Greek literature at Gaza, and law probably in Constantinople. In 527, he was appointed to travel as the secretary and legal assistant of Belisarius in his campaign against the Persians in Syria. He followed him from Syria to the Vandal wars in north Africa and to the Gothic wars in Italy. Procopius saw that he had the chance to emulate his two heroes, Thucydides and Herodotus. He too lived in a great age and was to be an eyewitness to the wars that would change its character. He modeled himself consciously on the methods and style of Thucydides; and when he first began writing the history of the wars, in 545–50, he copied the very first paragraph of *The History of the Peloponnesian War:* "Procopius of Caesarea wrote the history of the wars which Justinian, emperor of the Romans, waged against the barbarians both of the East and of the West . . . that the long years might not for lack of record, consign mighty deeds to oblivion, and altogether blot them out." [12] Thucydides served Procopius well. The reconstruction of the battles is vivid and exciting. Procopius's character studies, especially of Belisarius, are subtle and far-ranging. And for all his aim

[12] Ure, *Justinian and His Age,* p. 18.

to produce a panegyric of Justinian's great achievement, Procopius showed honesty, as for example, when he comments on the end of the Gothic wars. After describing how the Goths murdered all the Romans they came upon in their flight to the Alps, he adds: "Then indeed it was most plainly shown that when men are doomed to disaster even what seem to be successes always end in destruction, and that when they have got their heart's desire such success may bring ruin in its train. Thus for the senate and people of Rome this victory proved to be still more the cause of ruin." [13] It was discovered after Procopius's death that he had also written a secret history of the reign of Justinian, in which he used a skill at scurrilous invective, hidden in his public work, to blast the emperor as a bloodthirsty monster and his wife, Theodora, as a scandalous, rapacious, and sadistic adventurer. Untrustworthy as the *Secret History* may be, it provides a fascinating antidote to the official panegyrics as well as a useful glimpse into the dark corridors of the Great Palace. And even in the *Secret History*, the comments of the man who has seen the ravages of war have the ring of truth:

That Justinian was not a man, but a demon in human shape, as I have already said, may be abundantly proved by considering the enormity of the evils which he inflicted upon mankind. . . . He so devastated the vast tract of Libya that a traveller, during a long journey, considered it a remarkable thing to meet a single man; and yet there were eighty thousand Vandals who bore arms, besides women, children, and servants without number. . . . The natives of Mauretania were even still more numerous, and they were all exterminated, together with their wives and children. This country also proved the tomb of numbers of Roman soldiers and of their auxiliaries from Byzantium. . . . In time of peace or truce, [Justinian's] thoughts were ever craftily engaged in endeavoring to find pretexts for war against his neighbors. In war, he lost heart, without reasons, and, owing to his meanness, he never made preparations in good time; and, instead of devoting his earnest attention to such matters, he busied himself with the investigation of heavenly phenomena and with curious researches into the nature of God.[14]

The other historian of Justinian's age, Agathias, is better remembered for his elegiac poetry. Like all the bureaucrats, lawyers, business leaders, and courtiers of Constantinople, he wrote short, charming epigrams in a Greek style that went back a thousand years. A famous collection of thirty-seven hundred of these poems called the Palatine Anthology, which was made in the tenth century, is still much admired by students of Greek poetry; and in this anthology, about one-tenth of the poems were written by the upper crust of Byzantine society. Here are two examples:

[13] Ibid., p. 172.

[14] Procopius, *The Secret History of the Court of Justinian* (Athens: Athenian Society, 1896), pp. 149–51, 154.

You roll your eyes, dark fire's similitude;
Lips tipped with rouge ambiguously protrude;
In fits of giggles toss your glossy hair,
And flaunt your swaggering hands. I'm well aware.
But in your stiff heart swollen pride bears sway;
You have not softened, even in decay.

"Anacreon, you overdrank and died." "But I lived well;
You also, though you may not drink, will find your way to hell." [15]

Justinian's Building Program

Significantly enough, two of the most famous pieces of Byzantine writing, one in prose and one in verse, were called forth not by love or drink or war but by a building, the great church of Santa Sophia. In 559–60, Justinian ordered Procopius to write an account of the buildings he had erected throughout the empire, "lest posterity beholding the enormous size and number of them, should deny their being the work of one man." Justinian's building program exceeded that of any previous Roman emperor. Like other emperors, he had a program of public works—bridges, roads, border fortresses, walls, aqueducts, cisterns, warehouses, public baths, and law courts. As a Christian ruler, he built works of charity such as asylums, hospitals for the incurably ill, orphanages, schools, and monasteries. Since both

[15] *Translations from the Greek Anthology*, trans. Robert A. Furness (London: J. Cape, 1931), pp. 80, 83. By permission of the Estate of Robert A. Furness and Jonathan Cape, Ltd.

Church of St. Savior in Chora, Constantinople
Although much altered during the later Byzantine empire, this church dates back to the fifth century. Its chunky, indented façade and high, small domes are typical of the new style of ecclesiastical architecture adopted in the late sixth century, when the outer façade was divorced from the design of the interior.   Turkish State Tourist Office photo

San Vitale, Ravenna
Constructed under Justinian in 538–547, San Vitale is one of the most subtle spatial compositions in all church architecture. It combines the straight lines of the outer octagonal walls with the undulations of seven circular interior arcades. Alinari photo; Italian Government Travel Office photo

he and Theodora loved the waterfront of Constantinople and its nearby straits, he constructed churches at the finest viewpoints, and provided promenades beside the water for the citizens to enjoy. "Those who take their walks [at the new church of Anaplus]," wrote Procopius, "are charmed with the beauty of the stone, are delighted with the view of the sea, and are refreshed with the breezes from the water and the hills that rise upon the land." The Great Palace too was greatly extended, especially with the building of a new entrance hall called the Chalke, which was gorgeously decorated with mosaics of his triumphs in Africa and Italy. It was in church buildings, however, that Justinian exceeded himself. Procopius describes huge programs of church building in Mesopotamia and Syria; in Palestine, where Justinian paid special attention to Jerusalem; and in Armenia, the Crimea, the Balkans, Egypt, and north Africa. And though Procopius failed to describe Italy, Justinian built some of his finest churches in Ravenna. In Constantinople itself, however, the emperor's church building became a mania. He had already rebuilt seven churches before becoming emperor, and had probably given orders for construction of a new Santa Sophia before the Nika rioters helped him by burning the old one down. In all, he built or rebuilt thirty-four churches in Constantinople.

Santa Sophia

Justinian's church of Santa Sophia is the single finest achievement of all Byzantine civilization, and the only building so far mentioned in this book that rivals the Parthenon. Moreover, it still exists, almost exactly in the form in which it was completed in 537, five years after Justinian put his engineer-architects, Anthemius and Isidore, to work on its construction. Santa Sophia deserves a prolonged visit, even in these pages. Justinian spared no expense to build the Great Church, as it came to be called. The basic construction was the normal Roman use of brick and stone set in thick layers of cement. Almost no attempt was made to embellish the outside, of which the structural features were left to speak for themselves—the huge projecting buttresses on the north and south, the undulating rise of the superimposed domes on east and west. Inside, however, every available space was covered with carefully worked sheets of marble, fitted so skillfully as to blend one into the other and to emphasize the distinctive veins in each piece. In the Homeric form of epic poem that one of Justinian's court officials, Paul the Silentiary, wrote to celebrate Santa Sophia, he described the marbles:

Yet who, who even in the measures of Homer shall sing the marble pastures gathered on the lofty walls and spreading pavement of the mighty church? Those the iron with its metal tooth has gnawed—the fresh green from Carytus, polychrome marble from the Phrygian range, in which a rosy blush mingles with white, or it shines bright with flowers of deep red and silver. There is a wealth of porphyry too, powdered with bright stars, that has once laden the river boat on the broad Nile. You would see an emerald green from Sparta, and the glittering marble with wavy veins which the tool has worked in the deep breast of the Iassian hills, showing slanting streaks blood-red and livid-white. From the Lydian creek came the bright stone mingled with streaks of red. Stone too there is that the Libyan sun, warming his golden light, has nourished in the deep clefts of the hills of the Moors, of crocus color glittering like gold; and the product of the Celtic crags, a wealth of crystals, like milk poured here and there on a flesh of glittering black. There is the precious onyx, as if gold were shining through it; and the marble that the land of Atrax yields, not from some upland glen, but from the level plains; in parts fresh green as the sea or emerald stone, or again like blue cornflowers in grass, with here and there a drift of fallen snow—a sweet mingled contrast on the dark shining surface.[16]

A vast empire has never been praised in quite this way for the varieties of stone it is capable of producing! But the passage is worth rereading, because the architecture of the Roman Empire, West and East, of medieval Italy, and of the Italian Renaissance, cannot be understood unless one shares to some degree this feeling for the variety, and surprisingly enough, the emotional appeal of marble.

The altar was a table of gold, with an inlay of precious stones, sheltered by a vast conical canopy of silver. Byzantine textiles of silk, gold, and silver, embroidered with scenes of the life of Christ and the charitable deeds of Justinian, hung around the altar. Hanging chains of beaten brass, fitted with silver disks and thousands of candleholders of fine glass held cups of burning oil by night, so that the church itself acted as a beacon to mariners coming up the Bosphorus. And all this richness of decoration was lavished on a church of enormous size, 220 feet long by 107 feet wide in the central nave, with the dome 180 feet above the floor. But the decoration, so unlike the Parthenon, for example, would not alone have accounted for the impressiveness of this building. Its designers combined technical mastery of building skills—they were mathematicians as well as architects—with artistic subtlety of the highest form. Let us glance both at the plan on the following page and at the photographs of the interior of Santa Sophia on pages 247 and 281 to try to grasp what they were trying to achieve.

The plan shows that the architects combined two basic church forms: the rectangular basilica that we already saw in Sant' Apollinare Nuovo in Ravenna, and the centrally planned church. The distinction between these two types of churches is basic to all Christian architecture. The basilica is a rectangular building with the altar placed at the east end and the congregation, seated or standing, facing lengthways down the building. It can be made in the form of a cross when a transept is inserted near the east end.

---

[16] Cited in Philip Sherrard, *Constantinople: Iconography of a Sacred City* (London: Oxford University Press, 1965), p. 27.

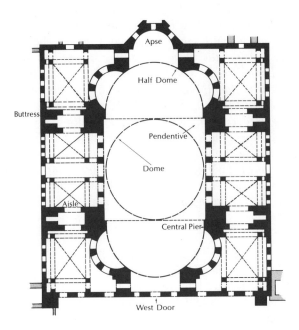

Ground Plan of Santa Sophia

The centrally planned church began with mausoleums, in which the grave was placed in the middle of a circular or octagonal building. Often the church took the form of a Greek cross, that is a cross with four arms of equal length, with a vaulted dome placed over the point where the four arms met. The plan of Santa Sophia shows that the building is almost a square, if one looks at the outside walls. In the center of the square is a dome built upon four enormous piers. So far, the building is centrally planned. However, to the east and west of the central dome are two half-domes, also rising from the four central piers, while to the north and south of the dome, two aisles have been built. The plan shows therefore that the architects deliberately created two different kinds of feeling for space inside the building. There is the longitudinal, or forward, drive, produced by the side aisles and by the rectangular share of the central space. Entering at the main west door, one expects one's glance to be directed toward the far east end of the building, as in a basilica. But the dome creates an entirely different feeling. The culminating point of the building is not the east end, but the center of the great dome. One's eyes automatically look up and around the dome, and one feels the urge that the architects worked to inspire—to move forward to the very center of the building. Then, one stands before the very dome of heaven, and all around in exciting symmetry are displayed the images of the beauty, grandeur, and harmony of God's universe. The great dome united all worshippers in a community under God. The photos show what the ground plan does not, that the architects succeeded in mak-

Interior, Santa Sophia, Constantinople
Great variation in lighting is achieved by the forty-two windows in the base of the dome and by the opening up of the solid masonry of the wall.
Turkish State Tourist Office photo

ing the dome appear to float, unconnected from the huge pillars that support it. "From the lightness of the building," wrote Procopius, "it does not appear to rest upon a solid foundation, but to cover the place beneath as though it were suspended from heaven by the fabled golden chain." [17] The device used by the architects was the pendentive. Once they had built the four huge round arches in a square, on top of the four central piers, they had to figure out how to rest the dome upon these arches, transferring the weight of the dome from there to the piers. To do this they filled in the space between the edges of the round arches and the base of the dome with

[17] Procopius, *Buildings of Justinian*, p. 9.

Air View of Santa Sophia, Constantinople
The plain exterior of Santa Sophia unsparingly reveals the structural framework of projecting buttresses and the half-domes by which the vast dome is supported. The minarets were added after the Ottoman conquest, but the rest of the building is substantially unaltered. The waterway to the left is the Golden Horn, that to the right the Bosphorus.   Turkish State Tourist Office photo

masonry, creating a spherical triangle called a pendentive, which looks weightless but in fact transfers the weight of the dome away from the round arches to the piers. Secondly, the architects pierced the base of the dome with forty-two windows, not only enhancing the impression of the separation of the dome from the rest of the building but permitting the constant play of sunlight, which is one of the most superb characteristics of Santa Sophia. "It is singularly full of light and sunshine," Procopius commented. "You would declare that the place is not lightened by the sun from without, but that the rays are produced within itself, such an abundance of light is poured into this church." Thus the appearance of the building was constantly changing as the shafts of sunlight shifted in its many windows; and "No one ever became wearied of this spectacle." This display of light was essential to a church dedicated to the second person of the Trinity, the abstract Wisdom of Christ.

Whoever enters there to worship perceives at once that it is not by any human strength or skill, but by the favor of God that this work has been perfected; his mind rises sublime to commune with God, feeling that He cannot be far off, but must especially love to dwell in the place which He has chosen; and this takes place not only when a man sees it for the first time, but it always makes the same impression upon him, as though he had never beheld it before.[18]

[18] Ibid., pp. 6–7, 11.

Justinian, like Pericles, knew what he had created; and according to a tenth-century description that still rings true, he exclaimed, after walking the length of the church to the altar on the day of the church's dedication, "Glory be to God, who has thought me worthy to finish this work. Solomon, I have outdone thee!"

Constantinople After Justinian

While a new form of civilization was being created in western Europe during the Middle Ages, two great and totally different civilizations continued to flourish on the European continent and at times to influence the development of medieval Christendom—the Byzantine civilization on the southeastern tip of Europe and the Moslem civilization on the southwestern, in Spain and Portugal. Moslem Spain will be discussed in the next chapter. Let us glance briefly here at the fortunes of Constantinople after Justinian's death.

By the mid-sixth century, the character of the Byzantine monarchy, the sources of its military and economic strength, the nature of the Greek Orthodox Church, and even the appearance of Constantinople had been given a definitive form. In spite of the evolution of eight centuries, the Byzantine empire in the fifteenth century was recognizably the same society as that under Justinian. One can realize the amazing achievement of continuity this is if one contrasts Victoria's England with that of William the Conqueror, which also represents the evolution of eight centuries, or even if one contrasts Rome at the time of Justinian with Rome at the time of Michelangelo.

Justinian's policy of reconquest in western Europe had weakened the empire in men and money; but the remaining resources of the empire were gathered for a long and ultimately victorious war against the Persians, which destroyed the Sassanid empire but left the Byzantine monarchy too weak to save large parts of its own empire from the many new waves of invaders that were threatening. All the territory won by Justinian in Italy, except Ravenna and the south coast, was taken by a new Germanic tribe, the Lombards, in the seventh century. The Visigoths soon regained control of southern Spain. Slavs and Bulgars penetrated the Balkans and settled. But above all, the Arab followers of Mohammed seized half of the Byzantine empire—between 634 and 647, they took Syria, Palestine, and Egypt, whose inhabitants, weary of taxation and persecution for heresy, made no effort to oppose them. In 670–697, they took north Africa, the first of Justinian's conquests, and moved on from there into Spain. Their fleet raided the Sea of Marmara, and on several occasions their armies reached the walls of Constantinople itself. They were finally driven back after the siege of 717–718 by a new dynasty of Byzantine emperors, the Isaurians (717–867). The Isaurians reestablished the empire's finances, or at least of what was left of the empire: Asia Minor, the Balkans, and the southern tip of Italy. The new stability encouraged the appearance of a new period of cultural achievement through the late ninth and tenth centuries.

The Macedonian dynasty (867–1081) brought a new wave of economic prosperity, favored by developing trade relations with the new states of western Europe. It spread the Greek Orthodox religion to the Bulgars, the Russians, the Croats and Serbs. Its newly built fleets again controlled the waters around the empire. Constantinople's artisans in silk and metalwork again dominated the European market. From the end of the eleventh century, however, the slow but seemingly inexorable downfall of the empire began. The Normans drove the Byzantines from the whole of southern Italy by 1071. The Crusaders struck two damaging blows. First, after sacking Constantinople during the Fourth Crusade in 1204 and then occupying it, they enabled the Venetians and other Italians to set up almost a stranglehold on Constantinople's trade. Second, the opening of new trade routes between western Europe and the Near East through Palestine broke Constantinople's monopoly of the Asiatic trade. When, after sixty years, a Greek emperor finally drove out the "Latin emperors" imposed by the Crusaders, he took possession of a ruined, starving, and depopulated city. The Byzantines therefore lacked the strength to hold out against the Ottoman Turks, the last of a series of Turkish tribes who had been moving westwards through central Asia since the tenth century. Throughout the fourteenth century, the Ottoman Turks, who had taken possession of all the Arab lands of the Near East, moved to encircle Constantinople. From Anatolia, they attacked the Balkans, taking Adrianople in 1347. They transformed the tiny city into their new capital, at a distance of only fifty miles from Constantinople. By 1390, they held all the Balkans and had reached the Danube. They besieged Constantinople in 1397, again in 1422, and began their final assault in April 1453.

More than seventy thousand battle-hardened Turkish troops armed with gigantic cannon besieged a city held by only seven thousand soldiers. Few documents are more moving than the last letter sent by the last East Roman emperor, Constantine XI, to his assailant, Sultan Mohammed II:

As it is clear that you desire war more than peace, since I cannot satisfy you either by my protestations of sincerity, or by my readiness to swear allegiance, so let it be according to your desire. I turn now and look to God alone. Should it be his will that the city be yours, where is he who can oppose it? If he should inspire you with a desire for peace, I shall be only too happy. However, I release you from all your oaths and treaties with me, and, closing the gates of my capital, I will defend my people to the last drop of my blood. Reign in happiness until the All-just, the Supreme God, calls us both before his judgement seat.[19]

---

[19] Sherrard, *Constantinople,* pp. 127–28.

Le siege du grant · turc auec · ij · deles pricipaulx coseilles
Le siege du capiteine gñal de la turquie

Capture of Constantinople by the Turks in 1453
Bibliothèque Nationale, Paris

The city fell at dawn on May 29 when the Turks finally succeeded in getting a small group of men over the top of the land walls. At midday the young sultan rode with his court through a city given over to pillaging, across the forums along Middle Street, to the Church of Santa Sophia. There he dismounted, picked up a handful of soil which he scattered on his head to humble himself before his god, and in Santa Sophia, he listened to the first Moslem prayer recited from the pulpit. He then moved on to the

Sultan Mohammed II, by Gentile Bellini
This fine example of Venetian portraiture was painted twenty-seven years after Mohammed II's capture of Constantinople in 1453.
Turkish State Tourist Office photo

Great Palace, where, seeing the cobwebs spreading across its ruins, he murmured the lines of an old Persian poem: "The spider has woven his web in the imperial palace/And the owl has sung a watch-song on the towers of Afrasiab." At the age of twenty-three he had destroyed an empire that had lasted for 1,123 years.

SUGGESTED READING

Philip Sherrard has combined superb photography with a wealth of contemporary quotations to create a marvelously poetic but historically valid portrait of the city in *Constantinople: Iconography of a Sacred City* (1965). Glanville Downey, an outstanding Byzantine historian, makes many provocative judgments but succeeds very well in re-creating the character of the age in *Constantinople in the Age of Justinian* (1960). For the building programs of the emperors and their significance, one should consult Michael Maclagan, *The City of Constantinople* (1968) or John E. N. Hearsey, *City of Constantine 324–1453* (1963). Dean A. Miller's *Imperial Constantinople* (1969) is well documented but marred by jargon. Cyril Mango, *The Brazen House: A Study of the Vestibule of the Imperial Palace of Constantinople* (1959) demonstrates the archaeological methods by which knowledge of the imperial palace and its surrounding buildings has been obtained.

For the life of Justinian, John W. Barker, *Justinian and the Later Roman Empire* (1966) is solid, with emphasis on military and religious questions, and contains a good list of primary sources. P. N. Ure, *Justinian and His Age* (1951) is unbalanced and opinionated, but makes very rich use of contemporary writings.

There are many excellent surveys of Byzantine history. Charles Diehl, *Byzantium: Greatness and Decline* (1957), by a French historian, is a first-class summary, even if slightly outdated in places. It contains an indispensable bibliography by Professor Peter Charanis for additional study. Steven Runciman, the doyen of British historians of Byzantium, provides an elegant study, which packs an incredible amount of information into a short space, in *Byzantine Civilization* (1956). His earlier *Byzantine Empire* (1925) still makes good reading. For a narrative with emphasis on religious problems, see Joan Hussey, *The Byzantine World* (1957); for cultural background, see Speros Vryonis, Jr., *Byzantium and Europe* (1967); for political intricacies, see George Ostrogorsky, *History of the Byzantine State* (1956), translated by Joan Hussey. Jack Lindsay, *Byzantium into Europe* (1952) makes use of wide knowledge of primary sources, especially literature, and brings such topical studies as Faction and Circus to life. Tamara Talbot Rice, *Everyday Life in Byzantium* (1967) is quite scholarly and gives many fascinating details. For example, she points out that one of the most popular imports from Asia in the sixth century was sets of chessmen and checkers. In *The Byzantines and Their World* (1973) Peter Arnott makes rich use of contemporary writers.

Dmitri Obolensky shows the extent of Byzantine influence upon the Slavic peoples, especially in the Balkans, in *The Byzantine Commonwealth: Eastern Europe, 500–1453* (1971), while Deno J. Geanakoplos, *Byzantine East and Latin West: Two Worlds of Christendom in Middle Ages and Renaissance* (1966) discusses the Byzantine influence on the West.

André Grabar has written two gorgeously illustrated books on Byzantium's art: *Byzantium from the Death of Theodosius to the Rise of Islam* (1966), which covers architecture, painting, sculpture, sumptuary arts, and art industries, and *Byzantine Painting* (1953), which includes studies of the mosaics of the Great Palace in Constantinople, St. Mark's in Venice, and the Palatine Chapel in Palermo. David Talbot Rice, *The Art of Byzantium* (1959) is short and well illustrated with color photos of paintings and metalwork.

Once again, the ancient writers are the most vivid. Procopius's *The Secret History of the Court of Justinian* has attracted many translators; the Palestine Pilgrims' Text Society put Procopius's *Buildings of Justinian* (1897) in the hands of its peregrinating members. The Hakluyt Society of London published *The Christian Topography of Cosmas Indicopleustes* for its armchair travelers. Robert A. Furness has translated selections from *Greek Anthology* (1931). Ernest Barker, *Social and Political Thought in Byzantium* (1957), covers the whole sweep of the city's political science.

On the Turks who overthrew the Byzantine empire, see P. Wittek, *The Rise of the Ottoman Empire* (1954) and especially the work of the leading Turkish historian Halil Inalcik, *The Ottoman Empire: The Classical Age, 1300–1600* (1973) which deals with the rise of the Ottoman cities. On the events of 1453, see Stephen Runciman, *The Fall of Constantinople* (1965).

Chronicle of Events   *The Middle Ages*

600–1500

	Islam	Catholic Church	European Political History
600	Mohammed (c. 570–632) 622 Hegira to MEDINA Orthodox Caliphate (632–661) 641 Capture of ALEXANDRIA Ummayad Caliphate (661–750) 674–678 Siege of CONSTANTINOPLE		Decline of Merovingian dynasty in France
700	711 Moslem invasion of Spain 717 Moslems driven back from CONSTANTINOPLE 732 Moslems halted at Tours Abbasid Caliphate (750–) in BAGHDAD Ummayad rule in CORDOBA, Spain (756–1031) Harun-al-Rashid (786–809)	c. 722–754 Missions of St. Boniface in eastern Germany 756 Donation of Pepin	Charles Martel (714–741) 732 Battle of Tours 754 Pepin Kings of the Franks Charlemagne (768–814) Foundation of new capital at AACHEN
800	826 Arab landing on Crete 827 Arab landing in Sicily		800 Charlemagne crowned emperor Louis I, emperor (814–840) 843 Division of empire at Treaty of Verdun Invasions by Norsemen and Magyars

	France	England	Germany	Catholic Church	Other European States
900	911 Norsemen settle in Normandy Decline of Carolingian rulers	Anglo-Saxon rule		910 Foundation of Monastery of Cluny Reform movement in Church	c. 880–912 Oleg establishes state at KIEV in Russia
			Saxon Dynasty (916–1024) Henry I (916–936) Otto I (936–973) Expansion into eastern Europe; Ottonian renaissance 962 Otto I crowned emperor Otto II (973–983)		955 Magyars defeated at battle of Lechfeld. Settle in Hungary.
	Capetian Dynasty (987–1328) Hugh Capet (987–996)		Otto III (983–1002)		Vladimir, prince of Kiev (978–1015). Conversion of Russia to Greek Orthodox Christianity
1000	Consolidation of Capetian domain		Henry II (1002–1024) *Salian Dynasty* (1024–1125) Conrad II (1024–1039) Henry III (1039–1056) Henry IV (1056–1106)	Leo IX (1049–1054) 1059 Election of pope by College of Cardinals begins	Norman conquest of Southern Italy and Sicily. Capital at PALERMO

France	England	Germany	Catholic Church	Other European States
	1066 Invasion of England William, Duke of Normandy *Norman Dynasty (1066–1154)* William I (1066–1087) Building of Norman castles			
Abelard (1079–1142)	1086 Domesday Book William II (1087–1100)		Gregory VII (1073–1085) 1075 Investiture contest begins 1077 Emperor at Canossa	
			St. Bernard of Clairvaux (c. 1090–1153) 1096–1099 First Crusade	1099 Crusaders capture JERUSALEM Crusader states in Palestine
Louis VI, The Fat (1108–1137)	Henry I (1100–1135) Development of common law	Henry V (1106–1125)	1120 Order of Knights Templars founded 1122 Concordat of Worms	
1133–1144 Invention of Gothic architecture at St. Denis Louis VII (1137–1180)	*Angevin Dynasty (1154–1399)* Henry II (1154–1189)	*Hohenstaufen Dynasty (1138–1254)* Frederick I, Barbarossa (1152–1190)	1147–1149 Second Crusade	

1100

France / Paris	England	Empire	Church & Crusades	Other
1163 Notre Dame cathedral in PARIS begun	1170 Murder of Becket	1176 Battle of Legnano	St. Francis (1182-1226)	1187 Moslems recapture JERUSALEM
Philip II, Augustus (1180-1223) Conquest of Normandy and Anjou City Wall around PARIS	Richard I, the Lionhearted (1189-1199)	Henry VI (1190-1197) 1194 Henry VI crowned king of Sicily	1189-1192 Third Crusade	
	John (1199-1216)		Innocent III (1198-1215)	
c. 1200 University of PARIS chartered	Magna Carta (1215) Henry III (1216-1272) Building of Westminster Abbey LONDON	Frederick II (1215-1250)	1202-1204 Fourth Crusade 1204 Crusaders sack CONSTANTINOPLE	
			1216 Dominican Order founded	
			1218-1221 Fifth Crusade	
Louis VIII (1223-1226)			St. Thomas Aquinas (1225-1274)	
Louis IX (1226-1270)			1228-1229 Sixth Crusade 1233 Inquisition established	1241 Mongols take KIEV Flemish wool-manufacturing cities at greatest power (BRUGES, GHENT, BRUSSELS)

1200

France	England	Germany	Catholic Church	Other European States
Sainte Chapelle built in PARIS Philip III (1270–1285)			1248–1254 Seventh Crusade	
	Edward I (1272–1307) Pacification of Wales	Fragmentation into feudal principalities Rudolf of Habsburg, emperor (1273–1291)		
Philip IV, the Fair (1285–1314)	1295 Model Parliament		Boniface VIII (1294–1303) 1296 Bull Clericis Laicos	Rise of Ottoman Turks Decline of PISA
			1302 Bull Unam Sanctam 1305–1378 Babylonian Captivity in AVIGNON	
	Edward II (1307–1327) Edward III (1327–1377)			1323–1328 Peasants' revolt in Flanders
Valois Dynasty (1328–1589) 1337–1453 Hundred Years' War	Lancaster and York Dynasties (1399–1485) Geoffrey Chaucer (c. 1340–1400)			
1347 Black Death 1356 Battle of Poitiers	1347 Black Death	1347 Black Death 1356 Golden Bull named seven electors of Holy Roman Emperor		
1358 Jacquerie Charles V (1364–1380)			Thomas à Kempis (1370–1471)	Philip the Bold of Burgundy (1364–1404)

Charles VI (1380–1422)

1381 Peasants' Revolt

Great Schism (1378–1417)

1380 VENICE defeats GENOA
Jan van Eyck
(c. 1380–1440)

Henry V (1413–1422)

Hanseatic League weakened

1414–1418 Council of
Constance
1415 Burning of
John Huss

1415 Battle of Agincourt

Duke Philip the Good of
Burgundy (1419–1467)

Charles VII (1422–1461)
1431 Joan of Arc burned

1453–1485 Wars of the
Roses

1453 Ottoman Turks
capture CONSTANTINOPLE;
and 1456 ATHENS
Duke Charles the Bold of
Burgundy (1467–1477)
Lorenzo de' Medici rule in
FLORENCE (1449–1492)

Louis XI (1461–1483)

1485 Battle of Bosworth
Field
Tudor Dynasty
Henry VII (1485–1509)

Isabella, Queen of Castile
(1474–1504)
Ferdinand, king of Aragon
(1479–1516)
1492 Expulsion of Moors
from Spain
1492 Columbus discovers
America

Maximilian I emperor
(1493–1519)

7 / *The Early Middle Ages, 600–1000*

At the end of the sixth century, when Constantinople was at the height of its power and prosperity, the Germanic states in the West, as we saw in Chapter Five, were small, primitive, and poverty-stricken. During the next four centuries these states suffered repeated attacks of two new waves of invaders, and, in reaction to the invasions, developed a new form of economic structure known as manorialism and a new kind of political administration called feudalism.

The first wave of invaders consisted of Moslem Arabs, who crossed from north Africa into Visigothic Spain in 711 and penetrated into central France. Although they were pushed back to the Pyrenees after their defeat near Tours by the Frankish leader Charles Martel in 732, they controlled most of Spain and Portugal for the next four centuries and were not finally defeated until 1492. In Spain they created a flourishing urban civilization in such centers as Cordoba, Toledo, Seville, and Granada, exerting great influence upon both the economic and cultural life of all Europe.

Following the repulse of the Moslem invasion, the Franks in their turn attempted to create a powerful empire by bringing the neighboring Germanic states under their control. Charles Martel's son Pepin seized the Frankish throne for himself; and his son, Charlemagne (reigned 768–814), through annual wars of conquest, was able to extend his rule from France to the Elbe in the East and beyond Rome in the South. From his new capital

Mosque of Cordoba   Spanish National Tourist Office photo

city of Aachen in western Germany, which he considered a second Rome, he encouraged an ephemeral cultural revival we call the Carolingian renaissance; and he was even crowned "Emperor of the Romans" by the Pope in the year 800.

After Charlemagne's death in 814, a second series of invaders destroyed even the modicum of political stability and economic prosperity that his rule had made possible. New attacks on Sicily and southern Italy were mounted by the Moslems from north Africa. Savage Asiatic invaders known as Magyars drove on horseback into Germany, Italy, and France, and finally settled in Hungary. Equally vicious Norsemen, or Vikings, swept from Scandinavia in their long-prowed boats to ravage the coasts of northern Europe and eventually settled in parts of Scotland and England, in Normandy, and in Sicily and southern Italy.

During this period of disorder, the Germanic rulers' power disintegrated. In place of centralized state control, government and defense came to be accomplished at local levels in a system of relationships known to later historians as feudalism. By the year 1000, this system not only had evolved a complex legal structure but also underlay the government of the new states then evolving in France, England, and Germany. Meanwhile, in the universal chaos, commerce and manufacturing largely ceased for all but local needs. Towns became unnecessary, for either governmental or economic purposes, and urban life virtually disappeared from the European continent except in the Moslem cities of Spain and in the Byzantine empire. Most of Europe's inhabitants fell back on the agricultural village or hamlet as the nucleus of their social and economic life. As the agricultural historian Georges Duby has pointed out, the student of this period does not have to "consider the problem, so pressing in succeeding times, of the relationship between town and country." The city had temporarily given precedence to the village.

Historians have recently proven, however, that in spite of the conditions of disorder, the agriculture of this period was far from stagnant. In fact, an agricultural revolution took place in crop rotation, in the use of tools and animals, and in the variety of foodstuffs planted. The resultant increase in production made possible, for the period after 1000, an important growth in population. Thus, while the city declined, agriculture advanced, preparing and directly contributing to the revival of commerce and the restoration of city life.

In this chapter, we shall trace, first, the origins of Moslem civilization and its expansion into Europe through Spain; second, the resurgence of Frankish power in the empire of Charlemagne; third, the destructive impact of the second wave of invasions by Moslems, Magyars, and Vikings; fourth, the formation both of the political system called feudalism and the economic system called manorialism; and finally, the nature of the medieval agricultural revolution.

Mohammed and the Civilization of Islam

Mohammed (c. 570–632) and the Religion of Islam

Arabia did not figure large in the history of civilization before the sixth century, except to send wave after wave of Semitic invaders from its forbidding deserts and mountains to seek a better life among the cities and irrigated plains of the Fertile Crescent. Most of its inhabitants were desert nomads, except for small numbers of sophisticated traders who grouped in cities in the oases along the caravan routes. Mohammed was born in Mecca, the most important of these trading cities, and spent his early life in the caravan trade, traveling widely through Arabia and probably north into Palestine and Syria, where he became acquainted with the beliefs of both Christians and Jews. He was an astute businessman, married the wealthy widow whose business he had managed, and might have led a wholly unexceptional life had he not begun at the age of forty to see visions. Mohammed believed he saw the Angel Gabriel, who ordered him to reveal the will of God, in part by "reciting" the words of God revealed to him in his visions. These revelations continued for twenty years, and were collected in the Moslem holy book, the *Koran*. The message Mohammed had to teach was

Detail of Wall Panel, The Alhambra, Granada
The words of the Koran and nonrepresentational design, often of intricate geometrical patterns, formed the basis of the stucco decoration that covered the walls of Moslem palaces.   Spanish National Tourist Office photo

very simple. There is only one god, Allah, who can never take human form; he will judge all mankind in a terrible Day of Judgement; while awaiting that day, men must lead a decent life along the lines indicated by Allah's last and greatest prophet, Mohammed.

Mohammed preached the new faith, which he called Islam, or "abandonment," to the will of God, among the people he knew in Mecca. But most of the city's leaders attacked him for his opposition to their polytheism, especially as the great black meteorite in the center of the city was the main goal of pagan worship in Arabia. In 622, however, Mohammed was invited to mediate the disputes of feuding tribes in Medina, the second

ISLAM, 570–1492

c. 570	Birth of Mohammed
622	Mohammed's Hegira (flight) to MEDINA
630	Mohammed's capture of MECCA
632	Death of Mohammed
632–661	*Orthodox Caliphate* (MEDINA; MECCA)
	Abu Bakr 632–634
	Omar 634–644
	Othmar 644–656
	Ali 656–661
636	Conquest of Syria
637	Capture of JERUSALEM
	Defeat of Persia
641	Capture of ALEXANDRIA
654	Conquest of Cyprus and Rhodes
661–750	*Ummayad Caliphate* (DAMASCUS)
698	Capture of Carthage
711	Invasion of Spain
717	Defeat at Constantinople
732	Defeat near Tours by Charles Martel
750–1258	*Abbasid Caliphate* (BAGHDAD)
756–1031	*Ummayad Caliphate in Spain* (CORDOBA)
800–909	*Aghlabid Dynasty in Tunisia* (KAIROUAN)
910–1171	*Fatimid Caliphate in Egypt and Palestine* (CAIRO)
1055	Seljuk Turks establish protectorate in BAGHDAD
1096–1099	First Crusade
1147–1149	Second Crusade
1189–1192	Third Crusade
1232–1492	*Nazarite Dynasty in Spain* (GRANADA)
1258	Mongols Sack BAGHDAD
c. 1350	Rise of Ottoman Turks
1453	Ottoman Turks capture Constantinople
1492	Completion of Catholic reconquest of Spain

Major Islamic cities appear in capital letters.

largest city of Arabia, and he decided to take "flight," or *hegira,* there. All Moslem history has since been dated from the Hegira, because in Medina, Mohammed was able to give Islam a political base. As chief magistrate of Medina, Mohammed elaborated the rules that were to govern the daily life of believers in Islam, and laid down five basic requirements for all believers: ritual prayer five times a day; belief in one god, Allah; fasting from dawn to dusk during the month of Ramadan; a pilgrimage at least once in a lifetime to Mecca; and almsgiving. To support the overcrowded community of Medina, Mohammed sent marauding parties to raid the caravans passing to Mecca; and after several indecisive battles, he led a successful expedition to capture Mecca in 630. War against the pagans was justified as *jehad,* or holy war, for the conversion of the unbelievers. By the time of Mohammed's death in June 632, Moslem rule extended over two-thirds of Arabia, and had reached the southern edge of Palestine.

The Orthodox Caliphate, 632–661

After the Prophet's death, Islam was faced by two great difficulties. An enduring method of regulating the succession to Mohammed had to be found; and if expansion was to continue, the military strength would have to be raised to defeat the two great empires, Byzantium and Persia, that held Islam penned up in the Arabian peninsula. Mohammed had left the basis of the new religion—the sayings revealed to him by Allah, which were to be collected in the *Koran;* his own sayings, called the *hadith,* dealing with the detailed rules for everyday conduct; and the *sunna,* or custom, a description of the life of Mohammed himself, which set an example for the faithful. But Mohammed had ignored the problem of making permanent in a political form the theocracy of Islam. His closest companions settled the question temporarily by appointing Abu Bakr, one of his oldest and most trusted followers, as his "successor," "deputy," or "representative," that is, as *caliph.* Abu Bakr was succeeded by Omar (reigned 634–644), who had been a companion of Mohammed's on the Hegira, and by Othman (reigned 644–656), another early follower of the Prophet. Mohammed's son-in-law Ali was caliph from 656–661. In Islamic history, these four rulers are known as the Orthodox Caliphate.

During his two-year rule, Abu Bakr was preoccupied with crushing the revolts of the Arab tribes, who felt that Mohammed's death had dissolved the political control of Islam. The second caliph, Omar, settled both basic problems. He regulated the claims of the army by listing the soldiers on the *diwan,* a payment sheet naming the contribution they were to receive from the public treasury instead of conquered lands. He increased the state domain by confiscating conquered land, and the state treasury by imposing tribute on those who surrendered voluntarily to his armies. Above all, he turned the Bedouin tribesmen under their superb Arab generals against disaffected provinces of the Byzantine and Persian empires. With little opposition from the inhabitants, the armies of Islam destroyed the great cavalry of

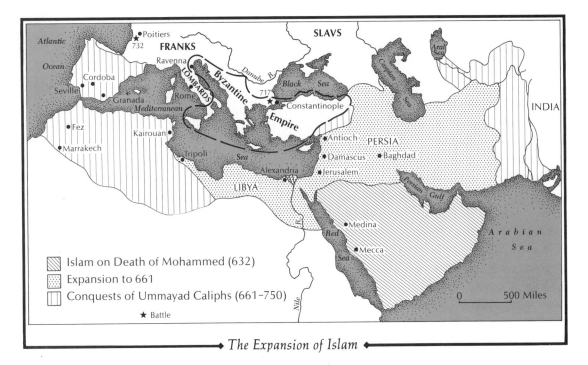

The Expansion of Islam

Byzantium and Persia, riding nimbly around them on their desert ponies; and before Omar was assassinated, they had captured Palestine, Syria, Mesopotamia, Persia itself, and Egypt.

The death of Omar marked the end of the first great period of Islamic expansion. A vast migration of Arabs into the conquered territories took place, perhaps half a million establishing themselves throughout the Fertile Crescent and in Egypt. Overpopulation in Arabia that had been a significant factor in the military expansion was thus relieved, and also the endurance of Arab control of this empire was assured. Unlike Justinian's conquests, the conquests of Islam were to be lasting because they involved not only conversion to the religion of Islam but also the bodily settlement of a new ruling class. Omar's successor, Othman, of the Ummayad family, was a kindly, pious man unresistant to the demands of his near relatives and unsuited to the rigorous demands of the caliphate; and he too was murdered. The succession of Mohammed's son-in-law Ali precipitated civil war with the governor of Syria, Muawiya, who was a member of the important Ummayad family. Ali in turn was murdered, and Muawiya set about restoring stability to the Moslem Empire.

The Ummayad Caliphate, 661–750

The caliphate remained in the hands of the Ummayad family for almost a century, in spite of revolts of the Shi'ites who held that only the descendants of Ali had the right to succeed the prophet and that the Ummayads were usurpers. The Ummayads revived the expansionist drive, using it to whip up religious fervor and the unifying desire for booty. They were foiled in several attempts to capture Constantinople, but they did extend their control into central Asia and western India, along the coastlands of north Africa, and into Spain. It is often suggested that the Arabs intended to link up the forces driving from the west through Spain with those driving into the Byzantine empire somewhere in central Europe, thus completing the Arab control of the whole Mediterranean. But they were now overextended. When the Byzantine armies used Greek fire, an explosive mixture shot through copper tubes, the Moslems abandoned the attempt to capture Constantinople in 717; and in 732, defeated near Tours by the cavalry of the Frankish leader Charles Martel, they withdrew to south of the Pyrenees. In this way, the Arabs established the northwestern and northeastern boundaries of their conquests, which would not be surpassed until the empire of Islam was taken over by the Seljuk Turks; and the caliphs settled down to digest their conquests.

Perhaps most important of all, the Ummayads had recognized that the center of Islamic power was no longer Medina in Arabia, which was now on the periphery of their empire. They moved their capital to Damascus in Syria where, under Byzantine influences, they sponsored a vast building program and encouraged artists, artisans, and scholars in the creation of Islam's own culture as well as the study of early cultures of the eastern Mediterranean. Moreover, they turned their Arab followers into great city builders in the less developed regions between the deserts of Arabia and the more settled portions of their conquests in Palestine and Syria.

The Abbasid Caliphate, 750–1258

The Ummayads did not survive to see the height of the cultural boom they had inaugurated. They were overthrown in 750 by the Abbasid family, the descendants of the uncle of Mohammed, who transferred the capital from Syria to a newly founded city, Baghdad in Iraq. The only member of the Ummayad family to escape the Abbasid sword fled to Spain, where he was recognized as the rightful emir. During the next two centuries, Islam saw an extraordinary intellectual boom, whose centers were the two capitals of the rival caliphates, Abbasid Baghdad and Ummayad Cordoba. Both eventually exerted a beneficial effect on the development of Western culture, the lesser center, Cordoba, probably exercising a greater influence because of its geographical accessibility.

Under such Abbasid rulers as Harun-al-Rashid (reigned 786–809), the character of Islamic rule changed. The caliph withdrew into Oriental seclusion, with all the pomp and ritual of the Persian and Byzantine courts. He abolished the distinction between Arab Moslem and non-Arab Moslem, making all eligible both for office in the royal bureaucracy and a share in

Cordoba from the River Guadalquivir

Already prosperous under the Romans, Cordoba became one of the wealthiest and most cultured cities in Europe when chosen in the eighth century as the capital city of the Ummayad caliphate in Spain.

Spanish National Tourist Office photo

the duties and profits of the army. Moslem life was thus open to the influences of the earlier civilizations— of the conquered territories, Byzantium and Persia, and even of Greece. Possession of the Fertile Crescent brought great economic resources in agriculture, in cereals, olives, and dates. The outer provinces of the empire in Africa and Asia supplied gold and silver, copper, iron, and precious stones. New crops were introduced, such as sugar cane and cotton from India; and silk manufacture was continued in Syria, where Justinian had started it. Captured Chinese soldiers introduced the art of paper-making, which soon spread throughout the empire. Islam now controlled the great trade routes between Asia, Africa, and Europe, including the Red Sea, Persia, and the caravan routes through Bokhara and Samarkand; and it opened up new routes across Russia by the great rivers of the Don and Volga, to trade with Scandinavia. In the tenth and eleventh centuries, however, weak Abbasid rulers were unable to maintain their power, and the empire broke apart. The Ummayads in Spain had never recognized the caliphate in Baghdad. Now a large number of new dynasties established themselves throughout the empire. For a brief period the glory of Islamic culture sparkled from a galaxy of new capitals—Kairouan in Tunisia, Cairo in Egypt, Fez in Morocco, Cordoba in Spain, Palermo in Sicily, Bokhara and Samarkand in Transoxiana. But this disintegration was ended in large part when the Abbasids became the willing captives of the Seljuk Turks in the mid-eleventh century.

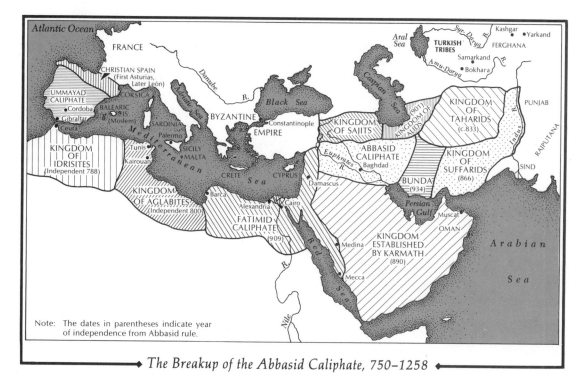

The dates in parentheses indicate year of independence from Abbasid rule.

The Breakup of the Abbasid Caliphate, 750–1258

First Effects of Islamic Conquests on the West

The influence of this Arab expansion on Western civilization went through two clear phases. The first, from the beginning of the Moslem conquests through the eighth century, was largely negative. The conquest of Syria, Palestine, and Egypt obviously struck an enormous blow to Christianity. When the Arab conquests began, the whole of the Mediterranean basin, north and south, was Christian. When the conquests stopped, the whole of north Africa and the Near East was permanently lost to Christianity. From the Christian point of view at least, this was a tragedy, particularly the loss of Christ's own birthplace to the infidel. Christian hatred of the Moslem acted throughout the Middle Ages as a poison in a religion based on brotherly love. It led to condonement of the slave trade in Moslem captives. It inflamed for eight hundred years the war for the Christian reconquest of Spain. It caused the waste of the Crusades in the eleventh, twelfth, and thirteenth centuries, which diverted the labor, power and precariously small resources of Europe to the chimera of reconquering Palestine. During the years of the conquests and immediately afterwards, Mediterranean trade inevitably dwindled, affected by war, Christian and Moslem unwillingness to maintain direct economic contact, Arab piracy, and the Byzantine empire's use of its naval power to isolate the lost provinces of Syria and Egypt from trade with the Franks.

The Cultural Impact of Islam on the West

Once the Arabs had stabilized their empire, and had transformed a state of mounted warriors in constant motion into a settled bureaucratic state, their influence on the West was largely beneficial, even though the Arabs were not interested in what the Europeans might teach them. "The peoples of the north," wrote a tenth-century Arab geographer, "are those for whom the sun is distant from the Zenith. . . . Cold and damp prevail in those regions, and snow and ice follow one another in endless succession. The warm humor is lacking among them; their bodies are large, their natures gross, their manners harsh, their understanding dull and their tongues heavy." The achievements of five hundred years of medieval scholarship made no better impression. "We have heard of late that in the lands of the Franks, that is, the country of Rome and its dependencies on the northern shore of the Mediterranean, the philosophic sciences flourish," wrote a well-informed Arab scholar. "But God knows best what goes on in those parts." The Europeans, however, never lost their interest in the Near East. Trade of Byzantium with its possessions in Italy had never been entirely broken off; and these cities—Venice, Amalfi, Gaeta, Salerno, Bari—after first profiting from a virtual monopoly of the Byzantine trade, began to open up a lucrative commerce with Islam itself. The Jews, however, acted as the main intermediary. A famous passage from an Arab geographer of the ninth century described Jewish traders from the south of France:

[*They*] *speak Arabic, Persian, Greek, Frankish, Spanish, and Slavonic. They travel from west to east and from east to west, by land and by sea. From the west they bring eunuchs, slave-girls, boys, brocade, castor-skins, marten and other furs, and swords. They take ship from Frank-land in the western Mediterranean sea and land at Farama, whence they take their merchandise on camel-back to Qulzum, a distance of twenty-five parasangs. Then they sail on the eastern* [*Red*] *Sea from Qulzum, to Al-Jar and Jedda, and onward to Sind, India and China. From China they bring back musk, aloes, camphor, cinnamon, and other products of those parts, and return to Qulzum. Then they transport them to Farama and sail again on the western sea. Some sail with their goods to Constantinople and sell them to the Greeks, and some take them to the king of the Franks and sell them there.*

Sometimes they bring their goods from Frank-land across the western sea and unload at Antioch. Then they travel three days' march overland to Al-Jabiya, whence they sail down the Euphrates to Baghdad, then down the Tigris to Ubulla, and from Ubulla to Uman, Sind, India and China.[1]

During the ninth and tenth centuries, therefore, European trade across the Mediterranean revived, and the cities of Europe soon began to revive also.

From the Arabs, a vast range of new products and manufactures en-

---

[1] Bernard Lewis, *The Arabs in History* (London: Hutchinson's University Library, 1958), p. 90.

tered Europe, mainly through Spain, though the Crusaders also later brought back many things from the Holy Land. The Arabs introduced rice, sugar cane and cotton, oranges and lemons, thus changing the distinctive character of Mediterranean agriculture from its reliance on olives and vines. Paper manufacture came to Spain through Morocco, and made possible the invention of the printing press in Germany in the fifteenth century. Arab handcraft produced the great steel blades of Toledo, the leather of Cordoba, and heavy silks that rivaled those of Byzantium.

In Spain, the Europeans undertook the study of not only the achievements of Islamic culture but the Greek heritage too. The Ummayads established their capital in Spain at the bridgehead on the river Guadalquivir, in the town of Cordoba, which in the ninth and tenth centuries was second only to Constantinople among the cities of Europe. Cordoba had perhaps half a million inhabitants, three thousand mosques, three hundred public baths, great libraries filled with Arabic and Greek manuscripts, numerous hospitals and medical schools, and a great university attached to the mosque that rivaled those of Cairo and Baghdad. Moreover, Christian, Jew, and Moslem lived side by side in a toleration enforced by the caliph, thus making fairly easy prolonged residence by Christian students from the

Air View, Cordoba
The city plan of Arab Cordoba is preserved in the maze of narrow streets surrounding the vast square of the mosque's outer walls. Spanish National Tourist Office photo

The Giralda of Seville
Originally a minaret, the Giralda was preserved as a belltower when the mosque of Seville was torn down to make way for a Gothic cathedral. Built in 1196, it displays the delicate tracery that the Arabs attained by use of red brick. The top floor, in Renaissance style, was added in the sixteenth century. Spanish National Tourist Office photo

northern countries. This tradition of learning was carried on by the smaller Moslem states that succeeded the caliphate: Seville, until its capture by the Christians in 1248; and Granada, the last stronghold of the Moslems in Spain.

Islamic Philosophy, Science, and Medicine

The transmission of Arab learning was thus made in the most direct way possible. Christians came to get it for themselves. And in the state of El-Andalus, or Moslem Spain, the achievements of the whole Arab world, including those of faraway Baghdad, were available for study. According to an English chronicler, Pope Sylvester II (Gerbert of Aurillac) learned a surprising variety of subjects in Spain:

Gerbert, coming among these people, satisfied his desires. There he surpassed Ptolemy with the astrolabe, and Alcandraeus in astronomy, and Julius Firmicus in judicial astrology; there he learned what the singing and flight of birds portended; there he acquired the art of calling up spirits from hell: in short, whatever, hurtful or salutary, human curiosity had discovered.

The greatest number of Christians came to study classical books that had been brought from the East, even though many were in Arabic translation. Cordoba had its center for translation from Greek into Arabic; and later the city of Toledo, once in Christian hands, became the main center in Europe for the translation into Latin of Arabic translations from the Greek. In this indirect way, many of the greatest manuscripts of Athens, including much of Plato and Aristotle, entered medieval Europe. Christian scholars were also interested in the philosophical writings of great Arab writers, especially those who had divorced their philosophy from religion by basing their writings on classical Greek philosophy. The most important of all these writers for Christians was Averroës (1126–1198), a protégé of the caliph of Marrakech. Averroës was admired by Christians for a massive commentary that he wrote on the works of Aristotle, which was required reading in the University of Paris. His assertion that religion was an allegorical way of expressing philosophical ideas and the emphasis that he put on reason as a method of attaining philosophical truth led some of his admirers into the heresy, called Averroism, of ignoring the truth of revealed religion. For ignoring the truth of Islam's revealed religion, Averroës's writings in Arabic were burned by the caliph; Saint Thomas Aquinas thundered against the Christian Averroists, although he himself followed many of the writings of Averroës.

The impact of Moslem science and medicine was less controversial. The greatest medical writer of the Middle Ages was Avicenna, whose textbook on medicine was the main one studied in European universities for several hundred years. And it was an Arab physician in Spain who told the Christians that the Black Death of the fourteenth century was not an act of God but a disease spread by contagion:

To those who say, "How can we admit the possibility of infection while the religious law denies it?" we reply that the existence of contagion is established by experience, investigation, the evidence of the senses and trustworthy reports. These facts constitute a sound argument. The fact of contagion becomes clear to the investigator who notices how he who establishes contact with the afflicted gets the disease, whereas he who is not in contact remains safe, and how transmission is effected through garments, vessels and earrings.[2]

While the Arab contribution to medicine was largely one of saving what was already known, the Arabs did make advances in the use of drugs, especially herbs. Many Arabic medical terms have entered the English language, though not always with the original medicinal purpose implied. *Julep, syrup, soda,* and *alcohol* were originally medical terms. From Arab scientists, European scholars took our present system of numerals, which are not Arabic

[2] Philip K. Hitti, *History of the Arabs from the Earliest Times to the Present* (New York: St. Martin's Press, 1964), p. 576.

but which had been brought by the Arabs from India; the study of algebra, itself an Arabic word; and the study of astronomy.

Islamic Art and Architecture in Spain

Islamic art and architecture were admired but rarely imitated. It is impossible to mistake a piece of Islamic art. The Court of Lions of the Alhambra, a Persian carpet, Damascus tiles, Baghdad silk, or a Cairo pitcher of rock crystal could not be mistaken for the work of any other culture. The reason for this is that all Islamic art is dominated by the Koran and the Arabic language. The Koran laid down the religious ceremonies that were to be followed by Moslems and hence the primary building in all Moslem architecture, the mosque, was developed in a set pattern to satisfy these functions. Ritual group prayer, including prostration, is prescribed. Hence the house of prayer is a broad, carpeted room where worshippers can assemble in lines; and it has two outstanding architectural features, an empty niche called a *mihrab*, indicating the position of Mecca, and a pulpit on a staircase from which prayer can be led. Since ablution before prayer is required, there is a large open-air court with fountains and washbasins. For the muezzin to call the faithful to prayer, a tower called a minaret was added later. From the simple temple of palm branches that Mohammed constructed to the Taj Mahal, the principles of the mosque remain the same, and can be seen in great splendor at Cordoba.

The entrance to the Cordoba mosque was a wide courtyard, the Patio of the Orange Trees, where the Moslems washed. Rows of orange trees in the court were prolonged inside the building by lines of Roman and Visigothic columns, set in a series of eleven parallel naves crossed by a similar number of aisles. Originally there was no outer wall between the court and the interior, and court and mosque were linked by the lines of trees and columns. As each ruler felt the need for a larger mosque, he simply added a few more aisles, so that the ultimate sense was not of being in a building with a central core but rather of walking through a colorful and somewhat confusing forest of porphyry, jasper, and marble beneath arches composed in alternate bands of red brick and white stone. The tragedy of all Spanish history is symbolized in this mosque. In 1523, the cathedral clergy, with the permission of Emperor Charles V, hacked out a large space in the center of the mosque, removing sixty columns, and built there a complete Christian church in the shape of a cross. When Charles V saw what they had done, he was appalled. "You have built here what you or anyone else might build," he said, "but you have destroyed what was unique in the world."

It is in the Alhambra palace in Granada, however, that one understands the predominance in all Islamic art of decorative ornament cut in low relief. The Koran and more especially the Sunna forbade the representation of living beings, especially human beings and animals. Although this proscription was later evaded, most Moslem art was based on decoration by

Entrance Gate, Mosque of Cordoba

This lavishly decorated gateway of the eighth century illustrates the decorative use made by Arab architects of the horseshoe arch. Stylized flower patterns were traced in stucco, while diamond patterns in the square frame are composed of colored tiles and mosaics. Spanish National Tourist Office photo

The Catholic Church Within the Mosque of Cordoba

The flamboyant Gothic church erected in the heart of the Arab mosque symbolizes the final triumph of the seven-hundred-year long Spanish Crusade, and appears ponderous and overdecorated in comparison with the simplicity of the Moslem arches. Spanish National Tourist Office photo

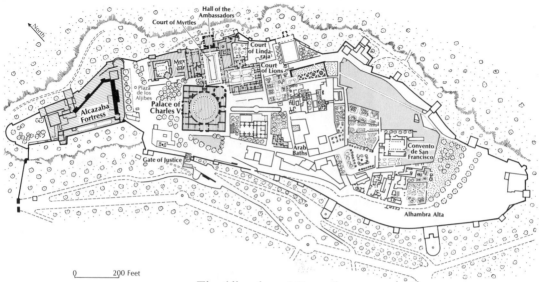

The Alhambra of Granada

use of forms not deriving from nature, and on the use of the Arabic language, especially quotations from the Koran, as the principal form of decoration. The result of this kind of concentration for more than fourteen centuries was an amazing variety of decorative forms in all types of art and handicraft—in leather, steel, ivory, textiles, carpets, wood, stone, stucco, pottery, and glass.

The Alhambra was the fortified palace of the Nazarite dynasty, which ruled Granada from 1232 to 1492. It stands on a tall hill on the edge of the town, commanding broad views in every direction. From the distance it looks like a typical medieval fortress, with bare crenelated walls, rough and primitive, waiting for the Christian invasion that was bound to come across the snowy heights of the Sierra Nevada. The palace was divided into three parts. Administration and justice was carried on in the *mexuar,* the first part a visitor entered. The mexuar led to the Court of Myrtles, a long narrow patio richly decorated at one end with a series of round arches on delicate columns, with a huge reflecting pool in the center, beyond which was the Hall of the Ambassadors. Here the enthroned sultan received official visitors, amid one of the most beautiful creations of Islamic craftsmanship. Although the room was two stories high and thirty-seven feet square, every flat space on walls, floor, and ceiling was covered with a scintillating pattern of sculptured plaster, tile, or cedarwood. Motifs used by Moslem craftsmen included geometrical designs like squares, circles, ellipses, and cones; more complicated patterns of swirls, scrolls, cusps, and stars; leaves, flowers, birds, animals; and strange stalagmite formations and long borders of Arabic script. In the Court of Lions, where the harem was situated, the art of decoration fused with the exquisite use of the Moorish arch into an unrivaled composition of colors and shapes. The grey gravel of the courtyard

The Hall of the Ambassadors, The Alhambra of Granada
The sultan received important visitors in this sumptuously decorated hall. The stucco and tile that covers every space in the 75-foot high room displays all the favorite motifs of Moslem decorative art. Spanish National Tourist Office photo

Exterior View, The Alhambra of Granada
In the fifteenth century, the Alhambra was the defense bastion of the last remaining Arab dynasty in Spain. Its vast fortifications give little hint of the delicacy of the interior rooms and courtyards of the red-tiled palace in the foreground. Spanish National Tourist Office photo

contrasted with the white of the hundred and twenty-four marble columns, the fretwork above them, and the muted red tile of the roof, while from every passageway the tile and stalactite roofs shimmered with the reflected sunshine. Finally in a last cypress-shaded patio overlooking the valley of Granada, the Nazarite dynasty inscribed their own farewell to the jewel they had created:

> *I am not alone, for a delightful garden can be contemplated from this spot.*
> *Such a place has never before been seen.*
> *This is the palace of crystal, he who looks on it will believe he regards the*
> *   mighty ocean and will be filled with fear.*
> *All this is the work of Imán Ibn Nasar, may God keep his grandeur for*
> *   other kings.*
> *His forebears in ancient time were of the most noble, giving hospitality to*
> *   the Prophet and his family.*[3]

Charlemagne and the Carolingian Empire

In the sixth and seventh centuries, many of the states created by the Germanic tribes from fragments of the Roman Empire, such as the Visigothic state in Spain or the Ostrogothic state in Italy, lost the power to control and defend their subjects, and proved easy prey to new invaders. The most important exception was the kingdom of the Franks, which was able to halt the Moslem advance at Tours in 732. Of all the Germanic peoples, the Franks were the most aggressively self-confident. Their tribal law began: "The illustrious tribe of the Franks, established by God the Creator, brave in war, faithful in peace, wise in their counsels, of noble body, of immaculate purity, of choice physique, courageous, quick and impetuous, converted to the Catholic faith, free of heresy." Many but by no means all of these qualities had been displayed by Clovis, who at the end of the fifth century had brought most of France and the southern part of Germany under his control; but his family, the Merovingians, had proved to be "rois fainéants," do-nothing kings. In the words of Charlemagne's biographer, Einhard, "The wealth and power of the kingdom was in the hands of the Prefects of the Court, who were called Mayors of the Palace, and exercised entire sovereignty. The King, contented with the mere royal title, with long hair and flowing beard, used to sit upon the throne, and act the part of a ruler, listening to ambassadors, whencesoever they came, and giving at their departure, as though of his own power, answers which he had been instructed or commanded to give."[4]

---

[3] F. Prieto-Moreno, *Granada,* trans. John Forrester (Barcelona: Noguer, 1957), p. 19.

[4] A. J. Grant, ed., *Early Lives of Charlemagne* (London: Chatto and Windus, 1926), p. 8.

The tough Frankish virtues were exemplified instead by a new family that had built up vast landed estates in the region of eastern Belgium and, through sheer ability in administration, battles, and intrigue, had kept the office of chief minister, or mayor of the palace, in their hands for several generations. The greatest rulers of this family, Charles Martel, his son Pepin, and his grandson Charlemagne, all followed a similar policy. They sought to unify the Frankish kingdom by canalizing the warlike energies of the local lords on their own behalf. They tried to extend Christianity in the area that could be exploited for taxes and new fiefs, to the pagan tribes of Frisia and Saxony. They struck an alliance with the Catholic Church, supporting the pope in Italy against the Lombards and granting rich lands in the newly Christianized territories to new bishops, accepting in return the religious sanction of their political authority and the collaboration of the clergy in bureaucracy and educational tasks of the kingdom. And they attempted to drive back the Moslems, first blocking their advance into France, and then beginning the long reconquest of the Iberian peninsula. Pepin abolished Merovingian rule by asking the pope the loaded question, "What should be done with kings who were living in the kingdom of the Franks without exercising royal authority?" The pope had replied, in an equally disingenuous way, that "it was best that those be named king who exercised the highest authority." With this sanction, Pepin had packed the last Merovingian king off into a monastery, and was crowned king of the Franks himself, in 754, and he left to Charles, whose exploits soon won him the title of "the Great" (Charlemagne), an adequate treasury, large family estates, effective cavalry, and a papal alliance that could be used both to repress internal discontent and to bless external aggression.

Charlemagne's Character and Military Policy

Charlemagne strode uninhibited into the rough Germanic world, determined to dominate it as a new King David. In a society where physical prowess was the basis for prestige, Charlemagne excelled. In the stylized court of Constantinople, Justinian could get away with being thin and sallow. According to Einhard, Charlemagne was a warrior's king:

His body was large and strong; his stature tall but not ungainly, for the measure of his height was seven times the length of his own feet. The top of his head was round; his eyes were very large and piercing. His nose was rather larger than is usual; he had beautiful white hair, and his expression was brisk and cheerful; so that, whether sitting or standing, his appearance was dignified and impressive. . . . His step was firm and the whole carriage of his body manly, his voice was clear, but hardly so strong as you would have expected. He had good health, but for four years before his death was frequently attacked by fevers, and at last was lame on one foot. Even then, he followed his own opinion rather than the advice of his doctors, whom he almost hated, be-

**Sixteenth-century
Portrait of Charlemagne
by Albrecht Dürer**
Deutsche Zentrale für Fremdenverkehr

*cause they advised him to give up the roast meat to which he was accustomed,
and eat boiled instead.*[5]

Charlemagne was constantly at war. Every year in the spring his army
would gather for the annual campaign. He defeated the Lombards in Italy,
and took the title King of the Lombards. After thirty years of fighting the
Saxons were finally subdued. The defeat of Bavaria brought his kingdom to
the upper Danube, from which he mounted a great campaign against the
Hunnish people called the Avars.

The latter campaign was as profitable for Charles as Justinian's attack
on the Vandals, and for similar reasons. He was able to seize from the
Avars all the booty they had been accumulating in a century of depreda-

[5] Ibid., pp. 37–38.

tions, especially the large tribute in gold that had been paid by Constantinople. It was said that fifteen wagonloads of gold, silver, and precious clothing were sent back to Charlemagne's capital after the defeat of the Avars; but his armies left a desolation. Einhard wrote:

How many battles were fought there, and how much blood was shed is still shown by the uninhabited condition of Pannonia [Hungary], and the district, in which the palace of the Kagans was, is so desolate that there is not so much as a trace of human habitation. All the nobles of the Huns were killed in this war; all their glory passed away. Their money, and all the treasures they had collected for so long were carried away, nor can the memory of man recall any war waged by the Franks by which they were so much enriched, and their wealth so much increased.

The Talisman of Charlemagne
Carolingian jewelry, like this charm supposedly worn by Charlemagne, favored heavy settings of gold and large gems. German Information Center photo

Charlemagne was unable to win the major victory he sought against the Moslems in Spain, but he did establish a foothold on the southern slopes of the Pyrenees, from which the reconquest could be continued. By these conquests, he established an empire that ran from the southern Pyrenees, the Mediterranean shore of France, and central Italy, to Hungary in the East and southern Denmark in the North.

Aachen, Charlemagne's New Imperial Capital

Charlemagne could see, after his conquests, only two rulers who could compare with him—the Abbasid caliph in Baghdad and the Byzantine emperor in Constantinople. He was aware of how greatly inferior the Franks were in culture to both those empires; and Caliph Harun-al-Rashid helped remind him by sending as presents "monkeys, balsam, nard, unguents of various kinds, spices, scents, and many drugs, all in such profusion that it seemed as if the East had been left bare so that the West might be filled," and an elephant called Abul-Abaz, which became Charlemagne's special delight. Although Charlemagne enjoyed the primitive Frankish life—he disliked luxurious foreign clothes, ate simple food, lived like a clan leader surrounded by his relatives, and refused elaborate ceremonial—he was determined that his own empire should rival that of Constantinople. Like Constantine, he ordered the building at Aachen in western Germany of a new capital, as a second Rome and a new Athens. (Constantine had already built a second Rome, but Charlemagne was not prepared to call his a third.) Charlemagne picked Aachen because he liked the hot springs, and because of its central position in his dominions. It had few other advantages, however, and was abandoned as a capital soon after his death. Like Constantine, however, Charlemagne stood on a high spot, and designated the place for his forum, his senate, the theater, the baths, and the aqueduct. He brought in architects and artisans from his whole kingdom. To obtain antique columns and mosaics, he even asked the pope to let him demolish the walls

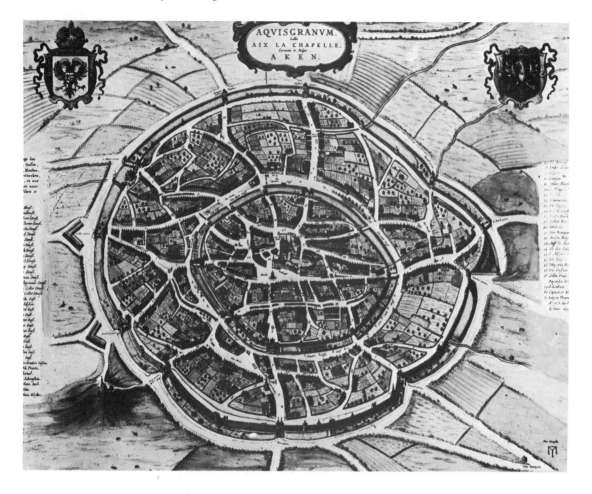

Sixteenth-Century City Plan, Aachen

The successive enlargements of Aachen may be easily distinguished in this sixteenth-century drawing. Charlemagne's small settlement is grouped around the Palatine Chapel, in the very center of town. German Information Center photo

and floors of the palace in Ravenna. But what he created was worlds removed from another Constantinople. In Aachen, there was merely a large palace, surrounded with walls like a country villa, and linked by a long colonnade with an octagonal Palatine Chapel. Around the palace, homes for the officials and scholars of the palace and the palace clergy were built; and merchants established their warehouses to supply the king.

The most ambitious building was the chapel. Charlemagne had never visited Constantinople but he had asked his ambassadors for exact descriptions of the churches there; and in the lands he had conquered from the Lombards, he possessed the finest church Justinian had built in Italy, San Vitale in Ravenna. He sent his architects to use that church as a model. The contrast between San Vitale and Charlemagne's Palatine Chapel is, however, revealing of the difference in character of the two empires. The octagonal ground plan and the three superimposed colonnades are similar. But Charlemagne's architect simply neglected to include the curving apses that in San Vitale create a sense of undulation, of eddying motion accentuated by the play of darkness, semidarkness, and light. He also did away with the columns that in San Vitale go from ground to dome, replacing them on the first floor with eight huge base pillars split from the upper floors by a heavy pediment. And yet the marble columns, the alternating colors of the reliefs, and the glimpses of sparkling mosaic behind, give al-

**Interior of Charlemagne's
Palatine Chapel at
Aachen**
Bettmann Archive

most a nostalgic reminder of the Byzantine beauty of Ravenna. The church is a Frankish interpretation of the Byzantine style, emphasizing strength and solidity rather than lightness and elegance. A value system can be seen in the treatment of space.

The Carolingian Renaissance

Charlemagne pursued his emulation of Constantinople by ordering a rebirth of culture. "Because it is our obligation to improve constantly the condition of our churches," he wrote in one law, "we are anxious to restore with diligent zeal the workshops of letters which are almost deserted because of the negligence of our ancestors, and we invite by our own example all who are able to learn the practice of the liberal arts." He established new schools throughout his kingdom. He brought the English scholar Alcuin to head the palace school in Aachen; and Alcuin's division of education into the *trivium,* of grammar, rhetoric, and dialectic, and the *quadrivium,* of arithmetic, geometry, music, and astronomy, became the basis for education throughout the rest of the Middle Ages. Large numbers of manuscripts of the Bible, the Church fathers, and classical writers were copied; and his

Cover of the Ashburnham-Lindau Gospel, Ninth Century
This is one of the finest examples of jeweled book covers from the Carolingian period. The Pierpont Morgan Library, M. 1 front cover

scholars developed the modern form of handwriting, called Carolingian minuscule. Charlemagne himself labored manfully but in vain to learn how to read and write, and kept his writing tablets under his pillow. For all his efforts, however, Charlemagne's court produced no great writers. If Aachen was not a second Rome, it was even less a new Athens.

Charlemagne's Revival of the Roman Empire

The most important requirement for Charlemagne in his determination to equal Byzantium was, however, to be named Roman emperor. The chance came in 799–800 when the pope had fled from Rome to seek safety with Charlemagne, and the throne in Constantinople was held by a woman. Charlemagne was under pressure from many sides to profit from this situation. Alcuin told him he was now superior to both pope and Byzantine emperor. Representatives of the opposition in Constantinople asked him to become emperor there. The church synod tried to persuade him that a woman could not hold the throne of Constantinople, and that therefore the empire could be re-created in the West. On Christmas Day, 800, while Charlemagne was praying during mass in Saint Peter's, the pope placed a crown on his head and the people in the church acclaimed him: "To Charles Augustus crowned by God the great and peaceful emperor of the Romans, life and victory!" Nothing was clear about this coronation, either then or now. Einhard said that Charlemagne did not wish to be crowned, but this was probably untrue. He may have been displeased by being crowned by the pope, since it appeared that the Church was naming the emperor. The murky relationship to Byzantium was not cleared when the Franks persuaded the Byzantine emperor to recognize the Frankish king as emperor, but not as Roman emperor, since that left uncertain what he was emperor of. To Charlemagne, however, at the very minimum the title implied that he was the equal of the emperor in Constantinople, and it led to centuries of animosity between the two powers. It also gave the Germanic rulers the title to rule in Italy, and led them into four hundred years of wasted effort in their attempts to hold onto an empire on both sides of the Alps, a goal that brought them into direct conflict with the increasingly ambitious papacy.

The fragility of Charlemagne's achievement was soon revealed. The desire of the local lords to throw off the burdensome controls of the central government were facilitated by the division of the empire at the Treaty of Verdun in 843 among his three grandsons. The western third and eastern third of the empire were later to develop into the modern countries of France and Germany. But the central section, which was taken by the eldest grandson together with the imperial title, lacked all unity, since it consisted of a variegated band of peoples and topography running from Holland in the North to Italy in the South. The central kingdom was divided again and again for the rest of the century, while the eastern and western kingdoms, although nominally united under their kings, were in the control of the feu-

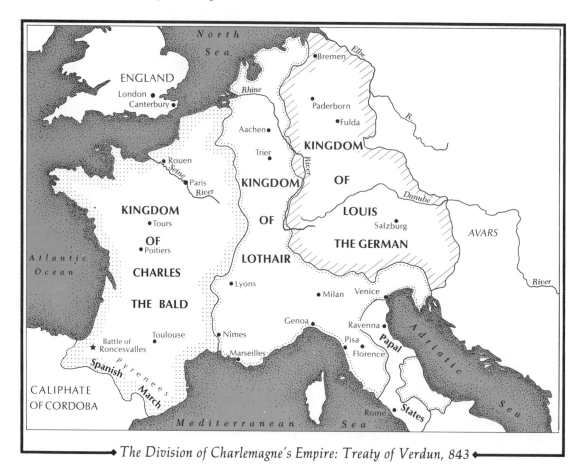

The Division of Charlemagne's Empire: Treaty of Verdun, 843

dal lords. This fragmentation of authority made the whole of western Europe an easy prey to new invasions by Moslems, Magyars, and Vikings.

Invasions Renewed: Moslem, Magyar, Viking

The new invasions from South, East, and North lasted for more than two centuries. Under their impact, the populations of western and central Europe completed their withdrawal to the village, the basic cell of civilized life, which they had begun during the Germanic invasions.

The renewed attacks by the Moslems were mounted by the emirs of the North African states who struck by sea to capture most of the important islands of the Mediterranean, including Sardinia, Corsica, Sicily, and Crete. From southern Italy, they mounted plundering raids, burning the Benedictine monastery at Monte Cassino and sacking churches on the outskirts of Rome itself. They even attacked Provence in southern France. By the

Invasions of the Moslems, Magyars, and Vikings: 9th to 11th Centuries

tenth century, however, they began to weaken, and the Byzantine emperor was able to retake southern Italy. In the eleventh century the city-states of Genoa and Pisa captured the islands of Sardinia and Corsica, while Sicily was taken from Moslem control by the Normans.

The Magyars were a nomadic tribe of mounted warriors, possibly related to the Turks, who entered Europe from the East and struck through the Danube valley. For almost half a century they roamed with little resistance through southern Germany, across Alsace almost to Paris, southwards past the Alps, and in a great loop along both coasts of Italy. They were fi-

Viking Ship
The "long ship" of the Vikings carried about 30 oarsmen and could hold up to 90 warriors, whose painted shields were hung on either side of the vessel. With such ships, the Vikings struck without warning at any of the coastal towns of Europe.
Royal Norwegian Embassy Information Service, 825 Third Avenue, New York, N.Y. 10022

nally halted by the German emperor Otto I at the battle of Lechfeld in 955 and compelled to settle in Hungary.

Probably driven by overpopulation at home, the Vikings, or Norsemen, of Scandinavia first began to attack the northern coasts of Europe in the eighth century. In their long boats, which they propelled by oar and sail, they could attack any part of Europe with impunity. They arrived in total surprise, drove inland along the rivers, and withdrew with the plunder of church and village. They showed no respect for the manuscript collections of the monasteries, depriving us of an irreplaceable source of historical documentation by burning them. In the ninth century, they renewed their attacks along the North Sea coast of Germany, Holland, and France, and on eastern England and Scotland. But soon their expeditions crossed the dangerous northern waters to Iceland, Greenland, possibly even to America, while others sailed south from the Faeroe islands to attack northern Scotland and Ireland. One group from Sweden established itself in the Russian trading town of Novgorod, and sent an expedition along the Dvina and Dnieper rivers to the Black Sea and on to attack Constantinople itself. In the West, the Vikings soon ceased to return home from their annual expeditions, but instead established winter quarters on island bases at the mouths of the Thames, Seine, and Loire rivers, and later on the mainland. For a time they controlled most of northern England; and in 911, they accepted the French king's offer of the land at the mouth of the Seine, a province that was renamed Normandy. From there, the Norman Duke William mounted a successful invasion of England in 1066. He killed its Saxon king, and made himself king instead. Shortly after, other mercenary Norman knights wrested Sicily from the Moslems and southern Italy from the By-

Cathedral of Cefalú, Sicily
After overthrowing the Arab rulers of Sicily in the late eleventh century, the Normans erected massive churches in romanesque style, regardless of its unsuitability to the Mediterranean climate. The cathedral at Cefalú on the north coast was begun in 1131 by Roger II, the grandson of the island's conqueror. Italian State Tourist Office photo

zantines. Although the Vikings were at length absorbed into the native populations, especially after they had accepted Christianity, the effect of two centuries of their raids was to undermine the political stability of all the successor states of the Carolingian empire. Their invasions, combined with those of the Moslems and Magyars, forced native populations to develop new economic and governmental institutions of a localized character, in order to survive the period of disorder. Those institutions were feudalism and manorialism.

Feudalism

The word feudalism has been used by historians in various ways during the past three hundred years to describe the institutions of European society in the period from the ninth to the fourteenth century, although the word was never used by people who lived in the Middle Ages. The word is derived from the Latin word feodum, or fief, which was the piece of land a lord granted to his retainer. For a long time, the whole political and economic structure of the central Middle Ages was referred to by historians as feudalism. In this chapter, however, we shall follow the contemporary, more restricted use of the word to refer only to the system of government which had come into existence by the end of the invasions of the ninth century, in which defense, justice, and even the provision of the most elementary public services were carried out by lords related to each other not by common service to the state but by private, personal ties established by contract.

Origins of Feudalism as a System of Government

Feudalism as a system of government evolved slowly and with wide variations in different parts of Europe during the six centuries following the breakup of the Roman Empire in the West. Only in the eleventh century, and then only in the several states of northern Europe, did feudalism attain full development as a legally organized and binding set of political relationships. As a result it is possible to see in this long development the amalgamation of institutions deriving from several different societies, and it is impossible to say that feudalism derived primarily from the one or the other.

Two basic feudal ideas probably derived from the Roman Empire. From the bands of clients who waited on the powerful elite in late republican and early imperial days may have come the notion that a freeman could commend himself to a lord in return for protection and material support, while the lord or magnate in the Roman colonate of the third and fourth centuries exercised powers of administration similar to those later exercised by a feudal lord over his manor. In the Germanic tribes, the chiefs had bands of warriors with whom they consulted and who owed personal loyalty and service. The concept of doing military service in return for the grant of land may have originated in the eighth century, when Charles Martel distributed confiscated church lands to endow a number of cavalrymen he enlisted to help drive back the Moslems from France. At that time he adapted the system of the "cataphract," or the "enclosed" or armored man on a great horse, which the Byzantines had taken from the Persians, to the conditions of eighth-century Europe. The great horse was just what its name implied, a specially bred animal valued as the equivalent of four oxen or six cows, capable of carrying the knight and his heavy armor, shield, sword, and long iron-tipped lance; and this horse became an even more effective weapon in the eighth century with the use of the foot-stirrup, which enabled the warrior to strike his opponent with the combined force of his own muscles and his horse's charging body. These separate institutions—the personal relationship of vassal and lord, the tenure of land in return for service, and the performance of the duties of governmental administration by the warrior class—had been welded into a distinctive form of government by the tenth century.

The Lay Vassal

This feudal government was constructed like a pyramid, a hierarchial structure to assure the main functions of government. At the base of the pyramid were thousands of lay lords who lived on their own manors. Each local lord provided justice in his own court, protected the inhabitants of the manor from disorder within and attack from without, and organized the few public services like maintenance of roads. What was unique about this system was the nature of the lord's ties with those above him in the political hierarchy. In theory, every lord was the vassal of another, higher lord, from whom he held his land. The grant of land was at first called a *beneficium*, or benefice, but by about 1100 it was usually called a *feodum*, or fief. In return for his fief, the knight owed his suzerain, who was the person who had granted him the fief, a well-defined number of duties. He had to appear, on horseback and in armor, at his own expense, to fight for his lord—usually for forty days a year. If he had been given a fief so big that it could be subdivided to support several knights, then he had to appear with that specific number of knights and the servants they needed. He owed his lord a financial gift or aid on three occasions: when the lord's eldest son was knighted, when his eldest daughter was married, or if the lord had to be ransomed. He had to offer hospitality to his lord and his retinue as they traveled around the suzerain's possessions and he had to appear at the lord's court when summoned to give council or to share the trial of one of his peers, or equals. In return, the suzerain provided the fief on which his vassal lived, protected him when necessary from outside attack, and provided justice for him in his court. Moreover, the right of the vassal's family to inherit his fief

Ekkehard and Uta, Naumburg Cathedral
The so-called Naumburg Master transferred to this wonderful secular portrait of the founders of the cathedral the skills he acquired in study of the Gothic sculpture of France. Few statues more beautifully capture the self-assurance of the knightly class at the height of its prestige. German Information Center photo

came to be recognized, on the condition that his heirs paid an inheritance tax or relief, which often amounted to a year's revenue from the fief.

This relationship of lord and holder of the fief was later converted into a moral obligation by the ceremony of homage and fealty. The vassal knelt before his lord, put his hands, with palms together, between his lord's hands, and swore to become his man (homage) and to be faithful to him against all men (fealty). This oath established a relationship of mutual trust that was fundamental to feudal society. All the great medieval poems glorified this relationship, especially the *Song of Roland*, written about 1100, when the feudal relationship had been fully elaborated. As Roland led a rearguard action for the defense of Charlemagne's main army in the dangerous pass of Roncesvalles in the Pyrenees, the poet has Roland tell his friend Oliver, "For his lord man should suffer great hardships, should endure extremes of heat and cold, should lose his blood and his flesh. Strike with thy lance! And I will strike with Durendal, my good sword which the king gave me. If I die, may he who has it be able to say that it belonged to a noble vassal." [6] And after the action, looking around on the dying warriors who have sacrificed themselves, Charlemagne gives them the highest praise possible. "Lord barons, may God have mercy on you! May he grant all your souls rest in Paradise! May he set them amidst the Holy flowers! Never have I seen better vassals than you." [7]

The ceremonial of knighthood developed rapidly from the eleventh century. It began with the Christianization and the romanticizing of the ceremony of becoming a knight. From early childhood, the son of a lord was put into training for that day. He was apprenticed to another lord, in whose service he moved from duties like helping put on armor and leading the horse, through mock battles with other apprentices, to full-scale charges with armor and lance. Usually at twenty or twenty-one he took a purifying ritual bath, prayed all night in the church, took confession and communion, and was finally admitted to the fraternity of knights by his lord, who presented him with his sword. In one medieval poem, the young man is taking a quick nap after his night's vigil in the church when his uncle arrives.

"Come, Fromondin, get up. You must not sleep too long, good sire. The great tournament ought already to be forming." The young man leaped from his bed on hearing the voice, and the squires entered to serve him. They quickly booted and clothed him. In the presence of all, Count William of Montclin girded the sword on him with a golden belt. "Dear nephew," he said, "I enjoin thee not to trust false and dissolute men; given a long life thou shalt be a mighty prince. Always be strong, victorious, and redoubtable to all thy enemies. Give the vair and gray to many deserving men. It is the way to attain honor." "Everything is in God's hands," answered Fromondin. Then they led him to a costly horse. He mounted him with an easy bound, and they handed him a shield emblazoned with a lion. [8]

Knighthood's high standards were rarely achieved, however. Vassals often deserted their lords, and indeed the practice of permitting a man to hold land from two or more lords often compelled him to decide which of the two he would let down. Many lords oppressed their peasants, and were

---

[6] C. Stephenson, *Medieval Feudalism* (Ithaca, N.Y.: Cornell University Press, 1942), p. 22.

[7] Joan Evans, *Life in Medieval France* (London: Oxford University Press, 1925), p. 101.

[8] Cited in A. Luchaire, *Social France at the Time of Philip Augustus* (New York: F. Ungar, 1957), pp. 345–46.

The Rider of Bamberg
One of the few free-standing equestrian statues of the Middle Ages, this figure was completed for the cathedral of the south German city of Bamberg in 1245. German Tourist Information Office photo

little better than armed robbers who stole the animals, crops, money, and even the clothes of their neighbors. One French abbey complained that their noble neighbor had broken down their fences, seized eleven cows, cut down their fruit trees, tied up their servants, and at various times helped himself to tunics, capes, cheeses, stockings, and shoes of their servants. Tournaments held in peacetime were vicious bloodlettings, in war the sack of a city was an open invitation to pillage and murder.

The Church as Feudal Lord

As a great landholder, the Church had to become part of this system of rights and obligations. Throughout the Middle Ages, the Church came to hold an increasingly large portion of the land. The pope himself claimed direct ownership of most of central Italy as the result of the Donation of Pepin in 756, a gift of land from the Frankish king Pepin, confirmed by his son Charlemagne. In the rest of Europe, the Church's possessions were the result of vast gifts of land made by kings or lords for the foundation of abbeys or churches, of smaller bequests by laymen left in the hope of winning spiritual salvation, of the opening up of new land by the religious orders, and of the voluntary renunciation of land and freedom by free peasants. In the mid-eleventh century, for example, the monastery of Marmoutier in France recorded a renunciation of this kind:

Be it known to all who come after us, that a certain man in our service called William, the brother of Reginald, born of free parents, being moved by the love of God and to the end that God—with whom is no acceptance of persons but reward only for the merits of each—might look favorably on him, gave himself up as a serf to Martin of Marmoutier; and he gave not only himself but all his descendants, so that they should for ever serve the abbot and monks of this place in a servile condition. And in order that this gift might be made more certain and apparent, he put the bell-rope around his neck and placed four pennies from his own head on the altar of St. Martin in recognition of serfdom, and so offered himself to almighty God.[9]

By the thirteenth century, the Church held perhaps one-quarter to one-third of the land of Europe. Its primary function was of course to carry out its religious duties, which encompassed most of the educational and charitable work of the age as well as pastoral and devotional duties. But where the Church held land directly from a lay lord, it had to fulfill the same obligations as any lay vassal, that is to use the produce of the land to support armed knights for his lord's military service. Since churchmen themselves were not permitted to kill or even to sentence to death in the courts, they solved the problem by employing laymen to lead their knights or carry out their duties of justice. But there was little doubt that the Church's involvement with the political and military obligations of feudal society acted as a detriment to its spiritual role.

The Role of Monarchy

The kings both suffered from, and profited from, this system. In fact, by the tenth and eleventh centuries, the king very often controlled less territory and people than the great vassals who nominally owed him allegiance. In France, for example, the Counts of Paris, who were kings of France from 987 on, controlled far less territory than such great vassals as the Dukes of Normandy and Brittany or the Counts of Anjou and Flanders. The kings, moreover, exercised no direct control over their own subjects in the feudal estates of their great vassals, but for the acquisition of money or soldiers had always to use their vassals as intermediaries. This situation however was inevitable in the actual absence of royal power during the invasions; and feudal government provided, at little expense, a minimum of security and services for the mass of the population. On the other hand, the system provided the potential for the diffusion of royal power. Theoretically and legally, the king was the head of the feudal pyramid. He possessed certain

[9] R. W. Southern, *The Making of the Middle Ages* (London: Arrow Books, 1962), pp. 98–99.

rights throughout his kingdom—which he could best enforce when his independent wealth derived from his own domain was greater than that of his individual vassals. For this reason, one major goal of the French royal family was to increase their own personal domain by any means they could. In England, the Norman kings took care to retain the legal ownership of all land in their kingdom which they held by right of conquest in the invasion of 1066; but they also retained vast estates in their own possession, which gave them military strength, and they prevented their vassals from consolidating geographically the territories they had been granted. Moreover, from Germanic tradition the king possessed a kind of religious mystique, which was reinforced by his coronation by the Church. He also was regarded as the ultimate interpreter and enforcer of law and justice. As kings increased in strength, they slowly increased their legal prerogatives and interference within the domains of their vassals. This increase in royal power, however, took place largely in the eleventh and twelfth centuries.

Manorialism

When, in the tenth century, Gerbert of Aurillac left the glittering cities of Moslem Spain to return to Catholic Europe, the contrast must have been startling. The Europe he was entering was a society of villages. The old cities had decayed, the new towns were still in their infancy. While Cordoba had half a million inhabitants, Paris had only twenty thousand. In England and most of Germany there were no towns at all.

In the conditions of disorder of the ninth and tenth century, the majority of Europe's inhabitants could support themselves economically only by agriculture. The peasant was the principal producer, and in most places, the only one, and he had to support the other two classes of medieval society, the warrior and the churchman. In the words of a thirteenth-century poet:

> *The work of the priest is to pray to God,*
> *And of the knight to do justice.*
> *The farm worker finds bread for them.*
> *One toils in the fields, one prays, and one defends.*
> *In the fields, in the town, in the church,*
> *These three help each other*
> *Through their skills, in a nicely regulated scheme.*[10]

Recent historical research has thrown new light on the economic and social forces that shaped the medieval village; and it has shown the great variety of villages that existed in different parts of Europe and the vast

[10] Cited in Evans, *Life in Medieval France*, p. 35. Author's translation.

changes in population, agricultural technique, and commercial exchange of agricultural products that revolutionized medieval rural society. The older picture of the "typical" and seemingly unchanging medieval village is no longer tenable.

Several theories are offered regarding the origin of the medieval village, which as a unit of production came to be called from the seventh century a *mansus*, or manor. One theory assumes that free Germanic tribesmen were compelled to hand over their land to a lord, who became its owner, and in return extended his protection and gave back the land for the peasant's use with certain obligations required. A second theory holds that the manor was the outgrowth of the colonate system of the late Roman Empire, in which the slaves and the tenant farmers had merged into an unfree class that possessed customary rights to the land they worked, under control of the local magnate. Finally, it has been suggested that the great variety of status that existed within the hierarchy of the medieval village, stretching from slave to freeman, was due to the survival of innumerable traditional classifications existing in the different tribal societies that intermingled with the Roman society during the invasions. Whatever its origin, the medieval manor possessed certain distinctive features of social structure and land cultivation, which are basic to an understanding of medieval society.

Social Structure of the Manor

The peasant's legal status prescribed the way in which he would support his lord. There were innumerable gradations of peasant status, extending from the slave to the landowning freeman. But by the tenth century, most peasants had become, willingly or unwillingly, serfs. A serf was not a slave; he was not the property of another man. But neither was he free. He was tied to the land that he worked, and could be passed from one lord to another with the land. What made his situation tolerable, however, was that custom or legal contract, usually respected by his lord, laid down the work he must do for the lord and the amount of land that he held for his own use. The estate book of an abbey outside Paris has survived from the ninth century, giving a detailed description of that abbey's holdings and the people who worked them. Among them was a freeman called Bodo:

Bodo a colonus [freeman] and his wife Ermentrude a colona, tenants of Saint-Germain, have with them three children. He holds one free manse containing eight bunaria *and two* antsinga *of arable land, two* aripenni *of vines and seven* aripenni *of meadow. He pays two silver shillings to the army and two hogsheads of wine for the right to pasture his pigs in the woods. Every third year he pays a hundred planks and three poles for fences. He ploughs at the winter sowing four perches and at the spring sowing two perches. Every week he owes two labor services and one handwork. He pays three fowls and fifteen*

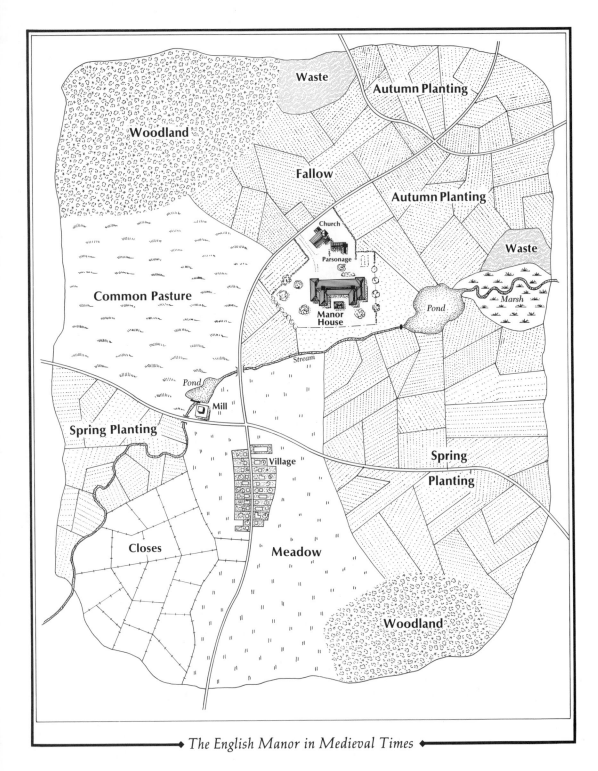

The English Manor in Medieval Times

eggs, and carrying service when it is enjoined upon him. And he owns half of a windmill, for which he pays two silver shillings.[11]

The serfs and the freemen alike, therefore, in return for their land, produced a surplus for others: by giving labor, usually three days a week and more in times of harvest, and by paying directly from their own produce. Charlemagne had a little island in a Bavarian mountain lake, with several tenants on it, each of whom had to pay him annually eighty-four pecks of grain, four hogs, two pullets, ten eggs, five pints of linseed, and five pints of lentils. Land in a village was divided between that kept for the lord, usually the better land, and that of the peasants. It was also divided according to use. Some was meadow, for grazing the animals; some in vines; some in woodland, where fuel could be gathered and hogs put out to forage, but only with the lord's permission; and most was ploughed. In most of northern Europe this arable land was worked in two, or after the eighth century, three huge fields, cultivated in rotation. The holdings of each man were scattered, in half-acre or one-acre strips, throughout the fields, which ensured that everyone got a fair share of good and bad land alike. All the villagers worked together on the fields. They agreed communally what should be planted, and the times of planting and harvest. The harvest was divided up accordingly to the amount of land held by each man. Individual initiative was thus discouraged. Extra work on one's strips, clearing of weeds, or carting in of fertilizer did not enable a man to increase his share of the common harvest.

Life for the peasant was hard and probably brutalizing. He lived in a one-room hut, usually with a beaten dirt floor, holes in the wall for windows, and an open wood fire for heat. He slept on verminous straw or, if fortunate, on a rough wooden bed. Candles were hard to obtain, so the peasant would retire at dark or after the evening meal. Pure water was hard to obtain, and the peasant usually drank beer or wine if he could. Meat was a rarity, but there were vegetables and black tough bread. Women's life was possibly even harder than men's. Families were large, pregnancy frequent, and infant mortality very high. Women were expected to work in the fields with their families at times of harvest, and to work in the plot near the house otherwise. They made the rough clothing for the family, and prepared the meals. Single women found that they or their would-be husbands had to pay for them to be allowed to marry off their own manor. Widows had to gain their lord's permission to marry, as a guarantee that the labor services would be paid on land she might have inherited. Occasionally, the lord of a manor forced unwilling couples to marry, to ensure that the able-bodied workers would stay on his manor. In a heartbreaking glimpse of peasant life in England, the medieval poem *Pierce the Ploughman's Crede* depicts a family group at work in the fields. The husband, "bemired in mud

---

[11] Eileen Power, *Medieval People* (Harmondsworth, England: Penguin, 1951), p. 183.

almost to the ankle," is driving a team of heifers so feeble that every rib could be counted.

His wiif walked him with, with a longe gode,
In a cutted cote cutted full heyghe,
Wrapped in a wynwe-schete to were hire fro
    weders,
Barfote on the bare iis that the blod folwede.
And at the longdes ende lay a litell crom-bolle,
And thereon lay a litell childe lapped in cloutes,
And tweyne of tweie yeres olde upon a-nother
    wyde,
And all they songen o songe that sorwe to heren;
They crieden alle a cry,—a carefull note.
The sely man sighede sore, and seide:
    "children, beth stille."

His wife walked beside him with a long goad
In a shortened cote-hardy looped up full
    high
And wrapped in a winnowing-sheet to protect
    her from the weather.
She went barefoot on the ice so that the
    blood flowed.
And at the end of the row lay a little
    crumb-bowl,
And therein a little child covered with rags.
And two two-year-olds were on the other side,
And they all sang one song that was pitiful
    to hear:
They all cried the same cry—a miserable
    note.
The poor man sighed sorely, and said, "Children,
    be still." [12]

This is a winter picture, and it must be set against the security and occasional pleasures that life on the manor brought. A good year's harvest might give the peasant the chance to buy a few necessities in the neighboring town. The round of agricultural labor was broken by festivals like harvest or planting, with ale-drinking and dancing. Traveling players would visit the church to present a morality play from time to time. But there is no point in trying to present an idyllic picture of country life before the indus-

[12] Cited in H. S. Bennett, *Life on the English Manor: A Study of Peasant Conditions, 1150–1400,* © 1967, Cambridge University Press.

trial revolution. Life was hard; but the existence of the manor gave the peasant a minimum of support.

The Medieval Agricultural Revolution

Conditions of life for the medieval peasant would have been far harder if there had not been extremely important improvements in agricultural productivity that were the result of changes in agricultural methods introduced between the sixth and ninth centuries. Perhaps the first improvement was the shift in many parts of northern Europe from a primitive scratch-plough, consisting of a conical, or triangular, share that scratched a furrow in light soil to a heavy wheeled plough. The scratch-plough was adequate for the thin soil of most of the Mediterranean region, and was used by the Celtic tribes and the Germanic invaders on the chalky upland soils of northern Europe until the seventh or eighth centuries. Then, however, pressure of population combined with growing evidence of the greater fertility of the heavy, well-watered alluvial soil of the plains and valley made it imperative to open up large stretches of undeveloped clay soils. The heavy plough, equipped with wheels, cut into these heavy soils with a vertical knife called a coulter, a flat ploughshare that sliced the earth horizontally, and a moldboard that turned over the turf to the side. To pull so formidable an instrument, the peasants had to assemble a team of eight oxen; and to use it

Ploughing in the Late Middle Ages
In this French illuminated manuscript, several of the technological innovations of the medieval agricultural revolution can be seen—the horse-collar and blinkers, the wheeled plough, the metal coulter, and the mouldboard.
The Pierpont Morgan Library, M. 52 F. 6 enlarged detail

effectively they had to farm communally. A second improvement was the use of the horse in place of the oxen. The horse can work longer hours and pull heavier weights than an ox; but until the ninth century, it could only be used for light loads because the method of harnessing was a yoke that strangled him under heavy loads. A new horse-collar enabled the animal to pull loads four or five times heavier. When a nailed iron horseshoe was fastened to the horse's brittle hoofs at the end of the ninth century, the peasant had in one animal transport to his field, an animal for ploughing, and driving-power for his wagon, which itself was also improved in design. The third big change was the shift, in the eighth or ninth century in northern Europe, from the two-field system to a three-field system. Under the two-field system, one field was left fallow while the other was planted in winter wheat. When the land was divided into three fields, one field only was left fallow, one was ploughed in the fall and planted with rye or winter wheat, and one was ploughed in the spring and planted with oats, barley, or vegetables. The new system increased productivity by one-half, diversified the crops planted, provided oats as fodder for horses, spread the ploughing through different parts of the year, and lessened the likelihood of famine. Among the great additions to the diet of the medieval peasant was vegetable protein, especially that from peas and beans. "It was not merely the new quantity of food produced by improved agricultural methods," Lynn White, Jr., has concluded, "but the new type of food supply which goes far towards explaining, for northern Europe at least, the startling expansion of population, the growth and multiplication of cities, the rise in industrial production, the outreach of commerce, and the new exuberance of spirits which enlivened that age [after 1000]." [13]

Effects of the Agricultural Revolution

The most immediate result of the improvement in farming methods was an increase in population, which itself compelled the medieval farmer to bring more land under cultivation. The increase in population was slight until the eleventh century, evidently owing to long periods of decimation of the village population through disease and especially the raids of invaders. But from about 1000 to 1300 there was a steady increase of the rural population. The only country for which fairly accurate figures are available is England. The population counted by the Norman conquerors in 1086, which was recorded in the Domesday Book, was just over one million. Two hundred years later it had risen to almost four million. Similar growth was probably achieved in most of western Europe during the same period, as more stable political conditions were achieved.

The expanding population fed itself in part by opening up new lands on the edge of the original village settlements, cutting into the surrounding forest or wilderness land for new fields, and turning cattle and sheep loose

[13] Lynn White, Jr., *Medieval Technology and Social Change* (Oxford: Clarendon Press, 1962), p. 76.

to graze on the fallow. The most important move was a vast colonization of the forest, marsh, and scrub land through the founding of new villages. The pioneers of this movement of reclamation were not the older monastic orders, like the Benedictines, but the newer orders, like the Cistercians, who deliberately sought solitude in the uninhabited wastes. In addition, speculating lords combined to found new villages, providing money or connections with the land-granting authorities at court and often the serfs as well to settle the land. The serfs who were brought to the new settlements usually had to render far less in customary dues than those who remained in the older villages, to encourage them to undertake the tough work of forest clearing or of marsh drainage. It is possible that in some of the new villages the serfs were able to throw off their nonfree status completely, and that the existence of such free villages led to a lightening of the burdens on the serfs who remained behind, lest they flee to the wilderness. Serfdom nevertheless remained the normal condition of the peasantry until the great depopulation of the fourteenth century (see Chapter 10) increased their bargaining power with their lords.

Agricultural expansion was at the root of the great economic revival of the eleventh, twelfth, and thirteenth centuries. The landlord class, both clerical and lay, profited greatly from the increase in production, partly by receipt of money rents but mostly by charges for grinding the peasants' grain in the landlord's mill and from direct appropriation of part of the peasant's harvest. According to Georges Duby, "This explains why so many religious houses flourished, why the aristocracy was so prosperous, civilization and material culture made such vigorous progress." The sale of agricultural surplus in foodstuffs and wine provided work for a large class of commercial middlemen, and of course at the same time supplied the growing cities where they lived. Thus the medieval rural economy came to possess some at least of the characteristics of capitalism—production for the market instead of for subsistence, acquisition of capital in money available for reinvestment to increase future profit, improvement in productivity through greater capitalization per worker, exploitation of technology and power, and so on. The presence of such factors in the economy of the countryside in the Middle Ages has led medieval historians to deny that a capitalist revolution occurred at the time of the Renaissance in the fifteenth century, and to argue that a gradual transformation of economic practice extended from at least the eleventh century to the seventeenth. The transformation of the village had prepared the way for the revival of the city.

SUGGESTED READING

The life of Mohammed and the history of the early expansion are authoritatively related in the well-illustrated *Muhammed and the Conquest of Islam* (1968) by Francesco Gabrieli, and the whole panorama of Arabic history and civilization is summarized in Bernard Lewis, *The Arabs in History* (1960). The most basic study, and one exceptionally detailed, is Philip K. Hitti, *History of the Arabs from the Earliest*

Times to the Present (1964). The West's debt to Islam, especially in architecture, literature, and philosophy is discussed in a series of specialized essays in Thomas Arnold and Alfred Guillaume, eds., *The Legacy of Islam* (1931). David Talbot Rice, *Islamic Art* (1965), is a fine short introduction in English; Georges Marçais, *L'Art musulman* (1962), a historical survey in French, with fine illustrations and succinct commentary. Moslem Spain receives an overly romantic treatment in Edwyn Hole's *Andalus: Spain Under the Muslims* (1958) and a more scholarly treatment in W. Montgomery Watt, *A History of Islamic Spain* (1965).

In French, there is a good survey by E. Lévi-Provençale, *Histoire de l'Espagne Musulmane* (1950). In spite of a tendency to excessive generalization, Anwar G. Chejne, *Muslim Spain: Its History and Culture* (1974) is valuable for political history and for art and architecture. Short lectures by an expert on Islam are an excellent introduction to the very great lesson that the Muslims taught Christian Europe, in W. Montgomery Watt, *The Influence of Islam on Medieval Europe* (1972). The continuity in Spain after the Christian reconquest is emphasized by Robert I. Burns, *Islam Under the Crusaders: Colonial Survival in the Thirteenth Century Kingdom of Valencia* (1973). Northern Spain is treated fully in H. V. Livermore, *The Origins of Spain and Portugal* (1971).

Contemporary writers still make exciting reading on the history of the Franks. Gregory of Tours, *History of the Franks* (1916), edited by Ernest Brehaut, covers the do-nothing kings. The indispensable life of Charlemagne by Einhard and the dispensable but entertaining life by the Monk of Saint Gall are edited by A. J. Grant, in *Early Lives of Charlemagne* (1905), but many other translations are also available. The best synthesis of the Carolingian achievement is Heinrich Fichtenau, *The Carolingian Empire* (1957); the revival of learning is described with fine illustrations by Donald Bullough, *The Age of Charlemagne* (1965), and in M. L. W. Laistner, *Thought and Letters in Western Europe A.D. 500–900* (1957).

General introductions to the early Middle Ages are given by J. M. Wallace-Hadrill, *The Barbarian West: The Early Middle Ages, A.D. 400–1000* (1962), and in the fresh, lively interpretation of R. W. Southern, *The Making of the Middle Ages* (1953). Christopher Brooke, *Europe in the Central Middle Ages, 962–1154* (1964), has new documentation and is solid in style. The origin and development of manorialism is excellently treated in M. M. Postan, ed., *The Cambridge Economic History of Europe, vol. 1, The Agrarian Life of the Middle Ages* (1966), while the vast recent research on the manor is presented in detail in Georges Duby's challenging *Rural Economy and Country Life in the Medieval West* (1968). The pioneering work of the great French historian Marc Bloch, *Feudal Society* (1961) merits careful reading.

Postan's own brilliant work should be sampled in *Essays on Medieval Agriculture and General Problems of the Medieval Economy* (1973), and *Medieval Trade and Finance* (1973). He is especially revealing on the introduction of the money economy and on demographic change. On the Anglo-Saxon agrarian systems, see H. P. R. Finberg, ed., *The Agrarian History of England and Wales, vol. I part 2. A. D. 43–1042* (1972).

The technological aspects of the medieval agricultural revolution are detailed, and their effects analyzed, in Lynn White, Jr., *Medieval Technology and Social Change* (1962). White also summarizes his views on the impact of technology throughout the Middle Ages in an essay in Carlo Cipolla, ed., *The Fontana Economic History of Europe, vol. I, The Middle Ages* (1972), which also contains useful essays on towns by Jacques Le Goff and on industry by Sylvia Thrupp. Quantification and economic theory are used with great effect in Douglass C. North and Robert P. Thomas, *The*

Rise of the Western World: A New Economic History (1973), which is especially good on the later Middle Ages. For the early Middle Ages, see R. Latouche, *The Birth of Western Economy* (1966), and R. H. Bautier, *The Economic Development of Medieval Europe* (1971).

The most modern interpretations of feudalism are documented in David Herlihy, ed., *The History of Feudalism* (1971). Older studies that are still useful include F. L. Ganshof, *Feudalism* (1961), C. Seignobos, *The Feudal Regime* (1902), and C. Stephenson, *Feudalism* (1962). Elizabeth A. R. Brown teaches caution in the use of the word feudalism in an invaluable survey of its past usage, in "The Tyranny of a Construct: Feudalism and Historians of Medieval Europe," *American Historical Review*, (October 1974), pp. 1063–1088.

On the Magyars, see C. A. Macartney, *The Magyars in the Ninth Century* (1930). For the Viking invasions, see J. Brondsted, *The Vikings* (1963). Charles H. Haskins, *The Normans in European History* (1915) is still useful, but David C. Douglas, *The Norman Achievement, 1050–1100* (1969) is more up-to-date though still full of admiration.

8 / Feudal Monarchy in the West, 1000–1200

In the tenth century, the infant states of Europe were still a source of amusement to the Byzantine emperor. "The soldiers of thy master," he told Liudprand of Cremona, the envoy of the German emperor Otto I, "do not know how to ride, nor do they know how to fight on foot; the size of their shields, the weight of their breastplates, the length of their swords, and the burden of their helmets permits them to fight in neither one way nor the other. . . . Their gluttony also impedes them for their God is their belly, their courage but wind, their bravery drunkenness."[1] Within a century, however, a Byzantine emperor was appealing in desperation for Christian armies from the states his predecessor had despised to mount a crusade that would save Constantinople from the armies of the Seljuk Turks that had overrun the Holy Land; and three centuries later, crusading armies from western Europe had pillaged Constantinople itself.

The revival of the European states after the chaos of the invasions of the ninth and tenth centuries was carried out under monarchies whose power was based upon the feudal system of government. Aided both by the great increase in food productivity due to the technological innovations of the agricultural revolution and by the revival of urban life and long-distance commerce, the monarchs of France, England, and Germany sought to solidify their authority through the creation of strong, efficient political

[1] *The Works of Liudprand of Cremona*, trans. F. A. Wright.

Durham Cathedral National Monuments Record

and legal institutions. The future political history of Europe was shaped by the widely different results these rulers achieved.

In France, in the ninth century, the division of the kingdom into semi-autonomous feudal principalities was far advanced, and the task of creating a centralized, unified government appeared almost insurmountable. For three centuries, however, the Capetian dynasty worked painstakingly to extend their power from their original holdings as Counts of Paris in the Ile de France over much of the present-day French state. By use of their feudal rights, alliance with the Church and the cities, and when necessary military force, they slowly brought first their own domain and then many of the feudal principalities of France under their control. Particularly under the great rulers Philip II and Louis IX, they created an efficient bureaucratic organization, a highly respected system of courts and traveling judges, and a productive fiscal organization. By the end of the thirteenth century, the Capetian dynasty had laid the foundations for a centralized absolutism.

In England, the conquest of the island by the Norman Duke William in 1066 ensured that the feudal institutions introduced would support rather than challenge the powers of the king. For a century and a half, the powers of the king grew. Revenues, based upon feudal dues and an efficiently collected land tax, were greater than those available to other feudal monarchs. The king's control over justice was widely respected as a result of the development of the common law under kings Henry I and Henry II. Such institutions of central government as the Exchequer and the Chancery had been created from the king's own household. In 1215, however, faced by the abuse of his powers and the neglect of his duties by King John, the feudal lords and certain leading churchmen reasserted the rights of vassals against the monarchy and, in the Magna Carta, stated the important principle that the king is under the law. England, however, did not break into feudal principalities; but with the growth of the institution of Parliament in the late thirteenth and fourteenth centuries, the kings were compelled to admit important segments of their population into governmental decision-making.

Germany, by contrast, possessed in the tenth century the most powerful monarchy with rights based upon feudal institutions. But by the middle of the thirteenth century, even the power of the German ruler had disintegrated, and Germany had broken up into hundreds of feudal principalities governed by lay lords, city bourgeois, or great ecclesiastics. Two reasons explained this breakdown of monarchical power in Germany. Almost every ruler, once appointed emperor, became obsessed with the ambition to dominate Italy, and in Italian adventures squandered both the wealth and military strength needed to maintain control of turbulent German vassals. Italian ambitions brought the German emperors into conflict with the papacy at a time when the reform movement in the Church had given the pontiffs not only the desire to end lay interference in clerical affairs but also to assert their own superiority over lay rulers. The German emperors thus became enmeshed in the Investiture conflict with the popes in the eleventh and twelfth centuries, over the right of emperors to control the nomination of high church officers in their own dominions and, in the later twelfth and thirteenth centuries, in an open power struggle for hegemony in Italy. This conflict ended with the ruin of the emperor and the consequent fragmentation of political power in Germany.

These long and complicated power struggles are of great significance for the development of western Europe. By the fourteenth century, the inhabitants of England and France had lived so long in their own separate, politically integrated societies and were developing characteristics of behavior so similar within the disparate societies that they thought of themselves as distinct from one another by "nationality." The basic political institution of modern society, the nation-state, had begun to emerge. At the same time, the French and English were formulating two of the principal patterns of government of the nation-state—centralized absolutism in France and representative democracy in England. In Germany and Italy, however, owing to the dispersion of political power, the sense of political community developed only in smaller local units. Both the German and Italian peoples were united as nation-states in the second half of the nineteenth century; but it can be argued that their greatest contribution to civilization was made within the decentralized political units. The Italian Renaissance was the product of the small city-states of the fourteenth and fifteenth centuries (see Chapter 11). The German Reformation was born in the small principalities and autonomous cities of sixteenth-century Germany; and the great German music and literature of the eighteenth and early nineteenth centuries was sponsored by the many small courts that were later to be swallowed up in the process of unification under Prussia.

The Capetian Monarchy in France

In the chaotic ninth century there seemed little chance that France would be united under a strong monarchy. When Charlemagne's empire had been divided in 843 at the Treaty of Verdun, the western third of the empire, known as the kingdom of the West Franks, passed to his grandson Charles the Bald. But this territory never became a unified state. Charles the Bald's successors were increasingly incompetent, and two of the Carolingian line were even deposed by their vassals. The grant of Normandy to the Viking leader Rollo in 911 by King Charles the Simple as a method of purchasing a minimal security from further attack was perhaps the most egregious example of the monarchy's weakness, but it was one of many. By the end of the ninth century, the kingdom of the West Franks had broken up into a congeries of feudal principalities, large and small, which owed only the most nominal allegiance to the monarchy. Most of the medieval history of

Knights on Horseback. Stained-Glass Lunette, 1246–1248
Although this scene illustrates the Book of Judith, the French artist has depicted the knights of his own day, with heavy armor and lances prepared for battle. Philadelphia Museum of Art. Photograph by A. J. Wyatt, Staff Photographer

France is concerned with the efforts, which were ultimately successful, of the king to bring the feudal principalities under his control.

The most powerful and efficient of these feudal states was the Duchy of Normandy, whose Scandinavian rulers imposed a highly regimented feudal order upon the whole province. Because the ducal rule was imposed by force and with relative speed, the rulers were able to make uniform demands upon each fief, especially in the number of knights owing for military service. This system made it possible for Duke William to raise the powerful army that conquered England in 1066; and there too the speed and completeness of the conquest made it easy for William to create a feudal hierarchy in which the king's powers were recognized in fact as well as in principle. After 1066, the rulers of Normandy drew upon the wealth of England to strengthen their forces in Normandy, and they thus represented an even greater threat to the king of France. To the west of Normandy lay the County of Brittany, which had been settled by Celtic immigrants from England in the fifth century. Speaking their own Celtic language of Breton, separated in ethnic background and in way of life and indeed by geography from the Franks, the inhabitants of Brittany resisted vigorously any closer ties to the rest of France; and the province did not finally become part of the French royal domain until 1532. To the east of Normandy lay the rich, well-governed County of Flanders, which is now part of Belgium and eastern France. The count of Flanders had thrown off almost all subservience to the king of France, and coined his own money, maintained his own courts, regulated commerce, and protected the church's activities. He governed through a number of military districts organized around strong castles; many of these castle-cities, especially Ghent, Bruges, and Ypres, were to develop into the most prosperous wool-manufacturing and trading cities of the Middle Ages.

The Loire valley was broken up into a number of smaller states, of which the most important was the County of Anjou. Although well-governed and rich in agriculture, these smaller states sought to maintain their autonomy through well-planned marriage alliances. The most important of these occurred in 1152 when Count Henry of Anjou, who was already duke of Normandy and the main claimant to the English throne as a result of his father's marriage into the English royal family, married the former wife of the French king, Eleanor of Aquitaine. Eleanor brought him as dowry the vast Duchy of Aquitaine in the southwest of France. When Henry became king of England in 1154, he controlled greater territories in France than did the king of France himself.

Among the many other principalities, the most important were the County of Toulouse in the south, which profited from its access to the reviving trade of the Mediterranean through the ports of Languedoc; the Duchy of Burgundy, on the eastern border; and the County of Champagne. It was, however, one of the weakest principalities that was to be the eventual unifier of France.

In 987, the great feudal lords decided to revive the Frankish habit of electing their king. They chose Hugh Capet, Count of Paris, whose royal domain of the Ile-de-France was so small that it did not seem to provide any challenge to their independence. The Capetian dynasty which, in this ignominious way, replaced the Carolingian line, was to reign in France for the next three hundred years, during which time it created the basis of centralized monarchy.

The first six Capetian kings (987–1188) worked pragmatically to strengthen their power inside the Ile-de-France, without attempting any important interference with their vassals. Their first and most important achievement was to establish the continuity of their own hold on the monarchy itself: Each king reigned for a long period; each had his own son crowned before dying himself. The Capetians' second achievement was to gain complete control of their own personal domain, in order to turn it into the base from which they could mount a military campaign necessary to bring the rest of the kingdom under their rule. The monarch most responsible for completing the destruction of opposition within the Ile-de-France

THE CAPETIAN DYNASTY

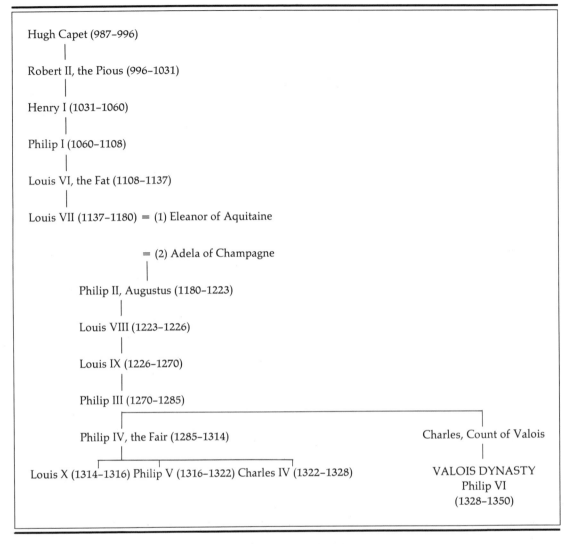

Hugh Capet (987–996)
|
Robert II, the Pious (996–1031)
|
Henry I (1031–1060)
|
Philip I (1060–1108)
|
Louis VI, the Fat (1108–1137)
|
Louis VII (1137–1180) = (1) Eleanor of Aquitaine

= (2) Adela of Champagne
|
Philip II, Augustus (1180–1223)
|
Louis VIII (1223–1226)
|
Louis IX (1226–1270)
|
Philip III (1270–1285)

Philip IV, the Fair (1285–1314)　　　　　　Charles, Count of Valois
|　　　　　　　　　　　　　　　　　　　　　　　　|
Louis X (1314–1316) Philip V (1316–1322) Charles IV (1322–1328)　　VALOIS DYNASTY
　　　　　　　　　　　　　　　　　　　　　　　　　　　　　Philip VI
　　　　　　　　　　　　　　　　　　　　　　　　　　　　　(1328–1350)

was Louis VI (reigned 1108–1137) known accurately as Louis the Fat. Louis saw that the fortunes of the monarchy were dependent upon an alliance with the Church and with the rising towns. For his chief administrator he chose the able Abbot Suger of the Abbey of Saint-Denis on the edge of Paris who was not only a subtle statesman but a man of great artistic talent and ambition as well. He led his armies in defense of monasteries or towns that complained of oppression by local feudal lords; and he used feudal law to compel the lords to appear in his courts, where they were frequently stripped of their possessions. Finally, he began the process of creating a loyal bureaucracy, drawn from the Church and the poorer nobility, which could administer justice and supply him with soldiers and taxes. His greatest triumph, however, appeared to be the marriage of his son Louis VII (reigned 1137–1180) to Eleanor of Aquitaine, which for a brief time brought the monarchy control over that duchy. Louis VII, however, deeply distrustful of his wife's supposed infidelities and disturbed by her failure to give him a son, had their marriage annulled, and thus, as we saw, provoked the union of the Duchy of Aquitaine to the possessions of the king of England.

Philip Augustus

The position of the Capetian kings was revolutionized by Philip II (reigned 1180–1223), known to his contemporaries as the Conqueror and to posterity as Augustus. Philip was one of those crafty, ambitious medieval kings who respected the feudal bond sufficiently to be able to profit from it and who served the Church with sufficient devotion to enlist it in his own service. By exploiting the moral rules of both feudalism and Church, he prepared the transformation of the French monarch's power as supreme lord in a feudal hierarchy to absolute monarch governing by divine right. This condition was achieved during the sixteenth and seventeenth centuries. Philip's father had died when he was fifteen, and during the following ten years he had experienced the most practical political training Europe could offer: a tour of the Italian city-states and a stay with the pope in Rome; a Crusade to the Holy Land; a personal feud with Richard the Lion-Hearted, King of England; and an uprising led by one of his most powerful vassals. From being a

Bust of Philip Augustus
The sculptor of this limestone portrait head was clearly aware of the need to portray Philip as a worthy successor to Charlemagne. Realism had to be sacrificed to regality. The Metropolitan Museum of Art, Fletcher Fund, 1947

high-spirited, active teen-ager with a mop of untidy hair and a love of hunting, he matured into a quiet, self-controlled commander of men, with a parsimony of language and a perhaps overly cynical understanding of the actions of his subjects and his enemies. He impressed his contemporaries as being a worthy successor to Charlemagne, a real king: "A fine man, well proportioned in stature, with a smiling countenance, bald, a rubicund complexion, inclined to eat and drink well, sensual . . . far-sighted, obstinate, rapid and prudent in judgement, fond of taking the advice of lesser people." [2]

For his whole reign, Philip fought to increase the territory under the direct rule of the kings of France, and he succeeded in tripling the royal domain. His principal objective was to reduce the territory controlled by the king of England, and to do so he used guile, treachery, legalism, and violence. He intervened in the numerous family quarrels within the English royal family, supporting a revolt of the sons of Henry II against their father and later supporting John against his elder brother King Richard I. Only when John became king of England (reigned 1199–1216) was Philip able to make any territorial gains at the expense of the English king. Profiting from the psychotic inefficacy of John, who had quarreled with his own barons and with the pope at the very time that the French were preparing an attack on Normandy, Philip declared that John had broken his feudal vows to him and therefore forfeited all his territories in France to the French king. Philip's cynical use of his feudal rights to justify the invasion of Normandy is illustrated in the letter the pope sent to John in support of Philip's action:

As you have taken away, without justice or reason, the castles and lands of men who consider them as his [Philip's] fief, Philip, as higher suzerain, driven by the complaints of the victims, has demanded, not once but many times, that you make reparation; you have promised but have done nothing and you have crushed the prostrate further. He has borne with you more than a year awaiting the satisfaction he has asked for. With the advice of his barons and subjects he has fixed a certain term for you to appear in his presence to do as the law demands without any withdrawal; although you are his liege subject, you have not appeared on the appointed day or sent any representative but have treated his summons with nothing but contempt. As a result, he has met you in person and warned you in his own words, for he does not wish to make war if you show yourself what you should be towards him. You have been unwilling to satisfy him. [3]

After two years of stiff fighting Philip conquered Normandy, and he took for himself most of the lands of the English king and of the Norman lords

[2] Cited in Charles Petit-Dutaillis, *The Feudal Monarchy in France and England: From the Tenth to the Thirteenth Century* (London: K. Paul, Trench, & Trübner, 1936), p. 214.

[3] Ibid., p. 218.

COUNTY OF FLANDERS

English Channel

Meuse R.

Seine River

DUCHY OF NORMANDY

COUNTY OF CHAMPAGNE

Paris

ILE-DE-FRANCE

COUNTY OF BRITTANY

COUNTY OF MAINE

DUCHY OF ANJOU

Loire

COUNTY OF BLOIS

DUCHY OF BURGUNDY

Atlantic

Ocean

COUNTY OF POITOU

COUNTY OF LA MARCHE

COUNTY OF AUVERGNE

River

DUCHY OF AQUITAINE

Garonne

DUCHY OF GASCONY

R.

Rhône River

LANGUEDOC

COUNTY OF PROVENCE

COUNTY OF TOULOUSE

Mediterranean

Sea

Royal Domain, 1180

Acquisitions of Philip Augustus, 1180–1223

Acquisitions of Louis VIII and Louis IX, 1223–1270

Expansion of the Capetian Monarchy, 1180–1270

who remained in England. By 1206, he had taken all the English possessions in France except Aquitaine. After showing how the feudal bond could be used to justify territorial annexation, at the end of his life Philip showed how service of the Church through participation in a Crusade could be equally profitable. In 1223, he sent his son Louis to crush the Albigensian heresy, whose leaders held that the world was a battlefield of the forces of light and darkness and that the corrupted Catholic Church was a servant of the latter. After horrible massacres in the name of religion, the Capetians completed the incorporation of the County of Toulouse in their kingdom through a marriage alliance.

Finally, Philip greatly improved the bureaucratic administration located in Paris. He began by transforming his household officers into governmental officials. His chamberlain, seneschal, butler, and constable, although not yet highly specialized in the tasks assigned them, gathered round them a staff of civil servants, who formed the nucleus of future governmental ministries. By calling in his greatest barons and bishops to give him advice and support on important occasions at a meeting of the Curia Regis, or King's Court, he developed a body with at least some of the characteristics of a legislature. And perhaps most important of all, Philip sent out paid officials, called baillis, to supervise local administration and justice. Drawn from the poorer nobility, the middle class, and the Church, these professional servants were a direct instrument of the king against the feudal lords. He even succeeded in putting together a royal income from a form of taxation, based on the demand for "loans," from groups like the Jews; special tithes to support crusades; and monetary payment in lieu of military service. Philip, in short, succeeded in using his feudal rights to expand vastly the territories of the kingdom of France and to form a centralized administration to control his kingdom.

The Norman and Angevin Dynasties in England

For all prehistory, and indeed for a good deal of history, England stood on the outer fringes of the known world, backward and poverty-stricken. The four-hundred-year Roman occupation left a superficial veneer of Latin culture, a few technical advantages like a decent road system, and a population that was unwilling and unable to fight in its own defense. When the Romans pulled back their garrisons to defend Rome itself from the Visigoths, England was invaded and conquered with relative ease by the Germanic tribes of Angles, Saxons, and Jutes, who drove the unfortunate Celtic inhabitants back to the western edges of the island, to Cornwall, Wales, and Lancashire. The great Anglo-Saxon achievement was the colonization of England, for it was the invaders who cut down the primeval forests and opened up the heavy clay soil of central England to cultivation. In spite of pressure from the Vikings after their invasions in the ninth and tenth centuries and their settlement in the North and East and along the northwestern coast of England, the Anglo-Saxons also gave England several institutions of great importance for its future political and legal development. For purposes of local government, they divided the country into thirty-four shires, administered by a local earl and bishop and by a royal representative called a sheriff (shire-reeve). In the shires and their subdivisions, the hundreds, there were local courts recognizing the king's authority; and there was a central council, called the witan, of all the great landholders, churchmen, and royal officials, and a national militia, called the fyrd. Upon these Anglo-Saxon foundations, Duke William of Normandy, who conquered the island in 1066, imposed the most developed form of feudalism.

The Norman Kings, 1066–1154

The Norman conquest is graphically portrayed in the famous Bayeux tapestry, with its seventy-two scenes embroidered in eight colors of wool on a huge sheet of linen. In this astonishing survival the whole bloody brutality of the conquest is displayed unflinchingly, and perhaps even with a certain relish. The fleet of Norman ships, with prows like the Viking vessels of earlier invaders, is seen crossing the Channel to England, with a favoring gale in their sails and the knights' horses docilely lined up, the whole length of the ships. Then there is the battle of Hastings (1066), with a seething mass of knights in battle—some impaled on spears, others lunging with

THE NORMAN AND ANGEVIN DYNASTIES IN ENGLAND

NORMAN DYNASTY

William I, the Conqueror (1066–1087)

| Robert, Duke of Normandy | William II, Rufus (1087–1100) | Henry I = Matilda (1100–1135) | Adela = Stephen, Count of Blois |

Geoffrey of Anjou — = Matilda — Stephen (1135–1154)

ANGEVIN DYNASTY

Henry II (1154–1189) = Eleanor of Aquitaine

Richard I (1189–1199)   John (1199–1216)

Henry III (1216–1272)

Edward I (1272–1307)

Edward II (1307–1327)

Edward III (1327–1377)

Edward, the Black Prince

Richard II (1377–1399)

great broadswords through a tumultuous mass of upended horses. Finally, there are the somewhat more peaceful scenes of the imposition of Norman rule, with the building of the great castles that were to ensure that the Saxons would never rise again.

Crowned as King William I (reigned 1066–1087), the "Conqueror" set about ensuring that his hold on England would not be challenged from within or without. Like Charlemagne, he already had the reputation of being a warrior-king, unattractive in appearance but enormously tough and ruthless. According to the twelfth-century chronicler, William of Malmesbury:

He was of just stature, extraordinary corpulence, fierce countenance; his fore-head bare of hair: of such great strength of arm, that it was often matter of surprise, that no one was able to draw his bow, which himself could bend when his horse was on full gallop; he was majestic, whether sitting or stand-ing, although the protuberance of his belly deformed his royal person; of excel-lent health, so that he was never confined with any dangerous disorder, except at the last; so given to the pleasure of the chase, that as I have before said, ejecting the inhabitants, he let a space of many miles grow desolate, that, when at liberty from other avocations, he might there pursue his pleasures. . . . His anxiety for money is the only thing for which he can deservedly be blamed. This he sought all opportunities of scraping together, he cared not how.[4]

William of Malmesbury even claims that the king brought on his own death by his determination to avenge a sarcastic remark that the king of France had made about him:

Not long after, in the end of the month of August 1087, when the corn was ripe on the ground, the clusters on the vines, and the orchards laden with fruit in full abundance, collecting an army, he entered France in hostile manner, trampling down, and laying everything waste: nothing could assuage his irri-tated mind, so determined was he to revenge this injurious taunt at the expense of multitudes. . . . Exhilarated by this success, while furiously commanding his people to add fuel to the conflagration of the church of Mantes, he approached too near the flames, and contracted a disorder from the violence of the fire and the intenseness of the autumnal heat. Some say, that his horse leaping over a dangerous ditch, ruptured his rider, where his belly projected over the front of the saddle.[5]

The new king moved at once with great force against the Saxon in-habitants of the island. The few remaining glimmerings of resistance were quickly extinguished, William himself leading his armies into the North

[4] William of Malmesbury, *Chronicle of the Kings of England* (London: 1847), p. 308–309.
[5] Ibid., p. 310.

Tower of London
The Normans kept the defeated Anglo-Saxons submissive by erecting a large number of castles. Rectangular towers, like that in London, were surrounded by earthen ramparts and wooden or stone palisades, and were unassailable with the primitive siege weapons of the eleventh and twelfth centuries.   British Tourist Authority photo

and West. To maintain control he built a number of castles, most of them in strategically located cities such as Dover and Rochester, that commanded the route from Normandy to London, Lincoln, and York on the old Roman road to Scotland, and Exeter in the West. Tall, unadorned keeps surrounded by tall walls and an outer defense ditch rose in the middle of the city where hundreds of houses were pulled down to make space. The keep of the Tower of London rose 118 feet, that of Colchester 152 feet high. These bare towers were symbolic of the occupying force that systematically deprived the old Saxon nobility of its lands and turned the Saxon peasantry into a uniform class of unfree serfs.

To keep control over his own Norman lords, William declared himself, according to feudal law, the sole owner of the conquered country. From him

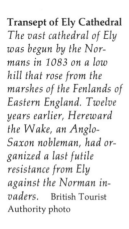

Transept of Ely Cathedral
The vast cathedral of Ely was begun by the Normans in 1083 on a low hill that rose from the marshes of the Fenlands of Eastern England. Twelve years earlier, Hereward the Wake, an Anglo-Saxon nobleman, had organized a last futile resistance from Ely against the Norman invaders. British Tourist Authority photo

both lords and churchmen were to hold their possessions. Only on the borders, where defense required the establishment of powerful territorial units, did William grant his vassals large, contiguous estates. Generally, his most important vassals were given lands scattered throughout the kingdom, and thus were unable to unify their forces to rival the king's. Although he did not immediately remove many of the Saxon bishops from their lands, William appointed no Saxon to an English bishopric; and he brought one of the leading clerics of Normandy, Lanfranc, to be his archbishop of Canterbury. The new church officials set out to impress the Saxon English with their cathedrals almost as effectively as William did with his castles; and there is an obvious similarity in the effect of the great, bare aisles of the Norman cathedrals. Nothing in Anglo-Saxon England had remotely resembled these enormous churches that the Normans raised as both cathedrals and monasteries. The Normans had already become great church builders only a century after their arrival in Normandy, as seen in the abbeys of Caen. In England, possessing greater wealth and labor, the Normans erected some of the largest and, one is tempted to say, strongest churches in Europe. Plainness, power, and decisiveness—all great Norman characteristics—can be seen in such a splendid transept as that of the cathedral of Ely illustrated on the opposite page.

Almost as impressive a monument to Norman thoroughness and efficiency is the Domesday Book, which William's commissioners completed in 1086. William had collected a land tax on several occasions, using the precedent of the Danegeld paid to Saxon kings for defense against the Vikings; but he was apparently unsatisfied with the results. Therefore in 1085 he ordered a survey of the whole kingdom, to determine how much tax could be assessed. Each locality was compelled to report its land area in arable, forest, and pasture, the number of plow-teams and mills, its workers and their possessions, and even the smallest numbers of farm animals. Moreover, they were to compare the situation that existed before the Conquest with that of the year 1086. The result was a historical document of incomparable importance for our understanding of the Middle Ages and a financial record of immediate and unparalleled value for the Norman kings. By the end of William's reign, England not only possessed the most regimented, feudalized society in Europe; its kings disposed of financial resources unavailable to kings in richer but less organized states.

William I's son, William Rufus or William II (reigned 1087–1100) was equally tough and money-grubbing; but since his father had given Normandy to his older brother Robert, he wasted much time and resources in vain efforts to seize Normandy for himself. This preoccupation of English kings with the maintenance or the acquisition of territories in France continued, to England's detriment, until their last continental possession, the French town of Calais, was taken from them in 1558. William II's younger brother Henry proved a more dangerous rival than the effete Robert; for when the king died of a hunting accident, Henry rushed from the forest where some suspected he had participated in the supposed accident to seize the treasury and the crown for himself. Shortly after, he campaigned against Robert in Normandy, and within six years had imprisoned him and reunited Normandy and England.

King Henry I (reigned 1100–1135) is better known, however, for the unglamorous work of creating an effective royal bureaucracy and the beginnings of an impartial and uniform legal system. Since he continued the practice of commuting as many as possible of the services due him from his vassals into money payments, he used part of his royal household as a treasury called the Exchequer after the checkerboard table on which the officials rendered their accounts. Another group of servants under the royal chancellor formed the Chancery where detailed public records were kept. Henry I also developed the king's control over local justice by sending out officials called itinerant justices to hear pleas throughout the kingdom. These justices compared their decisions on their return to the king's court, and were thus able to achieve uniformity in the principles they followed. In this way, they contributed to that reliance upon precedent and case law that is perhaps the preeminent feature of the English common law.

Henry I's only son died in a shipwreck; and Henry failed in his efforts to get the great English vassals to support his daughter Matilda as his successor. After his death, England was plunged into feudal anarchy, with the nobility's support divided between Matilda and her husband, Geoffrey of Anjou, and Stephen, a nephew of Henry II. The details of the fighting, in which Stephen eventually prevailed, are unimportant, but the overall chaos, in which each lord built castles to control the regions where his own possessions lay, and made military alliances like an independent potentate, is an indication of the hazards the feudal system presented in the absence of a powerful personality as king. The chronicles of the period fully reflect the distress of these years "when Christ and his Saints were asleep;" and the people as a whole were relieved to find that their new king, Matilda's son Henry II (reigned 1154–1189), was prepared to act incisively to control the anarchy.

The Angevin Kings, 1154–1399

Henry II began his reign from a position of strength. He had inherited Anjou from his father and Normandy from his mother. Stephen, whose own son had been killed, had even recognized him as the legitimate heir to the throne of England. And his wife Eleanor of Aquitaine had brought him that rich Duchy in southwestern France. He was later able to marry his son to the heiress of Brittany and two of his daughters to the kings of Castile and Sicily. He at once brought the rebellious nobility of England to obedience, destroying their castles and often confiscating their possessions.

Henry II's most lasting contribution to England was his development of the common law. Building on the earlier work of Henry I, he greatly increased the use of itinerant justices, whose task was to handle cases in the shire courts in a uniform manner. Moreover, in civil cases, he made considerable use of the jury, a group of twelve local people who were called in to give evidence on which they were supposed to have personal knowledge and who were sworn (juré) to tell the truth. The itinerant justices made constant use of the juries, both to accuse suspected criminals and to testify to the state of royal order and finances in the area where they lived. In the thirteenth century, after the Church had forbidden trial by ordeal or by combat, decisions in criminal cases were also passed to juries, which thus became one of the central institutions of the English juridicial system. The advances in legal practice under Henry II were further solidified at the end of his reign with the composition of the first great textbook of English law, the 'Treatise on the Laws and Customs of England' attributed to the royal Justiciar Glanville.

Henry II was less successful in his attempts to cow the Catholic Church. Determined to lessen the powers of the separate ecclesiastical courts, which claimed the sole right to try clerics, he demanded in 1164 that clerics guilty to crimes like murder should be punished in the royal courts. His old

Murder of Archbishop Thomas Becket
In this thirteenth-century miniature, Becket is shown kneeling at the high altar of Canterbury Cathedral as three knights wearing chain mail lunge at him with their broadswords.
Courtesy of the Trustees of the British Museum

friend, Thomas Becket, whom he had named archbishop of Canterbury in the hope of having an ally in the heart of the Church, refused this demand; and after a long trial of strength, Henry, in an unthinking outburst of rage, asked—rhetorically, as he thought—"Who will rid me of this pestilent cleric?" Four knights, taking him at this word, then murdered Becket in front of his altar in Canterbury Cathedral in 1170. Becket was made a saint, and Canterbury became the major goal of English pilgrims, but the final result was a compromise. The Church continued to receive immunity from the royal courts, and the king still exercised the right of picking the principal churchmen in the kingdom.

The stability of the administrative machinery created by Henry I and Henry II was proven during the reign of Richard I (reigned 1189–1199), the Lionhearted. Richard spent most of his reign abroad, either crusading in the Holy Land or in captivity in Europe, but the government functioned well in his absence. After the repression of the first months of Henry II's reign, most of the feudal barons had accepted his rule with equanimity, and few had joined in the rebellion led by his wife and sons. The reign of Richard's brother John (reigned 1199–1216) compelled them, however, not only to take a stand in support of their rights but to think out a constitutional justification for their actions. John, a mean, suspicious, and unskillful ruler, infuriated many of his leading vassals by failing to respect his role in the feudal contract, at the very time that Philip Augustus in France was preparing to strip him of as many as possible of his possessions in France. John frequently punished his barons without respecting their right of trial. To pay for his constant wars with Philip Augustus, he squeezed every source of income possible from abuse of his rights as suzerain. At the same time that he was enraging his barons, he challenged the English church. When he refused to accept the pope's nominee as archbishop of Canterbury, the pope placed all England under an interdict, forbidding the holding of any church services. John himself was later excommunicated. When Philip Augustus prepared to depose him by force, John capitulated to the pope, and won forgiveness by promising to hold England from him as a fief. The English barons, however, accompanied by many leading churchmen, had lost patience, and in 1215 they took up arms to compel him to accept a long statement of their rights known as the Magna Carta.

Most of the chapters of this famous document were specific limitations on the king's power to abuse his feudal privileges, by his control over heiresses, for example, and his use of scutage and his exorbitant charges for inheritance of fiefs. But several of the clauses, although intended solely to safeguard the rights of the highest ranks of the barons, were to be interpreted, in the constitutional struggles of the sixteenth and seventeenth centuries, as guarantees of the basic rights of all English citizens. The right of a representative parliament to control taxation was held to be contained in the clause: "No scutage or aid, save the customary feudal ones, shall be levied except by the common consent of the realm." And the right of a man to be tried by a jury of his fellow citizens according to the established processes of law was found in the clause: "No freeman shall be taken or imprisoned or dispossessed, or outlawed, or banished, or in any way destroyed, nor will we go against him, nor send upon him, except by the legal judgement of his peers or by the law of the land."

The Origins of Parliament

The weakness of John's son, Henry III (reigned 1216–1272), and his expensive favoritism to foreign adventurers welcomed by his mother, brought the English nobility into revolt on several occasions during his reign. No longer satisfied with the assertion of their rights, the nobles began to create administrative devices to ensure the respect for those rights by the king. In 1258, they refused to grant money until the king accepted the Provisions of Oxford, by which a council of barons was to help him govern. Five years later, they again revolted; and in 1265, after two years of skirmishing, their leader Simon de Montfort sought broader support for the rebellion by calling to a "parliament" not only the lords but the local "knights of the shire" and representatives of the towns. Although the king refused to recognize this body, the principle of representation had been established. The rebellion was crushed shortly afterwards by the king's son Edward, and Simon de Montfort was killed. Edward then ran the government for his father until he succeeded to the throne in 1272.

Edward I (reigned 1272–1307) was the last of the great administrators of the English medieval monarchy, and he attempted to carry on the work of Henry II. Like him, he began his reign by bringing the nobles into submission, stripping them of their private courts of justice, restoring their duty of direct loyalty to him rather than to an intermediary lord who had divided up his lands, and especially by destroying their castles. He at-

Harlech Castle, Wales, c. 1285
The finest surviving medieval castles were built by Edward I to hold down the newly conquered Welsh. Harlech consists of an inner castle, or donjon, marked by the twin towers on the right of the photo, and an outer wall also strengthened with round towers. British Tourist Authority photo

tempted to bring peace to the borders and to extend the size of his kingdom by the successful pacification of Wales and by the unsuccessful effort to defeat the Scots. Finally, to raise the revenue for this energetic policy, Edward called together in 1295 all the groups he wished to tax, in his Great Council. There had been several precedents for such an assembly in England. The Anglo-Saxon kings had had the privilege of consulting their principal subjects in the witan; and the Norman kings had frequently used the *curia regis* or king's council. Edward, however, followed the example of Simon de Montfort in admitting the principle of representation. For the first time, a Great Council or Parliament summoned by the king included all the groups later to be represented in parliament, and for that reason the assembly of 1295 has been called the Model Parliament. The precedent had been set, even though Edward rarely repeated his gesture. During the following two centuries, the higher clergy and more important vassals separated from the representative members of the council to become the House of Lords, while the knights of the shire and the burgesses joined in the House of Commons. The contest between king and parliament for supremacy did not occur, however, until the seventeenth century (see Chapter 15). Thus, while the French monarchy was gaining ever greater control over its subjects, finally emerging as Europe's most centralized monarchy, the English kings, after creating a powerful state in their own right, were forced to share the exercise of power with their subjects.

Germany Under the Saxon and Salian Emperors

The Saxon Emperors

The eastern section of Charlemagne's empire, taken by Louis the German after the Treaty of Verdun of 843, differed markedly in character and population from the western section that was to become the kingdom of France. The part that was to be the main body of Germany had always been outside the boundaries of the Roman Empire and lacked the civilizing influence and, in particular, the urbanizing influence of Roman rule. Much of the land was still covered with dense forest and, in the North, with wide marshes or barren heaths. Low but rugged mountain ranges separated North from South and helped the tribes maintain a kind of seminational separation with a sense of their own distinctive character. Moreover, life remained constantly menaced by the exposure to the invaders from the East; in fact, along the whole eastern border lay a line of military marches, or Marks, organized principally by Charlemagne to hold off not only the Magyars but also such marauding tribes as the Wends or the Sorbs. As Carolingian power diminished in this area, power was taken, or rather seized, by Carolingian administrators and military leaders who took for themselves the title of duke. By the end of the ninth century, Germany was divided into

German Principalities

Kingdom of Italy

Kingdom of the Two Sicilies
(Acquired 1186)

◆ *Germany and Italy Under the Hohenstaufen Emperors* ◆

five great duchies—Lorraine, Saxony, Franconia, Swabia, and Bavaria. The dukes were aware of the fragility of their position on the invasion frontier of Europe. Unlike the great vassals in France, who chose Hugh Capet as king because his weakness was no threat to their own power, the German dukes—when the last Carolingian died in 911—chose Conrad of Franconia, who had given tangible proof of his strength by wiping out his rivals in Franconia and whose duchy was itself extremely powerful. Conrad I (reigned 911–918), however, proved a military failure, and on his death the throne passed to a far more effective ruler, Henry the Fowler from the northern duchy of Saxony. The Saxons were at that time the great warriors of Germany. They had fought for many years to hold off the armies of Charlemagne, and even after their incorporation into his empire had been compelled to defend the empire against Vikings from the North and the many Asiatic invaders from the East. Henry I (reigned 919–936) determined to bring the duchies under his control. Franconia, which had supported his designation as king, eventually passed into the personal rule of his son. New dukes loyal to the king were appointed in Swabia, Bavaria, and Lorraine, after rebellions had been crushed. And the forces of his whole kingdom were united to push German control eastwards into the lands held by the Slavs.

Henry's son Otto I (reigned 936–973), known as the Great, carried on his father's policy with even greater effectiveness. He made his own brother Bruno archbishop of Cologne, because that gave him control over the Duchy of Lorraine. He extended his own royal estates throughout the five duchies, so that he possessed his own financial and military resources within the territories where possible disaffection might occur. From the Church he drew a large corps of reliable administrators; and he strengthened both the Church and royal authority by taking under his own legal protection many of the Church lands and monasteries. This system worked to the mutual benefit of Church and state as long as the pope accepted the king's nominees to the principal German bishoprics. It took Otto almost twenty years before he felt Germany had been brought under monarchical control. He then devoted the rest of his reign to expanding German influence in eastern Europe and in attempting to create for himself a renewed Roman empire that would include Italy.

German expansion to the east, the so-called *Drang nach Osten*, became one of the most important factors in all European history, and was not finally reversed until the end of the Second World War. Otto had stabilized the Hungarian border by his victory over the Magyars at Lechfeld in 955. He then extended the system of fortified colonies begun by Henry I beyond the Elbe river, where vast fertile lands lay open to the eager grasp of the military leaders. The Slav population, he believed, once subdued, could be used for labor. The scheme was blessed by the Church as a method of converting the heathen, and monks and clerics quickly followed the armies into the subjugated lands. Most important of all, the German kings encouraged

SAXON, SALIAN, AND HOHENSTAUFEN DYNASTIES IN GERMANY

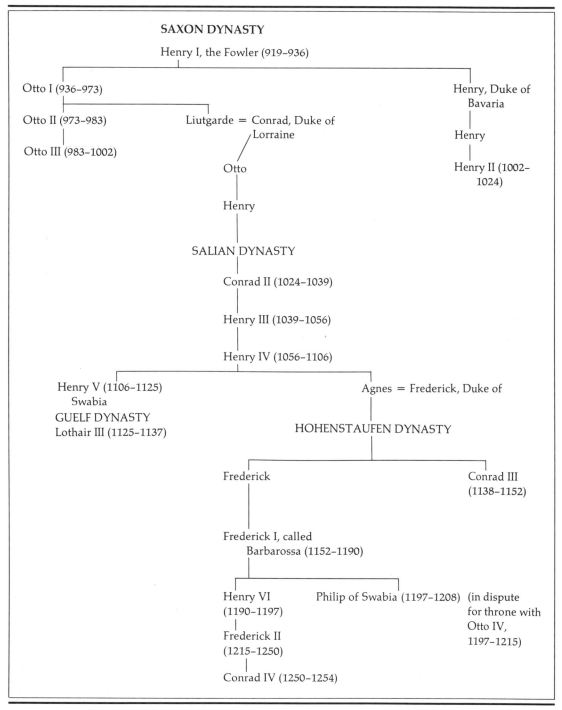

SAXON DYNASTY

Henry I, the Fowler (919–936)

Otto I (936–973)   Henry, Duke of
                                                                              Bavaria

Otto II (973–983)   Liutgarde = Conrad, Duke of
                                                        Lorraine   Henry

Otto III (983–1002)
                                             Otto   Henry II (1002–
                                                                                            1024)

                                             Henry

                                  SALIAN DYNASTY

                                  Conrad II (1024–1039)

                                  Henry III (1039–1056)

                                  Henry IV (1056–1106)

Henry V (1106–1125)   Agnes = Frederick, Duke of
Swabia
GUELF DYNASTY   **HOHENSTAUFEN DYNASTY**
Lothair III (1125–1137)

                      Frederick   Conrad III
                                                                              (1138–1152)

                      Frederick I, called
                          Barbarossa (1152–1190)

                      Henry VI   Philip of Swabia (1197–1208)   (in dispute
                      (1190–1197)   for throne with
                                                                                                  Otto IV,
                      Frederick II   1197–1215)
                      (1215–1250)

                      Conrad IV (1250–1254)

German Expansion Eastwards, 1000–1300

city building in the lands near the Elbe as an instrument of Germanization. Hamburg, founded in 834, and Magdeburg, founded in 805, were the key cities in this process. But the excessive greed and cruelty of the German settlers provoked the Slavs to desperate revolt, and by the end of the tenth century the process of expansion had been temporarily halted.

The siren call of Italy seduced the German rulers for the next three centuries. Otto I had already intervened in Italy in 951, when the widow of the Lombard King appealed to him for protection against an unwelcome suitor: Otto had solved the problem by marrying her himself, and had thus enlarged his claim to rule in Italy. In 961, answering an appeal for help from

St. Michael's Church, Hildesheim
This Benedictine abbey was built in 1001–1033 by the reforming bishop Bernward. The heaviness of the walls is lightened by the four round towers appended to the two transepts, an architectural oddity that was not adopted outside the German-speaking countries.
German Information Center photo

the pope, who was embroiled with rivals from among the Roman nobility, Otto entered Italy from Bavaria across the Brenner Pass. At Pavia, he first had himself crowned king of Italy; then, moving on to Rome, in February 962, he was crowned emperor of the Romans by the pope, in direct emulation of the coronation of Charlemagne. The title of emperor had come to mean so little under the later Carolingians that it had not been adopted by a German ruler since 924. Now Otto's ambitions were clear. He did not intend to recreate the empire of Charlemagne, even though his coronation was a reenactment of the ceremony on Christmas day in the year 800. He was, however, laying claim to the Middle Kingdom, which had been given, along with the imperial title, to Charlemagne's grandson Lothar at the Treaty of Verdun in 843. By combining the Middle Kingdom with the eastern section of Charlemagne's empire, which he already held, he proposed to create a powerful state commanding most of central Europe but freed from the complications of the struggles in France. The ambition seemed realistic, in view of the ease with which Otto had conquered Italy. But he and his successors should have been aware that Italy presented them with a double problem that would sap their energies and resources to no lasting benefit:

Otto I
This tenth-century ivory plaque shows the emperor offering a model of Magdeburg Cathedral to Christ. The Metropolitan Museum of Art, Gift of George Blumenthal, 1941

the turbulent hatred of the Italian population for the German overlord and, even more important, the determination of the pope eventually to assert his supremacy over the emperor on whom he was temporarily dependent. One year later, Otto I had overthrown the pope by force, and appointed his own nominee as pope. Rome itself was brought into submission through a siege. The degradation of the city was a poor augury for German imperial rule, as Benedict of a nearby monastery of Saint Andrea witnessed:

Rome was surrounded by the people of the Lombards, the Saxons, and the Gauls, in a great circle, so that none dared to go beyond the walls. Fire and sword caused great famine in Rome, and the hearts of the people quailed within them because their strength was brought to naught. There was but one voice among them from the least to the greatest. Forced by dire need, they took Benedict the pope [the rival to Otto's nominee] and gave him into the hands of the emperor, and said to one another: "It is better for one alone to die for all, that we may save all other lives from destruction by hunger." The emperor sent the pontiff to the most sacred seat, amid the praises of the Roman people. . . .

Woe unto thee, Rome, oppressed and trodden under foot by so many nations! Thou art taken captive by the Saxon king, thy people are put to the sword, thy strength is brought to naught. Thy gold and thy silver are carried away in their purses. The mother thou wast—a daughter thou hast become. What thou hadst, thou hast lost. Thou art despoiled of thy former strength. . . . Now thou art plundered and utterly despoiled by the Saxon kings. . . . Now the people of Gaul have encamped in the midst of thee. Thou wast too beautiful.[6]

Both Otto II (reigned 973–983) and Otto III (reigned 983–1002) were obsessed with the goal of bringing all Italy under their rule. Otto II was defeated in his attempt to annex the Byzantine possessions in the South. His son, Otto III, after his coronation in Rome in 996, established his home on the Aventine Hill. There, influenced by his mother, a Byzantine princess, he adopted the fashions of Constantinople. In a palace high above the Tiber river, surrounded by ancient Christian basilicas, he maintained punctilious court ritual and had himself served by consuls, senators, prefects, chancellors, and other assorted functionaries. In himself he saw united the Saxon, the Roman, and the Greek. In 998, Otto III placed on his seal the inscription *Renovatio imperii Romanorum* (The Restoration of the empire of the Romans), and two years later he went to Aachen to make the personal acquaintance of the first reviver of the empire. At the imperial palace of Charlemagne, one chronicler wrote:

He was in doubt where the bones of Charlemagne lay, and so he had the floor of the Palatine Chapel breached, and ordered workmen to dig where he thought they were. In due course the bones were found seated on the royal throne. Otto removed the golden cross which hung on Charles' neck, and such of the clothes as had not crumbled to dust, and the rest were interred with great devotion.[7]

The last Saxon emperor, Henry II (reigned 1002–1024) was compelled to return to Germany to deal with a revolt of the German nobility, but he was only able to raise the necessary military strength from his supporters in the Church by granting greater privileges and territories to them. The moment Germany was pacified, however, he had to return to Italy to put down a serious revolt among the vassals of the North. Like his predecessors, he had found that Italian ambitions had made it impossible for him to focus his attention on his German possessions.

The baleful results of this preoccupation with the extension of the Ger-

---

[6] Cited in J. H. Robinson, *Readings in European History* (Boston: Ginn and Co., 1904), I, 254–55.

[7] Thietmar of Merseburg, *Chronicon*, IV, 47. 29, cited in Christopher Brooke, *Europe in the Central Middle Ages, 962–1154* (London: Longman's, 1964), p. 172.

manic empire into Italy were not, however, to be fully felt until the twelfth and thirteenth centuries. When one compares the state of affairs under the Saxon emperors in the tenth century with that in France and England, one realizes the enormous advances the Saxons achieved. The German feudal lords were curbed. An efficient system of frontier defense was created along the troubled valleys of the Elbe and upper Danube. A cultural revival (perhaps *birth* is more accurate) was encouraged in the great monasteries of Saxony and Burgundy, especially in Hildesheim. Historical chronicles and lives of the bishops were composed in the monastic schools. Manuscript illumination emulated the work of Byzantium. Churches modeled upon Charlemagne's chapel in Aachen were built in the nearby towns of Nijmegen and Liège, and at the end of the century more massive churches in Romanesque style were built in Magdeburg and Hildesheim. Some writers have even spoken of this period of German culture as the Ottonian renaissance.

Nevertheless, the ambitions of the Saxon kings proved double-edged. They succeeded in subduing their feudal nobility only so long as they themselves mustered sufficient personal wealth and strength to do so. The feudal principalities remained potentially disruptive to imperial unity. The Saxon kings struck an effective alliance with the Church, using the clergy in secular administrative tasks and as leaders of a cultural renaissance commanded from above. They endowed great monasteries like Hildesheim with rich lands, favoring the ambitious building efforts of those communities with their patronage of art and scholarship. They occasionally used their power over the papacy to ensure the election of clerics of high scholarship and moral standards. But the error of the Saxon emperors lay in being deluded by dreams of reviving Rome. Constant campaigns were necessary to secure German power in Italy, against Romans, Byzantines, Moslems, and Normans; and this distracted successive dynasties from the work of both defending the borders of Germany and maintaining the obedience of the German feudal lords. Understandably, the emperor's power was extremely vulnerable when, to his surprise, he was challenged by the papacy which, for two centuries, had been a malleable instrument of imperial ambitions.

The Early Salian Emperors

For the first three quarters of the eleventh century, German prosperity grew, thanks to innovative emperors of the Salian dynasty from Franconia. Under Conrad II (reigned 1024–1039) and Henry III (reigned 1039–1056), the Ottonian system of administration was consolidated. The great duchies began to lose some of their regional separatism, and the flow of trade and culture between North and South created bonds of self-interest and comprehension. The foundation of large numbers of new monasteries in the eastern parts of Germany also broke down the isolation of the more backward regions along the military frontiers. New towns expanded along the trade routes linking the great river valleys. Bamberg and Nuremberg, for example, lay along the routes joining the Danube to the Main. From the economic and social point of view, perhaps the most important change was the vast movement to colonize the forest lands within the country that had previously resisted the efforts of would-be farmers; new settlements were hacked from the woodlands in the Taunus to the west of the Rhine and in the uplands of Swabia and Thuringia. With a growing population and an expanding economy, ruled by efficient kings, Germany became the most powerful European state. Poland and Bohemia were forced to acknowledge its overlordship. Hungary lay under its influence. Italy was quiescent. And as King of Arles, the German emperor felt his power extend even into the southeast of France.

This satisfactory situation continued for the first two decades of the rule of Henry IV (reigned 1056–1106). Then, suddenly, in the words of Geoffrey Barraclough, "at the very moment of Henry's most sweeping success [the suppression of a Saxon revolt] a new and mightier adversary took up arms. Under the leadership of Gregory VII, the papacy declared war on the German emperor and on the whole established system of German imperialism." At the end of this struggle, the German state had been reduced to fragments.

The Conflict of Emperors and Popes

The Reform of the Church

The papacy's determination to reassert the authority of the Church over the lay power was the sequel to the great reform program carried through in the Church in the ninth century. At the time of the breakdown of the Carolingian empire, the Church's moral standards had slumped badly. Monasteries had fallen away from the disciplined simplicity of life laid down by Saint Benedict, partly because of the riches bequeathed them, partly because of the nonspiritual duties given them by the state. Bishoprics, regarded as feudal fiefs with military and fiscal obligations, had come under the direct control of great lords who appointed their own friends and relatives to office, or sold them to the highest bidder. The rich bishopric of Narbonne in southern France was bought by a noble in Provence for his ten-year-old son. Later, the seller complained to a church council that the new bishop, once an adult, "arrogant as a devil, unexpectedly provoked me to anger and harassed me and built castles against me and made cruel war on me with a vast army so that on account of him almost a thousand men were slaughtered on both sides." The new kind of bishops ignored the idea of priestly celibacy, took wives or concubines, and even passed on the bishopric to their sons. The corruption undoubtedly spread even to the popes themselves, who spent much of their time engaging in endless quarrels among the petty factions in Rome itself.

In reaction to the corruption in the Church, reform was demanded from both outside and inside the Church. As we saw, the Saxon emperors had overthrown popes, not least because they disapproved of their moral standards. Great nobles who were sincerely concerned with the decline in monastic standards founded new monasteries wherein the austerity and discipline prescribed by Saint Benedict could be restored. The most important of these monasteries was the Abbey of Cluny in Burgundy, founded in 910 by the Duke of Aquitaine. By its charter, the monks of Cluny were to recognize no outside interference in the running of the monastery or in the choice of abbot, except from the pope alone. These monks founded daughter houses and accepted older monasteries into their order, all the while maintaining a centralized control headed by their abbot, which enabled them to enforce strict discipline. Their main goals were the return to poverty, though not to manual labor, and a new emphasis on prayer and liturgical ceremony, combined with the overthrow of secular interference and especially the end of simony, the crime of selling church offices. Cluny's influence was especially great in France and Belgium, while monasteries in Lorraine—sponsored by the emperor and German nobles—carried the monastic reform movement into Germany.

From the monasteries, reform spread to the papacy itself, primarily through the intervention of Emperor Henry III. Faced with three churchmen all claiming to be the rightful pope, Henry forced the appointment of a fourth, a German reformer, after he had deposed the three quarreling pontiffs. For the rest of the eleventh century, the papacy was in the hands of reformers, who were mostly Germans; and the emperor was startled to find himself the main object of the pope's reforming zeal.

The reforming popes began with the most glaring examples of corruption within the Church, vigorously attacking simony (the sale of ecclesiastical preferment), clerical marriage, and clerical concubinage. Pope Leo IX (1049–1054) went personally to councils in France and Germany where he dramatized the seriousness of the pope's determination to cleanse the Church by deposing and excommunicating bishops who disregarded his warnings. Shortly after Leo's death, largely under pressure from the papal adviser Hildebrand, the selection of pope was removed from the influence of both the emperor and the Roman nobility by the decree of 1059 ordering the pope's election through the College of Cardinals in Rome. Hildebrand also struck an alliance with the Norman knights of southern Italy, who promised their military support in the event of a conflict between the pope and the German emperor. The Church was further strengthened by a renovation of the whole clerical bureaucracy, a more skillful exploitation of Church wealth, and the strategic use of the ultimate weapon of excommunication. Excommunication enabled the pope to deny any man the support of his peers in this world and the heavenly host in the next. Even an emperor who would risk damnation was unwilling to chance the consequences of excommunication in this life.

The Crusades

The most dramatic expression of the revived prestige of the Church was the Crusades to reconquer the Holy Land. In 1095 at Clermont in central France, Pope Urban II called on the knights of Christendom, and especially those of France, to "enter upon the road to the Holy Sepulcher; wrest that land from the wicked race, and subject it to yourselves." He had been begged for aid by the Byzantine emperor, whose army had been defeated in Asia Minor by the Seljuk Turks; and he expected to achieve the submission of the Eastern Orthodox Church to Rome in return for aiding the Byzantine emperor in reconquering Asia Minor. The Seljuk Turks had also captured Jerusalem in 1071, and were making it more difficult, though by no means impossible, for pilgrims to visit the places associated with Christ's life and death in the Holy Land. Nevertheless, pilgrimages to the Holy Land, which brought not only the excitement of foreign travel, the possibility of commercial transactions, and large-scale remission of sins, had become so pop-

Meeting of Christian and Saracen
In this somewhat anachronistic version, the fifteenth-century artist has portrayed the Crusaders in the puffed doubloon and tight hose of the contemporary courtier. The Pierpont Morgan Library

ular by the eleventh century that even the rumors of Seljuk obstructionism were enough to rouse widespread fury in Europe. For participating in the Crusade, the pope also offered the opportunity for wealth and territorial rule, as well as automatic absolution of sins to those killed in battle; and to those disturbed by the unruly conduct of the knights at home, he offered a way of getting them gainfully occupied in distant lands at the expense of the infidel and of thus securing the Peace of God at home. The response to his appeal was enthusiastic. After a year's hectic organization, three large armies set off for Constantinople, from which they were to attack Syria and Palestine. Most of the knights were from France and the western parts of Germany, but recruits came from almost every state of Europe. No kings participated, but several leading feudal nobles, including Count Baldwin of Flanders and Duke Robert of Normandy, led large numbers of their personal followers. During the three years (1096–1099) of fighting in Asia Minor and the Holy Land, individual leaders began to cut out dominions for themselves: Baldwin of Flanders took Edessa; Prince Bohemond, Antioch; and after the bloody capture of Jerusalem in 1099, the Crusaders handed to Godfrey of Bouillon the hastily created kingdom of Jerusalem.

It seemed that the First Crusade had thus been a startling success, given the enormous difficulties of military operations so far from western Europe. The Crusaders intended to hold the Holy Land by building vast castles even more elaborate in defense works than those in Europe, and they received a

Castle of Krak des Chevaliers
To hold the lands reconquered from the Moslems, the Crusaders erected enormous castles embodying the most recent techniques of fortification. Krak controlled much of northern Syria.
Roger–Viollet

constant reinforcement of knights from newly organized military orders like the Knights Templar and the Knights Hospitaler. Moreover, they were determined to make the new possessions a profitable economic concern, by granting trading privileges to the major Italian cities. Venice, Pisa, and Genoa were thus encouraged to become the intermediaries who could sell the products of the Holy Land and the goods brought there from the East to the ready markets in western Europe.

Within twenty years, however, Moslem power had been revived under a Syrian prince; and when Edessa fell, Saint Bernard took it upon himself to preach the Second Crusade (1147–1149). Although the French king and the German emperor both took part, the Crusade was a dismal failure. The Crusaders were defeated outside Damascus, and returned home in disarray. The Third Crusade (1189–1192) was provoked by the military successes of Saladin, the Moslem ruler of Egypt who succeeded in reconquering the Holy Land, including Jerusalem itself. This time, the kings of England and France and the Holy Roman Emperor all set off for the Holy Land. The German emperor drowned in a river on the way; the French and English kings bickered constantly, especially when their armies failed to recapture more

Jerusalem
When the Crusaders captured Jerusalem in 1099, it was a predominantly Arab city dominated by two seventh-century mosques, el-Aksa and the Dome of the Rock. Today, the skyline is a mixture of Christian, Moslem, and Jewish buildings. Trans World Airlines photo

than a few coastal cities. The English army was finally left alone to conclude a truce with Saladin that gave pilgrims the right to visit Jerusalem. Richard ended his ill-fated journey by being captured for ransom in Austria. This debacle ended the true crusades, that is, the genuine attempt to recapture the Holy Land.

The Fourth Crusade (1202–1204) was a totally different affair. Although its original purpose was supposedly to recapture Jerusalem, the Venetians who provided transport first diverted the expedition to capture the Adriatic island of Zara for themselves, as payment for their services. Then, in return for promises of financial aid for their attack on the Holy Land, the Crusaders agreed to aid a pretender to the Byzantine throne by conquering Constantinople. Their motives were mixed. The pope still nourished the hope of reuniting the Greek Orthodox and Catholic churches. Unless they took this opportunity of gaining financial and military support promised by the pretender, the Crusaders saw no way of waging a successful campaign against the Moslems. The Venetians wanted a monopoly on Byzantine trade for themselves. The pretender was installed on the throne in 1203, after Constantinople had been taken without much difficulty. But popular resistance to him prevented him from keeping his promises, and in 1204 the Crusaders seized Constantinople a second time. They had agreed in advance on how they would divide up the Byzantine empire among themselves; and they sacked the city mercilessly.

The results of the Fourth Crusade were disastrous. Many of Constantinople's greatest art treasures were destroyed in the looting. Its citizens were confirmed in their conviction that reunion of their Greek Orthodox Church with the Catholic Church was impossible. The Byzantine empire was divided among the city's occupants; and when the emperor installed by the Crusaders was driven out by Emperor Michael VIII Palallogus, the ruler of the tiny state of Nicaea, in 1261, the restored empire was a debilitated remnant huddled around the shores of the Aegean Sea and could offer little resistance to the growing attacks of the Ottoman Turks. Finally, the Crusaders had been distracted from the Holy Land, and all future attempts to reconquer it were doomed from the start. Only Frederick II succeeded in gaining possession of Jerusalem, by diplomatic bargaining; and he held it for less than fifteen years. By the end of the thirteenth century, the Crusaders had been ousted from their last foothold in Palestine.

The Crusades were thus notable for their ineffectiveness. They were proof of the extraordinary but ephemeral exploits possible when the Church and feudality combined in a common enterprise. They furthered the taste for eastern luxuries and enriched the supplier. But they did not recapture the Holy Land for more than a short time. They greatly weakened Byzantium as a bulwark of Europe against invasion by the Moslems. They brought little knowledge of Arab culture. And the obvious materialism of the later Crusaders brought discredit on the papacy as the original sponsor of the Crusades.

Conflict of Pope and Emperor: The Investiture Contest

The pope's challenge to the emperor reached its most dramatic form when Hildebrand, who had already been running the papal government since 1054, was acclaimed as Pope Gregory VII (1073–1085). Within two years, Gregory had laid down a clearly thought out program that not only would have removed the Church from secular control but also made impossible the formation of a centralized monarchy in Germany by the emperor Henry IV (reigned 1056–1106). In February 1075, he issued a decree banning lay investiture. He thus attacked the power of the emperor at its most crucial point in the feudal age, the right of a lord to invest every new vassal with his benefice, in the symbolic ceremony that implied the lord's right to service from his vassal in return for the land. Previously, the Church had willingly supplied men and money in return for the land, and had allowed the emperor to hand each new bishop his ring and staff as proof that they would continue to keep this bargain. When Gregory forbade the bishops to go through with this ceremony, the emperor feared eventual refusal to supply his income and his army. In March, 1075, Gregory followed up his challenge to lay investiture with an even more threatening document known as the *Dictatus Papae.* The document is regarded by most experts as an accurate representation of the pope's views at the opening of his conflict with the emperor. The pope, Gregory stated, with the cutting logic that marked both his character and his intellect, "alone can depose or reconcile bishops . . . it is lawful for him to depose emperors . . . he can absolve from their fealty the subjects of wicked rulers." Far from demanding the mere separation of church and state, Gregory in short had claimed the supremacy of the pope over lay rulers.

The conflict was colorful. The German bishops, under Henry's persuasion, wrote to the pope: "Since you have degraded your life and conduct by multifarious infamy, we declare that in the future we shall observe no longer the obedience which we have not promised to you." Henry ordered him to give up the papacy, in a letter that began: "Henry, King not by usurpation, but by pious ordination of God, to Hildebrand, now not Pope, but false monk." THe pope's reply was immediate: "I take from King Henry, son of the Emperor Henry, who has risen against your Church with pride unheard of, the government of the whole kingdom of the Germans and the Italians, and I free all Christian people from any oath they have made or shall make to him, and I forbid any to serve the king. . . . I bind him with the chain of anathema."[8] Both his clergy and nobles deserted Henry, on hearing of his excommunication; and to save his throne, in 1077 Henry rushed across the Alps in midwinter to the papal palace at Canossa where he waited as a penitent in the snow for three days. The pope had no choice but to give him absolution, for fear of losing his own moral prestige. Gre-

---

[8] Theodor E. Mommsen and Karl F. Morrison, eds., *Imperial Lives and Letters of the Eleventh Century* (New York: Columbia University Press, 1967), pp. 149–50.

gory himself described the scene in a letter to those who had supported him:

When, after many delays and after much consultation, we had, through all the envoys who passed between us, severely reprimanded him for his offenses, he at length came of his own accord, accompanied by a few followers, with no hostility or arrogance in his bearing, to the town of Canossa, where we were tarrying. And there, laying aside all the trappings of royalty, he stood in wretchedness, barefooted and clad in woolen, for three days before the gate of the castle, and implored with profuse weeping the aid and consolation of the apostolic mercy, until he had moved all who saw or heard of it to such pity and depth of compassion that they interceded for him with many prayers and tears and wondered at the unaccustomed hardness of our heart; some even protested that we were displaying not the seriousness of the apostolic displeasure but the cruelty of tyrannical ferocity.

At last, overcome by his persistent remorse and by the earnest entreaties of those with us, we loosed the chain of anathema and received him into the favor of our fellowship, and into the lap of the holy mother Church. . . .[9]

Gregory's triumph was short-lived. Absorption with political power lost him the support of many Church reformers; and his reliance on the unscrupulous Normans soon made him their captive—literally, since he died as a virtual prisoner in a Norman castle, after his allies had pillaged Rome itself. He had also weakened the power of the papacy's most effective ally, the emperor himself, by inviting the German lords to revolt against him. The chaotic fighting between nobility, imperial armies, and Normans dragged on for almost fifty years. Only in 1122 was a compromise reached between the new emperor Henry V (reigned 1106–1125) and a less ambitious pope, at the Concordat of Worms. By this agreement, the investiture ceremony was split into two parts. The emperor no longer invested the new bishop with the ring and staff that symbolized his spiritual authority, and thus technically he gave up the right of lay investiture. But bishops were to do him homage for their lands, and by refusing to receive such homage he could in effect veto their appointment.

Frederick Barbarossa: The Conflict of Pope and Emperor Renewed

The struggle between pope and emperor continued throughout the twelfth and first half of the thirteenth centuries. At the end of it, Germany had been reduced to a misgoverned patchwork of over five hundred feudal principalities, the once flourishing island of Sicily was a ruins, the last member of the imperial family of the Hohenstaufen executed, and the papacy, which had sacrificed its spiritual prestige in the defeat of the emperor, about to be-

[9] Cited in Robinson, *Readings,* pp. 282–83.

come the physical captive of the French monarchy. This bloodletting occurred, paradoxically enough, while the civilization of medieval Christendom was reaching its height—not in Rome but in Paris.

When Henry V died without a son, the German princes picked Lothair III (reigned 1125–1137), the Duke of Saxony, to be emperor in preference to Henry's nephew, Conrad, Duke of Swabia. Their choice precipitated civil war between the factions, in which the only gainers were the smaller princes seeking greater power in their own principalities. For the next century, Germany was split between the adherents of Lothair's faction, who were called Guelfs, and the Ghibellines, who supported Conrad's family, the Hohenstaufen. (The names were also adopted in Italy shortly after, a Ghibelline meaning a supporter of the emperor and a Guelf a supporter of the pope.) Lothair himself saw the need to end this chaos, and he named Conrad to succeed him as emperor (reigned 1138–1152). These unhappy rivalries finally seemed to be resolved with the succession of Conrad's nephew, Frederick Barbarossa or Redbeard (reigned 1152–1190), since his father was Ghibelline and his mother Guelf. Frederick added to these advantages a warrior's physique, a statesman's mind, and unbending determination; he was, in short, the only medieval emperor to compare with Charlemagne or Otto the Great.

Frederick's plan was clearly conceived—he proposed to consolidate the royal domain which stretched from southern Germany across Switzerland and into northern Italy as a central nucleus of monarchial power. Beyond that area, he sought reliable allies and servants. His policy therefore required that he should pacify the outlying principalities of Germany, especially Guelf Bavaria, and win friends among the increasingly wealthy cities of the Rhine and Main valleys. In Italy, it was essential that the north Italian cities, which were organized as autonomous communes, should be enlisted as obedient allies and sources of revenue. If possible, Frederick was willing to work with the pope, as he showed when he went to Rome to be crowned. If a workable friendship was not possible, he was prepared to use force against the pontiff. What distinguished Frederick from many of the earlier emperors was his cold recognition that his position was not dependent upon any spiritual qualities implied by his title or indeed his coronation by the Church but upon the right of conquest. In a superbly phrased letter to the Roman nobility, which had had the gall to imply that they had the right to offer him the throne, all the power of the emperor's character is evident:

You have related the ancient renown of your city, and have extolled the ancient state of your sacred republic. Agreed! Agreed! In the words of your celebrated author, "there was once virtue in this republic." "Once," I say. Would that we could truthfully say "now." But Rome has experienced the vicissitudes of time. . . . First, as is known to all, the vigor of your nobility was transplanted to the royal city of the East [Constantinople]. . . . Then came the Franks . . . who took away by force the remnants of your freedom. . . We have

*turned over in our mind the deeds of modern emperors, considered how our sa-
cred predecessors, Charles and Otto, wrested your City with the lands of Italy
from the Greeks and Lombards, and brought it within the frontiers of the
Frankish realm, not as a gift from alien hands but as a conquest won by their
own valor . . . I am the lawful possessor.*[10]

Frederick had identified three enemies: the dissident nobility of Germany, the turbulent communes of northern Italy, and the reformed papacy.
Yet Frederick's policy united all three against him. One of his greatest errors was to announce, at the Diet of Roncaglia in 1158, that he had the right
to name the city governor, collect city revenues, and administer city justice
in the Italian communes. In the ensuing war, he besieged the city of Milan
for three years, and then ordered it totally destroyed. This act of savagery
merely persuaded the other cities of the necessity of allying with the pope
and Frederick's German rivals. At the battle of Legnano in 1176, Italian
footsoldiers won a crushing victory over Frederick's feudal horsemen, and
Frederick was compelled to recognize most of their demands. For the last
years of his life, he attempted with some success to pacify Germany
through accommodation with the princes. By then it was already too late for
the achievement of a unified state in Germany under a Hohenstaufen
emperor.

The last phase of the Hohenstaufen struggle with the papacy was completely different from the investiture contest, and even from the battles of
Frederick I with the papacy in northern Italy—for one reason. Frederick I's
son Henry VI (reigned 1190–1197) had inherited the kingdom of Sicily as a
result of his marriage to its Norman heiress. Henry VI, and even more his
son Frederick II (reigned 1215–1250), conceived of an empire stretching
from northern Germany to Sicily, that would dominate the eastern Mediterranean and hold both Byzantine and Moslem at bay. But such a vision was
even more frightening to the papacy than Frederick Barbarossa's plans, because their territories in central Italy would be surrounded by imperial possessions. Sicily moreover was a possession that could only reinforce the
Italian infatuation of the German emperors. The rich, almost semitropical,
island had never lost its contacts with the trade of the East, as a possession
either of Byzantium or of the Arabs; and under the Normans it had received
good government and new wealth from plunder. Sicily was a jewel to be-
dazzle any northern monarch—with the unspoiled Greek temples of Agrigento and Selinunte, the Roman theaters of Syracuse and Taormina, the Byzantine mosaics and the Arab fountains of the great cathedral of Monreale,
the massive Norman churches seemingly transplanted from the East Ang-
lian marshes to the cliffs of the Mediterranean shore—and Frederick II was
peculiarly susceptible to their charms. During his minority he had seen

---

[10] Cited in Geoffrey Barraclough, *The Origins of Modern Germany* (Oxford: Basil Blackwell, 1966),
p. 171, n.1.

Germany once again dissolve into internecine warfare among the princes, and he had learned to hate Germany's "long winters and sombre forests," and its "muddy towns and rugged castles." [11] In his long reign he spent only nine years there, satisfied to win recognition from the princes by leaving them the substance of power. In Italy he struggled during most of his reign to bring the northern cities into submission, and he even occupied most of the papal states for a while. In Sicily itself, he ruled as the descendant of all its past conquerors, speaking all the languages of his island—Italian, Greek, and Latin, as well as German and French—continuing the scientific interests of its Moslems, and learning from its multiracial society a tolerance that the pope found close to heresy. He swore to go on a Crusade, but found crusading methods so repugnant that on his first expedition to the Holy Land he turned back as soon as he was out of sight of land, and on the second he took possession of Jerusalem by negotiation instead of battle. His ambition to create a powerful state in Italy, his oblivion to excommunication, and his denial of the supremacy of the papacy brought on him the hatred of almost every pope of his reign. By the 1240s the pope was supporting an anti-emperor in Germany and an alternative king for Sicily; and after Frederick's death the pope gave the island to Charles of Anjou, the brother of the French king, and excommunicated Frederick's bastard son Manfred, to whom Frederick had bequeathed Sicily. Charles defeated and killed Manfred in 1266, and two years later beheaded in the main square of Naples the last Hohenstaufen, the fifteen-year-old grandson of Frederick II.

Thus, while the English and French monarchies were successful in creating centralized states wherein a sense of national homogeneity could grow, the German emperors, diverted from their affairs in Germany by their ambitions in Italy and their conflict with the papacy, saw their realm break into hundreds of fragments. Both Germany and Italy were to remain disunited until the nineteenth century. It was to be in the great feudal monarchies that had overcome the feudal tendency to fragmentation, and especially in thirteenth-century Paris, that medieval civilization was to reach its greatest heights.

SUGGESTED READING

Sidney Painter gives a useful introduction to the monarchies of France, England, and Germany in *The Rise of the Feudal Monarchies* (1951).

On the French kings, the standard work is R. Fawtier, *The Capetian Kings of France* (1960). The literary sources are entertainingly mined by A. Luchaire, *Social France at the Time of Philip Augustus* (1929) and Joan Evans, *Life in Medieval France* (1925).

G. O. Sayles, *The Medieval Foundations of England* (1948), is a masterly survey of English constitutional history, which comes to life more effectively, however, by a

---

[11] Ibid., p. 220.

reading of the documents collected in C. Stephenson and F. G. Marcham, eds., *Sources of English Constitutional History* (1937), or D. C. Douglas and G. W. Greenaway, eds., *English Historical Documents, 1042–1189* (1953). Douglas also has a good life of the great Norman, *William the Conqueror and the Norman Impact upon England* (1964). On the later English kings, one should consult C. Petit-Dutaillis, *The Feudal Monarchy in France and England: From the Tenth to the Thirteenth Century* (1964), S. Painter, *The Reign of King John* (1949), and F. M. Powicke, *King Henry III and the Lord Edward* (1947). David Knowle's *Thomas Becket* (1971) is short and stimulating, if excessively unfavorable to Henry II. Amy R. Kelly, *Eleanor of Aquitaine and the Four Kings* (1950) throws light on the dynasties of both France and England. On the making of the English legal system, see Alan Harding's good survey of recent research, with documents, in *The Law Courts of Medieval England* (1973), or return to admire the brilliance still glittering in F. Pollock and F. W. Maitland, *History of English Law Before the Time of Edward I* (1923). On Parliament, see P. Spufford, *Origins of the English Parliament* (1967); G. L. Haskins, *The Growth of English Representative Government* (1948); and Bryce Lyon, *Constitutional and Legal History of Medieval England* (1960). On English economic development, M. M. Postan is lucid and completely authoritative in *The Medieval Economy and Society: An Economic History of Britain, 1100–1500* (1972.)

Geoffrey Barraclough, *Medieval Germany, 911–1250* (1938), is still the best study of the Holy Roman Empire in the Middle Ages, but it can be supplemented by J. Bryce's classic *The Holy Roman Empire* (1904) and J. W. Thompson's *Feudal Germany* (1928). E. Kantorowicz, *Frederick the Second, 1194–1250* (1931) is an idiosyncratic life by a great historian, but fortunately it can be replaced by, or at least compared with, the superb biography by Thomas Curtis Van Cleve, *The Emperor Frederick II of Hohenstaufen: Immutator Mundi* (1972).

The growth in strength of the papacy is analyzed in W. Ullman, *Growth of Papal Power in the Middle Ages* (1955) and its use in the investiture contest in G. Tellenback, *Church, State and Christian Society at the Time of the Investiture Contest* (1940). The conflicts are surveyed, with a fine choice of documents, in Brian Tierney's *The Crisis of Church and State, 1050–1300, with Selected Documents* (1964). Geoffrey Barraclough, *The Medieval Papacy* (1968) is incisive and short. On the major popes, see A. J. MacDonald, *Hildebrand, A Life of Gregory VII* (1932); M. Baldwin, *Alexander III and the Twelfth Century* (1968); Sidney R. Packard, *Europe and the Church Under Innocent III* (1927); and L. E. Elliott-Binns, *Innocent III* (1931). On other aspects of the medieval church, see H. C. Lea, *A History of the Inquisition of the Middle Ages* (1922) and W. L. Wakefield and A. P. Evans, *Heresies of the High Middle Ages* (1969).

On the Cluniac revival, see Joan Evans, *Monastic Life at Cluny* (1931). In spite of its geographical limitations, a vast amount can be learned on the whole monastic movement from David Knowles, *The Monastic Order in England* (1951). For a balanced summation of the role of the Church, see R. W. Southern, *Western Society and the Church in the Middle Ages* (1970).

For a new approach to the Crusades, one could begin with the Arab version, presented in Francesco Gabrieli, ed., *Arab Historians of the Crusades* (1969), but the more familiar accounts of Villehardouin and Joinville in Frank Marzials, ed., *Memoirs of the Crusades* (1933) are more exciting. Good histories of the Crusades are now available in almost every length. The best full treatment is Stephen Runciman, *A History of the Crusades* (1951–54), vols. I–III. Shorter treatments include René Grousett, *The Epic of the Crusades* (1970) and Hans E. Mayer, *The Crusades* (1972). Much use of lovely contemporary illustrations gives immediacy to the short but reliable text of Joshua Prawer, a professor at Hebrew University, Jerusalem, in *The World of the Crusaders* (1972). On the methods of fighting in the Crusades, see R. C. Smail, *Crusading Warfare, 1097–1193* (1956); on the fortifications the Crusaders erected, see T. S. R. Boase, *Kingdoms and Strongholds of the Crusaders* (1971). The establishment of new states in the lands conquered by the Crusaders provides us with one of the best examples of feudal government, as can be seen in J. La Monte, *Feudal Monarchy in the Latin Kingdom of Jerusalem* (1932); Jonathan Riley-Smith, *The Feudal Nobility and the Kingdom of Jerusalem, 1174–1277* (1973); and D. C. Munro, *The Kingdom of the Crusaders* (1935). For the role of Constantinople in the last Crusades, see Dino J. Geanakoplos's "Byzantium and the Crusades, 1261–1453", which comprises chapters 2 and 3 in K. Setton, ed., *A History of the Crusades* (1975).

Finally, why not browse through the photographs in W. Douglas Simpson, *Castles from the Air* (1949)? Few things bring home the character of the life of the feudal nobility better than those massive piles of stone.

I am in Paris, in this royal city, where the abundance of nature's gifts not only captivates those who live there but invites and attracts those who are far away. Even as the moon surpasses the stars in brightness, so does this city, the seat of royalty, exalt her proud head above all other cities.—A provincial churchman, on visiting Paris in 1190

9 / The Paris of Saint Louis

The charm of medieval Paris was the harmony of city and countryside. "She is placed in the bosom of a delicious valley," wrote a visitor from the provinces, at the end of the twelfth century, "in the center of a crown of hills enriched with the gifts of Ceres and Bacchus. The Seine, that proud river which comes from the east, flows there through wide banks and with its two arms surrounds an island [the Ile de la Cité] which is the head, the heart, and the marrow of the whole city." Already the quarters of the city were developing a distinctive character according to that aspect of the city's life that had become centered there: "Two suburbs extend to right and left, the smaller of which would be the envy of many another city. These suburbs communicate with the island by two stone bridges; the Grand Pont toward the north in the direction of the English sea, and the Petit Pont which looks toward the Loire.

Saint Louis French Cultural Services

384

Royal Palace and Sainte Chapelle Giraudon

The first, broad, rich, and commercial, is the scene of feverish activity, and innumerable boats surround it laden with merchandise and riches. The Petit Pont belongs to the dialecticians, who pace up and down disputing. In the island adjacent to the king's palace, which dominates the whole town, the palace of philosophy is seen where study reigns alone as sovereign, a citadel of light and immortality." [1]

[1] Cited in Thomas Okey, *The Story of Paris* (London: Dent, 1906), pp. 69–70.

The Paris of Saint Louis

Period Surveyed	Reign of Louis IX, 1226–1270
Population	100,000–150,000
Area	1 square mile
Form of Government	Feudal monarchy. Administration through royal household and Curia Regis (King's Council, with specialized officials for law and finances)
Political Leaders	Louis IX; Blanche of Castile (mother of Louis IX); Charles of Anjou (brother of Louis IX)
Economic Base	Royal, ecclesiastical, and university revenues. Commerce in luxury goods. Manufacturing (textiles, jewelry, crystalware, armaments)
Intellectual Life	Philosophy (Alexander of Hales, Bonaventura, Thomas Aquinas)
Principal Buildings	Wall of Philip Augustus; Louvre; Royal palace on Ile de la Cité; Sainte Chapelle; Notre Dame Cathedral; Monastery of Saint Germain des Prés
Public Entertainment	Ludi theatrales (morality plays). Tournaments of knights. Minstrels. Soccer
Religion	Catholic. Some Jews

The special character of medieval Paris was formed by the joint efforts of bourgeoisie, monarchy, Church, and university. The bourgeoisie were concentrated on the right bank of the river, between the busy docks and the new wall of Philip Augustus. Although Paris was not one of the great economic centers of thirteenth-century Europe compared, for example, to Venice or Bruges, study of the origins of its prosperity as a commercial and

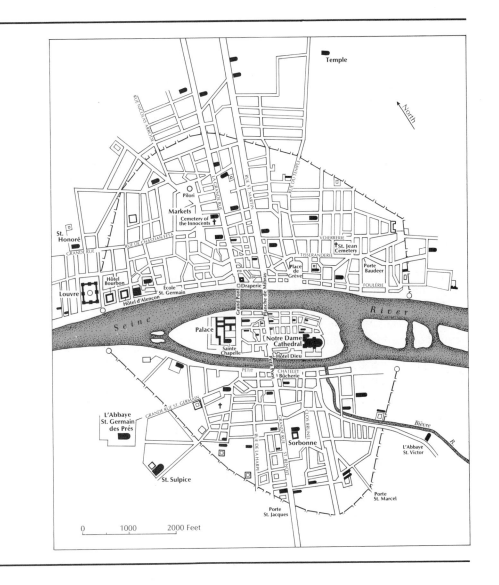

manufacturing center gives us insight into the great network of trade among the new or reviving cities of Europe that developed from the tenth century on. However, when we turn to the achievements of monarchy, Church, and university, we are dealing with medieval civilization at its most consummate. In the great palace on the western half of the Ile de la Cité, King Louis IX (reigned 1226–1270) established a model of feudal monarchy so rigorous in its morality, efficient in its administration, and yet appealing in its humanity that its superiority was recognized not only in France but also throughout Europe. The Catholic Church in Paris and the surrounding cities of the Ile-de-France, enriched and strengthened by the benefactions and support of monarchy and feudal lords, exercised as great if not greater influence on the lives of all segments of society as in any other part of Europe; and its importance was recognized throughout Christendom, not least by the papacy itself. The outward expression of the French Church's grandeur, material and spiritual, was the great series of Gothic cathedrals, of which Notre Dame de Paris is one of the most superb examples. But the greatness of the French Church was also expressed in the University of Paris, the dominant force on the Left Bank of the city; in philosophy, the most revered of all medieval fields of knowledge, Paris was supreme.

Bourgeois Paris

Although Paris never became one of the major commercial or manufacturing centers of Europe in the Middle Ages, it could never have developed to its size and complexity had it not profited from the great revival of commerce and manufacturing in old and new urban centers in Europe from the tenth century on.

Revival of the Mediterranean Cities

Trade in Europe had dwindled to a mere trickle by the end of the Viking invasions of the ninth and tenth centuries; and except for a small nucleus of clerical or lay administrators the great cities had been largely abandoned. There has been much dispute among historians over the causes and extent of this urban decline, especially since the Belgian historian Henri Pirenne suggested in *Mohammed and Charlemagne,* published in 1935, that the principal factor was the closing of the Mediterranean to western traders by the Arab conquests of the eighth century. Pirenne's thesis implied as a corollary that trade would only revive once the Mediterranean had again been opened to Christian commerce. Most critics of Pirenne agree that two factors must be emphasized. Western trade was dependent upon an active short-distance commerce, essentially the exchange of a surplus of agricultural goods for such basic supplies as salt or iron and for simple manufactured goods like clothing or tools. In the period of the invasions, stretching

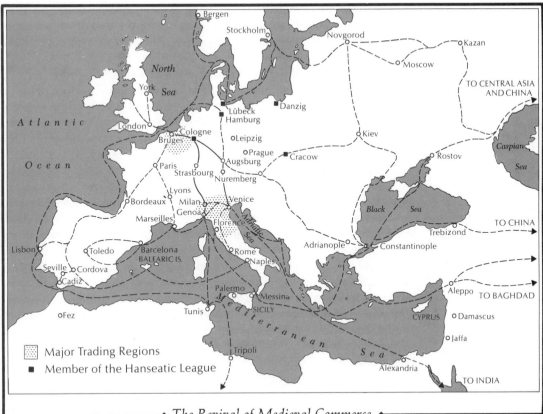

The Revival of Medieval Commerce

from the first Teutonic incursions through the Viking attacks, this form of exchange had broken down. Neither local nor long-distance trade was therefore possible, and the village had perforce to become self-sufficient. As we saw in Chapter 7, however, the improvement in agricultural techniques, combined with the establishment of security through feudal government, led to the production of an agricultural surplus, a growing population, and the revival of manufacturing for a local market. By the eleventh century, Europe once again possessed a surplus in food and manufactured goods that it could trade for non-European products. The second generally accepted criticism of Pirenne is that he failed to realize that trade with the East had never entirely ceased. Even in the worst days of the ninth century, there had been a demand from the great lay lords and from the Church for such products as silks, jewels, and spices; and these had been supplied from Constantinople which, in spite of the Arab conquests in the Mediterranean, had continued to trade in Asian products, shipping them into Europe through Italian ports like Amalfi, Bari, and especially Venice. When Europe was again in a position to expand its long-distance commerce, these Italian cities were the natural intermediaries.

Until the fifteenth century, no European city rivaled Venice in commercial importance. Built on several hundred tiny islands in the lagoons north of the Adriatic Sea, Venice was protected from inland attacks by two miles of water and storms in the Adriatic by the reef that formed its lagoons. Although its citizens at first made only a small living from salt and fish, Venice soon profited from its easy access to the growing cities of the Po valley. Over the Brenner Pass, its traders reached with relative ease the mineral resources of Austria. Down the valley of the Inn, its merchants joined the trade routes of southern Germany and the shipping lines of the Rhine valley which led to the Low Countries. The Venetian fleet, constantly enlarged from the tenth century on, was used not only to transport goods but also as an instrument of Venetian expansion. It was used in support of Constantinople's struggle with the Normans of Sicily in the eleventh century, for the conquest of territory down the Dalmatian coast of the Adriatic, and for the transport of Crusaders. After the fleet had provided passage for the knights of the Fourth Crusade in the conquest of Constantinople in 1204, Venice acquired virtually autonomous control of a part of the city. By the end of the thirteenth century, Venice was second only to Constantinople in wealth. It had a population of at least one hundred twenty thousand. And since power was concentrated in an oligarchy of about two hundred merchant families whose names were listed in the Golden Book, Venice possessed an astonishingly durable and stable form of government. Genoa and Pisa, on the western coast of Italy, broke Venice's monopoly of the Eastern trade by aiding the Crusaders; and they too built up trading routes from Syria and Palestine along the Mediterranean shores and northwards into continental Europe. But the main efforts of Genoa and Pisa were devoted to opening up the western Mediterranean to Christian commerce. During the eleventh century, they drove the Arabs out of Sardinia and Corsica, and made the seas between Italy and the expanding ports of Marseilles in southern France and Barcelona in Spain safe for their shipping. The prosperity of Pisa and Genoa lasted as long as they cooperated. At the end of the thirteenth century, however, Pisa was defeated by Genoa which, in its turn, was defeated by Venice in 1380. By then, the stimulus to commerce, manufacturing, and banking had spread from the coastal cities into the interior of Italy, and such cities as Florence, Siena, Lucca, and Milan were beginning to rival the ports in size and prosperity.

The Commerce of Northern Europe

Trade in the luxury goods of the East such as pepper, ginger, silk, and cotton was certainly the quickest way to make a profit in goods of small bulk. The trading cities of the Mediterranean, however, also supplied more mundane and bulkier items for their own citizens and for the inland cities: wheat, salt, fish, sweet wine of Cyprus, hides, dyestuffs, alum, raw wool, and cloth. In the North of Europe, these bulky items predominated in the trade of the commercial cities. In the Baltic region, furs, timber, salt fish, pitch and tar, hemp, and potash passed through Kiev and Novgorod and through the German cities planted along the Baltic coast, such as Riga, Königsberg, Stettin, and especially Lübeck. The export of wool preoccupied the merchant class of London. The wine of Gascony was the principal item traded in Bordeaux. Increased opportunities in national and international trade led many cities to concentrate on manufacturing specialized goods, for which they became famous throughout the continent. Toledo produced the finest sword blades; Arras, lace and tapestry; and Cordoba, leather goods. But the most important item by far was cloth, whose manufacture was concentrated in two principal regions: the Low Countries, particularly Flanders, and Florence and the neighboring towns of central Italy.

The Flemish Cloth Trade

The wealth of Flanders was due to a double advantage: its position as the northern terminus of the trade route by which eastern goods were brought north by Italian merchants, and as the manufacturer of the best woolen cloth in the world. The Low Countries, like northern Italy, had a favorable geographical position. Many navigable rivers led into France and Germany—the Rhine, the Maas, the Oise, the Marne. Their ports lay at the midpoint of the North Sea coast, with easy contact with England, northern and western France, and the Baltic. The flat, well-watered fields were rich in dairy produce, providing beef, milk and cheese for the city dwellers and more items for export. The fairs of Champagne in France, where most trade between northern and southern merchants took place through the thirteenth century, were only a short overland journey. By the end of the thirteenth century, almost every Flemish town had mastered the complicated technique of clothmaking, and each was known for its own dis-

The Cloth Hall, Ypres
This hall, constructed in c. 1260–1380, was one of the finest examples of the adaptation of the Gothic style to secular buildings. Official Belgian Tourist Bureau photo

tinctive brand—for instance, scarlet of Ghent, the lightly woven *rasch* of Arras, and the finely woven *saie* of Bruges.

For each stage of the process of manufacture, a specialized group of workers was formed. The first group prepared the wool by sorting, beating, washing, carding, and combing it. Then it was spun on a spinning wheel, usually by women. Next workers called warpers prepared the spun wool arranging it in threads of the right thickness and length, after which two weavers worked the threads onto a loom. Finally, the cloth had to undergo fulling—a wearisome process of beating and cleaning carried out in a trough with fuller's earth—and stretching. Dyeing was carried out at any part of the process. Before being sold, the fabric was subjected to further treatment such as raising the nap and shearing. On these processes, the whole social structure of the wool manufacturing towns was founded. The key person in the whole process was the cloth merchant, who owned the raw material and put it out at each step of the process to different groups of workers, establishing wages and profits to his own advantage. The cloth merchants controlled the city through powerful guilds and by participation in city government. Hated by many of their workers, these men were challenged by the most powerful of the craftsmen, the weavers. Again and again, the weavers rose in bloody but abortive riots, only to be forced back into sullen subjection.

The Economic Function of Paris

Paris had first been settled by a few fishermen who beached their ships on the three little islands in the center of the river Seine. That original site had expanded into a genuine city when the Romans made it the center of their road system and administration in northern Gaul. Lutetia, as they called it, became a flourishing city with arena, baths, temples, and palace. But abandoned by the Roman armies in the fifth century, it was preserved from total extinction only by the Catholic Church, which had established a bishopric there in the third century. As elsewhere in Europe, most of the Roman buildings fell into ruin, the arena and baths to the south of the river were covered with grass and bushes, and the major churches were isolated from each other by marshes and fields. After a brief revival under Charlemagne, Paris turned to agriculture for sustenance and to the counts for protection against the Viking invasions. Paris was easy prey for the black-prowed boats of the Norsemen, who from their island redoubt at Oisselin at the mouth of the Seine would sack it on their way to invade the richer towns of Burgundy. It was only at the price of a two-year siege in 885–887, followed by the grant of the whole province of Normandy to the invaders, that the Counts of Paris were finally able to gain a respite. From that point on, however, Paris reasserted its economic importance.

The settlement of merchants in Paris starting in the tenth century illustrates the process of town growth that took place throughout Europe. With the concurrent revival of trade in agricultural produce, local manufactures, and eastern luxuries, merchants in increasing numbers began to travel along the old roads again, especially along the Roman roads, whose superb construction preserved them as Europe's main highways for almost two millennia. Most of these merchants must have moved off the land with the growth in population, although many were aliens like the Jews, who never did fit into the servile pattern of village society. Travel with goods for trade was frequently dangerous, and the merchants sought protection at night in castles or monasteries. Here they often traded as well, establishing permanent settlements near the walls. They also picked advantageous locations for trade at fords or bridges, or where principal highways crossed, especially if the walls of a preexisting city could still be utilized. In time, their settlement became so dense that they often had to move outside the walls of the fortress, monastery or city, to what was called the "faubourg" (the area outside the bourg or original settlement); and this new settlement was then surrounded by a new wall. This pattern was followed in Paris and in many other cities such as London, Cologne, and Florence. A totally different pattern of urban development occurred when a feudal lord or king decided to found a new town (*ville neuve* in French or *Neustadt* in German). Here fortifications and church would be built, a street plan laid down, and settlers enticed by promises of freedom from feudal obligations and the right to sell property, including land, freely.

Paris offered many advantages to the merchant class. It lay on one Roman road from southern France to Britain and Flanders. Its easily navigable river carried goods from eastern France to the English Channel. It possessed not only a bishopric but several wealthy monasteries; and from the end of the tenth century, it was the most important seat of the Capetian kings of France. Above all, its walls still survived from Roman days. Merchants attracted by these advantages first settled on the major island, the Ile de la Cité, but soon spread over to the right bank where the river was widest and offered the finest docking facilities, and where by chance no important churches owned property. Thus, very early in Paris's history, the right bank took on the character it has never lost, as the commercial and industrial sector of the city.

At first, the commerce was of a very small scale. The king ordered all trade in basic foodstuffs to be carried on where the main bridge from the Ile de la Cité, the Grand Pont, met the right bank, thus forcing the grouping of the butchers, bakers, and fishmongers next to the money changers whose stalls were already set up along the bridge. But local commerce was soon supplemented with long-distance trading, when the king permitted the holding of a fair, the Foire du Lendit; and with the fair came a great expansion of banking facilities, first run by Jews and then by the Lombard bankers. With the great development of royal power in the twelfth century, the newly wealthy king was joined in Paris by large numbers of feudal lords, while the equally prospering churches and monasteries increased their recruitment and their consumption. Thus the trade in staples dwindled in importance in comparison with the market for luxuries. Many were manufac-

A Shopping Street in Medieval Paris
Most shopkeepers lived above their stores, which opened onto the narrow, winding streets; though sometimes paved, they had no sidewalks and little provision for wheeled traffic.   Bibliothèque Nationale, Paris

tured in Paris itself. The tailors of linen robes were so swamped with orders that they worked night and day shifts, and were still compelled to recruit foreigners to help them meet their orders. Skilled craftsmen worked to produce jewelry in gold and precious stones, dagger handles, crucifixes in ivory and wood, and crystalware. Others catered to less aesthetic tastes. Barrel makers provided containers for expensive wines and perfumed water; sword and lance makers and saddlers met the needs of the men at arms. Yet again the luxury market was a stimulus to long-distance commerce, in the cloths of Flanders and Tuscany, the silks of Byzantium, or the spices of the Orient. Many of these goods were obtained at the fairs of Champagne, where the Parisian merchants sold their luxury cloths, jewelry, and goldwork; and thus Paris was able to share easily in the great North-South trade of the twelfth and thirteenth centuries.

Parisian Guilds

From the tenth century on, the merchants of the reviving cities had formed themselves into guilds for their own protection, for the maintenance of standards, and for works of charity and piety. When the towns were still small, most of the town merchants tended to join together in one "merchant guild," but from the twelfth century on men of the same craft joined together in a "craft guild." In Flanders and Italy, the guilds frequently sought greater independence from their local lord; and in some cases, like Florence, they joined to run the city themselves. But in France the guilds very early struck an alliance of mutual convenience with the king, who regarded them as a reliable source of royal revenue and of support against his feudal nobility, and in return granted them monopolistic trading privileges and the right to elect their own officers. The most important of the early guilds in Paris was the "hansa of the merchants by water," the shipowning guild to which the king gave the monopoly of the carrying trade on the Seine. Other guilds quickly followed—the mercers, the bakers, the dagger makers, the goldsmiths, the fishmongers, and many more. Many received a royal charter granting a monopoly in Paris. They all enforced strict standards in their craft or trade, controlled the recruitment of apprentices and the employment of journeymen or day laborers, and provided social services for their members. Until the middle of the thirteenth century, this system worked well in Paris. Relative harmony existed between the great mass of artisans and the few extremely wealthy merchants who shared with the king in the work of government. (Philip Augustus entrusted the royal treasury and the

The Grand Pont, Paris
In this detail from an illuminated manuscript of about 1317, a shepherd drives his flock through the covered section of the bridge, while a boatman unloads provisions. Bibliothèque Nationale; Ms. Fr. 2092

royal seal to six bourgeois when he went on a crusade in 1190.) After the death of Louis IX in 1270, however, the tendency of the guild masters to take larger numbers of apprentices and journeymen and to block their advancement into the masters' ranks led to great social friction. The journeymen in particular came to form a class with many of the characteristics of the later industrial proletariat—little prospect of advancement, no personal capital, frequent unemployment, and subsistence wages at best. Throughout the fourteenth and fifteenth centuries, the Parisian working class frequently erupted into riots against the well-to-do bourgeoisie; but they themselves could also be mobilized by bourgeois leaders in movements against the king that were almost revolutionary in character. In 1357–1358, for example, Etienne Marcel, the provost of the merchants of Paris, was able to bring the whole city into insurrection against the dauphin in the hope of winning important concessions for the representative assembly, the States General, during the Hundred Years' War with England.

During the age of Louis IX, however, these conflicts still seem distant. Paris congratulated itself on having achieved not only prosperity but social harmony.

Paris as the Capetian Creation

In spite of its economic importance, Paris was above everything else a royal city, the capital of "la douce France." It was the presence of the royal government and the determination of the kings to mold the city into a capital worthy of their realm that made the greatness of Paris.

The Urban Projects of Philip Augustus

The Count of Paris had been chosen king of France in 987. But the first six Capetian kings did not regard Paris as their capital, even though Robert the Pious rebuilt the old Roman palace on the western end of the Ile de la Cité. The court remained peripatetic. Lacking a regular income, it moved around, living off the hospitality of the king's vassals and carrying the government records and treasure with it. It was Philip Augustus who determined to make Paris into a worthy capital of the kingdom he had so vastly expanded by his conquests. At his accession, Paris was a small squat town, of perhaps fifty thousand inhabitants. It had an old wall, built in Roman times but regularly repaired; its streets were thick in mud; sanitation was nonexistent. Although the king's palace on the western end of the Ile de la Cité had been rebuilt less than two centuries before, living conditions even for the king were very primitive. Whenever the king left town for a long trip, one of his usual acts of charity was to bequeath the straw spread on the palace floor to the local hospital. The palace itself had fortified rectangular walls, about a

The Ile de la Cité and the Latin Quarter
In this eighteenth-century drawing, several of Paris's great medieval churches dominate the skyline–the cathedral of Notre Dame (upper left), the Sainte Chapelle in the center of the palace buildings on the island, and the monastery of St. Germain des Prés (lower right).
Turgot plan

hundred yards in length, with a tall circular tower in the central courtyard where the king kept his armaments. In the living quarters he had only three principal rooms: a large dining hall, used for public meetings of his major vassals, banquets, and reception of important visitors; a private dining room; and an oratory. One chronicler reports that Philip's first idea for the improvement of his city occurred to him one afternoon as he looked out from the palace windows:

He was strolling in the great royal hall thinking over affairs of state and came to the Palace windows from where he often looked out on the River Seine as a diversion. The horse wagons, crossing the city and cutting up the mud, stirred up a stench which he couldn't stand and he decided on a difficult but necessary piece of work which his predecessors had not dared to initiate because of the

The Louvre
The original Louvre palace, built by Philip Augustus on the western edge of the city, was embellished in the midfourteenth century with the fanciful towers and turrets seen in this illustration from the early fifteenth-century Book of Hours *of the Duc de Berri.* Giraudon

crushing expense. He summoned the burgesses and the provost of the city and ordered by his royal authority, that all the roads and streets of the city should be paved with strong, hard stone.[2]

Only the roads leading to the city gates were paved, however, and the rest of Paris remained glutinous and odoriferous.

Four years later, Philip decided to erect a new city wall. By this act, he shaped the topography of Paris for centuries. The wall ran in two great semicircles, one on the right bank of the Seine and one on the left enclosing an almost circular area about one mile in diameter. The wall was more than ten feet thick and from seven to twenty feet high, broken by sixty-seven round towers and twelve gates. The wall on the right bank, which was built first to protect the business section of the city, took eighteen years to finish; the wall on the left, which safeguarded the intellectual riches of the university, took fifteen. Once completed, the wall influenced the history of the monarchy itself. The strongest fortress of the Capetian kings was now no feudal castle set apart in the countryside, but the capital city itself, defensible only with the aid of the citizens. The alliance of the king and middle classes of Paris led inevitably to the grant of commercial privileges and to a preferential position for Paris over the other cities of France. The wall itself was also a form of real estate development similar in character to the founding of "new towns," the famous *villes neuves.* Philip's wall did not merely surround the populated part of Paris but included large areas of meadow, vineyard, and marsh, which delighted owners were soon selling as building lots and making fortunes.

Philip's third building project, erection of a fortress called the Louvre on the right bank just outside the new wall, appeared to be an obvious bastion protecting against attack where the Seine entered the city; a chain was stretched across the river at that point each night. But Philip intended to do more than defend his burghers. He paid for the fortress himself, kept in it the most important state prisoners, much of the state treasure, and his main supply of weapons. Although he continued to live in the palace on the Cité, he had his own fortress independent of a Parisian population that could turn fickle or even menacing to the monarchy. The Louvre was not only part of the defense of Paris; it could become in time of need the king's refuge from Paris. Already the physical separation of the king from a distrusted people, that led Louis XIV to shift his whole court from Paris to Versailles in the seventeenth century, was glimpsed.

Character of Saint Louis

The achievement of Philip's grandson, Louis IX (reigned 1226–1270), was to make the French monarchy the most admired in Europe for its combination

---

[2] Charles Petit-Dutaillis, *The Feudal Monarchy in France and England: From the Tenth to the Thirteenth Century* (London: K. Paul, Trench, and Trübner, 1936). p. 199.

of religious fervor and political astuteness; and as the prestige and power of the monarchy rose, Paris itself experienced a continuing influx of people from all over France and indeed all Christendom, who hoped to benefit in one way or another from the richness of its life.

Both Louis' grandfather Philip and his mother, Blanche of Castile, impressed upon Louis from his early childhood a respect for religion. Blanche trained him in constant devotions and attendance at church sermons, and frequently informed him that she would prefer him to die rather than commit mortal sin. In early youth, Louis was a tall, good-looking gallant with fine blond hair, and at least a moderate interest in the manly pleasures of hunting and female companionship. But ill health, which wracked him for his whole life, beginning with erysipelas and compounded by recurrent malaria and anemia, was worsened by his own asceticism, and it played a part in driving him to the consolation of religion. His Crusade to the Holy Land in 1248, a disastrous failure during which he was captured and saw hundreds of his knights and his own brother die, deepened his sense of his own sin and of his responsibility to the Church. "If only I could suffer alone the opprobrium and the adversity," he told a bishop who tried to console him, "and my sins should not recoil on the universal church, then I could bear it with equanimity. But woe is me, by me all Christianity has been covered with confusion." [3] By the age of forty, he was thin, bald, deathly sick, and occasionally petulant, but suffused with an aura of spirituality. More and more, his devotion reached to extremes. He scourged himself with little iron chains, lost himself in mystical trances for hours prostrate on the stone floor of the palace, personally served meals to lepers, washed the feet of the blind, wore hair shirts next to his skin, and struck without qualm at heresy. For all his kindliness, he declared that "the business of a layman, when he hears the Christian religion defamed, is to defend it with his sharp sword, and thrust his weapon into the miscreant's body as far as it will go." "I have heard him say," his biographer Joinville wrote, "that he would he were marked with a red-hot iron himself if thereby he could banish all oaths and blasphemy from his kingdom." It was evident during his lifetime that France was governed by a saint, a fact that the Church officially corroborated twenty-seven years after his death.

Political Achievements of Saint Louis

What really impressed the thirteenth century was that such religious devotion could be accompanied by solid political achievement. According to Joinville, "the great love that he had for his people appeareth in his saying to my lord Louis, his eldest son, in a dire idleness that he had at Fontainebleau: 'Fair son,' said he, 'I beseech thee to make thyself beloved of the

[3] Cited in Margaret Wade Labarge, *Saint Louis: Louis IX, Most Christian King of France* (Boston: Little, Brown, 1968), p. 145.

Sire de Joinville Offers His Life of Saint Louis to the King of Navarre *Joinville's biography was prized in the thirteenth century as a guide to pious living for feudal monarchs.*   French Embassy Press and Information Division photo

people of thy realm; for in sooth I had liefer have a Scot come from Scotland and govern the people of this realm faithfully and well, than that thou shouldst govern it manifestly ill.' " To Louis, good government implied first of all the extension of impartial justice through the king's powers of legal decision. He dramatized his own interest very effectively. After attending church, he would sit on the foot of his bed with his courtiers around and deal with cases that required his intervention. Or in the summer, with unusual attention to his dress—he wore a coat of camlet, a sleeveless surcoat of linsey-woolsey, a mantle of black silk round his neck, and a coronal of white peacock's feathers on his head—he would sit on carpets in his palace garden by the Seine and pronounce judgment. Of more importance for the future, however, he also had the legal specialists among the members of his Curia Regis devote themselves full time to studying precedent-making law cases and to giving legal decisions themselves. These professional lawyers became known as the Parlement de Paris, which developed into the principal law court of France. Moreover, the habit of recording legal decisions led to the accumulation in the palace of huge quantities of legal documents, whose organization required the recruitment of a large staff of bureaucrats, who helped swell the growing civil service on the island. Many more cases were transferred to Paris for judgment, while Louis's own impartiality was so admired that he was often called to arbitrate cases from outside his own kingdom.

Other members of the Curia Regis began to specialize in financial matters, auditing the accounts of the king's bailiffs, so that also in the palace there appeared the nucleus of the Chambre des Comptes, the king's exchequer. Efficient financial auditing was essential because Louis possessed a large and growing income: the new royal properties seized under Philip, forced loans, taxes on foreigners like Jews or Italian bankers, feudal aids paid by the lords, presents collected from bishops or cities, all had brought the monarchy considerable financial resources. It is characteristic of Saint Louis that, after satisfying the normal functions of government and waging as little war as possible with his Catholic neighbors in Europe, he spent the greater part of his income in the service of religion, especially through his two Crusades, his expensive collecting of relics, and his sponsorship of church building. This was foremost in Joinville's mind as he reported the king's death:

A pitiful thing, and one worthy to be wept over, is the passing of this saintly prince, that kept his kingdom in such holy and righteous fashion, and made such fair almsgiving therein, and instituted therein so many fair ordinances. And even as the scribe that hath made his book illumineth it with gold and blue, so did the said King illumine his realm with the fair abbeys that he there built, and with the great plenty of hospitals and houses of Preaching Friars and Grey Friars and other religious that are named above.[4]

Paris and the Glorification of God Through Art

Medieval art and architecture reached their summit in Paris in the thirteenth century because as has occurred at a few crucial moments in the development of civilization, the right patrons appeared just as a new style of art was ready to be born. More specifically, the French king and the leading churchmen of Paris and the Ile-de-France were ready and able to spend vast sums of money on art and architecture at the very moment when the principal components of the Gothic style had been invented but not yet combined into a distinctive art form.

The early religious history of Paris does not differ much from that of the other great cities of Europe. It had its requisite share of saints and martyrs. The two whose cult exercised the greatest influence on the city were Saint Denis and Saint Germain. Saint Denis, the first bishop of Paris, was tortured by the Roman occupiers in the third century and taken for execution to a hill, now called the Mount of Martyrs (Montmartre), north of the city. His calmness so annoyed his guards that they cut off his head at the bottom of the hill, but the saint picked up his head, washed it in a fountain, and walked on for four miles before he collapsed and was buried. A small

---

[4] Jean Sire de Joinville, *The History of St. Louis,* trans. Joan Evans (London: Oxford University Press, 1938), pp. 227–28.

pilgrimage church was built to guard his relics; but in the seventh century the Frankish king founded an important Benedictine abbey with vast land-holdings and the right to hold a lucrative fair annually. From this time on almost all the kings of France were buried in the monastery of Saint Denis, thus ensuring its continuing importance and prosperity. Another bishop of Paris in the sixth century, Saint Germain, succeeded in persuading the king to invade Spain to bring back the relics of Saint Victor, and to found a well-endowed Benedictine monastery like that of Saint Denis to hold the relics. When Saint Germain himself was buried in this church just outside Paris, so many miracles occurred among the pilgrims visiting it that he too was canonized, and the church renamed Saint Germain des Prés. In this way two of the richest and most important churches in France were founded. By the time of Charlemagne, Paris possessed a whole galaxy of saints, most of

Saint Germain des Prés, Paris
This fine Romanesque tower survived the destruction of most of the other buildings of the great monastery that occurred during the French revolution.   French Embassy Press and Information Division photo

them canonized bishops of Paris; a network of parish churches; and, largely as a result of the Church's collaboration with the monarchy in the work of government, a large number of highly prosperous abbeys. Rather surprisingly however, during the great period of church building in the tenth and eleventh centuries that followed the reestablishment of relatively peaceful conditions after Norman invasions, Paris and Ile-de-France achieved very little of real note in art and architecture. The style we call Romanesque was developed by the Normans in Normandy and England; in Germany; and in most provinces of France except the Ile-de-France. Since, however, the great style of the Ile-de-France, Gothic, is a logical progression from the achievements of the Romanesque style, we must glance briefly at what happened to architecture in the three hundred years that separated the building of Charlemagne's palace church in Aachen and the rebuilding of the abbey of Saint Denis, where the Gothic style began.

Purpose of Medieval Church Building

From the middle of the tenth century, the building of vast new churches became common throughout western Europe, for many reasons. The restored prestige of the Church following the Cluniac reform movement persuaded kings, lords, and townspeople to make large gifts of land or money to the Church, frequently for the specific purpose of improving the house of God and thereby, presumably, their own standing both with the Church and with God. The churchmen too, following the example of Cluny in its extravagant rebuilding as well as its reform program, sincerely believed that the service of God required the erection of ever more grandiose buildings, for the building was a physical representation of the Christian religion. It was in the form of the cross on which Christ had died. Sculptures and stained glass graphically represented, for literate and illiterate alike, the Biblical story and frequently the non-Biblical representation of the punish-

The Last Judgment, Facade, Bourges Cathedral
The saved are being separated from the damned by the Archangel Michael, who weighs the souls with his balance. The cauldron of hell is kept boiling by demons with bellows.
French Embassy Press and Information Division photo

ments of hell and the rewards of paradise. Increasing ritual—the habit of daily mass, the visible presentation of the body and blood of Christ at the high altar, the display of the relics of the patron saint, the complex music of the liturgy, the long processions of richly garbed clergy—all this required a finer and larger house. There were more mundane reasons, however. The central church in town was a meeting place for all townspeople for conversation, business transactions, and even restrained flirtation. It became a theater where visiting players presented morality plays. Competition, too, crept in. Rivalry among cities enabled bishops to draw on huge gifts not only from kings and feudal princes but from guilds or individual artisans and even from the peasantry. The very poorest volunteered their labor where money was lacking. Bishop competed with bishop and abbot with abbot, especially during the building of the Gothic cathedrals of the Ile-de-France when the competition was simply defined as who could build highest and widest without the church falling down.

The Romanesque Style

Large size had thus to be achieved by variation on the cruciform ground plan. In the Romanesque cathedral, large size was achieved mainly by bulk of masonry. Walls were immensely thick, and supported by sturdy but-

The Church of the Madeleine, Vézelay *Founded under the inspiration of Cluny, the abbey of Vézelay was located on the pilgrimage route to St. James's shrine in Spain.* French Embassy Press and Information Division photo

tresses built straight against the building. Windows were kept small, to reduce the pressure on the wall. No attempt was made at first to roof with stone, but instead a painted wooden roof was erected. What gave the buildings their beauty was the subtle use of the round arch which, appearing in different forms in the three or four stories of the nave, introduced a variety and a sense of movement towards the east that lightened the solidity of the masses of stone. The separation of the bays, by a purely decorative column of stone that ran from floor to ceiling, introduced a vertical drive. But it was in solving the problem of erecting a stone vaulted roof that the early style of Romanesque was transformed. The barrel vault of Vézelay, echoing the pattern of the mosque of Cordoba, was superseded by the far more complex ribbed vaulting of Durham in England (see p. 343). The rib vault consisted of two round arches intersecting diagonally. The advantages were already obvious at Durham. It was easier to build; each ribbed vault could be erected separately and the thin masonry filling between the ribs added later when the mortar of the ribs had set. This invention made possible that most attractive of all architectural styles, Gothic, which was invented in the building of the Abbey of Saint Denis outside Paris by Abbot Suger in 1133–1144.

The Criticisms of Saint Bernard

In the years when the great Romanesque churches were building, the Abbey of Saint Denis had not escaped the corruption and preoccupation with worldly goods that had sapped the reforming drive of Cluny; and the two abbeys alike came under the scourging tongue of Saint Bernard (c. 1090–1153), abbot of Clairvaux, the leader of the new reforming order of Cistercians. The Cistercian order had been founded in Burgundy in 1098 to restore the discipline of the order of Saint Benedict. Its monks had set the example by going into the wilderness to labor, practice celibacy, and live in total simplicity. But Bernard's overwhelming personality, the power of his preaching, his letters, and the example of his own life, made him the self-appointed arbiter of the moral and intellectual standards of western Europe, Paris not least. He was determined that no breath of heterodoxy should enter the University of Paris, and fought victorious duels with his intellectual superiors like Abelard. And in monastic affairs, he not only set himself as the disciplinarian but as the judge of artistic taste as well. He had lampooned the sculptural excesses of Cluny, in a memorable condemnation that showed his understanding as well as his condemnation of the medieval sculptor:

In the cloisters, under the eyes of the brethren engaged in reading, what business has there that ridiculous monstrosity, that amazing mis-shapen shapeliness and shapely mis-shapenness? Those unclean monkeys? Those fierce lions? Those monstrous centaurs? Those semi-human beings? Those spotted tigers? Those fighting warriors? Those huntsmen blowing their horns? Here you be-

Gargoyles of Notre Dame, Paris
French Embassy Press and Information Division photo

hold several bodies beneath one head; there again several heads upon one body. Here you see a quadruped with the tail of a serpent; there a fish with the head of a quadruped. There an animal suggests a horse in front and half a goat behind; here a horned beast exhibits the rear part of a horse. In fine, on all sides there appears so rich and amazing a variety of forms that it is more delightful to read the marbles than the manuscripts, and to spend the whole day in admiring these things, piece by piece, rather than in meditating on the Law Divine.[5]

To Saint Bernard, the abbey of Saint Denis seemed in even worse condition. It had become the "workshop of Vulcan" and "a synagogue of Satan"; and this condition he blamed exclusively on its abbot, Suger. "It was at your errors, and not at those of your monks," he wrote to Suger, "that the zeal of the saintly aimed its criticism. It was by your excesses, not by theirs, that they were incensed. It was against you, not against the abbey, that arose the murmurs of your brothers. You alone were the object of their indictments. . . . In fine, if you were to change, all the tumult would subside, all the clamor would be silenced."[6] Although Suger had been the adviser and friend of King Louis VI and King Louis VII and was to be regent of France during the Second Crusade, he could not ignore a direct blast from such a mentor. He reformed his abbey by disciplining its monks and cutting down its extravagant standard of life. But, far from accepting Bernard's artistic stipulations, he challenged them in theory and in practice.

[5] Erwin Panofsky, *Abbot Suger on the Abbey Church of St. Denis and Its Art Treasures* (Princeton: Princeton University Press, 1946), p. 25.
[6] Ibid., p. 10.

(Left) **The Chalice of Abbot Suger**
This chalice, used in administration of the sacrament in the Abbey of Saint Denis, was made in 1140 of gold inset with jewels. Widener Collection, National Gallery of Art

(Right) **The Choir and Transept, Basilica of Saint Denis**
The originality of Abbot Suger's choir lay in the combination of rib vaults, pointed arches, and flying buttresses. French Embassy Press and Information Division photo

Abbott Suger's Rebuilding of Saint Denis Monastery

Suger loved all the decorative arts of the Middle Ages—the painted frescoes, the cast bronze doors, the exquisite carving in gold, and above all the working of precious stones. In his memoirs on his administration of the abbey, he argued that the contemplation of such works of art brought a man closer to God, and moreover followed Biblical precedent:

Often we contemplate, out of sheer affection for the church our mother, these different ornaments both new and old . . . then I say [quoting Ezekiel], sighing deeply in my heart: "Every precious stone was thy covering, the sardius, the topaz, and the jasper, the chrysolite, and the onyx, and the beryl, the saphire, and the carbuncle and the emerald." . . . Thus, when—out of my delight in the beauty of the house of God—the loveliness of many-colored gems has called me away from external cares, and worthy meditation has induced me to reflect, transferring that which is material to that which is immaterial, on the diversity of the sacred virtues: then it seems to me that I see myself dwelling, as it were, in some strange region of the universe which neither exists entirely in the slime of the earth nor entirely in the purity of Heaven.[7]

He obtained his jewels in the most diverse manners. He shamed royal or episcopal visitors into giving him the jewels off their rings to decorate his

[7] Ibid., pp. 63–65.

altar, and he maliciously reported that he was able to buy "an abundance of gems" from monks of three reforming abbeys. He "thanked God and gave four hundred pounds for the lot, though they were worth much more."

Suger's principal work, however, was his rebuilding of the abbey itself. The work, he argued, was made necessary by the vast crowds flocking to see the relics of Saint Denis and the Nail of the Cross. Women, he said, had to walk to the altar on top of the heads of men! He at first intended to send for some of the marvelous marble columns that he had seen in the baths of Diocletian in Rome, but at the last minute the Lord revealed suitable stone in a quarry only twelve miles away. "Whenever the columns were hauled from the bottom of the slope with knotted ropes," he said, illustrating the community involvement in the actual building of the Gothic cathedrals, "both our people and the pious neighbors, nobles and common folk alike, would tie their arms, chests, and shoulders to the ropes, and acting as draft animals, drew the columns up; and on the declivity in the middle of the town the diverse craftsmen laid aside the tools of their trade and came out to meet them, offering their own strength against the difficulty of the road, doing homage as much as they could to God and the Holy Martyrs." [8] To find trees tall enough for the beams of the outer roof, he related that, after a sleepless night of worry, he went himself to one of the abbey's forests, and after searching all day, found twelve trees of the right size, the exact number needed. The work was completed in eleven years, and his new church was consecrated in the presence of the king and twenty bishops in 1144. Immediately, his contemporaries realized that he had revolutionized architecture; and many of those bishops returned home burning with desire to pull down their own cathedrals and erect even finer basilicas than Suger's.

The Invention of Gothic Style

What Suger had done was to combine in a new way three forms already known—the pointed arch, the rib vault, and the flying buttress. The pointed arch created a soaring sense of upward motion in the vertical line of the wall. Construction of the rib vault in the form of a pointed arch allowed roof vaults to be built over any form of rectangle, whereas a vault of round arches could be built only over a square. The flying buttress enabled the architect to do away with the thick stonework of the Romanesque wall and to use the space for large windows, which Suger, who loved color and brightness, filled with the first important stained glass windows.

Immediately after the construction of Saint Denis, the powerful archbishop of Sens began his own Gothic cathedral, and shortly after, the cathedral of Canterbury was begun by an architect from Sens. Then the bishop of Noyon, beginning his cathedral fifteen years later, added an extra story to the nave wall, the triforium, and this brought his roof up to eighty-five

---

[8] Ibid., p. 93.

Flying Buttresses, Notre Dame, Paris

The flying buttress transfers the thrust of the stone roof from the thin nave wall downwards and outwards, enabling the architect to open up the walls into huge stained-glass panels. French Embassy Press and Information Division photo

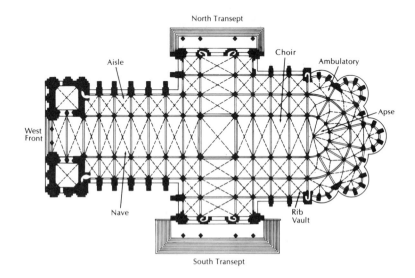

Ground Plan of a Gothic Cathedral: Chartres

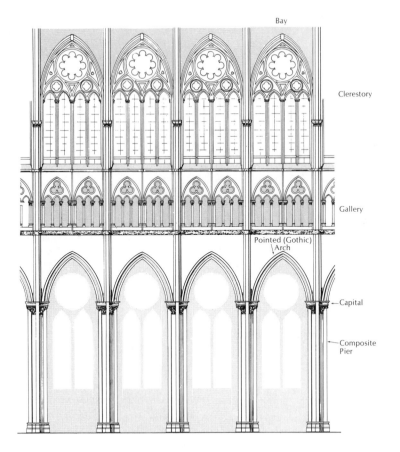

Nave of a Gothic Cathedral: Amiens

feet in height. He had reached the height of one side aisle of the Basilica of Maxentius. Then came the cathedral of Senlis, in much the same style, followed by Laon in 1165. Laon marked a big change in Gothic naves, because the architect did away with the composite pier. The ground floor of the nave became a line of identical columns, and the impression was no longer projected of the nave divided into a series of separate bays. For the first time, the spatial sensation of the onward horizontal drive toward the high altar was uninterrupted. This was the point Gothic architecture had reached when the best known of all Gothic cathedrals, Notre Dame de Paris, was begun by Maurice de Sully, bishop of Paris.

Notre Dame de Paris

Maurice, like Suger, was a church-made man, the son of a poor peasant family singled out for tough intellectual training and rapid advancement. Both a scholar and an administrator, he lacked Suger's interest in national politics. For his thirty-six years as bishop, his chief interest was to build a

Notre Dame Cathedral, Paris

The use of flying buttresses to support the nave and choir permitted the architect to fill the wall space with intricate designs of stained glass.

Trans World Airlines photo

cathedral worthy of the capital city of France and of his own ambition. At that time the finest church in Paris was the monastery of Saint Germain des Prés, an impressive Romanesque building with a recently completed Gothic choir. But the bishop himself had only a small dilapidated Carolingian church. Plans for the cathedral were drawn up in consultation with King Louis VII, whose palace abutted the site of the new church. Louis, aware that the reputation of the monarchy required that his cathedral exceed any previously built, approved the extraordinary dimensions Maurice had planned—130 yards long, with a nave 115 feet high, 30 feet higher than any previous cathedral, and room for more than ten thousand people inside. The architecture too was innovative. The transept was moved almost to the middle of the church, and a double ambulatory was constructed around the nave and choir. The effect was to unify the whole interior, which no longer appeared broken into separate units. And at Notre Dame the great program for the outer decoration of the building advanced the art of Gothic sculpture enormously. The sculpture became an integral part of the architecture of the building and not merely surface embellishment, while the figures themselves moved from a highly stylized, spiritual form of representation to ever more appealing realism. The west facade of Notre Dame, planned and begun under Maurice and completed in 1250, is one of the most complex and harmonious compositions of the Middle Ages, blending sculpture and architecture.

The Last Achievements of High Gothic

But even Notre Dame de Paris could be excelled. When the cathedral of Chartres, a small country town to the southwest of Paris, burned down in 1194, the bishop sought even greater height and width: five feet higher and six feet wider. The big gallery and triforium window that darkened the original nave of Notre Dame were done away with and huge stained glass windows turned the nave into a wonderland of light. Here at Chartres, medieval stained glass presented the whole history and message of the Christian Church. To produce these pictures in glass, the artist built up the window of small pieces of glass joined together by strips of lead. The glass was colored with metal oxides in a melting pot, producing color of absolute purity. For variety, pieces of white glass were fused with pieces of colored glass, producing the so-called flash glass; and to show figures and faces, a way of applying a mixture of iron oxide and powdered glass to produce lines and shade was invented. The artist usually painted a picture, reproduced it in pieces of glass, joined the pieces in their lead framework, and then put the whole window inside an iron frame, which could be lifted into place in the stone tracery. The result was a new art form. The light playing through glass of different thicknesses and color produced a jewel-like splendor, which modern artists have been unable to recapture.

South Facade, Chartres, c. 1210–1220
The figures of Saints Paul, John, James the Great, James the Less, and Bartholomew form one small part of an intricate composition spreading across three doorways of the south facade. French Embassy Press and Information Division photo

Amiens Cathedral
The nave and choir of Amiens Cathedral, 470 feet long and 140 feet high, were begun in 1220, for the principal bishop of the province of Picardy.
French Government Tourist Office photo

The competition continued. Begun in 1211, the cathedral of Rheims, where the French kings were crowned, reached 125 feet; that of Amiens, begun in 1220, attained 140; and the one at Beauvais, begun in 1247, was 157 feet high. Here at last Saint Bernard's invective against the waste of effort by these cathedral-building bishops seemed justified. The choir of Beauvais fell down the moment it was finished. Rebuilt, it fell again; and although it was repaired, the church was left unfinished, a monument to a style that could advance no further.

At the moment when the building of Beauvais was beginning, Saint Louis created the last of the great Gothic churches of Paris. In 1238, Louis had acquired the Crown of Thorns from the Emperor Baldwin of Constantinople, who had pledged it as security for a loan from a Venetian patrician; and soon after, Louis had bought a piece of the True Cross, a broken fragment of the Holy Lance, the Holy Sponge, the Holy Blood, a piece of the Reed, and even a little stone from Christ's sepulcher. Louis immediately ordered the further expense of a chapel in the palace grounds that would be specially built for the safekeeping and display of the relics. The result was the lovely Sainte Chapelle, the Gothic building in which the architect has come closest to achieving the ideal of a wall composed entirely of stained glass.

In the twelfth and thirteenth centuries Paris came to be dominated by the buildings of the Church. As well as the monuments on the Ile de la Cité, there were thirty parish churches, twenty-nine major convents, several huge hospitals, five houses for lepers, and many houses for the orders of mendicant friars. But the most important area in which religion dominated the life of Paris, and Paris dominated the life of Europe, was in the university.

(Left) **The Exterior and** (Right) **the Lower Chapel, Sainte Chapelle, Paris** *Constructed by Louis IX in 1243–1248 to hold the Crown of Thorns and other relics, the chapel stood in the center of the Capetian palace.* French Embassy Press and Information Division photos

The University: Paris as the Intellectual Capital of Europe

Throughout the twelfth and thirteenth centuries, students from all over Europe swarmed to Paris to enjoy the intellectual excitement of the hard-argued debates between the great masters of philosophy and theology who taught at its cathedral school and, after 1200, at its newly chartered University. Already the student's district, known as the Latin Quarter after the language in which instruction was given, was acquiring that endearing character of boisterous irreverence that it has never lost. One visitor from the provinces in the thirteenth century was astounded at the sheer number of pupils:

Never before at any time or in any part of the world, whether in Athens or Egypt, had there been such a multitude of students. The reason for this must be sought not only in the beauty of Paris itself, but also in the special privileges which King Philip and his father before him had conferred upon the scholars. In this great city the study of the trivium and the quadrivium, of canon and civil law, as also of medicine, was held in high esteem. But the crowd pressed with special zeal around the professorial Chairs where Holy Scripture was taught or where problems of theology were resolved.[9]

The Organization of the University of Paris

The University of Paris became the pattern of organization for all the universities of northern Europe. The word university (*universitas* in Latin) was first used in the twelfth century to describe a collective organization similar to a guild formed either by a group of students or teachers. In Bologna, Italy, students particularly interested in the study of law had gathered in large numbers and, believing themselves exploited by teachers and towns-people alike, they had formed associations for their own protection. In a short time, they were able to both bring down their rents and discipline their professors. Among the many regulations they imposed was a fine on the professor for poor class attendance by his students, on the ground that he must be teaching badly, and a requirement that he get permission from the students before leaving town. By contrast, the University in Paris was the guild of teachers. In 1200, in a charter regarded as the founding document of the university, they obtained from Philip Augustus the right to be free from any interference by lay officers of the state. In 1207, they were recognized by Pope Innocent III as a *Universitas magistrorum et scholarium* (University of professors and students). Finally, the professors sought to throw off even the controls exercised over them by the cathedral. In 1229, when both Church and city authorities failed to make redress for the mur-

---

[9] Guillaume Le Breton, cited in Ernest Barker, ed., *Golden Ages of the Great Cities* (London: Thames and Hudson, 1952), p. 97.

der of a number of students after a tavern brawl, they suspended their lectures and took jobs in universities elsewhere. (Half the universities of Europe were formed by similar dispersions of teachers and students. Cambridge, for example, was begun by a dispersion of students and faculty from Oxford.) Neither King Louis IX nor the pope wanted to see the leading Christian university disappear, and they at once confirmed the privileges of masters and students of the university. The papal bull was notable for the effusiveness of its appreciation of the university:

Gregory, the bishop, servant of the servants of God, to his beloved sons, all the masters and students at Paris—greeting and apostolic benediction.

Paris, the mother of sciences, like another Cariath Sepher, a city of letters, stands forth illustrious, great indeed, but concerning herself she causes greater things to be desired, full of favor for the teachers and students. There, as in a special factory of wisdom, she has silver as the beginnings of her veins, and of gold is the spot in which according to law they flow together; from which the prudent mystics of eloquence fabricate golden necklaces inlaid with silver, and making collars ornamented with precious stones of inestimable value, adorn and decorate the spouse of Christ. . . . Accordingly, it is undoubtedly very displeasing to God and men that any one in the aforesaid city should strive in any way to disturb so illustrious grace.[10]

The chancellor of the cathedral was therefore ordered to grant a license to teach to anyone accepted by the masters' guild, whose claim to run the university was henceforth undisputed by the clergy of Notre Dame. The pope's bull also laid down other recommendations of continuing significance. The summer vacation was not to exceed one month. Students were not to carry weapons. "Those who call themselves students but do not frequent the schools, or acknowledge any master, are in no way to enjoy the liberties of the students."

By this time, the curriculum of the university had been formalized. All students began by spending five or six years in the Faculty of Arts, during which they studied the trivium (grammar, logic, and rhetoric) and the quadrivium (arithmetic, geometry, astronomy, and music). Only about a third of the students completed the arts course, at the end of which they were granted a degree of master of arts and admitted to one of the three higher faculties: theology, canon law, and medicine. A student of theology had many years of exacting study ahead: four years of lectures on the Bible; two years on Lombard's *Sentences*, a summary of theological questions; two years as a lecturer himself on the Bible, and a year on the Sentences; and a final five years of study, before receiving the degree of doctor of theology.

For many students, the years of study were made tolerable by the corporate life. The arts students were divided into four "nations," France, Pi-

[10] Cited in David Herlihy, ed., *Medieval Culture and Society* (New York: Walker, 1968), p. 217.

cardy, Normandy, and England, to which students from all over Europe were assigned. Most countries of central and eastern Europe were grouped under England. National compatibility brought students to rent houses together, drink together, and fight together. They went around, wrote one observer, "saying that the English are drunkards and have tails; that the French are proud, soft, and womanish; the Germans mad and indecent in their feasting; the Normans stupid and boastful; the Picards traitors and fair-weather friends. . . . And because of such wrangling they often proceed from words to blows." Their unruliness made them heartily disliked by the law-abiding citizens of Paris, and led to frequent street battles. It was partly to discipline the students as well as to give charity to the deserving poor among them that benefactors in the thirteenth century began to found colleges where students could be lodged and supervised. Robert de Sorbon, whose college developed into the principal school of the university and gave its name, the Sorbonne, to the present school of arts and sciences, reminded his scholars of the advice of Saint Bernard: "There is as much difference between reading and studying as there is between an acquaintance and a friend." [11]

The influence of the University was greater than that of any other medieval institution of learning. Its pattern of organization was copied by almost every new university north of the Alps and, in fact, by many in southern Europe also. Its students, who were drawn from most of the European nations, returned home to positions of power in both Church and state. A degree from the University of Paris, in theology, law, medicine, or merely in the arts, was a guarantee of advancement within the royal civil or the ecclesiastical hierarchy. Finally, the faculty of the University assured its preeminence in European thought by the sparkling intellectual achievement in philosophy and theology of the professors who taught there. During the thirteenth and fourteenth centuries, every great name in the history of European philosophy appeared on the faculty of the University, among them Alexander of Hales, Albert the Great, Bonaventura, Thomas Aquinas, Roger Bacon, and William of Occam. Much of Paris's keen appeal to students lay in the opportunity to witness firsthand the dramatic development and exposition of the philosophical theories of its professors.

The Battle of Realists and Nominalists

At the beginning of the twelfth century, the teachers of the sparsely attended cathedral school were expounding a philosophy, established by the Church Fathers around the fall of the Roman Empire, to which little had been added in five centuries. This philosophy, called Realism, adopting a late interpretation of Plato's theory of ideas, held that reality was a series of ideas, or universals, such as justice and humanity, that existed in the mind

[11] Cited in Joan Evans, *Life in Medieval France* (London: Oxford University Press, 1925), p. 165.

of God. Particular things, such as an act of justice or an individual person, were only important or real because of the existence of the universals. This theory fitted nicely into the Catholic Church's determination to monopolize truth and to deny reason a primary role in the understanding of truth. Belief was held necessary to an understanding of truth. "I do not try to understand in order to believe, but I believe in order to understand," said the great Realist thinker Anselm (c. 1033–1109). In the period of questioning that began in the early twelfth century, this doctrine came under attack by the Nominalists, who held rather contemptuously that universals were just names, a "breath of the voice," and that individual things were of primary importance and reality. Thus, the Nominalists could imply, somewhat unwisely, that the three parts of the Trinity were real, and that Christians were therefore worshipping three gods rather than one, a doctrine that the Church hurriedly condemned as heretical. This philosophical battle between Realists and Nominalists, and the later battles of the thirteenth century over the interpretation of Aristotle, were deeply exciting to medieval students and teachers and of direct concern to the highest authorities of the Church. Philosophy dealt with matters of faith and thus of salvation, which in the Middle Ages was the supreme form of knowledge.

Peter Abelard

Paris first became a magnet for that vast horde of students who roamed from city to city to hear the most widely acclaimed professors, when Peter Abelard (1079–1142), at the age of twenty-four, challenged the Realistic teaching of the leading professor in the cathedral school and, with a flash of brilliant logic, compelled him publicly to change his views. To many students, Abelard was a charismatic figure, a precocious master of the instrument of logic, irreverent to accepted theory and theorists, humorous in his exposure of error—in all, a humane cleric, as shown by his relations with the sixteen-year-old Heloise, whose tutor and lover he became. His students followed him in fascination on the many occasions when his quarrels compelled him to seek new places to teach; and they made the scalpel of his logic, the syllogism, the principal instrument of philosophical surgery for the rest of the Middle Ages. Logic he expressed in a book called *Sic et Non,* in which he laid out 158 problems, with authorities for and against, leaving the reader to come to his own conclusions. In philosophy he leaned toward a modified form of Nominalism, accepting the Nominalist view that the individual is real but holding that universals were concepts, that existed also, but solely in the mind of the person perceiving them. Abelard's uncompromising use of reason won him the incomprehension and hatred of Saint Bernard, who accused him variously of being tainted with the heresies of Arianism, Pelagianism, and Nestorianism, and who had many of Abelard's propositions condemned by church council in 1141. Abelard died one year later and was buried in the convent where Heloise had become prioress.

The Franciscan and Dominican Friars

Both the organization and philosophy of the University masters were shaken early in the thirteenth century by the establishment in Paris of the newly founded orders of mendicant friars, the Franciscans and the Dominicans. Both orders were started as further attempts to bring the Church back to the primitive ideal of poverty, from which even the Cistercians had fallen. Saint Francis (1182–1226), the son of a wealthy merchant of Assisi in central Italy, had experienced a deep religious conversion after years as a spendthrift and soldier; on the rocky slopes of the Apennine Mountains of Umbria, he had gathered around him a small group of disciples who followed him in living in total simplicity, begging their food and shelter, and preaching the unadorned gospel of God's love and the brotherhood of all living creatures. To Saint Francis, learning was unimportant; example and eloquence were all. When he died, his order had five thousand members; half a century later, two hundred thousand.

The Dominicans were founded by a Spaniard, Saint Dominic, who was appalled by the spread of heresy through the south of France, and independently reached the same conclusion as Saint Francis: that the corruption within the Church and the heresy without could only be halted by the foundation of a new order devoted to poverty and preaching. But Dominic, challenged by highly educated leaders of the Albigensian heretics, saw from the start that his Dominicans would have to be the masters of theological learning, but not of "secular sciences or liberal arts except by dispensation."

Established in Paris, like the Dominicans, in the 1220s, the Franciscan friars ignored their founder's warning against study, and rivaled their black-robed competitors in the pursuit of philosophy and in the acquisition of the professorial chairs that previously had been monopolized by the masters' guild. The masters objected strenuously to the friars' refusal to accept the guild's discipline and to suspend their lectures in solidarity with the masters during their conflicts with the Paris government. After a long battle involving excommunications, appeals to the pope, muggings of friars in the streets, and a threat by the masters to dissolve the University, a compromise was finally reached, permitting the friars to become professors of theology on condition that they follow the university statutes and the master's oath. The conflict was important in that it recognized the central position of the friars in higher learning, but also strengthened the institutional character of the University.

For these Dominican and Franciscan scholars, the study of philosophy and theology had been transformed by the diffusion in Europe of a vast range of writings of classical Greece, from the Toledo translation school, Sicily, and Constantinople, including most of the works of Aristotle then known and commentaries on them by Arabic and Jewish scholars in Spain. What fascinated thinkers most was the majesty and range of Aristotle's writings, covering everything from biology to poetry. The first reaction of the conservative professors of the University was one of terror at the dam-

age that study of Aristotle's speculations could do to the faith of the students and the reputation of their professors; and in 1210, the reading of Aristotle's works on natural philosophy was banned under pain of excommunication. Philosophy was rescued from this impasse and Christianity converted from Plato to Aristotle by the greatest thinker of the Dominican order, Saint Thomas Aquinas.

Saint Thomas Aquinas (1225–1274)

Aquinas, the son of an Italian nobleman, had studied in the Benedictine monastery of Monte Cassino and in the University of Naples. He arrived in Paris in 1245 to work through the course of study in the faculty of theology under the fine Aristotelian scholar, Albert the Great. Although he was called to the papal court in 1259, he returned to teach again in the University of Paris from 1269–1272, during which time he composed a good part of his finest book, *Summa Theologica*. In breadth and subtlety, no Catholic thinker has excelled Aquinas, and in the nineteenth century he was officially recognized by the pope as the standard of orthodoxy in Catholic study of philosophy. Aquinas set out to harmonize the writings of Aristotle with the basic dogmas of the Christian Church, by the use of the dialectic. His famous proof of the existence of God begins:

Our consideration of God shall fall into three parts, for we shall consider (1) whether there is a God, (2) how he exists, or rather, how he does not exist, and (3) those things which pertain to his actions, that is, his knowledge, will and power.

Considering the first point, three things will be investigated: (1) whether it is self-evident that God exists, (2) whether his existence can be proved, and (3) whether there is a God. . . .

Aquinas's vast learning stimulated other professors to violent disagreement. Once again, scintillating debate enlivened the lecture halls. The Franciscans in particular challenged his abandonment of Plato and his promotion of reason above a mystical understanding of God; and at the end of the century, Duns Scotus and William of Occam were able to rally most of the professors of Paris to reject Aquinas in favor of a reassertion of Nominalism. Since, however, they rejected reason rather too enthusiastically, both Scholasticism and probably religion too suffered as a result.

The University of Paris thus represented everything that was most idiosyncratic and typical about medieval culture. It harnessed a vast apparatus of learning in support of doctrines whose truth was taken as self-evident. It rewarded research, but insisted that its results enhance what was already known. It established stiff mental training, but circumscribed it in the study of a fixed group of authoritative texts. It did little or nothing to further an interest in natural science, technology, or the fine arts. It turned higher learning into a predominantly vocational training for three careers, churchman, lawyer, and doctor. And it gave a restricted corporation of teachers so tight a monopoly of stylized learning that innovation outside, and even within, the established fields was only possible after an attack on the institution itself. The University of Paris was both as unnecessary and as intellectually justifiable—and for roughly the same reasons—as the Cathedral of Notre Dame. They were the supreme achievements of an age of faith.

SUGGESTED READING

Maurice Druon's *The History of Paris from Caesar to Saint Louis* (1969), though slightly romantic, can be consulted for lack of an up-to-date scholarly study of thirteenth-century Paris. Thomas Okey, *The Story of Paris* (1925), and Hilaire Belloc, *Paris* (1923), are useful for some background detail of an anecdotal kind. In French, however, René Héron de Villefosse, *Histoire de Paris* (1948) is very sound; Edmond Faral, *La Vie quotidienne au temps de Saint Louis* (1942) fills in the social history of the period. Roger Dion et al., *Paris: Croissance d'une capitale* (1961) approaches the problem of urban growth from the viewpoint of recent urbanistic studies. Louis Hautecoeur, *Paris* (1972), vol. 1, pp. 47–74, is an ambitious attempt to link the architectural development of the city to its wider history. In complete contrast, Virginia W. Egbert, using the small illuminations illustrating the Grand Pont and Petit Pont in the *Legend of St. Denis* of 1317, has created a delightful survey of Parisian social life in *On the Bridges of Medieval Paris* (1974). Pierre Couperie has illustrated the urban development of Paris throughout its history, with a series of maps and excellent accompanying photographs, in his *Paris Through the Ages* (1971).

More general studies on the revival of cities in the Middle Ages include Henri Pirenne's masterly *Medieval Cities* (1925), and his *Belgian Democracy* (1915), which deals fully with the Flemish wool cities. Urban documents are collected in John H. Mundy and Peter Riesenberg, *The Medieval Town* (1958). The pattern of trade is illustrated with documents in Robert S. Lopez and I. W. Raymond, *Medieval Trade in the Mediterranean World* (1955), and synthesized in H. L. Adelson, *Medieval Commerce* (1962) and R. S. Lopez, *The Commercial Revolution of the Central Middle Ages, 950–1300* (1971).

The life of Saint Louis is charmingly described in Margaret W. Labarge, *Saint Louis: Louis IX, Most Christian King of France* (1968), which contains a good chapter on Paris, pp. 155–68. Jean de Joinville's biography, *The History of St. Louis* (1938) is well translated by Joan Evans. Regine Pernoud's life of Louis's mother, *La Reine Blanche* (1972) is a serious biography, in spite of the difficulty of documenting Blanche of Castile's life, and of course tells much about the son. Joseph R. Strayer, *The Albigensian Crusades* (1971) illustrates the lengths to which the Capetian rulers went to serve the Church and extend their own dominions.

The art of medieval Paris is exhaustively covered. The ideal way to begin is to let Abbot Suger tell his own story, in Erwin Panofsky, ed., *Abbot Suger on the Abbey Church of St. Denis and Its Art Treasures* (1946). George Henderson, *Gothic* (1967) explains all aspects of Gothic expression in art and architecture. One can then turn to the more specialized studies of Notre Dame Cathedral, especially the evocative description by the architect Allan Temko, *Notre Dame of Paris* (1955) or the beautifully illustrated volumes by Pierre du Colombier, *Notre Dame de Paris: Mémorial de la France* (1966) and Yves Bottineau, *Notre Dame de Paris and the Sainte-Chapelle* (1965). Robert Branner, *St. Louis and the Court Style in Gothic Architecture* (1965) studies the creation of a specifically Parisian style of architecture in the middle of the thirteenth century.

The University of Paris is superbly examined by Gordon Leff, *Paris and Oxford Universities in the Thirteenth and Fourteenth Centuries: An Institutional and Intellectual History* (1968), and the character of student life on the Left Bank can be tasted in Hastings Rashdall, *The Universities of Europe in the Middle Ages* (1936), vol. 1, pp. 269–84. The influence of the University of Paris on the other universities can be followed in Alan B. Cobban, *The Medieval Universities: Their Development and Organization* (1975).

Gordon Leff summarizes the course of medieval philosophy in *Medieval Thought: St. Augustine to Ockham* (1958). Other useful surveys are David Knowles, *The Evolution of Medieval Thought* (1962); Frederick N. Artz, *The Mind of the Middle Ages* (1962) and Frederick C. Copleston, *Medieval Philosophy* (1952). The story of Abelard is best approached through his *Letters* (1926) or Etienne Gilson's *Heloise and Abelard* (1951).

Finally, in view of the paucity of good books in English on Paris in the Middle Ages, it is instructive to glance at the parallel development of London. Here one can reliably consult Ralph Merrifield, *Roman London* (1969); Timothy Baker, *Medieval London* (1970); Gwyn A. Williams, *Medieval London from Commune to Capital* (1970); Christopher Brooke and Gillian Keir, *London, 800–1216: The Shaping of a City* (1975); D. W. Robertson, Jr., *Chaucer's London* (1968); and Sylvia Thrupp, *The Merchant Class of Medieval London* (1962). What a pity that the thirteenth century seems to be the most neglected period of Parisian history!

10 / *The Transformation of the Medieval Synthesis*

In the two centuries following the death of Saint Louis, medieval civilization, which had reached its most sparkling synthesis in thirteenth-century Paris, was slowly transformed. The fascination of the fourteenth and fifteenth centuries is in the reaction of a medieval civilization still intellectually and artistically vigorous to the impact of manmade and natural disaster that destroyed more than a third of the continent's population and provoked an economic recession that lasted more than a century.

From about the year 1000 Europe had undergone an invigorating revival that affected every aspect of life. The economy had prospered, both in the countryside and in the growing cities, and population had expanded. Effective government had been restored under the institution of feudal monarchy in many parts of the continent. The Church had renewed its spiritual and intellectual vigor, and its prestige had enabled it to encroach with considerable success upon the prerogatives of the lay powers. Under the ubiquitous influence of the Church, a brilliant, relatively homogeneous culture, embracing all aspects of creativity from architecture to medicine, had been formed. This flourishing civilization was severely shaken in the fourteenth and fifteenth centuries by a series of disasters with which all study of this period must begin. The three scourges were famine, plague, and war. The most obvious effect was the vast reduction in population which, in western Europe at least, forced the virtual abandonment of the manorial system and the remaining obligations of serfdom.

King's College Chapel: Vault and Organ   Photographed by Michael Pentland. Jarrold & Sons Ltd., Norwich

In these conditions of economic crisis, the basic institutions of the three centuries preceding were greatly changed in character. First, the papacy found that its increase in material wealth had weakened its spiritual prestige, so that in a test of strength with the lay rulers it could no longer bring spiritual weapons to bear as the decisive factor. Pope Boniface VIII tangled with French King Philip IV in a struggle to enforce papal supremacy over the French clergy and lost the battle. From 1309 to 1378, the papacy resided in Avignon under French influence in what was known as the Babylonian Captivity and, even after returning to Rome, the prestige of the papacy declined further with the election of rival popes by warring cardinals. Attempts to restore papal dignity by reforms pressed in church councils in the fifteenth century were of little avail. Thus, in the fourteenth and fifteenth centuries, the papacy ceased to be the predominant institution of Europe.

Second, the feudal monarchies that had been created between the tenth and thirteenth centuries changed in character. New techniques of war, especially the use of the longbow, pike, and gunpowder, made the armored knight an anachronism in battle; and, instead of relying upon a territorial nobility to administer local government, the "New Monarchs" developed regular monetary revenues and employed highly trained civil servants. The most notable of these monarchs were Louis XI of France, Henry VII of England, and Ferdinand and Isabella of Spain.

Third, in response to the economic recession, the cities carried through major reforms in business techniques and embarked upon new forms of commercial and industrial activity. As a result, the cities moved to the forefront as the creators, and spenders, of wealth; and the creative activity of this period is owing to the patronage of the urban middle classes rather than to Church or monarchy.

The Dance of Death: Famine, Pestilence, and War

No image was more common through all the art and literature of the late Middle Ages than that of death. Even if we did not possess clear evidence of population decline from tax records, monastic account books, wills, registers of vital statistics, and studies of town topography and rural depopulation, the new ubiquity of the depiction of bodily decay would lead us to suspect a continuing and catastrophic threat to the people of Europe throughout the fourteenth and fifteenth centuries. The meticulous absorption with the details of human putrefaction would compel us to imagine a society in constant terror.

In the lyric poetry of the Parisian François Villon, there is a recurrent lament for "the snows of yesteryear," for the beauty that passes too soon.

Death makes him tremble, turn pale,
His nose curves, his veins swell,
His neck bursts, his flesh melts,
His joints and tendons grow and swell,
Feminine body, who are so tender,
Smooth, soft, and so precious;
Must all these evils await thee?
Yes, or you must go to heaven alive.[1]

The Three Living and the Three Dead, c. 1345
These pages from the psalter and prayer book of the Bonne of Luxembourg reveal the fascination with sudden death that pervaded much of the popular art of the fourteenth century.   The Metropolitan Museum of Art. The Cloisters Collection 1969

Bishops commissioned tombs in which their own bodies were portrayed being eaten by worms. In the tiny parish churches of Bavaria, the wood carver Tilman Riemenschneider depicted an emaciated Christ writhing in physical agony in the throes of death. And in the widely circulated *danse macabre*, the dance of death, printed on the newly invented woodcut of the late fifteenth century, dancing skeletons carried away men of every character and condition, with robed churchmen and landowners being perhaps the most favored.

[1] J. Huizinga, *The Waning of the Middle Ages* (London: E. Arnold, 1924), p. 133.

Demographic Catastrophe

The facts justify the image. The population of Europe began to decline from the beginning of the fourteenth century, sank rapidly by as much as a third in the second half of the fourteenth century, and only returned to the level of the year 1300 by the early sixteenth century. The earliest scourge was the elemental fact of starvation. On several occasions, the staple wheat crop was destroyed by summers of abnormally high rainfall, as in 1314–1316. Much of the new land brought under cultivation in previous centuries to meet the needs of the growing population was marginal, and it began to lose its productivity at this time. Deforestation, lack of fertilization, and omission of periods of fallow turned much land to dust, and brought the inevitable consequence of flooding. The first general famine from 1315 to 1317, for example, killed ten percent of the inhabitants of the Flemish city of Ypres; and while localized famines could be mitigated by import of food from unaffected regions, famines affecting most of Europe occurred every few years throughout the fourteenth and fifteenth centuries. In prosperous southern France, there were eleven famines, many of them lasting several years.

In 1347, the weakened population was hit by a second scourge, pestilence—the Black Death, a combination of bubonic and pneumonic plagues that was brought to Europe through Constantinople through fleas on infected rats. Within two years it had spread north from Italy as far as Scotland, striking with seeming capriciousness. In one English village, it killed seventy-four people, in the neighbor village only five. But neither city nor countryside was spared. In Florence, probably fifty thousand died out of a population of eighty thousand; an abbey in the east of England lost half of its tenants. Most historians agree that about one-third of Europe's population perished, and horribly. According to the Florentine writer, Boccaccio (1313–1375), who described in his *Decameron* the flight of a group of Florentine gentry to the countryside, where they amused themselves relating frequently bawdy tales while waiting for the plague to subside:

In its early stages both men, and women too, acquired certain swellings, either in the groin or under the armpits. Some of these swellings reached the size of a common apple, and others were as big as an egg, some more and some less. . . then the appearance of the disease began to change into black or livid blotches, which showed up in many on the arms or thighs and in every part of the body. And just as the swellings had been at first and still were an infallible indication of approaching death, so also were these blotches to whomever they touched. . . . Oh, how many palaces, how many lovely houses, how many noble mansions once filled with families of lords and ladies remained empty even to the lowliest servant! Alas! How many memorable families, how many ample heritages, how many famous fortunes remained without a lawful heir! [2]

[2] Cited in David Herlihy, ed., *Medieval Culture and Society* (New York: Walker, 1968), p. 217. Trans. by David and Patricia Herlihy.

Worse, the plague kept recurring at least once a generation, especially in the big cities. London, which had twenty outbreaks in the fifteenth century, was to suffer its worst epidemic as late as 1665. Fear of plague was perpetually in the background of men's thoughts, and could be played upon by such preachers of repentance as the Florentine monk Savonarola, who threatened, "There will not be enough men left to bury the dead; nor the means to dig enough graves. . . . Men will pass through the streets crying aloud, 'Are there any dead? Are there any dead?'"[3]

Coupled with the scourges of famine and pestilence in medieval litanies was the curse of war. In a sense the whole feudal system had been a preparation for war, or at least for defense; but in the fourteenth and fifteenth centuries men were conscious of war in much the same way that they were conscious of the plague, as a recurring disaster from which no locality was free and whose moment of impact could never be foreseen. In the southeastern part of Europe, the Turks were advancing into the Balkan peninsula, capturing not only the rough lands of the Bulgars and Serbs but the great centers of European culture, Constantinople in 1453 and Athens three years later. In the 1460s their expansionist drive took them into the plains of Hungary, and in 1480 they landed on the heel of Italy itself. Further to the north, the princes of Muscovy were engaged in the campaigns that culminated at the end of the fifteenth century in the throwing off of the yoke of their Tartar overlords. Northern Germany and the eastern shore of the Baltic were ravaged by the continuing crusade of the Teutonic knights for the establishment of Christianity and their own territorial aggrandizement in the lands of the Slavs. The long, bitter struggle of the Catholic kingdoms to reconquer the Iberian peninsula from its Moslem invaders was completed only in 1492. Throughout western Europe there was civil strife—in the cities between the lower classes and the well-to-do patriciate, in the countryside between the peasants and their landlords. Noble family fought against noble family, some struggles, like those between the houses of York and Lancaster in England, developing into civil wars for control of whole kingdoms. The effort of the French kings to oust the English from their vast possessions in southwestern and northern France produced the dreadful destruction of the Hundred Years' War. And finally, perhaps affecting the peasantry most of all, there was simple brigandage—by great mercenary bands employed by the Italian cities, by nobles down on their luck, by peasants in desperation.

War itself did not kill vast numbers of people, although pitched battles frequently decimated the nobility. (In contrast with later wars, the nobleman in armor did the fighting rather than commanding from a safe distance behind the lines.) War destroyed the productive capacity of city and country alike, and thereby added to the likelihood of famine and the inability of trade to lessen the impact. Marauding armies destroyed livestock, burned

---

[3] Cited in Margaret Aston, *The Fifteenth Century: The Prospect of Europe* (New York: Harcourt, Brace & World, 1968), p. 15.

The Building and the Destruction of Troy
In this illuminated manuscript of about 1410, the moral lesson of the fall of Troy is made more graphic by the depiction of Troy as a fifteenth-century French city.
Philadelphia Museum of Art

fields, pulled down farmhouses and mills; peasants fled, many never returning. Precariously collected surpluses of wheat or wool were commandeered; and the lack of capital, even by lords, made it impossible to restore these depredations. The result was a demoralized society. A contemporary reported on the condition of France in the middle of the Hundred Years' War:

The affairs of the realm went from bad to worse, the public weal came to an end and brigands appeared on every side. The nobles hate and despise the villeins, they care no more for the good of the King or of their vassals; they oppress and despoil the peasants of their villages. They no longer trouble to defend the country: to tread their subjects under foot and to pillage them is their only care. From this day the land of France, hitherto glorious and honored throughout the world, became the laughing-stock of other nations.[4]

Rural Adaptation to Population Decline

Under the pressure of this disastrous population decline, the basic institutions of medieval society changed profoundly; and the change was most palpable in the most fundamental of all medieval institutions, the manorial system. The obligations of serfdom had already been greatly re-

---

[4] Joan Evans, *Life in Medieval France* (London, Oxford University Press, 1925), p. 188.

duced in the twelfth and thirteenth centuries, as serfs were given special privileges in return for their cooperation in opening up new land and as landlords found it more productive to commute labor dues to monetary payments with which they could hire more willing laborers. The institution of serfdom itself was already, in western Europe at least, beginning to disappear. As a result of the fall in population in the fourteenth and fifteenth centuries, this process was accelerated. There was a migration of the peasantry from the land into the cities, which increased the rural depopulation still further and also increased the wages the remaining laborers could demand. There was a falling demand for basic foodstuffs, whose price remained stable or declined slightly at a time when the cost of luxuries and manufactured goods was increasing sharply. The landlords' predicament was thus very acute. Many of them made great efforts to avoid making concessions to the peasantry. Some ecclesiastical estates attempted to impose stricter legal ties to prevent their laborers from leaving the land. In England, Parliament passed law after law to keep down wages. In western Europe these efforts provoked three great peasant rebellions in the fourteenth century: in Flanders in 1323–1328; around Paris, in the Jacquerie of 1358; and near London, in the Peasants' Revolt of 1381. In all three, religious reformers inflamed the peasantry against the Church; all three were justified by their leaders as attempts to throw off the unjust burdens imposed on the

The Jacquerie, Paris in 1358
Armored knights hurl the bodies of the defeated guildspeople into the Seine. In the background are the buildings of the royal palace and the Sainte Chapelle. Bibliothèque Nationale, Paris

peasant to feed classes who "prayed" and "fought"; and in every case a discontented city—Bruges, Paris, or London—provided leaders and artisan support. All three rural revolts were hopeless from the start, and their repression was bloody. In France alone, twenty thousand peasants were killed. Yet if those immediate revolts failed for lack of leadership, money and weapons, and realizable goals, the transformation of the agrarian system nevertheless could not be stopped. Only in eastern Europe beyond the Elbe river was the nobility powerful enough to force the peasantry to remain on their lands. In western Europe, the medieval manor was doomed.

The west European landlord was compelled to adjust to market conditions by changing the nature of his farming methods and choice of crops. The most obvious change was a reallotment of land use to the production of crops other than wheat, which would require less farm labor or would fetch a higher price on the market. In England, in particular, much land was devoted to sheep-herding, which was a lucrative agricultural sector as long as the English manufacture of cloth was expanding. In France and Germany, viticulture was expanded to meet greatly increased demand largely because the fall in price of breadstuffs left more money available for such luxury items. In England, a similar rise in the consumption of beer made the growing of barley profitable. Barley was also used as fodder for the larger herds of cattle that were raised for meat and for butter and cheese. Not all these stratagems paid off, however. The demand for English wool went through periods of expansion and slump, and the periods of decline provoked considerable social distress. Those, however, who attempted to meet their difficulties by renting out their land found themselves in an even worse posi-

Rent Day, by Pieter Breughel (c. 1525–1569). Burghley House Collection

tion. So much land was available that little income could be obtained from rent. Rents were long-term and fell in real value as money was inflated—and kings were often guilty of debasing the currency and thus reducing the income from leased land. Very frequently nobody was found to lease the land, and it reverted to pasture or to waste. Here in part is the explanation of the abandonment of large numbers of villages; in England alone, perhaps one-fifteenth of all villages were abandoned.

Reaction Against the Papal Monarchs

The Papal Monarchy

Nothing more clearly signified the breakdown of the medieval synthesis than the decline in the prestige of the papacy and indeed of the whole hierarchy of the Catholic Church. At the end of the thirteenth century the Church enjoyed a commanding position in the spiritual and cultural life of Europe, and after its triumph over the German emperors it wielded considerable influence in the political sphere as well. The means the Church used to obtain this position of predominance and the use it made of it, however, sapped its spiritual vitality, and even weakened the faith most Europeans had come to accept unquestioningly in the importance of the Church to the well-being of society.

During the thirteenth and early fourteenth centuries, the popes built a material power that was the envy of many lay rulers. Increasingly, they claimed universal powers of judicial administration, and the fees derived from it. They had a large income from a multitude of sources, such as feudal dues from their own holdings, tribute from many monasteries, the first year's income of many newly appointed clergymen, and from the time of the Crusades a very productive tax on the annual income of all churches. They maintained large armies, often of mercenary soldiers. And they constantly interfered in the international relations of the European states, seeking to arbitrate territorial disputes over royal inheritances or joining in national wars of one Catholic king against another. This increase in the pope's powers had several noxious effects on the Church. First, it diverted the pope from his religious duties. He found himself spending his time adjudicating legal cases, many of which were concerned with squabbles over the financial aspects of church appointments. He was responsible for the expenditure of vast sums for such nonreligious purposes as the maintenance of armies at war, the functioning of a luxury-loving court in Rome or Avignon and the building of huge papal palaces as well as ever grander churches. And he had to recruit and supervise a large centralized bureaucracy. The attempt to carry out in Rome or Avignon the tasks better left in the hands of the local clergy alienated the local priesthood as well as their laity, and encouraged a sense of nationalism among the churchmen of countries like

England, France, and Germany. The popes themselves, of course, were not alone responsible for the decline in the standards of the clergy. Church positions had long been regarded as livings for younger sons of anyone from kings down to impoverished knights. The clergy had long been guilty of nepotism, that is, seeking positions for their relatives in the hierarchy. Orders devoted to poverty, chastity, and obedience had frequently forgotten their vows, and made reform movements necessary. But in the fourteenth and fifteenth centuries, the decline in the Church's observance of its spiritual duties, accompanied and worsened by an indulgence in its ambition for material power, led to a widespread disgust with the institution and its members.

The Conflict of Boniface VIII and Philip the Fair

The first proof of the decline in the pope's power in relation to the secular rulers occurred when Pope Boniface VIII (1294–1303) challenged the ruthless French king Philip IV (known as the Fair, reigned 1285–1314) in his determination to exercise fiscal and judicial control over the clergy in France. In 1296, Philip IV had ordered the French clergy to pay him a special tax to support his war against England. In response to complaints from the French church, the pope, ambitious but unrealistic, issued the bull *Clericis Laicos* forbidding such taxation on the clergy without papal consent and threatening excommunication of rulers who ignored the bull. Philip replied by banning the export of gold and silver from France. Boniface, finding that the papacy was in danger of losing an important source of its revenues, then compromised by admitting that the king could levy such taxes in an "emergency." Three years later, when Philip attempted to try in the secular courts a French bishop accused of treason, the pope returned to the offensive. The clergy could only be tried in clerical courts, Boniface reaffirmed, and taxation of the clergy did require papal consent. A battle of claims and counterclaims ensued. In the bull *Ausculta Fili*, the pope claimed the power of interfering in the internal affairs of a secular state. The French king replied by calling together the first assembly, or Estates General, representing not only the nobility and the clergy but the middle classes as well; and this assembly came out strongly in his support. The pope then broadened his claims with the famous bull *Unam Sanctam* of 1302, in which he laid out the doctrine of the "two swords," the material and the spiritual. "Both the material and spiritual swords are in the power of the Church. . . . It is fitting moreover that one sword should be under the other, and the temporal authority subject to the spiritual power. . . . We, moreover, proclaim, declare, and pronounce that it is altogether necessary to salvation for every human being to be subject to the Roman Pontiff."

Philip had no intention of undergoing the humiliation of the Emperor Henry IV at Canossa. Instead of seeking papal forgiveness, he sent an army to Italy to bring back the pope to France to be tried for such crimes as heresy and sorcery before a church council. The troops seized Boniface briefly before being driven off by the outraged townspeople where he was staying; but the pope's prestige had been broken, and he died shortly afterwards. The new pope, who held office for one year only, absolved Philip of all blame; and, in 1305, Philip's pressure helped assure the election of a Frenchman as pope, Clement V (1305–1313).

The Babylonian Captivity and the Great Schism

Clement V at first attempted to establish his court in Rome, but finding Rome in disorder in 1309 he settled instead in southern France at Avignon, a fief of the kingdom of Naples which the papacy eventually purchased. Clement V and the next six popes, who also lived in Avignon, were not prisoners of the French monarchy, as has often been asserted. Some of them brilliantly helped to further the powers of the papal monarchy by increasing its revenues and its judicial powers, improving its bureaucracy, and building up its armies. Nevertheless, during the so-called Babylonian Captivity, from 1309 to 1378, when the popes resided at Avignon rather than in Rome, a chauvinistic dislike of the papacy spread throughout every country except France, and perhaps a cynical contempt grew even there. Papal ambitions became intolerable to most Catholics when it appeared that the pope was favoring France at the expense of the rest of Christendom. All seven popes who resided in Avignon were French. All filled the papal bureaucracy and the college of cardinals with Frenchmen. The English and Germans in particular complained about the large sums the Church raised in their countries to spend in France, and found it particularly infuriating that the new palace in Avignon was being built by the most extravagant of these popes at the very time that the Black Death was rampant.

The Palace of the Popes, Avignon
The enormous fortresslike palace was constructed in eighteen years (1334–1352) during the Babylonian Captivity of the papacy. Samuel Chamberlain photo

The return of the papacy to Rome in 1378 only worsened matters. Partly out of fear of the Roman mob, who invaded the conclave of cardinals during their election of a new pope, the cardinals elected an Italian, Urban VI, who to their horror started destroying their privileges and their incomes, and who even created twenty-five new cardinals at once. The French cardinals and one Spanish cardinal then left Rome and elected another pope, who took the title of Clement VII and established himself in Avignon. (In official papal terminology, certain of the Avignon popes are regarded as anti-popes, and thus the great Renaissance cardinal Giulio de' Medici was able to take the title of Clement VII in 1523). For the next thirty-one years there was a pope and a college of cardinals in Avignon, and another pope and college of cardinals in Rome. The Church dissolved into confusion. Both the popes interfered in local wars as a means of bringing more provinces to recognize the legality of their election, both increased their demands for money, and each denounced the other as a usurper. This disturbing spectacle even united the English and French for a time in unsuccessfully demanding that both popes abdicate; and the French clergy tried to coerce the Avignon pope into compliance by refusing him revenues. The faculty of the University of Paris called for a church council that would settle the disputed succession to the throne of Peter, but when a council in Pisa in 1409 appointed a third pope without being able to persuade the other two popes to resign it merely increased the confusion. Only in 1417 did the Council of Constance put an end to the Great Schism, with the appointment of Martin V, and the deposition or resignation of the other three. But it was too late to save the reputation of the pontiff, at least as long as he clung to the methods of the papal monarchy.

The literature of the fourteenth and fifteenth centuries teemed with protest against the state of the Church. To Petrarch, the Avignon papacy was the "whore of Babylon." Dante subjected popes to the punishments of hell—upside-down burial, exposure roped and nude. The popular storytellers of France, in their *fabliaux*, or fables, displayed the clergy as seducers and tricksters. But it is in *The Canterbury Tales* of Geoffrey Chaucer (c. 1340–1400), a subtle, humorous portrayal of a fourteenth-century group of pilgrims journeying to the shrine of Saint Thomas in Canterbury, that we have the most polished condemnation of a clergy guilty not of big misdeeds but of myriad crimes of omission. The Prioress is pretty, well-mannered, and sentimental; but where her rosary should have been, she wears a golden pendant:

And ther-on heng a brooch of gold full sheene,	And on it hung a brooch of shining gold,
On which was first i-written a crowned A,	On which was written a crowned *A*,
And after Amor vincit omnia.	And after *Amor vincit omnia.*

The monk was a handsome horseman,

A manly man, to been an abbot able.	A manly man, to be an abbot able.
Ful many a deyntee hors hadde he in stable;	Full many a dainty horse he had in stable;
And whan he rood men myghte his brydel heere	And when he rode men might hear his bridle
Gynglen in a whistlynge wynd als cleere,	Jingling in a whistling wind as clear,
And eek as loude, as dooth the chapel belle,	And also as loud, as does the chapel bell,
Ther as this lord was kepere of the celel.	There where this lord was keeper of the cell.

The friar was a jovial fellow, always a success with the ladies.

He knew the tavernes well in every toun,	He knew the taverns well in every town,
And everich hostiler and tappestere	And every inn-keeper and barmaid
Bet than a lazar or a beggestere.	Better than a leper or a beggar.

And already, in the flaxen-haired, smooth-faced Pardoner, with his wallet full of relics and piping hot pardons from Rome, we can see the unscrupulous Tetzel, whose activities two centuries later drove Martin Luther to his first blast against the papacy:

For in his male he hadde a pilwebeer,	For in his bag he had a pillowcase
Which that, he seyde, was oure lady veyl;	Which was, he said, our Lady's veil;
He seyde he hadde a gobet of the seyl	He said he had a piece of the sail
That Seint Peter hadde, whan that he wente	That Saint Peter had, when he went
Upon the see, til Jhesu Crist hym hente.	On the sea, until Jesus won him over.
He hadde a croys of latoun, ful of stones,	He had a cross of latten, decorated with stones,
And in a glas he hadde pigges bones. . . .	And in a glass he had pig's bones. . . .
Upon a day he gat hym moore moneye	In a day he could make more money
Than that the person gat in monthes tweye;	Than the parson could in two months.

*And thus with feyned flaterye
     and japes
He made the person and the
     peple his apes.
But, trewely to tellen atte laste,
He was in chirche a noble
     ecclesiaste.*
	And thus with feigned flattery
	     and tricks
	He made fools of the parson and
	     his people.
	But last, to tell the truth,
	In church he was a noble
	     ecclesiastic.[5]

Failure of the Conciliar Movement

How was the Church to be saved from this corruption? As at earlier periods of ecclesiastical decline, reformers were not lacking; for the Church's power of survival has been its capacity to regenerate itself from within. The Church hierarchy proposed an institutional answer—restrict the papacy's powers by making it subject to the general councils of the Church, to which all Catholic bishops would be summoned. The justification for this proposal, elaborated in the University of Paris, was that the doctrines of the early Church had been worked out in church councils, like that at Nicaea, and that God would continue to protect such gatherings from error, when they spoke in proper consideration of the past teaching of the Church. Moreover, the reformers held, when the council met, one primary task should be the reform of abuses in the Church that the pope had been unwilling or unable to remedy. The high point for the supporters of conciliar theory was reached in 1415 at the Council of Constance, when the prelates declared: "The Council of Constance, an ecumenical council, derives its power direct from God, and all men, including the Pope, are bound to obey it in matters of faith, of ending the schism, and of reforming the Church in head and in members."

The only achievement of the council, however, was to end the schism. The popes refused to cooperate in reform measures whose main purpose appeared to be to reduce papal revenue, and they continually denied on principle the supremacy over them of Church councils. The clergy themselves had a vested interest in maintaining the perquisites that indeed provided the larger portion of the revenues with which to administer their dioceses. The laity, who were not officially represented at the councils, were unable to pressure the priests; and the councils, lacking lay members, could hardly claim to be restoring democracy in the Church. As a result, the conciliar movement got little popular support; and the Council of Constance, faced by John Huss (1369?–1415), a genuine reformer who had roused the masses of Bohemia to religious frenzy, fell back on repression. Huss was called to the council on a safe-conduct pass, condemned as a heretic, and burned at the stake. What really destroyed the conciliar movement, however, was that everybody present at the councils was playing politics. The

[5] Author's translation.

pope concluded a series of agreements with the governments of the nation-states, without regard to the council's opinions. The Avignon and Rome factions bargained. Cardinals maneuvered in their dealings with the pope on one hand and the bishops on the other. The popes were thus able to ride out the swell of reforming ardor, but they failed to channel the vast out-pouring of religious emotion arising out of the miseries of pestilence and war.

Revival of Catholic Mysticism

This perfervid piety, based on a mystical desire for communion with God, was, however, expressed on an enormous scale throughout Europe, and it found expression in some of the most beautiful pieces of religious literature ever composed. At times, the furor of religious emotion led directly into heresy condemned by the Church, as with the English reformer John Wycliff (c. 1328–1384) and his followers the Lollards, or with John Huss and the Hussites, who had to be beaten into submission by large armies. At times it led to direct abuse of the Church leadership, such as occurred in this denunciation by Catherine of Siena (1347–1380):

They love their subjects for what they can get out of them and nothing more. Their share of the Church they spend entirely on their own garments, loving to go delicately apparelled, not as clerks, and religious, but as lords and courtiers. They take pains to have fine horses, and many vessels of gold and silver for the adornment of their dwellings, possessing that which cannot be ultimately retained, with much vanity of heart; and with the disordinate vanity their heart swells, and they place all desire in food, making of their belly their god, eating and drinking without restraint, so that they promptly fall into an impure and lascivious life.[6]

But most of the mystical leaders remained within the Church, and some, like Catherine herself, in spite of their vituperation against the institutional Church, were canonized after their death. They made so many followers in the Church that many new and influential congregations of monks and friars or of lay people were formed, with such revealing names as the Friends of God or the Brethren of the Common Life. From all parts of the continent and all sections of the Church came the expression of a great desire for the immediate realization of God's presence. From the Franciscans in Italy came the heartbreaking religious poem *Stabat Mater*:

Stabat mater dolorosa	There his grieving mother stood
Iuxta crucem lacrymosa,	Weeping beside the cross
Dum pendebat filius	On which her son was hanging.

[6] *The Dialogue of the Seraphic Virgin, Catherine of Siena,* trans. Algar Thorold (London: K. Paul, Trench, Trübner, 1896), p. 264.

Marienaltar, Bad Mergentheim, by Tilman Riemenschneider (c. 1460–1531)
German Tourist Information Office photo

Cuius animam gementem
Contristantem et dolentem
Pertransivit gladius.

Through her suffering soul,
Compassionate and tortured,
Pain struck like a sword.[7]

The German Dominican Eckhart taught of the divine spark in a person's mind that united everyone with God: "The eye with which I see God is the eye with which God sees me." From Sweden came Saint Bridget, whose revelations were read all over Europe. But amid the multitude of books of devotion, the most admired—and the most widely read Christian book after the Bible—was the *Imitation of Christ* by the Flemish monk Thomas à Kempis (1379–1471). Thomas à Kempis had no time for dogma: "What will it profit thee to dispute profoundly of the Trinity, if thou be devoid of humility, and art thereby displeasing to the Trinity?" he asks. And he had no room for the organized Church: "Consider that you and God are alone in the universe and you will have great peace in your heart." The appeal of his book, however, was in the simple, direct prayers he suggests with which the Christian can talk to God.

[7] Author's translation.

*How can I bear this miserable life unless thy mercy and grace strengthen me?
Turn not away thy face from me, delay not thy visitation. Withdraw not thou
thy comfort from me, lest my soul "gasp after thee as a thirsty land." Lord,
teach me to do thy will, teach me to walk humbly and uprightly before thee, for
thou art my wisdom, who knowest me in truth, and knewest me before the
world was made and before I was born into the world.*[8]

The mystics thus helped the faith in the Christian religion during the period
of disenchantment with the institutions of the Christian Church. Because
there was no decline in the numbers or enthusiasm of Christian believers,
the need for a reform of the institutions of the Church appeared more necessary than ever. This reform took place in the two reformations—the Protestant Reformation of the early sixteenth century and the Catholic Reformation of the second half of the sixteenth century. Seen in this context, the
similarity in the writings of Thomas à Kempis, Martin Luther, and Ignatius
Loyola is not surprising.

Feudal Monarchy Transformed into the "New" Monarchy

The crises of the late Middle Ages also transformed the feudal monarchy.
By the beginning of the sixteenth century, large parts of western Europe
were governed by a very different form of state from that of the thirteenth
century, whose ideal we saw in the reign of Saint Louis. Operating under a
new set of assumptions about the duties and powers of government and
about the position of the citizen in relation to government, the rulers of
France, England, Spain, Burgundy, and some of the principalities of Germany and Italy had created the modern form of state. The basis of this state
was the assumption that *sovereignty* is possessed by the central government—
and sovereignty means the right and ability to control the lives and property of the citizens of the state for the purposes of the state, through taxation, law courts, civil servants, diplomacy, and making war. The great
change was the movement from the feudal conception of the state, in which
the power of the king derived from the personal allegiance of a hierarchy of
vassals, to a conception of the state in which the political relationship is reduced to one of governor and governed. During the following three centuries, the internal political struggles and the striving of all political theorists was to be devoted to the question of the extent to which the governed
can, or should, retain control over the governor. But such control was only
made possible when, as a result of the changes of the late Middle Ages, the
feudal concept of political rule was jettisoned.

---

[8] Thomas à Kempis, *The Imitation of Christ* (New York: P. F. Collier and Son, 1909), cited in
Herlihy, *Medieval Culture*, p. 404.

The Feudal Nobility in Western Europe

The first prerequisite for the transformation of feudal monarchy was, of course, the decline in the power of the feudal lords. Here many factors worked in favor of the king. The value in battle of the armored knight was ended by the long bow, the pike, and gunpowder. In the great battles of the Hundred Years' War, Crécy, Poitiers, and Agincourt, the lines of French knights charged again and again into a hail of arrows from the long bows of the English archers, and fell helpless, pinioned by their writhing mounts and heavy armor until dispatched by the knives of the English foot-soldiers. Sir John Froissart's *Chronicles,* the classic portrayal of the bravery and pan-ache of the feudal knight in these wars, is also a documentation of his anachronism as a warrior:

Poitiers (1356): [The Prince of Wales] addressed his troops as follows: "My gallant men, we are only a few against the might of our enemies, but do not let us be discouraged by that. Victory goes not to the greater number, but where God wishes to send it. If we win the day, we shall gain the greatest honor and glory in the world. If we are killed, there will still be the King my father, and my noble brothers, and all your good friends, to avenge us. I therefore beg of you to fight manfully today; for please God and Saint George, today you will see me act like a true knight."

Soon afterwards the fighting became general. The battalion under the French marshals advanced before those troops who were intended to break the line of the English archers; and it entered the lane where the hedges on both sides were lined with the archers, who began shooting with such deadly aim from both sides that the horses would not go forward into the hail of bearded arrows, but became unmanageable and threw their riders, who were then unable to rise in the confusion. . . . Seldom can a body of good fighting men have been so totally and speedily defeated as the battalion of the marshals of France, for they fell back on each other so fast that the army could not advance. . . . The English archers were certainly of infinite service to their side, and caused great havoc. For their shooting was so accurate and so well concerted that the French did not know which way to turn, as the archers kept on advancing and gaining ground.[9]

The use of the pike, a long pole topped by a sharp metal head with point and curving blade, made it suicidal for a knight to charge at full tilt against the bristling barbs of a line of pikemen. But above all gunpowder was even-tually to sweep away the great horse. Small guns were probably used at Crécy, and artillery was quickly developed into a mobile weapon of even greater use in sieges of castles than in fixed battles.

---

[9] John Froissart, *Chronicles,* trans. J. Jolliffe (London: Collins, 1967), pp. 167–68.

The Cult of Chivalry

At this very moment, when the lord was in economic difficulties as landowner and was losing his role as warrior, the whole cult of the knight received a curious transfiguration in the most blatant, the most colorful, and in a sense the most pathetic attempt to perpetuate medieval cultural ideals—*chevalerie*, or chivalry. The less the knight counted in battle, the more he indulged in the sport of the tournament, which became a glorious, stylized spectacle of gorgeously robed lords and ladies seated beneath floating pennants and multicolored awnings to watch the combat of lords whose handcrafted plate armor was in itself a work of art. The tournament had become a nostalgic entertainment, essential, however, to the role-playing demanded by society of its new hero, the perfect knight. The ideal of the virtuous knight, devoted to the unselfish service of God and his lord and to the worship of some idealized woman, was developed to an inordinate degree by the poets, storytellers, and historians of the period because the nobility reveled in it; and it was encouraged for their own purposes by kings and princes, who found in it a method of domesticating the nobles and of glamorizing the gift of knighthood in the eyes of their middleclass supporters. The king of England founded the Order of the Knights of the Garter; the king of France, the Order of the Star; and Philip the Good, Duke of Burgundy, the most glamorous of all, the Order of the Golden Fleece. By inheritance, marriage, and conquest, Philip had put together a rich, new state controlling the prosperous towns of Flanders and the fine agricultural lands of eastern France; and he attempted by the magnificence of his court's chivalry to make up for his state's lack of a history. Enormous banquets, elaborate costumes, grandiose tournaments, and above all the ritual of the Knights of the Golden Fleece gave to his court a fairy-tale quality. Chivalry became in these two centuries a charming, expensive, and time-consuming avoidance of reality by a nobility that had lost its original function.

Yet the pageantry of chivalry should not lead us to dismiss the continuing importance of the nobility in its later functions. Great nobles remained a powerful force in the constitutional development of the western kingdoms. They could still put large armies into the field, as the noble families who fought the Wars of Roses in England or the great houses who disputed the French throne in the late fifteenth century showed. Many were able to turn from the role of cavalryman to that of professional commander; and indeed it became extremely common for younger sons of the nobility to become professional soldiers. In some European countries, like Germany, the nobility retained control of the officer corps until the twentieth century. The nobility also found a role for themselves in the courts of the centralizing monarchies. They not only provided the companionship, and indeed the social setting, against which the new role of kingship could be dramatized. They provided much of the personnel of civil and ecclesiastical administration, such as diplomats, ministers, and abbots. And many were eventu-

Ritter Hans von Rodenstein, Tomb in Fränisch-Grumbach, and Jörg Truchsess von Waldburg, Tomb in Waldsee
By the fifteenth century, the feudal lord no longer presented the terrifying image of the armored soldier (left) but the glamorous and almost effete figure of the hero of chivalry (right).   German Tourist Information Office photos

ally able, in the reviving economy of the late fifteenth and sixteenth centuries, to turn their estates once again into profitable productive enterprises. Chivalry for the nobility of western Europe was a phase of psychological readjustment to the passing of the great horse and with it their accustomed position on the battlefield.

Continuing Power of the Feudal Nobles in Eastern Europe

In most of eastern Europe, however, the landowners gained a position of supremacy from which they were not ousted until the twentieth century, thus setting all Europe east of the Elbe river on a course completely divergent from that of western Europe. In eastern Germany and Poland, in Bohemia, Hungary, and Rumania, the landowning nobles solved the problem of a declining population by simply tying the peasant more firmly than ever to the soil and by exploiting their farms for the production of marketable surpluses, especially wheat. The number of days a peasant had to work for his lord was vastly increased, in some areas from one day a year to one day a week. The lords forced from weak kings the right to administer their own lands free of any interference from the central government. Poland became the supreme example of noble misrule. Its king was elected by the nobles. The assembly of nobles was responsible for legislation, which it passed by unanimity, and was hence frequently paralyzed by the disagreement of a few lords. The country only survived by the accidental choice of an occasional good king and by the weakness of its neighbors; and in the eighteenth century, it paid the price of centuries of noble misgovernment by being partitioned among Russia, Austria, and Prussia. The prototype of the east European landed gentleman was, however, the German aristocracy, who controlled the lands of the North German plain to the east of the Elbe until forcibly dispossessed after the Second World War. This group of frugal, self-righteous, caste-conscious martinets added to their landholdings, fought off state interference with the peasantry of their lands, and provided a conservative phalanx of army officers and bureaucrats and occasional government ministers first to the Prussian state and then to a unified Germany. It seemed, however, very possible that western Europe too, with the solitary exception of the city-dominated regions of the Low Countries and northern Italy would follow the same pattern of development, particularly because of the constant wars in which they were engaged.

The Hundred Years' War (1337–1453)

Both the French and English monarchies suffered greatly from the Hundred Years' War. It ran through four distinct phases beginning in 1337 when king Edward III (reigned 1327–1377) of England laid claim to the throne of France. In 1337, the possessions of the English king in France, which under the Angevin rulers (see pages 349–51) had included vast areas in northern and southwestern France, were reduced to a coastal strip of Aquitaine. When the last Capetian king Charles IV died in 1328, Edward III glimpsed an opportunity to reestablish English power in France. The French claimant to the throne, Philip of Valois who became king Philip VI (reigned 1328–1350) was the grandnephew of king Philip IV; Edward III of England was grandson of Philip IV through his mother, and insisted that he therefore had the better right to the French throne, ignoring the traditional law in France that inheritance did not pass through the female line.* The immediate cause of the outbreak of fighting in 1337 was, however, the attempt of king Philip VI to raise greater revenues from the rich wool-manufacturing towns of the County of Flanders over which he was suzerain. The Flemish merchants appealed successfully to the English king for support, since England was the principal supplier of wool and the main market for the products of the cities of Flanders. The first phase of the war (1337–1364) was a

---

* This so-called Salic law had in fact been in disuse in France, and was revived by the lawyers of Philip VI. It remained the law of succession in France for all future monarchs.

Entry into Paris of Louis II, Duke of Anjou
The twin towers of Notre Dame dominate the small city of Paris in this fifteenth-century illuminated manuscript by Louis Bruges.   Bibliothèque Nationale

series of English victories. At the battle of Sluys in the English Channel in 1340, the English established their control over the sea routes to France. Then, at Crécy in 1346 and at Poitiers in 1356, the French knights on horseback were massacred by English soldiers armed with pike and longbow. King John II (reigned 1350–1364) of France, who had succeeded Philip VI, was captured at Poitiers and held in England for ransom. During these disasters, as we saw earlier in the chapter, the misery of the French peasantry brought them to revolt against their own nobility in the Jacquerie in 1358, while the population of Paris under their provost Etienne Marcel attempted to use the Estates General, representing the different classes in France, to restrict the powers of the monarchy.

The second phase of the war (1364–1380), in which the French gradually reasserted their power, coincided with the reign of Charles V (reigned 1364–1380) of France, who compelled the Estates General to grant him adequate revenues for carrying on the war; and the tough general Bertrand du Guesclin was able to win back most French territory except the coastline. During the third phase of the war (1380–1429), France was handicapped by rulers who were weak and incompetent or even periodically insane. The two most powerful feudal princes of France, the duke of Burgundy and the duke of Orléans, vied for control of the monarchy; and when the English king Henry V (reigned 1413–1422) invaded France, the duke of Burgundy joined him. Henry easily defeated the forces of the French king at the battle of Agincourt (1415), and the Burgundians captured both the mad king Charles V and his capital city. His son, the dauphin, however, continued to hold southern and central France and to maintain a royal court at Bourges. A Parisian noted in his journal that year:

Alas, never, I think, since the days of Clovis the first Christian King, has France been as desolate and as divided as it is today. The Dauphin and his people do nothing day or night but lay waste all his father's land with fire and sword and the English on the other side do as much harm as Saracens. . . . And the poor King and Queen have not moved from Troyes since Pontoise was taken, where they are with their poor retinue like fugitives, exiled by their own child, a dreadful thought for any right-minded person. . . . Everything was so dear in Paris that not even the most intelligent of its inhabitants could find enough to live on. Bread especially and firewood were dearer than they had been for two hundred years and so was meat.[10]

Consolidation of the New Monarchy in France

It was at this lowest point in the fortunes of the French monarchy that the foundations of the "new monarchy" were laid. The force that made possible a change in the character of the monarchy was nationalism, a new form of loyalty that transcended the local loyalty of, for example, a Parisian for his city or a Norman for his province. The war's fourth and last phase (1429–1453) began with the mysterious appearance of Joan of Arc, the peasant girl who, after raising the siege of Orléans for the dauphin and persuading him to be crowned in Rheims in 1429, was seized by the Burgundians, then tried for heresy and condemned to death by burning by a court of the Inquisition. Nationalism was far less important as a stimulant to military ardor than as a solvent of the opposition to the more down-to-earth measures that the former dauphin, crowned King Charles VII (reigned 1422–1461), saw necessary to drive the English out of France. In 1439, the king persuaded the Estates General to grant him the *taille*, and annual tax on individual citizens collected by the king's own agents, and with it he created a professional army, the *compagnies d'ordonnances*, composed of cavalry and mounted archers backed later by mercenary foot soldiers recruited from all over Europe. Charles had taken the crucial steps in creating the new form of state. He had a regular, expandable income and a standing army; and by 1453, he had succeeded in sweeping the English out of all France except the port of Calais.

The consolidation of the powers of the French king was carried much

---

[10] Janet Shirley, ed. and trans., *A Parisian Journal, 1405–1449* (Oxford: Clarendon Press, 1968), pp. 146–48.

Louis XI, King of France (Reigned 1451–1483)
French Embassy Press and Information Division photo

further by Louis XI (reigned 1461–1483), a mean, underhanded, down-to-earth, farsighted ruler. In the account of his reign, *The Memoirs*, written by the statesman Philip de Commines, we are fortunate in possessing not only a fine narrative but also description of the political theory of the new monarchs. In the famous Chapter Ten, "A digression concerning some of the virtues and vices of King Louis XI," Commines stated bluntly the doctrine that Machiavelli was to repeat a generation later, that the virtues and vices of princes should be judged by their contribution to the well-being of the state and not by commonplace morality:

Of all the princes that I ever knew, the wisest and most dexterous at extricating himself out of any danger or difficulty in time of adversity, was our master King Louis XI. He was the humblest in his conversation and dress, and the most painstaking and indefatigable in winning over any man to his side that he thought capable of doing either mischief or service. Though he was often refused, he would never give over a man that he wished to gain, but still pressed and continued his insinuations, promising him largely, and presenting him with such sums and honors as he knew would gratify his ambition. . . . He was naturally kind and indulgent to persons of mean estate, and hostile to all great men who had no need of him. Never prince was so easy to converse with, nor so inquisitive as he, for his desire was to know everybody he could and indeed he knew all persons of any authority or worth in England, Spain, Portugal, and Italy, in the territories of the Dukes of Burgundy and Brittany, and among his own subjects; and by those qualities he preserved the crown upon his head, which was in much danger by the enemies he had created to himself upon his accession to the throne. But above all his great bounty and liberality did him the greatest service.[11]

Louis XI still squeezed higher taxes from his subjects, and by spending as little as possible built up a considerable treasury. He increased the size of the army, and tried not to use it, seeking to defeat his opponents by diplomatic guile and by subsidizing their other enemies rather than by fighting himself. Most of the territories that had been granted to members of the royal family, as semi-independent principalities called *appanages*, were brought back under the control of the crown. But his most important achievement was to prevent the dukes of Burgundy from achieving their ambition of converting their territories into a new kingdom stretching from the Channel to Switzerland by incorporation of Alsace and Lorraine. The state of Burgundy had known half a century of prosperity under Duke Philip the Good (1419–1467), and its court at Bruges was the most glamorous in Europe. "The subjects of the house of Burgundy were at that time very wealthy," wrote Commines, "by reason of the long peace they had enjoyed, and the goodness of their prince, who laid but few taxes upon them;

[11] Andrew R. Scoble, ed., *The Memoirs of Philip de Commines* (London: G. Bell, 1886), I, 59–60.

so that, in my judgment, if any country might then be called the land of promise it was his country, which enjoyed great wealth and repose, more than ever it had since; and it is now probably three and twenty years since their miseries began." [12] This misery had been inflicted on them by the ambitions of Duke Charles the Bold (reigned 1467–1477) and the unrelenting enmity of Louis XI. Louis financed the mercenaries of the Duke of Lorraine and the armies of the Swiss confederation in their wars against Charles; and, although the French armies had not themselves fought, France annexed the duchy of Burgundy itself, when the states of Burgundy were partitioned soon after Charles's death in battle with the Swiss in 1477. Looking back on the suffering of the wars and the startling reversal in the fortunes of Burgundy, Commines commented on the role of monarchical power:

The brutishness and ignorance of princes are very dangerous and dreadful because the happiness or misery of their subjects depends wholly upon them. Wherefore, if a prince who is powerful and has a large standing army, by the help of which he can raise money to pay his troops, or to spend in a luxurious way of living, or in anything that does not directly tend to the advancement of the common good, and if he will not retrench his outrageous extravagances himself, and those courtiers that are about him rather endeavor to flatter and applaud him in everything he does, than to dissuade him from doing ill (for fear of incurring his displeasure), who can apply any remedy in this case but God alone? [13]

Establishment of Tudor Rule in England

In two other countries of western Europe, England and Spain, feudal monarchy was also transformed into the "new" monarchy by the end of the fifteenth century. In many ways, English history ran parallel to that of France during the fourteenth and fifteenth centuries. National feeling was stimulated by the Hundred Years' War, first by the great victories and then by the shock of the expulsion from France, and by revulsion from the financial exactions of the pope, especially during the residence in Avignon. The kings sought allies in the local gentry, whose position had been strengthened by the acquisition of new lands at the time of the Black Death, and in the city middle class, both of whom were represented in the lower house of Parliament, the House of Commons. The greater nobility, especially relatives of the royal family, profited from the weakness of young or inefficient kings, to create territorial principalities for themselves, to organize paid professional armies of their own, and at times to put their own candidate on the throne. During the thirty years of the Wars of the Roses (1455–1485), the great nobility split into two factions. One faction supported the house

---

[12] Ibid., I, 12–13.
[13] Ibid., I, 382–83.

THE LANCASTER AND YORK DYNASTIES IN ENGLAND

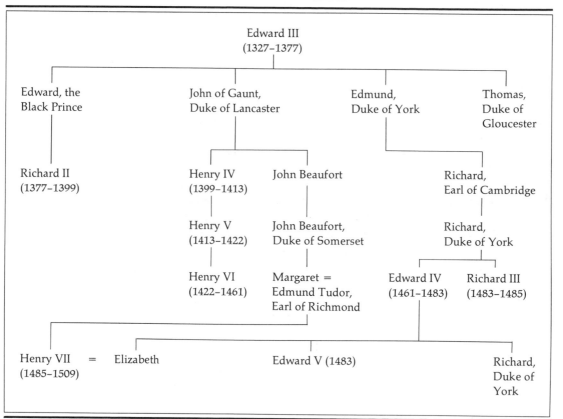

Edward III
(1327–1377)

Edward, the Black Prince

John of Gaunt, Duke of Lancaster

Edmund, Duke of York

Thomas, Duke of Gloucester

Richard II
(1377–1399)

Henry IV
(1399–1413)

John Beaufort

Richard, Earl of Cambridge

Henry V
(1413–1422)

John Beaufort, Duke of Somerset

Richard, Duke of York

Henry VI
(1422–1461)

Margaret = Edmund Tudor, Earl of Richmond

Edward IV
(1461–1483)

Richard III
(1483–1485)

Henry VII = Elizabeth
(1485–1509)

Edward V (1483)

Richard, Duke of York

of Lancaster, the descendants of Henry Bolingbroke who had seized the throne and proclaimed himself king Henry IV (reigned 1399–1413), and whose symbol was a red rose; during the long reign of the weak-minded king Henry VI (reigned 1422–1461), the barons of this faction had been able to exploit the kingdom for their own self-interest. A second faction, equally self-interested, supported the claim to the throne of the house of York, whose symbol was the white rose; and in 1461 they placed the efficient but dissolute Edward IV (reigned 1461–1483) on the throne. Although Edward IV attempted to reassert the powers of the monarchy over taxation, the royal courts, and local government, the nobles continued to skirmish throughout the country and to build themselves huge, heavily fortified castles. On Edward IV's premature death at the age of forty, his young son Edward V was deposed and imprisoned in the Tower of London by Richard, Duke of Gloucester, his uncle who made himself king Richard III (reigned 1483–1485). The long years of chaos and murder were finally brought to an end when Henry Tudor, the Lancastrian claimant to the throne, invaded England from France, defeated Richard III at the battle of Bosworth Field in

Tomb of King Henry VII and Queen Elizabeth, Westminster Abbey, London
Italian artists were brought to England to sculpt the royal tomb in the style of the Florentine Renaissance, although the chapel where the first Tudor monarch is buried is an outstanding example of English late-Gothic vaulting.   National Monuments Record

1485, and had himself proclaimed King Henry VII (reigned 1485–1509). Henry married the heiress to the house of York, thereby ending the rivalry of the two houses, and immediately set about ending the anarchic independence of the feudal nobility.

Henry VII was the first of the "new" monarchs in England. He profited from the fact that the old noble families had virtually wiped each other out. He formed a new class of career bureaucrats from the middle classes and the Church, and turned over most local administration to the local gentry in their role as justices of the peace. Like Louis XI, whom he resembled in many ways, he built up his treasury by exploiting feudal dues, judicial fines, forced loans, and trade customs, and by seeking peace abroad. While recognizing the importance of Parliament, he consulted it as little as possible, only on rare occasions asking it for money. Henry was typical of the new style of monarch, even in death. He was buried in a tomb of Italian Renaissance style beneath the Gothic vaults of Westminster Abbey.

The Reforms of Ferdinand and Isabella in Spain

In Spain, the transition was carried out by Ferdinand, king of Aragon (1479–1516), and his wife, Isabella, queen of Castile (1474–1504). Their first problem was the disunity of the country. During the long reconquest of the peninsula from the Moors, the territories won back had been divided into several independent kingdoms—Portugal, Castile, Aragon, and Navarre—with the Moors holding on to a last foothold in the southeast in the Kingdom of Granada. Within the kingdoms, the nobility had vast land grants and a tradition of autonomy and bellicosity. The towns had won a limited

Portugal   Aragon
Castile   Granada
Navarre

Bay of Biscay

FRANCE

Pamplona
KINGDOM OF NAVARRE
Ebro

León (882)

Saragossa (1118)   Barcelona (801)

Atlantic Ocean

Oporto   *Douro*

Valladolid

KINGDOM

(1083) Madrid   KINGDOM OF ARAGON

(1085) Toledo

OF

Valencia   BALEARIC ISLANDS (1224 to 1232)

Lisbon (1147)   *Tagus*

Guadiana

Badajoz (1228)   CASTILE

Cordoba (1236)   Murcia (1243)   *Mediterranean Sea*

(1492)
Granada

Guadalquivir   KINGDOM OF GRANADA

Seville (1244)

Cadiz (1250)

Notes:
1. The dates in parentheses indicate year of Christian reconquest of Moslem cities or territories.
2. The heavy line marks the southern extent of Christian reconquest by 1100.

◆ *The Christian Reconquista of Spain* ◆

independence. And racial and religious differences presented a further barrier to national unity; Portuguese, Castilians, Catalans, Basques, and Moors all spoke their own languages, while Jews and Moors followed their own religions or a superficial version of the Christianity of the persecuting majority. The war against the Moors, which was completed in 1492 with the conquest of Granada, had, however, given the Christians of the peninsula a sense of common purpose. The marriage of Ferdinand and Isabella in 1469 united the two largest kingdoms permanently; and the "Catholic Monarchs" quite successfully wiped out most religious differences by expelling all Jews and Moors who refused conversion and by turning the Inquisition in search of heresy among Catholics. Moreover, they acquired the two most important prerequisites of new monarchs of the times, a large income and an efficient army. Castile's revenue was expanded thirty times, especially from a ten percent tax on commercial transactions; this eventually, however, did enormous damage to Spanish prosperity. The army was based on a combination of pikemen and soldiers armed with sword and javelin, backed by soldiers with guns called *arquebuses,* and it was effectively used in curbing the independence of the great nobles. Unauthorized castles were torn down and royal lands taken back, but the nobles were courted with high-sounding titles and ceremonial honors at court.

To Machiavelli, whose book *The Prince* was an accurate summation of the political methods of the new monarchs and whose applicability made the book favored reading of such new monarchs as Henry VIII of England, Ferdinand of Aragon was a model ruler:

Nothing makes a prince so much esteemed as great enterprises and setting a fine example. We have in our time Ferdinand of Aragon, the present King of Spain. He can almost be called a new prince, because he has risen by fame and glory, from being an insignificant king to be the foremost king in Christendom; and if you will consider his deeds you will find them all great and some of them extraordinary. In the beginning of his reign, he attacked Granada, and this enterprise was the foundation of his dominions. He did this quietly at first and without any fear of hindrance, for he held the minds of the barons of Castile occupied in thinking of the war and not anticipating any innovations; thus they did not perceive that by these means he was acquiring power and authority over them. He was able with the money of the Church and of the people to sustain his armies, and by that long war to lay the foundation for the military skill which has since distinguished him. Further, always using religion as a plea, so as to undertake greater schemes, he devoted himself with a pious cruelty to driving out and clearing his kingdom of the Moors. . . . Under this same cloak, he assailed Africa, he came down on Italy, he has finally attacked France; and thus his achievements and designs have always been great and have kept the minds of his people in suspense and admiration and occupied with the issue of them. And his actions have arisen in such a way, one out of the other, that men have never been given time to work steadily against him.[14]

The late Middle Ages had created a new form of state and a new ideal of ruler; and the political and economic, and indeed the cultural leadership of Europe was very quickly to pass to them. Yet during the period when the new monarchies were sharpening their weapons, literally as well as metaphorically, the greatest achievements of Western civilization were to be sought in the cities—those of the northern European seaboard, of western and southern Germany, and especially of Italy.

The Urban Response to Economic Recession

Evidence of Economic Recession

The cities of Europe were even more vulnerable to the impact of famine, plague, and war than the countryside. Much evidence points to a widespread economic recession that struck the cities from the early fourteenth until the midfifteenth century. The population of cities, which had been growing rapidly until the early fourteenth century, either stabilized or in

[14] Machiavelli, *The Prince,* trans. W. K. Marriott (London: Dent, 1908), pp. 173–74.

most cases dropped considerably. Barcelona's population dropped by two-thirds. Narbonne's was reduced by more than ninety percent. Most cities revived after the Black Death but very few had reached their previous height by the end of the fifteenth century. Physical proof of the diminution of population was provided by the virtual end of construction of city walls in Italy after 1300 and in France and Germany after 1400. The production of the most basic manufacturing industry of the Middle Ages, woolen cloth, had to cut back drastically to take account of the reduction of market. Production of the great Flemish cloth city of Ypres fell from 90,000 pieces annually about 1310 to 25,000 sixty years later. The sale of raw wool was drastically reduced at the very time that many farmers were converting their land to sheep farming to economize on the use of labor; and the effect of oversupply was to reduce prices from the beginning of the fifteenth century. Competition thus became more cut-throat between the countries producing woolen cloth and, as so often in times of recession, governments fell back on restrictions on imports of manufactured cloth and on exports of raw materials. In Flanders in particular, this form of trade war was clear proof of the sharpness of the recession. Restrictive rules were also applied by the guilds in an attempt to keep down the wages of their workers, as a method of remaining competitive in the smaller market. One cause of the great wave of urban riots that affected all parts of Europe in the late fourteenth and fifteenth centuries was the resentment of the journeyman laborers against these wage regulations; but they were fueled by the determination of the poorer artisan groups, who themselves formed guilds in large numbers in this period, to share in the privileges of the well-to-do guilds, whose members formed the governing patriciate of the cities. Frequently the guilds sought the support of the king, as in France and to some degree in Spain, in winning monopoly positions in their city or their region, so as to limit output and throw competitors out of business. When one looks at patterns of trade, the recession is equally visible. Study of such widely separated ports as Marseilles, Genoa, and Dieppe shows that international trade may have dropped as much as three-fifths from its peak, a far higher percentile drop than that in Europe's population. Clearly, certain areas were more directly affected by the disorder of the wars than others. The great fairs of Champagne, for example, barely survived the wars between the Flemish cities and the French king and the Hundred Years' War.

The indisputable evidence of economic recession that the historian finds in price indexes, parish registers, and company and city archives seems to contradict what a visitor to Europe still can see with his own eyes. Throughout the continent, during this period of recession, both large and small cities were being embellished not only with cathedrals and parish churches but with city halls, guildhalls, wool halls, burghers' houses, charity hospitals, and old folks' homes. To take just a few outstanding examples, in 1356 the citizens of Ulm began to build the tallest spire in Europe only a decade after being hit by the Black Death; the intricate Gothic town

Spire of Ulm Cathedral
This late Gothic spire, built in 1356, was 630 feet high, and the tallest in Europe. German Tourist Information Office photo

hall that dominates the central square of Brussels was begun in 1401; London's elaborate Guildhall, where the Lord Mayor was elected, was started in 1411, in the middle of the Hundred Years' War; and the great patrician palaces of Florence, built by merchant bankers such as the Rucellai, the Medici, and the Davanzati, were all constructed during the century of economic recession.

From Russian Novgorod and Norwegian Bergen to Catalan Barcelona and Byzantine Thessalonica, the profits from trade and manufacturing were poured into an urban civilization that is one of the glories of the late Middle Ages, and in this widespread urban vigor, two regions predominated, the Low Countries, with the city of Bruges as its jewel, and northern Italy, with Venice the brightest in a whole galaxy of cities. Bruges, with its soaring church towers, the flamboyant Gothic of law courts and town hall contrasting with the sober rectitude of its brick homes, and its fantastic belfry

City Plan of Bruges, 16th Century

Bruges was a canal city like Venice, though on a smaller scale. The waters of the river Zwyn can be seen flowing through the city and around the outer walls.

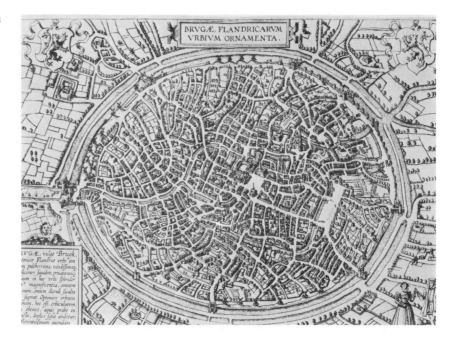

rising 350 feet above the flat Flemish plain, was an impressive setting for the pageantry of the court of Burgundy. It struck the young English wool merchant John Paston as a fairyland: "I heard never of none like it, save King Arthur's Court." And as for Venice, by the fifteenth century the most romantic city in Europe, it appeared to observers as another Constantinople or a new Rome. The French chronicler Philip de Commines, who visited the city just as the gleaming white Gothic arcade of the Doge's Palace was being erected beside the lagoon, thought it "the most triumphant city I have ever seen." How then is one to explain the contrast between the statistics of adversity and the physical evidence of prosperity?

One explanation is that in some ways the very demographic decline was profitable to the surviving city dwellers. In areas where there was relative freedom from marauding armies, the reduced city population was able to feed itself from the surrounding countryside, and did not have to seek food supplies from a long distance. Moreover, the decline in grain prices enabled them to satisfy their needs with a smaller proportion of their income, and this in turn gave them more to spend on manufactured products of the towns themselves. Individual manufacturing sectors may have profited from chance consequences of the rural changes. Hides, for example, became cheaper because of the increased number of cattle raised in place of grain growing; and the tanner could afford to process a larger number of hides at one time by soaking for long periods in oak bark and water. Timber fell in price, and thus increased the profitability of metallurgy. Better sites for fulling mills became available as former grain mills were abandoned on streams. It also appears that one psychological result of the plague was to discourage saving, and to encourage purchase of luxuries in manufactured goods, clothing, and foreign imports. The towns obviously profited, since the reduced number of workers were producing at the same or even a lower level of efficiency than before, forcing prices even higher. In England the price level for several basic foodstuffs fell from a level of 100 in the period 1261–1350 to an index of 99 in the following fifty years, while the price index of metals went up to 176, of textiles to 160, and of manufactured agricultural implements to 235. Wages for building craftsmen almost doubled at the same time. There is thus considerable evidence of prosperity resulting from the plague in some cities at least.

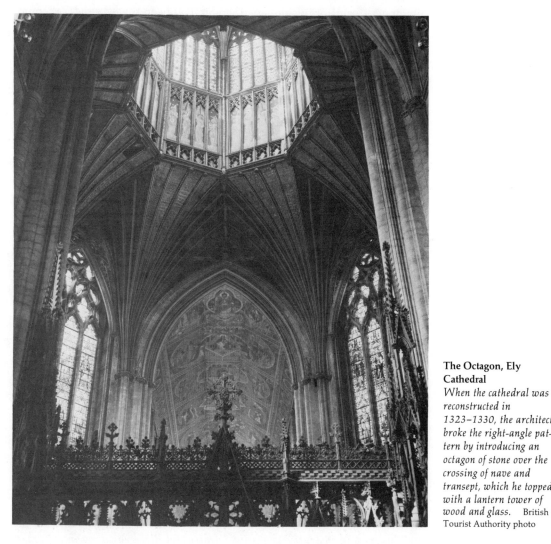

The Octagon, Ely Cathedral
When the cathedral was reconstructed in 1323–1330, the architect broke the right-angle pattern by introducing an octagon of stone over the crossing of nave and transept, which he topped with a lantern tower of wood and glass. British Tourist Authority photo

New Techniques of Business

More far-reaching in its effects was the ability of the merchant class to adapt itself to conditions of recession by inventing far more efficient techniques for carrying on business, by developing new and greatly expanding old sources of wealth, and by profiting from the opening to commerce and manufacturing of new geographical areas.

In the first place, far more effective methods of conducting business were invented, mostly in Italy, and then carried north by representatives of Italian companies. By the end of the thirteenth century, the typical merchant who brought his merchandise with him had been replaced by the merchant who conducted business from the home office; and this change involved a different organization of the business firm. Previously one of the commonest forms of business partnership had been the *commenda*, a temporary partnership in which several merchants pooled their capital and sent one of the partners to conduct a trading mission; at the mission's end the partnership was dissolved and the profits shared out. The obvious inefficiency of constantly reforming business partnerships was first remedied in associations lasting several years, which employed resident agents in the city where the firm's goods were to be traded. These agents could be either independent merchants working for a large number of companies or else the representative branches of a large home company. Meanwhile, the organization of companies through which capital could be accumulated for reinvestment became more formal. The most successful companies in Italy were family firms where relatives pooled their savings, appointed a senior partner to run the enterprise, took shares in the company in proportion to the amount they had invested, and often invited outside capital as well. In Florence almost all the major companies were controlled by families, such as the Bardi and the Peruzzi in the fourteenth century and the Medici in the fifteenth. Even self-made millionaires like Francesco Datini of Prato had started out aided by the financial backing of their relatives. The collapse of a number of overextended firms after the Black Death, when royal and noble debtors were more than usually tempted to renege on their loans, led most of the larger companies to organize their different commercial and industrial ventures, and their overseas branches, as independent partnerships. In 1455, for example, the Medici set up a partnership for trade in Bruges, and signed a contract to send Angiolo, son of Jacopo Tani, to run it, under strict regulations:

Piero, Giovanni, and Piero Francesco de' Medici are to invest L 1,900 groat; Gierozzi de' Pigli, L 600 groat, and Angiolo Tani, L 500 groat, besides his personal (service). And the latter is bound to conduct (business) and to stay in residence in Bruges and in the neighborhood (in order to attend) faithfully to all (business) that he shall see and understand to be to the honor, advantage, and welfare of the said compagnia *in accordance with mercantile custom, and to all orders and instructions of said Medici and Pigli, engaging in legitimate*

trade [and in] licit and honest contracts and exchange. . . . Said Angiolo prom-
ises and obligates himself not to do business for himself or to have business
done in his own name or in the name of others, directly or indirectly in the city
of Bruges nor in any other place. . . . Further, said Angiolo promises and obli-
gates himself not to gamble or have [someone else] gamble in any game of zara
or cards, with dice or with anything else during the life of this said com-
pagnia, under the penalty of L 100 groat for each instance. . . . And let it be
understood he will incur the same penalty and disgrace any time he keeps any
woman at his quarters at his expense.[15]

Written records naturally accumulated with the conduct of much business
by correspondence, and with regulation of far-flung and variegated business enterprises from the home office. Much of the correspondence was
connected directly with business deals. Tommaso Portinari of the Medici
office in Bruges, reporting in 1464, had a sorry tale for Cosimo de' Medici,
the senior partner: "Our profits, as you will see, are very low this year, and
expenditures have been high. . . . Let the new year bear the rest of the liabi-
lities. We have made a good start in it and we shall continue in such a way
that I hope that, through God's grace, we shall partly recoup the losses of
the past. And, besides, we shall make it our care as far as possible to elimi-
nate debtors and to move to a clean slate."[16] Other letters were veritable
diplomatic newsletters, indicating how much the profits of the bigger companies were bound up in the political fortunes of the European governments. Where business leaders actually ran the government, as in Florence
and Venice, news bearing on business was sent directly through their ambassadors, while the most comprehensive collection of news reports was
made by the vast Fugger enterprise in Augsburg. French financier Jacques
Coeur was so keen to have immediate political information that he built
openings for carrier pigeons into the roof of his great mansion in Bourges.

But the most important development in record keeping was also the
most down-to-earth, the invention of modern methods of accounting. The
replacement of clumsy Roman numerals with Arabic numerals made bookkeeping simpler and faster. The adoption of double-entry bookkeeping, the
balancing of debit and credit accounts, became common in the fourteenth
century, making it possible to ascertain immediately both the profitability
of a potential enterprise and, more importantly, the financial health of one's
own firm. Accurate bookkeeping made more feasible the transfer of large
sums of money from place to place without use of currency or bullion. The
instrument used was the bill of exchange, by which one branch of a company promised to pay a specific sum of money, often in another currency,
through one of its branches or an agent. The bill of exchange could be used
by pilgrims, by the Church when collecting its income from other countries,
or by merchants settling accounts; and its vast use left the way open for

[15] Robert S. Lopez and Irving W. Raymond, *Medieval Trade in the Mediterranean World* (New
York: Columbia University Press, 1955), pp. 206–208.
[16] Ibid., p. 404.

profit making by firms dealing in letters of credit, since there was not only a charge for the service but profiteering on changes in exchange rates or on loaning out the money deposited.

Improved accounting methods thus enabled businesses to diversify their activities by engaging in banking. In their commercial activities they extended and sought credit, on which interest was made, after a certain verbal accommodation with the Church's laws against usury. The deposits of large sums of money in return for letters of credit, the profits made from currency exchange, the role of certain companies as tax collectors for the papacy or the monarchies, and many other activities brought huge amounts of capital into the hands of the merchants, who became moneylenders and bankers, especially to princes with urgent needs of large sums of money. The Emperor Charles V had gained his election as Holy Roman Emperor in 1519 borrowing 543,000 florins from the Fuggers, in order to exceed the bribes being offered to the electors by the kings of France and England. Two of Florence's principal companies, Bardi and Peruzzi, however, were ruined in 1343 when the English king refused to pay one and a half million florins he owed them. Banking nevertheless remained a primary source of income for merchant companies throughout Europe, in spite of its risks, and was at the basis of every great fortune put together in the late Middle Ages.

Besides commerce and banking, the merchants also diversified their industrial activities or even shifted into wholly new forms of production. Increased mining of iron ore and other raw materials, in southern Belgium, and in Austria and Hungary, led to foundation of the metallurgical industry, and to investments in armaments and firearms production. Milan, finding its woolen industry in a state of decline, shifted into armaments production, and reached the point where it could outfit a small army in a few days. Liège, in the Low Countries, developed an iron industry, and then specialized in gunmaking. The prosperity of many cities in the Low Countries, endangered with the growth of woolen industries in Italy and England, was saved by production of new types of cloth, such as linens like the cambric of Cambrai, or by concentration on enterprise hitherto of minor importance, such as the wheat commerce in Ghent. But frequently trade shifted from the old established cities, where guild restrictions crushed out new enterprise and imposed unacceptable financial burdens on commerce, to newer towns. Among the regions of greatest expansion in the fifteenth century were south Germany and Switzerland. They developed new industries like textiles and began to engage in banking, in order to service the growing markets of eastern Germany, Hungary, and Poland. The new wealth paid for the walls and fine middle-class homes of the lovely towns of northern Bavaria, such as Nördlingen and Rothenburg, and especially Augsburg and Nuremberg. In England, the wool trade brought wealth to the villages of Somerset and East Anglia, where the wool merchants erected parish churches like that of Long Melford, as grandiose as many cathedrals.

The Fuggerei, Augsburg
The Fuggers, reputed to be the richest family in Europe in the early sixteenth century, endowed an almshouse for old people of their native city of Augsburg which is still in operation. German Tourist Information Office photo

Panorama of Bamberg
Bamberg was an ecclesiastical state, governed by its powerful prince-bishop, whose four-towered cathedral dominates the city. German Tourist Information Office photo

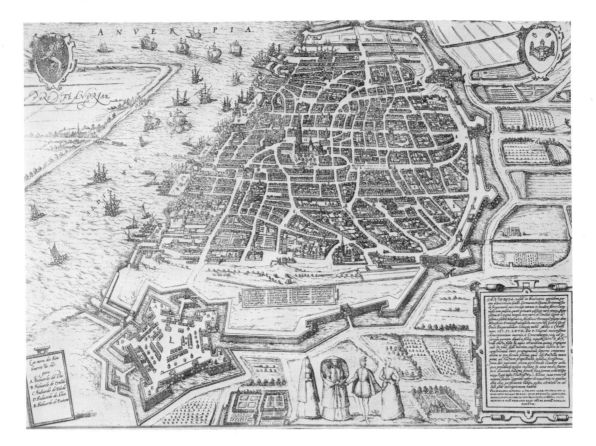

City Plan of Antwerp
Antwerp, on the River Scheldt, was the leading financial center of northern Europe in the sixteenth century. The wealthy guilds erected elaborately decorated houses on the central square, from which they could supervise the work of the city government.

And in the Low Countries the most significant change was the gradual shift of the banking and commercial center for northern Europe from Bruges to the more dynamic city of Antwerp.

Finally, merchants took more drastic measures for ensuring the continuance of their prosperity. Shipping routes were changed to take account of the rise of unfriendly empires, disturbances of war, or changes in maritime technique. The Venetians, for example, began to obtain their spices and other Asian goods from Syria and Egypt rather than from Constantinople and the Black Sea, while the Catalans developed new trade with northwest Africa. From the beginning of the fourteenth century, the Italians adopted new forms of ships, the single-masted cog, suitable for bulky cargoes, and the great galley, operated under sail on the open sea but capable of entering harbor propelled by oarsmen and defended from pirates by bowmen; and annual convoys of these ships were sent from Venice and Genoa to Flanders, stopping on the way to call at the ports of Spain and north Africa. These convoys were so secure that many merchants did not even use the newly invented marine insurance for their cargoes. These great fleets infused new life into the economy of Italy and the Low Countries. Yet perhaps the most important step taken by the merchants was to prepare their cities for war and territorial expansion. In the fourteenth century, the Venetians abandoned the tradition of isolation from the mainland that had served them well and began to conquer a land empire that by 1400 included the lower Po valley and the nearby Alpine chain. In this way, they safeguarded their food supply and the control of the passes into south Germany, but only at the expense of long wars and growing dependence on mercenary armies. The Hanseatic League, a union of over seventy cities along the coast of the North and Baltic seas under the leadership of Lübeck and Hamburg, developed a powerful navy, with which they compelled Denmark to open the entrance to the Baltic to Hanseatic ships. In all these ways, the cities preserved their prosperity through recession and boom; and with their wealth they financed the great artistic creations of this period.

The Culture of the Late Middle Ages in Flanders

Though cultural achievements spread throughout Europe—the perpendicular style of late Gothic architecture in England, the burgher houses of the Hanseatic League, the sharply realistic wooden sculpture of south Germany, the illuminated books of Burgundy, the icon-covered cathedrals

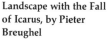

Landscape with the Fall of Icarus, by Pieter Breughel
By the sixteenth century, the great galley of the previous century had evolved into the high-sterned galleon seen at anchor. The peasant turning over the chalky soil of the hillside can use a much lighter plough than that developed in the early Middle Ages for clay soils (compare illustration, p. 337). Belgian National Tourist Office photo

The Garden of Delights, by Hieronymus Bosch (1450?–1516)
Not all Flemish painters had the serenity of Jan van Eyck. Bosch peopled his canvases with wildly imaginative scenes of grotesque people and animals. King Philip II of Spain loved his style, and bought many of his paintings.
Museo del Prado, Madrid

of the Moscow Kremlin, the songs and masses of the Parisian composers like Guillaume de Machaut—it was in the cities of Flanders that late Gothic culture reached its highest peak, and it was in Italy that medieval culture gave way to the vibrantly new style of the Renaissance.

In the late fourteenth and fifteenth centuries, the artists of the Low Countries, especially Flanders, made great advances in almost every form of aesthetic creation. Their architects created city halls, belfries, and town houses in late Gothic style. Their writers produced moving works of mystical devotion. Churches rang to the masses of Guillaume Dufay of Cambrai. Claus Sluter and his followers sculpted dramatic altarpieces. But it was in painting that Flanders was supreme in the north of Europe, and Bruges was its artistic capital. In Bruges patrons abounded, the most important being the Duke of Burgundy, who moved his court there in 1419. The cloth merchants favored religious paintings with which to endow the churches, especially triptychs for the high altar, which featured the donor amid groupings of saints and apostles, whereas the foreign colony of resident agents who traded and banked for great Italian companies or the Hanseatic League preferred portraits of themselves, although as the fame of the Flemish artists spread to Italy these agents occasionally commissioned works for patrons in Florence or Milan. Two of the finest Flemish paintings are of Italian merchants, Jan van Eyck's *Giovanni Arnolfini and His Wife,* and Hans Memling's *Tommaso Portinari,* whose financial report to his home office we just quoted. Painters from all over the Low Countries settled in Bruges where, as members of the painters' guild, they ensured that the Flemish style, once created, would remain intact for over a century.

Tommaso Portinari, by Hans Memling (c. 1440–1494)
Portinari was the Medici agent in Bruges.   The Metropolitan Museum of Art. Bequest of Benjamin Altman, 1913

Donor with His Patron, St. Peter Martyr, Attributed to the Master of the St. Lucy Legend (Active 1475–1500)
Fifteenth-century artists often depicted the saints in company with the donors of the painting. The spires of Bruges can be seen in the distance.   Los Angeles County Museum of Art, Gift of Anna Bing Arnold

The genius most responsible for the triumph of this style was Jan van Eyck (c. 1380–1441). With Van Eyck, artists began to enjoy a new and higher status in society. He went on diplomatic missions for the duke, making portraits of possible candidates for the ducal hand. He was proud of his position, had his servants wear ducal livery, and broke with the still prevailing habit of artistic anonymity by signing his paintings. He usually inscribed *Als ich kann* (As best I can), with mock humility; in the Arnolfini portrait, in which he showed himself in the convex mirror, he wrote "Jan van Eyck was here." Van Eyck's technical contribution was in his mastery of oil painting, a technique which for centuries he was considered to have invented. As the Italian writer Vasari explained in the midsixteenth century, "To practice this method of painting one must proceed as follows: when one wishes to begin—having coated the panel or other surface with glue and plaster, having polished it and applied four or five layers of mild glue—one grinds the colors with nut oil or linseed oil (nut oil is better, for it yellows less); and having thinned them thus, they need no further treatment before being applied with the brush." The process, however, was much slower and more painstaking than that used today, because Van Eyck had to apply each color like thick glue, and then stroke it with his brush into the right thickness for the modulation of tone he was seeking. The end result, however, was a jewellike sparkle that has endured for five centuries.

A glance at a couple of Van Eyck's paintings will explain why art historians are divided between those who call him a late medieval painter and those who want to see in him the beginning of the northern Renaissance. The latter find the coming of a new conception of art and humanity in Van Eyck's realism, in his portrayal of human beings, building interiors, and landscape. In the portrait of Arnolfini, Van Eyck is interested in character. He explores the details of the Italian merchant's face, contrasting its white narrowness with the full, round hat he is wearing, emphasizing the flattened ears, the heavy lids, the heavy skin between the nostrils—a totally competent, self-controlled, perhaps even ruthless leader of the bourgeoisie. Even more striking however is the affection of the painter for the detail of material objects: shoes scattered on the floor, the ermine edging of the gown of Arnolfini's wife, fruit ripening in the sun, the intricate bronze candelabra, and the interior scene reflected in the mirror. Then there is the sense of perspective, made palpable by the framework of the window to the left and the bed on the right, a sense of receding space that Van Eyck frequently created by opening up his rooms through windows or porticoes to vast landscapes dotted with ships and towers and tiny people.

But Van Eyck and the Flemish painters who followed him for the next century were not men of the Italian Renaissance, either in technique or thought. The painters of the Italian Renaissance, as we shall see in the next chapter, had a theoretical basis for their work in Neoplatonism—they were out to present the unseen "ideas" of the universe, in the Platonic sense, through pictorial representation. The Flemish artists delighted in the ap-

**Giovanni Arnolfini and
His Wife by Jan van
Eyck, 1434**
The Granger Collection
photo

**Virgin and Child with
Saints and Donor by Jan
van Eyck (c. 1380–1441)**
*To the left of the Virgin is
St. Barbara, to the right
St. Elizabeth of Hungary.
The kneeling donor is Jan
Vos, prior of a Carthu-
sian Charterhouse near
Bruges.* Copyright The
Frick Collection, New York

pearance of the things they could see, and presented a visual experience of a given moment in time. They worked instinctively to find the technique necessary: perspective, for example, was the result of observation by a craftsman, not of application of a theory of optics. Again, the anatomy was seen from outside the skin, and not, as in the Italian works, a presentation of thoroughly understood physiology. As a result, the Flemish paintings still seem stylized, or "primitive," from the way the people stand or move their bodies, and from the treatment of internal space. Their realism is far from photographic. The philosophy of the painters was thoroughly medieval, moreover. Van Eyck saw symbolism in all the material objects he inserted so lovingly in his paintings. In the Arnolfini painting, the little dog represents faithfulness; the fruit, the lost paradise of the garden of Eden; the beads of crystal and the mirror, purity and innocence; and the one lighted candle in the chandelier, Christ as the light of the world. For Van Eyck, the world was a whole. Every scene, the combination of the smallest objects and the broadest landscapes, must be an experience of the overall harmony of God's creation, almost in the same way as a Gothic cathedral. For the Flemish painters, the world of fifteenth-century Flanders was still the world of a living Christian faith. In Van Eyck's depiction of Prior Jan Vos praying next to the Virgin and Child, and in Roger van der Weyden's portrait of the Virgin at the foot of the cross as a Flemish matron in a Gothic church, one does not have the feeling, as with many Italian paintings, that the religious story is an excuse for a secular painting. On the contrary, by making the scene contemporary, the Flemish painters emphasized the relevance of the Christian story. It is revealing that when the emperor Charles V retired into the seclusion of a Spanish monastery to devote himself to a life of prayer and contemplation, he took with him only one painting, by Roger van der Weyden.

Throughout the fifteenth century, the artists of Flanders, like Hugo van der Goes, Hans Memling, and Gerard David, continued to produce masterpieces in the tradition established by Van Eyck. The contemporary changes in Italian painting had little influence on them; what interchange there was went from north to south. Hence the swan song of the Middle Ages lasted until the economic decay of Bruges and Ghent could no longer be ignored. From the beginning of the sixteenth century, the cultural life of the Low Countries began to move northward in the wake of its economic prosperity, first to Antwerp and then in the seventeenth century to Holland.

SUGGESTED READING

Among the general surveys of the late Middle Ages, Denys Hay, *Europe in the Fourteenth and Fifteenth Centuries* (1966) avoids narrative in favor of an excellent, original analysis of the nature of society. Wallace K. Ferguson, *Europe in Transition, 1300–1520* (1962) is sound and extensive, and has surveys of music and painting.

Louis Halphen and Philippe Sagnac, eds., *La Fin du Moyen Age* (1931) is still useful for its articles by such great French historians as Edouard Perroy and Augustin Renaudet and the Belgian historian Henri Pirenne. Margaret Aston, *The Fifteenth Century: The Prospect of Europe* (1968) is well illustrated, treats Europe as a whole, and is especially useful on the diffusion of knowledge and on travel.

An admirable synthesis of recent research on the economic recession of the late Middle Ages is given by Harry A. Miskimin, *The Economy of the Early Renaissance, 1300–1460* (1969) and by Raymond de Roover, *Business, Banking, and Economic Thought in Late Medieval and Early Modern Europe* (1974). Fuller and more specialized accounts are provided in the second edition of the *Cambridge Economic History of Europe*—vol. 1 (1966) dealing with agriculture, vol. 2 (1952) with industry and trade, and vol. 3 (1963) with economic organization and policies. The studies of northern European trade by M. M. Postan and of southern European trade by R. S. Lopez in vol. 2 are particularly useful. On individual countries, see J. Vicens Vives, *An Economic History of Spain* (1969); Gino Luzzato, *An Economic History of Italy from the Fall of the Roman Empire Until the Beginning of the Sixteenth Century* (1961); and Sidney Pollard and David W. Crossler, *The Wealth of Britain, 1085–1966* (1968). The great changes in the agrarian economy of Europe during the high Middle Ages and the crisis of the late Middle Ages are described, with great variety of new documentation, by Georges Duby, *Rural Economy and Country Life in the Medieval West* (1968) and by B. H. Slicher van Bath, *The Agrarian History of Western Europe, A.D. 500–1850* (1963).

The effects of the Black Death are analyzed in P. Siegler, *The Black Death* (1969) which concentrates on England.

On the Papal Monarchy, see G. Mollat, *The Popes of Avignon, 1305–1378* (1963) and Walter Ullmann, *The Origins of the Great Schism* (1948). For the efforts to reform the Church through the councils, see Brian Tierney, *Foundations of the Conciliar Theory* (1955) and J. H. Mundy and D. M. Woody, *The Council of Constance* (1961). The psychological impact of the disasters of the fourteenth century can be seen in Philippe Aries, *Western Attitudes Toward Death: From the Middle Ages to the Present* (1974). The popular piety which was in part a reaction to the crisis is studied in Robert Lerner, *The Heresy of the Free Spirit in the Later Middle Ages* (1972); and Norman Cohn's two books, *Pursuit of the Millenium* (2nd. ed., 1964) and *Europe's Inner Demons: An Inquiry Inspired by the Great Witchhunt* (1975).

The changes in political organization that culminated in the "new monarchies" are discussed in Arthur J. Slavin, ed., *The New Monarchies and Representative Assemblies* (1964); but the most graphic account is Philip de Commines, *The Memoirs.* Joseph R. Strayer draws mostly upon the evolution of the English and French monarchies in his brilliant summation, *The Medieval Origins of the Modern State* (1970), which should be contrasted with the model-building of Charles Tilly, ed., *The Formation of National States in Western Europe* (1975). On the French monarchy, see P. S. Lewis, *Later Medieval France: The Polity* (1968) and P. S. Lewis, ed., *The Recovery of France in the Fifteenth Century* (1971). On Spain, see Roger Highfield, ed., *Spain in the Fifteenth Century (1369–1516): Essays and Extracts by Historians of Spain* (1972).

For individual monarchs, see P. Champion, *Louis XI* (1929); S. B. Chrimes, *Henry VII* (1973); on the Burgundian dynasty, the uneven biographies by R. Vaughan, *Philip the Bold* (1962), *John the Fearless* (1966), *Philip the Good: The Apogee of Burgundy* (1970), and *Charles the Bold* (1973).

The best survey of the Hundred Years War is still E. Perroy, *The Hundred Years War:* (1951). C. T. Allmand, ed., has provided a good source book, *Society at War:*

The Experience of England and France During the Hundred Years War (1974) while John Barnie searches for the impact of the war on such intangibles as nationalism in *War in Medieval English Society: Social Values and the Hundred Years War, 1337–99* (1974).

R. S. Lopez and I. W. Raymond have collected fascinating documents on all aspects of medieval commerce in *Medieval Trade in the Mediterranean World: Illustrative Documents* (1955). First-class monographs on individual cities, especially Italian cities where documentation is superabundant, are numerous. See especially D. Herlihy's two studies, *Pisa in the Early Renaissance: A Study of Urban Growth* (1958) and *Medieval and Renaissance Pistoia: The Social History of an Italian Town* (1968); William K. Bowsky, *The Finance of the Commune of Siena, 1287–1355* (1970); J. K. Hyde, *Padua in the Age of Dante* (1966); and Robert Brentano, *Rome Before Avignon* (1974). Josiah Cox Russell has attempted to use quantitative techniques to demonstrate the significance of regions dominated by a city or cities in the economic structure of medieval Europe, in his *Medieval Regions and Their Cities* (1972).

Among many excellent studies of the medieval city, the German cities receive unusually full treatment in Fritz Rörig, *The Medieval Town* (1967). The basic work on the Hanseatic League is Philip Dollinger, *The German Hansa* (1970). Henri Pirenne, *Medieval Cities* (1956) is still the standard treatment of the Belgian cities, but it should be backed up with the more specialized D. Nicholas, *Town and Countryside: Social, Economic, and Political Tensions in Fourteenth-Century Flanders* (1971).

The Belgian cities are most usually approached through their art, and up-to-date social and political studies are regrettably rare. William Gaunt, *Flemish Cities: Their History and Art* (1969) is a gorgeously illustrated attempt to link urban influences to style of painting. Joseph van der Elst, *The Last Flowering of the Middle Ages* (1944) is succinct and informative on Flemish painters. Jacques Lassaigne and Giulio Carlo Argan, *The Fifteenth Century, from Van Eyck to Botticelli* (1955) treats Flemish and Italian painting as part of one Renaissance. François Cali, *Bruges: The Cradle of Flemish Painting* (1964) has fine photographs and an evocative account of the development of art in Bruges, with special attention to the influence of folk religion. E. Gilliam-Smith, *The Story of Bruges* (1905) is old-fashioned but rich in detail.

Chronicle of Events

From the Renaissance to the Overseas Discoveries

1400–1650

Italy	Germany	England	France	Spain and Portugal	International/Other European Powers
1397 Foundation of Medici Bank in FLORENCE	Rise of cities in central and south Germany (AUGSBURG, NUREMBERG, FRANKFURT)	Henry IV (1399–1413)	Hundred Years' War with England (1337–1453)	Last phase of *Reconquista* of Spain from Moslems	
1402 d. Giangaleazzo, Visconti of MILAN					
1408 Donatello's *David*		Henry V (1413–1422)	1415 Defeat by English at Battle of Agincourt	1415 Portuguese take CEUTA	1414–1418 Council of Constance
				1419 Henry the Navigator of Portugal moves to Sagres	1417 Martin V pope; end of Great Schism
				1419 Portuguese discover Madeira	
1421 Brunelleschi's Foundling Hospital, FLORENCE		Henry VI (1422–1461)			

1400

1425

1426 Masaccio's frescoes in Brancacci chapel, FLORENCE

Cosimo de' Medici in power in FLORENCE (1434–1464)

1434 Brunelleschi's dome on Florence cathedral completed

1429 Charles VII crowned king at RHEIMS

1431 Joan of Arc burned at stake in ROUEN

1434 Portuguese round Cape Bojador

Ivan III, Tsar of Russia (1462–1505)

1450

c. 1450 Invention of printing

Period of urban prosperity in central and south Germany

Tilman Riemenschneider (c. 1460–1531)

Veit Stoss (1445–1533)

1453 End of the Hundred Years' War

Wars of the Roses (1455–1485)

1460 d. Henry the Navigator in Portugal

Louis XI (1461–1483) Foundation of the New Monarchy

1462 Platonic Academy founded in FLORENCE

Italy	Germany	England	France	Spain and Portugal	International/ Other European Powers
Dominance of Lorenzo de' Medici in FLORENCE (1469–1492)					Charles the Rash, Duke of Burgundy (1467–1477)
1478 Pazzi uprising in FLORENCE 1478 Botticelli's *Primavera*				John, King of Portugal (1481–95)	c. 1480 End of Tartar yoke in Russia
1484 Strozzi palace in FLORENCE		*Tudor Dynasty* Henry VII (1485–1509)	Charles VIII (1483–1498)	1487–88 Bartholemew Dias rounds Cape of Good Hope 1492 Columbus discovers New World	Pope Alexander VI (1492–1503)

1475

1492 Conquest of Granada; expulsion of Moors from Spain

Manuel the Fortunate, King of Portugal (1495–1521)

1498–99 Vasco da Gama voyage to India

Pope Julius II (1503–1513)

1509 Erasmus's *Praise of Folly*

Maximilian I, Holy Roman Emperor (1493–1519)

1494 d. Pico della Mirandola

1494–1498 Dominance of Savonarola in FLORENCE

Italian Wars (1494–1559)

Hans Holbein (c. 1497–1543)

1497 John Cabot's voyage to Newfoundland

Henry VIII (1509–1547)

1505 Michelangelo's *David*

1510 d. Botticelli

1511 Luther's visit to ROME

1512 Medici restored to power in FLORENCE

1500

Italy	Germany	England	France	Spain and Portugal	International/Other European Powers
1513 Michelangelo's Sistine Chapel painting completed 1513 Machievelli's *Prince*					Pope Leo X (1513–1522)
	1517 Luther attacks indulgences Charles V, Holy Roman Emperor (1519–1556)	1516 More's *Utopia*	Francis I (1515–1547) Renaissance in France 1515 Victory at Marignano in Italy		
1520 d. Raphael	1520 Luther excommunicated 1521 Luther at Diet of Worms 1524–1526 Peasants' War		1519 Chateau of Chambord in Loire valley begun	1519–1522 Magellan circumnavigates the globe 1519–1522 Cortés conquers Mexico for Spain 1521 Revolt of the comuneros in Spain	1519 Zwingli in ZURICH
1528 Castiglione's *Courtier*					1529 Siege of VIENNA by Turks

1525

1530 Pizarro conquers Inca empire in South America for Spain				1534–1541 Michelangelo's *Last Judgment*
	1531–1539 Break with Catholic Church; dissolution of monasteries		1534–1535 Anabaptists in Münster	
1531 d. Zwingli	1540 Thomas Cromwell executed		1546 d. Luther 1546–1547 Schmalkaldic War 1547 Battle of Mühlberg	
Ivan IV, the Terrible, Tsar of Russia (1534–84) Calvin in GENEVA (1536–1564) 1540 Jesuit order founded	Edward VI (1547–1553)			
1545–1547 First session of Council of Trent; beginning of Catholic Reformation	Mary (1553–1558); Catholic reaction	Dominance of Catherine de Médicis (1555–1589)	1555 Treaty of Augsburg	
1551–1552 Second session of Council of Trent 1553 Servetus burned at GENEVA				

1550

Italy	Germany	England	France	Spain and Portugal	International/ Other European Powers
1558 Dome and Nave of St. Peter's, ROME, begun	Ferdinand I, Holy Roman Emperor (1558–1564)	Elizabeth (1558–1603) 1559 Act of Supremacy	1559 Treaty of Cateau-Cambrésis (France, Spain)	Philip II, King of Spain (1556–1598) 1561 Madrid becomes capital of Spain	
1564 d. Michelangelo 1568 Jesuit Church in ROME begun 1571 d. Benvenuto Cellini	Maximilian II, Holy Roman Emperor (1564–1576)		1562–1598 Wars of Religion 1572 Massacre of Saint Bartholomew in PARIS	1564 Spanish drive French from Florida 1571 Spanish defeat Turks at Battle of Lepanto	1562–1563 Third session of Council of Trent 1568 Revolt of Netherlands begins
		1577–1580 Drake's voyage around the world		1580–1640 Portugal under Spanish rule	1584–1613 Time of Troubles in Russia 1584 Assassination of William of Orange

1575

1585 ANTWERP taken by Duke of Parma

1602 Dutch East India Company founded

1610 Plan of the Three Canals, AMSTERDAM

1604 Cervantes's *Don Quixote*

Henry IV (1589–1610)
1593 Henry IV converts to Catholicism

1598 Edict of Nantes

Louis XIII (1610–1643)

1585 Troops sent to aid revolt in Netherlands
1585 Shakespeare moves to LONDON
1588 Defeat of Spanish Armada

1595–1600 Shakespeare's principal comedies

1601–1609 Shakespeare's principal tragedies

James I (1603–1625)

1605 Gunpowder Plot
1607 JAMESTOWN, Va. founded

1600 Giordano Bruno burned in GENEVA

1600

Italy	Germany	England	France	Spain and Portugal	International/ Other European Powers
1629 Bernini appointed architect of St. Peter's, ROME	1618 Thirty Years' War begins Ferdinand II, Holy Roman Emperor (1619–1637) 1625 Danish King Christian IV invades Germany 1630 Swedish King Gustavus IV invades Germany Ferdinand III, Holy Roman Emperor (1637–1657)	1620 Pilgrim Fathers land in Massachusetts Charles I (1625–1649) 1628 Assassination of Buckingham 1629–1640 Charles I's personal rule 1638–1639 Scottish wars	1614 Meeting of Estates General 1624–1642 Cardinal Richelieu, principal minister	1614 d. El Greco 1616 d. Cervantes 1625 d. Lope de Vega	1631 Rembrandt arrives in AMSTERDAM

1640 Portugal throws off Spanish rule

Louis XIV (1643–1715)

1642–1648 Civil wars

Frederick-William I, the Great Elector of Prussia (1640–1688)

1648 Treaty of Westphalia

I cannot believe that my Antonio Loschi, who has seen Florence, or anyone else who has seen it, can deny that it is the flower, the most beautiful part, of Italy—unless he is utterly mad. What city, not merely in Italy, but in all the world, is more securely placed within its circle of walls, more proud in its palazzi, more bedecked with churches, more beautiful in its architecture, more imposing in its gates, richer in piazzas, happier in its wide streets, greater in its people, more glorious in its citizenry, more inexhaustible in wealth, more fertile in fields?—Coluccio Salutati, Invective Against Antonio Loschi of Vicenza. *Cited in Paul Ruggiers,* Florence in the Age of Dante *(Norman: University of Oklahoma Press, 1964), p. ix.*

11 / *The Florence of Lorenzo de' Medici*

In the fifteenth century, the citizens of Florence were conscious of living in an age of great artistic and intellectual achievement. To the business leader Matteo Palmieri, it was a rediscovery of Rome: "Now, indeed, may every thoughtful spirit thank God that it has been permitted to him to be born in

this new age, so full of hope and promise, which already rejoices in a greater array of nobly gifted souls than the world has seen in the thousand years that have preceded it." To Poliziano, the translator of Homer, Florence was a reborn Athens: "Greek learning, long extinct even in Greece itself, has come to life and lives again in Florence. There Greek literature is taught and studied, so that Athens, root and branch, has been transported to make her abode—not Athens in ruins and in the hands of barbarians, but Athens as she was, with her breathing spirit and her very soul."

Lorenzo de' Medici Alinari photo

Florence Alinari photo

For almost a century, Florence dominated the cultural movement that we call the Renaissance. Its scholars and authors—among many, Bruni, Poggio, Ficino, Pico della Mirandola—took the lead in the revival of Greek and Latin culture and the creation of a new literature in both Italian and the classical languages. Its painters—Masaccio, Uccello, Ghirlandaio, Botticelli, Leonardo da Vinci—mastered the geometry of perspective, learned to portray the human anatomy in unmatched accuracy and beauty, and gave to pagan and secular subjects a prominence at least the equal of religious themes. Its sculptors—Ghiberti, Donatello, Luca della Robbia, Michelangelo—broke with the Gothic tradition, and at times surpassed even their classical models in physiological accuracy and psychological insight. Its architects—Brunelleschi, Michelozzo, Alberti—revived the motifs of impe-

The Florence of Lorenzo de' Medici

Period Surveyed	Fifteenth century, especially rule of Cosimo de' Medici (1434–1464), Piero de' Medici (1464–1469), and Lorenzo de' Medici (1469–1492)
Population	50,000–70,000
Size	2.34 square miles
Form of Government	Republic. Signoria of 9 priors as executive; advisory councils of 12 buonomini and 16 gonfalonieri; Council of the Seventy and Council of the Hundred added to original constitution under Medici; Council of the People and Council of the Commune as legislative assemblies. Manipulation of electoral process by Medici to maintain their control
Political Leaders	Albizzi family in early fifteenth century; Medici family from 1434
Economic Base	Woolen manufacturing; banking; international finance; tax collecting for papacy; artisan crafts
Intellectual Life	Humanists (Bruni, Ficino, Pico della Mirandola); painters (Masaccio, Uccello, Ghirlandaio, Botticelli, Leonardo da Vinci); sculptors (Ghiberti, Donatello, Luca della Robbia, Michelangelo); architects (Brunelleschi, Michelozzo, Alberti)
Principal Buildings	Cathedral; Palazzo della Signoria; Palazzo del Podestà; churches (Santa Croce, Santa Maria Novella); Foundlings' Hospital
Public Entertainments	Open-air music; dancing; street horse-racing; chivalric tournaments; religious plays; church processions
Religion	Catholic; Monasticism (Dominicans, Franciscans, Carmelites); millenarianism (Savonarola)

rial Roman building, and transformed the style into something wholly original by their own innovations in technique. These literary and artistic geniuses of fifteenth-century Florence created the culture of the Renaissance. We no longer, however, speak of the Renaissance as a self-contained cultural movement. These men were not working detached from their own society, stashing away their manuscripts in some penurious garret, like so many Romantic writers of the early nineteenth century, until the public would be ready for them. They were admired, lionized, and well paid by the wealthy merchant class that controlled the Florentine government, to whose values with regard to religion, moneymaking, politics, and even people they appealed and at times catered.

If definitely not isolated from society and its concerns, neither was the

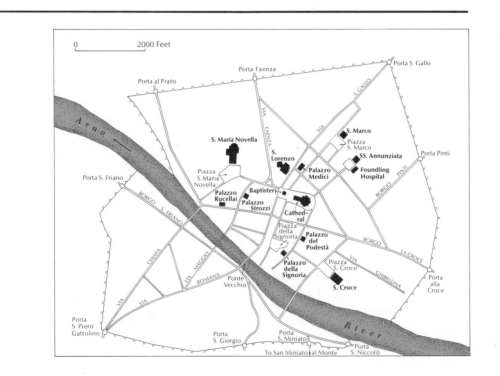

Renaissance, as earlier believed, a closed, almost static period—stretching through the fourteenth and fifteenth centuries—that broke decisively with the Middle Ages. The individualism, the irreligion and amorality, the admiration of Greece and Rome, even to some extent the secularism, which for

◆ *Italy at the Time of Lorenzo de' Medici* ◆

at least half a century after the publication of Jacob Burckhardt's *Civilization of the Renaissance in Italy* (1860) were held to initiate Renaissance society and to be the origin of modern society, existed already in the Middle Ages. The view that capitalism originated in the merchant cities of Italy in the fourteenth and fifteenth centuries has also been rejected. Medieval agriculture made great productive advances through revolutionary technological changes, and rural society achieved a money economy well before 1300. At that same time, the medieval cities had already become accustomed to the accumulation of liquid capital and its reinvestment for profit, large-scale commercial and financial enterprise, and even the division of those engaged in manufacturing into employer and employee classes. Thus, many of the features once considered typical of the Renaissance have been shown as widely present in the Middle Ages. Moreover, many features considered typical of medieval society are now recognized to have continued to exist in full force during the Renaissance. It is true that respect for clerical institutions was at a low ebb, but religious piety and also intolerance were present at all levels of Italian society, as can be seen in Florence's receptivity to the apocalyptic outbursts of Savonarola and the deep faith of Michelangelo, to take only two examples. The northern Renaissance has never been considered secular. And unless one recognizes the continuance of strong religious commitment during the fifteenth and sixteenth centuries, one cannot understand why the Protestant Reformation should have occurred after the Renaissance rather than before. Finally, the hierarchical organization of society was still respected, both in the relationship of the guilds within the cities and in the long if somewhat indistinct series of gradations in the countryside from landless laborer to great noble.

Nevertheless, even if we regard the achievements of the fourteenth and fifteenth centuries, in Italy at least, as the culmination of trends long present in European society, it is clear that to live in fifteenth-century Florence was to be at the heart, one might almost say in the maelstrom, of a consciously recognized period of human achievement. The humanist Coluccio Salutati was outraged that Antonio Loschi from Vicenza dared call Florence the dregs of Italy rather than its "one and only glory":

What city has been more active in professions, more admirable, generally, in all things? What city without a seaport ships out so much goods? Where is business a greater enterprise, or richer in variety of stuffs, or carried on with more astuteness and sagacity? Where are men more illustrious? And—let me not be tiresome—more distinguished in affairs, valiant in arms, strong in just rule, and renowned? Where can you find a Dante, a Petrarch, a Boccaccio? Tell me, I beg you, oh infamous monster, to what place, to what men can you assign the highest place of honor in Italy, if you say that Florence is the off-scouring of Italy? [1]

---

[1] Cited in Paul Ruggiers, *Florence in the Age of Dante* (Norman: University of Oklahoma Press, 1964), pp. ix–x.

Renaissance creativity reached its height in the last third of the fifteenth century; and it was the personality and power of Lorenzo de' Medici, whose position as unofficial ruler of Florence and head of its richest banking and mercantile company made him the supreme patron of art and letters, that stimulated the final and highest flowering of Florentine genius. Unlike earlier members of his family, Lorenzo neglected business in favor of politics and the intellectual life. Supported by a restricted alliance of wealthy patrician families, he manipulated the electoral process in Florence to keep political control in his own hands; and he used his power to give Florence thirty years of political stability and diplomatic quiet. He and the patrician families poured their wealth and energy into the cultural life. Their newly built palaces were vast monuments of the new style in architecture. The churches they patronized were filled with the paintings and sculpture of the contemporary artists they favored. And the philosophy of Neoplatonism was developed by Marsilio Ficino and the group of scholars whom the Medici gathered in their Platonic academy in the hills near the city. Two years before Lorenzo died, below Ghirlandaio's fresco in the Church of Santa Maria Novella, an inscription was added that summed up the self-congratulation of the Florentines at having lived in such an age: "Florence fair and noble through her victories, her great works, her crafts and houses, enjoys abundance, health and tranquillity."

Early History of Florence

Florence was a latecomer among medieval cities. Although it had been founded during the consulship of Julius Caesar as a typical garrison and administrative center for the provinces, laid out like all such foundations on the square gridiron plan of a military camp, it had developed very little during its first twelve centuries of existence. It was fifty miles from the sea, on a river, the Arno, which, although it flooded large parts of the city twice every century, shrank to an unnavigable stream each summer. Although it commanded one of the main roads crossing the rugged Apennines from Milan and Venice to the south, it was too far inland to profit from the most important north-south highway that ran through Lucca and Siena. Its desire to monopolize the seaborne and landborne trade of central Italy brought Florence inevitably into conflict with Pisa, Lucca, and Siena for several centuries. Yet for a small city—in 1172, Florence covered only 200 acres and had a population of under 25,000—it did have certain natural advantages. The river provided ample water not only for household use but in the large quantities needed for an expanding textile industry. The plain around the river and the nearby foothills provided wheat, olives, and grapes, although Florence had to assure its wheat supply from the midthirteenth century by a close alliance with Naples.

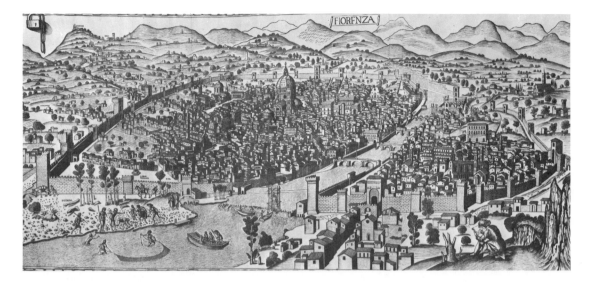

In the general prosperity of the eleventh and twelfth centuries, Florence slowly revived as a trading center, and began in a small way the finishing of woolen cloth. As late as 1200, however, Florence was very little different from any of the small hill towns of the Apennines and relatively backward in comparison to the cities of the Lombard plain. Led by a peculiarly Florentine coalition of merchants, bankers, and landowners, the citizens had won autonomy from the local feudal aristocracy and their bishop. Governed as a "commune" by an executive of twelve consuls and an assembly ostensibly representing all the citizens, they had twice rebuilt their city walls and had financed a spate of church building in a specifically Florentine Romanesque style that was to exert great influence on the fifteenth-century Renaissance. In the church of San Miniato al Monte, on a hill overlooking the city, and in the octagonal baptistery in the center of town, Tuscan architects revived Roman forms such as the round arch, the Corinthian capital, and the pedimented window, with a simplicity and fidelity to the original style lacking in other Romanesque architecture; but by the use of marble in contrasting colors—white and black at San Miniato, white and green in the baptistery—they gave an austere strength and elegance to the line of the building that remains a distinctive feature of all later Florentine building. So striking is the connection in style between these twelfth-century buildings and those of the fifteenth century that historians have called the Romanesque period of building the Proto-Renaissance.

Florence in 1490
Looking up the Arno River, the observer sees on the left the major churches and government buildings, on the right the textile-manufacturing suburbs. Alinari photo

Economic Advances in Thirteenth-Century Florence

During the thirteenth century, Florence spurted to a leading position among Europe's cities, with a prosperity firmly based on textile manufacture and sales, banking, and tax collection. Many factors contributed to this boom.

Cathedral Square, Florence

The ecclesiastical heart of Florence is composed of the twelfth-century baptistery, the belltower designed by Giotto in the fourteenth century, and the cathedral which was completed in 1434 with the addition of Brunelleschi's dome. Italian Government Travel Office photo

The Florentines had shared only a small part in the maritime expansion throughout the Mediterranean undertaken by such great port cities as Venice, Genoa, and Pisa, and they had thus avoided the costly rivalries that were eventually to sap the vitality of many of these cities. They had come late to the industry of wool manufacturing, and had been able to profit from the advances achieved first in the cities of Flanders. During the twelfth century, most woolen goods sold by Florence were manufactured from imported cloth merely refinished in Florence. But during this period of apprenticeship, the Florentines had discovered their own natural talents for design and perfection of finish, and by the midthirteenth century their cloth exceeded in quality that of almost all other European cities. At the same time, they were helped by the decline of the Flemish cities, whose competition fell off rapidly in the last years of the thirteenth century. To perfection of the product, the Florentines added skill in marketing and the procuring of raw materials for production. They concluded favorable arrangements with Spanish and English producers of high-quality wool for direct import of their best product, and they employed their commercial outlets in western Europe and the eastern Mediterranean for aggressive selling of their finished cloth. Finally, they developed banking skills, especially in international finance, which they put into the service of the popes and the rulers of Naples after the papal, or Guelf, faction inside Florence had defeated the imperial, or Ghibelline, faction. By the early years of the fourteenth century, a number of important Florentine banking and commercial companies, such as Bardi, Peruzzi, and Scali, were operating throughout Europe as international bankers, tax collectors for the papacy, and financial administrators of the whole kingdom of Naples and Sicily.

Florence's second wall, built in 1172, had enclosed only 200 acres. Its third wall, begun in 1284, enclosed 1500 acres, to provide living and working space for a population that was soon to reach 90,000, a number exceeded only by Paris, Venice, Milan, and Naples. Giovanni Villani, a chronicler with an unusual taste for statistics and an even more unusual reliability, chose the year 1338 to demonstrate the "greatness and state and magnificence of the Commune of Florence." That year, he wrote, Florence had 25,000 citizens fit to bear arms; its churches numbered 110, including 30 hospitals with more than 1,000 beds for the poor and sick; 200 workshops produced more than 70,000 pieces of cloth worth 1.2 million gold florins; and the Florentines consumed 4,000 oxen and calves, 110,000 sheeps, goats, and pigs, and 70,000 quarts of wine.

[Florence] within the walls was well built, with many beautiful houses, and at that time people kept building with improved techniques to obtain comfort and richness by importing designs of every kind of improvement. [They built] parish churches, and churches of friars of every order, and splendid monasteries. And besides this, there was no citizen, whether commoner or magnate, who had not built or was not building in the country a large and rich estate with a very costly mansion and with fine buildings—much better than those in the city—and in this they all were committing sin, and they were called crazy on account of their wild expenses.[2]

The Florentine Patriciate

The Renaissance was in a direct sense the creation of, or at very least was created for, the urban aristocracy, or "patriciate," of Florence. This class combined economic wealth, political influence, social prestige, and artistic patronage. It will therefore be helpful, in order to understand why this class sponsored a cultural movement permeated with new values in art, liter-

---

[2] Robert S. Lopez and Irving W. Raymond, *Medieval Trade in the Mediterranean World* (New York: Columbia University Press, 1955), pp. 71–73.

ature, scholarship, political theory, and even perhaps in ethics, if we examine separately the economic, the political, and the social evolution of this class during its rise in the thirteenth, fourteenth, and fifteenth centuries.

The Economic Power of the Patriciate

The wealthy merchants of the city were organized in seven great guilds, known as the *arti maggiori*. Up to the midfourteenth century, the most important was the wool-finishing guild, the Calimala, named after a street of ill fame where its shops clustered. The guild's members or their agents purchased the cloth of northern Europe at the fairs of Champagne or in the Flemish cities, shipped them overland on packhorse to Provence, and then by sea to Pisa for transshipment to Florence. There they either sold them at once for shipment to other parts of Italy or the eastern Mediterranean, or put them out for dyeing and finishing by carefully supervised specialists in Florence. The Calimala had a highly organized network of trade throughout Europe; the members ran their own inns and postal service, negotiated toll reductions and guarantees of safe passage, and severely punished those who cheated them, especially the artisans in Florence itself.

During the early fourteenth century, the wool-manufacturing guild, called the Lana, eclipsed the Calimala in economic and political power. Buying raw wool in England and Spain, contracting for the production years ahead of time, seeking the dyestuffs of the East, recruiting labor from all northern Italy, the merchants of the Lana built up a highly capitalized industry employing thirty thousand workers in some two hundred companies. Concentrating on higher-quality production for the luxury market, in a period of thirty years they doubled the value of their sales, marketing their products aggressively throughout Europe and the Mediterranean. Throughout the fourteenth century, the wealth of the Lana was the basis of Florence's prosperity; and it was against the oligarchy of merchants controlling the guild that the workers, both the skilled dyers who possessed a little capital in their own tools and workshops and the great proletarian majority of poverty-stricken carders, combers, beaters, spinners, and weavers, revolted sporadically. Their most successful uprising, the Ciompi revolt of 1378, brought a temporary improvement of wages and recognition of the right to organize; but within four years, the old predominance of the Lana's inner circle was restored. In Renaissance Florence, as in Periclean Athens, there was a large, disenfranchised laboring class who saw little of the cultural pleasures of their employers and rulers other than the public monuments they raised.

The third of the great textile guilds, the Seta of the silk manufacturers, expanded in the fifteenth century as wool manufacturing began to decline under increased competition from England and new centers in the Netherlands and Italy itself and with the shift in society's taste toward silk and brocade. Here again the Florentine genius for anticipating shifts in consumer trends and for catering to them helped maintain the city's prosperity.

An aggressive foreign policy also served the needs of the textile guilds. The acquisition of the ports of Pisa and Leghorn at the beginning of the fifteenth century enabled the Florentines for the first time to build a fleet, and to trade directly with northern Europe and the eastern Mediterranean.

The fourth of the great guilds, and ultimately the one in which the greatest concentration of wealth in the hands of individual families occurred, was the Cambio, comprising the bankers. Commerce had given great opportunities to the merchants to engage in banking as a sideline, in the selling of bills of exchange, the changing and transferring of foreign currency, and the extending of credit. From the thirteenth century through the fifteenth, the most important client of the Florentine bankers was the papacy, which entrusted them with the collection of the vast papal revenues from all over Europe; but they also engaged in far more risky ventures with national sovereigns, supplying loans to be covered by future taxation that were often repudiated. The greatest of the Florentine banking companies, however, was the Medici. In little over a century, they had succeeded in expanding a little capital brought from farming property in the mountains near Florence into a large commercial, manufacturing, and financial enterprise valued at 90,000 florins. They had one silk and two wool-manufacturing companies in Florence; their bank in Florence boasted eight branches in the major trade centers of Europe, including Bruges, London, and Venice. For most of the fifteenth century they were the main papal bankers, and the papacy gave them a lucrative monopoly on the mining of alum at Tolfa. The Medici were therefore represented in the Lana, Seta, and Cambio guilds, and Lorenzo himself was a member of all three; but by befriending the lesser guilds during the Ciompi uprising, they won a reputation they never lost for being the friend of the poorer classes of the city against the oligarchy.

The other three guilds of the *arti maggiori* were the furriers' guild, the guild for doctors and apothecaries, and the guild for judges and lawyers. Thus there existed a uniquely Florentine alliance of the intellectual classes with the economically powerful; and the lawyers and judges played so important a part in a city excessively litigious and in a bureaucracy deeply concerned with the distribution of the tax burden that it was good sense to welcome them into the self-interested circles in power.

Finally, the more mundane but still profitable professions of butchers, locksmiths, wine merchants, bakers, and so on, were organized as the lesser guilds, or *arti minori*. They made up the bulk of the lower middle class, and were usually given a minor share in political power to prevent their throwing in their lot with the poor.

The Political Evolution of the Patriciate

Control of political power in Florence followed changes in economic power, to a large degree. In the eleventh and twelfth centuries, the Florentine business classes, like those of the other northern and central Italian cities, established an independent city government known as a commune, which took over from the feudal and ecclesiastical lords such city functions as the administration of justice and defense. In the thirteenth century, the Calimala guild took the lead in completing the ouster of the nobility and in establishing a republican form of government dominated by the members of the great guilds. Throwing in their lot with the Guelf supporters of the papacy against the Ghibelline supporters of the emperor, the Calimala and other great guilds first won equality with the nobility and then seized power in 1282. The constitution, called the Ordinances of Justice, which they wrote in 1293, barred both the nobility and the laboring classes from political power. Out of the six thousand guild members who were given the franchise, only about one-third ever held an administrative or legislative post. The principal executive body was the Signoria, a group of nine priors elected for two months only, which also had the power to initiate legislation. During their term the Priors lived in the Palazzo della Signoria on the city's central square, where they were waited on by large numbers of serv-

Palazzo della Signoria, Florence

A fortress inside the city, the Palazzo della Signoria was begun in 1299 as the seat of the chief judge and the priors.   Italian Government Travel Office photo

ants in green livery, treated to the finest in food and wine, and entertained by a permanent staff of musicians, singers, and jesters. The priors were advised on policy by twelve *buonomini* representing the four quarters of the city and by sixteen *gonfalonieri* (literally, banner bearers), but there were also two legislative assemblies known as the Council of the People and the Council of the Commune, which could veto but not initiate legislation. This was clearly a complicated administrative system in which power appeared to be spread more widely than, for example, in the oligarchy of Venice. Through manipulation of the scrutiny, the method of establishing through a commission those eligible for office, the control of the Signoria was, however, kept tightly in the hands of the great guilds; and it has been shown that in the 1330s almost three-quarters of the priors were chosen from the Calimala, the Lana, and the Cambio guilds.

After surviving a number of attacks in the early fourteenth century when the Florentines voluntarily called in foreign princes to defend them, the republican system was tested even more thoroughly in the second half of the century when the city split into warring factions. The more conservative faction, representing the interests of the great guilds and headed by the Albizzi family, was opposed by a popular alliance of artisans and newly rich or *gente nuova,* headed by the Ricci family. After the Ciompi uprising of 1378, the republic was controlled by the popular faction for three years, until the wealthy older families reasserted their power; and from 1382 until 1434, Florence was governed by a far more conservative patrician regime than it had known for a century.

During the crucial early years when the Renaissance culture was being created in Florence, this conservative oligarchy gave the city much-needed stability. Republican forms were preserved. The lesser guilds retained their customary two seats in the Signoria. Large numbers of immigrants to the city were absorbed without great dislocation, and the disfranchised workers displayed an enthusiastic patriotism for the city republic to which they felt they belonged. The members of the ruling patriciate undoubtedly served themselves in office, influencing the tax rolls in their own favor or manipulating foreign policy to serve their commercial interests. They also ensured that they would maintain their hold by restricting communal office to those who had paid, or whose fathers had paid, taxes continuously for thirty years. But they gave unstintingly for their time and energy, if not always of their money, in the city's service. Eventually, however, the ruling class divided into factions whose disputes over policy were exacerbated by family quarrels. In the 1430s, during an unsuccessful military campaign against the city of Lucca, one faction headed by Rinaldo degli Albizzi was opposed by another faction headed by Cosimo de' Medici. In 1434, when Rinaldo unwisely sought a showdown with Cosimo, he lost because Cosimo possessed the great financial resources of the Medici bank which he had used to win clients among the patriciate and the artisans, and friends among the mercenary captains hired by Florence. From 1434, the faction of the patriciate

Cosimo de' Medici, Possibly from an Original Bas Relief by Andrea del Verrocchio (1435–1488)   Palazzo Medici-Riccardi, Florence. Alinari photo

headed by Cosimo de' Medici was the unofficial government of Florence. The dominance of Cosimo's family was continued by his gout-afflicted, conscientious son Piero (1464–1469), by the multifaceted genius of his grandson Lorenzo (1469–1492), and for a brief, troubled time by his great-grandson Piero (1492–1494).

The Social Character of the Patriciate

This patriciate, economically wealthy and politically powerful, created in Florence a form of upper-class society whose values differed markedly from those of other Italian cities. Considerable research in recent years has been lavished in efforts to establish those features in the "social world" of this patriciate that made Florence the incubator of the early Renaissance. The consensus appears to be, in Gene Brucker's words, "the flexible character of the society and its institutions, and the fruitful balance between tradition and innovation."[3]

The primary Florentine social institution was the family, conceived so broadly as to be almost a clan. Each family preserved in written and oral records a history of its past activities and greatness which, although often romanticized, acted as a unifying force. Probably deriving from the days of

[3] Gene Brucker, *Renaissance Florence* (New York: Wiley, 1969), p. 256.

the family towers, when in the twelfth and thirteenth centuries each family possessed a fortress-home within the city itself, each of the main patrician families lived within a tightly restricted area of the city, often on one street or square. An individual's social status and usually also his ability to win political office depended upon the status of his family; and this status was determined by wealth, proven antiquity, possession of high city office in the past, and ties, especially marriage ties, with other important families. In this way, the patrician family set out to be the safeguard of the city's continuity and at the same time the barrier against the intrusion of new men whose wealth lacked the respectability of age. But the very features that established the status of a family were those that fluctuated most frequently in Florence. Family wealth continually varied according to the vicissitudes of the international markets, the impact of war, and the recurring scourge of plaque. Political fortune was even more capricious, as a result both of external intervention or internal revolution. Thus a patriciate that prided itself upon preserving the continuity of communal tradition was in fact continually forced to accept innovation; and, as we shall see, the most crucial characteristic of the Florentine Renaissance was the ability to innovate while reviving past tradition, both classical and Florentine.

The Patriciate as Patron

Until about 1420, the patriciate's patronage of artists and intellectuals was to a large extent exercised through their guilds and through the city government controlled by the guilds. After 1420, however, when the effects of the continentwide recession began to be felt, the corporate spirit became far less strong among the Florentine patriciate. The guilds declined in importance, as did political associations like the Parte Guelfa, which had led the battle against the Ghibellines in the thirteenth century. Families and increasingly, individuals, took over the stimulus and support of Florentine cultural life. One historian has gone so far as to suggest that the hard economic conditions of the fifteenth century led the patriciate to regard "the increased value of humanistic culture as an economic investment," because culture admitted them into the elite group in society.[4] Because of this patronage, the Renaissance began in Florence rather than in any other Italian city around the turn of the fifteenth century.

First, the Florentine patriciate gave generous recognition, both in financial reward and social prestige, to the work of the humanists and artists. Many of the leading scholars and lawyers were members of patrician families. Others, who grew wealthy through their own achievements, without family ties to the patriciate, were able to reinvest their money in land and business. Artists succeeded in gaining acceptance of their claim to be mas-

---

[4] Robert S. Lopez, "Hard Times and Investment in Culture," in Wallace K. Ferguson et al., *The Renaissance* (New York: Harper and Row, 1962), p. 48.

ters of the liberal arts, intellectual workers, that is, instead of master crafts-men like those, for example, who built the medieval cathedrals; and the competition for their services, both from inside Florence and from outside patrons, naturally increased their cost. The city recognized the political importance of the scholars by appointing four great humanists in succession as city chancellors, the most highly paid executive position in the city administration. Teaching posts, artistic jobs, tax exemptions, and even state funerals were showered upon them. And the patronage was carried out

Lady with a Nose-Gay, by Andrea del Verrocchio (1435–1488)
Verrocchio was a sculptor, painter, silversmith, and engineer. Among the many artists trained in his workshop was Leonardo da Vinci. Museo Nationale, Florence. Alinari photo

through the 1420s by wealthy guild members or city administrators, and after the 1420s mainly by individual or family patrons.

Secondly, the patrons used their patronage of art and letters to assure their own continuing fame with posterity. The most obvious examples were the funeral chapels, mausoleums, and tombs, which rank among the greatest works of Florentine art. Brunelleschi designed the chapel for the Pazzi; Michelangelo, the mausoleum for the Medici. In the Church of Santa Maria Novella, where many prominent families were buried, the donors were frequently portrayed by the artists as witnessing the crucifixion or taking part in scenes from the life of John the Baptist or other saints. Ghirlandaio in fact portrayed not only the merchant Tornabuoni and his wife but all their friends and relatives as well. Appreciative biography also was suitably rewarded, as when the prominent bookseller Vespasiano turned his hand to writing short lives of over a hundred "illustrious men" of his own time, "that their fame may not perish." Vespasiano's life of Cosimo de' Medici, though informative on Cosimo's attitudes, is most valuable for illustrating the traits for which a Medici would wish to be remembered:

He was well versed in Latin Letters, both sacred and secular, of capable judgment in all matters and able to argue thereupon. . . . He had a great liking for men of letters and sought their society. . . . He understood his own disposition which made him discontented with low estate, and made him seek to rise out of the crowd of men of small account. . . . Now Cosimo, having applied himself to the temporal affairs of the state, the conduct of which was bound to leave him with certain matters on his conscience—as is the case with all those who are fain to govern state and take the leading place—awoke to a sense of his condition, and was anxious that God might pardon him, and secure to him the possession of his earthly goods. Therefore he felt he must needs turn to pious ways, otherwise his riches would be lost to him. . . . I once heard Cosimo say that the great mistake of his life was that he did not begin to spend his wealth ten years earlier because, knowing well the disposition of his fellow-citizens, he was sure that, in the lapse of fifty years, no memory would remain of his personality or of his house, save the few fabrics he might have built.[5]

The Florentine patron, however, subsidized the new culture and believed it would assure him immortality because his own values and perceptions were attuned to those of the new culture. From his life as a merchant and banker, he had come to accept and to manipulate the material world, especially of course as a source of the wealth he sought for himself and admired in others. He had learned to admire human individuality in both appearance and character, a necessary accomplishment in an administrator who must appoint representatives to work for him at the ends of the

---

[5] Vespasiano, *Renaissance Princes, Popes and Prelates* (New York: Harper Torchbook, 1963), pp. 213–14, 218–19, 222–23.

continent or make loans whose repudiation would ruin him. He had learned to love quality, in the appearance of newly dyed cloth, in the language of a state proclamation, in the foliage of a landscape; and in the give and take of Florentine society, where merchants, politicians, and intellectuals circulated freely in the greater guilds, he had come to appreciate the intellectual sharpening encouraged by the serious interplay of fine minds. Florence, like Athens, effervesced with the sparkle of the exchange of ideas in large numbers of structured groups, organized around a philosopher like Salutati or Ficino, or a merchant like Palla Strozzi. The Florentine patriciate too, faced with the problems of governing a state, had decided that history had lessons for the present, and that in particular the Roman republic provided the most useful parallels for the Florentine republic. In short, the Florentine patrons were ready for, and able to support, an art and literature that would beautify their daily lives, glorify their city, preserve their memory for posterity, stimulate their intellects, and even teach practical lessons in government.

Florentine Culture in the Late Middle Ages

In order to appreciate the innovative genius of the Florentine Renaissance that began at the beginning of the fifteenth century, we must first glance back at the city as it was in the late Middle Ages.

The Buildings of Medieval Florence

Until about 1400, Florence remained essentially medieval in appearance. Architecturally, its two predominant characteristics were its fortifications, including both the city walls and the private and public palaces, and the Italian-Gothic style of its churches. The third city wall, built in 1285 mainly to enclose within its protection the newer middle-class and manufacturing districts that had grown up as a result of the wool trade, ran for five miles, forty feet high, six feet thick, with seventy-three towers each one hundred feet high. Behind this massive wall the city's brown, crenelated palaces and homes were tightly squeezed, reaching skyward for space and protection in a panorama of balconied towers and belfries. Two self-contained fortresses stood out from the rest, both strikingly resembling the country castles of the feudal nobility. In 1250, following their first victory over the Ghibelline nobility, the patriciate began the construction of a Palazzo del Podestà, now the Bargello museum, as a residence for the chief magistrate of the newly reformed city government; and in 1299, after the final middle-class victory was signaled by the issuing of the Ordinances of Justice, the great guilds built the Palazzo della Signoria to house the priors and the city's councils. It is hard to imagine a greater contrast with the open spacious facade of the

Doge's Palace in Venice, looking outward to the sea that was its only defense. The two centers of municipal power of medieval Florence were built for defense by a government fearful of a revived feudal nobility, of factions within itself, of its own proletariat, and of attacks from without by local enemies like Siena or marauding foreigners like the king of France. As we shall see, even at the height of the Medici popularity, the palaces built in Renaissance style for the merchant oligarchy never lost this appearance of a defensive bastion turned in on itself against the dangers of the streets.

The city's great churches were even more closely connected to the guild republic. The cathedral, begun in 1294, was also to be a symbol of the pride of the new Signoria: "The Florentine Republic, soaring ever above the conception of the most competent judges, desires that an edifice should be constructed so magnificent in its height and in its beauty that it shall surpass anything of the kind produced in the time of their greatest power by the Greeks and Romans." The cathedral was begun by the city, using poll taxes and death duties as well as voluntary contributions, but responsibility for its construction passed for a while to the silk guild and then to the Lana; its building proceeded most quickly during the Albizzi oligarchy. By the end of the fourteenth century, it was complete except for the vast cupola, which was proving to be not only financially but architecturally beyond the city's capacity. At the same period of patrician prosperity, two orders of friars were able to raise vast funds for rebuilding their churches, Santa Maria Novella in the west of the town for the Dominicans, and Santa Croce in the east for the Franciscans, to make them more suitable for the eloquent preaching for which the friars were admired. Both were well patronized by individual wealthy families, the bankers, like the Spini and the Peruzzi, for example, taking a special interest in Santa Croce. These great churches, with their broad spacious naves, their calm open spaces, their strong emphasis on the horizontal line, and their bare whitewashed walls, were something new in Gothic style. They totally lacked the sheer upward drive and the mysterious complexities of the great Gothic cathedrals of France. Already they were rational and intellectually appealing, and thus point toward the Renaissance style; but they and the government buildings and the great family palaces were still undisputably Gothic. For all its distinctive features, the architecture created before 1400 for the great capitalist families of Florence was still medieval.

Dante and Petrarch

Precisely the same character of individuality within the medieval concept of the style and purpose of culture, was possessed by the great artists and writers of Florence before the fifteenth century. Dante Alighieri (1265–1321) created in his *Divine Comedy* a masterpiece that has been compared to the writings of Aquinas as a summation of all medieval knowledge. It is an allegory describing Dante's journey through hell, purgatory, and paradise, during which he meets the souls of hundreds of the great, the infamous, and the blessed, from Judas Iscariot to Saint Peter; and from the great writers of antiquity, to the medieval saints, and finally to a number of Florentine citizens he knew personally. In his Ptolemaic description of the spheres of the universe, his scholastic classification of virtues and vices, and his vision of punishment and salvation, Dante was thoroughly medieval. What marked his individuality and influenced future writers was his superb mastery of the Tuscan dialect of Italian, which he chose to use instead of Latin; his presentation of separate human beings with all their peculiarities and distinctive flaws or merits; and his delicate if somewhat idealized passion for Beatrice, whom he presents leading him through paradise. And like so many writers in imperial Rome, he looked back to a purer Florence, in the days before the great migration of workers into the clothmaking suburbs had overwhelmed the original citizens.

The great poet Petrarch (1304–1374) showed a similar love of classical culture, both in the buildings of imperial Rome and the writings of Greek and Latin authors. Petrarch was a professional writer, who was well paid for his work; and he was a favorite guest in most of the courts of Italy and especially in the papal court at Avignon. He was most admired, and he most admired himself, for his Latin writings, which included a series of *Letters to the Ancient Dead,* such as Homer, Livy, and Cicero. But his lasting influence, like Dante's, was due to his poems in Italian, especially the beautiful sonnets to Laura; his love of landscape; and his sense of individual psychology, especially his own. He was worshipped during his lifetime, crowned poet laureate in both Rome and Paris, and regarded as the arbiter of both classical scholarship and vernacular literature. Recent scholars have even called him the first modern man. But Petrarch's writings were like the Gothic churches of fourteenth-century Florence; they were beginning to part company with the Middle Ages, but had not yet done so. Petrarch, for example, reproaches Cicero for engaging in Rome's civic troubles, and gives him a piece of Christian advice: "Oh, how much more suitable would it have been if thou, philosopher as thou wast, hadst grown old in rural surroundings, and there hadst meditated upon eternal life and not upon this trifling existence below!" He courted the Laura of his sonnets for twenty-one years, in the manner of medieval chivalry. And after climbing the Mont Ventoux in southern France to see the view, an enterprise whose difficulty he grossly exaggerated, he pulled out a copy of Augustine's *Confessions,* which chastened him by falling open at the lines: "And men go to admire the high mountains, the vast floods of the sea, the huge streams of the rivers, the circumference of the ocean, and the revolutions of the stars—and desert themselves."

Giotto

It is hard, however, for Florence to take much credit for Dante and Petrarch. Dante had enrolled as a "Florentine poet" in the guild of doctors and

apothecaries, and had served as a prior in 1300; but as a result of getting involved in the internecine fighting of the Guelf party, he was exiled in 1302
at the age of thirty-seven, and spent the rest of his life in exile. Petrarch was
the son of a Florentine exile, and he too spent most of his life outside Florence. With the painter-architect Giotto (1266–1336), Florence was more
generous. Giotto's great contribution to Italian painting was summarized by
the Renaissance art historian Vasari, who wrote that Giotto "became so
good an imitator of Nature that he totally banished the rude Greek [Byzan-
tine] manner, restoring art to the better path adhered to in modern times,
and introducing the custom of accurately drawing living persons from life."
For the first time in the history of painting, the critic Bernard Berenson later
claimed, Giotto left behind the flat, decorative, but unrealistic style derived
from Constantinople, whose goal had been the presentation of the spiritual
world, and introduced the tactile sense, painting figures that we sense in
our fingers and palms.

In the witty, self-confident, worldly Giotto, Florence found an artist it
could idolize. His commissions came from the wealthiest citizens, especially
the Bardi and the Peruzzi, for whose private chapels in Santa Croce he
painted the great frescoes of the lives of John the Baptist and Saint Francis.
And near the end of his life, the city named him master mason of the cathedral, because "in the whole world no one better could be found in this and
many other things." He rewarded them with the lovely campanile that
stands beside the cathedral, a soaring Gothic tower sparkling with red,
white, black, and green marble.

Thus, Florence was still a thoroughly medieval city at the end of the
fourteenth century in spite of the great economic changes it had undergone;
and its skyline as seen from the neighboring hilltown of Fiesole would have
confirmed this fact, revealing the turreted walls, the crenelated towers of
the palaces of the Signoria and the Podestà, the tall family homes built like
fortresses, Giotto's gleaming campanile. Around the turn of the next century, however, Florence enjoyed nothing less than an artistic and cultural
revolution.

The Early Florentine Renaissance, 1400–1430

In the last quarter of the fourteenth century, Florence produced remarkably
little that was innovative in art or literature. Petrarch died in 1374, Boccaccio the following year. Dante and Giotto had been dead long since.
Then, all at once, masters of a new style appeared simultaneously in almost
every form of creativity, launching Florence on a century of greatness that
can only be compared to Athens in the fifth century B. C. In 1413, Donatello
finished his statue of Saint Mark for the linenmakers' guild, restoring to figure sculpture its independence from architecture, and he followed up with

an even greater achievement three years later, his superb statue of Saint George for the armorers' guild. With these works, Donatello began a new tradition in marble sculpture that culminated in the work of Michelangelo. In 1421, Brunelleschi built the Foundling Hospital, a building that transmuted Roman architectural forms into the totally new Renaissance style. In 1426, Masaccio began the frescoes of Saint Peter in the Brancacci Chapel, in which the perspective, color, and anatomical and psychological realism indicated the appearance in full maturity of the "grand style" of the Renaissance. And in the aftermath of the successful repulse in 1402 of the aggression of the Milanese duke Giangaleazzo Visconti, the leading scholar-statesmen of Florence, such as Chancellor Leonardo Bruni, began proclaiming a new set of cultural and political values, which we call "civic humanism," that were fundamental to both the writings of the humanists and the political activity of the city's leaders. In writings about the Roman republic and especially about Cicero, they drew the conclusion that the Florentine republic had inherited the task of independence and freedom in Italy, especially through the participation in its civic life of both economic and intellectual leaders. By the 1420s, every educated man in Florence was aware that a revolution was under way among artists and intellectuals; and it is to the credit of the guilds and individual merchants that they opened their purses to the innovators.

Brunelleschi's Break with Medieval Architecture

In no sphere was the break with the Middle Ages more clear, or more deliberate, than in architecture. Brunelleschi had trained as a goldsmith and a sculptor, and in 1401 had been bitterly disappointed at coming in second in the competition to sculpt the bronze door of the Baptistery. Ghiberti won, and spent the rest of his life producing the two great doors that still prove the excellent judgment of the jury of the Lana guild. Brunelleschi went off to Rome with the young Donatello and began to study Roman ruins, measuring the columns, arches, and vaults to work out the mathematical principles that guided the Roman architects. On his return to Florence, he won the competition organized by the Lana for an architect sufficiently skilled to complete the dome of the cathedral, which, spanning 150 feet, was the largest undertaking of its kind since the construction of Santa Sophia in Constantinople. Brunelleschi constructed a steep, octagonal cupola, 308 feet high, using an inner and outer shell whose thrust upon the supporting drum was contained by inner chains. He thereby gave the Florentine skyline its dominating feature; but his dome was still distinctively Gothic in appearance and technique. The white ribs of the dome form a curving Gothic arch, for example, and the technique of the inner and outer shell was used in Gothic cathedrals and not in Roman vaulting.

At the very same time, however, Brunelleschi designed the Foundlings' Hospital for the silkweavers' guild, for their charity home for abandoned

Joshua at the Taking of Jericho, from the Baptistery Doors, by Lorenzo Ghiberti (1378–1455)
When Michelangelo saw these doors, he declared that they were worthy to be the Gates of Paradise.
Philip Gendreau

children. For the facade, he used Roman motifs, nine round arches set on delicate Corinthian columns, with a firm architrave running the whole length of the building, and nine pedimented windows centered above the arches. This building was the first in Renaissance style. It combined an understanding of the Roman style with a fascination for the mathematical basis of proportion and the treatment of space. But with the Foundlings' Hospital Brunelleschi had also made an important contribution to urban planning, the theory and practice of which was to take an enormous leap forward in fifteenth-century Florence. The medieval city, and thus most of Florence, had grown up in unplanned confusion. In a very pragmatic way, the Florentine government had attempted to remedy this in the fourteenth century, using the destruction of the homes of exiled families, for example, to create the great but irregular open space in front of the Palazzo della Signoria, and demolishing other buildings so that the cathedral would "be encircled by beautiful and spacious streets." The Foundlings' Hospital formed one side of one of the great Renaissance squares (literally square, this time) harmonizing with the old church opposite and later balanced with two sixteenth-century buildings. This square represented the perfect combination that the Florentine architect Alberti theorized should be at the base of all urban construction: *commoditas,* or functionalism, and *voluptas,* or delight for the senses. The Florentines balanced the two; the baroque architects two centuries later sacrificed commoditas to voluptas.

Early Renaissance Painting and Sculpture

So great was the impact on painting of the brief career of Masaccio, who was killed in 1428 at the age of twenty-seven, that every artist in Florence studied his paintings for the next century. Masaccio, they said, had taken over from where Giotto had stopped. The brilliant young man had mastered Giotto's art of painting monumental figures, outstanding in their impression because they were unencumbered by unnecessary details of background, and he had the same ability to make his figures appear as living human beings. But he had gone further, so that he is generally recognized to be the first great Renaissance painter. Masaccio's fresco *The Expulsion from the Garden of Eden* perfectly illustrates his different technique. He had mastered the presentation of figures in space, using what is called atmospheric perspective; he had used changes of tone in the vague, misty atmosphere separating the angel from Adam and Eve to suggest their separation in space. He had mastered the technique of creating the impression on the observer of glimpsing a scene from a specific distance, so that a visual impression was produced rather than a minutely detailed, almost microscopic, portrayal such as Van Eyck wished to achieve. Above all, however, Masaccio was interested in the individual and his emotions; the panic and the sense of despair of Adam and Eve have never been more graphically depicted. In *The Expulsion,* and indeed in most of his paintings, Masaccio sought to show the impact on individuals of moral reality in a particular historical setting; and so even though his subjects were taken from the Bible, he was not so much interested in the question of divine salvation as of human responsibility on earth.

Masaccio was undoubtedly influenced by the work of Donatello (1386–1466), the greatest Italian sculptor before Michelangelo. Donatello had determined to represent in sculpture the appearance of the human anatomy in all its forms: the movement of children at play, the gentle modesty of the virgin, the restrained strength and physical hardening of the mercenary captain, even the first ravages of death on the corpse. To do this, he learned nothing from medieval statues, much from ancient Roman work, and most from personal observation. To the mastery of anatomical presentation, he added psychological insight into the individuals he portrayed, a skill that can be seen in his bust of Niccolò da Uzzano. One of the most curious buildings in Florence was the church of Orsanmichele, built as a grain market with storage rooms upstairs for the stockpiles kept by the city for famine or war, and as a chapel, and simultaneously as a showcase for statues of the patron saints of the city's guilds. Here the patronage of the newest in sculpture by the guilds was most evident. The Calimala had Ghiberti sculpt John the Baptist, while Donatello created his Saint Mark for the linen dealers and Saint George for the armorers. The Saint George excels any surviving Roman statue and can be favorably compared with any Greek. It represents a young man in his twenties, tall, slender, intelligent,

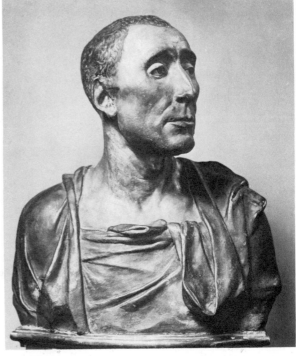

**Niccolò da Uzzano, by
Donatello (c. 1386–1466)**
*The self-confident Floren-
tine business leader is
presented in the robe of an
ancient Roman patri-
cian.*   Museo Nazionale,
Florence. Alinari photo

**The Expulsion of Adam
and Eve from the Garden
of Eden, by Masaccio
(1401–1428)**
*This fresco forms part of
the great series Masaccio
painted for the Brancacci
chapel in Florence when he
was twenty-four years
old.*   Chiesa del Carmine,
Florence. Alinari photo

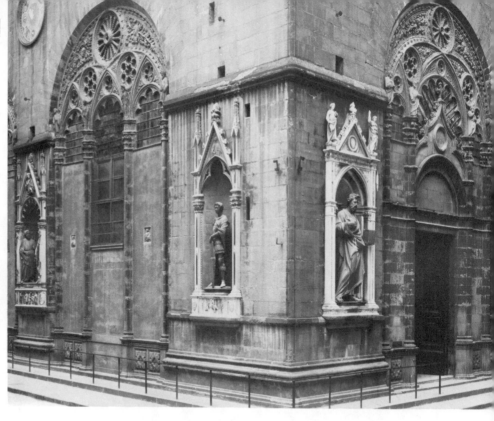

St. George, by Donatello
The armorers' guild commissioned Donatello to portray St. George for their niche on the outside of the Orsanmichele chapel. The original statue is in the Bargello Museum. Alinari photo

and quietly strong. The body has the repose and balance of perfect physical control, calm but ready for instant action. Donatello's Saint George is not a feudal knight; he is a classical hero reborn.

The Florentine Humanists

The influence of classical learning and admiration for it were greatest among Florence's scholars and writers who studied history, moral and political philosophy, poetry, rhetoric, and grammar and are known collectively as humanists. The influence of Latin had been strong throughout the Middle Ages. Legal study derived largely from Justinian's code; all students in the early years at the university read deeply in Horace, Livy, and Cicero. Greek culture, too, played an important role, as Aristotle did in the work of Aquinas. But in the fourteenth and fifteenth centuries, the attempt to appreciate and use the classical legacy took new form. First, it involved technical progress in the method of study. Although Latin was well known, the Greek language had to be learned, largely without the help of dictionaries, grammar books, and graduated texts; and an important start was given by professors from Constantinople who came to teach in either the schools or the University of Florence, or privately. In the half-century before the fall of Constantinople to the Turks, many of that city's leading scholars came to Italy as refugees, bringing with them manuscripts of classical books largely unknown in western Europe. The search for manuscripts was conducted throughout Europe by scholars in detective fashion, as they burrowed through the confused collections of old and remote monasteries or persuaded their patrons to invest in the purchase of rare manuscripts. The texts, both the well-known and the new, were then exposed to searching analysis, especially on linguistic grounds, to establish authentic texts free of forgery, later additions, and incorrect copying. This examination invariably demanded far more than linguistic diligence; it required a deep insight into the nature and events of classical civilization. Only an understanding of the political character of first-century Rome, for example, made it possible for the humanists to grasp that Cicero actually believed that the intellectual ought to fling himself wholeheartedly into politics. Petrarch could not conceive that any philosopher in his right mind would waste his time in this way, and so he was unable to penetrate to the essence of Cicero's message. Much of the educational curriculum of Florence was remodeled under the influence of the humanists to emphasize classical studies, history, philosophy, rhetoric, and grammar; and as tutors to the wealthier families, the humanists inculcated in the future leaders of the city a lifelong and in many cases deeply felt absorption with the classics. About 1420, one merchant advised his sons to study the Bible, but also: "Every day for at least an hour, read Virgil, Boethius, Seneca and other authors. . . . Begin your study with Virgil. . . . Then spend some time with Boethius, with Dante and the other poets, with Tully [Cicero] who will teach you to speak perfectly, with Aristotle who will instruct you in philosophy." [6]

Scholars have been disputing for more than a century the importance of these humanists. Burckhardt believed that they had discovered in their study of the Greek and Latin classics the key to a new individualism completely in contrast with the group mentality characteristic of the Middle Ages, an individualism that expressed itself in love of nature, interest in the personality and the physical nature of the human being, and paganism and amorality. Toward the end of the nineteenth century, several important works argued that medieval scholars had already found in their study of the classics everything distinctive that Burckhardt saw in the Renaissance humanists, that these humanists were deeply influenced by medieval religious ideas, and that in fact they were not of much significance as innovators. The contemporary view is something of a compromise, although expressed with variety and subtlety. One significant group emphasizes that humanism is best seen as an educational movement concentrating on the curriculum in the Italian universities called *studia humanitatis*, comprising history, literature, and language rather than the philosophy and theology central to medieval scholasticism. This is a useful but excessively narrow view. For Florence itself, the most valuable analysis was offered by Hans Baron, who showed that Florentine humanism in the last half of the fourteenth century was still medieval in character, favoring a contemplative life isolated from

[6] Cited in Gene Brucker, *Renaissance Florence* (New York: Wiley, 1969), p. 240.

politics, leaving government to despots, and seeking an ideal in the Roman Empire. After the emotional crisis around 1400, when Florence feared it would fall to the armies of the Milanese Giangaleazzo Visconti, the humanists became aware, according to Baron, of the values of freedom and individualism, of political activity, and, as a corollary, of the ideals of the Roman republic. Their thinking turned to the character of Florence itself, which they explored in histories of the city and in studies of its political character. In this way, they were in fact the precursors of modern ways of thought in political theory and history, and, by their acceptance of vernacular literature, in writing as well.

Contribution of the Medici

After the brilliant revolution in art and letters of the 1420s, Florence seemed to mark time for a decade. Masaccio's meteoric career had ended in a street brawl. Ghiberti continued to labor on at the baptistery doors, Brunelleschi to apply the style he had perfected before 1420 to new churches and chapels. But in general there were few commissions for architects and sculptors. The wool guilds were facing increased competition in their export markets, and were spending less freely. Commissions for painting were going to those who practiced the colorful but anachronistic style called international Gothic; and many who had mastered the new techniques of perspective and anatomical accuracy reverted to the overly pretty approach espoused by

The Annunciation, by Fra Angelico
This delicate fresco stands at the head of the stairway leading to the monks' cells in the Dominican convent of San Marco in Florence.   Italian Government Travel Office photo

painters like Gentile da Fabriano, Fra Angelico, and Benozzo Gozzoli. But the pause in the city's intellectual drive was due above all to political and military troubles. The oligarchy headed by the Albizzi family had created great internal enmity by imposing crushing taxation to pay for ill-judged wars, especially with Milan. Florence, wrote one chronicler, "abounded with men filled with envy and pride, and with other abominable vices." "In this bad world of ours," wrote another, "nine hundred out of every thousand are living like sheep, with their eyes bent on the ground and their minds full of folly and evil thoughts."

The Basis of the Medici's Power

The champion for the discontented was Cosimo de' Medici, whose banking fortune gave him the means to challenge the Albizzi; and in 1434, after the Albizzi had unsuccessfully attempted to end his popularity by exile, he was called back by popular vote and a government of his supporters rushed into power. For the next sixty years, the Medici were the unofficial but acknowledged rulers of Florence. "You are the arbiter of peace, of war, of the laws," the pope told Cosimo. "Of kingship you have everything but the name." The city's democracy had entered a totally new phase. Very little was changed in the formal structure of government; and Cosimo himself held elected office only once—for six months as gonfaloniere—during the thirty years of his supremacy. What few changes there were gave a greater impression of democracy. But from behind the scenes Cosimo manipulated the whole electoral system. The Signoria and the gonfalonieri were picked by hand by reliable "assemblers," from purses in which only the names of Medici supporters were placed. The opposition to the Medici occasionally tried to reinstate the system of appointing officials by lot, but in each case the Medici soon restored their own reliable system. The oligarchy under the Medici was far more restricted in size than it had been before 1434. Some opponents were exiled; others executed, although infrequently. Incipient opposition was nipped in the bud by application of crushing taxation. A large clientele was maintained by careful dispersal of the benefits of office; the working classes were appeased with public entertainments like colorful tournaments, by munificent gifts to charity, and especially by internal peace and stability. The Medici were therefore so firmly entrenched that power passed without incident on Cosimo's death in 1464 to his son Piero, and, on Piero's death in December 1469, to his son Lorenzo de' Medici. Lorenzo noted in his diary on the day of his father's death:

Although I was very young, being twenty-one years of age, the principal men of the City and of the State came to our house to condole with us, and to persuade me to take charge of the City and the State, as my father and grandfather had done. I consented to do so, but unwillingly, because considering my

The Procession of the Wise Kings, by Benozzo Gozzoli (1420–1497)
This fresco was painted in 1459–1460 in the chapel of the Medici Palace. Lorenzo (just off photo to right) is followed by his father and uncle and other relatives. Alinari photo

youth, the responsibility and danger were great—in order to protect our friends and property, since at Florence life is insecure for the wealthy without control of the government.'' [7]

Under Lorenzo, government became more conservative. A restricted group of patrician families sought to hold onto power, and succeeded in putting down internal opposition that ranged from occasional negative votes in the councils to the Pazzi uprising of 1478 in which Lorenzo's brother was assassinated. These families were satisfied to maintain their economic standing rather than to seek rapid expansion. Some new fortunes

[7] Cited in Ernest Barker, ed., *Golden Ages of the Great Cities* (London: Thames and Hudson, 1952), pp. 124–25.

were made. Cultivation of the silkworm in southern Italy had made the country virtually self-sufficient in raw silk, with Florence the main manufacturer. Florentine merchants were challenging the Venetians in the spice trade of the eastern Mediterranean. Banking was still the basis for new fortunes, especially as the decline of the Medici bank, due to the lack of business acumen in Lorenzo and his representatives in the foreign branches, was leaving opportunities open for aggressive new companies. But the general pattern was of caution and avoidance of risk, with both economic and political stability as the highest goal. Francesco Guicciardini presented a fulsome description of the age's ideal if not of its reality just before Lorenzo's death brought the purportedly idyllic period to an end:

The city enjoyed perfect peace, the citizens were united and in harmony, and the government so powerful that no one dared oppose it. The people every day delighted in shows, revelries and other novelties; they were well fed, as the city was plentifully supplied with victuals, and all its activities flourished. Men of intellect and ability were contented, for all letters, all arts, all talents were welcomed and recognized. While the city within was universally enjoying the most perfect peace and quiet, without her glory and reputation were supreme because she had a government and a leader of the highest authority. . . .[8]

The Palaces of the Patriciate

The establishment of this restricted, conservative plutocracy through which the Medici governed was complete by the beginning of the 1440s; and the Florentine Renaissance again leaped to creative heights. The direction of its leap, however, was clearly dictated by the Medici and the small number of extremely wealthy families in their coterie. In no place is this more obvious than in architecture. For the next half-century, the principal buildings erected in Florence were private palaces of the merchant princes—massive, rusticated facades rising foursquare from the narrow streets, Renaissance fortresses on the outside, Renaissance pleasure gardens within. Brunelleschi had taught Florence to adopt Roman motifs, like the triumphal arch, the column, the orders of capitals, and the cornice; and this style had been ideal for churches and hospitals, especially for those many facades designed as triumphal arches. But how was one to adapt this style to the building of houses? Brunelleschi's design for a palace for Cosimo was so grandiose that he rejected it. The task instead was given to Michelozzo (c. 1396–1472), whose answer to the problem of building a house front in Renaissance style was to use dressed stone in three parallel bands. The ground floor had huge, rough blocks with three massive, round-arched doorways; the second floor had smoother, rectangular blocks, with ten round-arched windows di-

---

[8] Francesco Guicciardini, *History of Italy and History of Florence,* trans. Cecil Grayson (New York: Twayne, 1964), p. 1.

vided by delicate columns; and the third floor was built of completely smooth stone, topped by a heavy Roman cornice. The interior courtyard was a complete contrast, a light, colonnaded cloister, onto which all the main rooms of the palace faced. Thus, Michelozzo established the pattern that was followed for the next century by the merchants of Florence and the cardinals of Rome. At the time when the city's humanists were abandoning their civic preoccupations and turning inward with such philosophies as Neoplatonism, the patriciate was turning its back on the city and creating, behind impregnable walls, a center of princely elegance, and these palaces were built with total disregard for the convenience of their less influential neighbors. One diarist, whose shop overlooked the building site of the great Strozzi palace, complained:

Palazzo Strozzi, Florence
Begun in 1484 by one of the richest merchant families, the palace is a fine example of the Florentine use of rusticated stone blocks and heavy cornices to produce a massive but balanced facade.
Italian Government Travel Office photo

20th August. (1489). They finished filling in the foundations on this side, in the Piazza de' Tornaquinti. And all this time they were demolishing the houses, a great number of overseers and workmen being employed, so that all the streets round were filled with heaps of stone and rubbish and with mules and donkeys who were carrying away the rubbish and bringing gravel; making it difficult for anyone to pass along. We shopkeepers were continually annoyed by the dust and the crowds of people who collected to look on, and those who could not pass by with their beasts of burden. . . .

15th May (1491). That Filippo who was building the above-mentioned palace died; and he did not see it carried up even as far as the lanterns. . . . One sees how vain are the hopes of transitory things! It appears as if we were master of them, but in reality it is the other way about; they are master of us. This palace will last almost eternally: has not this palace mastered him then? [9]

Renaissance City Planning

To many architects this way of building, hacking out space from medieval streets to create palaces whose grandeur could only be properly appreciated if seen at the end of a properly planned vista, was very frustrating. They began to design ideal streets, and later ideal cities; they then incorporated these designs in theatrical scenery, or used them as illustrations in books that popularized their ideas. Very rapidly, they diffused the conception of the planned, symmetrical city that was to dominate urban design for the next three centuries. The Florentine architect Filarete (c. 1400–c. 1465), designed a complete model city, called Sforzinda, for the Milanese ruler Francesco Sforza; and his plan, with its straight streets, planned vistas, mathematically regulated piazzas, and interrelated functions of the principal buildings laid down the principles that were to transform such great cities as Rome and Paris and to inspire the beautiful "new" cities of the seventeenth and eighteenth centuries, like Nancy, Karlsruhe, Bath, and above all Washington, D.C. and St. Petersburg. According to Filarete,

After the completion of the citadel, the prince had the arrangement of the inner city explained.

At the center, laid out east and west, is the principal square or piazza, 150 braccia wide and 300 braccia long. Each small square of the plan equals one square stadio. At the eastern end of the piazza is the principal church. Opposite, on the west, is the princely palace. On the north the square of the merchants, 99¾ × 187½ braccia (¼ × ½ stadio) joins the Piazza. On the south is the great market, 125 × 250 braccia (⅓ × ⅔ stadio), where the food will be sold. At the west of this I will erect the palace of the captain of police. In this way he will be separated from the royal palace only by a street. South are

⁹ Luca Landucci, *A Florentine Diary*, trans. Alice De Rosen Jervis (London: Dent, 1927), pp. 48, 51–52.

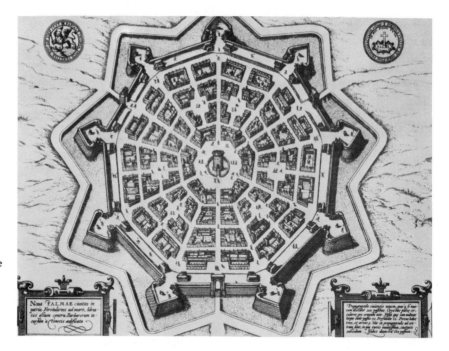

Palma Nova, Near Venice
The nonagonal city was constructed by the city-planner Scamazzi in 1593, to defend Venice from attack by land.

the baths and brothels, west the inns and taverns; . . . In order to limit noisy waggon traffic and to provide greater convenience for the inhabitants, we will surround the Piazza and other markets with navigable canals and make every other principal street a porticoed water-canal.[10]

Such utopian canal cities were to be built not in Italy but in Amsterdam, Copenhagen, and Gothenburg. Sforzinda never progressed beyond the pages of Filarete's treatise on architecture.

These ideal cities, like the exterior facades of the palaces and the interior plans of the churches, were complete in themselves. Nothing could be added or subtracted without destroying the symmetry of the plan. This was a basic, new contribution by Renaissance planners to the treatment of space in both individual buildings and the city that marked a complete break with the Middle Ages. The Gothic cathedral or the medieval city could be continually remodeled and added to; and as they grew, they absorbed the additions harmoniously. The Renaissance creations were intended to remain unchanged.

Neoplatonism and Ficino

The great new palaces became the center of the artistic and intellectual life of Medician Florence. Partly it was a question of patronage. The palaces in

[10] Elizabeth G. Holt, *A Documentary History of Art* (New York: Doubleday, 1957), I, 244–46.

town and the country houses needed frescoes, oil paintings, and sculptures. In a more direct way, the palaces dominated and directed the artists and intellectuals. In the Medici garden of San Marco, Lorenzo began a school of sculpture amid his collection of ancient statues; and it was there, according to one probably apocryphal story, that Lorenzo recognized the genius of the young Michelangelo, who was brought to live in the palace until his patron's death two years later. The greatest influence, however, was that exercised by the so-called academy. Apparently Cosimo was so deeply impressed by the Greek scholars who attended the Council of Florence that he decided to make the "new philosophy" available to Italians by funding a program of translations and study. To take charge of the program he picked a talented young man called Marsilio Ficino, brought him to live in the palace, and in 1462 when his studies were complete, set him up in a villa just outside town with an income and a collection of Greek manuscripts. Ficino was charming, intelligent, and hard-working; and as Cosimo had intended, the villa, or academy as it came to be called, provided a center where the patriciate met with Florence's finest humanists and artists for discussion of the innumerable themes that Plato and his followers had written about. Thus, Ficino's views of Plato—expounded for thirty years to a group that included merchant princes like the Medici and the Rucellai, painters like Botticelli, architects like Alberti, and humanist-philosophers like Pico della Mirandola—spread across Europe through his letters and the publication of his writings, and became the basic philosophy of the Florentine Renaissance.

Ficino first translated Plato into Latin; and on completing his task in 1472, he turned to the works of the most famous follower of Plato, Plotinus, who lived in Egypt and Rome in the third century A. D. Ficino's own commentaries, whose influence lasted into the nineteenth century, intermingled the original doctrines of Plato and the "Neoplatonism" of Plotinus. The central concepts of this amalgam exerted a direct appeal on the artists and writers who attended the academy, and thus Ficino's philosophy came to be embodied in the painting and literature of Lorenzo's Florence. Ficino adopted Plato's theory of ideas, but assumed that these eternal ideas that constitute the only reality existed in the mind of God. People, he felt, had an inner drive toward God, in whom all goodness and truth existed. Unfortunately, humankind had become separated from God in some distant calamity, but had not lost the urge to return to that original glory, to achieve reunion even in this life with that former state of being in what was called "ecstasy." Two human emotions in particular were regarded as proof of this urge toward God, the desire for beauty and the drive toward love. A person seeking beauty or love was thus on the way to achieving communion with the divine.

Ficino had thus helped change the character of humanism, and had made it more suitable for an age when political activity was increasingly restricted to the Medici allies in the patriciate. Earlier humanists in the fifteenth century as we have seen had called upon Florence's intellectuals to be active in the life of the city; and their cultural interests had been predominantly in the political and moral sciences that were of direct importance to the civic life. Ficino was, in Eugenio Garin's words, "the first great Quattrocento (fifteenth century) Florentine prototype of the court philosopher in all its luxuriant and recherché style." He was used by the Medici not only to bring luster to themselves as the patrons of philosophy but to preach a doctrine that turned intellectuals away from the active life toward contemplation of their own inner life. As a result, humanism moved from the exposition of the virtues of republican activism to reach eventually a depiction of the perfection of the courtier.

Ficino's message was carried into the world of poetry by Angelo Poliziano (1454–1494), a young scholar of Greek and Latin who was chosen by Lorenzo as the tutor of the Medici children and as a lecturer at the University of Florence. He first became known in Florence at the age of sixteen as the translator of Homer into Latin, and he wrote poetry both in elegant Latin and sparklingly fresh Italian. In his great lyric play *Orpheus*, Poliziano gave an image of the singer of songs, the poet, as the educator who leads humanity to the understanding of the ideas that, in the philosophy of Plato, lie at the heart of the universe. He singles out Dante and Petrarch as the geniuses whom Florence has nurtured:

> *Nor would I desist from paying tribute to Dante,*
> *who with fair Beatrice to guide him*
> *sped through the nether and upper realms*
> *to the loftiest peaks of the mountains;*
> *and Petrarch who renews the triumph of love;*
> *those who in ten days create a hundred tales*
> *and those who reveal the origins of an obscure love.*
> *Hence, eternal glory reflects forever upon you,*
> *inexhaustible in genius, unsurpassed in art,*
> *Mother Florence!* [11]

Poliziano's close friend Giovanni Pico della Mirandola (1463–1494) sought to broaden the humanistic inquiry in Florence to encompass all human knowledge. He was wealthy enough to travel to many of the leading universities of Europe to study, and he purchased so many books that his library became one of the finest in Florence. He mastered not only Latin and Greek, but Hebrew and Arabic as well. At the age of twenty-three, he defended in public debate in Rome a list of 900 philosophic theses, some of which the Catholic Church was to find questionable in orthodoxy. His most important contribution to the actual debate, however, was his introductory

---

[11] Cited in Eugenio Garin, *Portraits from the Quattrocento,* trans. Victor A. and Elizabeth Velen (New York: Harper and Row, 1972), p. 183.

speech, known as the *Oration on the Dignity of Man* which was one of the noblest expressions of the Florentine Renaissance. All men, Pico argued, possess in themselves part of the divine idea. Their greatness and uniqueness lies in the fact that they have been given the potential by God of making themselves into anything that they wish. The highest achievement of man in moulding himself, however, is seen in the life of the pure contemplator, "unconscious of his body, withdrawn into the sanctuary of his mind . . . a most majestic spirit dressed in human flesh." Thus, for Pico also, admiration of man's achievements does not lead back to the active but to the contemplative life.

The Cult of the Courtier

These ideas that were current in late-fifteenth-century Florence were brought together as a program of behavior in *The Book of the Courtier* by Baldassare Castiglione (1478–1529), which was written, not for Florence but for the little princely court of Urbino. This book, the finest eulogy to Platonic, or rather to Neoplatonic love, ostensibly portrays a series of conversations among courtiers at Urbino, in which the light-hearted but learned participants discuss what constitutes the attributes of the ideal courtier. The group agrees on a long list of qualities the courtier should possess: noble birth, efficiency in arms and sport, knowledge of the classical and humanistic writings in both Latin and Greek, a flair for poetry and art, fidelity to his prince. But the last word is spoken by Cardinal Bembo, who lifts the courtiers from their down-to-earth concept of love to the highest quality the perfect courtier should seek, the striving of the human soul for beauty:

A kiss may be said to be rather a coupling together of the soul than of the body, because it hath such force in her, that it draweth her unto it, and, as it were separateth her from the body. For this do all chaste lovers covet a kiss, as a coupling of the souls together. And therefore Plato the divine lover saith that in kissing his soul came as far as his lips to depart out of the body. . . . But among these commodities the lover shall find another yet far greater, in case he will take this love for a stair, as it were, to climb up to another far higher than it. The which he shall bring to pass, if he will go and consider with himself, what a strait bond it is to be always in the trouble to behold the beauty of one body alone. And therefore to come out of this so narrow a room, he shall gather in his thought little by little so many ornaments that meddling all beauty together he shall make a universal conceit and bring the multitude of them to the unity of one alone, that is generally spread over all the nature of man. And thus he shall behold no more the particular beauty of one woman, but a universal that decketh out all bodies.[12]

---

[12] Baldassare Castiglione, *The Courtier*, trans. Sir Thomas Hoby (1561) (London: Dent, 1928), pp. 315, 317–18.

**Primavera, by Sandro
Botticelli (1444–1510)**
Alinari photo

Botticelli and Ideal Love

In painting, the same idea was expressed in the *Primavera* of Sandro Botticelli (1444–1510). The picture is an allegory representing the coming of springtime. In the center, the goddess Venus presides over a green forest glen where young girls in diaphanous gowns are dancing unrealistically, and a self-possessed but enigmatic Flora is scattering flowers on all and sundry. The picture is an idealization of a real woman, Simonetta Vespucci, a charming, intelligent young woman who, though married, was idolized by Lorenzo's brother Giuliano and by the whole Medici circle, with the unrequited admiration prescribed by chivalric convention and Neoplatonic philosophy alike. Simonetta died young, of tuberculosis; Giuliano was murdered two years later to the day by the Pazzi conspirators. Botticelli, painting his *Primavera* in the year of Giuliano's death, depicts a spring that is sadly beautiful, a meditation on an ethereal beauty that has already joined the divine. Simonetta is Venus, just as she is the naked goddess arising from the sea in Botticelli's equally lovely picture, *The Birth of Venus.*

Florence After Lorenzo

Lorenzo himself died in 1492, at the age of only forty-four. His early death gave a special poignancy to the most famous poem among the many delightful lyrics he himself wrote:

Quant' è bella giovinezza	How sweet is youth,
Che si fugge tuttavia:	Yet it flies from us.
Chi vuol' esser lieto, sia,	Be happy now, if you wish to be happy.
Di doman non c' è certezza.	One cannot be sure of tomorrow.[13]

Yet it is doubtful if the Magnificent Lorenzo could have prolonged for much longer the Florentine domination of the Renaissance. The city's economy was wavering, and the Medici bank itself was near ruin. Political rivalries and the military weakness of the Italian states were an invitation to the intervention of the powerful military forces of the new monarchs of France and later of Spain. From the 1450s, the reviving papacy in Rome and the wealthier cardinals began tempting away from Florence many of the artists and intellectuals, by more ambitious and better-paying commissions. Forgotten Florence, of the artisan masses and the visionary religious leaders, was to find in the monk Savonarola a leader who would persuade them to reject the books and the paintings of their past century and to remember that their city should be not a new Rome or a new Athens but rather a new Jerusalem. Lorenzo could hardly have stemmed so insistent a tide of change. Perhaps there was an irony in the words of his former enemy, King Ferrante of Naples: "This man has lived long enough for his own immortal fame, but not long enough for Italy."

For two years after Lorenzo's death in 1492, his son Piero struggled to maintain the Medici regime unchanged. In November 1494, however, the French king Charles VIII, with an army of 40,000 men, invaded Tuscany with the ultimate goal of conquering Naples. Piero at first unwisely opposed him, but then tried to appease him with the surrender of Pisa and several important fortress towns. In rage, the Florentine population rose against him, expelled the Medici family and its principal supporters, and restored republican government on a more broadly representative basis. For the four years from 1494 to 1498, however, the principal influence in Florence was the preaching of the Dominican monk Savonarola. Savonarola strongly favored the broadened democratic representation, and he spoke out constantly on behalf of the poorer classes of the city. He sincerely saw himself as the prophet of a great religious revival that would purify the church. Seizing upon old Florentine traditions which saw their city as the favorite instrument of God's destiny, where liberty, justice, and piety were united, Savonarola sought popular support for his transformation of Lorenzo's inward-looking city into the vanguard of Europe's religious renovation. Savonarola had made too many enemies, however, both among the patricians who had supported the Medici and in the Catholic Church itself. Pope Alexander VI, whom he had denounced, excommunicated him in 1498. A new group of priors, dominated by his enemies, had him tortured into confession and burned him at the stake in the center of the Piazza della

---

[13] Author's translation.

David, by Michelangelo
This vast statue by the twenty-six year old sculptor was placed in the central square of Florence in 1505 to remind the restored Republic to defend liberty in the name of the lord.   Galleria dell' Accademia, Florence. Alinari photo

Signoria. In 1512, the Medici were recalled from exile—to establish a regime that made no further concessions to the city's republican inclinations.

The years of the restored republic, from 1494 to 1512, witnessed the last important achievements of the Florentine Renaissance. After the rejection of Savonarola, for a brief time, the city resumed its role as artistic patron and as the school of Italy's greatest geniuses. In 1503, the city government, in its last great commissions, gave Michelangelo the task of sculpting a David for the square in front of the Palazzo della Signoria. And the city consigned to Michelangelo and Leonardo da Vinci the carrying out of two huge frescoes for their new council hall; unfortunately, neither artist completed more than the preliminary draft cartoon. But it was increasingly clear that Florence could no longer compete with Rome. Raphael had left in 1508; Michelangelo in 1512; Leonardo in 1513. The great age of Florence was over.

The High Renaissance in Rome

For the first half of the sixteenth century, Rome, not Florence, dominated the Renaissance; and, transplanted to the city of the popes, the Renaissance changed character. If Florence had been its springtime, Rome became its summer (and Venice, in the second half of the sixteenth century, was its autumn.)

Function of Sixteenth-Century Rome

Rome's principal economic base was the papacy. The Papal States were mismanaged agriculturally, and contained no important trading or manufacturing city. Rome itself was off the main commercial routes, possessed only branch offices of banking or trading companies centered elsewhere, and manufactured nothing. During the residence of the popes in Avignon and the chaos of the Great Schism that followed, the city declined dramatically. When the pope finally returned to reside in Rome, one humanist wrote, he "found Rome in such extreme decay that it hardly seemed a town at all, with shaky and tumbling houses, temples destroyed, empty streets. . . .

Woodcut of Rome, from Sebastian Münster's Cosmographiae (1544)
In the upper right is the original cathedral of St. Peter's, in the center the Pantheon dome.
Bildarchiv d. Ost. Nationalbibliothek, Vienna

Palazzo Farnese, Rome
Michelangelo completed San Gallo's great palace constructed for Cardinal Alessandro Farnese, who later became Pope Paul III. The travertine stone for the façade was taken from the Colosseum.
E. Richter-Rome

The faces of the inhabitants themselves bore the sad marks of want and misery. No trace remained of the beauties of ancient Rome." [14] In less than a century, however, a long line of ambitious, intelligent, and frequently ruthless popes totally transformed the character of Rome, making it once again one of the most beautiful cities in the world. They made the city wealthy by restoring to Rome the administration of the vast papal income from all over the continent and by inventing new methods to increase that income; and they made Rome the artistic capital of Europe again. They deliberately sponsored the High Renaissance, as the guilds and patrician families of Florence had sponsored the Early Renaissance; and they unwittingly, as we shall see, provoked, in reaction to their financial exaction and their secularism, the Protestant Reformation.

The popes did nothing to make Rome a self-supporting economic unit. It existed as a service center, supplying the needs of the papal court and throngs of Christian pilgrims and tourists. Almost all the money needed to finance the lavish building and artistic programs and the luxurious court life of the pope and cardinals had to be found outside Rome; and the amount needed was growing astronomically. As artists passed from the status of master craftsmen to masters of the liberal arts and finally, as in the case of Michelangelo, to semidivine beings, they commanded increasingly high fees. Botticelli received 38 florins for an altarpiece; two generations later, Titian commanded 2,000. The enormous scale of papal projects made them forbiddingly expensive. Michelangelo spent seven months in the

[14] Cited in Barker, *Golden Ages, p. 137*

quarries of Carrara merely to pick the marble for the tomb of Julius II; it took him three years to paint the ceiling of the Sistine Chapel, which is 134 feet long; and Raphael seriously proposed the restoration of what was left of ancient Rome. The great palaces, like Raphael's Cancelleria or San Gallo's Palazzo Farnese, were far larger even than the palaces of the Medici or the Strozzi in Florence. Moreover, the papacy was posing as the military arbiter of Italy. Pope Alexander VI (1492–1503) spent large sums for the armies of his son, Caesar Borgia, who was attempting to create a Borgia family domain in the papal states. Pope Julius II (1503–1513), with his white beard streaming over his armor, led the papal armies himself against the Venetians and the French. The Medici popes, Leo X (1513–1522) and Clement VII (1523–1534), used Church funds to aid their family in Florence's internal and external struggles. To meet these vast expenses, the popes had

Moses, by Michelangelo (1475–1564)
Michelangelo designed a tomb with forty statues for the mausoleum of Pope Julius II, but completed only four, including this colossal figure of Moses— which resembles Julius. Italian Government Travel Office photo

squeezed their traditional revenues: the income from landholding in the Papal States, the fees for "providing" a benefice, the "annates" exacted on other appointees to Church office, "voluntary" gifts, and judicial fees. But the rebuilding of Saint Peter's forced Leo X to sanction a continentwide sale of pardons, or indulgences, which provoked Martin Luther's first challenge to papal authority.

Art of the High Renaissance

The character of the High Renaissance corresponded to the wishes and interests of the popes and cardinals. The achievements of Rome were primarily in the visual arts. Very few important writers emerged from the Vatican library or papal court, in history, politics, philosophy, creative literature, or religion; and the Church actively discouraged speculative work in science. Many of the activities that had most interested fifteenth-century Florence seemed unimportant in Rome, among them the fresh delight in nature, the fascination with self-awareness, the cultivation of ideal love. The predominant characteristic of the Roman Renaissance was its monumentality. Rome was a world capital, not a provincial trading city like Florence. The churchmen sought a magnificent background of churches, palaces, streets, fountains, stairways, paintings, and clothing that would enhance their grandeur. All creative activity adopted a careful formalism. The direct delight in the portrayal of nature was abandoned, to be replaced by conscientious, geometrically planned compositions intended to illustrate large and uplifting themes, such as the truth of Transubstantiation in Raphael's famous fresco known as *Disputa*. This formalism required that everything should be balanced and harmonious. Color should be rich and full, utterly satisfying, rather than a stimulus to the imagination or a disturbance of the emotions. In a *Madonna* by Raphael, one is calmed by the harmony of color and composition. A Botticelli allegory, by contrast, is a stimulus to the imagination in the unreality of its coloring and the swirling action of its figures. Above all, a universalism pervaded the art of the High Renaissance, especially its religious paintings, which was probably due to the adaptation of the Neoplatonist theory of ideas expounded by Ficino to the teachings of the Church. Leonardo's well-known fresco, *The Last Supper*, in Milan, is usually taken to be the first example of this new style. He portrays a moment in time, in which Christ announces that one of his disciples will betray him. But the disciples are expressing a variety of universal emotions—guilt, recognition of impending catastrophe, awareness of divinity.

The Supremacy of Michelangelo

It was Michelangelo (1475–1564), however, who towered over Renaissance Rome, inspiring awe and occasionally fear in the terrible majesty of his temper, the boldness of his conception, the superhuman discipline of his

Pietà, by Michelangelo
The deeply moving statue of the Virgin Mary holding the body of Christ was carved by Michelangelo when he was only twenty-five. St. Peter's Basilica, Rome. Alinari photo

working habits, and the greatness of everything he created—poems, drawings, statues, paintings, buildings. Throughout his life, Michelangelo sought to express his deep Christian piety by the application of the teachings of Ficino, which he had learned at the circle of Lorenzo. "Had my soul not been created Godlike," he wrote, "it would seek no more than outward beauty, the delight of the eyes. But since that fades so fast, my soul soars beyond, to the eternal form." By the time he was twenty-eight, he had already created in sculpture one of the finest expressions of the concept of youth, his *David*, and of the sorrow of death, his *Pietà*. Called to Rome by Julius II to decorate the ceiling of the Sistine Chapel, he made the project a manifesto of the Neoplatonic conception of the long struggle of the soul to reach reunification with the divine, a scheme he had already envisaged for the unfinished tomb of Julius II. At one end of the ceiling is the Drunkenness of Noah, representing the human soul totally imprisoned in the material flesh; at the

Ceiling of the Sistine Chapel, Rome, by Michelangelo
The panel in the top-center represents the expulsion from Eden, the panel in the bottom-center the creation of Adam. Italian Government Travel Office photo

opposite end, above the altar, is complete spirituality, God the Creator; and in the center is the superb Creation of Adam, the spirit of God infusing man with life. And all around are figures of sibyls and prophets, linking the world of antiquity with Christianity.

Julius II died shortly after completion of the Sistine ceiling, and his successor, Pope Leo X, the son of Lorenzo de' Medici, sent Michelangelo back to work in Florence. There he designed a funeral chapel for the Medici family, and began to sculpt a series of allegorical figures to accompany his sculptures of the Medici dead. Again, the whole composition is a search for the eternal ideas. One Medici portrays the active life, and below him are the figures of Day and Night; another represents the contemplative life, and he is accompanied by the indecisive figures of Dawn and Dusk. In 1543, he returned to Rome, where he became superintendent of the Vatican buildings; the great monuments he created in his role still dominate the skyline of Rome. For the summit of the Capitol Hill, he designed a harmonious three-

Model for the Dome of St. Peter's, Rome, by Michelangelo
Although Michelangelo later designed a more squat dome, this original design for a soaring dome was finally constructed in 1590.   Alinari photo

Detail from the Last Judgment, in the Sistine Chapel, Rome, by Michelangelo
Alinari photo

sided court and a long stairway focusing on the ancient equestrian statue of the emperor Marcus Aurelius. At the age of seventy-two, he redesigned Saint Peter's in the form of a Greek cross, using colossal pillars to hold up a magnificent, steeply soaring dome. Although he later reduced the dome in height, he died when only the drum had been completed; and the architect who took over the construction reverted to Michelangelo's original design.

This Rome of Michelangelo's later years was no longer the city of the serene, balanced art of Raphael's day and of the self-satisfied, self-indulgent complacency of the Borgia and Medici popes. The papacy was fighting des-perately the most challenging heresy in its existence; and Michelangelo's art expressed the new tensions. From the 1520s, a sense of discord, of disharmony deliberately invoked, could be felt in his buildings and sculptures in Florence. He indulged in a kind of contorted violence, seen in the writhing figures of the vast fresco of the *Last Judgment* on the back wall of the Sistine Chapel, painted in the late 1530s. Finally, he relapsed into deep despair. His last three sculptures all represent the *Entombment of Christ,* one of them intended for his own tomb; all are infinitely sad, the old man's final meditation on the pathos of old age and death. "Let there be neither painting nor sculpture," he wrote, "to calm the soul that gives itself up to that Divine Love which stretched out His arms from the cross to comfort us." [15]

> *Nè pinger nè scolpir sia più che quieti*
> *L'anima volta a quell'Amor Divino*
> *Ch'aperse, a prender noi, 'n croce le braccia.*

As he wrote, Protestants and Catholics were massacring each other in the name of the Savior.

SUGGESTED READING

The changing concept of the Renaissance is described in the fine historiographical study by Wallace K. Ferguson, *The Renaissance in Historical Thought* (1948). The role of the Greek and Roman classics in the Renaissance is documented by R. R. Bolgar, *The Classical Heritage and Its Beneficiaries* (1954); and Paul Oskar Kristeller concentrates on the position of Plato and Aristotle in the writings of the humanists in *The Classics and Renaissance Thought* (1955) and in his essay in the fine collection edited by Wallace K. Ferguson, *Facets of the Renaissance* (1963). The role of the humanist as teacher of civic skills and virtues is explained in the erudite study of Hans Baron, *The Crisis of the Early Italian Renaissance: Civic Humanism and Republican Liberty in an Age of Classicism and Tyranny* (1955). The social history of the Renaissance can be tasted in John Gage's fresh and entertaining *Life in Italy at the Time of the Medici* (1968). David Herlihy shows the use that can be made of the relatively abundant statistical data to illustrate the pattern of birth, marriage, and death in "The Tuscan Town in the Quattrocento: A Demographic Profile," *Medievalia et Humanistica,* new series, no. 1 (1970), pp. 81–109.

The history of the medieval city is well treated in Daniel Waley's beautifully illustrated *The Italian City-Republics* (1969) and in J. K. Hyde, *Society and Politics in Medieval Italy: The Evolution of the Civil Life, 1000–1350* (1973). Anthony Molho edits an excellent collection of documents illustrating the attitudes of the merchant of the late Middle Ages, *Social and Economic Foundations of the Italian Renaissance* (1969). Luzzato's *Economic History of Italy* (see Chapter 10) is a conveniently short survey by a great Italian economic historian.

---

[15] Author's translation.

Florence is perhaps best served with Gene Brucker's masterly synthesis *Renaissance Florence* (1969). Ferdinand Schevill, *History of Florence* (1936), is full on detail but has been outdated by the new wave of Florentine studies in recent years. On Florentine government, one should consult Gene Brucker, *Florentine Politics and Society 1343–1378* (1962); Marvin B. Becker, *Florence in Transition* (1967–68), which studies the relation of the ideals of fourteenth-century Florence and its style of government; and Nicolai Rubinstein, *The Government of Florence Under the Medici (1434–1494)* (1966), a technical and authoritative account of the Medici's manipulation of the Florentine constitution. On Lorenzo himself, Cecilia M. Ady, *Lorenzo dei Medici and Renaissance Italy* (1962) is short and popular in style; Ferdinand Schevill, *The Medici* (1960) is excessively long and not always reliable. The city's topography is nicely described in Paul G. Ruggiers, *Florence in the Age of Dante* (1964). For a delightful social survey, packed with trenchant extracts from primary sources, see J. Lucas-Dubreton, *Daily Life in Florence in the Time of the Medici* (1961). The patriciate's role as patron in the economic depression of the Renaissance is analyzed in the suggestive essay by Robert S. Lopez, "Hard Times and Investment in Culture," in Wallace K. Ferguson *et al., The Renaissance* ((1962); and the details of individual commissions are mentioned in August C. Krey's essay, "A City That Art Built," in *History and the Social Web* (1955), pp. 135–73. Lauro Martines, *The Social World of the Florentine Humanists, 1390–1460* (1963) surveys the positions of humanists in Florentine society in terms of wealth, public office, and public esteem. Anthony Molho, *Florentine Public Finances in the Early Renaissance, 1400–1433* (1971) is especially good on the fiscal crisis of 1430–1433, which led to Medici hegemony. Lauro Martines *et al., Violence and Civil Disorders in Italian Cities, 1200–1500* (1972) contains essays on Florence by Brucker and Herlihy. Donald Weinstein discusses the millenarian aspects of Savonarola's interaction with Florentine civic traditions in his brilliant study, *Savonarola and Florence: Prophecy and Patriotism in the Renaissance* (1970). For wider perspective, see C. Trinkhaus, ed., *The Pursuit of Holiness in Late Medieval and Renaissance Religion* (1974).

On Florentine humanism, see the suggestive books of Eugenio Garin, *Italian Humanism* (1965), and *Portraits from the Quattrocento* (1972), as well as George Holmes, *The Florentine Enlightenment, 1400–50* (1969), which also covers the humanism of the papal court.

The art of the period is superbly illustrated, with a suggestive text that seeks the philosophical implications of the paintings, in Jacques Lassaigne and Giulio C. Argan, *The Fifteenth Century: From Van Eyck to Botticelli* (1955). F. Hartt, *History of Italian Renaissance Art* (1969) is a good synthesis. Linda Murray's *The High Renaissance* (1967) is particularly useful on Michelangelo's later work in Florence. The artists speak for themselves in Elizabeth Gilmore Holt, *A Documentary History of Art*, vol. 1, *The Middle Ages and Renaissance* (1957), but few achieve the self-advertisement of Benvenuto Cellini's fascinating *Autobiography* (many translations).

Among the liveliest primary sources, there are Villani, *Chronicle* (1906), Agnolo Guicciardini, *History of Italy and History of Florence*, edited by John Hale (1964), and Niccolò Machiavelli, *History of Florence and of the Affairs of Italy* (1960). For political and literary background on these writers, see Felix Gilbert, *Machiavelli and Guicciardini: Politics and History in Sixteenth-Century Florence* (1965.)

The two most famous and widely read books of Renaissance Italy are *The Prince* (many translations) of Machiavelli and *The Courtier* (many translations) of

Baldassare Castiglione. But for a panorama of telling, if flattering, lives of the important men of Florence, one should browse in Vespasiano, *Renaissance Princes, Popes and Prelates* (1963). The view from below is presented by Luca Landucci, *A Florentine Diary,* translated by Alice De Rosen Jervis (1927). Finally, for a superbly interpretive survey, enjoy Robert S. Lopez, *The Three Ages of the Italian Renaissance* (1970).

12 / The Protestant and Catholic Reformations

When the splendor of Renaissance Rome was viewed by visiting Germans, it provoked not admiration but disgust. Martin Luther, an Augustinian friar and teacher of theology, visited Rome in 1511. He ran like "a mad saint through all the churches and catacombs," went on his knees up the Holy Staircase where Christ supposedly mounted to Pilate, and "almost regretted that my father and mother were still living, for I would have liked to redeem them from purgatory with my masses." Later in life, he claimed that he would not have exchanged that trip for any amount of money. "Otherwise I would not believe what I saw with my own eyes. Godlessness and evil are great and shameless there. Neither God nor man, neither sin nor modesty, are respected. So testify all the pious who were there and all godless who returned worse from Italy."[1] This reaction was hardly surprising, in view of the great wave of religious emotion that had been sweeping across northern Europe for the past half-century (see Chapter 10), to which the secularized papacy seemed oblivious.

What is fascinating, on the other hand, is the positive reaction of Italians who visited the great cities of South Germany where the Protestant revolt was to receive crucial early support. Pope Pius II was greatly impressed on his trip through Germany in the midfifteenth century:

[1] Hans J. Hillerbrand, ed., *The Reformation: A Narrative Related by Contemporary Observers and Participants* (New York: Harper, 1964), p. 25.

Luther and Friends (detail), by Lucas Cranach the Elder (1472–1553)
At center is John Frederick, Elector of Saxony. Others left to right, are Martin Luther, John Oecolampadius, Huldreich Zwingli, and Philipp Melanchthon. The Toledo Museum of Art. Toledo, Ohio, Gift of Edward Drummond Libbey

Never has Germany been richer, more resplendent, than today. . . . Without exaggeration it may be said that no country in Europe has better or more beautiful cities. They look as fresh and new as if they had been built yesterday; and in no other cities is so much freedom to be found. . . . When one comes from Lower Franconia and perceives this glorious city [Nuremberg], its splendor seems truly magnificent. Entering it, one's original impression is confirmed by the beauty of the streets and the fitness of the houses. The churches . . . are worthy of worship as well as of admiration. The imperial castle proudly dominates the town, and the burghers' dwellings seem to have been built for princes. In truth, the kings of Scotland would gladly be housed so luxuriously as the common citizen of Nuremberg.[2]

By the late fifteenth century, south and central Germany and the neighboring cantons of Switzerland felt no sense of inferiority before the economic or cultural or, especially, religious achievements of Italy; and it was here, in a region shaped like an irregular diamond, with the cities of Wittenberg, Augsburg, Geneva, and Frankfurt at its four points, that the religious revolt against Rome began. In this region, the Protestant leaders found that combination of circumstances that could turn a reform movement into a religious revolution. Rich, populous, armed, and deeply religious, the imperial cities, princely states, and federated Swiss cantons were determined to throw off all restrictions on their freedom of action. "Poor Germans that we are—we have been deceived! We were born to be masters, and we have been compelled to bow the head beneath the yoke of tyrants," Luther cried to a receptive audience.[3] But such a sentiment was open to a wide variety of interpretations. Almost everyone had a tyranny he wanted to throw off: peasants felt oppressed by landlords, laborers by masters, guildsmen by merchant bankers, princes by the emperor, cities by the local bishop, scholars by scholasticism, the pious by the papacy. Once the revolt against the Catholic Church began, it gained momentum rapidly because all groups desiring change saw in the confusion of the conflict their own opportunity for bettering their condition.

The Protestant revolt went through three rather clearly marked stages. First, the leaders developed theologies at variance with the teachings of the Catholic Church, and thus came into opposition to the Church on a doctrinal basis. The most important leaders of the Protestant Reformation were Martin Luther, who developed his views while teaching theology at the University of Wittenberg and broke with the papacy after criticizing the sale of indulgences in 1517; Huldreich Zwingli, a priest in the cathedral church of Zurich in Switzerland, who persuaded the city council to adopt his teachings in 1522–1525; and John Calvin, a Frenchman who wrote the first draft of his famous book *The Institutes of the Christian Religion*, published

---

[2] Cited in Will Durant, *The Reformation* (New York: Simon and Schuster, 1957), pp. 298, 155.

[3] Henry Bettenson, ed., *Documents of the Christian Church* (New York: Oxford University Press, 1947), p. 278.

in 1536, in France but elaborated on it constantly during his domination of the Swiss city of Geneva in 1536–1564.

Second, each of these theologians found a territorial base in which to found new churches for the practice of their doctrines and from which they could withstand the first attempt of the papacy and its lay supporters to suppress these doctrines. Luther established himself under the protection of the elector of Saxony, and was supported by many princes and free cities of central and southern Germany. Zwingli soon gained followers in the richer and more urbanized cantons of Switzerland. Calvin was able to turn the city-state of Geneva into a theocracy during the period of his domination.

Third, the new doctrines were spread widely throughout Europe and

Europe at the Time of the Protestant Reformation

the European colonies overseas from this original territorial base. Lutheranism was propagated in north Germany and the Scandinavian countries by the middle of the sixteenth century, and even made inroads into the Austrian possessions of the Holy Roman Emperor. Zwinglianism's spread into the rural cantons of Switzerland was halted with the death of Zwingli in battle in 1531, but believers in a radical offshoot of Zwinglianism called Anabaptism founded communities in many parts of eastern Europe and North America. Influenced by the advance of Lutheranism in Germany, the English king Henry VIII founded the Anglican church as his own brand of Protestantism. Calvin became the greatest proselytizer of all, and his admirers spread Calvinism to Scotland, the Netherlands, parts of France and England, and—in the form of Puritanism—to the New England colonies.

The successes of Protestantism stimulated a reformation within the Catholic Church, which used to be called the Counter-Reformation but is now usually known as the Catholic Reformation. It began with a thorough reform of abuses within the Church and culminated in a counterattack against Protestantism with the weapons of persuasion and force. The Catholic Reformation was partly successful in reducing the territorial spread of Protestantism; but bitter fighting between Catholic and Protestant continued until a compromise of exhaustion was reached in 1648 at the end of the Thirty Years' War.

Protestantism: Establishment of a Theological Base

Luther's Character and Religious Development

When Martin Luther attacked the sale of indulgences in 1517, he believed he wanted to reform abuses. His action began the Protestant Reformation, however, because he had already developed a theology that was unacceptable to the Catholic Church, Then, and at all the turning points of his life, Luther expressed surprise at his own actions and their consequences:

That I became a baccalaureus [B.A.] and magister [M.A.], but afterwards took off the brown cap, giving it to others; that I became a monk which brought shame upon me as it bitterly annoyed my father; that I and the Pope came to blows; that I married an apostate nun; who would have read this in the stars? Who would have prophesied it? [4]

Yet Luther's character and intellect combined to make him a religious revolutionary and not a reformer. He was successful because he preached his revolution in a receptive place and time.

Luther might have followed his father's wishes and become a prosper-

[4] Hillerbrand, *The Reformation*, p. 22.

ous lawyer if he had not been absorbed by a sense of sin and unworthiness before God. His father had given up peasant farming for a more profitable career, leasing a couple of smelting furnaces in Saxony, and he had sent his son to the University of Erfurt in the confident expectation that he would take a law degree when he had completed his bachelor's and master's degrees in liberal arts. Shortly after enrolling as a law student, Luther was knocked to the ground by a bolt of lightning and, in terror, he promised St. Anne, the patron saint of the local miners, that he would become a monk. The thunderclap was a useful excuse for warding off the rages of his father—a temper that Martin inherited and that gave him a good deal of courage in the conflicts ahead—and his inclination was to seek salvation by the time-tested method of mortification of the flesh through extreme monasticism. While studying with great concentration for the doctor of theology degree, which he received in Wittenberg in 1512, he tried every method he could think of to reduce his unworthiness before the wrath of God: fasting, private chastisement, long vigils, confessions. Nothing worked. "I was a good monk, and I kept the rule of my order so strictly that I may say that

Luther's Room, Wittenberg
German Information Center photo

if ever a monk got to heaven by his monkery it was I," he said later. "If I had kept on any longer, I should have killed myself with vigils, prayers, reading, and other work." [5]

By 1512, Luther was beginning to feel that while the institutionalized Church did not have the answer, the Bible did. As professor of the Holy Scriptures at Wittenberg from 1512 on, he began to lecture on the Bible: the Psalms for two years, Saint Paul's Epistle to the Romans for two years, Saint Paul's other letters for three, and then again the Psalms. During this long period of immersion in the Biblical text, he slowly began to realize that he was approaching the question of salvation from a completely false direction, relying entirely on his own efforts or "works" to justify himself in the eyes of his righteous God. He claimed that one day, in the tower of the Wittenberg monastery, he found the answer he had been seeking his whole life, justification by faith that Saint Paul had explained in the Epistle to the Romans:

I did not love a just and angry God, but rather hated and murmured against him. Yet I clung to the dear Paul and had a great yearning to know what he meant.

Night and day I pondered until I saw the connection between the justice of God and the statement that "the just shall live by his faith." Then I grasped that the justice of God is that righteousness by which through grace and sheer mercy God justifies us through faith. Thereupon I felt myself to be reborn and to have gone through open doors to paradise. The whole of Scripture took on a new meaning, and whereas before the "justice of God" had filled me with hate, now it became to me inexpressibly sweet in greater love. This passage of Paul became to me a gate of heaven. [6]

What Luther seems not to have realized at the time was that he had rejected several basic tenets of the Catholic Church: the need for a Christian to do good works before he could be saved (rather than after being saved, as Luther later asserted); the role of the Catholic hierarchy as the intermediary between the believer and God; and recognition of the source of religious truth equally in the teachings of the Church and in the Bible.

Luther's Break with the Catholic Church

The power of Luther's emotions and intellect had combined to make him a first-rate teacher of a fresh theology in a provincial university on "the dirty outskirts of the west," as he himself said. His strength of will and his bull-necked courage drove him to accept the consequences of his theological development: the break with Rome and the division of Christianity.

[5] Roland Bainton, *Here I Stand* (New York: Abingdon Press, 1950), p. 45.

[6] Ibid., p. 65.

The incident that began his conflict with the Church was his criticism of the sale of indulgences in Germany. The papacy held that, owing to the special goodness of the lives of Christ and the saints, there existed a treasury of merit that the popes could draw upon to reduce the punishment in purgatory of those who had sinned. An indulgence or pardon could be issued to those truly penitent, or on behalf of those already dead. In practice, this indulgence was usually given to those who made a financial gift to the agent supplying the indulgence. A particularly glaring example of abuse of this custom occurred in 1517 when Albert of Hohenzollern, who was already Archbishop of Magdeburg, agreed to pay the pope a huge installation fee in return for being permitted to become Archbishop of Mainz as well. He borrowed the money from the Fugger banking house in Augsburg, and was permitted by the pope to recoup his finances by dispensing, that is, by selling, indulgences in Germany. Half of the proceeds from the sales were to go to Albert to repay the Fuggers, the other half to the pope for the rebuilding of St. Peter's cathedral in Rome. The agent, Tetzel, was particularly venal in his methods of persuading people to make gifts in return for the indulgence; and Luther, who acted as a parish priest in Wittenberg, was furious to find that many of his parishioners had purchased indulgences from Tetzel. On October 31, 1517, Luther fastened to the door of the castle church 95 Theses, for public, academic debate. The way in which Tetzel behaved roused Luther's temper. In Thesis No. 27 he wrote: "They preach only human doctrines who say that as soon as the money clinks into the money chest, the soul flies out of purgatory." Luther also asserted that pouring out money to build Saint Peter's was a waste of German income. The pope was lending his authority to financial extortion. The German public applauded these sentiments for their sharp criticism of abuses, and circulated copies of the Theses. But Luther had gone much further. He had denied the pope's control over purgatory; he had rejected the doctrine of "superfluous merit," by which for the benefit of sinners the pope could dispose of extra credit created by especially good lives like Christ's or the saints'; and above all he had argued that the whole system was damaging because by making a man complacent, it prevented him from achieving the complete contrition that precedes salvation.

The unorthodoxy of Luther's views became clearer during the next three years as the Church examined his writings and their author; and the more Luther argued with the exponents of Catholic orthodoxy, the more rebellious he became. Archbishop Albert of Mainz, who had precipitated the whole crisis, sent a copy of the Theses to Rome for examination, but the urbane Leo X, the son of Lorenzo de' Medici, was happy to leave the matter in the hands of the Augustinians. "Monks bickering as usual," he remarked. Luther appeared before his order at Heidelberg, and won even more followers, including Martin Bucer, who made Strassburg Protestant. When the elector refused to send him to Rome for trial, he was examined in Augsburg by a learned Italian cardinal, whose reliance on papal and scholastic pronouncements and writings seemed to Luther to be in conflict with the teachings of the Bible. Finally, in a debate in Leipzig in 1519, he took on the leading conservative theologian, the Dominican friar Johann Eck, who succeeded in getting Luther to admit his support for some of the views that Huss had been burned for advocating. Luther once again was stimulated to further study of the Scriptures and of the early history of the Church, which confirmed him in in the correctness of his own views. The papacy, meanwhile, had spent six months studying Luther's writings. In June 1520, it found forty-one of his propositions heretical, gave him sixty days to recant, and ordered his writings burned. The language of the bull, *Exsurge Domine* (Arise, Oh Lord), was a mixture of fury and perplexity:

Arise, Oh Lord, and judge thy cause. Be mindful of the daily slander against thee by the foolish, incline thine ear to our supplication. Foxes have arisen which want to devastate thy vineyard, where thou hast worked the winepress. A roaring sow of the woods has undertaken to destroy this vineyard, a wild beast wants to devour it. . . .

As regards Martin; dear God, what have we failed to do, what have we avoided, what paternal love did we not exercise, to call him back from his errors. [Had he come to Rome], we believe, he would have come to himself and recognized his errors. He would not have found at the Roman curia as much error as he charges, listening unduly to the false rumors of evil men.[7]

Luther, who was not even aware that the bull had been issued, was pouring out a series of short books that not only proved him a heretic but the avowed leader of a revolt against the pope, whom he now openly referred to as the Anti-Christ. In *An Address to the German Nobility*, he called on the secular rulers to reform the Church from top to bottom. In *The Babylonian Captivity of the Church*, he argued that the sacraments, administered by a monopolistic church hierarchy, prevented the individual believer from reaching God through an act of faith. He wrote his own version of the doctrine of transubstantiation; and he threw out five of the seven sacraments of the Catholic Church. "The breach is irreparable," Erasmus commented. On receiving the pope's bull, Luther quickly penned a reply, *Against the Accursed Bull of the Anti-Christ,* and gathering together a group of friendly students and professors at the Wittenberg gate, he presided over the burning of a copy of the canon law, a few books by minor theologians, and the papal bull. "Perhaps the papal incendiaries will become aware that it is no outstanding achievement to burn books which cannot be repudiated by argument," he wrote the same evening.

Luther at the Diet of Worms

Since Luther was protected by the elector of Saxony, the Church authorities appealed to the new Holy Roman Emperor, Charles V (reigned 1519–1556),

[7] Hillerbrand, *The Reformation,* pp. 80, 83.

The Emperor Charles V on Horseback, by Titian (c. 1490–1576)
Painted in 1548, the emperor is shown attacking in the battle of Mühlberg (1547), in which he defeated the German Protestant forces and captured the Elector of Saxony.   The Granger Collection

to take action. But Charles too was unable to act against the wishes of the German princes and cities, and he reluctantly agreed to summon Luther before a meeting of the imperial diet at Worms in October 1521. Luther had originally hoped that the young emperor would heed the appeal in his address to the German nobility. At Worms, in a classic confrontation with Charles V, he learned his error. Asked if he would recant, Luther gave his most famous speech:

Since your Imperial Majesty and Lordships demand a simple answer I will do so without horns or teeth as follows: Unless I am convinced by the testimony of Scripture or by evident reason (for I trust neither in popes nor in councils alone, since it is obvious that they have often erred and contradicted themselves) I am bound by the Scripture which I have mentioned and my conscience is captive to the Word of God. Therefore I cannot and will not recant, since it is difficult, unprofitable and dangerous indeed to do anything against one's conscience. God help me. Amen.[8]

[8] Ibid., p. 91.

The emperor's reply the next day was equally compelling:

You know that my ancestors were the most Christian Emperors of the illustrious German nation, the Catholic kings of Spain, archdukes of Austria, and the dukes of Burgundy, who all were, until death, faithful sons of the Roman Church. Always they defended the Catholic faith, the sacred ceremonies, decretals, ordinances and holy rites to the honor of God, the propagation of the faith and the salvation of souls. After their deaths they left, by natural law and inheritance, these holy Catholic rites, for us to live and to die following their example. . . .

It is certain that a single monk errs in his opinion which is against what all of Christendom has held for over a thousand years to the present. According to his opinion all of Christendom has always been in error. To settle this matter, I am therefore determined to use all my dominions and possessions, my friends, my body, my blood, my life and my soul. . . . I am resolved to act and proceed against him as a notorious heretic, asking you to state your opinion as good Christians and to keep the vow given me.[9]

After the Diet of Worms, Luther did not shift from the theological position he had worked out during the previous decade. Though he refined his teaching in voluminous writings, he was compelled by circumstances to move on to his next task, the establishment of an institutional church in the face of the counterattack that Charles had promised.

Zwingli and the Reformation in Zürich

During the years that Luther was teaching in Wittenberg, Huldreich Zwingli was working out his own brand of Protestantism in the rural parishes of German Switzerland, and from 1519 as people's priest in the main church of Zürich. A kindly, optimistic man, he first became enthusiastic about the writings of Erasmus and the other Christian humanists, which he read while studying liberal arts at the universities of Vienna and Basel. While working for twelve years as a parish priest, he followed Erasmus in protesting the abuses in the Church, especially the sale of indulgences, and he studied the Greek New Testament of Erasmus. When he took up his work as preacher in Zürich, he turned at once to explaining the life of Jesus from Saint Matthew's gospel, and in six years covered the whole New Testament. Like Luther, and without Luther's aid, Zwingli claimed, he had reached the point where he believed the Scriptures alone contained religious truth, and that the Catholic Church's hierarchy and ceremonial were unnecessary; and he had accepted the doctrine of justification by faith as explained by Saint Paul and seized on by Luther. In 1522–1525, he persuaded the city council of Zürich to renounce papal authority, to abolish the Catholic Mass, do away with images and relics, take out the stained glass

[9] Ibid., p. 94.

windows and the organs from the churches, and institute a simplified service of prayer and preaching. Zwingli had thus proposed a Swiss version of church reform, accompanied by a good deal of nationalistic oratory, which the widely based oligarchy in the Zürich city council found acceptable. His doctrines were spread rapidly through the wealthier cantons and the larger cities, although they made little progress in the central rural cantons.

The Lutheran princes of Germany saw that the survival of the new churches in face of the Catholic counterattack that was gathering strength in the late 1520s would be aided by an alliance between the Zwinglian cantons and the Lutheran forces in Germany. As a prerequisite for this fusion, in 1529 they persuaded the leading Lutheran theologians, Luther and Melanchthon, to meet with Zwingli and his main supporters from Strassburg and Basel, at the newly founded Protestant university of Marburg, to hammer out a theological agreement. At Marburg, it became obvious that the differences were irreconcilable, as well as the personalities. Zwingli had deviated from Luther's views as early as 1522 by sanctioning the conversion of the city council into a kind of theocracy, with power over doctrine and the duty to enforce the Christian life. During the next six years, the Zürich council instituted a marital court that used espionage and denunciation to purify morals, used confiscated church property to run a state welfare system, doled out excommunications, drowned Anabaptists for heresy, and thus provided a model for the theocracy Calvin was soon to create in Geneva.

But the basic cause of the break with Luther was the interpretation of the meanings of the communion service. Zwingli had become convinced that Christ had instituted the ceremony of partaking of bread and wine solely as a memorial service, as the "Lord's Supper," and that Christ was not physically present in bread and wine at the moment of Communion. Luther held that while the Catholic interpretation was wrong in that the bread and wine did not turn into the body and blood of Christ, Zwingli was also wrong, in that Christ was present in the actual bread and wine. Luther made it clear that he had come to Marburg "to point out the basis of my faith and point out to the others where they err." To emphasize his point, he wrote in chalk on the table, *Hoc est corpus meum* (This is my body). As to Zwingli's scruples about eating Christ's body, Luther retorted: "If he [Christ] ordered me to eat manure, I would do it, since I would altogether know that it would be to my salvation. Let not the servant brood over the will of his Master. We have to close our eyes." The meeting broke up in failure. Two years later, in 1531 when the first open fighting broke out between Catholic and Protestant, Zwingli could raise only twenty-five hundred men against the forces of the Catholic cantons, and died unregretted by Luther. Zwinglianism, however, survived in western Switzerland and in Strassburg, until its followers agreed to a series of doctrinal compromises with the Calvinists, which enabled them in 1566 to form one reformed church.

The Theology of John Calvin

The third of the great Protestant theologians, John Calvin (1509–1564), regarded Zwingli as a poor theorist; but Calvin recognized always that his own basic teachings were drawn from Luther. Calvin was born at Noyon in northern France, and like Luther was set by his father to study law for its financial prospects. At the University of Paris, he took the regular courses in liberal arts, which gave him a grounding in medieval philosophy, and at two provincial schools he learned both law and the linguistic tools of humanism. His first book, a commentary on Seneca's *Treatise on Clemency*, was an ethical work entirely in the tradition of Christian humanism. He soon abandoned the law, and returned to Paris to align himself with the university scholars who were expressing an open sympathy for Lutheranism. At that time, he wrote later, "God by a sudden conversion subdued and brought my mind to a teachable frame, which was more hardened in such matters than might have been expected from one at my early time of life." Forced to flee with other suspected Lutherans, he spent three years as a fugitive in the French provinces and in Basel, meeting leading reformers and working on his masterpiece, *The Institutes of the Christian Religion*, which he published in its first edition in 1536 and reworked and expanded for the rest of his life. *The Institutes* was a clear, incisive summary of the Christian religion as Calvin conceived it. At the age of twenty-seven, he had already reached the theories and mastered the style that made his book more influential than anything Luther, or any other sixteenth-century Protestant, ever wrote.

Like Luther, Calvin recognized the Bible as the sole source of knowledge of God. He held that man was totally unworthy and could achieve nothing through his own works; and only through prayer could he approach God, whose grace had been shown through the death of Christ on the Cross. But he went further than Luther in his emphasis on the terrible majesty of God and the unintelligible expression of His absolute power. He believed the most incomprehensible and most terrifying act of God to be predestination—the determination by God in advance, for all time, of who shall be saved and who shall be damned.

Predestination we call the eternal decree of God by which He has determined with Himself what He would have to become of every man. For . . . eternal life is foreordained for some and eternal damnation for others. Every man, therefore, being formed for one or the other of these ends, we say that he is predestinated to life or to death.[10]

This was a "horrible decree," Calvin admitted, since nothing anyone did could alter fate and since a supposedly merciful God was damning all ex-

---

[10] John T. McNeill, *The History and Character of Calvinism* (New York: Oxford University Press, 1954), p. 210.

cept a small minority of mankind, the "elect." It did have its advantages, however. It convinced Calvin's followers to respect the three tests he suggested as possible means of discovering one's status in God's plan, "a confession of faith, an exemplary life, and participation in the sacraments of baptism and the Lord's Supper"; and it gave those who thought they were chosen one of the elect absolute confidence in pursuing a difficult life of self-denial.

The task of the elect was to establish their church on earth, as the visible, if ephemeral, expression of the true universal church that includes all the elect of God who have ever lived or who will ever live. Every Calvinist thus had the feeling of being part of an eternal organization; the visible church was essential to help a person through the misery of earthly life on the way to true happiness after death. For Calvin the tasks of this visible church impinged on the secular tasks of the state. In the holy commonwealth that he envisaged as the ideal religious and political community, every member would be striving to serve the glory of God. The regulations of the church were to extend into affairs normally considered the province of the lay authority, such as moral conduct, education, eligibility for state office, and business ethics. In case the state refused to recognize, or persecuted, the Calvinist Church, Calvin had created a form of church organization that could exist in spite of the state—a self-governing ministry of pastors, deacons, teachers, and elders, under whose guidance a small elite of the elect could continue to serve God.

Finally, Calvin laid down his own version of the godly life for the layperson. He rejected the medieval notion of the higher quality of priestly life over laylife. One could serve God in any vocation. Hard work and thrift were signs of service to God. Personal wealth accumulated through thrift and industry was not for Calvin a sign of godliness, nor was poverty a sign of the carelessness of God's will, although later Calvinists frequently took up these views; and belief in them probably contributed to the advances of capitalism in northern Europe during the next two centuries. To Calvin, "prosperity like wine inebriates men, nay even renders them demented"; the prosperous were to use their wealth for their neighbors and for the Church. The excellent care of the sick and the aged in Geneva under Calvin showed his concept of the use to be made of the products of diligence.

The Protestant Reformation was begun by three superb theologians, not by social or political revolutionaries. They offered variants of a way to worship God that was incompatible with Catholicism. But in the sixteenth century, the way a man worshipped God was not regarded as his own affair. It had vast effects on his political allegiance, the disposition of his income, the class relationships within his society, his education, and his cultural tastes. Changes in religion therefore provoked vast changes in many other spheres, and would be blocked unless a powerful enough segment of those affected desired not merely religious change but political, economic, social, and cultural change as well.

Protestantism: Establishment of a Territorial Base

Four characteristics prepared the region lying between Wittenberg, Frankfurt, Geneva, and Augsburg for its role as the territorial base of the early Protestant Reformation: (1) It was wealthy, and thus able to withstand coercion from without. (2) It was composed of several hundred political units, whose governments were prepared and able to use a declaration of religious independence as a means of increasing their political independence and, frequently, their internal cohesion. (3) Renaissance humanism of a decidedly Christian character had made great progress in the newly founded universities, fostering an intellectual attack on scholastic learning and Church abuses. (4) A deep Christian piety, an almost excessive religiosity, expressed in religious art, the cult of saints, and the reform-minded monastic orders, made the secularism of the Church and its abuses increasingly intolerable.

The Sources of German and Swiss Prosperity

The prosperity of this region increased continually throughout the fifteenth century, and reached its height in the first decades of the sixteenth century. Its location, sprawled across the major trans-European trade routes, provided a first impetus. Goods moving to the Netherlands from Venice passed through Augsburg, Ulm, and Strassburg. Products from the Baltic cities crossed Saxony to link with the routes along the Rhine and down the Danube. Geneva lay on the route from Genoa to Paris, and commanded the opening in the Alps where the Rhône River flowed to the manufacturing city of Lyons and southward to the Mediterranean port of Marseilles. Textile manufacturing had begun, though not on a scale comparable with Italy's. Linen was made in Saxony, woolen and silk goods in Augsburg and the nearby Bavarian towns. Nuremberg, one of the three greatest cities in Germany, supported many of its thirty thousand inhabitants by shipping all over Europe the products of its artisans, who ran through a whole gamut from mirror and comb makers to the famous gold- and silversmiths. Even little Zürich, with only five thousand inhabitants, added the sale of weapons manufactured locally to its primary economic function as a center where iron ore was exchanged for salt, wine, and foodstuffs.

Far outshadowing trade and manufacturing as the source of the region's wealth, however, were mining and banking. A few of the mines were in the region itself. The elector of Saxony enjoyed a large income by granting out the right to work his copper and iron mines; and it was here that Luther's father made the moderate fortune that enabled him to pay Luther's university fees and to appear at his son's ordination with fifty horses. The prosperity of Erfurt's twenty thousand citizens, and the money that enabled them to found their own university, where Luther studied liberal arts, was

St. Ulrich's, Augsburg
German Tourist Information
Office photo

the product of the mining industry. Even more profitable were the silver, iron, and copper mines of Hungary and the Tyrol, whose exploitation was entrusted by the Habsburg imperial family of Austria to the Fuggers and other bankers of Augsburg, as security for loans. The Fuggers almost achieved a monopoly on European copper production, and ruthlessly forced up prices, to the impotent fury of their customers, while another Augsburg merchant established a profitable monopoly on quicksilver. The determination of the princes of Germany to ban such monopolies was one factor mak-

**Peasants Dancing, by Albrecht Dürer
(1471–1528)**
German Information Center photo

ing difficult an alliance between them and the cities, even when both had embraced Protestantism.

Finally, the banking center of Europe had been moved decisively from Florence to southern Germany by the beginning of the sixteenth century. The capital of the Fugger company was ten times that of the Medici bank a century earlier; and the Fuggers were only one, though the greatest, of the banking families in Augsburg. The Höchstetters, the Welsers, and the Baumgartners were making loans to princes only a little less large than the 543,000 florins Charles V borrowed from the Fuggers to bribe his way to election as Holy Roman Emperor in 1519. As bankers, the German merchanthouses established themselves in Antwerp, the new commercial center of northern Europe, where they could avoid the guild restrictions that were stifling Bruges and the more southern centers. They gained a monopoly in the supply of colonial goods to Germany from the newly acquired possessions of Spain and Portugal in America and Asia, and they won from the papacy the right to collect its income from most of central Europe. A Fugger agent even accompanied the priests who were selling indulgences.

The general prosperity of the towns was shared, though to a lesser degree, by the food producers of the countryside who, even in this region of great cities, constituted three-quarters of the population. The Black Death had helped destroy the institution of serfdom. The town provided a large market for cash crops and wool. Cities like Strassburg acted as export centers for agricultural produce, like the wine of the Rhine valley. And many peasants profited from possessing long-term, fixed leases in a time of rising prices.

Protestantism, in short, was to strike root in a region of great economic strength, a strength on which it would draw in facing the great counterattack mounted by the Catholic Church and its lay supporters.

Progress of Lutheranism in the German Cities

Politically, the disunity of Germany was a powerful factor in enabling Protestantism to gain an early foothold. In the sixteenth century, Germany consisted of twenty-five hundred different units of government, but most of these were tiny scraps of land controlled by imperial knights. Over three hundred larger states, controlled by the Church, the princes and counts, or the imperial cities, were pressing for almost total freedom from the political controls of the one power they recognized in theory, the Holy Roman Emperor. At the end of the fifteenth century, they proposed to the emperor a reform program that would have established common imperial institutions, such as a federal tax and a court of justice, but which was unacceptable to him for the controls it established over his policy-making power. The larger princely states and the wealthier cities then continued the conversion of their territories into smaller versions of the states created by the "new monarchs" in France, England, and Spain—with more rational boundaries, effective armies, secure incomes, cooperative subjects, and increased independence of external authority. This autonomy, and the desire for further independence from pope and emperor, made many German cities and princely states receptive to Protestantism.

The German cities responded quickly and enthusiastically to Luther. The influence of the university faculty soon brought Wittenberg to abandon Catholic worship, dissolve the monasteries, and permit marriage of the clergy. The much larger city of Erfurt followed; and the Protestant wave swept along the north coast through the great Hanseatic cities from Hamburg and Bremen as far as Danzig and Riga. Heidelberg acted as the catalyst for many of the smaller cities along the Rhine. But the main strength of the movement lay in the imperial cities of the south. In Nuremberg, the humanist business leader Lazarus Spengler, and a circle of friends that included Albrecht Dürer and the poet Hans Sachs, pushed the city council to accept Lutheranism in 1525. The city itself was already uproariously Protestant, according to the papal legate:

**Sixteenth-Century
Nuremberg**

**Twentieth-Century
Nuremberg**
*Heavily restored after the
bombing of the Second
World War, the profile of
Nuremberg is again that
of the sixteenth century,
its hilltop crowned by the
Imperial Castle.*   German Information Center
photo

*In this city the sincere faith in Christ is utterly abolished. No respect is paid
either to the Virgin Mary or to the saints. They ridicule the Papal rites and
call the relics of the saints bones of men who have been hanged. In Lent they
eat meat openly. Confession is neglected, as they say it should be made only to
God. They generally communicate under both forms. They make a laughing
stock of Pope and Cardinals by circulating drawings and caricatures. In short,*

they consider Martin their enlightener, and think that until now they have been in darkness.[11]

In Strassburg, whose peripheral location in Germany gave it little respect for the emperor and whose population had long resented the wealth and independent authority of the Church within its walls, the call to abolish the Mass, given by the subtle reformer Martin Bucer, was finally carried out in 1528 by a coalition of intellectuals, city magistrates, and lower clergy. In Augsburg, the wealthiest of all the south German cities, Lutheranism made its first converts among the workers and guild masters. Anabaptist preachers made converts during the peasants' revolt, but were soon rooted out, while the well-to-do of the city government turned, with some notable exceptions, to Zwinglianism. By 1530, a predominantly Lutheran form of church service was being followed. By the end of the 1530s, two-thirds of the German cities were Protestant.

Hieronymous Holzschuher, Bürgermeister of Nuremberg, by Albrecht Dürer
Dürer painted the Bürgermeister in 1526, one year after he had presided over the city's official adoption of Lutheranism. German Information Center photo

Within this general pattern of receptivity to the doctrines of Protestantism, there were significant variations, however. Certain cities and certain classes felt themselves tied to the cause of the emperor by economic necessity. The city of Nuremberg, even after it had become Lutheran, felt its local power and its widespread commerce to be dependent on its alliance with a strong emperor; and it therefore refused to join in the alliance of Protestant cities formed to hold off the emperor's attempt to reconvert them to Catholicism by force. Even though most of Augsburg turned Protestant, the Fuggers remained Catholic, only to be ruined later in the century when the Spanish Phillip II of Spain repudiated his debts. Class tension, between the three main groups of patriciate, guild masters, and poor artisans, was often expressed in religious terms. The workers were often attracted to the more radical forms of Protestantism, such as Anabaptism, although they occasionally remained Catholic when their masters turned Protestant. The masters would frequently follow one form of Protestantism when the city patriciate adopted another, as in Augsburg. Thus for economic and social reasons, there was a readiness in the German cities to reject the Catholic Church; but the manner of its rejection had infinite variation.

Lutheranism in the Princely States

Of the major German states, several were firmly tied to the Catholic Church. The three richest states in the west of Germany were ruled by the archbishop-electors of Cologne, Mainz, and Trier; the largest contiguous landholdings in the empire, stretching from Silesia to the Tyrol, were the property of the emperor himself. Between 1520 and 1540, all the other powerful princely states, with the one exception of Bavaria, joined the Protestant cause. The lead was taken by the elector of Saxony and the landgrave

[11] Gerald Strauss, *Nuremberg in the Sixteenth Century* (New York: Wiley, 1966), p. 174.

George the Pious of Brandenburg, by Lucas Cranach the Elder
George II, the Hohenzollern elector of Brandenburg, accepted Lutheranism in 1539. John G. Johnson Collection, Philadelphia

of Hesse. Frederick the Wise, of Saxony, who had already spent on the University of Wittenberg the money he had collected for a papal Crusade, probably saved Luther from oblivion by refusing to extradite him to Rome after he first challenged the papacy over indulgences; and four years later, when Luther was under papal excommunication and imperial ban, he gave him sanctuary in his castle at the Wartburg. The Saxon electors embraced both the advantages and the risks of Lutheranism. Church property was secularized, and much retained for their own profit. A single state church, which recognized the supremacy of the prince, was set up, with the agreement of Luther. But in 1547, Frederick's nephew was defeated at the Battle of Mühlberg, and rather than give up Lutheranism, abdicated as elector. Hesse's adherence to the Protestant cause was more flamboyant. Landgrave Philip joined the Lutherans in 1526, and became the foremost organizer of their military alliances. He took for himself two-fifths of the proceeds from the dissolution of Hesse's monasteries, persuaded Luther to let him commit bigamy, led the Protestant princes in their quarrels with the emperor, and almost lost his throne when he too was captured at Mühlberg. In the 1520s, Saxony and Hesse were joined by Schleswig, Brunswick, and the Duchy of Prussia; and in the 1530s, by Nassau, Pomerania, and the very important states of Württemberg and Brandenburg.

Spread of Protestantism to the Swiss Cities

In Switzerland, the political independence of the cantons had been won from Austria in two centuries of warfare that had begun in 1291 when three cantons first joined together in a defensive league, the nucleus for the future Swiss confederation; this warfare culminated in their defeat of both Burgundy and Austria at the end of the fifteenth century. By then, although the thirteen federated cantons were nominally part of the Holy Roman Empire, they already controlled their own internal affairs free of interference from the emperor and their own common legislature, which controlled only external relations. The Catholic Church in Switzerland was unusually corrupt and tolerant, and in any case had little power over the political authorities, who began several years before the Reformation to interfere in the running of the Church. It was therefore quite easy for the city council of Zürich to accept the changes in doctrine and form of worship proposed by Zwingli, which had by 1525 made it a Protestant city; and preachers from Zürich were soon able to convert the other two leading cities of the confederation, Basel and Bern, and to influence Strassburg and the cities of southwestern Germany. Bern extended its protection to the city of Geneva, in its conflict with its ruling bishop and his ally the Duke of Savoy, and made it an official ally, though not yet a member, of the Swiss confederation. Bern's aid enabled the citizens of Geneva to expel their bishop in 1535, and to follow a brand of Protestantism preached by the French reformer Guillaume Farel, who the next year invited another French reformer, John Calvin, to settle in the city. In short, the Protestant Reformation was established in Switzerland in those cantons dominated by cities. It sustained its principal defeat when the rural, Catholic cantons took arms against Zürich and in 1531 defeated the city's forces and killed Zwingli himself. While Calvinism later replaced Zwinglianism in the Protestant areas of Switzerland, it was never able to penetrate the rural cantons that had refused the teaching of Zwingli.

Thus, economic and political factors combined in Germany and Switzerland to enable Protestantism to establish a territorial base very rapidly. The cities provided the intellectual drive that spread the ideas of the reformers. But the princes supplied the muscle that in the long run was to spell the difference between survival and annihilation of Protestantism.

Christian Humanism

Cultural vitality accompanied economic prosperity and the search for political independence, helping in one more way to prepare for Protestant acceptance. The most direct influence was exerted by the Christian humanists. Knowledge of Italian humanistic studies had been brought to the North of Europe by scholars who had studied in Italy and by merchants whose business ventures had brought them into the humanistic circles patronized by the Italian merchant bankers. But above all, the printing press had made possible the diffusion of the newly discovered classical works and the revised versions of better known works, as well as the original writings of Italian scholars. Printing by use of movable metal type had been perfected in Mainz on the Rhine around 1450, and had soon been taken up in the cities of south and central Germany like Strassburg, Augsburg, and Nuremberg. It was first used in Italy in 1467, and by the end of the century the Aldine Press in Venice was sending north large numbers of inexpensive editions of the classics. Nevertheless, German technicians continued to dominate printing throughout Europe, and Germany remained the greatest publisher of books. Printing made the great towns of Germany and Switzerland aware of the humanist attack on scholastic learning; it presented them with the Bible in vernacular long before Luther made his own translation; and above all it spread Luther's doctrines with revolutionary speed. Six million books in all had been printed by 1500; between 1517 and 1520, one-third of a million copies of Luther's writings were published. The printing press thus prepared an intellectual elite for Luther; but it also made his doctrines the basis of a popular revolution.

The irony of German humanism lies in the fact that the Dutch scholar Erasmus, who dominated German intellectual life in the first two decades of the sixteenth century and probably did most to prepare the intellectuals for Luther, finally refused to go along with Luther's revolutionary program. Erasmus was born in Rotterdam in 1466, educated at one of the newer monastic orders, the Brethren of the Common Life, and eventually became a priest, a step he later regretted. His later studies made him a master of Latin and Greek and the classical and Christian works in those languages. He became the foremost Biblical scholar in Europe by publishing a revised edition of the New Testament in Greek, with a Latin translation and notes; this was followed by similar editions of the Church Fathers. Luther lectured from Erasmus's New Testament at Wittenberg, and used it as the text for his great German translation of the Bible. Erasmus also became the most widely known satirist in Europe when he published in 1511 his *Praise of*

The September Testament, from the Workshop of Lucas Cranach the Elder *Luther's translation of the New Testament was illustrated with woodcuts like this, which shows the opening of the book of the Apocalypse.* German Information Center photo

Folly, a scintillating attack on almost all institutionalized banality, ecclesiastical or secular. His attitude about indulgences, placed in the mouth of Folly, makes Luther seem moderate:

What shall I say of such as cry up and maintain the cheat of pardons and indulgences? . . . By this easy way of purchasing pardons, any notorious highwayman, and plundering soldier, or any bribe-taking judge shall disburse

Erasmus by Hans Holbein (c. 1497–1543)
Erasmus was greatly admired by King Henry VIII, for whom the court painter Holbein painted several of the leading Christian humanists.
Courtesy of the Louvre, Paris

some part of their unjust gains, and so think all their grossest impieties sufficiently atoned for. So many perjuries, lusts, drunkennesses, quarrels, bloodsheds, cheats, treacheries, shall all be, as it were, struck a bargain for, and such a contract made, as if they had paid off all arrears and might now begin upon a new score. . . . Several of these fooleries, which are so gross and absurd as I myself am even ashamed to own, are practiced and admired, not only by the vulgar, but by such proficients in religion as one might well expect should have more wit.[12]

Erasmus expounded the "philosophy of Christ," a humane ethics derived from Christ's teaching and from ancient philosophy. He made the hierarchic Church seem irrelevant, attacked the political authorities for permitting the crime of war, and criticized the barriers of wealth and social distinction. Erasmus, many of his German admirers thought, should have had no difficulty in becoming a Lutheran. The gentle scholar, however, had no taste for heroic conflicts and no desire to break Christianity apart, and he remained a Catholic, in spite of the pressure put on him by the Protestant leaders to join them. "I seem to see a cruel and bloody century ahead," he wrote in 1527. "As things are, certain persons are not satisfied with any of the accepted practices, as if a new world could be built of a sudden. There will always be things which the pious must endure."[13] Many of his former admirers could not agree, and many of the humanists in the German courts and the universities accepted Protestantism at once. And the Lutheran Church was fortunate that the person most responsible for drawing up a systematic presentation of the new beliefs was Philipp Melanchthon, professor of Greek at the University of Wittenberg and a far more widely educated humanist than Luther.

The Religious Character of German Art

The revolt against the financial exactions and spiritual corruption of the Church in Germany and Switzerland was fueled by the deep piety of the region. The political leaders of the Protestant revolt were often profoundly pious men. Frederick the Wise of Saxony had over nineteen thousand relics, including the thumb of St. Anne. Mysticism was widely practiced. Many of the religious orders were uncompromising in observing their rule, particularly the Augustinian Eremites that Luther joined. And the religious art of the region magnified the emotional character of this attitude to worship.

German artists produced their finest work in the last half of the fifteenth and the first half of the sixteenth centuries; and its predominant character was a strong, passionate Christianity. The workshops of the city of Nuremberg, for example, produced an extraordinary group of sculptors of wood, bronze, and stone. The churches of Germany were filled with the altarpieces, the crucifixions, and the bronze reliefs of men like Veit Stoss and Peter Vischer, and hundreds of lesser artists—portrayals of Christ and the saints, some with bodies writhing in agony, faces transfigured with the realization of God's presence and man's inhumanity. After 1500, the paint-

---

[12] Desiderius Erasmus, *The Praise of Folly* (London: Reeves and Turner, 1876), pp. 82–83.
[13] Hillerbrand, *The Reformation*, pp. 425–26.

Sarcophagus of Henry II, and His Consort Kunigunde, Bamberg Cathedral, By Tilman Riemenschneider
German Tourist Information Office photo

ers were especially influential. They had absorbed the technical advances of the Italian Renaissance as well as the representational accuracy of Flanders; but they combined their interest in individual psychology with a late Gothic intensity of religious feeling. Many of the great painters accepted Luther's teaching at once. Lucas Cranach (1472–1553), the court painter of Wittenberg, has left a superb series of paintings of Luther at all stages of his progress from tormented theologian to disillusioned if world-renowned reformer. He also took employment as a skilled propagandist of Lutheranism by using the newly invented process of the woodcut, which could be reproduced in hundreds of copies on the printing machine, to spread the message of papal depravity. One of the greatest German painters, and without doubt the greatest printmaker, Albrecht Dürer, had already mirrored his age's spiritual uneasiness before Luther first spoke out. Dürer's *Melancholia* depicts a young, handsome woman, surrounded by the implements of creative work, like geometric instruments and woodworking tools; but, in spite of the wings on which she should soar, she is sunk to earth in total despair. In *The Knight, Death, and the Devil,* a Christian knight rides steadily toward a beautiful hilltop city; but we feel that when he has ridden on, death and corruption will still hold the field. Luther's teachings, Dürer wrote, "helped me out of great distress." He studied most of Luther's writings, and became a convert. In 1521, fearing that Luther had been put to death, he wrote in his journal:

The Knight, Death, and the Devil, by Albrecht Dürer
Los Angeles County Museum of Art, Graphic Arts Council Fund

I know not whether he lives or is murdered, but in any case he has suffered for the Christian truth. If we lose this man, who has written more clearly than any other in centuries, may God grant his spirit to another. His books should be held in great honor, and not burned as the emperor commands, but rather the books of his enemies. O God, if Luther is dead, who will henceforth explain to us the gospel? What might he not have written for us in the next ten or twenty years? [14]

[14] Bainton, *Here I Stand*, p. 192.

In this original political base, Protestantism withstood the first counter-attack of the Catholic powers; and from it, a great missionary drive spread the religious revolt to much of northern Europe.

Protestantism: Expansion from the Territorial Base

Early Spread of Lutheranism

Luther was fortunate that his principal enemy, Holy Roman Emperor Charles V, was never able to unite the Catholic states inside Germany with the Catholic powers in the rest of Europe, to crush the Protestant cities and princely states. Charles was overburdened by the extent of his empire. In Spain, he faced opposition from the cities. The turbulent Sicilian nobility ignored his wishes. The Netherlands nobility was virtually self-governing. The treasure pouring in from Mexico and Peru was causing ruinous inflation. Even the Catholic princes of Germany were unwilling to strengthen the emperor with increased arms and money as the price of defeating Protestantism. Enemies outside were even more dangerous. The French king allied with German Protestants against Charles. The Turkish sultan, Suleiman the Magnificent, was campaigning in Hungary and threatening Vienna itself. Even the pope regarded Charles as a threat to his temporal power inside Italy. Charles's political and military difficulties made possible Luther's successes.

Lutheranism was soon organized to take advantage of this situation. In his writings and his magnificent translation of the Bible, Luther had made a scriptural religion enormously appealing. The thrust of the language, its homey metaphors, its humor, its vigor, and especially its clarity won many converts. In the 1520s, he organized a Lutheran form of worship, with the sacraments of baptism and the Lord's Supper, preaching and reading the Bible in the vernacular, and a great deal of lusty choral singing; and after sanctioning the suppression by the princes of the peasants' revolt, he recognized the power of the prince as the "highest bishop" of the territorial Lutheran churches. The Lutheran Church thus became subordinated to the state administration, and in practice it became necessary for the citizens of a state to accept the Lutheranism of their prince or emigrate. To Luther, this church-state relationship was unimportant in comparison with the advantage of bringing the Word of God to all citizens; but to princes outside Germany who were seeking to increase their own control over their subjects, it made Lutheranism additionally attractive.

Knowledge of both the new theology and new church organization was spread primarily by the printing presses. Lutheran books were sent into France, for example, from publishers around its borders, in Antwerp, Basel, and Strassburg. But the German universities, especially Wittenberg, played an important part in training and inspiring the preachers who would carry Luther's message home. Of the sixteen thousand students who went to Wittenberg from 1520 to 1560, one-third were foreigners; among them were future leaders of the Reformation in Denmark, Sweden, and Finland. Universities abroad were particularly receptive to Luther's doctrines. An important Lutheran circle was formed in the University of Paris; the University of Cambridge first grasped its role as the main exponent of Protestant theology in England when a small group of theologians began to meet in 1520 to discuss Luther's theories; the University of Cracow turned many Polish nobles Protestant. The first urban groups to accept Luther's doctrines outside Germany were the transplanted colonies of German merchants along the Baltic. In the Hanseatic cities, the German merchants became missionaries. From Danzig, Riga, Reval, Königsberg, and Bergen, they brought Lutheranism with their trade goods.

In Scandinavia, adoption of Lutheranism suited the political purposes of the kings. The Catholic Church was wealthier and more exacting there than even in Germany; ambitious young rulers were seeking to give to Norway, Sweden and Denmark a national cohesion after the breakup of the disastrous Union of Calmar under Denmark. At the Diet of Vesterås in 1527, King Gustavus I of Sweden used the threat of abdication to compel the confiscation of most church property and the free worship of Lutheranism. In 1593, a national synod definitively adopted Lutheranism as the Swedish national church. The Danish king broke with the Catholic Church in 1527 and began to seize church lands. A decade later, in consultation with Luther, a national church was created. Since Norway and Iceland were both provinces of the Danish crown, Lutheranism was introduced there without much preliminary proselytizing. Finland, which was under the rule of Sweden, was greatly affected by the nearby Hanseatic cities and by its own Michael Agricola, who after studying in Wittenberg for three years published a Finnish translation of the Bible and created a form of Lutheran worship in keeping with Finland's own religious traditions.

The Anabaptists

Zwinglianism never penetrated very far beyond the immediate neighborhood of Zürich, owing to the untimely death of its founder, although Zwinglian doctrines had some effect as far afield as Budapest and Cambridge. One offshoot of the Zwinglian Church, the Anabaptists, was, however, destined to have widespread and troubled propagation. Several of Zwingli's followers attempted in 1523–1525 to push him into more rapid religious reform, based on a literal interpretation of the Bible. Believing in free will, they denied the doctrines of predestination and justification by faith; and they demanded that baptism should be delayed until adults had "learned repentance and amendment of life" and, as intelligent believers, had committed their lives to God. The Zürich authorities threatened them with death for "rebaptizing" (they called themselves Baptists, but the authorities called them "re-Baptists," or Anabaptists, since rebaptism was punishable by death under the Justinian Code). Nevertheless, on January 21, 1525, their leader Conrad Grebel baptized a former priest, who then proceeded to baptize fifteen others present. As the movement spread, the persecution by torture and the execution—by burning, hanging, or drowning—that followed was due far more to the Anabaptists' determination to live apart from church and state than to the one fact of adult baptism. By their strict biblical interpretation, the Anabaptists determined that they could not take part in public affairs, do military service, offer resistance if attacked, take oaths, own private property, drink alcohol, or pay war taxes. According to a Swiss chronicler:

Their walk and manner of life was altogether pious, holy, and irreproachable. They avoided costly clothing, despised costly food and drink, clothed themselves with coarse cloth, covered their heads with broad felt hats; their walk and conduct was altogether humble. . . . They carried no weapon, neither sword nor dagger, nothing more than a pointless bread knife, saying that these were wolf's clothing which should not be found on the sheep. They would never swear an oath, not even upon demand of the government. And if anyone transgressed, he was excluded by them.[15]

Driven out of Zürich, the Anabaptists sought refuge in nearby cities, especially tolerant Strassburg, and finding the government of Moravia (part of present-day Czechoslovakia) willing to permit them to lead their own way of life, thousands emigrated there, to form Bruderhofs, or communes, in which they held all property in common. Their creed appealed especially to village peasants and artisans. But in 1534–1535, extreme Anabaptists under the leadership of a demented fanatic took control of the city of Münster in west Germany and, during a long siege by its archbishop, introduced communal ownership of property and polygamy. The excesses cast disfavor on the more sober Anabaptists and persecution by Catholic and Protestant alike reached great depths of cruelty and depravity. Nevertheless, the Anabaptists were revived by the Dutchman Menno Simons (1496–1561); and his followers, returning to the scriptural simplicity of the early Anabaptists without any of the excesses of the Münster episode, founded the communities of Mennonites that spread to the United States and Canada and eastwards to Poland, Hungary, and Russia.

The Reformation in England

The Reformation in England was only slightly influenced by Luther. In the fourteenth century, the heretical Lollards, the followers of John Wycliff, had

---

[15] Roland Bainton, *The Reformation of the Sixteenth Century* (Boston: Beacon Press, 1952), pp. 100–101.

already denounced the pope's control of the Church and many Catholic doctrines. Christian humanism had found some of its most talented exponents in London, especially Sir Thomas More, a close friend of Erasmus and lord chancellor under Henry VIII. The rising middle class was hungrily eyeing the possessions of the Church; these composed almost one-third of the arable land in England. And the new Tudor dynasty, which had seized power through victory in the Wars of the Roses, proposed to profit from the long-standing objection to papal interference in English affairs to use religious sanctions in support of its own attempt at absolutism. England could therefore have followed the Danish example, creating its own national brand of Lutheranism, or the French example, negotiating a concordat with the papacy that would recognize a national brand of Catholicism. The second Tudor king, Henry VIII (reigned 1509–1547) chose a third way, however. He was a curious mixture of conservatism and modernity, of principle and flexibility. He wrote a book condemning Luther, for which the pope called him *Fidei Defensor* (Defender of the Faith); and he consistently refused to change the forms of Catholic worship. He apparently became sincerely worried in 1525 that God was punishing him for marrying his brother's widow, Catherine of Aragon, by not giving him a son; and he requested, in time-honored fashion, that the pope annul his marriage. Since Catherine was the aunt of Emperor Charles V, the pope procrastinated; and Henry finally determined to sever the Catholic Church in England from Rome, make himself its pope, and incidentally have his own archbishop of Canter-

(Left) **Thomas More, by Hans Holbein the Younger (c. 1497–1543)** *The humanist and lawyer was still in Henry VIII's favor when painted in 1527. Eight years later he was beheaded for refusal to accept the Act of Supremacy.*

(Right) **Thomas Cromwell, by Holbein** *Cromwell, who had been largely responsible for the execution of More, was beheaded for treason himself in 1540.* Both photos copyright The Frick Collection, New York

Henry VIII (Reigned 1509–1547)
In the last years of his life, ravaged by disease, Henry became increasingly distrustful of even his closest associates, as the artist shows.

bury annul his marriage. Between 1531 and 1539, working through a collaborative parliament, he broke the opposition within the English church, cut off all financial payments and legal appeals to Rome, and by the Act of Supremacy made himself "supreme head" of the Church of England. His archbishop, Thomas Cranmer, one of the finest writers and sincerest Protestants of the sixteenth century, obligingly annulled the marriage to Catherine and married him to his secret love, Anne Boleyn, who gave him yet another daughter, Elizabeth, and was beheaded for this inadequacy. The members of Parliament were rewarded by being given a major share of the spoils from the dissolution of the monasteries—whose supposed evil-doing was unmasked by the king's vicious minister Thomas Cromwell—and were incidentally linked materially to the king in their commitment to the Anglican Church. When Henry died in 1547, the new church was still Catholic in character; but already the wide diffusion of the Bible in English was preparing many people for an acceptance of Protestantism on the continental pattern. During the regency of Edward VI (reigned 1547–1553), Cranmer introduced his book of prayer, which, in its revised form, was directly influenced by the continental reformers, and his Forty-Two Articles defining the Anglican faith that accepted the sole authority of the Bible and justification by faith. After the brief attempt of Mary (reigned 1553–1558) to restore Catholicism, Elizabeth (reigned 1558–1603) returned to a moderate Protestantism that was acceptable to the majority of her subjects.

Geneva: City of the Saints

Anglicanism was not a proselytizing religion; it was a state church that extended only to the colonies of the English state. By contrast, Calvinism was organized from the start to win converts. In Calvin's theology, the movement had a body of teachings more international in their appeal than Luther's. But the most important instrument for transmission of Calvin's message was the city of Geneva. Calvin arrived in Geneva in 1536, intended to spend one night on his way to Strassburg. Persuaded by a "dreadful imprecation" of his fellow Frenchman, Guillaume Farel, that God had put his hand out to stop him, he agreed to stay in Geneva to help organize the Protestant Church there. After two years, he and Farel were expelled; but they returned in 1541. From then until his death in 1564, Calvin dominated the city.

Character of City Life in Calvin's Geneva

During Calvin's hegemony, Geneva produced no great art, music, or nonreligious literature. No fine buildings were erected, and as the outer suburbs were pulled down for defense purposes and the population squeezed together behind its magnificent fortifications, Geneva became less attractive. "There were many pleasant buildings within the city which have been torn down," a contemporary reported, "either to protect the city against her enemies or to remove Papist superstitions; in sum, her beauty has been diminished in order to augment her power." [16] The only buildings still surviving from Calvin's day are the churches, and these were medieval. The city did not enjoy a wave of economic prosperity until the seventeenth and

[16] E. William Monter, *Calvin's Geneva* (New York: Wiley, 1967), p. 3.

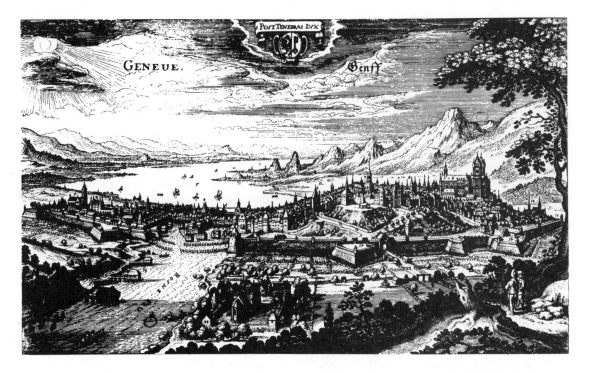

Geneva in the Seventeenth Century
The city is built on both banks of the Rhône River at the point where it emerges from Lake Geneva. The tall Gothic building at the right is the cathedral of St. Peter.

eighteenth centuries; and Calvin's influence encouraged only one new industry, though an important one—book publishing. Even within Geneva, Calvin's ideal of government was slowly jettisoned after his death. Nevertheless, Geneva was the single most influential city in sixteenth-century Europe, because it was the achievement in real life of the ideal of the Christian commonwealth, the model Christian community. It inspired love or hatred, never indifference. According to John Knox, the fiery preacher who converted Scotland to Calvinism:

[In] Geneva . . . I neither fear man nor am ashamed to say that this is the most perfect school of Christ that ever was in the earth since the days of the apostles. In other places, I confess Christ to be truly preached; but manners and religion to be so sincerely reformed, I have not yet seen in any other place.[17]

To the great poet of the French Renaissance, Ronsard, it was the instigator of civil war and sedition:

A town set in the fields of Savoy
which, by fraud, drove out its former rulers,
the miserable abode of every apostasy,
of stubbornness, pride, and heresy.[18]

[17] C. R. N. Routh, *They Saw It Happen in Europe* (Oxford: Basil Blackwell, 1965), p. 277.

[18] Monter, *Calvin's Geneva,* p. 232.

After years of struggle with its recalcitrant citizens, Calvin succeeded in enforcing his ideals of Christian conduct. A consistory, composed of twelve lay persons picked from the elders of the church, was "to keep watch over every man's life, to admonish amiably those whom they see leading a disorderly life, and where necessary to report to the assembly which will be deputized to make fraternal correction." Meeting weekly with the pastors of the church, the elders called in spies and informers. Private immorality, from playing cards to sunbathing naked, was sharply punished, sometimes by humiliating public penance, at other times by whipping. Punishment for blasphemy was the piercing of the blasphemer's tongue. Dancing, swearing, rude songs, lavish clothing, overcharging a customer, drunkenness, laughter in church—all were punishable offenses, with no one spared. The death penalty was pronounced unsparingly on a great variety of offenses, though most executions were of suspected heretics. Two or three witches were burned each year. The Spanish physician and theologian Servetus, who had already been persecuted by the Catholics, was burned at the stake for criticizing the doctrine of the Trinity. Usually, however, those excommunicated by the church were banished.

Calvin also believed the church should take positive action for social betterment. While provision of daily services by a well-educated clergy was its initial function, the church was also to supervise poor relief, run the city hospital, look after orphans and widows, and keep the town clean. The city too was to extend its responsibility to those Calvinists forced to flee from their own countries for their faith. Refugees at times were said to equal the number of permanent inhabitants of Geneva; and many settled permanently, bringing skills like silk-weaving that were to make the city prosperous for the next two hundred years. Others came to learn from Calvin and the example of the city he had shaped, with the intention of creating Christian commonwealths in their own countries. They found in Geneva little national churches, of which the most important were the English, the Italian, and the Spanish, while the French, by far the greatest in number, almost swamped the Genevan church itself. To train the youth of Geneva and the many students from abroad, Calvin founded the Genevan Academy, taking one of the two chairs of theology himself. Its alumni included the councilors of William the Silent of the Netherlands and of King Henry IV of France. Geneva, with some justification, came to be regarded as the training school for a revolutionary underground.

Finally, under Calvin, Geneva provided the example of a theocracy. The church did not govern Geneva; Calvin conceived of the secular arm's acting in harmony with the spiritual to ensure enforcement of God's will. He therefore took steps to see that the secular power respected God's will. He preached a special sermon before elections. In the early years, he strongly supported the political faction sympathetic to the church, which eventually banished or executed its leading opponents. By 1553, Geneva had a civil government that was perhaps even more Calvinist than Calvin; and thus the cooperation of state and church that Calvin envisaged became a reality.

The Expansion of Calvinism

From Geneva, Calvinism spread rapidly. It was accepted by the elector of the Palatinate in nearby Germany, and he made the University of Heidelberg into an additional training school for Calvinist missionaries. Isolated congregations were formed in other parts of Germany, but Calvin made no effort to convert Lutherans. Members of the Polish nobility were converted, and some progress was made in Hungary and Bohemia. In France, however, the pastors who had been sent from Geneva made many converts among the middle classes of the trading cities and also won over some of the highest members of the nobility. By 1560, there were perhaps half a million Calvinists in France, who possessed a close-knit network of churches and were beginning to arm in preparation for the showdown they could see in the offing. In the Netherlands, Calvinism spread into the French-speaking provinces of what is now Belgium, feeding on the hatred of Spain and of the Catholic Church in the big cities like Antwerp and Ghent, but moving only slowly into the northern provinces, whose revolt against Spain the Calvinists were eventually to lead.

Calvinism's most startling triumph was in Scotland. John Knox returned to Scotland from Geneva in 1559 as the pastor of a northern city church; and through his sermons he succeeded in making Calvinism the ally of Scottish nationalism, which was in fever against the rule of Mary Stuart. With the help of Elizabeth of England, the Scots rose against Mary and the troops sent to her aid by France; Mary fled to England where she became Elizabeth's captive, while the Scottish Calvinists installed her infant son James as king in her place. In 1560, the Scottish Parliament broke all ties with Rome, and adopted a Calvinist declaration of faith drawn up by Knox. A system of church government, derived from Geneva, was organized throughout the country, which rigidly enforced many of the moral regulations of the City of the Saints. Scotland was the first country to approximate the gloomy discipline of Geneva.

Finally, Calvinism began to penetrate without much difficulty into the broad-based Anglican church. During periods of religious persecution in England in the last years of Henry VIII and under his daughter Mary, English refugees went to Geneva, Zürich, and Strassburg, and returned with strongly Calvinist views. When life became unsafe in the continental cities, many reformers took refuge in England, and were even given teaching positions at Oxford and Cambridge. From Scotland, the powerful influence of Knox reached southward. As a result, a strong Puritan movement inside the Anglican Church sought to push it closer to the Genevan ideal. Only in the early seventeenth century, however, did a minority of the Calvinists decide that separation from both the Anglican Church and England was the only solution, and seek to found in New England their own Genevas.

The Catholic Reformation

"In many countries obedience to the Pope has almost ceased," a Venetian ambassador noted in the midsixteenth century, "and matters are becoming so critical that, if God does not interfere, they will soon be desperate."[19] A century later, not only had the expansion of Protestantism been halted but many wavering areas had been firmly brought back to the Catholic faith, while the Catholic Church itself was reformed, vigorous, doctrinally self-assured, and culturally ascendant.

The first efforts made by the Catholic Church to meet the Protestant threat had been tardy and ill-chosen. The pope had made a hero out of Luther by an excommunication that had no teeth and by answering his Scripture-based theology with a reassertion of the authority of the Church. Reliance on the force of Emperor Charles V and the German Catholic princes had created a counterforce in the Schmalkaldic League of German princes and cities; and a decade of fighting had ended in the Peace of Augsburg (1555), in which the Catholics had been compelled to recognize, by the famous principle *cuius regio eius religio,* that the ruler of each German state had the right to choose Lutheranism or Catholicism as his state's religion.

Reforms Within the Catholic Church

To stop the Protestant advance, the Church had first to reform itself. Several of the popes who faced Luther made efforts to stop the sale of Church offices, reform the bureaucracy in Rome, and make Church justice more rapid and less fiscally motivated; but real progress was made after the turn of the century when the popes were appointed, not from the rich Italian families but from the poorer families who saw their ideal in the austerity of Spanish Catholicism. By the end of the sixteenth century all the glaring abuses had been rooted out. Far more important, however, was the renewal of the spiritual fervor of the Church. Rather than accept the humanistic revival sought by Erasmus and Thomas More and the vast number of scholars who remained faithful to Catholicism, the Church turned again to its rich mystical tradition, setting against the Protestant emphasis on man's impotence and depravity the conception of man's perfectibility, achieved in part through his own actions and his own deliberate search for God through contemplation. The inspiration again came from Spain, from mystics like Saint Teresa of Avila and Juan de la Cruz; and its most influential exposition, the *Spiritual Exercises,* was written by Ignatius Loyola (1491–1556), a Spanish soldier turned religious general.

Loyola was the most important figure of the Catholic Reformation.

[19] V. H. H. Green, *Renaissance and Reformation* (London: E. Arnold, 1964), p. 177.

Badly wounded at the age of thirty, after years of riotous living and military campaigning, he started reading devotional books during his long convalescence. He himself explained later that in reading the life of the Lord and the lives of the saints, he paused to think and reason with himself, "Suppose that I should do what Saint Francis did, what Saint Dominic did?" During the next year, withdrawing to a cave in the eastern mountains of Spain, he felt he experienced God; and from his experiences he set out to show others how to do so. The *Spiritual Exercises,* which he then began to write, laid down a four-week course of disciplined meditation, by which the believer was brought in slow stages to subordination of his will, understanding of the worthlessness of the body, horror at the depths of sin, and finally realization of the sublimity of Christ's passion.

The person taking the exercises was directed to specific meditations five times a day—at midnight, on rising in the morning, before or after Mass, at Vespers, and an hour before supper. Among the subjects Loyola allowed for meditation were "death and other punishments of sin." A nineteenth century version of the meditation on death suggests clearly the atmosphere in which the exercises could be conducted:

A few moments after your death. Your body laid on a funeral-bed, wrapped in a shroud, a veil thrown over your face; beside you the crucifix, the holy water, friends, relatives, a priest kneeling by your sad remains . . . the public officer who writes in the register of the dead all the particulars of your decease. . . .

The day after your death. Your inanimate body enclosed in a coffin, covered with a pall, taken from your apartment, sadly carried to the foot of the altar. . . . Consider well the dismal field where the eye sees nothing but tombs; this open grave where they are laying your body. . . .

Some months after your death. Contemplate this stone already blackened by time, this inscription beginning to be effaced; and under that coffin which is crumbling bit by bit, contemplate the sad state of your body.[20]

Loyola also concluded that the Church needed a spiritual army in its service, a new order that would be organized on military lines, owing total obedience to the pope and its own superior, the general. In 1540, the pope recognized his followers as the Society of Jesus, or Jesuits, and gave it the task of combating Protestant heresy in Europe and spreading Catholicism among the heathen. Loyola imposed long years of study of theology and classical learning, so that the Jesuits used education as their primary weapon. Their universities, colleges, and seminaries were founded throughout Europe, and were soon sending out missionaries who were as feared in the Protestant countries as Geneva-trained missionaries were in the Catho-

---

[20] *Manresa, or The Spiritual Exercises of St. Ignatius* (New York: Catholic Publication Society, n.d.), Third Exercise on Death.

lic states. As preachers, the Jesuits won over the masses by simple, telling sermons. As confessors in the royal courts, they began to influence national politics. As missionaries, they fanned out around the globe; their famous saint, Francis Xavier, travelled to Goa, in India, to the pearl-fishers of the Comoro Islands, to Malaya, and Japan.

Missions were backed by repression. In 1542, the pope made the Inquisition an institution with powers throughout the Church of discovering heretics and handing them over to the state for punishment. The zeal of the Inquisition—its use of torture, of secret trials, of extraordinary minutiae of evidence, of informers, and of infamous burnings—soon wiped out Protestantism in Spain and Italy. Its *Index of Forbidden Books*, first issued in 1559, which included all the works of Erasmus, made it extremely difficult for heretical books to circulate in Catholic countries, and was the first effective censorship since the invention of printing. But both the Inquisition and the *Index* strengthened the Protestant will to resist and the Protestant conviction that the pope was an Anti-Christ; and unlike the Jesuits, they were probably harmful to the cause of Catholicism.

By calling the Council of Trent, which met in 1545–1547, 1551–1552, and 1562–1563, the papacy finally recognized that its central battle with the Protestants was doctrinal. Compromise had been considered, first on Erasmian lines and even, for a short time, by giving in to Luther on a few points; but it was rejected. The Council of Trent declared war on all Protestant doctrines, reaffirming in complete intransigence the traditional position of the Church: that councils, popes, and Church Fathers are a source of religious truth in addition to the Bible; that good works are efficacious in salvation; that purgatory exists and that indulgences can reduce a sinner's time there; and that there are seven sacraments, not just two.

A reinvigorated Catholic Church was therefore prepared for an uncompromising counterattack against Protestantism. In many ways the two sides were remarkably similar. They shared a belief in the absolute truth of their own version of religion and of their duty to use all means, including torture and execution, to bring sinners to righteousness. They regarded spiritual life as infinitely more important than the material, but they had found allies to whom religion offered political and economic advantage. But by the middle of the sixteenth century, the two sides had developed decisively different lifestyles. Geneva and Rome symbolize the gulf between the two. While the Genevans were smashing their stained glass windows, breaking the heads off statues, whitewashing their church walls, and enforcing an almost ostentatious austerity of daily life, Rome was embarking on a new artistic boom very different in character from the High Renaissance. Michelangelo, who had dominated Rome's art in the age of Julius II and the Medici popes, moved on to establish an equal dominance over the new art of the Catholic Reformation. In the 1530s, he had created the swirling violence of the *Last Judgment* in the Sistine Chapel; and, as a friend of Loyola, one of his last acts was to design the ground plan for the sensuously dramatic church of the Jesuit order in Rome. For a hundred years, the art of Rome became increasingly ornate, convoluted, sensuous, and emotional, with the development of the baroque style that was chosen by the Catholic Church to carry the message of its revival. Between Catholic and Protestant, there developed almost a physical revulsion, which accounts for much of the savage butchery of the next century.

SUGGESTED READING

Several good studies have been made of the urban influence in the Reformation. On the German cities, Hans Baron, "Religion and Politics in the German Imperial Cities During the Reformation," *English Historical Review,* July 1937, pp. 405–27 and October 1937, pp. 614–33; B. Moeller, *Imperial Cities and the Reformation* (1972); and Steven E. Ozment, *The Reformation in the Cities: The Appeal of Protestantism to Sixteenth Century Germany and Switzerland* (1975). Norman Birnbaum, "The Zwinglian Reformation in Zürich," *Past and Present,* April 1959, pp. 27–47, is an excellent social analysis of the appeal of Zwinglianism, with study of supporters and opponents. For a more detailed account, see Robert C. Walton, *Zwingli's Theocracy* (1971).

Among studies of individual cities, the best is Miriam U. Chrisman, *Strasbourg and the Reform: A Study in the Process of Change* (1967). Also good in relating economic background to religious change are Gerald Strauss, *Nuremberg in the Sixteenth Century* (1966) and E. William Monter, *Calvin's Geneva* (1967). Nuremberg and Geneva are also studied in several articles in Lawrence W. Buck and Jonathan W. Zophy, eds., *The Social History of the Reformation* (1972), which is particularly useful for Robert Kingdom's article on "The Control of Morals in Calvin's Geneva." See also Kingdom's article "Social Welfare in Calvin's Geneva, 1562" in *American Historical Review,* LXXVI, (1971), 50–69 and E. W. Monter's article, "Crime and Punishment in Calvin's Geneva," *Archiv für Reformationsgeschichte* (1973), pp. 281–87.

Much emphasis on social background, including city life, is given in A. G. Dickens, *Reformation and Society in Sixteenth-Century Europe* (1966) and Hajo Holborn, *A History of Modern Germany: The Reformation* (1967). For the comments of Pius II on Germany, *see Memoirs of a Renaissance Pope* (1959). On princes, see Francis L. Carsten, *Princes and Parliaments in Germany* (1959). For good textbooks, consult Harold J. Grimm, *The Reformation Era 1500–1650* (1968) and Lewis Spitz, *The Reformation Movement* (1972). Roland Bainton, *The Reformation of the Sixteenth Century* (1952) is too general, but his *Erasmus of Christendom* (1969) is sympathetic, well focused, and pleasantly readable.

Owen Chadwick, *The Reformation* (1964) is predominantly theological in orientation. V. H. H. Green, *Renaissance and Reformation* (1964) is clear and full. The broad European scene is covered in G. R. Elton, *Reformation Europe, 1517–1559* (1963). An interesting ecumenical reappraisal is made by Lewis W. Spitz *et al., Luther, Erasmus and the Reformation: A Catholic-Protestant Reappraisal* (1969). Excellent sources are presented in Hans J. Hillerbrand, *The Reformation in Its Own Words* (1964).

Luther's early life is described in Gordon Rupp, *Luther's Progress to the Diet of Worms* (1951), and is presented in psychohistorical terms by Erik H. Eriksen, *Young Man Luther: A Study in Psychoanalysis and History* (1962). Most traditional is James Atkinson, *Martin Luther and the Birth of Protestantism* (1968). Roland H. Bainton, *Here*

I Stand: A Life of Martin Luther (1960) is the standard biography, but it can be compared with works by a great French and a great German historian—Lucien Febvre's *Martin Luther: A Destiny* (1955) and Gerhard Ritter's *Luther* (1963).

The life of Zwingli is reliably presented in J. Courvoisier, *Zwingli: A Reformed Theologian* (1964). On the Anabaptists, see G. H. Williams, *The Radical Reformation* (1962), and Claus-Peter Clasen, *Anabaptism: A Social History, 1525–1618* (1972).

The English Reformation is solidly and usefully analyzed in David H. Pill, *The English Reformation, 1529–58* (1973), although the standard work on the period remains G. R. Elton, *England Under the Tudors* (2nd ed., 1974). Elton has also written an elegant biography of the scourge of the English monasteries, in *Reform and Renewal: Thomas Cromwell and the Common Weal* (1973). A reliable biography of Cromwell's master and nemesis is J. J. Scarisbrick, *Henry VIII* (1967). A. G. Dickens, *The English Reformation* (1964) is the work of a major scholar in the field.

With Calvin, it would not be amiss to plunge into *The Institutes of the Christian Religion* (many editions). For the man himself, see F. Wendel, *Calvin* (1963) or the overly appreciative Georgia Harkness, *John Calvin: The Man and His Ethics* (1931); for the movement he founded, see John T. McNeil, *The History and Character of Calvinism* (1954). On the relationship between religion and economic development by the capitalist class, see the statement of theme by Max Weber, *The Protestant Ethic and the Spirit of Capitalism* (1930) or R. H. Tawney, *Religion and the Rise of Capitalism* (1926), and then go to the thoughtful reappraisal of Kurt Samuelsson, *Religion and Economic Action* (1961). The economic activism of Calvin himself is demonstrated in W. Fred Graham, *The Constructive Revolutionary: John Calvin and His Socio-Economic Impact* (1971).

An excellent scholarly presentation by a Catholic historian of the Reformation in the Catholic Church is H. Daniel-Rops, *The Catholic Reformation* (1961), but the best short account is A. G. Dickens, *The Counter-Reformation* (1969). A fuller survey is presented in M. O'Connell, *The Counter-Reformation, 1560–1610* (1974). For the great Catholic figures, see P. Dudon, *St. Ignatius of Loyola* (1949); M. Suclair, *St. Teresa of Avila* (1953); and E. Alison Peers, *St. John of the Cross* (1946).

Two areas that have received much attention from historians in the past few years have been popular piety and charity in the cities and the problem of witchcraft. On the former, see Natalie Z. Davis, *Culture and Society in Early Modern France* (1975), which is especially useful for her study of Lyons; Brian Pullan, *Rich and Poor in Renaissance Venice* (1971); and C. Trinkhaus, ed. *The Pursuit of Holiness in Late Medieval and Renaissance Religion* (1974). Calvin's witchhunt was part of a wider European phenomenon, as can be seen in H. C. Eric Midelfort, *Witchhunting in Southwest Germany, 1562–1684* (1972) and Alan D. MacFarlane, *Withcraft in Tudor and Stuart England* (1970).

13 / *The Lisbon of Manuel the Fortunate and the Madrid of Philip the Prudent*

prosperity, and perhaps in some related way to cultural greatness, as it did for Portugal and Spain in the fifteenth and sixteenth centuries. Up to that time the Atlantic coast of Europe had been of little value to its inhabitants except for fishing and as the route of an occasional Crusade. Visiting Cape Finisterre in Spain, where Europe ends, as the name implies, the Bohemian Leo of Rozmital found:

One sees nothing anywhere but sky and water. They say that the water is so turbulent that no one can cross it and no one knows what lies beyond. It is said that some had tried to find out what was beyond and had sailed with galleys and ships, but not one of them returned.

As to inland Portugal, just to the south, it was dreadfully poverty-stricken.

One finds nothing to eat or drink for man or beast. This is because no roads are built there. It happens often that no traveller is seen there for four or five years. The people build in hollows in the mountains or under the earth. They go out very seldom, especially not at noon on account of the great heat, but work and do their business mostly by night. They live mostly on fruit and drink no wine.[1]

[1] Malcolm Letts, ed., *The Travels of Leo of Rozmital* (Cambridge: Cambridge University Press, 1957), p. 100.

Early Sixteenth-Century Portuguese Galleon   National Maritime Museum, Greenwich, England

Yet Spain and Portugal, which both had suffered economically throughout their history from their isolation on the periphery of the known world, were ideally located to launch the first great voyages of discovery in the North and South Atlantic Ocean. Their pioneering voyages, followed by the establishment of trading posts and the planting of colonies, were undertaken by Spain and Portugal at least a hundred years before the other countries of the Atlantic seaboard possessed the skills, the daring, the political stability, and perhaps even the desire, to seek a share in these lucrative ventures.

The lead was taken by the Portuguese monarchs of the house of Aviz, which sponsored the development of the necessary maritime technology and financed the first expeditions down the unexplored coast of Africa. Between 1419, when they discovered the island of Madeira and 1497–99, when Vasco da Gama rounded the Cape of Good Hope to discover the route to India, the Portuguese established trading and slaving centers on the Atlantic islands and the African coast. In 1509, a Portuguese expedition discovered Brazil. Ten years later, Magellan embarked on the first expedition to circumnavigate the globe. As a result of these voyages, Portugal acquired a trading empire that stretched from South America to Macao in China, and knew, perhaps for the first time in its history, the flush of material prosperity, which reached its height in the dramatic transformation of its capital city Lisbon during the reign of King Manuel the Fortunate.

The first expedition sponsored by Spain was Christopher Columbus's voyage of 1492, in which he discovered the Bahamas and several Caribbean islands. By 1530, however, Spanish navigators and military adventurers called *conquistadores* had established a vast new colonial empire in the Carib-

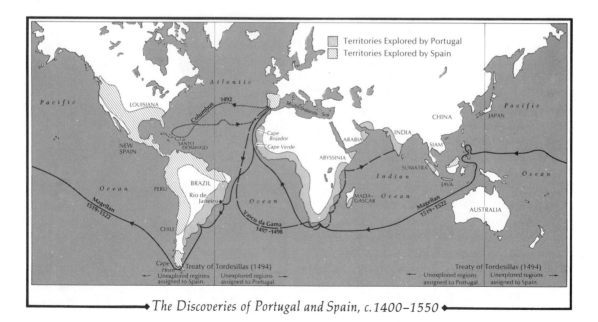

◆ *The Discoveries of Portugal and Spain, c. 1400–1550* ◆

bean and on the ruins of the Aztec empire in Mexico and the Inca empire in South America. Although in the Aztec capital of Tenochtitlán, which is now Mexico City, the Spaniards had acquired one of the most distinctive urban creations of all civilization, they totally leveled it to create in its place a beautiful but distinctively European form of city. From the agriculture and the mines, particularly of gold and silver, in their colonial empire, the Spanish derived a vast new source of wealth that poured into Spain to transform its economy and its society. Although the colonial trade was funneled through the southern port of Seville, it is to Madrid, the new Spanish capital chosen by King Philip II in 1561, that we must look to comprehend the blessing and the curse of colonial empire upon Spain.

The Lisbon of Manuel the Fortunate

When Lisbon was recaptured from the Moors in 1147, after more than four hundred years of occupation, it was a very different city from the flourishing Arab centers like Seville and Cordoba. According to an English Crusader who took part in the conquest, "The buildings of the city were so

closely packed together that, except in the merchants' quarter, hardly a street could be found which was more than eight feet wide. The cause of so great a population was that there was no prescribed form of religion among them, for everyone was a law unto himself; the most depraved elements from all parts of the world had flowed together as it were into a cesspool, and had formed a breeding ground of every lust and abomination."[2] The development of an elementary foreign trade in the thirteenth century, through the exchange of wine, salt, and dried fruits for cloth and luxury goods, brought a fairly rapid expansion of the merchant community; and the king made a sound choice

Manuel   Radio Times Hulton Picture Library

when he transferred his court there, establishing himself in the impregnable royal castle on one of the two high hills that loomed over the flat, rectangu-

[2] Cited in H. V. Livermore, *A History of Portugal* (Cambridge: Cambridge University Press, 1947), p. 75.

(Opposite Page)
Panorama of Lisbon in the Sixteenth Century
The new royal palace of King Manuel adjoins the quays on the Tagus River. The older streets of the Alfama quarter twist up the hills to the Castle of Saint George.
Bildarchiv d. Ost. Nation-albibliothek

lar business quarter by the riverfront. Lisbon was the natural capital of the country. It possessed the better of the country's two good harbors, easily accessible to the ocean on the slow-flowing waters of the broad Tagus River known to the citizens as the Sea of Straw. It lay on the country's north-south routes; it was easily defensible from attack by sea or land, as Napoleon was to discover later; and from the fertile plains beside the Tagus, it could initially feed itself. By the end of the fourteenth century, it had a population of about forty thousand. Lawyers, bureaucrats, and physicians numbered about a thousand; and the majority of the lay population were engaged in commerce, the artisan trades, or shipbuilding. The merchant guilds by 1385 had sufficient power to be able to force a change of dynasty, by recognizing John of Aviz, a bastard son of the previous king, as Defender of the Realm and shortly after as king, against the wishes of the aristocracy and the clergy.

The Lisbon of Manuel the Fortunate

Period Surveyed	Years of oceanic explorations between discovery of Madeira (1419) and voyage of Vasco da Gama (1497–1499), especially the reign of King Manuel I (1495–1521)
Population	100,000
Area	2.4 square miles
Form of Government	Absolute monarchy
Political Leaders	Prince Henry the Navigator; King John II; King Manuel I
Economic Base	Spice trade with India and Far East. Port services. Royal bureaucracy. Slave trade
Intellectual Life	Poetry (Camões); Painting (Nuno Gonçalves)
Principal Buildings	Jeronomos monastery; Tower of Belem; Royal Warehouse (Casa da India); Royal palace
Religion	Catholic

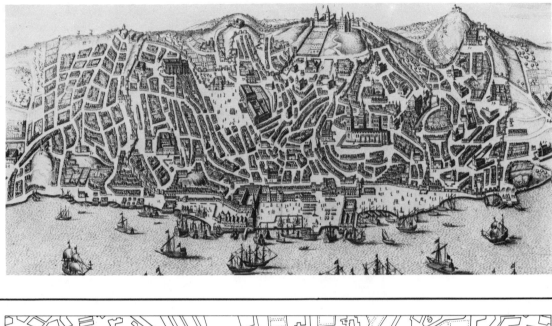

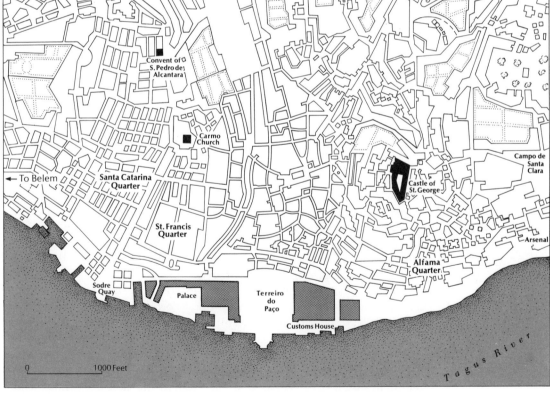

Convent of
S. Pedro de
Alcantara

Carmo
Church

To Belem →

Santa Catarina
Quarter

St. Francis
Quarter

Castle of
St. George

Campo de
Santa
Clara

Arsenal

Alfama
Quarter

Sodre
Quay

Palace

Terreiro
do
Paço

Customs House

Tagus River

0   1000 Feet

Prince Henry the Navigator, by Nuno Gonçalves
The panel of the Infanta *from the* Veneration of Saint Vincent *portrays the founder of Portugal's overseas empire and other members of the royal family.* Museo Nacional de Arte Antiga

Prince Henry the Navigator

John brought to Portugal an English alliance that has lasted to this day, the military strength to hold off the threat of Spain for two hundred years, and five talented sons. The third, known to foreigners though not to the Portuguese as Prince Henry the Navigator, was the brains and the will power behind Portugal's first great maritime discoveries. Henry was quiet, pious, and single-minded in his ambition to open up the coast of west Africa and the islands of the Atlantic to Portuguese trade and settlement. As a young man, he had taken part in an expedition against the Moslem city of Ceuta, across the straits from Gibraltar, which the Portuguese had kept as a garrison city surrounded by hostile Arabs; and there his imagination had been excited by the description of the great trade routes across the Sahara that met at Timbuktu, of the wide river basins of the Senegal and Niger, and of the legendary Christian empire of Prester John in Ethiopia.

To carry out a program of maritime exploration, Henry left the court of Lisbon, and moved to the southwest tip of Portugal, the rocky promontory of Sagres on Cape Vincent. Here ships creeping up the coast from Gibraltar met the full force of Atlantic gales and many, in Henry's own words, "departed this life and were thrown about these rocks and on the beach." It was, however, the point in Portugal nearest to Africa; it had a good harbor in the nearby town of Lagos, and offered no distraction from the essential tasks Henry set the circle of experts he gathered round him: ship design, chart-drawing, astronomical observation, and instrument making. At Sagres, he brought together and made available to his captains all the contemporary maritime technology: the charts called *portalani* that Italian and Catalan sailors had been using to show courses along accurately mapped coastlines in the Mediterranean, the compass and thirty-point compass card; and the astrolabe and quadrant for measuring altitude of heavenly bodies, as a means of finding latitude. His shipbuilders developed the *caravel*, a light maneuverable ship that replaced the oar-driven galleys, into a magnificent carrier for braving the open ocean, particularly when a combination of square and triangular, or lateen, sails was adopted late in the century. And he gave members of his own entourage specific tasks of exploration to carry out as captains of his vessels, sending them back patiently

A Portalano of the North and South American Coasts, 1555–1563
Bildarchiv d. Ost. Nationalbibliothek

PRINCIPAL VOYAGES OF DISCOVERY IN THE FIFTEENTH AND SIXTEENTH CENTURIES			
Year	*Explorer*	*Sponsor of Voyage*	*Area Explored*
1418–60	Various captains	Portugal (Henry the Navigator)	Madeira, Azores, west African coast to Cape Verde
1487–88	Bartholomew Dias	Portugal (John II)	African coast to Cape of Good Hope
1492	Christopher Columbus	Spain (Ferdinand and Isabella)	Bahamas, Santo Domingo
1493	Christopher Columbus	Spain (Ferdinand and Isabella)	West Indian islands
1497–98	John Cabot	England (Henry VII)	Newfoundland, Nova Scotia
1497–99	Vasco da Gama	Portugal (Manuel I)	Cape of Good Hope, Indian Ocean to Western India
1498	John and Sebastian Cabot	England (Henry VII)	Expedition lost at sea
1498	Christopher Columbus	Spain (Ferdinand and Isabella)	Trinidad, Venezuela
1499	Amerigo Vespucci	Spain (Ferdinand and Isabella)	Northeastern coast of South America
1500	Pedro Alvares Cabral	Portugal (Manuel I)	Brazil, Indian Ocean route to western India
1502 1504	Christopher Columbus	Spain (Ferdinand and Isabella)	Central American coast
1519–22	Ferdinand Magellan	Spain (Charles V)	First circumnavigation of globe. Cape Horn, Pacific Ocean
1524	Giovanni Verrazano	France (Francis I)	American coast from Virginia to Newfoundland
1533, 1534	Jacques Cartier	France (Francis I)	Quebec, St. Lawrence River
1577–80	Francis Drake	England (Elizabeth)	Circumnavigation of globe. Cape Horn, West coast of North and South America

until they had accomplished their goal. This patience was most evident in the primary task that had held up all exploration of the African coast, the rounding of Cape Bojador to the south of Morocco. The first voyages, which led to the rediscovery and settlement of Madeira and the Azores, were easily carried out, and profitable from the start, with the rapid development there of sugar and wine production. But Cape Bojador was thought of as the end of the known world, beyond which lay what the Arabs called the green sea of darkness, and a tropical sun so hot that it turned white men black. Cape Bojador was finally passed in 1434, and later expeditions pushed slowly down the flat, forbidding coast, through vicious gales and heavy waves, to reach Cape Blanco. From here, in 1441, one of Henry's captains brought back some gold dust and a group of Negro slaves, who were baptized and sold.

Goals of Portuguese Overseas Exploration

The motives driving Henry to this unrelenting activity, as outlined by his contemporary biographer Gomes Eannes de Azurara, are basic to all Portuguese and Spanish imperialism of the next two centuries:

You should note well that the noble spirit of this Prince, by a sort of natural constraint, was ever urging him both to begin and to carry out very great deeds. For which reason, after the taking of Ceuta he always kept ships well armed against the Infidel, both for war, and because he had also a wish to know the land that lay beyond the isles of Canary and that Cape called Bojador, for up to his time, neither by writings, nor by the memory of man, was known with any certainty the nature of the land beyond that Cape. . . . Seeing also that no other prince took any pains in this matter, he sent out his own ships against those parts, to have manifest certainty of them all. . . . And this was the first reason of his action.

The second reason was that if there chanced to be in those lands some population of Christians, or some havens, into which it would be possible to sail without peril, many kinds of merchandise might be brought to this realm, which would find a ready market, and reasonably so, because no other people of these parts traded with them, nor yet people of any other that were known; and also the products of this realm might be taken there, which traffic would bring great profit to our countrymen.[3]

Four further reasons, Eannes continued, were Henry's desire to discover the power of the Moslem enemy, to find if any Christian king such as Prester John would help him against the heathen, to spread Christianity to the heathen, and to follow the advice of his astrologers.

---

[3] Gomes Eannes de Azurara, *The Chronicle of the Discovery and Conquest of Guinea*, trans. C. R. Bagley and E. Prestage (London: Hakluyt Society, 1896), I, 27–29.

The combination of the crusading motive, so natural to the Portuguese and Spanish after centuries of effort in driving the Moslem peoples from their homelands, and missionary zeal was a prime driving force in all their imperial efforts. It won them papal support expressed in a series of bulls, giving plenary indulgences to those who died in Africa and granting to the Portuguese a monopoly from west Africa to the Indies of discovery, conquest, and trade. Genuine scientific interest in the fruits of geographical discovery was also a real factor. The journals of one of Henry's captains, Cadamosto, are a compendium of fascinating information on social customs, diet, trade patterns, clothing, climate, and so on. But even for Prince Henry, the economic motive was central, or at least became so when the potential profits were glimpsed. The monarchy granted Henry not only a monopoly on trade with all lands discovered by his expeditions but also monopolies on tuna fishing on the southern coast of Portugal, on sugar importation, and on the soap industry. He was thus the principal person to profit from the diversion of the gold deliveries away from the Sahara trade to Portuguese vessels and from the beginning of a large-scale slave trade with the chiefs of Senegal and Guinea. Henry, however, unlike the Lisbon merchants to whom he conceded trading rights, spent far more than he made on his voyages of exploration, and he died in debt.

The commercial and missionary value of the Guinea coast led Henry to establish at Arguin island the first European trading center and fortress overseas, a type of settlement that was to lead to the establishment of all the great European colonial empires. Exploration continued, and the Gambia River had been reached by the time of Henry's death in 1460. Henry had thus vastly increased the technical capacity of Portuguese ships, explored 1,500 miles of west African coast, made Madeira and the Azores flourishing Portuguese possessions, and established commerce with the west African tribes in slaves, gold, and ivory.

After Henry's death, the west African monopoly was given to a wealthy Lisbon merchant, who increased his fortune while sponsoring further expeditions down the African coast. They provided the disappointing discovery that the African coast turns south again at the mouth of the Niger; they had therefore not yet found a new sea route to the Indies. King John II (reigned 1481–1495), an able, enthusiastic and ruthless colonialist, then decided to send Bartholomew Dias on the great voyage in 1487, during which he discovered the Cape of Good Hope. His most famous decision, however, was his refusal to finance Christopher Columbus when the Genoese navigator proposed that he discover a route to India by sailing due west across the Atlantic. The opening of the sea route round Africa to give Portugal the chance to break Venice's hold on the Asian spice trade was in the short run a far more lucrative course; it was John's most important contribution to Portugal. His successor, King Manuel the Fortunate (reigned 1495–1521), was to see the plan succeed to perfection.

Panel of the Archbishop, by Nuno Gonçalves (Active 1450–1471) *Gonçalves's most famous painting, his many-paneled* Veneration of Saint Vincent *of about 1460, portrays not only the royal family but the leading knights, monks, bankers, doctors, and even beggars of fifteenth-century Lisbon.* Courtesy Museu Nacional de Arte Antiga, Lisbon

Transformation of Lisbon Under Manuel the Fortunate

During Manuel's reign, Lisbon was changed as completely as Athens under Pericles. The opening of the west African trade had already begun to transform both the economic and social character of the city. Lagos had soon been abandoned in favor of the far better harbor of Lisbon, and along the wharfs of the Ribeira Velha huge warehouses and shipbuilding yards had been constructed in the very heart of the city. While there had been little stimulus to manufactures, the merchants had become specialized in the import of those European goods needed for barter in Africa, such as woolen cloth from Britain, copper and lead from Germany, and cereals from northern Europe, and in the sale of oddities like parrots and monkeys, and more important items like slaves and west African pepper. A permanent slave market on the waterfront sold one hundred fifty thousand Negro slaves before 1500, and the household slave became common in the well-to-do homes of Lisbon. The mass of the laborers in Lisbon had gained almost nothing from the voyages, and they remained turbulent and violent, especially in their occasional massacres of Jews; and the monarchy spent most of the year wandering among its palaces in the quieter and more salubrious countryside.

Manuel, however, was determined to make Lisbon into a genuine royal capital, a Renaissance city embellished from the wealth of its overseas commerce. He moved the court from the uncomfortable medieval citadel on the steep Alfama Hill down to the water's edge, with his windows overlooking the incoming shipping. He combined aristocratic grandeur with commercial astuteness. The upper floors of the palace were devoted to a stylized court life, in which the members of seventy-two noble families joined him in a round of receptions, banquets, balls, and concerts. "Every Sunday and saint's day he dined and supped with music of pipes, sackbuts, horns, harps, tambourines, fiddles and on special festivals with drums and trumpets that all played each one after its kind while he ate," his chronicler remarked. But the ground floor of the palace was reserved for the *Casa da Mina,* the offices and storehouse where the king controlled his monopoly of Guinea gold that was coined into the *cruzados,* the gold coin used to pay for Portugal's imports. Not content with one palace, Manuel built lavishly throughout the city, erecting other palaces and churches, and encouraging the nobility and religious orders to do the same.

Establishment of the Portuguese Colonial Empire

Manuel's greatest monument, the Jeronomos monastery at Belem a little way down the Tagus, was built to celebrate the greatest achievement of his reign, the opening of the sea route to India by Vasco da Gama in 1497–1499. Manuel was well aware that secret voyages in the South Atlantic sent out by King John had brought Portuguese sailors to the point where they were prepared technically for a major expedition to India itself; and he may have had a report on trading conditions in the Indian Ocean ports prepared by a spy who actually reached the kingdom of Prester John in Ethiopia. Like everyone else in Lisbon, he had been shocked when Columbus sailed into the Tagus in 1493 with the claim that he had discoverd India by sailing west. He determined to profit at once from the Treaty of Tordesillas (1494), by which the Spanish and Portuguese had agreed that land and sea west of a line passing 360 leagues to the west of Cape Verde Islands and joining the poles should be Spain's sphere of exploration and all to the east of that line Portuguese; for the treaty had given the Portuguese a free hand in the Indian Ocean. He picked Vasco da Gama, a tested sailor in his thirties, to take charge of four ships, two of which were specially built for the voyage, and a crew of 170. They were supplied with the most up-to-date nautical equipment, a treatise on seamanship, stone pillars to place as signs of overlordship, and surprisingly unsuitable goods for trade and inadequate presents for Indian princes. In exploration they were masters, in trade they still had much to learn of the East. After spending the night in vigil at a little church in Belem, da Gama and his crew marched in ceremonial procession to the shore, amid a great crowd who knew quite well the importance of the voyage for Lisbon's future.

The Tower of Belem
This tower in Manueline style was built, on the beach from which Vasco da Gama set sail in 1497 for India, to defend the mouth of the Tagus River. Heyward Associates, Inc. photo

Da Gama first followed the well-known route to the Canaries and west Africa; but after a few days in the Cape Verde islands, he struck far out into the Atlantic, and in a great semicircular voyage that kept him out of sight of land longer than any previous sailor—from August to November 1497—he reached the southern tip of Africa. Proceeding up the Arab-controlled coast of east Africa, as far as present-day Kenya, he found a superb Indian pilot who brought him easily to the great spice port of Calicut on the Malabar coast of India. There was no great enthusiasm to hail him as the first European to sail to an Indian port. Two Spanish-speaking Arabs met his first landing party with he words: "What the devil has brought you here?" Their reply, "We have come to seek Christians and spices," provoked the deflating question, "Why does not the king of Castile, the King of France, or the Signoria of Venice send hither?" His trinkets and cloth despised, his presents contemptuously received, da Gama still succeeded in getting a cargo of pepper, cinnamon, and other spices; and after a harrowing year he returned to Lisbon in September 1499 with only two ships and two-thirds of his men. Manuel, however, had reason to be excited. Not only did the one cargo brought back cover his costs several times over, his sailors had found the sea route to the quickest source of wealth in his world, the provision of the spices that had made Venice the envy of Europe. He took the grandiose title of "Lord of Guinea and of the conquest of the navigation and commerce of Ethiopia, Arabia, Persia, and India"; he changed the name of the royal warehouse to the Casa da India, and took for himself the monopoly of the commerce in spices; and he made immediate plans to use force to break the Arab hold on the Indian spice trade.

A new fleet sent the next year under Pedro Alvares Cabral veered off course westward, and discovered Brazil before continuing to India. Annual fleets, heavily armed, engaged poorly armed Moslem ships without great losses; and from 1509, a carefully conceived network of ports controlling the Indian Ocean was conquered. "Golden Goa," seized from its sultan in 1510, became the principal Portuguese center on the Indian coast; and even more ambitious expeditions were sent to gain control of the entrance to the Persian Gulf by conquest of the city of Ormuz and to gain direct access to the spice trade of southeast Asia by seizure of Malacca, near present-day Singapore. From Malacca, it was an easy journey to Canton in China itself, and Portugal soon gained the right to establish a trading post at Macao at the mouth of the Canton River. The Portuguese thus acquired a sea empire, controlled by its fleets and linked over enormous distances by a chain of fortress cities and "factories."

Lisbon's Brief Prosperity

Lisbon was the heart of this empire; and by the death of Manuel, it had become perhaps the greatest entrepôt in the world. It had succeeded in gaining a monopoly, or at least a large share of the import trade in every African and Asian product desired in Europe: African gold and slaves, Madeira sugar, Indonesian pepper, Ceylon cinnamon, Ternate cloves, Chinese silk and porcelain, Japanese silver, Persian horses. And it had become a principal purchaser of the European products that would be sent out to the East. It had frequent sailings to Antwerp, through which it sold its tropical goods to northern Europe. It continued to grow throughout the century, until with a population of a hundred thousand, it was one of Europe's twelve largest cities. Lisbon itself, however, soon showed signs of the weaknesses of the empire. Supplying soldiers, sailors, administrators, and merchants for a world empire from a population of just over a million proved an excessive burden. Portuguese military strength was insufficient to maintain the claimed monopoly of spices in the Indian Ocean, when Venetian ships began to compete again in the 1520s. The Portuguese economy failed to profit fully from the opportunities of empire as a result of the lack of both a solid banking system to finance the mercantile ventures and the native industry to supply the demand for exports. Inflation inevitably followed the influx of Guinea gold and the collapse in export prices caused by an oversupply of spices and sugar. Manuel's Lisbon enjoyed a brief, heady period of glory, to be followed by deep disillusionment. "No beggars equal those of Portugal for strength of lungs, luxuriance of sores, profusion of vermin, variety and arrangement of tatters, and dauntless perseverance," wrote one eighteenth-century visitor.

The atmosphere of those years when a century of daring exploration suddenly paid off, or so it seemed, can be felt today in the monastery of Belem, amazingly preserved from the great earthquake of 1755 that destroyed the whole center of Lisbon, and in Portugal's greatest poem, the *Lusiads* of Luiz Vaz de Camões (1524–1580). Both were inspired by Vasco da Gama. Manuel devoted a fixed portion of his profits from the spice monopoly to erect a monastery in flamboyant Gothic style by the Tagus beach from which Vasco da Gama had sailed. A vast building, with fan vaulting and delicately carved columns, the Jeronomos monastery is most notable for its decoration in carved stone. All over the building, around windows and doorways, on roofs and walls, there is a lavishly exciting lacework of decorative motifs, many of which seem to come directly from the ships and lands they discovered—twisted ropes, shells, tropical foliage, coral, sea gulls, waves, fruits. The unique style was named Manueline; and in this style Manuel constructed the great funeral chapel for his family at Batalha, whose unfinished columns still symbolize the unrealizable dreams of the Lord of Guinea.

The *Lusiads*, published in 1572, is an undisguised, and wholly successful, attempt to rewrite Virgil's *Aeneid*, using the vehicle of the epic poem to describe the voyage of da Gama and the past glories of Portugal. Camões begins:

This is the story of heroes, who leaving their native Portugal behind them opened a way to Ceylon, and further, across seas no man had ever sailed before. They were men of no ordinary stature, equally at home in war and in

The Cloister of Batalha Monastery
The fretwork of stone-carving in the Manueline style recalls the exquisite carving of the Indian temples that Portugal's navigators had just visited. Manuel planted the cloister garden with luxuriant semitropical plants that trailed over the carvings.   Author's photo

dangers of every kind: they founded a new kingdom among distant peoples, and made it great. It is the story too of a line of kings who kept ever advancing the boundaries of faith and empire, spreading havoc among the infidels of Africa and Asia and achieving immortality through their illustrious exploits. If my inspiration but prove equal to the task, all men shall know of them.

Let us hear no more then of Ulysses and Aeneas and their long journeyings, no more of Alexander and Trajan and their famous victories. My theme is the daring and renown of the Portuguese, to whom Neptune and Mars alike give homage. The heroes and the poets of old have had their day; another and loftier conception of valour has arisen.[4]

Yet one feature of Camões's poem has made the Portuguese wonder if he was serious about his whole epic, a speech he gave to an old man who, watching da Gama depart from Belem, condemned the whole idea of the Indian voyage. Perhaps the great poet had understood what a Lisbon observer wrote in 1608:

The price of the brilliant discoveries, the bravery and endurance, was that as we went forward in the discovery of the world, the cultivation of Portugal grew worse and the rural population diminished. . . . If we consider what is to be seen in this city [of Lisbon] from the East Indies: spices, amber, pearls, precious stones and other things of great esteem, and gold from the mines it will be seen to exceed greatly what could have been imported by the fleet of Solomon. Yet all this wealth from the conquests, in India, which brought to Lisbon parrots in golden cages, gave us no fields in which to sow or to pasture cattle, or laborers to cultivate fields. On the contrary, it took away those who might have served us in this. . . . I do not put much faith in Indian things. Let men occupy themselves with the things that they have at home.[5]

Tenochtitlán and the Conquest of the Americas

During the first half of the sixteenth century, while Portugal was acquiring a commercial empire in Africa and Asia, its powerful neighbor and rival Spain was acquiring a very different but equally lucrative empire in the Americas. Spain's colonial empire was organized around two great cities. In Spain itself, Seville, the Atlantic port on the river Guadalquivir, was given a monopoly of the American trade and rose as a consequence to be the fifth largest city in Europe, with a population by 1588 of one hundred and fifty thousand. In New Spain, the area roughly equivalent to modern Mexico,

---

[4] Luiz Vaz de Camões, *The Lusiads,* trans. William C. Atkinson (Harmondsworth, England: Penguin, 1952), p. 39.
[5] J. B. Trend, *Portugal* (London: Ernest Benn, 1957), p. 146.

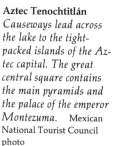

Aztec Tenochtitlán
Causeways lead across the lake to the tight-packed islands of the Aztec capital. The great central square contains the main pyramids and the palace of the emperor Montezuma. Mexican National Tourist Council photo

The Tenochtitlán of Montezuma

Period Surveyed	Reign of emperor Montezuma (1502–1520) and Spanish conquest of Mexico (1519–1521)
Population	80,000
Area	5 square miles
Form of Government	Despotic emperor; empire of subordinate tribes owing tribute to Aztec central government
Economic Base	Agriculture in valley of Mexico; tribute from empire (food, raw materials, money); manufacturing (cotton clothing, feather goods, goldsmith work); central market
Intellectual Life	Monumental sculpture; pyramids; astronomy
Principal Buildings	Palace of Montezuma; Great Temple; causeways; aqueducts
Public Entertainment	Religious festivals (including human sacrifice); military celebrations of victory; dancing; music; games of chance
Religion	Polytheism (especially Quetzalcoatl, Tlaloc)

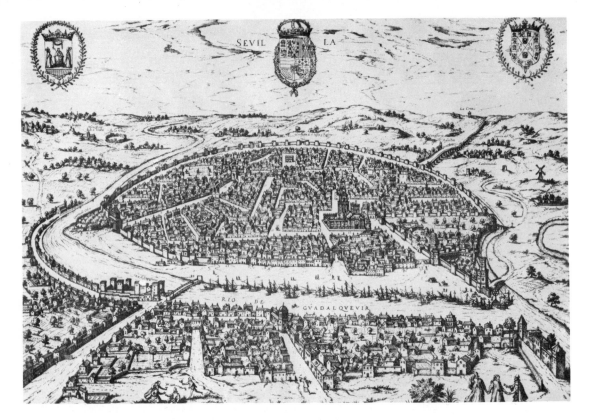

Sixteenth-Century Seville
The fleets from America cluster in the docks of the river Guadalquivir. In the center of town is the huge Gothic cathedral, with its belltower that was once the minaret of the Arab mosque.

Guatemala, and the southern United States, Tenochtitlán, the capital city of the Aztec emperor Montezuma, was renamed Mexico and made the administrative center of the Spanish possessions. During the sixteenth century it had the astonishing population of over a hundred thousand. In comparison with these vast, flourishing cities, Madrid was a provincial backwater, favored by the monarchy only for the excellent hunting nearby and the stimulating weather of its dry uplands. Madrid became the capital of Spain, and consequently a boom town, in 1561, when the absolute monarch Philip II decided to move court and bureaucracy there permanently; and owing to its function as ceremonial and administrative capital, it soon became the cultural and more slowly the financial capital of Spain.

The Voyages of Christopher Columbus

This new phase in Spain's history began dramatically in 1492. King Ferdinand of Aragon and Queen Isabella of Castile, whose marriage had unified most of Spain, had completed the reconquest of the peninsula from the Moslems by capturing Granada in January. Three months later, they agreed to send Christopher Columbus, a Genoese sea captain, to sail westward across the Atlantic to "discover and acquire islands and mainland in the

Ocean Sea," by which they meant Japan and China. Their motives were mixed. If Columbus reached the East, they hoped to begin missionary work and to win new military aid in their continuing crusade against the Moslems. They would win control of the Asian spice trade before the Portuguese, and might well restore the financial stability of the monarchy. A large crusading army, keyed up with the intense fervor of the Granada campaign, was ready for a new Crusade and new spoils. Finally, the Spaniards had already acquired colonial experience in settling the Canaries, and were profiting from the production of sugar and wine by a subjugated native population. They were prepared to do the same in any new islands Columbus might discover.

It was Caribbean islands and not the Asian mainland that Columbus did find when he made his first landfall on October 12, after thirty-three days of uneventful sailing from the Canary Islands. That exciting day, when Europeans first set eyes on America, is described in Columbus's *Journal*:

Thursday, October 11th/ He navigated to the west-south-west; they had a rougher sea than they had experienced during the whole voyage. They saw petrels and a green reed near the ship. Those in the caravel Pinta *saw a cane and a stick, and they secured another small stick, carved, as it appeared, with iron, and a piece of cane, and other vegetation which grows on land, and a small board. Those in the caravel* Nina *also saw other indications of land and a stick loaded with barnacles. At these signs, all breathed again and rejoiced. . . . Two hours after midnight, land appeared, at a distance of about two leagues from them. They took in all sail . . . and kept jogging, waiting for day, a Friday, on which they reached a small island of the Lucayos, which is called in the language of the Indians "Guanahani." Immediately they saw naked people, and the admiral went ashore in the armed boat. . . . When they had landed they saw very green trees and much water and fruit of various kinds. The admiral called the two Captains and the others who had landed . . . and said that they should bear witness and testimony how he, before them all, took possession of the island, as in fact he did, for the King and Queen his Sovereigns.*[6]

Columbus made the best of what he found—the medicinal plants, the gold plugs the natives wore in their noses,the many unknown fruits, the tractability of the islanders—but pressed on to his real object, Japan, which he thought must be a nearby island. From the Bahamas, he moved to Cuba and Hispaniola; but with his flagship wrecked, he was forced to return to Spain. He found a favoring wind to the north of his outward route and fought stormy weather to reach the Azores and Lisbon, before he was finally able to dock in Seville in March. He was convinced that he had found the Indies, and remained so until his death. Ferdinand and Isabella wisely decided to

---

[6] *The Journal of Christopher Columbus* (London: Anthony Blon and the Orion Press, 1960), pp. 22–23.

settle the islands at once; and they sent Columbus back the same year with seventeen ships and twelve hundred colonists. On his second trip, he explored the south coast of Cuba and discovered Jamaica; but the settlement in Hispaniola was rebellious and mishandled by Columbus. On his third voyage in 1498, he found Trinidad and the mouth of the Orinoco River in Venezuela; but the Spanish monarchs had replaced him as governor, and he was sent home in irons by his successor. He was given one more expedition in 1502, in which he explored Costa Rica and the coast of Honduras; but, dismissed from all governmental power and disappointed in his hope of finding the spice islands, Columbus withdrew to embittered but wealthy retirement.

By then, the Spaniards had concluded that he had found a new and extremely large continent, and that they ought to profit from what he had found rather than lament what he had not. Settlers were sent in large numbers to the West Indian islands, where they caused death to the natives by the introduction of infection and by overworking them. The little gold was soon exhausted; and the islands became a source of tropical products like sugar cane for Europe and a launching point for expeditions to the mainland. The most important settlement made was on the Isthmus of Panama, the town of Darien planted by Balboa. He was the first of the great Spanish conquerors, or *conquistadores,* and in 1513 led the exploring party that first sighted the Pacific Ocean. It had become clear that fortunes could be made from pearl-fishing, slavery, and gold; and Magellan's great voyage in 1519–1522 under Spanish sponsorship, that took him around Cape Horn and across the Pacific to the Moluccas, only served to discourage the Spanish from challenging the Portuguese monopoly in Asia. The Straits of Magellan, it was clear, could not be turned into a reliable trade route, since it took Magellan himself thirty-eight days to get through the towering seas of Cape Horn.

Aztec Mosaic Mask
Masks held a special place in the cultures of prehispanic Mexico. This mask of turquoise mosaics, with mother-of-pearl teeth and eyes, probably dates from the fifteenth century.
Mexican National Tourist Council

Conquest of Mexico

From 1519 to 1550, the Spanish concentrated on acquiring a land empire in Central America and South America. In 1519, Cortés led an expedition of six hundred men, with sixteen horses, a few cannon, and thirteen muskets from Cuba to the coast of the mainland at Vera Cruz. "We came here to serve God and the king, and also to get rich," wrote one of his footsoldiers. Their minds filled with the glamorous stories of the last chivalric novels, their ambition stimulated with the prospect of social advancement within the nobility of Spain, their greed whetted with the rumors of the riches of the inland empire of the Aztecs, Cortés's men were ready to attack an empire of perhaps a million people. Cortés led them from the steamy jungles of the Caribbean coast up the steep escarpment that protected the valley of Mexico. The villages appeared increasingly prosperous as they advanced, and the signs of wealth and civilization grew. Finally, they saw to their

Tenochtitlan.

Meeting of Cortés with the Aztec Emperor Montezuma
From the so-called Lienzo de Tlaxcalla of 1555–1564. Courtesy of the American Museum of Natural History

amazement the vast lake city of Tenochtitlán, as large as most of the great cities of Europe and in many ways more attractive. Four days after he had beguiled the emperor Montezuma into permitting him and his men to enter the city peacefully, Montezuma led him and his captains to the top of the city's central pyramid and, according to Cortés:

. . . told him to look at the great city and all the other towns nearby on the lake and the many villages built on the dry land. . . . This great accursed temple was so high that from the top of it everything could be seen perfectly. And from up there we saw the three causeways that led into Mexico—the causeway of Iztapalapan, by which we had come four days earlier; the causeway of Tlacopan, by which we were later to flee, on the night of our great defeat . . . and that of Tepeyacac. We saw the aqueduct that comes from Chapultepec to supply the town with sweet water, and at intervals along the three causeways the bridges which let the water flow from one part of the lake to another. We saw a multitude of boats upon the great lake, some coming with provisions, some going off loaded with merchandise . . . and in these towns we saw temples and oratories shaped like towers and bastions, all shining white, a wonderful thing to behold. And we saw the terraced houses, and along the causeways other towers and chapels that looked like fortresses. So, having gazed at all this and

Great Temple of Tenochtitlán, Reconstructed by Ignacio Marquina
Courtesy of the American Museum of Natural History

reflected upon it, we turned our eyes to the great market-place and the host of people down there who were buying and selling: the hum and the murmur of their voices could have been heard for more than a league. And among us were soldiers who had been in many parts of the world, at Constantinople, all over Italy and at Rome; and they all said they had never seen a market so well ordered, so large and so crowded with people.[7]

Pre-Colombian Civilization in the Americas

Cortés had found one of the world's great cities. For the preceding fifteen hundred years the Indians of America had been creating a high quality of civilization, without benefit of contact with Asia, from which they originated, or with Europe or Africa. They had created a food surplus by cultivating native American plants, especially maize or corn, beans, squash, and potato. Cities had been built as elaborate ceremonial centers regulated by a large priestly group, who organized the peasant majority to carry out enormous manual tasks building temples and roads and irrigating the land.

[7] Jacques Soustelle, *The Daily Life of the Aztecs on the Eve of the Spanish Conquest* (London: Weidenfeld and Nicolson, 1955), pp. 10–11.

In these cities, stone sculpture, metalworking, astronomy, and engineering were developed; and often a certain amount of commercial exchange took place. By the fifteenth century, the Mayan peoples of Yucatán and Guatemala, perhaps the most creative of all the Indians in science and art, had broken up into quarreling states, and their temple complexes had been abandoned for centuries. In Peru, the Incas had consolidated a large number of city-states into an integrated empire, linked by miraculous roads and governed despotically and bureaucratically by the Great Inca from his capital of Cuzco. Unlike the Incas, who used their troops to maintain the cohesion of their empire, the Aztecs in Mexico went to war primarily to seize human victims for sacrifice to their insatiable gods, especially the infamous Quetzalcoatl. They overran the highly advanced tribes of the valley of Mexico in the thirteenth century, finding there vast pyramids like those of the vanished Toltecs; and borrowing ideas like all successful conquerors, on the islands created by a series of swampy lakes, they raised great pyramids of a similar kind.

The creation of the city was a task similar to that of building Venice in its lagoon. Land had to be created by dredging mud from the lake between lines of pilings; extra fields for food-growing were formed by piling sludge on floating platforms of reeds, as can be seen today in the floating gardens of Xochimilco; stone had to be brought in from a hostile countryside. But by 1519 they had created a beautiful, flourishing city. Its center was the great temple, where Mexico City's main square is today, a terraced building up which the captives were marched to the sacrificial stone to have their hearts cut out. Across from the temple was the vast imperial palace. Like

Aztec Drum
This very rare carved wooden drum was used in the ritual of Aztec religious processions.   Lowie Museum of Anthropology. University of California, Berkeley

Pyramid of the Sun, Teotihuacán
The ceremonial center of the Toltec religion was at Teotihaucán, about thirty miles from Mexico City. The Pyramid is 216 feet high, and its base covers ten acres.   Author's photo

the temple it was a complex of buildings, grouped around interior courts and broken by canals. "I went several times to the emperor's residence merely to look at it," one Spanish soldier remarked. "Each time I walked about until I was quite tired, but even so I never saw the whole of it." All these white-painted buildings, which housed hundreds of priests and visiting nobility, the law courts and public treasury, prisons, music school, and even a house of rare birds, were entwined with blossoming trees. For this conjunction of a priestly and warrior aristocracy, Tenochtitlán existed. Its third function, as marketplace, was satisfied by the canals and vast open squares, where merchandise from all over the valley was sold in carefully arranged aisles—gold and silver, feathers, slaves, shoes, foodstuffs, colors for dyeing, building materials, and medicines. And to facilitate communication, the whole city was laid out in regular rectangles, divided by broad, straight streets, one side of which was beaten earth, the other a canal. The countryside that supported this metropolis with food and sacrificial victims was exploited, receiving no benefits for the supplies exacted from it; and the Aztecs' neighbors were easily persuaded by Cortés to aid him against their overlords.

The Construction of Mexico City

The beauty of Tenochtitlán survived the arrival of Cortés for only two years. In an uprising provoked by the Spanish destruction of their temples, Montezuma was stoned to death by his own people; and Cortés lost one-third of his men while fleeing by night across the causeways. He returned in 1521, besieged the city for three months, and finally destroyed it block by block. The debris of houses and temples was pushed into the lake and street-canals, and a larger number of natives perished from an epidemic of smallpox than fell victim to the Spaniards' other weapons. The next year, Cortés decided to rebuild the city in the same location as the metropolitan center of the colony, "as the city was so renowned and was so important." An equally impressive Spanish city was soon erected, through the labor of thousands of Indians. One friar listed the city building as one of the ten plagues the Spanish had brought upon Mexico: "In the building of the great city of Mexico, more people worked during the first years than upon the Temple of Jerusalem. . . . The laborers carry everything on their backs; they drag great stones and beams with ropes; and in the absence of skill but abundance of hands, four hundred men are used to move the stone or beam when one hundred are necessary. It is their custom, when moving materials, that the crowds sing and shout, and these voices continued by night and day, with the great fervor of building the city in the early years." [8]

On the site of the Aztec temple, a vast new cathedral was built, around which a European nucleus was formed. A gridiron plan for the streets gave

---

[8] George Kubler, *Mexican Architecture in the Sixteenth Century* (New Haven: Yale University Press, 1948), I, 71.

guzmā.   michvacā.

Cortés's Attack on Mexico City
Cortés and his Indian allies attack the Aztecs in this Indian drawing from the so-called Lienzo de Tlaxcalla of 1555–1564.
Mexican National Tourist Council photo

an appearance of regularity and openness to the city that impressed English sailors brought there as captives: "The said City of Mexico," wrote one, "hath the streets made very broad, and right, that a man being in the high place, at the one end of the street, may see at the least a good mile forward." [9] It was a city conceived according to the urban views of Italian theorists like Alberti and Filarete and carried out by the absolute Spanish administration in a way that was impossible in Italy—uniform street facades, municipal water supplies, paved streets, city-supervised slaughterhouses and granaries, and a state university. But Mexico City was only the beginning of the Spanish urbanization of Mexico. Like the Romans, they created an empire of cities. Large numbers of cities were built in unsettled areas, with the deliberate purpose of segregating the Spanish settlers to avoid exploitation of the Indians. Others, like Vera Cruz on the Caribbean, were trading centers; many like Queretaro were for mining or manufacturing; and even more were missionary centers, founded by the mendicant friars to combine missionary work with economic development through Indian labor. This city building in sixteenth-century Mexico was the greatest example of successful urban planning between the time of the Roman Empire and the nineteenth century.

[9] Ibid., I, 75.

Cuzco in the Sixteenth Century
The Spanish conquistador Pizarro captured the Inca capital of Peru in 1533, and rebuilt the city, using the walls of Inca buildings as the foundations for his new Spanish city.

The Economy of the Spanish Colonial Empire

The economic basis of this new colonial empire was less sound than its urban planning. By 1550, the Spaniards had conquered all Mexico, Central America, and through the expedition of Pizarro in 1530, the huge Inca empire of Peru. By 1550, all the conquistadores had been relieved of their governmental duties, and a centralized administration had been set up by order of the government in Spain. The soldiers were rewarded by the grant of tribute rights in specified districts, which meant goods and, at first, labor from the Indians living there. In a few years, large estates were organized by the original conquerors and the new settlers from Spain and even by Indian rulers. Many of the inland estates concentrated on animal rearing, especially of cattle, sheep, and horses; some supplied the larger towns with cereals. The tropical regions turned to sugar and tobacco plantations, using Negro slaves whenever they could afford them. Most Indians, however, continued to work their old lands as they had always done, supplying the new lords with tribute as they had supplied their previous Indian masters. The Spaniards were, however, interested most in gold and silver. "I have not come here for such reasons [as God and faith]," Pizarro told a friar. "I have come to take away their gold." The first shipments were of the booty of the Aztec and Inca empires; and only too often the intricate works of art were melted down for easy shipment. Then came the washing of surface gold from stream beds, which was soon exhausted. Finally, from 1530, mines were sunk to dig out silver; and in the 1540s "silver rushes" were precipitated by the discovery of immensely rich veins of silver in central Mexico and of the fabulous mountain of silver at San Luis Potosí in Bolivia.

During the second half of the sixteenth century, the Spanish American colonies sent to Europe their tropical goods like sugar and tobacco, hides for the making of leather goods, and especially gold and silver. In return they were sent wine, oil, and flour, and manufactured goods like metal tools and cloth, and domestic animals. At the height of the trade in the middle of the century, 133 ships sailed from Seville for America in one year, a very large number by the standards of that time. This trade had enormous reper-

Taxco, Mexico
Founded in 1529 as a silver-mining center, the lovely Spanish colonial town boomed in the eighteenth century, when the twin-towered rococo church was built.
Author's photo

cussions on Spain. The effects were most obvious in Seville, whose merchant guild enjoyed the monopoly of the trade. Many new harbor installations were constructed. The local nobility broke the tradition of its class by entering trade. Manufacturing of soap, china, and cloth was developed for export. The merchants grew wealthy by accepting commissions to act as intermediaries for merchants in other parts of Spain and for foreign merchants who wanted a share in the Indies trade, and they built themselves sumptuous palaces in Moorish style. From Seville, the economic stimulus was transmitted to inland Castile, where it magnified the volume of exchange in the great fairs and the manufactures of a few of the towns. But Spain as a whole did not receive a great economic boost from the acquisition of empire, because after 1550 when the Americas were demanding vast quantities of manufactured goods, the Spanish economy—for reasons we shall consider—was not geared to such production. Moreover, the shipping of bullion, which was regarded in sixteenth-century economic theory as an ideal import, had very deleterious effects. The crown took one-fifth of all bullion imported into Spain, and regarded it as an inexhaustible source of income with which to pay for military adventures abroad. It failed to realize that the effect of the huge imports of silver into Spain and their subsequent expenditure in other parts of Europe was to raise the prices of the goods being bought and, in general, the cost of living not only in Spain but throughout Europe. During the sixteenth century, prices in Spain quadrupled, causing great suffering among the majority of the population who could neither understand the causes nor cope with the effects of the sudden fall in the value of money. At the same time, it discouraged productive enterprises when wealth could be made so easily from handling the bullion. While the Spanish crown obtained up to twenty percent of its revenues from the bullion trade, private citizens made two and a half times that amount.

Unfavorable Results of Spanish Colonialism

Thus, in 1550, the Spaniards were mistakenly congratulating themselves on conquest and exploitation of an empire that would maintain their supremacy in Europe for an unlimited time. Yet the balance sheet was already unfavorable. In the West Indian islands and their mainland colonies, they had destroyed old civilizations, and had begun through disease and overwork to decimate the Indian population. Accurate figures are impossible to obtain, but it has been calculated that the native population of Mexico declined from about eleven million at the beginning of the Spanish conquest to 2.5 million in 1600. The end of human sacrifice, the more humane treatment brought about by the intervention with the crown of indignant friars like Las Casas, and the enforcement of justice were poor compensations for such tragedy. Nor did a large population of Spaniards emigrate to fill the vacant land, as happened in the United States. (Not more than one hundred thousand emigrated from Spain in the whole sixteenth century.) Rather, a colonial oligarchy had taken possession of vast lands, and was encouraged through government policy to embark on a misguided economic policy based on mining of silver. In Spain, the economy had been distorted by inflation, and the monarchy had grown dangerously dependent on a maintenance of its revenues from the Indies for payment of its creditors, upkeep of its armies, and construction of its fleets. Yet the flow of bullion could only be continued if sufficient Indians or Negroes were found to work the mines, if the annual treasure fleets could elude the privateers from England, France, and Holland, and if manufactured goods could be bought in the north of Europe to ship to the colonies in return for bullion. During its golden age, Spain was in actual fact living on borrowed money and borrowed time.

The Madrid of Philip the Prudent

The choice of Madrid as capital of Spain in 1561 was a symbolic act as well as a matter of Philip II's personal preference for the dry, windy uplands of Castile. It gave notice that the king regarded Spain as a united country and not as a temporary union of separate kingdoms, and that he regarded Spain as the most important of his many possessions in Europe and America. By placing his capital in the mathematical center of Spain, an extremely remote location for a monarch who had need of constant communication by sea with places as far apart as Palermo, Amsterdam, and Lima, he indicated his absorption with his tasks as absolute ruler of Spain. "It was right" wrote a contemporary chronicler, "that so great a Monarchy should have a city which could function as its heart—a vital center in the midst of the body, which ministered equally to every state in time of peace and war." [10]

Phillip II   Courtesy Museo del Prado, Madrid

The Reign of Charles V

Philip intended to avoid the dispersion of effort and strength that had marked his predecessors' reigns. By marrying Ferdinand of Aragon, Isabella

[10] Cited in John H. Elliott, *Imperial Spain, 1496–1716* (London: Edward Arnold, 1963), p. 247.

THE HABSBURG DYNASTIC INHERITANCE

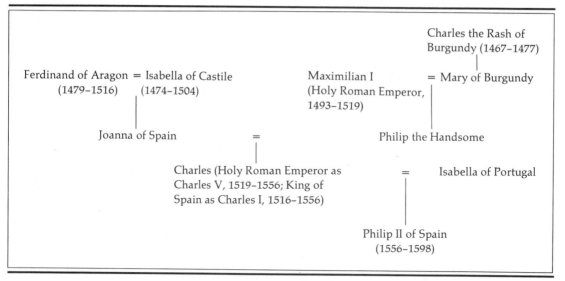

Ferdinand of Aragon = Isabella of Castile
(1479–1516)   (1474–1504)

Charles the Rash of
Burgundy (1467–1477)

Maximilian I   = Mary of Burgundy
(Holy Roman Emperor,
1493–1519)

Joanna of Spain   =   Philip the Handsome

Charles (Holy Roman Emperor as   =   Isabella of Portugal
Charles V, 1519–1556; King of
Spain as Charles I, 1516–1556)

Philip II of Spain
(1556–1598)

**Emperor Maximilian I, by
Albrecht Dürer**
German Information Center
photo

had done far more than unite most of Spain. She had involved Castile in the European struggles of Aragon—in the first place, a duel with France for control of the Pyrenees and the kingdom of Naples and Sicily. In 1494, Ferdinand had already been forced to send an army to drive the French from Naples. Dynastic marriages further increased Spain's entanglement. Ferdinand and Isabella married their daughter Joanna to Philip the Handsome, the son of the Austrian Emperor Maximilian I and Mary, the heiress of Burgundy; since Joanna was not the immediate heir to the Spanish throne, her marriage appeared at the time to be little more than finding her a wealthy and influential husband. But disease swept away all senior claimants to the thrones of Spain and Austria; and the son of Philip and Joanna, Charles, inherited half of Europe and most of the settled portion of the Americas. On his father's death in 1506, he had inherited the Netherlands. On Ferdinand's death in 1516, he had become ruler of Spain, Naples, and Sicily, and the Spanish colonies in America. In 1519, on the death of Maximilian, he became ruler of Austria and parts of South Germany, and was shortly after elected Holy Roman Emperor. He was then only nineteen years old.

The sympathies of Charles V were with Spain, and after his abdication in 1556 he retired to lead a life of monastic seclusion there. But his own upbringing and the nature of his empire made it impossible for him to place Spain at the center of his policy. He had been brought up in Belgian Flanders in the court of Burgundy, and never learned to speak Spanish well. One of his first tasks was to suppress a revolt of the Spanish towns, the rising of the comuneros in 1521; and during the following seven years when he learned to love Spain and its conception of Catholicism, he found him-

Picnic on the Banks of the Manzanares, by Francisco de Goya (1746–1828)
At the time of its choice as capital of Spain by Philip II, Madrid's 30,000 inhabitants were clustered on the hilltop around the fortress-palace. When Goya painted this scene in 1776, the wealthy aristocrats were emulating the luxury of the court of France.   Courtesy Museo del Prado, Madrid

self engaged in a series of enormously difficult struggles forced on him by other territorial responsibilities. As Holy Roman Emperor, he felt it his duty to take the lead of the Catholic princes in meeting the challenge of Luther and his princely and urban supporters; he was thus involved in a series of religious wars in Germany. As ruler of Naples and Sicily, he was involved in constant wars with the ambitious French King Francis I in Italy. As ruler of Austria, he was to bear the brunt of the drive of the Ottoman Turkish sultan Suleiman the Magnificent that brought the Turks to the walls of Vienna in 1529. In all these efforts, Charles expected Castile and the American empire to pay the main expenses, especially as he rapidly exhausted the

The Madrid of Philip the Prudent

Period Surveyed	Reign of King Philip II (1556–1598)
Population	30,000 (1561)
Area	0.25 sq. miles (1561)
Form of Government	Absolute monarchy, administration through royal councils; Cortés representative assembly for grant of revenue
Economic Base	Governmental bureaucracy; supply of court and nobility; bullion from empire; trade in wool
Intellectual Life	Painting (Titian; El Greco); drama (Lope de Vega); Novel (Miguel de Cervantes)
Principal Buildings	Escorial palace (outside city); Alcázar palace; monasteries (especially Descalzas Reales).
Public Entertainment	Religious festivals, including burning of heretics (auto-da-fé); theater
Religion	Catholicism. Rigorous application of teachings of Catholic Reformation (Inquisition; Index; burning of Protestants; strict supervision of remaining Arabs and Jews)

resources of the Netherlands and his credit with the German bankers. Charles V's European empire was thus an unwanted burden for the majority of his Spanish subjects, and he recognized it as such. As early as 1521–1522, he had transferred Austria and his German territories to his younger brother Ferdinand; and when he abdicated he passed to his son Philip what he regarded as a manageable empire—Spain and its American colonies, the Netherlands, Milan, Naples, and Sicily. It was intended to sweep away half a century of failure: the inability to crush the German Protestants, to win back Hungary from the Turks, to establish imperial control over the German principalities.

The Knight of Santiago (c. 1510–1520)
In Spain, the ideal of the Crusading knight was admired well into the sixteenth century, as this sepulchral image shows. Los Angeles County Museum of Art, The William Randolph Hearst Collection

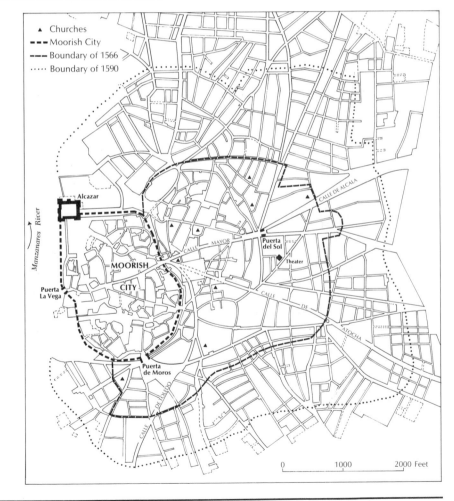

- ▲ Churches
- ▪▪▪ Moorish City
- ▬▬ Boundary of 1566
- ⋯⋯ Boundary of 1590

Manzanares River

Alcazar

CALLE DE ALCALA

Puerta del Sol

Theater

MOORISH CITY

CALLE   MAYOR

Puerta La Vega

CALLE   DE   ATOCHA

Puerta de Moros

CALLE DE TOLEDO

0   1000   2000 Feet

The Character of Philip II

Philip II (1556–1598) was uncompromisingly Spanish. In spite of his drooping Habsburg jaw, blue eyes, and fair hair, his Iberian rather than his German Habsburg ancestry was correctly remembered by his subjects. Once returned to Spain as king, he never again left the peninsula. He was an admirer, and himself an example, of the great Spanish virtues of personal dignity, of sobriety and frugality in daily life, and of religious devotion. Many of his traits were those of the better Spanish noblemen: a determination that justice should be done to the poor, a love of books and music, and a capacity for unremitting toil. But in Philip these characteristics were of worldwide importance. His desire to work hard was very soon equated, as a result of his acceptance of the doctrine of the divine right of kings, with the duty to do everything himself. His sense of duty to the Church, experienced at a time when the Catholic Reformation, under Spanish leadership, was attempting to turn back the Protestant tide, made him intolerant of heresy at home and abroad.

The choice of Madrid as capital and the construction nearby of the royal palace of the Escorial were the direct result of Philip's determination to run the monarchy on absolute, bureaucratic lines. Madrid, like Versailles under the French king Louis XIV, was a place where the nobility could be kept under supervision. The greater nobles were expected to build houses there; other citizens were expected to provide lodging for lesser nobles, a duty they avoided by building one-story homes. An elaborate court ceremonial provided time-consuming and meaningless tasks for his grandees, consumed their income, and kept them from plotting on their estates. The nobility were exempt from taxation, and also from attendance at the only representative institution, the Cortés, which met for the purpose of granting the king's demands for revenue. Philip governed through a series of councils, such as the Council of the Indies or the Council of Flanders, which were run by professional civil servants, usually from the lower nobility, but which were advisory only. All decisions, large and small, were made by Philip himself. The amount of papers he gathered around himself would alone have made a settled capital seem necessary; he assigned a special castle for their safekeeping at the beginning of his reign! He insisted on reading every dispatch from the remotest parts of the empire himself, and in commenting on it in his own handwriting. "If death should come from Spain," one of his representatives abroad commented, "we should all be immortal." Philip's slowness, however, was a matter of policy. "Time and I can beat any two opponents," he remarked. The result was ineffective government at a time when prompt decisions were needed, especially during the wars with the Dutch and the English.

Philip II's Religious Policy

Philip's satisfaction with the quiet languor of his administrative offices in the Alcázar palace was complemented by his pleasure in the religious char-

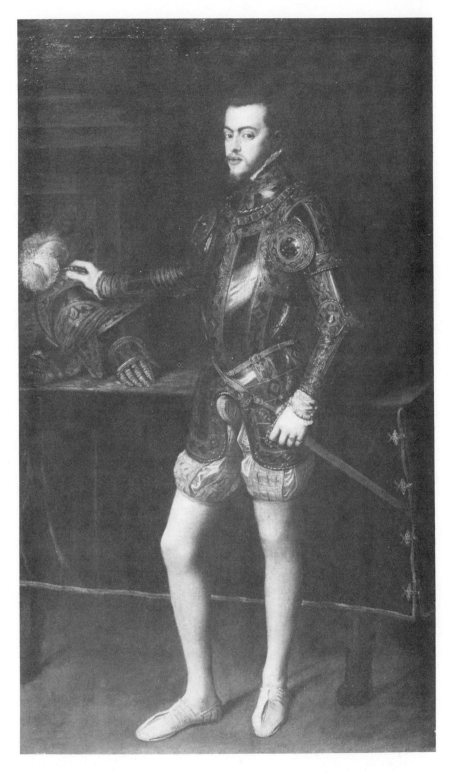

Philip II, by Titian
This portrait, painted when Philip was 24, was sent to Mary Tudor, Queen of England, to acquaint her with her future husband.   Courtesy Museo del Prado, Madrid

acter of his capital. One-third of the land of Madrid was held by the Catholic Church, and the skyline of the city was already rigid with the spires and domes of its convents and churches. This was, however, the church of the Catholic Reformation; in the first decade of Philip's reign, especially as a result of the closing sessions of the Council of Trent, the religious atmosphere in Spain stiffened. A vicious inquisitor-general was seeking heresy among the highest of Spain's nobility and churchmen. His greatest coup was to imprison the primate of Spain for seventeen years, and to find his writings guilty of heretical opinions. Stricter censorship was keeping out of Spain books as blameless as those of Sir Thomas More. For fear of contagion, all Spaniards were forbidden to study at foreign universities. The supposed discovery of cells of Protestants in Seville and Valladolid set off a wave of burnings that ended all danger of Lutheranism at home. When harsh treatment led the Moors of Granada to revolt, they were ordered transplanted throughout the rest of Spain. Converted Jews, who had not been expelled by Ferdinand and Isabella, were subjected to exceptionally strict supervision by the Inquisition. In all these measures, Philip gave the Church his fullest cooperation. Spanish Catholicism, in his mind, had to be maintained in its exceptional purity, unsullied by contact with the less pure faith of even the other Catholic countries of Europe.

The Escorial

In building the Escorial, Philip indulged both his taste for architecture and his absorption with the religious life. The building was to be a mausoleum for the remains of his father Charles V; a monastery for Hieronymite monks; and a royal palace. It was to be built in the shape of a gridiron, to commemorate the death by torture of Saint Lawrence, and was to rise on a bare rocky slope of the Sierra Guadarrama about twenty miles from Madrid. The palace was begun in 1563 and completed in 1584, mostly under the direction of Juan de Herrera. It was an exceptional building in many ways, and has rarely been admired. It was a temporary break with traditional Spanish architecture, which like the Portuguese architecture of the age of Manuel I was lavishly decorated and known as silverlike, or platteresque. The exterior of the Escorial has a bare classical simplicity, small windows providing almost the only breaks in the 670 feet of unadorned granite blocks. Its plan of a large number of inner courts was inspired by Filarete and by the great palace Diocletian had built in Dalmatia. It was to be a mausoleum totally unlike Michelangelo's Medici chapel, because the coffins of Philip's ancestors and successors were later ranged in the "Death House" like so many library shelves. The palace occupies only about one-quarter of the building, the greater part being the monastery of the Hieronymite brothers and the vast central church, derived rather inadequately from Michelangelo's dome of Saint Peter's. Philip was a connoisseur of architecture, took constant interest in the plans for the Escorial, and must be

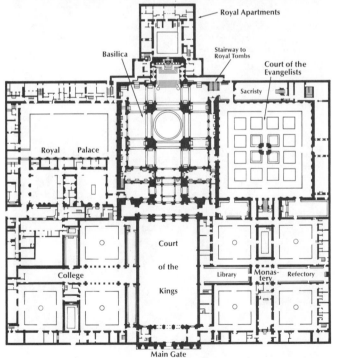

Royal Apartments

Basilica

Stairway to
Royal Tombs

Court of the
Evangelists

Sacristy

Royal   Palace

College

Court

of the

Kings

Library

Monas-
tery

Refectory

Main Gate

The Escorial
Pictured in a Dutch atlas of 1667, the Escorial's gridiron pattern to commemorate the death of St. Lawrence by torture is evident. Bildarchiv d. Ost. Nationalbibliothek, Vienna

Ground Plan of the Escorial of Philip II

held responsible for the frigid, ascetic character of the buildings and the life within. Perhaps the absorption with death that lingers in every part of the Escorial was only to be expected from a man whose life was filled with personal tragedies: his mother died when he was twelve, he outlived four wives, and his son and heir was a sadistic maniac who died while imprisoned by his father. The Escorial was a retreat for a permanently saddened man.

Spanish Painting: el Greco and Velázquez

Religion was not Philip's only consolation in the Escorial, however. Here he kept his great collection of paintings. He bought many of the colorful religious paintings being turned out in Venice, in the autumn of the Renaissance, and he appointed Titian an official court painter. Philip created among European royalty a new tradition of the court portrait, a dignified, often overflattering picture of the sovereign or his relatives, and especially of his eligible daughters, that could be placed in important public buildings, sent to fellow monarchs, or used to impress non-European royalty. Portraits of Charles V and Philip were even sent to the sultan of Turkey and the emperor of China. After Titian, there was no really great portrait painter until

The Empress Elizabeth of Portugal, by Titian
Elizabeth, daughter of King Manuel of Portugal, was the wife of Charles V. Titian painted the portrait from sketches nine years after her death in 1539. Courtesy Museo del Prado, Madrid

The Meninas, by Velázquez (1599–1660) *The little princess Margarita, with her two little ladies-in-waiting, or meninas, has burst into the painter's workshop while he, on the left, was painting the king and queen, who are visible in the mirror.*   Courtesy Museo del Prado, Madrid

Velázquez (1599–1660), who was court artist to Philip IV in the mid-seventeenth century. But Velázquez could not have created the amazing gallery of kings, queens, infantas, court jesters, popes, and dwarfs whose absolute honesty and penetrating insights still delight us if he had not inherited the achievements of a line of lesser men. For the Escorial itself, Philip turned mostly to Italians, bringing dozens to create the rather dull frescoes of palace, church, and tomb. In 1579, however, won over by two sketches he had been sent, Philip commissioned an *Adoration of the Holy Name of Jesus* from the greatest artist in Spain, an Italian-trained Greek from the island of Crete known as El Greco (1541–1614). El Greco had come to Venice where Tintoretto was creating turbulent movement by rejecting both natural presentation of the human body and harmony of background and color, but he had brought his own upbringing among the Byzantine tradition of Crete.

John the Baptist, by El Greco (1541–1614)
The painter has enhanced the sense of religious fervor by elongating the limbs and features of John and by depicting a turbulent silvery sky swirling around the vertical figure. Courtesy De Young Museum, San Francisco

Combining the two and infusing the new style with his own deep religious awe, he created a totally personal style that had made him highly favored with the Spanish clergy. Philip liked the *Adoration,* which showed the king, the pope, and the doge of Venice kneeling together and was interpreted by many as an augury of the great victory the Spanish fleet won over the Turks at Lepanto that year. El Greco was commissioned to paint the *Martyrdom of St. Maurice and the Theban Legion.* El Greco placed the actual decapitations in the background, portrayed the saint and his men in quiet dignity in the right foreground, and filled the upper third of the canvas with swirling, unnatural vermilions and ice-cold blues and yellows in a presentation of the moral suffering of martyrdom. It was one of his greatest paintings, and Philip disliked it so much that he never gave El Greco another commission. Fortunately, El Greco was able to return to his studio in Toledo, to which commissions poured in from more perspicacious patrons.

Spanish Literature: Lope de Vega and Cervantes

Philip was even more out of touch with the main delight of Madrid's citizens, the plays of Lope de Vega (1562–1625). Madrid had two regular theaters and eight companies of players, while itinerant companies worked all the theaters of Spain. The drama had begun with religious plays sponsored by the Church for special feast days, but with the opening of Madrid's first theater in 1579, the quite unsuccessful poet and dramatist Miguel de Cervantes (1547–1616) presented them with sober re-creations of Roman works. Shortly after, Lope de Vega erupted in the theatrical scene bringing life, spontaneity, romance, humor, and buffoonery. In short, like his contemporary Shakespeare, he wrote fine plays that pleased every section of his audience. He was too prolific; he wrote 1,500 plays, a hundred of them in twenty-four hours each. Yet he filled the state with real human beings in a panorama of Spanish society of his day. One of the favorite plays he wrote, *Fuenteovejuna,* portrayed a small Spanish town called Fuenteovejuna that had revolted and murdered its local official. The drama lay in the search for the culprit. But not a single villager broke faith with the others. To the famous question, "¿Quién mató al condestable?" (Who killed the constable?), every single one replied, "Fuenteovejuna."

Cervantes recovered from the disappointment of theatrical limbo by turning to novel writing. He had an adventure-filled life that provided him with plenty of material: wounded at Lepanto, imprisoned for five years by the Moors, tax collector in La Mancha, playwright in Madrid, prisoner for debt. Cervantes' overwhelming love for the foibles of humanity and his pity for its sorrows combined to make *Don Quixote* recognized immediately at its publication in 1604 as one of the world's great books and the quixotic knight as one of the most endearing characters of literature:

At a village of La Mancha, whose name I do not wish to remember, there lived a little while ago one of those gentlemen who are wont to keep a lance in the rack, an old buckler, a lean horse and a swift greyhound. . . . You must know that the above-mentioned gentleman in his leisure moments (which was most of the year) gave himself up with so much delight and gusto to reading books of chivalry that he almost entirely neglected the exercise of the chase and even the management of his domestic affairs. . . . Thus, with little sleeping and much reading his brains dried up to such a degree that he lost the use of his reason. His imagination became filled with a host of fancies he had read in his books—enchantments, quarrels, battles, challenges, wounds, courtships, loves, tortures and many other absurdities. . . . At last, having lost his wits completely, he stumbled upon the oddest fancy that ever entered a madman's brain. He believed that it was necessary, both for his own honor and for the service of the state that he should become a knight-errant and roam through the world with his horse and armor in quest of adventures. . . . [11]

[11] Miguel de Cervantes, *Don Quixote,* trans. Walter Starkie (New York: New American Library, 1957), pp. 15–17.

Philip died in 1598, the year when Lope de Vega's first play was produced, one year before the birth of Velázquez and six years before the publication of *Don Quixote*. The cultural greatness of Spain was already undeniable and was to become greater; but he left a country several times bankrupt; a colonial empire in demographic and economic decline; an exploited and exhausted peasantry; a privileged and bigoted nobility; a uniform, persecuting faith; and a string of imperial failures. For the cause and effect of these failures of a foreign policy inspired by the Catholic Reformation, one must look not to Madrid but to Amsterdam.

SUGGESTED READING

General treatments of Portuguese history, with full coverage of the Manueline period include H. V. Livermore, *Portugal: A Short History* (1973), which is particularly useful for political background and J. B. Trend, *Portugal* (1957). A. H. Oliveira Marques, *History of Portugal* (1972) is the most detailed and authoritative survey, although much useful material on social and intellectual background will be found in Stanley G. Payne, *A History of Spain and Portugal* (1973).

An interpretation of the effects of geography on Portuguese history is given by Dan Stanislawski, *The Individuality of Portugal: A Study in Historical-Political Geography* (1959). By far the best study of Portuguese society during the acquisition and organization of empire, and invaluable for its brief treatment of Lisbon, is C. R. Boxer's *The Portuguese Seaborne Empire, 1415–1825* (1969). The Portuguese overseas expansion is covered briefly but in a masterly way in J. H. Parry, *The Establishment of the European Hegemony, 1415–1715* (1961), which can be consulted for an introduction to the other colonial powers. Full and exciting details of the Portuguese voyages of discovery are related in Edgar Prestate, *The Portuguese Pioneers* (1933), and a pleasant biography of the great organizer of the voyages is Elaine Sanceau, *Henry the Navigator* (n.d.). Charles Verlinden, *The Beginnings of Modern Colonization* (1970), argues that the Genoese were the last colonizers of the Middle Ages and provide the transition to the colonial activities of Portugal and Spain through their ventures in the eastern Mediterranean. See especially his chapter on "The Italian Colony of Lisbon and the Development of Portuguese Metropolitan and Colonial Economy."

Daily life in Lisbon can be studied in two excellent books dealing with widely separated periods: A. H. Oliveira Marques, *Daily Life in Portugal in the Late Middle Ages* (1971) and Suzanne Chantal, *La Vie quotidienne au Portugal après le tremblement de terre de Lisbonne de 1755* (1962).

On Manueline art and architecture, see George Kubler and Martin Soria, *Art and Architecture in Spain and Portugal and Their American Dominions, 1500 to 1800* (1959). For a contemporary account of Portugal, see Malcolm Letts, ed., *The Travels of Leo of Rozmital* (1957).

Jacques Soustelle gives a fascinating account of the city under Montezuma in *The Daily Life of the Aztecs on the Eve of the Spanish Conquest* (1955). Two evocative accounts of the continent found by the Spaniards are Carl O. Sauer, *Sixteenth Century North America: The Land and People as Seen by Europeans* (1971) and Jorge E. Hardoy, *Pre-Colombian Cities* (1973). The impact on Europeans of the discovery of the continent of America is shown to affect every field of knowledge from anthropology to warfare, in the massive study edited by Fredi Chiapelli, *First Images of America: The Impact of the New World on the Old* (1976). The effect on Spain of its New World empire is the main focus of J. H. Elliott, *The Old World and the New, 1492–1650* (1970). For the economic structure of the new type of society that emerged, see Immanuel Wallerstein, *The Modern World-System: Capitalist Agriculture and the Origins of the European World-Economy in the Sixteenth Century* (1974).

The best contemporary accounts of the conquests of Cortés are Bernal Díaz del Castillo, *The True History of the Conquest of New Spain* (1890) and Hernando Cortés, *Five Letters 1519–1526* (1928). Extracts are given in J. H. Parry, ed., *The European Reconnaissance: Selected Documents* (1968). The situation two generations after the conquest is described in Alonso de Zorita, *Life and Labor in Ancient Mexico: The Brief and Summary Relations of the Lords of New Spain* (1963). The rebuilding of Mexico City is documented by George Kubler in *Mexican Architecture of the Sixteenth Century* (1948), which is illustrated with many contemporary maps.

The transformation of Seville is described in Ruth Pike, *Aristocrats and Traders: Sevilian Society in the Sixteenth Century* (1972).

A short account of Madrid's character under Philip II is given by R. Trevor-Davies, "Madrid Under the House of Austria," in Ernest Barker, ed., *Golden Ages of the Great Cities* (1952), pp. 191–212. A good history of the city in French is J. Lucas-Dubreton, *Madrid* (1962), but there is nothing comparable in English. Walks around Lope de Vega's haunts in Madrid are described in Joaquin de Entramasaguas, *El Madrid de Lope de Vega* (1959). On the Escorial, see Kubler and Soria, *Art and Architecture in Spain and Portugal*, cited above.

The best biography of Charles V is still Karl Brandi, *Charles V* (1939). For Philip II, see J. Lynch, *Spain Under the Habsburgs*, vol. 1, *Empire and Absolutism, 1516–1598* (1964).

On the overseas empire of Spain, it is best to begin by reading Cecil Jane's translation of *The Journal of Christopher Columbus* (1960), which could be followed up with the superlative biography of Samuel E. Morison, *Admiral of the Ocean Sea* (1942). Ernle Bradford's *Christopher Columbus* (1973) is a popularized account, but beautifully illustrated with paintings and old maps. J. H. Parry, *The Spanish Seaborne Empire* (1966) is particularly good on the role of Seville in the Americas trade. John H. Elliott, *Imperial Spain, 1496–1716* (1963) relates internal problems to overseas expansion. The policy of the Spaniards toward the indigenous inhabitants of their empire is judged objectively in L. Hanke, *The Spanish Struggle for Justice in the Conquest of America* (1949). The baleful effects of the importation of bullion can be observed in E. J. Hamilton, *American Treasure and the Price Revolution in Spain, 1501–1650* (1934). An overview of the economics of seaborne empire is given in the fine analysis of Ralph Davis, *The Rise of the Atlantic Economies* (1973).

Two older books that are still useful are R. Trevor-Davies, *The Golden Century of Spain, 1501–1621* (1958) and Jean Hippolyte Mariéjol, *The Spain of Ferdinand and Isabella* (1961). Antonio Dominguez Ortiz, *The Golden Age of Spain, 1516–1659* (1971) is especially good on the seventeenth century. Garrett Mattingley's *The Armada* (1959) not only describes the battle but re-creates the atmosphere of the Spanish court.

Finally, every student should immerse himself for a little while at least in the enormous erudition of Fernand Braudel's encyclopedic *The Mediterranean and the Mediterranean World in the Age of Philip II* (1972).

In this flourishing republic, this city second to none, men of every nation and every sect live together in the utmost harmony; and all they bother to find out, before trusting their goods to anyone, is whether he is rich or poor and whether he is honest or a fraud. —Baruch Spinoza

14 / The Amsterdam of Rembrandt

In 1610, the city fathers of Amsterdam approved the "Plan of the Three Canals," one of the most ambitious and most beautiful projects of urban planning ever undertaken. The city was to expand from 450 to 1,800 acres, to accommodate a population growing rapidly from an influx of refugees

Self-Portrait by Rembrandt
Bildarchiv d. Ost. Nationalbibliothek

from Spanish rule, of intellectuals and Jews enjoying freedom from persecution, and of workers and merchants seeking profit from the city's economic boom. The population had doubled since the beginning of the Dutch revolt against the Spanish in 1567, to reach fifty thousand in 1610; it doubled again in the next ten years; and by 1660, it was two hundred thousand. The genius of the team of men who provided for this growth—the director for city works and the city's master mason, carpenter, and sculptor—was to combine aesthetic sppeal, sanitation, and economic function. Three enormous semicircular canals were

Amsterdam in Winter, by Jan Abrahamsz Beerstraten (1627–1666)   Copyright the Rijksmuseun, Amsterdam

View of Amsterdam, c. 1611, by Claes Jansz Visscher
Courtesy the Rijksmuseum, Amsterdam

The Amsterdam of Rembrandt

Period Surveyed	Lifetime of Rembrandt (1606–1669)
Population	50,000 (1610); 100,000 (1620); 200,000 (1660)
Area	0.7 square miles (1610); 2.81 square miles (1630)
Form of Government	Federal government (Stadholder; States General representing seven United Provinces); oligarchic city government (sheriff, burgomasters, aldermen, councillors, known collectively as regents)
Economic Base	Merchant marine; principal commodity trader in Europe; overseas trading companies (East India Company; West India Company); financial services (Exchange Bank; Lending Bank; Stock Exchange); local foodstuffs
Intellectual Life	Painting (Rembrandt; Vermeer; Ruisdael; Cuyp; Steen); poetry (Vondel); philosophy (Spinoza); mathematics (Descartes)
Principal Buildings	Burgher homes on the Three Canals; North, South, East, and West churches; City Hall
Public Entertainment	Parades and dinners of civic guards; dances; banquets; skating
Religion	Calvinism; toleration of other religions, including Jewish

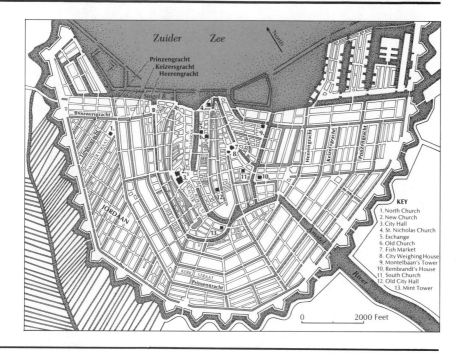

The West Church, by Jan van der Heiden (1637–1712)
Rembrandt was buried in this Calvinist Church on the Prinsengracht.
Bildarchiv d. Ost. Nationalbibliothek

dug by laborers around the old city. Radial canals made access easy between the new waterways and the rivers and canals of the central core. Building lots were created by driving wooden piles through the soft mud until they became firmly embedded in the hard sand below. Wide roadways were left in front of the houses, and planted with lime trees. At points where vistas linked, space was provided for four great churches, known respectively as the North, South, East, and West churches. The whole impression was one of a complex panorama of color, presented with controlled dignity rather than with the exotic exuberance of the Venetian canals. The rippling greens of the canal waters reflected bright red tiles, buff brick, green doors, white-framed windows, and blue slate stoops, providing a favorite subject for the city's well-patronized artists. Moreover, the city required that sanitation should be provided in every house, and it inspected drains and sewers. (Visitors still complained that the burghers threw their refuse into the canals, "which causes ill Scents and Fumes which is a nasty thing.") The canals enabled the business people to use their homes as warehouses, since the goods could be brought by small boat and lifted into the upper floors of the house by means of the block and tackle that jutted out from the gable. With greater volume, specialized warehouses could be built along the canals, with easy access to the port at the river mouth; and in Amsterdam even the warehouses had charm. "Among the large towns," wrote a French visitor, "Amsterdam is the most beautiful I have seen."

The Dutch, however, had not only created a unique city but also a unique way of life. They had accepted Calvinism, and fought for eighty years to be free of Spanish Catholicism, without turning Amsterdam into another Geneva. Religious toleration had given the world both a moral lesson and an example of the economic benefits of freedom of conscience. With no natural resources other than agriculture, they had made Amster-

Flower Still-Life, by William van Aelst (c. 1625–1688)
Van Aelst used flowers, leaves, ribbons, and vases to produce baroque compositions of undulating movement and scintillating color.   Courtesy of De Young Museum, San Francisco

dam the world's greatest trade center and an important manufacturer; and they had even turned constant war into a source of profit. Breaking into the colonial struggle a century later than the Portuguese and the Spanish, they had outstripped the former and equaled the latter; the Spanish treasure fleets were soon neglecting Lisbon and Seville and sailing on to the Netherlands. Its sober middle classes had turned their home life, perhaps more than even the Florentines, into a work of art; and their painters had responded by creating great works of art from the scenes of that life. "The name of Amsterdam became so famous," one contemporary reported, "that many people in distant countries believed it to be not a city but an entire country, and desired to form alliances with it."

The Revolt of the Netherlands

The Netherlands Under Charles V

The successful revolt of the seven northern provinces of the Netherlands against Spain made Amsterdam the predominant commercial center of northern Europe. When Charles V had inherited the Netherlands as part of his Burgundian territories, they consisted of seventeen provinces roughly equivalent to the present-day Netherlands, Belgium, and Luxembourg; their wealthiest cities were the textile towns of Flanders, like Ghent and Bruges, and the banking and trading metropolis of Antwerp. Amsterdam, by contrast, was smaller even than the other towns of the province of Holland, like Haarlem and Alkmaar. Its port, where the river Ij flowed into the huge inland sea of the Zuider Zee, had been created artificially on marshland. Expansion seemed uneconomical, and the location was inconvenient for both the North Sea trade and the overland commerce with Germany. The assembly, or States, of the province of Holland summed up their difficulties clearly in a petition to the emperor in 1548:

It is noticeably true that the province of Holland is a very small country, small in length and even smaller in breadth, and almost enclosed by the sea on three sides. It must be protected from the sea by reclamation works, which involve a heavy yearly expenditure for dykes, sluices, mill-races, windmills and polders. Moreover, the said province of Holland contains many dunes, bogs, and lakes which grow daily more extensive, as well as other barren districts, unfit for crops or pasture. . . . Consequently, the main business of the country must needs be in shipping and related trades, from which a great many people earn their living, like merchants, skippers, masters, pilots, sailors, shipwrights, and all those connected therewith.[1]

---

[1] Cited in C. R. Boxer, *The Dutch Seaborne Empire, 1600–1800* (New York: Knopf, 1965), p. 5.

This seaborne trade was largely with the Hanseatic cities of the Baltic, in beer, grain, timber, and especially herring; there was also trade in textiles and wine with western Europe. But the revolt known as the Eighty Years' War (1566–1648), stimulated an economic boom in Amsterdam for two reasons. The Spanish armies of the duke of Alva and his successors destroyed its rivals in the southern Netherlands, especially Antwerp, which was sacked in 1585; and political independence of the northern provinces alone gave Amsterdam the position of capital city of a country of two million people in all but name. (Amsterdam became the constitutional capital of the country in 1814, although most government offices remained in The Hague.)

The Netherlands had developed strong economic ties with Spain during the reign of Charles V; and only unwise measures of exploitation and repression, political and religious, under his son Philip II provoked the revolt. Two-thirds of the Netherlands' exports were sent to Spain, which was a ready market for finished cloth, metalwork and arms, cereals, and naval stores. In return the Spanish sent two-thirds of their wool exports to the Netherlands, as well as large amounts of their tropical products like spices and sugar. The Spanish had allowed the Netherlands' cities to gain greater profit from the trade of their empire than the cities of Spain itself. Moreover, Charles V had been satisfied to leave the feudal nobility of the Netherlands in control, provided that they gave him a satisfactory revenue from taxes they administered. Charles had even used moderation in his repression of Protestantism. Lutheranism had penetrated the southern Netherlands somewhat, and Calvinism considerably more when missionary work was undertaken in the French-speaking provinces from Geneva and Strasbourg. Philip II's mistake was to attempt simultaneously to reduce the political powers of the aristocracy, overtax the merchant class, and repress the Protestants. He thereby stimulated three revolts against him at once.

The Opening of the Revolt

In the first phase of the revolt, the high nobility of the Netherlands, led by Count Egmont and Count Horne and William the Silent, prince of Orange, attempted to prevent their own power being eroded by Philip's bureaucracy and to stop the religious persecution of the Inquisition. Although he was a Catholic, William spoke out in 1564 in favor of toleration. "However strongly I am attached to the Catholic faith," he told the council of state, "I cannot approve the princes attempting to rule the consciences of their subjects and wanting to rob them of the liberty of faith." Philip II, however, was determined to destroy both the political independence and the Protestant heresy of the Netherlands. As a result, the Catholic nobles found themselves supported by a spontaneous Calvinist uprising that began in 1566 in the textile towns of Flanders and spread rapidly northwards. In the "Calvinist Fury," the city mobs sacked the Catholic churches, destroyed paintings

◆ The Netherlands During the Revolt ◆

and statues, and turned many churches into Calvinist meetinghouses. So far the revolt had been largely centered in the southern Netherlands, and when the iconoclastic fever reached Amsterdam the merchant oligarchy took tough measures immediately to stop its excesses.

Failure of Spanish Repression

Philip forced the revolt into a second, more desperate phase by sending the tough, stupid duke of Alva to the Netherlands with a large Spanish army to extirpate Protestantism, break the nobility, and centralize in Brussels the rule of the seventeen provinces. Alva's legal instrument for dealing with rebels, both political and religious, was the Council of Troubles, nicknamed the Council of Blood, a commission of seven members with absolute powers of inquiry and punishment. The council arrested over twelve thousand people during its six years of activity, striking indiscriminately at Netherlanders of every class and religion and thus uniting the population in a common hatred of Spain. The counts Egmont and Horne were captured by trickery and executed. Alva then created a third opposition to his rule, in addition to the nobility and the Calvinists, by thrusting enormously heavy taxation on the merchant class. "A great deal remains to be done," he wrote to the king in 1568:

The towns must be punished for their rebelliousness with the loss of their privileges; a goodly sum must be squeezed out of private persons; a permanent tax obtained from the States of the country. It would therefore be unsuitable to proclaim a pardon at this juncture. Everyone must be made to live in constant fear of the roof braking down over his head. Thus will the towns comply with what will be ordained for them, private persons will offer high ransoms, and the States will not dare to refuse what is proposed to them in the King's name.[2]

In the southern Netherlands, Alva succeeded in breaking the opposition to Spanish rule, and he moved the council to Amsterdam, which was soon known as Moorddam, or Murderdam. The city government collaborated wholeheartedly in attacking the lesser merchants, since this self-perpetuating oligarchy had concluded that its own power was dependent on maintenance of Spanish rule. Amsterdam, however, was isolated in rebel territory. While Alva's army was ravaging the southern cities, many of the lower nobility and the merchant class had taken to the sea, joining with others who were little more than pirates, to harass the fleets coming from Spain. In 1572, these Sea-Beggars (a name they took from a derisive remark by a Spanish nobleman) seized the port of Brill commanding the mouth of the lower Rhine and in a few weeks were in control of all the provinces of Holland and Friesland except Amsterdam. This territorial conquest, supplied from the sea and protected from the Spanish armies in the South by the great rivers, estuaries, and network of dikes, was never lost. It was a natural fortress; and the Sea-Beggars at once gave it political cohesion by recognizing their allegiance to William of Orange, the patient, courageous statesman whose charismatic leadership fused the various motives for rebellion into a movement of national independence.

---

[2] Cited in Pieter Geyl, *The Revolt of the Netherlands, 1555–1609* (London: Williams and Norgate, 1932), pp. 102–103.

The Old Town Hall of Amsterdam, by Pieter Saenredam (1597–1665) *This intimate hall, which burned down in 1651, was replaced by a gigantic neoclassical building more fitting the pretensions of the city's merchant-oligarchy.*   Courtesy the Rijksmuseum, Amsterdam

The towns of the North had accepted the Sea-Beggars without much enthusiasm, as an alternative to the Inquisition and the Spanish sales tax; and Calvinist minorities engaged in a conquest of the city governments from within. The city government of Amsterdam withstood the pressure until 1578, although the city was surrounded by the rebels, the Zuider Zee blockaded, and foodstuffs dwindling. Then in May, the workers and shop-keepers of the city swarmed into the central market street, the Dam, in a violent demonstration against the city council and were joined by the citizen militia companies, those well-to-do burgher civic guards presented in Rembrandt's famous painting *The Night Watch.* In the "Alteration," as this municipal revolution was called, the city council and the leading churchmen were rounded up, put on board two ships, and set ashore on a distant dike. Exiled merchants poured back into the town, with large numbers of Calvinist refugees from the southern Netherlands. A new city government of moderate Catholics and Calvinists rapidly restored the city's economic life, and within seven years prosperity was so great that the first expansion beyond the old ramparts was undertaken. For a time it even appeared as though the whole of the Netherlands would be united under William of Orange. Alva, for lack of money, had been unable to put together an army that could defeat the North; and he had fled from Amsterdam by night to avoid his personal creditors. His successor, Don John, saw his own troops mutiny for lack of pay, and he himself died of typhus. For a brief period, both northern and southern Netherlands joined in the Union of Brussels; but the South soon withdrew. The southern nobility supported Spain against the mercantile oligarchies of the northern cities. Catholics in the South felt themselves threatened by the bellicose attitude of the Calvinists. Finally, Philip II sent a first-class general, the Italian duke of Parma. Parma drew on Spanish troops from the loyal southern provinces, and fought his way north, reducing the great Flemish cities one by one. Again, however, he was unable to break the river line north of Antwerp, even though Philip had engineered the assassination of William of Orange in 1584. With the help of a tiny army from England, the Dutch doggedly drove back every Spanish attempt to cross the Rhine.

The Independence of the Netherlands

During the following twenty years, Philip strained his resources. To stop English sailors from pillaging the Spanish fleets and ports in the American colonies, to end English support of the Dutch rebels, and to restore Catholicism in England, he sent an armada of one hundred and thirty ships from Lisbon to meet Parma's army in Flanders and attack London. Arriving a year later than originally planned as a result of a raid by Sir Francis Drake on Cadiz harbor, the Spanish ships were too ungainly to maneuver in reply to English attack. After moving slowly up the Channel in nine days of ineffectual skirmishes, they withdrew to the harbor of Calais. Drake, however, forced them out to sea again by sending fireships among them, and picked a number of them off individually when they panicked. A tempest forced the rest to flee around the north of the British Isles. Only half limped back to Spain. For the Dutch, the defeat of the armada provided a much needed respite; but the battles along the Rhine soon resumed. Under the leadership of a son of William of Orange, the Dutch won a few local victories. The truce of 1609 recognized that a standoff had been reached. The independence of the seven northern provinces, or Dutch republic, which had been claimed in 1581, was officially accepted by Spain; and after a renewal of fighting in 1621–1648, this recognition was again affirmed. For Amsterdam, however, prosperity had preceded peace by a quarter of a century. By 1609, the capitalism of Amsterdam was already a source of amazement and irritation to its rivals. Amsterdam, wrote a Frenchman, was "swollen with people, chock-full of goods, and filled with gold and silver." It was a surprising record after forty years of war.

Amsterdam Becomes the Hub of European Commerce

In the sixteenth century, Antwerp had been the center of European banking and international commerce. In the twenty-five years after its capture by the duke of Parma in 1585, that position had been taken by Amsterdam; and it

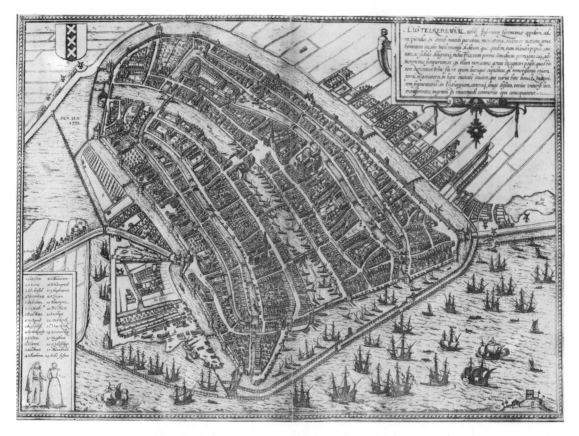

Panorama of Amsterdam, 1575

On the eve of its expansion in the Plan of the Three Canals, Amsterdam was protected by the sweep of the river Singel. Smaller ships could follow the Damrak into the center of the city.   Bildarchiv d. Ost. Nationalbibliothek, Vienna

held this preeminence for almost a hundred fifty years. "Here is Antwerp itself changed into Amsterdam," one refugee rejoiced. Rivals were determined to unearth the reasons for this metamorphosis. Dutch "riches and multitude of shipping is the envy of the present and may be the wonder of all future generations," wrote an English merchant in the midseventeenth century, "and yet the means whereby they have advanced themselves are sufficiently obvious and in a great measure imitable by most other nations, but most easily by us of this Kingdom of England."[3]

Economic Basis of Amsterdam's Prosperity

Many of the factors that aided Amsterdam's rise could have been turned to advantage by other great seaports. The refugees from Antwerp, with their capital and commercial skills, scattered to every port of northern and southern Europe from Danzig to Livorno, although a majority of them did settle in Amsterdam; and several of these cities could have competed for the des-

[3] Cited in Charles Wilson, *The Dutch Republic and the Civilisation of the Seventeenth Century* (London: Weidenfeld and Nicolson, 1968), p. 33.

perately needed role of kingpin in the highly developed network of European trade. Great profits could be made by shipping companies able to buy up the surplus grain of Poland and the eastern European cereal plains in order to supply the lands where famine threatened, notably southern Europe in the last decade of the sixteenth century and parts of western Europe through much of the seventeenth. The failure of Spain and Portugal to develop the industries that could supply export goods to their own empires left opportunities on a vast scale for other countries to supply the textiles, metalwork, armaments, furniture, rope, tar, and timber that would be exchanged for the bullion of the Americas. The decline of Spanish strength in the last years of Philip II and, especially, the weakness of the Portuguese during the union with Spain (1580–1640) left not only the treasure fleets but even parts of the colonial empire open to foreign seizure. The vast expansion of European shipping was a great opportunity for the country that could gain a semimonopoly on the naval supplies, especially wood and tar, which as a result of the great deforestation of western Europe completed in the sixteenth century had to be obtained from Scandinavia; and even greater results could be obtained by the sale or lease of fully equipped ships. It was, however, Amsterdam more than any other port of Europe that was ready to profit from these lucrative opportunities.

Amsterdam's first advantage was its superb merchant marine. Visitors spoke of a forest of masts along the city waterfront and were impressed that most of the ships were owned by Amsterdam merchants. Many had been built for the North Sea fisheries, which had boomed suddenly when the herring shoals had inexplicably moved from the Baltic into the North Sea in the sixteenth century. The herring, smoked or pickled, had become one of Holland's most important exports, as well as a principal food item for its own cities; and warships were sent out to defend the herring fleets as they ranged down the coasts of England and Scotland. Other ships specialized in the carrying trade of bulky goods, especially for the Baltic trade in cereals, timber, and copper and iron. In the 1590s, the Dutch invented an extremely important type of freight carrier, the flyboat, or fluit, which revolutionized the carrying trade. It was little more than a low-draught barge, manned by a few sailors and almost unarmed, that could be built quickly and cheaply and used for transport of goods. The flyboats made it possible for the Dutch to undercut all their rivals in freight rates, although some asserted that inhumanly low wages paid the crews was also a factor. With the beginning of interloping voyages to the Indies at the end of the sixteenth century, the Dutch also turned out larger ships that could make the long transoceanic voyages. By the midseventeenth century, they owned half the merchant ships in Europe.

Secondly, the Amsterdam merchants were prepared and able to trade in almost every commodity in world commerce; and the Amsterdam price lists, which were published weekly, became the reference prices for all parts of Europe. All commercial services were offered, including skilled classification of merchandise, credit facilities, insurance, brokerage, and rational legal treatment of commercial disputes. Goods traded through Amsterdam were handled with exemplary efficiency. Ships could be unloaded and filled again with purchases in a matter of days, which alone reduced the cost of doing business in Amsterdam as contrasted with more laggardly ports. But the variety of goods available was the greatest inducement to foreigners to buy in Amsterdam. It was Europe's biggest seller of wheat, naval supplies, armaments, and fish. It controlled most of the metal exported from Sweden, and of the wool from Spanish sheep, much of the salt from Denmark, and even a good share of the unfinished woolen cloth from England. Many of the goods brought into Amsterdam were raw materials or semifinished goods that could be turned, at a large profit, into finished goods for re-export. In Amsterdam and neighboring cities like Delft and Leiden, small manufacturing companies were created. In Amsterdam itself, unfinished cloth was dyed and dressed, beer brewed, glass blown, armaments cast, to-bacco cut, paper manufactured and books printed, jewels shaped, and leather dressed. Even the agricultural produce of the rich, wet fields around Amsterdam and the newly reclaimed land, or polders, fed the Amsterdam trade. The high-quality butter and cheese of the Dutch was exported, while low-quality butter and cheese was imported to feed the farmers who had produced the dairy products originally. But the greatest temptation, to which the Dutch succumbed in 1594 with the foundation of the "Company of Far Lands," was to break the spice monopoly of the Portuguese and Spanish.

Panorama of Amsterdam in the Seventeenth Century

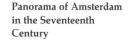

The Overseas Trading Companies of Amsterdam

The first fleet sent out by the new company used charts drawn up by Jan van Linschoten, a Dutchman who had spent several years in Goa in the service of the Portuguese archbishop there. Linschoten's book, *Itinerario,* with its detailed instructions for sailing to America and India, was significant in bringing both the Dutch and the English to open up the East Indies. The little Dutch fleet of four ships made its way as far as Java and the Moluccas, and brought back a moderately profitable cargo of pepper and mace. With direct access to the spice lands thus shown to be possible and the enormous difficulties of the Portuguese in maintaining their monopoly made obvious, large numbers of ships were sent from Amsterdam and the other Dutch ports. A few tried the route around South America but most sailed without trouble to the islands of Indonesia. Once again, Dutch commercial skills triumphed. They brought suitable goods for trade, such as armor, glassware, and toys; they traded honestly, and they made no attempt to proselytize. They did, however, compete with each other; and in 1602, they were pressured by the States General into forming one monopoly company, the United Netherlands Chartered East India Company. It was given a monopoly of Dutch trade between the Cape of Good Hope and the Straits of Magellan, and the right to make war and peace, build forts, capture foreign vessels, and coin money. Amsterdam, which subscribed half of the original capital, was dominant in the company, and its main offices and warehouses, which are still standing, were built in the city. The East India

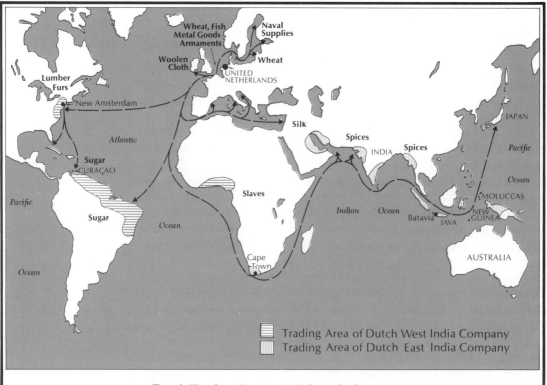

◆Dutch Trading Empire, Mid–17th Century◆

Company was soon sending annually a fleet to the spice islands, bringing back spices, silks, and cottons; and it quickly established treaties with the native princes and territorial claims, first on the Moluccas and then on the Indonesian archipelago. In Batavia on Java, they built their administrative and military capital, and used it to set up a trading empire among Asian states, from which they could also draw profit. They drove the Portuguese out of Malaya and Ceylon and massacred the last few English merchants in Amboina in the Moluccas, founded a trading post at Nagasaki to which the Japanese entrusted a monopoly of their export trade, and planted a settlement on the Cape of Good Hope as a supply center for their fleets traveling to the Far East. To the European goods available in their warehouses they had thus added pepper, cinnamon, nutmeg, cotton, silks, porcelain, tea, and coffee.

Nineteen years after the foundation of the East India Company, bellicose Calvinist elements founded the West India Company, to attack the trade, possessions, and ships of the Spanish in the western hemisphere. Its most spectacular achievement was the capture of the whole Spanish treasure fleet in 1628, as it lay at harbor in Cuba. It established a superb base for trade and marauding by taking the rocky island of Curaçao in the Caribbean, held the sugar-producing provinces of Brazil for several years, and sold slaves from west Africa in the Spanish colonies. Following Henry Hudson's exploration of the river subsequently named after him, the company attempted to found a colony of the New Netherlands, establishing a settlement called New Amsterdam on the tip of Manhattan island, and a trading post up the river at the site of present-day Albany. Only a few thousand settled, however, and the colony was seized by the English without trouble in 1664. New Amsterdam was renamed New York, and descendants of the original settlers like the Rensselaers and the Roosevelts quickly adapted to the new regime. The West India Company was soon torn with dissensions between the Amsterdam merchants and the southerners, especially as many of its ventures lost money; and it was eventually declared bankrupt.

Nevertheless, the two companies had won for the Netherlands a vast trading empire. The great Amsterdam poet Joost van der Vondel summed up their achievement with customary honesty. "For love of gain the wide world's harbors we explore," he commented.[4]

Amsterdam as Financial Center

Amsterdam's third advantage was the availability of large quantities of capital together with the means for its investment. The Amsterdam middle classes had been accumulating wealth all through the sixteenth century from the Baltic trade in grain and naval supplies; and to this was added the large patrimonies brought into the city by the refugees who moved there from the textile towns of Flanders and from Antwerp during the war with Spain. The Jews who were expelled from Spain and Portugal brought some capital, but were more significant for the wealth they created in the Brazilian sugar trade and, later in the century, by trading in shares. The English poet Andrew Marvell scorned this close identification of toleration and moneymaking:

Hence Amsterdam—Turk, Christian, Pagan, Jew,
Stable of sects and mint of schism grew:
That bank of conscience where not one so strange
Opinion but finds credit and exchange.[5]

The imperial trade conducted by the East and West Indian companies enriched many investors, notably the boards of directors; many of the rich homes along the new canals were owned by the famous Heeren ("Gentlemen") XVII and Heeren XIX, the seventeen directors of the East India Company and the nineteen directors of the West India Company. Others profited from war. According to one Amsterdam burgomaster, "It is known to

[4] Cited in Boxer, *Dutch Seaborne Empire,* p. 113.
[5] Cited in Wilson, *Dutch Republic,* p. 27.

all the world that whereas it is generally the nature of war to ruin the land and people, these countries [the Netherlands] on the contrary have been noticeably improved thereby." Amsterdam merchants supplied the armies of the dukes of Alva and Parma and later the armies of Louis XIV during the wars against the Dutch. They supplied ships for both sides in the war between Denmark and Sweden; and they fed both Roundheads and Cavaliers in the English civil war. By the end of the century, Amsterdam was the foremost supplier of all forms of military supplies; like Milan a century earlier, it had several stores that could equip an army of five thousand men. Finally, Amsterdam was also the center where the savings of hundreds of thousands of poorer people were invested. Land in the coastal provinces of Holland and Zeeland was scarce and expensive, and thus not a normal investment. Agricultural investment frequently had to be done by buying into companies attempting to drain the polders, which required a large-scale technological enterprise. Greater merchants were able to draw on the savings of their less well-to-do relatives when making investments in equipping East India men.

To enable wealth to be readily available for productive investment, the city of Amsterdam founded, and continued to supervise, the most efficient and reliable bank in northern Europe, the Amsterdam Exchange Bank. Money poured in from as far away as Russia and Turkey, as the continent's rich sought security for their fortunes. The bank's reputation, wrote an English nobleman, was "another invitation for People to come, and lodge that part of their Money they could transport, and knew no means of securing at home. Nor did [only] those people lodge Moneys here, who came over into the Country; but many more, who never left their own; Though they provided for a retreat, or against a storm, and though no place so secure as this, nor from when they might so easily draw their Money into any parts of the World." [6] Shortly afterwards, the city founded the Amsterdam Lending Bank, which offered loans to its best customers at three percent and soon succeeded in driving out the Italian moneylenders. Finally, there was the Amsterdam Stock Exchange, or Beurs, which was the center for trading in commodities. In its colonnaded courtyard, merchants from all over the world conducted the most concentrated trading in Europe. The Beurs, wrote Vondel,

> *Received the burghers' life breath*
> *From old and new side of the town*
> *All foreign blood that afternoons collected here*
> *Flowed in a single auricle*
> *Fed by many veins*
> *Giving life to the blood of the city.* [7]

[6] Cited in Violet Barbour, *Capitalism in Amsterdam in the Seventeenth Century* (Baltimore: Johns Hopkins University Press, 1950), p. 46.

[7] John J. Murray, *Amsterdam in the Age of Rembrandt* (Norman: University of Oklahoma Press, 1967), p. 60.

The city of Amsterdam, in short, was a superbly organized creator of wealth. Per capita, it had the highest income in Europe. Wealth, however, was far from being divided equally per capita.

Social Structure of Rembrandt's Amsterdam

The Grauw (The Rabble)

At the base of Amsterdam's society, as in all the large cities of seventeenth-century Europe, was the class whom the Dutch called the *grauw,* the dregs or rabble, whose miserable poverty comes alive in the etchings of Rembrandt. They varied from the old reduced to beggary to the unskilled day laborers who found occasional, badly paid work in the dockyards or warehouses. The reputed riches of Amsterdam and the ease of migration to the Netherlands brought into the slums a large number of the unfortunate from neighboring countries; and the Amsterdam upper classes lived in contempt and sometimes in fear of the temper of this mob. The grauw had turned on the Catholics before the revolt. After independence, members of the mob had lynched captains for losing sea battles and city fathers for supposed malfeasance. One of the wealthy burghers referred to them as "the sottish ill-natured rabble, who ever hate and are ready to impeach the aristocratical

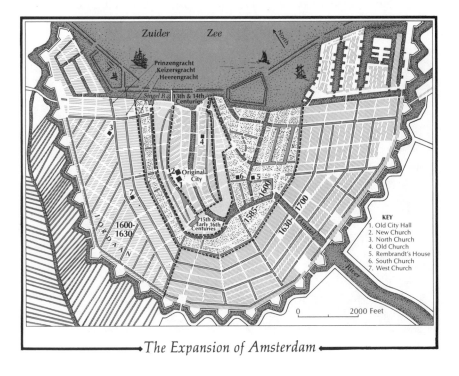

The Expansion of Amsterdam

rulers of their republic." They were a stratum almost totally alienated from the well-being of Dutch society. They could be aided by charity; the city of Amsterdam made a weekly distribution of money to the poor. Large numbers of orphanages, almshouses, and hospitals were founded by private individuals for the poor. But the most effective remedy was force. The poor were kept unarmed, while the wealthy joined in militia companies whose ostensible purpose was civil defense but who could be relied on to support the city government in the event of a mob uprising. Judicial punishment was harsh and fast. Criminals were branded with hot irons. Torture, the pillory, and executions by burning were common. A gallows stood at every entrance gate to the city. Prisons were rarely used; mutilation was cheaper. As a result, the grauw was usually submissive, if not entirely docile.

The Kleine Man (The Little Man)

The artisans and manual laborers of Amsterdam were known collectively as the *"Kleine man."* Most were members of guilds, or worked for guild members. A distinction was made between craft guilds, such as the furriers', and the guilds of the manual laborers, such as the beer carriers' or the herring packers' guilds. In spite of the large population, it was remarkable that only a small number of people actually gained membership in a guild. At the end of the seventeenth century, the furriers' guild had only 36 members. Even the cobblers' had only 658. But the number of professions was very large. There were, for example, spoon makers, shoelace makers, shuttle makers, drum makers, comb makers, and clasp makers, all of whom have

The Cloth Guild, by Rembrandt

left their names to some tiny alley in the city. Most guild members ran small establishments of six to ten workers. In the plan for the city's enlargement, the artisans were squeezed into the area called the Jordaan just beyond the three new canals. The land was left lower than the main city, without the fill or the same pilings. Streets followed the diagonal lines of the old fields, and were no more than eighteen feet wide, divided by tiny canals. The width of the block was only one hundred twenty feet, a size that could have fitted into many of the gardens on the more princely canals. Profits were made quickly as these houses were built for the Flemings, Poles, Huguenots, Jews, and the poorer native Amsterdamers. But the quarter developed a character of its own, a genuine class solidarity. Everyone called the other "aunt" and "uncle." Artists loved the familiarity of the society and the quaintness of the streets and chapels. Rembrandt, de Hoogh, and Hobbema all lived there for a while. And the streets were laced with almshouses, as the merchants gave recognition to the labor that nourished their enterprise. It was perhaps this sense of a common way of life, of genuine camaraderie, that took the sting out of social discontent in seventeenth-century Amsterdam.

The Middle and Upper Classes

Directly above the *kleine man* who lived in the Jordaan came the professional class, the ministers of the Calvinist Church, the lawyers, teachers, company bureaucrats, and members of the wealthier guilds. Immediately above them in social status were the landed nobility, who were a class apart in a society where commercial wealth was the highest recommendation. They maintained town houses whenever possible, occasionally intermarried with the wealthiest burghers, and took service with the state. But they could not adopt any of the pretensions of the French or English aristocrats: "Those that govern themselves with prudence and moderation and make themselves familiar with their inferiors are highly respected and popular, while those that are still and haughty are generally hated and despised," an English visitor noted.

The summit of Amsterdam society was a small group of enormously wealthy merchants. They included the Heeren of the big companies, wholesale merchants, large-scale manufacturers, and shipyard owners. They had been the leaders in the struggle against Spain; and from the truce of 1609 they had held tight control not only of the city government of Amsterdam but of the States General itself. These were the families who built the great houses that lined the three new canals—the Herengracht (Gentlemen's canal), Keizersgracht (Emperor's canal), and Prinzengracht (Princes' canal). At 123 Keizersgracht, for example, lived Louis de Geer, whose rapid acquisition of enormous wealth was due to his winning control of a large part of Sweden's armaments industry. De Geer's family had moved to Amsterdam from the Belgian mining town of Liège, and set up a munitions trade there

The Marriage Contract, by Jan Steen (c. 1626–1679)
Steen has transferred the Old Testament story of the marriage of Tobias and Sara to a setting in contemporary Holland.
Courtesy De Young Museum, San Francisco

in 1615. Three years later, in company with some other Amsterdam merchants, he made himself responsible for repayment of a large loan owed by the Swedish king to the States General, and in return was given mining concessions in Sweden. He virtually created the munitions industry in Sweden, and then branched out into timber, naval supplies, and the retail trade. His weapons were used by the Scottish covenanters, the English royalists, the Venetian mercenaries, the Turks, the Russians, the Portuguese, and the Dutch themselves. De Geer divided his time between Sweden and Amsterdam, where in 1634 he bought the House with the Heads, an elaborate example of Dutch Renaissance building, so-called because six Roman busts are affixed to the facade. It is colorful, picturesque, and playful, with a kind of Roman triumphal arch topping a foursquare functional home. This indeed was typical of the early seventeenth-century building in Amsterdam. The burgher homes made little contribution to the advance of architecture; external decoration was the main variant in the style. In the second half of the century, a severely correct classicism was introduced, beginning with the palatial city hall and spreading to the more majestic mansions, such as the Trippenhuis built in 1660 for de Geer's nephews.

Joris de Caullery, by Rembrandt (1606–1669)
One year after his arrival in Amsterdam, Rembrandt was commissioned to paint this ship's captain who later became a prominent wine merchant.   Courtesy De Young Museum, San Francisco

Canal House, Amsterdam
Dutch housebuilders achieved variety in simple facades by use of patterns in red brick and white stone and by ornamentation of the upper gables.
Netherlands National Tourist Office photo

**Gentleman in Black, by
Gerard Terborch
(1617–1681)**
*Terborch specialized in
small, finely finished portraits of the wealthy upper
classes of Amsterdam.*
Courtesy De Young Museum,
San Francisco

The Burgher Way of Life

What impressed foreigners about these wealthy burghers was the simple
dignity of their way of life, at least at the beginning of the century. The Calvinist Church discouraged ostentation; and the well-to-do were careful to
appear in public in dark, simple clothes, mostly black with an occasional
touch of violet. On special occasions, the men wore a ruff of stiffened lacework around the neck, while the women were able to enliven their appearance with a colored bodice and cloak. In the home, all furnishings were of
sturdy quality, ostentatious only in their solidity. The average room had
three main pieces of furniture, a table, chair, and wardrobe. Floors were of

tile or marble slabs, arranged in alternating colors; ceilings were of dark wooden beams, staircases so narrow and steep as to give one vertigo. Cleanliness was almost a fetish. Foreigners complained that the wives often failed to cook properly to avoid dirtying their sparkling pans. By the middle of the century, however, wealth had begun to erode the pristine simplicity of the way of life. According to the English consul in Amsterdam,

The old severe and frugal way of living is now almost quite out of date in Holland; there is very little to be seen of that sober modesty in apparel, diet, and habitations as formerly. Instead of convenient dwellings, the Hollanders now build stately palaces, have their delightful gardens, and houses of pleasure, keep coaches, wagons and sleighs, have very rich furniture for their horses, with trappings adorned with silver bells. . . . Yea, so much is the humor of the women altered, and of their children also, that no apparel can now serve them but the best and richest that France and other countries afford; and their sons are so much addicted to play that many families in Amsterdam are quite ruined by it." [8]

Expensive clothes in silk and velvet, elaborate sashes and swords, and feathered hats indicated an aping of the styles of the French court. "The grave and sober people [of Holland]," Sir William Temple noted, "are very sensible of the great alteration that now is in this country."

The Government of the Great Merchants

Sensitivity to the change in manners was increased by the changes in the well-to-do class's attitude to government. At the time of the revolt against Spain, the great merchants' theory of government had been quite simply the right and duty of the well-to-do to rule as an oligarchy. Amsterdam was governed by a sheriff, four burgomasters, nine aldermen, and thirty-six city councillors, known collectively as the regents. A small number of families held permanent control of the regents' positions in Amsterdam. Amsterdam dominated the provincial assembly for Holland; and Holland, which contributed more to the federal budget than the other six provinces combined, controlled the States General. The essential characteristic of this merchant oligarchy was its determination to place economic progress ahead of religious uniformity. The regents of Amsterdam regarded intolerant Calvinism as a threat to the city's prosperity, and they fought continually against the medieval restraints that the Calvinist Church attempted to place on economic enterprise. It was partly a matter of class feeling, since the preachers of the Calvinist Church came mostly from the lower middle class. But the regents were mainly concerned with preventing the creation of a theocracy like Calvin's in Geneva. Conflict between the regents and the extreme Calvinists came to a crisis in 1618–1619. The more liberal Calvinists, called Ar-

[8] Boxer, *Dutch Seaborne Empire*, p. 38.

Lazarus at the Rich Man's Door, by Esaias van de Velde (1591–1630) and Bartholomeus van Bassen (c. 1590–1652)
The Biblical story provides the artists with an excuse for displaying the luxury enjoyed by the wealthiest merchants of Amsterdam.   Courtesy De Young Museum, San Francisco

minians after a theological professor named Arminius who held only mild views on predestination, were defeated in the national synod by the dogmatic, persecuting Calvinists, and the regent who had supported them was executed in Amsterdam on trumped-up charges. But even apparently triumphant within the Church, the extremists found that they could do little to make the ruling class of Amsterdam accept their rule in any sphere other than the theological. Catholics were persecuted in theory but not in practice, and most continued to worship in private chapels built into the upper floors of the larger Catholic homes. Even church attendance was not required of Calvinists themselves, while attempts by the preachers to ban the theater, dancing, and drinking parties were completely unsuccessful. The most the regents would do was accept an appearance of Calvinist godliness. It is thus not correct to say, as has been frequently asserted since the publication in 1904 of Max Weber's *The Protestant Ethic and the Spirit of Capitalism*, that Amsterdam was a perfect proof that Calvinism encouraged the virtues basic to capitalist economic expansion. Amsterdam was not an

example of a city where extreme Calvinists controlled political and economic life.

The other challenge to the regents' oligarchy came from the House of Orange. The official position of William the Silent and his descendants was stadholder of one or more provinces and commander-in-chief of the armed forces. Their strength lay in family popularity with the poorer classes and in the support of the Calvinist preachers. Their eventual goal was to be recognized as kings. At times the stadholders intervened directly against the regents of Amsterdam, and appeared triumphant. After the victory over the Arminians, the stadholder Maurice (1584–1625) was able to force the regents to accept most of his wishes, including the formation of the West India Company. But after Maurice's death in 1625, the regents of Amsterdam refused to support his successor, Frederick Henry (1625–1647) in his plans to reconquer Antwerp, which they had no desire to see revived as a rival to Amsterdam. By extending the financial aid and naval resources of the city only to those of the stadholder which they approved, the regents were able to reestablish their influence over his policy. In the war between Denmark and Sweden, the munitions kings de Geer and the Tripps and their friends were able to force intervention on the side of Sweden in spite of the stadholder's desire to help Denmark; and in 1648 they brought an end to the long war with Spain, against the wishes of the stadholder. The new stadholder, Prince William II (1647–1650), laid siege to Amsterdam, which prepared to defend itself by cutting the dikes and calling out the garrison, but gave in to avoid the economic damage of a civil war. William II however died of smallpox on the eve of his triumph, and no new stadholder was appointed for twenty-two years. Only when French invasion threatened did the country turn again to the House of Orange for leadership, appointing William III stadholder in 1672. By then the character of regent government itself had changed.

The most noticeable sign of the decline of the quality of regent government was in nepotism and outright corruption. The regents filled all governmental and many commercial offices with their relatives and friends. Bribery became common at the lower ranks of the bureaucracy; and at the higher level political control was used to make diplomatic decisions, as intervention in the Dano-Swedish war was, for the purpose of serving the interests of individual companies owned by members of the regent class. But the more important transformation was the shift of the regents' economic interests from commerce into real estate and securities. From the middle of the century, the regents lived off their investments, and as a result showed less understanding of the needs of overseas commerce. A cleavage developed between them and the wealthy merchants, the class from which they themselves had originally come, with a resultant weakening of the city's prosperity and of its power. The decline in the quality of regent government was thus one factor among many that marked the middle of the seventeenth century as the beginning of Dutch decline.

Rembrandt and the Golden Age of Dutch Painting

The decline is perhaps most obvious in Dutch painting, because there was hardly a single great painting produced in Holland between the death of Rembrandt in 1669 and the appearance of Vincent van Gogh two centuries later. Dutch painting achieved a brief, superlative triumph of a duration almost exactly equivalent to the period of merchant oligarchy in Amsterdam.

The Roots of Dutch Art

The character of Dutch painting was strongly influenced by the society to which it catered. It was Protestant, in the negative sense that the painters were not asked, and were often forbidden, to paint great religious tableaux like those of the Italian Renaissance. All paintings had been removed from the Dutch churches, and the Calvinist ministers were not commissioning any new ones. Corporate commissions were given by the militia guilds, or *schutterij*, by the merchant guilds and professional guilds like those of the surgeons, and by the governing boards of orphanages and almshouses. Calvinist morality prevented the political leaders from being portrayed as burgomasters or city councillors, and thus the group portraits were always in their economic or social roles. Wealthy merchants commissioned portraits of themselves and their families; four of Rembrandt's finest paintings were portraits of the Tripp family. Finally, artists painted, for future sale in art dealers' shops or in open-air fairs and street stalls, everyday scenes that people of all classes from the wealthy even down to peasantry liked to hang in their homes as an additional piece of furniture. The subject matter was severely restricted, and artists made a name by specializing in a particular subject: landscapes, seascapes, and skyscapes; interiors of homes; gardens and backyards; city streets and squares; church interiors; still lifes; and in at least one instance, cows. These genre paintings had to be small enough to hang in the restricted wall space of a Dutch home, and wide enough in appeal to represent an investment that could be converted into cash without difficulty. The naturalist style was one method of achieving this.

In each of these specialized types of painting, one or two artists became preeminent, because they achieved so individual a quality to their work that simple scenes were transformed in their hands. In landscape painting, especially of gnarled trees blowing wild on days of cloudy sunshine, it was Jacob van Ruisdael. In portraits, conceived with a masterfully implemented air of gay and casual abandon, it was Frans Hals. In cows, it was Aelbert Cuyp. In the painting of interiors, the master was Jan Vermeer, who was second only to Rembrandt in his understanding and love of light. Vermeer's pictures are all deceptively simple—a cook pouring milk into a brown bowl from a porcelain jug, a girl reading a letter, a young lady at a spinet. In all, the technique seems to be the same. There is a window, often invisible, in one cor-

ner of the room, which lights up one or two figures in fairly mundane clothes doing some simple action in a barely decorated room. But the light has become the most important object in the picture. It sparkles in folds in a silk dress, flickers through creases in a wall map, vibrates in pearls in a necklace, or picks out the studs in the side of a chair. His paintings have the quality achieved in only the greatest art, of heightening our appreciation of the reality round us.

The realism of Dutch painting had several roots. It was a continuance of an uninterrupted tradition of accurate, detailed observation that began in Flanders in the fifteenth century with the Van Eycks. But a great advance in the technical skills of the scientist in seventeenth-century Holland was also

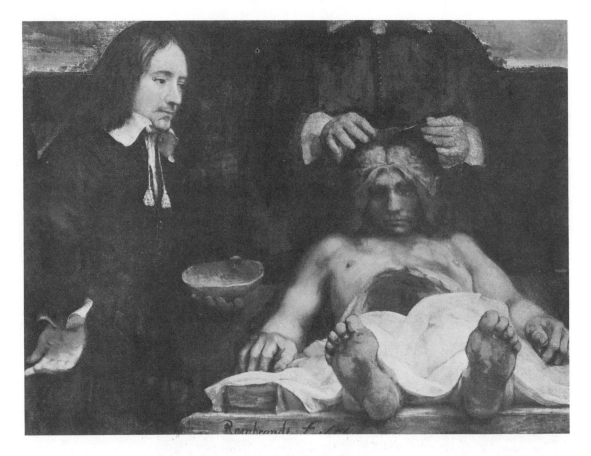

**Detail from The
Anatomy Lesson of Dr.
Deyman, by Rembrandt**
Courtesy Rijksmuseum,
Amsterdam

put to work by the artist. To aid navigation the Dutch invented the tele-
scope at the beginning of the seventeenth century. They developed great
skill in the making and polishing of lenses, and Amsterdam entomologist
Leeuwenhoek used them in the microscope to investigate such structures as
blood corpuscles and, of special interest to painters, drops of water. They
turned naturally to the nature of light. While the painters were exploring
every possible method for conveying the different character of light in
clouds, sunlit rooms, rich fabrics, or human features, a great Dutch scientist
suggested that light traveled in waves. Around the same time, the University of Leiden became one of Europe's centers of medical research that
made great advances in the study of anatomy. If the advantage of this
knowledge to painters was not obvious, it was made so by the startling
paintings of anatomical dissections that many painters undertook. The most
famous of all was Rembrandt's *The Anatomy Lesson of Dr. Deyman,* and his
heartbreaking etching *The Descent from the Cross* is truer to death than any of
the normal idealized views of a firm-limbed Christ being lowered to the
ground after his crucifixion.

The Young Rembrandt

Rembrandt was at once the greatest and the most individual of the Dutch painters; and his life is tied, more closely than that of any of the other painters mentioned, to Amsterdam. He settled permanently in the city in 1631 at the age of twenty-five, already equipped with the skills that brought rapid popularity among the wealthier patrons: a mastery of the depiction of light, an ability to bring motion to group scenes, and a psychological penetration in portraiture. He bought into an art dealer's partnership, and was at once introduced to the fashionable society of the three canals. Within months he had completed portraits of two rich merchants who were acquaintances of his art dealer. By 1639 he was wealthy enough to buy a large house and to have married Saskia, the daughter of one of the regents of the neighboring province, who became one of his favorite models. During the 1630s and 1640s Rembrandt rose to be the most popular painter in Amsterdam, showered with commissions by such families as the Tripps and by the merchant and militia guilds. Rembrandt thoroughly enjoyed Amsterdam's years of prosperity, made and spent a great deal of money, collected art himself, and until Saskia's death in 1642 filled their home with such exotic imports of the East India Company as Indonesian pottery, Japanese armor, and Arab swords. During these early years Amsterdam's patrician society accepted with admiration the changes that he made in the conventional portraits, the darkness behind the head that fills with light the longer one looks, the organized disarray of the figures in a group portrait, or the introduction of a moment of drama, as when Dr. Deyman slices open the scalp of the corpse he is dissecting. A myth is still spread that many of the militia members portrayed in Rembrandt's most famous group painting, *The Night-Watch,* were furious that his determination to create a dramatic scene had led to their subordination in the background and that they refused to pay him. Rembrandt was paid in full, however, and the painting was hung in a place of honor in the militia's guildhall. *The Night-Watch* marked Rembrandt's mastery of the baroque style in art. In particular, Rembrandt had used to the full the technique of *chiaroscuro,* the contrasting of light and dark developed in Italy in the sixteenth century. The figures are in surging movement through space, as the captain and his lieutenant move forward leading the congested mass of their civic guards outward toward the onlooker. Flags, drums, spears, halberds, and rifles create a sense of confused activity in the darkness. And the economy of color, lavished only on the red sash of the captain, the yellow uniform of the lieutenant, the dress of the little girl, and the pink velvet of the guard on the left, makes those few colors all the more dramatic.

The same baroque qualities of movement in space, contrast of light and shade, and dramatic coloring were present in the large number of religious paintings Rembrandt carried out during these years. At the time he was the only important painter in Amsterdam still interested in illustrating the

Bible; but many of his paintings were sold without difficulty. His great series of paintings of the passion of Christ was commissioned by the prince of Orange for his palace in The Hague. Rembrandt was also proving that similar effects could be achieved in etching, by drawing with a needle on a wax-coated plate on which nitric acid was poured to produce the printing-plate. Biblical scenes abounded; but he also produced sad little prints of crippled beggars, blind fiddlers, and lepers, of the human debris of the great city. Thus at the height of Rembrandt's fame, his central interest in deep human experience was already evident; but up to this point the taste of Amsterdam was able to grow with him.

The Night-Watch, by Rembrandt
Courtesy the Rijksmuseum, Amsterdam

The Tragedy of Rembrandt's Late Years

From the 1640s, Rembrandt and the patrons of Amsterdam grew slowly apart in their conception of art. Some wealthy merchants continued to patronize him to the end, and he never lost his reputation entirely. But he was not called on for any more lucrative group paintings until 1661; his painting for the city hall was rejected; and he was unable to sell more than a few of his religious subjects. The society of Amsterdam at midcentury was becoming more elegant, ostentatious, and superficial in its tastes. Even the painters of interiors found that the bare room with the simply dressed burghers

The Hundred-Guilder Print (detail), by Rembrandt
The Norton Simon Foundation, Los Angeles

**Self-Portraits, by
Rembrandt: Youth,
Middle Age, Old Age**
*Rembrandt painted many
self-portraits, tracing his
own journey from the exu-
berance of his early days
in Amsterdam through
personal tragedy to the final reconciliation with
life's burdens.*   Courtesy
De Young Museum, San
Francisco; Bildarchiv d. Ost.
Nationalbibliothek

had to be replaced with overelaborate decorations and Frenchified clothing. Rembrandt on the other hand was plunging deeper inside himself in his search for an art that would lay bare the depths of humanity. He was heartbroken at the death of Saskia, which was probably from tuberculosis. Commissions fell off, debts accumulated, and he was eventually declared bankrupt and forced to sell his house and art collection. His mistress, Hendrickje, was called before the Calvinist authorities for living with him; but she continued to stay with him until her death, also from tuberculosis, in 1663. His only son, Titus, died a year before Rembrandt himself. With tragedy piling up on him, Rembrandt's art became quieter, more subdued, and even more penetrating. Above all, in his self-portraits one can trace the passage of a deeply independent man from the despair of suffering, that tightens the skin around the mouth and fills the eyes with sadness, until a reconciliation with old age returns the glimmering of a smile to the face of a man in his last months of life.

From the Age of Gold to the Age of Periwigs

Amsterdam's Economic Decline

In Dutch history, the eighteenth century is often referred to contemptuously as the Periwig Age, when the once independent burghers copied French manners and modeled their society on the country that had driven them into decline. By then, economic disaster had affected much of the Netherlands. "Most of their principal towns are sadly decayed," wrote James Boswell in 1764, "and instead of finding every mortal employed you meet with multitudes of poor creatures who are starving in idleness." [9] Amsterdam alone retained its prosperity. Lovely new homes in restrained classical style were built along the three canals. The same number of ships docked along the Ij as in the midseventeenth century, and Amsterdam capitalists were pouring money into the purchase of government securities in all their neighboring countries. But the wealth no longer had a secure basis in commercial innovation, industrial productivity, and an expanding population. There was almost no change in the population of the Netherlands as a whole, nor of Amsterdam itself, between 1660 and 1800, while the population of France and England was booming. Throughout most of the eighteenth century, the total number of houses in Amsterdam remained stationary. Its industry declined in size, and many of its shipyards were idle for lack of orders. Its fishing fleet, which had made the herring fisheries a gold mine in the seventeenth century, was down to a quarter of its previous size. Its armaments makers were no longer supplying every army in Europe. Amsterdam was living precariously on the heritage of its golden age.

[9] James Boswell, *Boswell in Holland* (London: W. Heinemann, 1952), p. 288.

The reasons for the end of Amsterdam's economic expansion, and thus for its decline relative to such mushrooming cities as London and Paris, were partly the fault of the Dutch themselves. At its height, Amsterdam had laid far greater emphasis on overseas commerce than on industry. Money made in small-scale industry was invested in commerce; and the profits of commerce moved in the late seventeenth century into investments in land or securities. The movement of accumulated wealth worked against the coming of a large-scale industrial revolution. Moreover, the Dutch had permitted many of their skilled workers to be lured away by higher wages to other countries like Prussia or England, and they may have driven many out by their enormously high level of indirect taxation on everyday necessities. A Dutch worker paid three times as much in taxes as an English worker. The burden of taxes, and indeed a general impoverishment of the country, was due in part to wars in which the Dutch had engaged for profit. Their struggles with the Portuguese, their intervention in the Dano-Swedish war, their continual skirmishing with native dynasties and with European rivals in the Far East, their provision of convoys for their fleets in European waters to ensure "freedom of seas," were enormously costly.

It was, however, the advance of their rivals that destroyed Amsterdam's economic supremacy. The Dutch in the role of middleman had always been resented, while their concentration on finishing for resale raw materials or unfinished goods produced elsewhere left them vulnerable when other nations determined to take over their own manufacturing. Dutch freight declined when Britain and France built merchant navies in the eighteenth century, and achieved shipbuilding techniques in advance of the Dutch. The fisheries were invaded by large numbers of English, Scottish, Scandinavian, and Belgian vessels, who sold their catch at home or chose a new market for it in Hamburg. Dutch industry proved unable to compete with the luxury industries being founded in France with the financial support and control of the state; and it could not compete in price or quality with the mass production that began in England, especially in the textile industry, at the end of the eighteenth century. Even in agriculture, the Dutch began to fall behind the English as new productive techniques of capitalistic farming, the so-called agricultural revolution, were adopted in the eighteenth century.

Mercantilism

This increased competition need not have been so damaging if it had not been accompanied by acceptance by the English and French governments, and indeed by the Dutch themselves, of the economic theory called mercantilism. No one great theorist laid down the tenets to be followed, as Adam Smith was to do in the eighteenth century for free trade; and governments made only piecemeal efforts to apply the mercantilist views. Nevertheless, the opposition of England and France to the Dutch had an important theoretical basis. The mercantilist held that bullion, gold and silver, constituted national wealth. A country, to accumulate wealth beyond what could be dug from its own mines, had to export more than it imported, so that the difference would be paid in bullion. In short, a country had to strive for a favorable balance of trade. Moreover, the mercantilist felt that the amount of trade possible in the world was limited, and that therefore a country could only increase the amount of its trade at the expense of another country. "What matters this or that reason?" an English general commented shortly before England attacked the Dutch. "What we want is more of the trade the Dutch now have." Colonies and trade empires were necessary for supplying raw materials or trade goods that the home country could not produce, and they were to be kept as captive markets. Interlopers had to be kept out by force from a colonial, or commercial, monopoly overseas. The state was to intervene in the national economy to maintain quality production and to found new industries, and thus make possible greater exports; and the power of the state could be used to force open other countries' trade monopolies or to acquire colonies, if necessary, by war.

The Dutch were happy to follow mercantilism when it suited their purposes. They used force to keep control of the spice trade of Indonesia and the Moluccas and insisted that the mouth of the Scheldt be kept closed, to prevent the revival of Antwerp as a rival to Amsterdam. But they lacked the strong central government necessary for state direction of industrial production, and also the desire for one. Moreover, it became clear during their three wars with England (1652–1654, 1665–1667, and 1672–1674) and their war with France (1672–1678) that they would be the principal victim of the English and French conversion to mercantilism. English shipbuilding was stimulated by the government policy of requiring that imports be carried in an English ship or a ship of the exporting country. Tariffs in England and France were used to keep out Dutch goods, while subsidies were lavished on newly founded industries. In spite of the Dutch feat of sailing into the mouth of the Thames to destroy the British fleet in 1667, the Anglo-Dutch wars inflicted great damage on the Dutch economy; and the invasion by the French king Louis XIV in 1672 was only stopped by breaking the dikes and flooding the vast area from the Zuider Zee to the Rhine. War, while not destroying the prosperity of Amsterdam, had become a primary factor in sapping its expansive energies and diverting its resources to unproductive ends.

Amsterdam's hegemony had been brief, but it had left a number of valuable lessons to civilization: that toleration not only adds to the happiness of the greatest number but is good business as well; that a great city can be created in a small country of poor natural resources by skill in the provision of commercial and manufacturing services that larger, better endowed countries fail to supply; that a large city can quadruple in size in twenty years and become more beautiful in the process; and that restrained quality can be as great a virtue of civilization as exuberant magnificence.

SUGGESTED READING

Violet Barbour's *Capitalism in Amsterdam in the Seventeenth Century* (1950) is a short but incisive introduction to the city's economic life, and John J. Murray, *Amsterdam in the Age of Rembrandt* (1967) is a pleasant survey of its cultural growth. A superb short analysis of all aspects of Dutch civilization in the golden age, especially good on the Dutch influence abroad, is Charles Wilson, *The Dutch Republic and the Civilisation of the Seventeenth Century* (1968). For evocative essays by the great historian J. Huizinga, see his *Dutch Civilization in the Seventeenth Century and Other Essays* (1968).

C. V. Wedgwood provides a good introduction to the war with Spain in her biography *William the Silent* (1944). Primary sources are gathered in E. H. Kossman, ed., *Texts Concerning the Revolt of the Netherlands* (1974). The English contribution to the revolt is assessed in C. Wilson, *Queen Elizabeth and the Revolt of the Netherlands* (1974). Much fuller accounts are given in Pieter Geyl, *The Netherlands in the Seventeenth Century* (1961–1964) and in his two fine studies, *The Revolt of the Netherlands (1555–1609)* (1932) and *The Netherlands Divided (1609–1648)* (1936).

C. R. Boxer's *The Dutch Seaborne Empire, 1600–1800* (1965) is up-to-date, amply illustrated from contemporary sources, and full of information on Amsterdam as both an economic and a social unit. On Dutch agriculture, see J. deVries, *The Dutch Rural Economy in the Golden Age, 1500–1700* (1974). An interesting comparison of the social structure of Amsterdam and Venice is made by Peter Burke, *Venice and Amsterdam: A Study of Seventeenth Century Elites* (1974).

English visitors and diplomatic representatives wrote many accounts of the Netherlands, of which the best are Sir William Temple's *Observations Upon the United Provinces of the Netherlands* (1676) and W. Carr, *An Accurate Description of the United Provinces* (1691). The English poet Andrew Marvell wrote a splendidly vindictive poem called *Character of Holland,* which comments freely on Amsterdam, and which should be set beside the appreciative French view, Jean Parival, *Les Délices de la Hollande* (1662). The daily life of Amsterdam is revived with many contemporary references by Paul Zumthor in *Daily Life in Rembrandt's Holland* (1962).

As for Rembrandt himself, Joseph-Emile Müller, *Rembrandt* (1967) sticks closely to an analysis of artistic growth, while R. H. Fuchs, *Rembrandt in Amsterdam* (1968) discusses the painter's relationships with the city, especially its art patrons, theater, medicine, and religious communities. There are beautiful illustrations and a reliable text in Robert Wallace, *The World of Rembrandt 1606–1669* (1968), and authoritative treatment of Rembrandt and other Dutch painters, especially of the Rembrandt school, in Jakob Roenberg, Seymour Slive, and E. H. Ter Kuile, *Dutch Art and Architecture 1600 to 1800* (1966).

The influence of the unique geographical environment of the Netherlands is discussed in two excellent studies, Gerald L. Burke, *The Making of Dutch Towns: A Study in Urban Development from the Tenth to the Seventeenth Centuries* (1960) and Audrey M. Lambert, *The Making of the Dutch Landscape: An Historical Geography of the Netherlands* (1971).

Chronicle of Events

From the Baroque Era to the Age of Revolution

1600–1815

France and French Empire	Britain and British Empire	Germany	Other European Countries / International Events	Science and Technology / Culture
			1602 Dutch East India Co. founded	
	1603 d. Elizabeth James I (1603–1625)			1604 Cervantes's Don Quixote
	1605 Gunpowder Plot 1607 JAMESTOWN, Va. founded			
1608 QUEBEC founded 1610 d. Henry IV Louis XIII (1610–1643)			1610 Plan of the Three Canals, AMSTERDAM	1611 King James Version of the Bible 1614 d. El Greco 1616 d. Shakespeare; d. Cervantes
1614 Meeting of Estates General				
		1618 Thirty Years' War begins Ferdinand II, Holy Roman Emperor (1619–1637)	1618–1648 Thirty Years' War	1619 Inigo Jones's Whitehall palace in LONDON
	1620 Pilgrim Fathers land in Massachusetts			
1624–1642 Cardinal Richelieu principal minister				

France and French Empire	Britain and British Empire	Germany	Other European Countries / International Events	Science and Technology / Culture
	Charles I (1625–1649)	1625 Danish king Christian IV invades Germany		1625 d. Lope de Vega
	1628 Assassination of Buckingham			1628 Harvey proves circulation of the blood
	1629–1640 Charles's personal rule			1629 Bernini appointed architect of St. Peter's, ROME
		1630 Swedish king Gustavus Adolphus invades Germany		1630 d. Kepler
				1635 Foundation of French Academy 1636 Corneille's Le Cid

1642 d. Galileo; birth of Newton

1662 Palace of Versailles begun

1666 French Academy of Sciences

1667 Milton's *Paradise Lost*

1669 d. Rembrandt

1640 Portugal throws off Spanish rule

1648 Treaty of Westphalia

1667–1668 War of Devolution

1672–1678 Dutch War

Roman Emperor (1637–1657)

Frederick-William I, the Great Elector of Prussia (1640–1688)

1638–1639 Scottish wars
1640 Long Parliament
1641 Execution of Strafford
1642–1648 Civil wars

1649 Execution of Charles I
1649–1660 Puritan Commonwealth

1652–1654 First Dutch War
1653 Cromwell Protector
1658 d. Cromwell; Charles II (1660–1685); Restoration period

1665 Great Plague
1665–1667 Dutch War
1666 Great Fire

1672–1674 Third Dutch War

1642 MONTREAL founded

Louis XIV (1643–1715)

1661 d. Cardinal Mazarin; personal rule of Louis XIV begins

1669 Colbert principal minister; adoption of mercantilism

1650

	France and French Empire	Britain and British Empire	Germany	Other European Countries/ International Events	Science and Technology/Culture
1675	1683 d. Colbert 1685 Revocation of Edict of Nantes 1691 d. Louvois, minister of war	James II (1685–1688) 1688 Glorious Revolution; William III (1688–1702) and Mary (1688–1694)	Frederick I, Elector of Prussia (1688–1713) and King of Prussia (1701–1713) Reconstruction of royal palace in BERLIN by Andreas Schlüter	1678 Treaty of Nijmegen 1683 Turks besiege Vienna 1689–1697 War of the League of Augsburg Peter I, the Great, Tsar of Russia (1689–1725) 1697 Treaty of Ryswick	1679 d. Vondel 1687 Newton's *Principles* 1690 Locke's *Essay Concerning Human Understanding*
1700	Louis XV (1715–1774) 1715–1723 Regency of Duke of Orleans	Anne (1702–1714) George I (1714–1727) 1715 Uprising in Scotland 1720 Collapse of South Sea Company 1721–1742 Walpole leading minister	Frederick William I, King of Prussia (1713–1740)	1700–1721 Great Northern War 1713 Treaty of Utrecht	1704 d. Locke 1717 Watteau's *Embarkation for Cythera* 1722–1723 Bach's *Well Tempered Clavichord*

1726–1743 Cardinal Fleury, chief minister			
George II (1727–1760)			1727 d. Newton
			1728 Chardin's *Le Buffet*
			1728 Gay's *Beggar's Opera*
	1733–1735 War of Polish Succession		1733 Kay's Flying Shuttle
			1733 Voltaire's *Philosophical Letters*
1738 John Wesley begins Methodist movement		Frederick II, the Great, King of Prussia (1740–1786)	
	1740–1748 War of Austrian Succession	1740 Prussia invades Silesia	
	Elizabeth, Tsarina of Russia (1741–1762)		1743 Neumann's Vierzehnheiligen church
1745 Uprising in Scotland			1745 Sans Souci palace in POTSDAM begun
			1748 Montesquieu's *Spirit of the Laws*
			1749 Fielding's *Tom Jones*

			1751 1st volume of *Encyclopédie*
			1755 Soufflot's Pantheon in PARIS
	1756–1763 Seven Years' War		1756 birth of Mozart
			1758 Helvetius's *On the Mind*
George III (1760–1820)			1759 Voltaire's *Candide*
		1762 Russian army occupies BERLIN	1762 Rousseau's *Social Contract*
1763 Annexation of French possessions in India and North America			

France and French Empire	Britain and British Empire	Germany	Other European Countries / International Events	Science and Technology / Culture
1764 Expulsion of Jesuits				
1769 Birth of Napoleon Bonaparte	1765 Stamp Act			1769 Watts's patent for steam engine; Arkwright's water frame
				1771 Arkwright's spinning mill
Louis XVI (1774–1793)	1774 First Continental Congress		1772 First Partition of Poland	1774 Goethe's *Sorrows of Young Werther*
1774–1776 Turgot, controller of finances				
	1776 American Declaration of Independence		1776–1783 War of the American Revolution	1776 Adam Smith's *Wealth of Nations*
1778 Intervention in American Revolution				
1781 Dismissal of Necker after publication of budget	1783 Independence of American colonies		1783 Peace of Paris	
1783–1787 Calonne, controller of finances	1783 William Pitt the Younger, prime minister			
1787 Assembly of Notables				1785 David's *Oath of the Horatii*; Mozart's *Marriage of Figaro*
1789 Estates General meets; taking of Bastille				
1790 Civil Constitution of the Clergy				1790 Burke's *Reflections on the Revolution in France*
1791 Flight to Varennes of royal family				1791 d. Mozart
1791–1792 Period of constitutional monarchy				

1775

France	Britain	Germany / Prussia	International	Culture
1792–1795 Girondin ascendancy		1792 Prussia and Austria declare war against France	1792 beginning of Revolutionary war	1798 Malthus on population; *Lyrical Ballads* of Wordsworth and Coleridge
1793–1794 Reign of Terror	1793 Enters war against France		1793 First coalition against France	
1795–1799 Directory	1798 Nelson victory at Aboukir Bay		1793 Second partition of Poland	
1799 Coup d'état of Napoleon; First Consul			1795 Third partition of Poland	1800 Beethoven's First Symphony
1802 Napoleon Consul for life	1805 Nelson victory at Trafalgar	1805 Austrian defeat at Austerlitz	1802–1803 Temporary peace	
1804 Napoleon emperor	1806 d. William Pitt the Younger	1806 End of Holy Roman Empire	1806 Continental System	
		1806 Prussian defeat at Jena		
		1807 Stein chancellor of Prussia	1808 French invade Spain	
	1809 Wellington campaign in Spain		1809 Metternich Austrian chancellor	
	1812 U. S. A. declares war on Britain	1810 Hardenberg chancellor of Prussia	1812–1813 French invasion of Russia	
			1813 Battle of Leipzig	
1814 Napoleon abdicates Louis XVIII (1814–1824) 1815 Napoleon returns from Elba; Hundred Days			1815 Battle of Waterloo	

15 / *The Baroque City and Its Rulers*

In every period when civilization has achieved a kind of homogeneity, the city is the most revealing physical expression of the social and political realities of the age, or, to put it more bluntly, of the character and taste of the ruling classes. This was never more true than in the creation of the baroque city of the seventeenth and early eighteenth centuries.

The baroque city was created by remodeling and expanding existing cities, especially capital cities, on an enormous scale, or by creating totally new cities in equally magnificent proportions. Pope Sixtus V (1585–1590) completed the dome of Saint Peter's, the centerpiece of his city, and cut through the medieval and Renaissance fabric of Rome, long avenues linking in shimmering vistas great piazzas dominated by ancient Egyptian obelisks. At the Square of the Four Fountains, where the pope's architect ingeniously constructed a church the exact size of one of the piers of Saint Peter's, two long avenues crossed. One linked the monumental entrance gate to the city, which had been designed by Michelangelo, with the papal palace of the Quirinale. The other joined the ancient basilica of Santa Maria Maggiore with Santa Trinità dei Monti, from which the view extended over the whole of ancient Rome. The popes had become stage designers, and Rome was their theater. In Paris, the Bourbon kings, masters of a bureaucrat-designed absolutism, brought the shape of the city under the same discipline they were enforcing on society at large. The river front became a display of grandiose facades raised by royal decree, especially where the squat courtyard

The Ducal Palace, Karlsruhe German Tourist Information Office photo

St. Peter's, Rome
After the completion of Michelangelo's dome in 1590, the nave was lengthened, and in 1656 Bernini began the colonnades around the entrance square. TWA photo

of the Louvre palace was expanded in long pedimented galleries to link it with the tall pavilions of the Tuileries palace and the controlled vistas of the regimented gardens beyond. Great squares with inner gardens were built to provide apartments for the nobles—at first playful and jovial in red brick with yellow plastered motifs, as suited the taste of the popular King Henry IV, later grey and somber in massive limestone, reflecting the growing self-esteem of Louis XIII and Louis XIV. Where the river Neva emptied into the rain-drenched marshes of the Gulf of Finland, the autocrat of Russia, Tsar Peter I (reigned 1689–1725), laid the foundation stone for the new imperial capital of Saint Petersburg, which soon became a pastel panorama of palaces, schools, ministries, triumphal arches, monumental avenues, and geometric gardens. Even in London, amid the congeries of a medieval city rebuilt in all its confusion after the great fire of 1666, Christopher Wren raised the vast dome of Saint Paul's Cathedral. Frustrated in his desire to slap an orderly plan onto the city as a whole, he brought to the more amenable task of building suburban palaces the baroque ideals of orderly vistas and splendid facades.

The baroque city was the direct expression of the will of powerful monarchs or of privileged upper classes, who had succeeded in establishing their predominance in the power struggles of the sixteenth and seventeenth centuries. During this time, the politics of almost all the European states was concerned with a dialogue between the monarchy and the landed nobility and wealthiest bourgeoisie, who constituted the upper classes, a dialogue from which the majority of Europe's inhabitants were excluded. As a result of this dialogue, which ran the gamut from genuine debate over principles to all-out civil war, three major forms of monarchical government emerged. In Russia, the system of monarchical rule—strengthened by Tsar Peter I—was autocracy, the most extreme form of absolute monarchy in which almost no constraints upon the actions of the ruler can be imposed by the Church, the legal system, or constitutional bodies representing even the most influential of his subjects. The perfect urban expression of this form of monarchy was Peter's Saint Petersburg. In France, the second form of monarchy, absolutism, found its ideal form in King Louis XIV (reigned 1643–1715). In this type of state, the monarchy was able to weaken almost irreparably the medieval institutions, both constitutional and legal, that had existed to prevent the unfettered exercise of royal power, although the king continued to recognize the controls over his own actions exerted by the law of God, by traditional limitations on the functions of government, and by his need to compromise with the most powerful and wealthy nobles and bourgeois. In Paris and in Louis XIV's palace-city of Versailles nearby, we can observe both the strength and the limitations of this form of absolutism. In England, the upper classes gained political predominance against would-be absolute monarchs, and created a type of limited monarchy—or oligarchy—that functioned for their own benefit. The ideals of this oligarchy were reflected in the limited reconstruction of London after the great fire of 1666.

Yet we must be careful to avoid exaggerating the variations that exist within this urban culture and within the forms of government. The baroque style was the result of a fusion. It combined a wild emotional exuberance with a disciplined order, and particularly with a mathematical regulation of space. It joined the desire for order and the desire for freedom, the unrestricted imagination of the artist with the orderly experimental mind of the scientist, the sensuous religiosity of the South with the puritanical abnegation of the North. And the governments of the baroque age differ in degree more than in kind. France was not completely enslaved and England was not completely free. We are about to explore variations within a surprisingly unified culture, not unrelated societies.

In this chapter we shall first examine the functions served by the baroque city, and the style of city building developed to satisfy those functions. We shall then consider the three types of government developed in Russia, France, and England—autocracy, absolutism, and oligarchy; and in each case we shall see how the type of government influenced the form of city created.

Functions of the Baroque City

The Renaissance had merely modified the medieval city, changing the character of a few streets or squares and adding a few great palaces or churches to quarters that remained essentially medieval in character. Great new cities were conceived on paper, like those of Filarete, but were never completely built. But in the seventeenth and early eighteenth centuries, old cities were

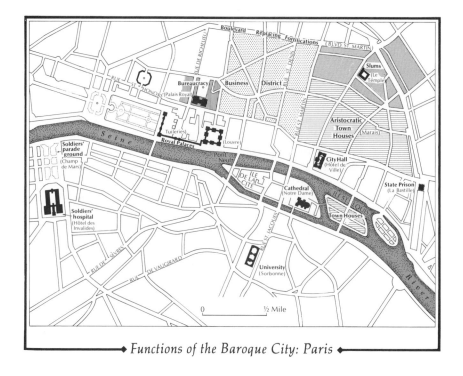

◆ *Functions of the Baroque City: Paris* ◆

transformed and vast new cities completed. The surprise of this period of city building was that the function of the new city and the style in which it was built were in perfect harmony.

The Palace

The most important function of the new city was to be the residence of the ruler and that small group of the upper classes who formed his court. It therefore required a palace or palaces and a large number of palatial houses in fairly close proximity. The palace served a kind of psychological function, impressing on the mass of the subjects their inferiority by the contrast of their own homes with that of the sovereign and emphasizing by physical separation their remoteness from political decision making. The most obvious separation occurred when the kings moved just outside their capital cities to palaces built as towns in themselves, as the French king Louis XIV did at Versailles or the Austrian empress Maria Theresa did at Schönbrunn. In these cases there was a ten- or twenty-mile walk for the common people of the city to glimpse even the outside of their sovereign's residence. But even where the palace was built as the central building of a city, as was more often the case, the architect used every trick he possessed to emphasize the separation from the rest of the city; the east facade of the Louvre palace in Paris, added by Louis XIV, has a ground floor so plain and forbidding that few would be attracted to approach closer. Were one tempted to go nearer, especially at the smaller palaces of the tiny German states or the houselike palace of the Danish kings, a permanent military detachment acted as a discouragement, or long rows of serrated grillwork provided a physical barrier. Louis XIV's chief minister, Colbert, summed up the purpose of palace building neatly: "In the absence of impressive acts of war, nothing marks the greatness of mind of princes better than the buildings that compel the people to look on them with awe, and all posterity judges them by the superb palaces they have built during their lifetime."[1]

The palace was the setting wherein an extremely complicated ceremonial was acted out. Every aspect of the ruler's day was exploited to provide time-consuming tasks for the court nobility, who were in many cases almost entirely excluded from the real exercise of political power. Louis XIV provided the model that was copied by almost every monarch of Europe. At his levée, or getting-up, for example, he expected all the courtiers to assemble outside his bedroom. The most privileged were admitted first to see him presented with holy water and to ask him favors. Then all were brought in to see him put on his clothes, and to note who was specially fa-

The Louvre Palace, Paris
The long facade facing the river Seine was constructed in the sixteenth century by Catherine de Médicis and Henry IV, to link the old courtyard of the Louvre palace with a new Tuileries palace that was destroyed in 1871.
French Embassy Press and Information Division photo

[1] E. A. Gutkind, *Urban Development in Western Europe*, vol. 5, *France and Belgium* (New York: Free Press, 1970), p. 115.

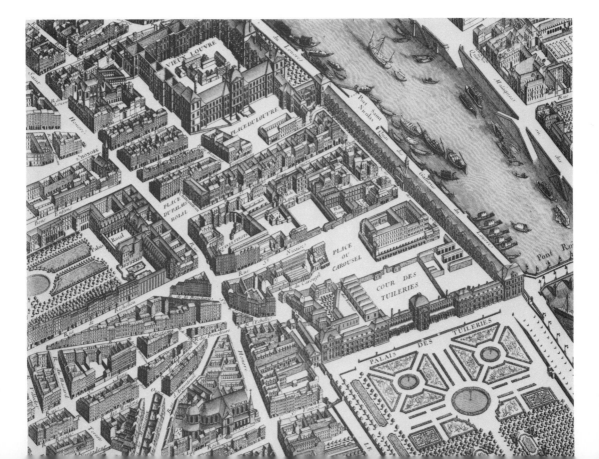

vored with the task of handing him his shirt. They stayed long enough to see him shaved, take a glass of wine and water, and say prayers. Finally they trailed after him to daily Mass. Such meaningless ceremonies enabled the king to exploit the vanity and ambition of his nobility, keep them in sight and thus unable to plot sedition, and sap their finances in conspicuous consumption. This artificial court life existed in the smallest courts, like that of Nassau, which controlled a principality of only a few thousand inhabitants; and it was enforced on even the most recalcitrant nobility. Peter compelled his nobles to look like Frenchmen by shaving them himself! (It should not be forgotten, however, that hardheaded economic calculations justified the decoration of the palace with the finest products of the country's handicraft and industry. Participants, both native and foreign, in the palace ceremonial were being subtly pressured to purchase for themselves similar examples of the country's glassware, tapestry, silver, and armor.)

The Bureaucracy

The palace also accommodated the bureaucrats who actually exercised the power of government; where the palace was insufficiently large for the growing horde of middle-class administrators required by the centralizing monarchs, special government ministries were erected nearby. The worldwide affairs of the Catholic Church were run from the Vatican palace, which expanded to include more than a thousand rooms, twenty courtyards, and eighty staircases. Government ministries in Versailles were concentrated around the entrance to the palace courtyard, where three vast avenues met in an arrowhead. Here, in carefully proportioned buildings, were the mansions for Messieurs des Bâtiments (buildings); Messieurs des Receveurs Généraux (tax collectors); and so on. Peter the Great decided to copy the bureaucratic pattern of Stockholm; and in the original design for Saint Petersburg, he assigned a frontage of the central Basil island in the Neva river to twelve identical government ministries. The idea of a governmental section of town, devoted to office buildings, was born with the baroque city; and only too frequently monotony was the architect's inspiration as well as the character of the bureaucrat's life.

Town Houses of the Aristocracy

The presence of the court required large numbers of houses for the aristocracy, built on a splendid enough scale for them to entertain each other. Peter insisted that every Russian noble build himself a house in Saint Petersburg, and forbade the use of stone for building anywhere else in Russia until his city was completed. French nobles demanded a town house separated from its neighbors by high walls, with an inner court surrounded by stables and offices, and frequently a broad garden behind the house. One of the most sumptuous examples of real-estate speculation occurred in Paris when a group of engineers, in return for building a bridge, were given the

right to drain the two little islands upstream from the Ile de la Cité and to sell off the resultant building lots. In a short time, the Ile Saint Louis became the favored quarter for nobles and lawyers, whose mansions rimmed the island and provided ever-changing views of the river and its traffic. In London, where aristocratic life was considerably less formal, most of the well-to-do lived in terrace houses; but from the seventeenth century on, they were built in squares. Not only did the square have the advantage of creating open space, which was turned eventually into a park of lawns and trees, but it established the class homogeneity of those who lived on the square by making the houses roughly the same in price, a triumphant distinction not even achieved on the Amsterdam canals.

The Army's Demands on the City

The army accompanied the monarch into the city, and was indeed the insurance of his power. "The name citadel is given to a particular part of a town, fortified on both the town and the country sides, and it is principally intended for the quartering of soldiers to keep the inhabitants of the town loyal in their duty," wrote one French theorist. The army required a fortified building or area as a center of operations in times of rebellion, and from which it could retake the city, a place that would symbolize to the citizens the power of the monarch. The slender spire of the Peter and Paul Cathedral marked for Saint Petersburg the fortress island where Russia's tsars held their political prisoners; in 1917 the taking of the fortress was one of the primary tasks of the Bolshevik revolutionaries. In London and Paris, medieval fortresses, the Tower and the Bastille, remained the principal royal garrisons; but vast numbers of barracks buildings also were put up. This was even truer in Berlin where almost a quarter of the population were soldiers.

The soldiers required parade grounds, which were created in the center of the town. The Champ de Mars, where the Eiffel Tower stands now, was the main parade ground in Paris. The English horse guards drilled on the wide sandy grounds behind Whitehall. Even in a city like Boston, Massachusetts, one of the principal uses of the common was for drilling the militia. To see soldiers on parade was one of the most popular free entertainments for city crowds; and when James Joyce, at the end of *Ulysses,* has Molly Bloom meditate on the regiments she has known, he is appealing to emotions that have been three centuries in the making:

I love to see a regiment pass in review the first time I saw the Spanish cavalry at La Roque it was lovely after looking across the bay from Algeciras all the lights of the rock like fireflies or those sham battles on the 15 acres the Black Watch with their kilts in time at the march past the 10th hussars the prince of Wales own or the Lancers O the lancers theyre grand or the Dublins that won Tugela.[2]

Molly felt something of the fascination of the French aristocrat Saint-Simon when he watched the mock battle rehearsed for Louis XIV on the plain outside Compiègne:

A wonderful sight—the vast army, cavalry, and infantry deployed, and the game of attacking and defending the city. But what struck me most, and remains as clear in my mind today after forty years, was the King on that rampart in supreme command over the whole army and that vast mass of myrmidons around him crowded on the rampart and spread out across the plain.[3]

The army wanted also triumphant avenues, long broad streets up which it could march in victory or simply in routine celebrations; and these streets also served the purpose of breaking up the rebellious lower-class quarters of the city into isolated islands that could be subdued individually, while the intersections of the new avenues, marked by a circle, or *rond point,* was an ideal point for placing artillery in time of insurrection.

New Fortifications

The wider and more effective range of cannons constricted the city enormously because new fortifications of a more complex and land-consuming

[2] James Joyce, *Ulysses* (New York: Random House, 1966), p. 749.

[3] Duc de Saint-Simon, *Louis XIV at Versailles,* trans. Desmond Flower (London: Cassell, 1954), p. 50.

size had to be constructed. The medieval wall was almost useless by the beginning of the seventeenth century, and military engineers were creating ever more ingenious patterns of masonry and earthworks to blunt the bombardment of artillery. But the new walls were so large that once constructed they could hardly ever be moved outward to accommodate increased populations. Space had to be found inside the city by giving up the gardens and orchards that had sweetened most medieval cities, by building upward to an average six stories and sometimes to ten, and especially by crushing the poor into ever more constricted quarters. Fortunately for Paris, Louis XIV decided that France was to be defended at its frontiers, where his engineer Vauban was constructing the most impregnable fortress cities in Europe. He allowed Paris to become an open city, turning the ramparts into boulevards and the city gates into triumphal arches; and when a wall was constructed at the end of the eighteenth century around a Paris that had doubled in area, its purpose was to enforce the collection of city import taxes, not defense. London, too, managed without a new city wall; but most capitals did not. Berlin, Copenhagen, Amsterdam, Vienna, Munich, Rome, were all restricted by their walls, the one advantage for the future being the easy conversion of the ramparts and their line of fire, or esplanade, into a green belt around the old city. The famous Ring of boulevards in Vienna is the product of such a conversion.

Needs of Business

The economic function of the city, even of those primarily administrative capitals, remained important. The need for a central machinery for handling the business transactions of the commercial revolution was met by the stock exchange and the banks. Wren made a new Royal Exchange, not Saint Paul's Cathedral, the focal point of his plan for the rebuilding of London. Peter gave the tip of Basil Island to the Bourse, which was rebuilt several times to give it the dominant role in the city's river facade. The proximate location of the stock exchange, the great banks, and the overseas trading companies led to the specialization of one area of the city in large-scale commercial transactions. In London, it was the "City," the area that lay between Saint Paul's Cathedral and the Tower of London, that developed the extraordinary mixture of specialized stores, stock traders, bankers, artisans, guildsmen, news reporters, shipping companies, artisans, and lawyers, that delighted such observers of humanity as Dr. Johnson in the eighteenth century and Charles Dickens in the nineteenth. Immediately below the City lay the docks, the other requirement of all the great commercial centers. Here again there was a great similarity in Europe's great cities. The same forest of masts could be seen in the Pool of London, in the Sea of Straw of Lisbon, or at the Elbe docks in Hamburg. Even the inland cities were dependent on water transport, and crowded docks were to be found on the Seine in Paris, the Moscva in Moscow, the Danube in Vienna and Budapest, and the Po in Milan. For all the large cities, one primary function of this shipping was to supply food and raw materials for its artisan classes, supplies usually brought from distant areas. The social peace of the city was dependent on the regular maintenance of this supply. When the Seine froze in 1788, preventing the arrival of food barges, it added directly to the misery of the lower classes that erupted in revolution the next year.

Church Building in the City

Library, Wiblingen Monastery, Germany
This colorful room illustrates the baroque use of simulated marble columns, writhing statues, and ceiling paintings that seem to open the room to the sky.   German Tourist Information Office photo

Finally, the requirements of religion had to be met, although churches rarely were the most important buildings constructed. At one extreme, there were churches that were deliberately conceived as the physical expression of great religious movements. The church of the Gesú in Rome was the triumphant assertion by the Jesuit order of the ambition of the Catholic Reformation; the four churches named after the points of the compass in Amsterdam represented a Calvinism that had won independence from Spain's repression; Saint Paul's in London is the most urbane expression of the ecumenical character of the Anglican Church. But frequently the

Hôtel des Invalides, Paris
This military hospital was founded by Louis XIV to house 7,000 disabled soldiers. The Emperor Napoleon was buried beneath the great dome. Interphototèque

churches served other purposes. The splendid domed church of the Invalides in Paris is, as its name suggests, attached to a military hospital, while the great Austrian and South German monasteries in which baroque architecture achieved its most fanciful forms seem more calculated to provide a wide range of aesthetic and worldly pleasures to the monks rather than to satisfy the code of Saint Benedict.

Thus, the urban planners had to provide for the requirements of a royal court and aristocracy, a well-to-do commercial bourgeoisie, a large military class and, to a minor degree, the churches. They presupposed the existence of a large laboring class, but rarely made provision for it.

The Style of the Baroque City

Meaning of Baroque

The style of the baroque city builder exactly suited the functions of the baroque city; and many of those who disapprove of the style are in reality disapproving of the function, as for example, nineteenth-century Protestants disapproved of the sensual appeal of Rome's Catholic Reformation churches. We must begin by removing the confusion of nomenclature. The word *baroque* originally meant odd-shaped, but it came to be applied to the architecture of Italy from the midsixteenth century on because that architecture too was characterized by unusual, extravagant shapes. This style

Saint Jerome, in Saint John Nepomuk Church, Munich
In a tiny chapel they built next to their own home in Munich, the Asam brothers, Cosmas and Egid, combined painting, sculpture, and architecture in a wildly dramatic composition celebrating the Trinity. German Tourist Information Office photo

was predominant in Italy throughout the seventeenth and much of the eighteenth centuries, and passed from there to Spain and Portugal and the Catholic states of Germany and Austria. The main characteristics of the style in architecture were movement and tension, theatricality, and emotionalism. Movement and tension were attained by use of undulating curves, sculptured figures, and vast, wildly colorful wall and ceiling paintings. Theatricality was created by constant employment of optical illusions, and by the combination of richly colored marbles, precious stones, stucco, and shining metals with statuary of unrestrained voluptuousness. Emotionalism was achieved through direct representation in exaggerated form of the sufferings of the saints or of the kindliness of the Virgin or simply by the appeal to the senses through color or form. Baroque eventually came to mean a series of specific tricks in architecture, sculpture, and painting. Facades were composed of two convex and one concave curve. Altars were designed like theatrical stages. Statues swarmed over walls and ceilings instead of sitting in well-defined niches. Ground plans were composed of ovals rather than squares or circles. Ceiling paintings gave the illusion of a building opening to the sky.

It is often said that the North of Europe rejected the baroque because its artists and patrons were repelled by these features of its style. Inigo Jones, the English king's architect at the beginning of the seventeenth century, wrote scornfully of the style of Rome: "Ye outward ornaments oft to be sollid, proporsionable according to the rulles, masculine and unaffected. . . . All thes composed ornaments the which Proceed out of ye aboundance of dessigners and wear brought in by Michill Angelo and his followers in my oppignon do not well in solid Architecture." [4] The answer of these Northerners, in England, France, and the Netherlands in particular, was to revert to what they considered pure classicism, by which they meant continuance of the style of the High Renaissance. This implied correct use of the orders of capitals, solid balance rather than movement in facades, simplicity and sobriety of interior decoration, and restraint in the use of color. What is important, however, is that the artists and architects of the North never achieved this classical ideal both because they never entirely rejected characteristics of baroque style and because they shared the intellectual ideals of the baroque age. For this reason it is justifiable to speak of the baroque city in both southern and northern Europe. Whether the motifs were those of Roman baroque or French classicism, the cities were baroque creations. Let us look more closely at what they had in common.

Principal Features of the Baroque Style

One should first note that the baroque artists and architects of Italy were admirers of geometry and mathematics, a taste that they inherited from the

---

[4] Cited in Nikolaus Pevsner, *An Outline of European Architecture* (Harmondsworth, England: Penguin, 1964), p. 309.

Renaissance that was greatly magnified by the scientific progress of the century. The city planners were fascinated by geometrical patterns, and they loved to work out abstractly all the variations possible in the planning of the city. In the simplest form, they worshipped the straight line, the search for the infinite, and from this they hit on the notion of the endless vista down a street of identical houses. They loved the intersections of straight lines, which could be opened out into traffic circles embellished with fountains or statues, or where vistas could be dramatically terminated with some impressive building. They elaborated squares, oblongs, ovals, and stars, which were all eventually tried in actual city building. This mathematical basis for the city was just as appealing in the North as in the South because the functions it served were the same. Everywhere the pedestrian was displaced along with the curved medieval streets, and the well-to-do in their carriages enjoyed the long avenues that on foot were both tiresome and tiring. The London squares, the half-star of the new city of Karlsruhe, even the canals of Amsterdam, carried on this baroque absorption with the geometrical ordering of space. The three avenues that converge at the entrance to the chateau of Versailles and those that meet in the Piazza del Popolo in Rome are virtually identical.

The desire for the infinite showed itself in many other ways in South and North. Mirrors became a favorite interior decoration, the most grandiose use of them being in the Hall of Mirrors in Versailles, the most important room in the whole kingdom of France. The ceiling painting was adopted in the North with almost no change of style, as when Louis XIV masquerading as Apollo floated over the heads of his courtiers, in the acres of canvases painted for Versailles by the court painter Le Brun. The vast

Royal Naval College, Greenwich
Designed by Christopher Wren (1632–1723) originally as a home for pensioned sailors, the college combines strict adherence to classical detail in the decoration of the buildings with a baroque freedom in the treatment of the twin towers. British Tourist Authority photo

Adoration of the Lamb, by Bacciccio (1639–1709) *In this sketch for a ceiling fresco in the Jesuits' church in Rome, Bacciccio used foreshortening of his figures to create the illusion of swirling movement in the heavens.* Courtesy the De Young Museum, San Francisco

formal gardens sought the merging of the artificial and the natural, preferably at the infinite horizon. The great palaces, whether at Munich, Hampton Court, or Versailles, made use of artificial canals to lead the eye out through receding forest to the far skyline.

Above all, it was in espousing baroque emotionalism that the artists and architects satisfied the desires of their patrons. Sheer size was emotionally impressive. The garden front of Versailles is six hundred yards long. It took the brass roof from the Pantheon to construct the huge twisted columns of Bernini's shrine over the high altar of Saint Peter's. The exuberance of Italy reached the North in such devices as the use of fountains and the decoration of parks or streets with writhing or soaring statues of pagan gods. Also, in the planning of interior space, the key was the use of the oval—for floor plans, ceiling paintings, and even niches in facades. The result of using ovals instead of squares or circles was a charming, vibrant elegance that the seventeenth- and eighteenth-century courtiers thought ideally suited their way of life. These patterns produced what is often called spatial polyphony, a weaving into an intricate pattern of several important lines of architectural emphasis. Christopher Wren was the great master of this art in England; and he used it fully when, after the Great Fire, he was given the task of drawing up new plans for fifty-one city churches. His ingenuity reached its greatest height in the church towers he created, an amazing variety of them within a simple form achieved by playing with

Fountain of the Rivers, Rome
Gianlorenzo Bernini (1598–1680) modeled his statues after ancient Roman river gods, in creating a centerpiece for Rome's oval Piazza Navona.   Italian Government Travel Office photo

geometric patterns. And this same quality can be felt in all the baroque cities, even when the most determined attempt has been made to use pure classical forms. The Paris and Versailles of Louis XIV, the London of Wren, the Saint Petersburg of Peter the Great, the Washington of the French city

Plan for Washington, D.C., by Charles L'Enfant (1754–1825)
L'Enfant's plan of 1791 for a gridiron pattern of streets, broken by diagonal avenues radiating from the White House and the Capitol, was not fully implemented until 1901. French Embassy Press and Information Division photo

planner Pierre Charles L'Enfant, the Rome of Bernini, all are unmistakably the products of the same age.

Autocracy in Russia

After examining the features of function and style that gave every baroque city a certain family resemblance, we turn now to the rich variations that existed within the pattern. In Russia, France, and England, we shall follow the rise of three different types of monarchical rule and the consequent variation in the form of urbanism adopted in St. Petersburg, Paris and Versailles, and London.

Origins of the Russian State

The most extreme example of the swing to absolute monarchy occurred in Russia. The first Russian state, governed from Kiev from the ninth to the midthirteenth century, had been at least as advanced as contemporary states in western Europe. It had given the Russians a common language written in the Cyrillic alphabet and a common religion, the Greek Orthodox faith it had accepted from Byzantium. While a powerful noble class of boyars clustered around the prince, the majority of the peasantry were probably free; and flourishing trade with Byzantium and to a lesser degree with the West supported a numerous merchant class in such cities as Pskov and Novgorod. This promising evolution was interrupted by the invasion of the Mongol tribes of Tartars led by Genghis Khan and his nephew Batu Khan who, after conquering most of Asia, swept into southern Russia and destroyed Kiev in 1240. The Tartars exercised overlordship over Russia for the next two hundred years, effectively cutting off Russia from its contacts

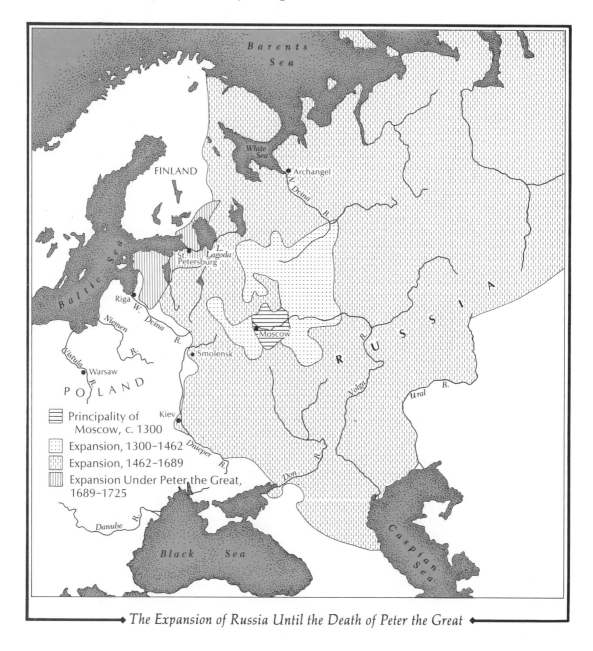

◆ *The Expansion of Russia Until the Death of Peter the Great* ◆

with the West and destroying its commercial ties except those through Novgorod. After the savagery of the initial conquest, the Tartars were satisfied to exact tribute in money and military recruits; but they left behind a tradition of autocratic government that was inherited by the native rulers whom they used as their intermediaries, especially the princes of Moscow. The city of Moscow was a relatively new creation, begun on the frontiers of settlement in the twelfth century; but by the fifteenth century its rulers had annexed so many surrounding territories that they possessed the most important principality under the Tartar ruler. By 1480, they were able to deny the Tartars their tribute and to confine them to three Khanates in the extreme south of Russia. The prince of Moscow, Ivan III (reigned 1462–1505), took the Byzantine emperor's title of *autocrat* after the fall of Constantinople, married the niece of the last East Roman Emperor, and supported the claim that Moscow had inherited the religious preeminence of Constantinople and was thus the Third Rome. At the same time he declared that Moscow had inherited the lands of the former Kievan state, which had extended to Lithuania and Poland; and in a series of wars, he seized from the Lithuanian prince huge territories extending westwards as far as Smolensk.

Moscow Under Ivan III

Ivan III was the true founder of Russian absolutism. He acted, like the Tartars, as though he were unimpeded in his exercise of power by the control of law. He controlled a state church that recognized him as its supreme authority. And he conceived of the landed nobles as a service aristocracy, who were to receive their privileges only to the extent that they served the state. To achieve this goal, he founded a class called *pomietchiks,* who were given lands for their lifetime in return for service to the tsar and in particular for their support against the hereditary aristocracy. He also began the custom, to be greatly expanded later, of tying the peasant to the land, so that he could not avoid working for the landlord or paying taxes to the state. The symbol of this new monarchy in the East of Europe, an area considered by most West Europeans as the extreme of barbarism, was the magnificent Kremlin, built for Ivan by architects brought in from Italy. The original fortress of Moscow had been built in the twelfth century on the junction of two rivers, in the triangular form favored for most Russian cities, and it had been extended a few times, usually in wood. But in 1485–1495, Ivan's Italian architects constructed the huge Kremlin walls that still exist, one and a half miles in length, sixty feet high, and fifteen feet thick, using a deep red brick and breaking the regular crenelation of the wall with riotously decorated watch and gate towers. They created inside, contrasting with the horizontal lines and rich color of the walls, a fantasy of cathedrals, not one vast church but six, brilliantly white and topped with a breathtaking array of onion-shaped domes whose gold leaf could be seen shining from miles away. And next to the cathedrals they built a palace for the metropolitan of

The Kremlin, Moscow
The cathedrals of Ivan the Great blend harmoniously today with the elaborate facades of the nineteenth-century palaces and the spare columns of the So-viet palace of congresses.
From M. Ilyin, *Moscow: Architecture and Monuments* (Moscow: Progress Pub., 1968), p. 15.

Moscow, the head of the Russian church, and a splendid palace for the tsar. In a period of twenty years they created one of the most beautiful complexes of buildings in the world, comparable in its harmony to the Periclean temples on the Acropolis.

The grandeur of this creation of Ivan III belied the real strength of Russian absolutism, however. The immense size of Russia, constantly being increased by conquest and eastward colonization, challenged any efforts at strict control, while encouraging the constant movement of peasants in search of better lands. The landed aristocracy resisted the tsar's attempts to control them so vigorously that Tsar Ivan IV the Terrible (reigned 1534–1584) determined to use violence to break them. He resettled many

Moscow aristocrats on the frontiers and gave their lands to the new service nobility. Thousands of the old boyars were executed, while a regime of terror, called the *oprichnina*, or separate kingdom, was loosed against the nobles. The oprichniks were the first grim secret police of Russia, blackclad sadists on black horses with a dog's head on their saddle who struck indiscriminately throughout central Russia. The reaction came during the reign of Ivan's idiot son, Russia's "Time of Troubles," when the nobles attempted to run the country as an oligarchy, the peasantry rose in agonized rebellion, and the Poles struck as far as Moscow itself. The compromise settlement in 1613, by which an undistinguished nobleman called Michael Romanov became tsar, did not restore in practice an absolutism that had never been challenged in theory. The legal enserfment of the peasantry in 1649 strengthened the control of the nobles. The patriarch of Moscow even claimed theoretical supremacy over the tsar. Taxation of the peasants brought an inadequate revenue for maintenance of an efficient military force, yet drove them into constant rebellions. Finally, a reaction against foreigners following the Polish invasion led to the isolation of foreign merchants and technicians in ghettos in the big Russian cities, so that the pernicious modernizing influences of the West could not destroy the old ways of Muscovy.

Aims of Peter the Great

The reign of Peter the Great (1689–1725) is a watershed in Russian history because he achieved efficient autocracy by linking it to the enforced modernization of the political, economic, and social structure of Russia. Peter grew up in the foreign quarter of Moscow, exiled from the Kremlin by the regent, and learned there a fascination with the technical achievements of the West, contempt for the determined resistance to progress of the Muscovite aristocracy, a distaste for the ambitions of the Orthodox clergy, and distrust of the intrigues of the palace guard, or *streltsi*. His admiration for Western technology was confirmed during his first visit to western Europe in 1697–1698. The many early defeats in the Great Northern War with Sweden convinced him of the superiority of the Swedish army and navy and also of the Swedish civil service. Traditional Moscow became for him the great obstacle to a modernized Russia. At first he attempted to change the ways of Moscow, compelling the nobles to wear Western dress, to shave their long beards, and to work in the government ministries. But in 1703 he captured the mouth of the Neva River, which enters the Gulf of Finland, a window on the West where he at once began to construct the new capital of Saint Petersburg. To build his city he reopened the dialogue with the Russian nobility. The peasantry was to be more firmly tied to the land; and the landowners were to discover a new way of life in the service of the state. They were to be educated in Western knowledge, in the Guards regiments, the Naval Academy, the artillery, and the engineering

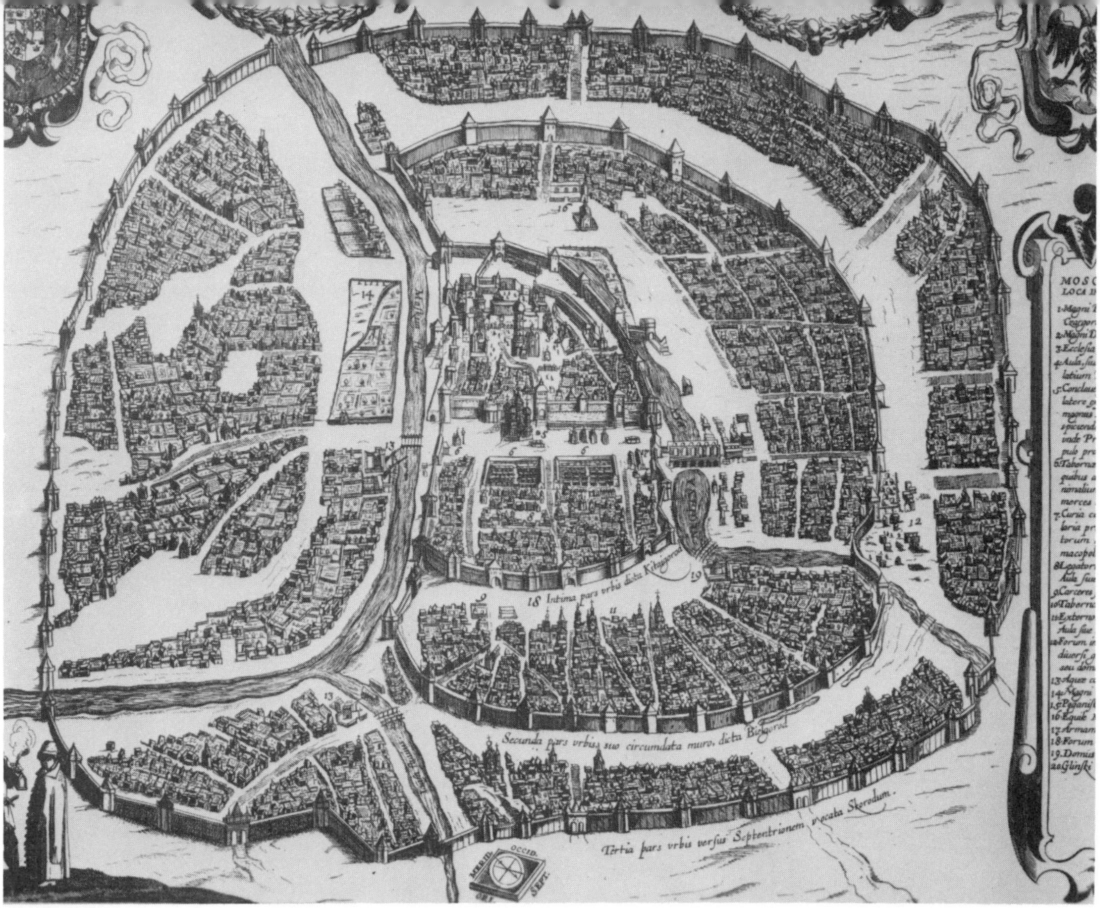
Intima pars vrbis dicta Kitaygorod
Secunda pars vrbis suo circumdata muro, dicta Bielgorod
Tertia pars vrbis versus Septentrionem vocata Skorodum.

Moscow in the Sixteenth Century
The inner fortress of the Kremlin is dominated by the Belltower of Ivan the Great. Just outside the wall rise the bulbous domes of St. Basil's cathedral.

schools. They were to be given a chance to rise through a Table of Ranks, by their service to the state in the military or civil service. And in Saint Petersburg, under the watchful eye of the tsar himself, they were to enjoy the amenities of European social life, whose economic requirements would be met by the forcible transfer of the merchant colony of Archangel.

The Creation of Saint Petersburg

Everything in Saint Petersburg, however, indicated the autocratic character of its founder. The site was sloppy marshland, where dysentery killed ten thousand of his first conscripted city builders. The nobility had to be compelled to leave the cold but salubrious climate of Moscow for the eternal drizzle of the Baltic coast; they were ordered to build homes whose size was assigned them by the police, after an inspection of their homes in Moscow. Tradesmen were moved into segregated streets, such as the Street of the Cannonmakers, the Street of the Armorers, and so on. The government ministries were grouped in identical pavilions on the central island, which Peter had hoped to turn into a new Amsterdam. The navy was given the island of Kronstadt, out in the river. The army had its barracks on the island of Saint Peter and Saint Paul, and later its parade grounds, as in Paris, on

The Admiralty, St. Petersburg, by G. A. Kochalov

The empress Catherine's vast Winter Palace was erected in the late eighteenth century next to the shipyards and naval headquarters of the Admiralty.

City Plan of Saint Petersburg in the Eighteenth Century

To the right are the regimented squares of Basil island; in the center the fortress-island of St. Peter and St. Paul; the street plan of the left bank, above, is focused on the Winter Palace and the Admiralty.

Проспектъ пъ низъ по Непъ рѣкѣ между зимнимъ Ея Императорскаго Величества домомъ и Академiею Наукъ.

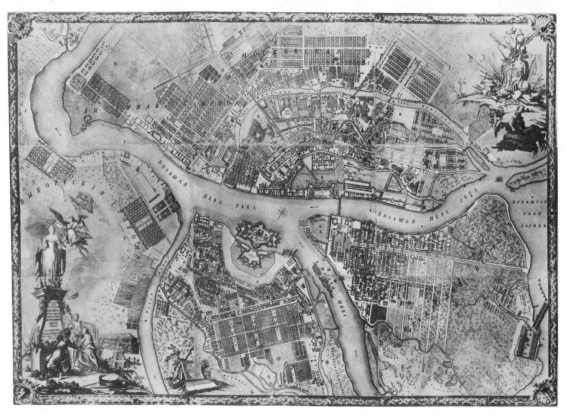

the Champ de Mars. During the next hundred years, Peter's successors shifted their model of urbanism from Amsterdam to Rome and Paris. On the south bank of the river, great baroque perspectives were opened up: the three avenues converging on the new Winter Palace, now the Hermitage Museum; the long facades of the imperial and aristocratic palaces along the river front, which remind the present-day viewer of Paris; gigantic squares and gardens; and everywhere the unifying force of color in the light yellow stucco that decorated all the buildings. Saint Petersburg was an artificial creation, the will of one man. It forced Russia headlong into the technology of the West, especially the military technology. But it split Russia between the autocracy and the part of the upper classes and bourgeoisie who had accepted West European ways and the vast majority of the population who remained untouched by them, except to provide the human and financial resources to pay for the modernization. Yet, because the modernization was the act of an autocrat, it was not the product of the drive of individuals working within a system that encouraged initiative, the secret of the West's dynamism.

Absolutism in France

Foundation of French Absolutism

The absolutism of Louis XIV in France, which was the model for the majority of European states in the seventeenth and early eighteenth centuries, was tainted by this same defect, but to a lesser degree. To start with, Louis did not have to work at such breakneck speed as Peter, because the foundations of French absolutism had been securely laid during the previous two centuries. At the end of the fifteenth century, Louis XI had left the monarchy a standing army, a large income from regular taxation, the undisputed right to legislate and to judge, the power of making war or peace, and the right of nominating bishops and abbots. Louis's successors for the next half-century, in spite of such wasteful wars in Italy as those waged by Francis I (reigned 1515–1547), ran France as a supreme example of the "new monarchy." This evolution was interrupted, although temporarily, by the Wars of Religion (1562–1598). The wars were only partly an attempt by the more fanatical of France's fourteen million Catholics to wipe out Calvinism, which was the religion professed by about one million of the country's most enterprising commercial and professional classes. The French kings attacked the Calvinists because they regarded their fortified cities and their superbly organized network of congregations as a threat to the absolute powers of the monarchy, especially in the outlying provinces. Three great factions of the nobility fought each other, and incidentally laid much of France waste, to gain control of the throne. The Queen Mother, Catherine

Two Chateaux of the Loire Valley: Chambord (above) **and Chenonceaux** (below)
In the fifteenth century the kings and aristocrats of France began to build country palaces for themselves along the Loire river and its tributaries. François I built Chambord in the middle of a vast hunting reserve, while Chenonceaux, which spans the Cher river, was a gift of Henri II to his mistress Diane de Poitiers.

de Médicis, controlled the policy of her three ineffective sons, Francis II, Charles IX, and Henry III, who reigned successively during the wars (1559–1589); she considered the measures to which she sank, including the murder of three thousand Calvinists in Paris on Saint Bartholomew's Day in 1572, as necessary for the protection of her family. The surprising result of the wars was, however, to strengthen the monarchy.

Henry IV, the Vert Galant

The victor in the wars, the Bourbon faction's leader Henry of Navarre, who became king on the assassination of Henry III in 1589, was a cynical, tough, and charming character, whose qualities were precisely what the monarchy required to end the chaos of the wars. He displayed his cynicism by three times converting from Calvinism to Catholicism—as a boy at court, at the St. Bartholomew's massacre, and four years after becoming king. Then, as a Catholic, he granted religious toleration to the Calvinists by the Edict of Nantes (1598), turning them in one stroke of the pen into the most loyal and productive segment of his population. He used force for ten years after his accession to crush the extreme Catholics and bring an end to Spanish intervention in France. And finally, by sheer charm—or rather by being himself the ideal Renaissance courtier, a combination of scholar, soldier, and lover—he created for himself the image of being the *vert galant*, the green gallant. This reputation of royal popularity was to serve the monarchy well in later years, although recent scholars have argued that during his actual reign Henry enjoyed far less popularity than was actually attributed to him by royalist propagandists.

The wars, moreover, had strengthened the monarchy in relation to any opposition. The nobility had killed off each other. The chaos had severely weakened the middle classes, forcing many Calvinists to emigrate and hampering the development of industry and commerce. The commercial classes in France, unlike those in England and Holland, were not in a position to make a claim for a share in political power, but rather sought the king as their sole guarantor against a return of feudal confusion. This attitude was expressed in a new political philosophy by a group called the *Politiques,* who held that royal sovereignty was the only guarantee of peace and internal order. Their great writer, Jean Bodin, in his influential *Six Books on the Republic,* argued that a true state only exists when it has a sovereign who exercises "supreme power over citizens and subjects, unrestrained by law"; that a king governs by the will of God, and is responsible only to God; and that the king is the sole maker of law, including, if he wishes, laws giving toleration to Calvinists. The wars, in short, had given the French monarchy a well-reasoned justification of its own pretensions to absolute power.

Henry IV and the Renovation of Paris

Perhaps most important of all, Henry made Paris a true capital city once more. Under Catherine de Médicis, Paris had been in a state of more or less

The Place des Vosges, Paris
Dutch influence is evident in the stone quoins and red brick facade of the square erected by Henry IV in 1605–1612.
Judy Poe photo

open rebellion against the monarchy, a city divided into isolated social groups alien to each other, tormented by disease and starvation, and ignored by an extravagant court. It had finally welcomed Henry in 1594, after he had become a Catholic for the third time. (He supposedly remarked, "Paris is worth a Mass"!) Henry in turn repaid Paris by beginning the process of making it a city worthy of the monarchy's new pretensions. First came work of restoration, the clearing of the garbage-piled streets, repair of ruined buildings, restoration of the water supply, rebuilding of the bridges. Then came the revival of commerce, aided by the policies of Henry's able financial minister Sully, whose frugality restored the reliability of government bonds and whose mercantilism encouraged the foundation of new industries in Paris. Last came the shaping of the city according to royal standards of taste, a practice that was to continue for almost three centuries and was to be responsible for the present-day appearance of Paris. "I would be very pleased," the king wrote Sully about a street being built on the left bank, "if you would see to it that those who are beginning to build in the aforesaid street make the facades of their houses all of the same [architectural] order, for it would be a fine ornament to see this street with a uniform facade from the end of the bridge." The tip of the Ile de la Cité set the standards for new urban groupings—a charming combination of grey stone bridge, uniform red brick houses with yellow stone facing, and tall slate roofs. In its triangular form and bold play of perspective, which led the eye to a strategically placed statue of Henry on horseback, it was already heralding the baroque city. Delighted with this first effort at urban planning, Henry created the first residential square, the Place des Vosges at the eastern, aristocratic edge of Paris; and he indicated the precise social character of the individual houses by selling off one side himself to chosen families who had been ennobled for legal and bureaucratic service.

Rule of the Cardinals

Henry's assassination in 1610 flung France back into chaos, as his wife struggled unsuccessfully to prevent the nobility from ignoring the nine-year-old King Louis XIII. The state treasury was shared out among them, and the provinces became virtually independent of the crown. To end this state of administrative anarchy, Cardinal Richelieu, the brilliant, secular-minded churchman who ran the government on Louis's behalf from 1624 to 1642, made use of the one class of bureaucrats he felt to be completely trustworthy, the traveling commissioners. These officials, renamed *intendants*, were given greatly expanded duties in running the taxation, law courts, and police in the provinces; and they remained the primary instrument of royal absolutism until the revolution of 1789. Under Richelieu, royal government was centralized round the person of the chief minister, who worked through his own appointees on the royal council and in the main government ministries in Paris and through the provincial intendants. Even the buildings of Paris showed this new emphasis, because just to the north of the Louvre, Richelieu constructed for himself the Palais Cardinal (now the Palais Royal), a large palace with a long rectangular and completely private garden. Around the Richelieu Quarter, all his top bureaucrats sought to build themselves homes in the same formal style as their patron's, the solid, luxurious buildings themselves a proof of the wealth that could come to the middle classes who served the crown faithfully. Richelieu's successor as chief minister, Cardinal Mazarin, was a clever, persuasive Italian who made himself the lover, and perhaps the husband, of Anne of Austria, the widow of Louis XIII. He attempted to run France on behalf of Louis's five-year-old son Louis XIV by relying entirely on the system created by Richelieu. He was challenged, however, by the Paris uprising known as the Fronde (1648–1652), which almost upset all the progress toward absolutism that the monarchy had made in the previous half-century.

The Fronde, so-called after the mud-throwing of Paris children, was an unplanned explosion of anger by all the classes in France who felt they had grievances against the monarchy. It began when a decade of poor harvests drove the peasantry into violent attacks on the tax collectors and the wealthy Parisians who were trying to buy up their lands cheap. It reached

Paris when the Parlement, which represented the rich lawyers and claimed
the right to register all royal edicts before they became law, demanded reform of the corruption caused by sale of government offices and a reduction
in the powers of the intendants. When the monarchy granted the Parlement's demands, the great nobles in turn took over. Paris was occupied by
noble armies, while in the rest of France private forces of aristocrats plundered and burned. Mazarin fled the country. The Paris mob terrified the
king, who was then thirteen, pouring into his bedroom in the palace and
forcing him to flee—perhaps the formative experience of his life, since it left
him with such distrust for Parisians that only a complete move of the government to Versailles could assuage it. Royal armies eventually defeated the
remaining noble armies, and both Louis XIV and Mazarin were able to return to Paris.

Opportunities Open to French Absolutism

The real results of the Fronde were not evident until the death of Mazarin
in 1661 left Louis free to run France his own way by becoming his own first
minister. Absolute monarchy had survived its most serious test; it remained
to be seen what use a conscientious despot would make of his powers. The
situation had never been more favorable for an ostentatious display of the
monarchy's powers. All France's rivals were in decline or disorder. England
had just emerged from civil wars. The Dutch were severely weakened by

naval wars with England and land wars with Spain. Spain itself could no longer raise the great armies and navies whose cost had brought Philip II into bankruptcy. The Thirty Years' War had left Germany an economic shambles, while the Hohenzollern family were just beginning to turn the state of Prussia into a major military force. Poland was in the hands of an anarchist nobility. Austria was distracted by a new attack of the Turks, who in 1683 were to besiege Vienna itself. France, by contrast, was the strongest and wealthiest state in Europe. It had a large population, eighteen million as compared with England's five million. Its agriculture was the most varied and prosperous in Europe, even though France had occasional times of famine. Richelieu had given it a strong navy and a renovated infantry that scored a landmark victory by defeating the Spanish at Rocroi in 1643. Above all, in spite of its continual social conflicts, France had a genuine national patriotism that expressed itself in veneration of the monarchy.

Louis believed sincerely that it was his duty to France and to God to profit from these advantages. Like the majority of Europeans of his day, he held that only through an absolute monarchy could order be guaranteed and the energies of the nation harnessed for the common benefit. In the memoirs he wrote for his son, he described the misery of peoples governed by popular assemblies and limited monarchies:

The more you grant it [the popular assembly], the more it demands; the more you caress it, the more it scorns you; and what it once has in its possession is retained by so many hands that it cannot be torn away without extreme violence. Out of so many persons who compose these great bodies, it is always the least sensible who assume the greatest license. Once you defer to them they claim the right forever to control your plans according to their fancy, and the continual necessity of defending yourself against their assaults alone produces many more cares for you than all the other interests of your crown, so that a prince who wants to bequeath lasting tranquility to his people and his dignity completely intact to his successors cannot be too careful to suppress this tumultuous temerity.

But I am dwelling too long on a reflection that seems useless for you, or that can at most serve you only to recognize the misery of our neighbors, since it is patent that you will reign in a state where you will find no authority that is not honored to derive its origin and its status from you, no body that dares to depart from expressions of respect, no corporation that does not see its principal greatness in the good of your service and its sole security in its humble submission.[5]

He proposed to set the example of hard work and conscientious attention to all duties, no matter how trival. As a child he had been taught to

---

[5] Louis XIV, *Mémoires for the Instruction of the Dauphin,* trans. Paul Sonnino (New York: Free Press, 1970), pp. 130–31.

hate the do-nothing kings of the Merovingian period, especially Louis the Idle; and his own characteristic sobriety, backed by a splendid physique, enabled him to combine the long hours of administration with a punctilious observance of the even more fatiguing round of court ritual. He was the only person at Versailles who was never bored; and he accepted discomfort as a matter of principle. Told that some of the fireplaces at Versailles would stop smoking if the chimneys were made taller, he replied that the smoke did not matter because the chimneys must remain invisible from the gardens. Food was brought several hundred yards and was cold when he ate it; wine froze in the glass. The king remained stoically indifferent. The essential factor was to maintain the majesty of kingship at whatever personal cost. In this work, Louis believed he was answerable to God, who had appointed him, and only to God. This theory, the divine right of kings, sustained him with a sense of self-righteousness, when it became evident even to his leading general that his wars were leading France into ruin. To the courtier Saint-Simon, Louis's conception of government seemed at the end to be the product of his personal failings, "his blindness, his pride in doing everything himself, his jealousy of experienced ministers and generals, his vanity in choosing only such leaders as could not be expected to earn credit for successes."

Military Aggression and Glory

Throughout his reign, Louis's main preoccupation was to achieve *la gloire*, military glory for France and the monarchy. The interior of Versailles is filled with florid portrayals of Louis's victories in his early wars; but in each case there is a material justification, such as the capture of a strategic fortress or the surrender of a rich city. In his first war, the War of Devolution (1667–1668) Louis sought glory by straightening the southward bulge in his border with the Spanish Netherlands, from which, he was told, an invader could reach Paris in four days. His second war, with the Dutch (1672–1678), was partly inspired by the mercantilist desire to destroy the commercial supremacy of the Netherlands, partly by the religious determination to wipe out one of the strongholds of Calvinism, and partly by continuing territorial ambitions on the Spanish possessions on his eastern frontier. For two years his armies were totally successful; but in 1674 the Dutch pierced the dikes to create a flooded barrier between the Rhine and Zuider Zee, and used the time they had gained to put together a coalition of European powers fearful of France's ruthless use of force in support of its growing ambition. To stop Louis's attempt at European hegemony in its early stages, the Dutch were joined by the English, the Spanish, and the Austrians, and several German states; the French were held to a stalemate; and peace was finally bought at the expense of the Spanish, by giving Louis a little more territory from the Spanish Netherlands and the valuable French-speaking province of Franche-Comté, which blocked the invasion route through the Belfort Gap.

Once peace was restored, legal chicanery was used to give France a pretext for seizing important cities in Alsace, including the important bridge town of Strasbourg. Luxembourg was occupied a little later. And in 1688 Louis's forces crossed the Rhine to subjugate the little German state of the Palatine, where they destroyed the elector's palace of Heidelberg. This action precipitated Europe into almost three decades of continuous war, in which France made no further territorial gains. In his third war, the War of the League of Augsburg (1689–1697), Louis faced again the powers that had foiled his attack on the Netherlands, and again was brought to a standstill. In 1700, he played for the greatest prize of his reign. He would risk war with the rest of Europe to enable his second grandson to inherit the whole Spanish empire that the dying Spanish king had bequeathed to him rather than to the other claimant, the second grandson of the Austrian emperor. In the War of the Spanish Succession (1702–1713), the French armies were defeated again and again, in Italy by the forces of Savoy and Austria and in Germany and the Spanish Netherlands by the English under the duke of Marlborough. With a national debt of three billion livres, the peasantry starving, and Paris on the verge of revolt, Louis agreed to the Treaty of Utrecht of 1713, by which Austria was to take most of the European possessions of Spain, including Milan and the Spanish Netherlands. Britain was to take Gibraltar and the island of Minorca and have a monopoly on the supply of slaves to the Spanish empire. Louis's grandson was to retain Spain

(Left) **Louis XIV's Passage of the Rhine, The Palace of Versailles, by Antoine Coysevox (1640–1720)** *Louis's triumphs in his early wars provided subject-matter of a suitably sycophantic nature for the fifty sculptors and painters who decorated the ceremonial rooms of Versailles.* Alinari photo

(Right) **The Garden Facade, The Palace of Versailles** *From the Hall of Mirrors in the second story of this facade, the king's control over nature itself could be seen in the geometrical patterning of woods and gardens around the palace.* French Embassy Press and Information Division photo

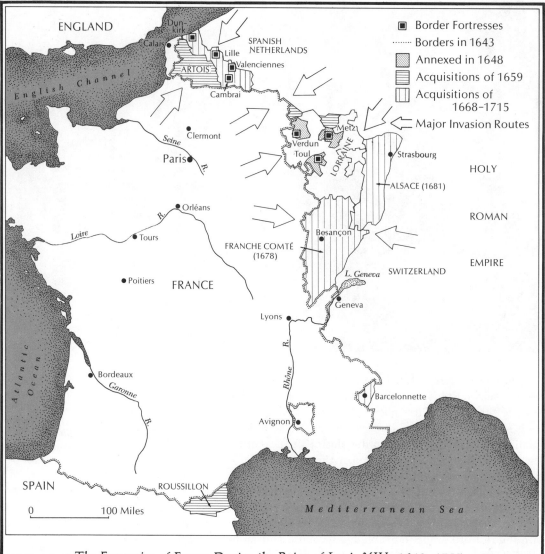

♦ *The Expansion of France During the Reign of Louis XIV, 1643–1715* ♦

and its overseas empire, but the thrones of Spain and France were never to be united. The establishment of the younger Bourbon line on the Spanish throne proved of almost no value to France during the next hundred years. The one worthwhile result of twenty-eight years of war was to establish a defensible frontier from the Channel to Switzerland.

Strengths and Weaknesses of the French Economy

In economic policy as in foreign policy, Louis's absolutism produced beneficial results only through the end of the Dutch war. Under the direction of his parsimonious finance minister, Colbert, tax collection was made more efficient and more just; internal barriers to trade were reduced. Roads and canals were constructed, including the Languedoc Canal that linked the Mediterranean and the Bay of Biscay. New industries, such as silk and glassmaking, were established. Overseas trading companies were founded. But mercantilism led Colbert into some drastic errors, such as a high tariff on Dutch trade and the even worse mistake of forbidding the export of wheat from France; and it led him to accept war as a necessary adjunct to commercial expansion. The wars, however, led to Colbert's own eclipse in the king's favor and to the rise of Louvois, the war minister, who though efficient as an army organizer only encouraged the king's provocation to the anti-French coalition. Colbert also could do nothing to make the king realize the economic contribution that the French Huguenots were making. During Colbert's lifetime, Louis attempted to convert Huguenots by billeting troops with them; and in 1685, two years after Colbert's death, Louis revoked the Edict of Nantes. To gain religious uniformity, which he felt essential to royal absolutism, he drove out of France one hundred thousand Protestants, who included many of France's finest artisans and business leaders, nine thousand sailors, six hundred army officers, and twelve thousand soldiers. In Europe, the persecution of the Huguenots aroused enormous indignation. In France itself, many thought it a shameful error. According to Saint-Simon:

The revocation of the Edict of Nantes, decided upon without the least excuse or any need, and the many proscriptions as well as declarations that followed it constituted a terrible plot which depopulated one-quarter of the kingdom, destroyed its commerce, enfeebled all parties, caused widespread pillage and condoned the dragonnades, allowed tortures and torments in which many innocent persons of both sexes died by thousands, ruined a numerous people, tore families to pieces, set relatives against one another in a fight for food and property, caused our manufacturers to move abroad, where they flourished and brought wealth to other States at our expense and enabled new and flourishing towns to be built, and gave them the spectacle of so remarkable a people being proscribed, stripped of their possessions, exiled, made to wander over the face of the earth without being guilty of any crime, seeking shelter from their own country.[6]

The Centralization of Culture

Only in the arts did Louis's centralization of all French life around himself produce an almost unblemished success; and it is the achievements of the writers, sculptors, painters, architects, and musicians of his reign that won it the lasting reputation of being France's golden age. Colbert himself had be-

---

[6] Cited in Maurice Ashley, *Louis XIV and the Greatness of France* (London: Hodder and Stoughton, 1964), p. 93.

Self-Portrait, by Antoine Coysevox
Coysevox, one of the most prolific baroque sculptors in France, has contrasted the firm serenity of his features with the motion of his swirling wig and the diagonal lines of his clothing. Courtesy De Young Museum, San Francisco

gun the process of retaining all patronage, and of laying down artistic standards, within the court. All painters were brought into an Academy of Painting and scientists into an Academy of Sciences. Intellectual life was dominated by the French Academy that had been founded by Richelieu. Colbert's admiration for Rome and his desire to make Paris a new Rome were evident everywhere—in the Louvre facade, in the antique subjects favored by the painters, in the triumphal arches at the city gates. But when Louis XIV began the expansion of the chateau of Versailles, both the focus and the style changed. Versailles itself became the training ground for the new architects, interior designers, sculptors, and painters. The new generation of artists was to be trained under the three great masters who were creating Versailles: Le Vau in architecture, Le Brun in painting, and Le Nôtre in landscape gardening. From Versailles, too, came the patronage of France's greatest comic playwright, Molière, and tragic playwright, Racine. Molière was an incisive but humane satirist, who made the court rock with laughter at the foibles of the excessively religious, in *Tartuffe;* of the social climber, in *Le Bourgeois Gentilhomme;* of learned women, in *Les Femmes Savantes.* And he could achieve the point at which the greatest comedy probes so deeply that it becomes tragedy, as in the scene from *L'Avare (The Miser)* in which the old miser turns almost demented at the loss of his money:

Thief! Thief! Murderer! Killer! Justice, just heaven! I am lost, I am killed!
Some one has cut my throat, some one has stolen my money! Who can it be?
What has happened to him? Where is he hiding? What can I do to find him?
Where shall I run? Where shall I not run? . . . My mind is troubled, and I
don't know where I am, who I am, and what I am doing. Alas! my poor
money, my poor money, my dear friend, they have taken you away from me!
And, since you have been taken away, I have lost my support, my consolation,
my job; everything is finished for me, and I have nothing more to do in the
world! Without you it is impossible to live. It is over, I am finished, I am dy-
ing, I am dead, I am buried. Is there no one who wants to bring me back to life
by giving me back my money? [7]

Racine, by contrast, was a superb poet who was able to build the classical
Alexandrine verse, with its strictly prescribed rhythms, into an almost musical form of evocation of deep psychological insights. In *Phaedra*, for example, Phaedra, the wife of Theseus, who is almost mad for the love of her
stepson, Hippolytus, attempts to reveal her passion to him:

> *Ah, yes. For Theseus*
> *I languish and I long, not as the Shades*
> *Have seen him, of a thousand different forms*
> *The fickle lover, and of Pluto's bride*
> *The would-be ravishers, but faithful, proud*
> *E'en to a slight disdain, with youthful charms*
> *Attracting every heart, as gods are painted,*
> *Or like yourself. He had your mien, your eyes,*
> *Spoke and could blush like you, when to the isle*
> *Of Crete, my childhood's home, he cross'd the waves,*
> *Worthy to win the love of Minos' daughters.*
> *What were you doing then? Why did he gather*
> *The flower of Greece and leave Hippolytus?* [8]

It was writers such as Racine who made it possible for a mediocre man like
Louis XIV to appear as a Sun King.

Oligarchy in England

A third type of monarchical rule, limited monarchy, was created in England
in the seventeenth century. Building upon the powers and the wealth they
had achieved under the Tudors, the English propertied classes, both the
landed gentry of the countryside and the merchant class of the cities, re-

[7] Author's translation.
[8] Racine, *Phaedra*, trans. R. Boswell (New York: Colonial, 1900).

jected the attempts of the Stuart kings to form an absolute monarchy on the French pattern. In its place they created a partnership, not of king and people but of king and well-to-do.

Rise of the Tudor Gentry

The classes who succeeded in limiting the monarchy had, almost without exception, grown wealthy under the Tudors. By the reign of Henry VIII, the old feudal nobility had almost disappeared and been replaced by new lords named by the Tudors from the rising class of gentry. The confiscation of the lands of the monasteries and the sale of crown lands had enabled many city merchants, government officials, and lawyers to become landed gentlemen; and they farmed their newly acquired lands with an eye to profit as well as social status. Some great families, intimately trusted by the Tudors, acquired huge portions of the land of the monasteries, and thereby laid the basis for their later demand for political power. Money was also being made in what some writers have called the first industrial revolution. Rapid advances were made in coal mining and in the use of coal as an industrial fuel; in metalworking, especially of brass, iron, and lead; in production of unfinished cloth; and in glassmaking. But the really dramatic rise to fortune was made by merchants in overseas commerce. Under Elizabeth, great trading companies were founded to open up trade with countries like Russia or with the East Indies. English ships were sent to find a northwest passage to China and ended by exploring the northeast coast of the North American continent. Other sailors plundered the Spanish possessions and treasure fleets in the Americas, and supplied African slaves to the Spanish colonies.

Henry VIII

Other companies like the Virginia company, founded in 1606, saw the settlement of English colonists in overseas plantations as a source of profitable investment; and the establishment of export crops, like tobacco in Virginia and sugar cane in the West Indian islands, helped the companies turn a belated but large profit for their stockholders. Thus, by the end of the sixteenth century there were a substantial number of landholders, industrialists, and merchants who felt economically independent of the crown, and who were prepared to demand greater influence in government when the policies of the crown were unsatisfactory to them.

The Age of Elizabeth

As long as the threat from Spain remained, Elizabeth had little opposition from Parliament, to which she turned for money for defense and administration. Indeed, the national struggle that culminated in the defeat of the armada, combined with a widespread sense of economic prosperity and power, produced a great feeling of national solidarity that, by some inexplicable alchemy, encouraged the genius of William Shakespeare (1564–1616). The culture of the Elizabethan age was just what a sturdy, exuberant, self-confident, and assertive people wanted—madrigals to sing, love poems to recite, gory tragedies to shudder at, bawdy comedies to rollick over, picturesque manors to be comfortable in. Without Shakespeare, it would have been little more than a charming and somewhat adolescent creation. But in Shakespeare, with his mastery of psychology, his superb sense of the stage, and above all his unparalleled poetry, drama reached its highest achievement. The language of Shakespeare (and the contemporary

Elizabeth I

Elizabethan Bedroom
The home of a prosperous family in Elizabethan England was often lined with small rectangular oak panels, while the ceiling plaster was designed in a system of ribs derived from Gothic architecture.
M. H. de Young Memorial Museum. Stone and Steccati photographers

translation of the Bible into English, the King James version) bestowed on English speech a rhythm and subtlety and an emotional significance that have never been lost. This language, taught to successive generations of schoolboys in England while students on the other side of the Channel were acquiring the sharp clarity of the logic of Descartes, played its role in the dangerous mutual incomprehension of the English and French peoples that underlay their willingness to fight each other throughout most of the seventeenth and eighteenth centuries. What could be more provocative of national pride than the beautiful lines Shakespeare put in the mouth of John of Gaunt, in his play *Richard the Second:*

> *This royal throne of kings, this sceptered isle,*
> *This earth of majesty, this seat of Mars,*
> *This other Eden, demi-paradise,*
> *This fortress built by nature for herself*
> *Against infection and the hand of war,*
> *This happy breed of men, this little world,*
> *This precious stone set in the silver sea,*
> *Which serves it in the office of a wall,*
> *Or as a moat defensive to a house*
> *Against the envy of less happier lands—*
> *This blessed plot, this earth, this realm, this England.*[9]

[9] William Shakespeare, *Richard the Second,* act 2, sc. 1.

At the very time that Shakespeare was writing these lines, Elizabeth had been compelled to appear personally in Parliament to overawe them into granting the revenues she asked, because the sense of national urgency aroused by the armada had subsided. Elizabeth could only appeal to the memory of great deeds done together and to their common pride in England: "I know that I have the body of a weak and feeble woman," she told the prostrate parliamentarians, "but I have the heart of a king, and of a king of England too." Thus, by sheer force of personality she kept the absolutism of her father in being until her death.

Constitutional Struggle Under the Early Stuarts

Her successor, King James I (reigned 1603–1625), was incapable of understanding the secret of Tudor absolutism, that it was a partnership for mutual convenience of king and well-to-do classes. He believed in divine right of kings, wrote a book explaining the theory, and lectured on it frequently to Parliament. "That which concerns the mystery of the King's power," he said, "is not lawful to be disputed; for that is to wade into the weakness of Princes, and to take away the mystical reverence that belongs unto them that sit in the throne of God." Unlike the French kings, however, the English monarchs did not possess a standing army, the right to tax, or a docile bureaucracy. They required parliamentary consent to raise troops and money other than their traditional revenues from customs and their own lands; and they were dependent on the gentry to carry out the administration in the local districts. Both James I and his son Charles I attempted to remedy this weakness, which was particularly apparent as the inflation of the price revolution ate into their traditional revenues. Between 1603 and 1640, almost all the possessing classes of England united against James I and Charles I because their methods of increasing revenue were regarded as constitutional innovations. This is the clearest theme in the English constitutional struggles of the seventeenth century. James I and Charles I attempted to raise revenues that would be independent of parliamentary control, by reviving feudal dues, taking forced loans, and levying payments that were taxes in all but name. They attempted to circumvent the regular administration by founding new bureaucratic councils that would be the instruments of their absolutism. In 1640–1642, both the House of Lords and the House of Commons joined to sweep away these pretensions to royal absolutism. The king's chief minister was executed; and laws were passed to ensure that Parliament should meet at least every three years and should control any extraordinary expenditures.

The Puritan Opposition

The constitutional issue was, however, deeply involved with the problem of Puritanism. The English Calvinists, or Puritans, had made many converts among the landed gentry of the East of England, in the University of Cambridge, and in the merchant class of London. The Stuart kings, like Louis XIV, sought religious uniformity, and not only refused the Puritan demands for change in the Church of England but actively persecuted them. Some fled to find toleration in Holland and in the settlement of Massachusetts; but most stayed behind to oppose the king in England. During the eleven years when Charles I governed without Parliament (1629–1640), he permitted his archbishop of Canterbury to restore extreme ceremonial within the Church and to enforce the use of the Anglican prayer book on the Calvinist Church in Scotland. The Scots reacted by going to war with England in 1638–1639, and their invasion forced Charles I to call Parliament to ask it for money. But the Puritans in Parliament, once they had helped destroy the king's attempt to create a constitutional absolutism, demanded in 1641 that the position of bishop be abolished and the Church of England remodeled on Calvinist lines. As a result of this controversy, the king found supporters among those who had opposed his absolutist pretensions but could not tolerate the radical religious changes proposed. In 1642, the king attempted to arrest the radical leaders in Parliament, and failing to find them, was forced to leave London to gather his supporters near the loyal city of Oxford. By August, both the king and Parliament were gathering armies for a trial of strength.

The English Civil Wars (1642–1648)

Historians are divided as to the motives that drove men to choose between king and Parliament. They agree on the geographical division; the South and East supported Parliament. Socially this implied that the great landowners and their laborers in the North and West supported the king, in opposition to the yeomen and lesser gentry of the East and the majority of the merchant class of the big cities. The majority of convinced Calvinists supported Parliament, loyal Anglicans, the king. And here again was a class basis to the decision, since the Calvinist support was among the lesser gentry and the merchants. But was the civil war a class war? There is no doubt that among extreme Puritans it was. The Diggers were a small group who believed in communal ownership of property; the Levellers demanded universal manhood suffrage, and were willing to resort to violence to destroy either royalist or parliamentary despotism. But it is difficult to prove that among the majority of the supporters of both king and Parliament, economic determinism, that is, class sympathy or materialistic motives, dictated the choice of loyalty. Men chose which side to fight for primarily in terms of religious or political loyalty. Many who approved of greater powers for Parliament simply could not bring themselves to fight against the anointed king; many who disapproved of Parliament's pretensions followed their Puritan faith in opposing the king. Brothers joined different sides, a fact that proves to many historians the inadequacy of an economic analysis of the struggle.

In the first phase of the civil wars (1642–1646), the Parliamentarians, or Roundheads, succeeded in defeating the undisciplined armies of the king. In the Puritan country squire, Oliver Cromwell, they found a great general, whose New Model Army, composed mostly of Puritan farmers, was a tough, fanatical force that destroyed the king's main forces at the battle of Naseby (1645) and soon after captured the king himself. Success, however,

The English Civil Wars

brought about the dissolution of the parliamentary side, and for the next fourteen years, they tried in vain to produce a viable alternative to royal government. In 1646–1648, Calvinist extremism in Parliament won Charles many supporters from among the parliamentary side; and Cromwell had to go to war again to defeat the new coalition of Scots, Anglicans, and disillusioned parliamentarians that Charles had succeeded in putting together. "We will cut off his head with the crown upon it," Cromwell announced; and in 1649, he did.

England became a Puritan republic, or commonwealth. Cromwell purged the Parliament to make it representative of the extreme Presbyterians, but finding them impractical fanatics, he felt compelled in 1653 to take over the state himself. "There was nothing in the minds of these men but overturn," he commented. But Cromwell himself as Lord Protector was even less able to put together a viable government, having as his only support the power of his own army. He could not solve the dilemma of combining rule of the godly, as Calvin proposed, and rule of the whole people, which he sincerely sought. He fought the Dutch at sea, at enormous expense to his own middle-class supporters, and he faced the continual burden of financing his fifty-thousand-man army. His financial exactions destroyed much of his support. The requirements of the godly, which involved as great a proscription of pleasure as in Calvin's Geneva, became increasingly irksome; and after Cromwell's death moderate leaders in the army itself decided to restore the monarchy as the only way to avoid chaos. Charles II, son of the executed king, was called back, on the explicit condition that the powers of the monarchy would be those defined in the constitutional settlement of 1640–1641.

The Restoration

The Restoration period (Charles II, reigned 1660–1685; James II, reigned 1685–1688) was the height of England's baroque age. In reaction against the drabness of the Puritan revolution, the revived aristocracy led by the pleasure-loving king engaged in all the sensual and emotional excesses, in life and in art. The theater was filled with convoluted tales of amorous intrigue, many of which were being acted out in reality in the court circles. All the foppery of Louis XIV's Versailles was introduced to aristocratic living, the wigs, the ribbons, the high-heeled shoes, the powder and lorgnettes and formalized politeness. But for all the artificiality, there were real achievements in Restoration culture. It produced England's finest composer, Purcell, whose opera *Dido and Aeneas* ranks with the best of the Italian operas of the period; England's greatest architect, Christopher Wren; and some passable poets, including Andrew Marvell. In 1667, the great Puritan poet John Milton published the finest of all baroque poems, alien in spirit to the court of Charles II but with a real affinity for the style of the Catholic Reformation in Rome with its swirling heavens filled with saints and angels, fallen or otherwise. In Milton are joined the color and drama of Bernini and the deep diapasons and complex harmonies of Bach, the perfect mingling of the arts that is so typical of the baroque ideal. Here is a baroque painting in words, the fall of Satan from the opening of *Paradise Lost:*

> . . . *Him the Almighty Power*
> *Hurled headlong flaming from th' ethereal sky*
> *With hideous ruin and combustion down*
> *To bottomless perdition, there to dwell*
> *In adamantine chains and penal fire*
> *Who durst defy th' Omnipotent to arms.*

James II, the rather stupid and excessively conscientious brother of Charles II, was unable to live within the framework of government set up in 1660, and he succeeded in uniting both Anglican and Puritan against him by attempting to restore Catholicism, by keeping a standing army, and by accepting French subsidies in place of taxes granted by Parliament. In 1688, the leading aristocrats in England invited the stadholder of Holland, William of Orange, who had married James's Protestant daughter Mary, to invade England, and hold the throne jointly with his wife. In a bloodless revolution, James was sent into exile—he was allowed to escape after he had

West Facade, St. Paul's Cathedral, London
The classic columns and triumphal arch of the lower stories of Christopher Wren's cathedral combine harmoniously with the baroque curves and niches of the side towers. British Tourist Authority photo

been captured, to avoid any bloodshed—and Parliament restored once again the constitutional situation of 1641. But this time the circumstances were different, since they were putting on the throne a man who had no right by birth. They were taking for themselves the role of nominating the king of England, ending by that act any pretense that future kings might have to govern by divine right.

Physical Evolution of London

This constitutional development has its urban counterpart in the physical development of London, whose contrast with Paris is itself graphic evidence of the divergence between the two monarchies. In 1619, the classicist architect Inigo Jones began the creation of a vast palace complex in Whitehall, that would eventually have run along the Thames north of Parliament, as the Louvre ran along the Seine. Work was interrupted by Charles's quarrel with Parliament over funds. It was taken up again at the end of the first fighting in the civil war, and broken off with the execution of Charles I in front of the barely begun palace. A new start was attempted again for a brief while until Charles II sought to avoid reliance on Parliament for his funds. The land intended for the palace was bought for private homes by members of the nobility. London was to be denied also the baroque town plan that Wren drew up for it after the fire of 1666 had destroyed most of the western part of the city. An absolute monarch might have enforced the plan, giving London its river terraces, its boulevards, and its monumental vistas. Private owners refused to pool their property, however, and rebuilt on the plots laid out in the Middle Ages. No power existed to subordinate private capitalism to public planning.

Garden Facade, Hampton Court Palace, by Christopher Wren
British Tourist Authority photo

Yet there was a compromise with the demands of the baroque city planner. The king was not reduced to a position of primus inter pares, like the stadholder of the Netherlands, whose palaces were only glorified town houses. His importance could be asserted on the edge of the city by rebuilding palaces like Hampton Court in the style of Versailles, and even in the parkland he owned in the center of town where avenues, as in Saint James's Park, could be laid out in geometrical patterns like Le Nôtre's. But the well-to-do dominated most of the city, and their baroque was the domesticity of the city square, created not by royalty but by real estate speculators. The

Royal Crescent, Bath
The superb terraces of the eighteenth-century spa town of Bath, a summer resort for the nobility of London, mark the high point of English city planning. British Tourist Authority photo

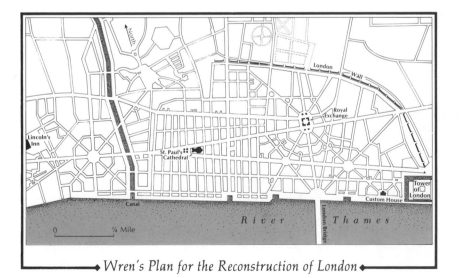

◆ *Wren's Plan for the Reconstruction of London* ◆

only requirement of the city government was that the new buildings should be in brick; and thus, in a century when the population of London grew from two hundred thousand to five hundred thousand, the predominant character of the city was that of the street or square, lined with three-to-four-story houses of undeniable comfort, which had cozily compromised with the demands of the baroque just as their inhabitants had equally satisfactorily compromised with the absolute demand of their monarchy.

SUGGESTED READING

Perhaps the best way to understand the baroque city is to begin with a specific city that was thoroughly remodeled according to baroque principles. Paris is a good example, seen through Orest Ranum, *Paris in the Age of Absolutism* (1968) or Leon Bernard, *The Emerging City* (1970). But one must turn again to Pierre Lavedan's *Histoire de l'urbanisme* (1941), vol. 2, or to Lewis Mumford's *The City in History* (1966), for a general survey of the principles underlying city building throughout Europe and its colonies.

The baroque style is described in Victor L. Tapie, *The Age of Grandeur: Baroque Art and Architecture* (1960), while the achievements of individual countries can be admired in H. Gerson and E. H. Huile, *Art and Architecture in Belgium, 1600 to 1800* (1960); Rudolf Wittkower, *Art and Architecture in Italy, 1600–1750* (1958); and Anthony Blunt, *Art and Architecture in France, 1500–1700* (1953). For music, see Manfred F. Bufkozer, *Music in the Baroque Era* (1947).

There are several good surveys of the politics of the baroque age, among them Henry Kamen, *The Iron Century: Social Change in Europe, 1550–1660* (1971), which employs economic quantification and is especially good on the recession of the first half of the seventeenth century; Carl J. Friedrich, *The Age of the Baroque, 1610–1660* (1952); Frederick L. Nussbaum, *The Triumph of Science and Reason, 1660–1685* (1953); John B. Wolf, *The Emergence of the Great Powers, 1685–1715 (1951)*; and Carl J. Friedrich and C. Blitzer, *The Age of Power* (1957). For the social background, on which much important research has been carried out recently, one might begin with the pioneering work of Pierre Goubert, *Beauvais et le Beauvaisis de 1600 à 1730* (1958). In addition, Marc Bloch's study *French Rural History* (1966), originally published in 1931, remains valuable.

The character of Moscow during the long struggles of the tsars to reaffirm their power during the conflict with the Tartars and after the overthrow of the Tartar yoke is evident in John Fennell, *The Emergence of Moscow, 1304–1359* and in the biographies of the great tsars, such as Harold Lamb, *The March of Muscovy* (1948) and J. L. I. Fennell, *Ivan the Great of Moscow* (1962). The battles for the throne are best covered in one of the general surveys, of which Nicholas A. Riasanovsky, *History of Russia* (1963) is among the best. C. Bickford O'Brien, *Russia Under Two Tsars, 1682–1689* (1952) prepares us for Peter, whose move to Saint Petersburg is explained in B. H. Sumner, *Peter the Great and the Emergence of Russia* (1951) and Harold Lamb, *The City and the Tsar: Peter the Great and the Move to the West, 1648–1762* (1948). The condition of the peasantry is the key to understanding Russian social history in Jerome Blum, *Lord and Peasant in Russia* (1961). James H. Billington, *The Icon and the Axe* (1966) is a stimulating interpretation of the whole of Russian cultural history. A sweeping overview is provided in Marc Raeff, *Imperial Russia, 1682-1825: The Coming of Age of Modern Russia* (1970).

On the creation of absolutism, by the immediate predecessors of Louis XIV, see Roland Mousnier's *The Assassination of Henry IV* (1972), whose title misleadingly conceals the book's broad treatment of the reign; V-L. Tapie, *Richelieu and Louis XIII* (1967); and A. D. Lubinskaya, *French Absolutism: The Crucial Phase, 1620-1629* (1968). The day-to-day absolutism of Louis XIV, with its minute regulation of noble life in Versailles, is described by Saint Simon, *Louis XIV at Versailles* (1963), translated by Desmond Flower, which is a good selection from his diaries. The whole life of France comes alive in W. H. Lewis, *The Splendid Century* (1953). For the Grand Monarque himself, good biographies include John B. Wolf, *Louis XIV* (1968) and Maurice Ashley's brief *Louis XIV and the Greatness of France* (1946). Pierre Goubert's, *Louis XIV and Twenty Million Frenchmen* (1970) describes public policy against an economic background, while his *Ancien Regime, 1600-1750* (1974) extends his study in time and space. Theodore K. Rabb, *The Struggle for Stability in Early Modern Europe* (1975) is a comprehensive survey of the political stress that brought about the creation of the new forms of state in the seventeenth century. There is no better way of understanding the impact of the absolutist government of France upon the countryside than to turn to E. LeRoy Ladurie's superb study of the peasantry of southwestern France, *The Peasants of Languedoc* (1974), which can be supplemented with Roland Mousnier's comparative analysis, in his *Peasant Uprisings in Seventeenth-Century France, Russia, and China* (1970).

David Maland, *Culture and Society in Seventeenth Century France* (1970) and J. Lough, *An Introduction to Seventeenth Century France* (1954) show the relationship of literature to society. Robert M. Isherwood, *Music in the Service of the King: France in the Seventeenth Century* (1973) is a learned study of the musicians of Louis XIV's court. On the palace of Versailles, see P. de Nolhac, *Versailles et la Cour de France: L'Art de Versailles* (1930). The highlights of the literature of the age can be sampled in Corneille, *Le Cid*; Molière, *The Miser*; and Racine, *Phèdre*.

Tudor English history abounds in fine biographies, perhaps because the people themselves were so excitingly expressive. J. J. Scarisbrick, *Henry VIII* (1968), and J. E. Neale, *Queen Elizabeth I* (1952) are superb. G. R. Elton explains the constitutional development under the Tudors in *England Under the Tudors* (1960), and A. L. Rowse makes *The Elizabethan Age* (1950-1955) one of the more colorful moments of history.

For the social background to the English constitutional struggles of the seventeenth century, one should turn to Lawrence Stone, *The Crisis of the Aristocracy, 1558-1641* (1965) and his *Causes of the English Revolution, 1529-1642* (1972), or to H. R. Trevor-Roper, *The Gentry, 1540-1640* (1953). Christopher Hill, *The Century of Revolution, 1603-1714* (1961) is a reliable survey, while his *World Turned Upside Down: Radical Ideas During the English Revolution* (1972) reveals the astonishing variety of radical movements that surfaced briefly in the 1640s and 1650s. After C. V. Wedgwood's biography *Oliver Cromwell* (1956) and her excellent studies of the revolutionary years, *The King's Peace, 1637-1641* (1955) and *The King's War, 1641-1647* (1959), one should consult Michael L. Walzer, *The Revolution of the Saints* (1965) for an explanation of the social origins of Puritan politics. George Rude, *Hanoverian London* (1971) describes the social structure of the capital after the establishment of the oligarchy in power. On the social stress within the English towns, see Peter Clark and Paul Slack, eds., *Crisis and Order in English Towns, 1500-1700* (1971).

Index

Aachen, 298, 317–20, 369, 370; *illus.* 318, 319

Abbasid dynasty, 303–304

Abelard, Peter, 419

Abraham, 38

Abu Bakr, 301

Acropolis, Athens, 74, 86–88, 92–93; *illus.* 74; *plan* 94

Actium, Battle of (31 B.C.), 163

Address to the German Nobility (Luther), 542

Adrianople, Battle of (378), 236

Aelst, William van, *illus.* 625

Aeneas, 138–39, 143

Aeneid (Virgil), 138–39, 143, 190–91

Aeschylus, 84–85, 104–106

Africa, exploration of, 578, 582–86, 590

Agamemnon (Aeschylus), 104–105

Agincourt, Battle of (1415), 447

Agora, Athens, 90–92, 128; *plan* 91

Agricola, Michael, 563

Agriculture, neolithic, 11, 14–15; in copper age, 17–18; Egyptian, 45–46; Athenian, 62; Roman, 151–52, 159–60, 214–17; Byzantine, 266–67; medieval, 298; 332–39, 430–32; *illus.* 337; Arab, 306–307; Norman, 352–53; pre-Colombian, 598–99; Dutch, 634; French, 693–95

Agrigento, 139; *illus.* 138

Agrippina, 183

Akkadians, 10, 20, 26

Alaric, 236

Alberti, Leon Battista, 505

Albigensian heresy, 351–52

Albizzi, 495

Alcuin, 320–21

Alexander, the Great, 120, 124–26, 129–30

Alexander VI (Pope), 521, 525

Alexandria, 120, 126, 129–33; *illus.* 130, 131

Alhambra. *See* Granada

Ali (Caliph), 301

Alva, Duke of, 627–30

America, discovery of, 594–96; Spanish empire in, 596–605; English colonies in, 705–706

Amiens Cathedral, 414; *illus.* 414

Amorites, 26

Amsterdam, expansion of, 620–26; under Charles V, 626–27; revolt of, 629–31; economic life in, 631–39; social structure of, 639–45; government, 645–47; painting in, 647–50; and Rembrandt, 651–55; decline of, 655–57; *illus.* 621, 622, 623, 624, 630, 631, 634–35, 643

Amun-Re, 47, 54, 126; *illus.* 56

Amunhotep III (Pharoah, Egypt), 54–55

Amunhotep IV (Pharoah, Egypt; Akhenaton), 55–57

Anabaptists, 563–64

Anabasis (Xenophon), 122–23

Angelico, Fra, 511; *illus.* 421, 510

Anglo-Saxons, 352–53

Anjou, 347

Anne of Austria, 693–94; *illus.* 694

Anselm, 419

Anthemius, 278

Antigone (Sophocles), 107–109

Antigonid dynasty, 126

Antioch, 120, 128, 220, 258, 262

Antioch, patriarchate of, 225, 228–30

Antony, Mark, 162–63

Antwerp, 462, 626–27, 632, 657; *illus.* 462

Anu (Sumerian god), 21, 22

Apuleius, 201–202

Aquinas, Saint Thomas, 309, 421–22

Arabia, 299–300

Arabs, expansion of, 283, 296–301; Orthodox Caliphate, 301–302; Ummayad Caliphate, 302–303; Abbasid Caliphate, 303–304; effects of on West, 305–308; cultural advances of, 308–10; architecture of, 310–11; in Spain, 311–14; renewed invasions, 322–23

Architecture, neolithic, 15–16; *illus.* 16; Sumerian, 22–23; *illus.* 21; Assyrian, 31–33; *illus.* 30, 33; Minoan, 65; Mycenaean, 66; *illus.* 66, 67; Persian, *illus.* 81; Doric, 93–98; *illus.* 71, 93, 95, 138; Ionic, 98; *illus.* 97, 98; Roman, 170–71, 174, 181, 183–85; *illus.* 169, 180, 184, 186, 204, 205; Ostrogothic, *illus.* 239; Byzantine, 276–83; *illus.* 238, 247, 271, 276, 277, 280, 281, 282; Turkish, *illus.* 271; Moslem, 310–14; *illus.* 271, 297, 304, 307, 308, 311, 313; Carolingian, 318–20; *illus.* 319; Norman, *illus.* 325, 355, 356; Romanesque, 404–406; *illus.* 343, 367, 403, 405; Gothic, 408–15; *illus.* 408, 410, 412, 414, 415; late Gothic, *illus.* 425, 457; Florentine Renaissance, 513–16; *illus.* 483, 490; Roman Renaissance, 526–30; *illus.* 524, 529; Portuguese, 588, 591; *illus.* 588, 589; pre-Colombian, 597–600; *illus.* 598, 599; Spanish, 612–14; *illus.* 613; baroque, 666–69, 677–81; *illus.* 667, 668, 671, 673, 676, 677

Areopagus, Athens, 76, 86

Arguin Island, Guinea, 586

Arianism, 228–30, 236

Aristophanes, 92

Aristotle, 113–14, 419; *illus.* 114

Arles, *illus.* 205

Armada, Spanish, 631

Arrian, 125

Asam brothers, *illus.* 678

Ashdad, 39

Ashkelon, 39

Assyria, 10, 20, 30–34; *illus.* 30, 32, 33

Athena Nike temple, Athens, 98; *illus.* 97

Athens, significance of, 60–64; summarized, 62; *plan* 63; physical setting of, 73–75, 88–90; constitutional development of, 75–76, 79–80, 86–88; in Persian wars, 80–85; under Pericles, 86–88; urban character of, 90–92; Acropolis of, 92–101; drama in, 101–110; philosophy in, 110–14; in Peloponnesian War, 114–17; Hellenistic, 120; Byzantine, 273; *illus.* 61, 74, 93, 95, 97, 99, 101

Athletics, Greek, 92; *illus.* 92

Attalos I (King, Pergamum), 128

Attalos III (King, Pergamum), 149

Attica, 68, 73–75

Attila, 237

Augsburg, 460, 548; *illus.* 460, 549

Augsburg, Peace of (1555), 571

Augustine of Canterbury, Saint, 232

Augustine of Hippo, Saint, 225–28

Augustus, (Emperor, Rome), seizes power, 162–63; rebuilding in Rome, 172; constitutional

714